THE
SOCIAL
DIMENSION

OF WESTERN CIVILIZATION

VOLUME 2

Readings from
THE SIXTEENTH CENTURY
TO THE PRESENT

FIFTH EDITION

THE
SOCIAL
DIMENSION

OF WESTERN CIVILIZATION

VOLUME 2

Readings from

THE SIXTEENTH CENTURY
TO THE PRESENT

RICHARD M. GOLDEN
University of North Texas

BEDFORD / ST. MARTIN'S
Boston ◆ New York

For Bedford/St. Martin's

Publisher for History: Patricia Rossi
Developmental Editor: Jessica Angell
Senior Production Editor: Michael Weber
Production Supervisor: Christie Gross
Marketing Manager: Jenna Bookin Barry
Art Director: Donna Dennison
Text Design: Anna George and ErinBen Graphics
Cover Design: Billy Boardman and Mark McKie
Cover Art: Avenue Clichy, Five O'Clock in the Evening, 1887, by Louis Anquetin. © 2003 Artists Rights Society (ARS), New York/ADAGP, Paris. Wadsworth Atheneum Museum of Art, Hartford, CT. The Ella Gallup Sumner and Mary Catlin Sumner Collection Fund.
Composition: the dotted i
Printing and Binding: Haddon Craftsmen, Inc., an R.R. Donnelley & Sons Company

President: Joan E. Feinberg
Editorial Director: Denise B. Wydra
Director of Marketing: Karen R. Melton
Director of Editing, Design, and Production: Marcia Cohen
Managing Editor: Erica T. Appel

Library of Congress Control Number: 2002110180

Manufactured in the United States of America.

4 3 2 1
f

For information, write: Bedford/St. Martin's, 75 Arlington Street, Boston, MA 02116 (617-399-4000)

ISBN-10: 0-312-39737-2
ISBN-13: 978-0-312-39737-1

Acknowledgments

PREFACE

When I began preparing the first edition of *The Social Dimension of Western Civilization* sixteen years ago (it was then called *Social History of Western Civilization*), many Western civilization textbooks tended to slight social history. I am delighted that more recent textbooks tend to devote more space to social history, including such topics as gender, daily life, cross-cultural exchanges, the impact of the environment, diet, dress, ethnicity, sexuality, marginalized groups, and the like. Nevertheless, survey textbooks covering centuries or millennia can barely scratch the surface of such subjects. Hence, *The Social Dimension of Western Civilization,* now in its fifth edition, presents readings that enable instructor and students to explore more fully, passionately, and in greater depth social history topics that textbooks necessarily discuss only briefly, if at all. My hope is that Western civilization textbooks whet students' intellectual appetite for social history, which this anthology of classic and very recent pieces can better satisfy.

As a history instructor over the past twenty-eight years, I have used a number of anthologies in the classroom, but their selections often assume a degree of background knowledge that the typical student does not possess. To make *The Social Dimension* better suited to students, I have sifted through hundreds of essays to find those that are both challenging and accessible, interesting and significant. To enhance the readability of the selected articles, I have included as footnotes more than six hundred glosses that translate foreign words or identify individuals and terms that students might not recognize. All these notes are my own unless otherwise indicated. Based on my experience, gloss notes are invaluable to students using anthologies.

A Western civilization anthology cannot be all things to all instructors and students. Nevertheless, I have consciously tried to make these two volumes flexible enough to work in a wide variety of Western civilization courses. The fifth edition's broader range of themes and its expanded notion of Europe should meet the needs of more instructors as the coverage is now more tightly correlated with survey texts. Some historians argue that Western civilization began with the Greeks, but I have included in Volume One a part on Mesopotamia, Israel, and Egypt for the courses that begin with those civilizations. In addition, both volumes now contain material on the sixteenth and seventeenth centuries because instructors and institutions divide Western civilization courses differently.

In this fifth edition, certain elements have been retained and strengthened while new features have been added. It is my hope that instructors will find this edition not only more flexible but also more helpful in sparking class discussions and making thematic comparisons among the essays.

New Readings. When I prepared this edition, as is the case every time I revise, there always seemed to be somewhere a more attractive article on every topic. While maintaining a balance between classical pieces in social history and those on the cutting edge of recent scholarship, I have changed seven of this volume's twenty-four essays and have added as well seven articles that are also in Volume One. I have based the substitutions and additions not only on my own searches but also on feedback from those instructors who have used previous editions. The new readings — on subjects such as French revolutionary women, letter writing, Gypsies, the Atlantic slave trade, rural women in Italy, German police in the Holocaust, and ethnic cleansing in Yugoslavia — reflect the active nature of historical scholarship today.

Social History Emphasis. Throughout the part introductions and the headnotes to each selection, I discuss the practice of social history — its growth and importance as well as its goals within the discipline. For each selection, I mention the types of sources the author used in order to show students that social historians consult a variety of evidence.

New Discussion Questions. I have frequently added questions to the headnotes that encourage comparative thinking by relating themes and issues across readings and to present-day collective attitudes and social conditions.

Topical Table of Contents. This alternate table of contents groups all the selections under the topics they discuss, enabling instructors and students to compare articles by theme.

Overlap of Articles between Volumes. To correspond better to a variety of course syllabi, Volume 2 now includes the last part of Volume One, on early modern Europe, so instructors may easily cover the material in either term.

Acknowledgments

Since I began work on the first edition in 1986, many people suggested essays to me, critiqued what I wrote, and helped in other ways as well. I thank Ove Anderson, Jay Crawford, Fara Driver, Patricia Easley, Phillip Garland, Laurie Glover, Tully Hunter, Christopher Koontz, John Leonard, Laurie McDowell, and James Sanchez. Especially generous with their time and comments on the first three editions were Philip Adler, Kathryn Babayan, William Beik, Robert Bireley, Richard Bulliet, Elizabeth D. Carney, Suzanne A. Desan, Lawrence Estaville, Hilda Golden, Leonard Greenspoon, Alan Grubb, Christopher Guthrie, Sarah Hanley, George Huppert, Thomas Kuehn, Charles Lippy, Donald McKale, Steven Marks, Victor Matthews, John A. Mears, William Murnane, David Nicholas, Thomas F. X. Noble, James Sack, Carol Thomas, and Roy Vice. Steven D. Cooley, Charles T. Evans, Anita Guerrini, Benjamin Hudson, Jonathan Katz, Donna T. McCaffrey, Maureen Melody, Kathyrn E. Meyer, Lohr E. Miller, Gerald M. Schnabel, Paul Teverow, Sara W. Tucker, and Lindsay Wilson reviewed the third edition or responded to questionnaires. Edward Coomes, Henry Eaton, Lee Huddleston, Terje Leiren, Marilyn Morris, Laura Stern, and Harold Tanner provided generous assistance with the fourth edition.

The following historians gave helpful feedback via questionnaires of reviews for the fourth edition of *The Social Dimension:* Ann T. Allen, University of Louisville; David Burns, Moraine Valley Community College; Leslie Derfler, Florida Atlantic University; John E. Dreifort, Wichita State University; Amanda Eurich, Western Washington University; William J. Events Jr., Champlain College; Marie T. Gingras, University of Colorado at Denver; Christopher E. Guthrie, Tarleton State University; Carla Hay, Marquette University; Daniel W. Hollis III, Jacksonville State University; John Hunt, Joseph College; Katharine D. Kennedy, Agnes Scott College; Thomas Kuehn, Clemson University; Joyce C. Mastboom, Cleveland State University; John McCole, University of Oregon; David Nichols, Clemson University; Philip Otterness, Warren Wilson College; Catherine Patterson, University of Houston; Dolores Davidson Peterson; Foothill College; Lowell Satre, Youngstown State University; Stephanie Sherwell, Charles County Community College; Malcolm Smuts, University of Massachusetts at Boston; Larissa Taylor, Colby College; Michael C. Weber, Northern Essex Community College; Michael Wolfe, Pennsylvania State University at Altoona; Anne York, Youngstown State University; and Ronald Zupko, Marquette University.

I thank as well the reviewers of the fifth edition: Anne Kelsch, University of North Dakota; Lawrence Langer, University of Connecticut; Lynn M. Laufenberg, Sweet Briar College; Michael R. Lynn, Agnes Scott College; Joyce M. Mastboom, Cleveland State University; Michael Richards, Sweet Briar College; Lynn Sharp, Whitman College; Richard L. Smith, Ferrum College; Andrea Winkler, Whitman College.

I have been fortunate in working with publishers and editors who show wonderful empathy for history and historians. My experiences have been completely positive, and I thank all the good people at Bedford/St. Martin's. Charles Christensen and Joan Feinberg, successively the company's presidents, and Denise Wydra, editorial director, have a feeling and appreciation for both books and the book market. For the fifth edition, Jessica Angell, developmental editor, has been efficient and thoughtful; Michael Weber, senior project editor (who had, as acquisitions editor, contracted with me sixteen years ago to do the first edition of this anthology with St. Martin's Press) has been his usual professional self; and Patricia Rossi, publisher for history, and Jane Knetzger, director of development, have proved knowledgeable and creative. Marcia Cohen, director of editing, design, and production, and Erica T. Appel, managing editor, expertly guided the production process; Christie Gross, production associate, and Brianna Germain, editorial assistant, were of great assistance. Donna Dennison, art director, and Billy Boardman, design associate, created the beautiful covers, and Fred Courtright smoothly handled the permissions.

Denis Paz, an eminent social historian who is more familiar with this anthology than anyone else, has given me for all five editions his perspectives as a historian and a professor. His help has been invaluable.

Finally, I have been blessed with the support of my wife, Hilda, and my three children — Davina, Irene, and Jeremy. They have sharpened my perception of social life and have always given me their love. I dedicate this book to them, as well as to my granddaughter, Isabella.

CONTENTS

PART ONE

EARLY MODERN EUROPE
Sixteenth and Seventeenth Centuries

PART TWO

THE OLD RÉGIME

PART THREE

THE NINETEENTH CENTURY

PART FOUR

CONTEMPORARY EUROPE

TOPICAL TABLE OF CONTENTS

CRIME

DISEASE AND DEATH

ETHNICITY / PEOPLEHOOD

FAMILY

FOOD

GENDER

POPULAR MENTALITIES AND COLLECTIVE ATTITUDES

RELIGION

RURAL LIFE

SEXUALITY AND THE BODY

TERRORISM, VIOLENCE, AND WAR

URBAN LIFE

WORK AND ECONOMIC LIFE

INTRODUCTION

The selections in this volume deal with the social history of Western civilization from the sixteenth century to the present.[1] Social history encompasses the study of *groups* of people rather than focusing on prominent individuals, such as kings, intellectual giants, and military leaders. Over the last four decades, social historians have examined a host of topics, many of which are included here: the family, gender, sexuality, disease, everyday life, death, social and ethnic groups, entertainment, work, leisure, popular religion and politics, criminality, the experience of soldiers in war, economic conditions, and collective mentality (the attitudes, beliefs, and assumptions held by a population). Social history, then, sheds light both on previously neglected areas of human experience and on forgotten and nameless people, including minorities and those at the bottom of the social scale. Indeed, some recent historians, perhaps a bit too optimistically, endeavor to write "total history," which aims to cover all aspects of people's lives.

Social historians take an analytical approach instead of the narrative and chronological approach generally used by biographers and traditional political historians. Social historians do not attempt to celebrate the heroes and heroines of a nation's history, although that is precisely the type of "feel good" history that many in the public wish to read and to see taught in school systems. They do not glorify any Alamos. Instead, their goal is to re-create and make known the lives of ordinary people.

In taking this approach, social historians have expanded their research beyond diaries, personal and government correspondence, and court documents to include such sources as police reports, trial records, tax rolls, census schedules,

---

[1] There are a few references in this volume to ancient dates. Current standard scholarly practice is to use the era designations B.C.E. ("before the common era") and C.E. ("of the common era") where formerly B.C. ("before Christ") and A.D. (*anno Domini*, "in the year of the Lord"), respectively, were used. Here the current standard style has been employed where relevant in the headnotes and footnotes; in the readings texts themselves, however, whatever style the authors of the readings used has been retained.

writings by people in the lower classes, conscription lists, parish registers, marriage contracts, wills, church records, government commissions, records of small businesses, newspapers and magazines, popular literature, oral histories, songs, and material artifacts. By using such a variety of sources, social historians are able to reveal the private and public lives of people in all social groups. The headnotes to the articles in this volume mention some of the types of sources historians have consulted as they strive to explain the social past. Some students may, of course, choose to seek out primary sources and other evidence to research some of the topics covered here, and they may indeed arrive at different conclusions from those of the historians.

Many of the articles treat similar themes, as is shown in the topical table of contents, and students can readily relate topics in various articles. Questions in the headnotes may link readings to one another so that students may also begin to make comparisons across centuries, cultures, and geographical areas. These questions will also help students make connections to material in their textbooks and in lectures. It is important to make such comparisons in order to place subjects in perspective and to discern causality and change over time.

Unlike traditional political history, social history rarely begins or ends with specific dates. The problem of periodization, always a thorny one, is especially difficult for social historians, who often study topics that can be understood only as long-term developments. Thus, infanticide, though surely declining in frequency in the late-nineteenth century, cannot be understood without looking back to antiquity and to the Middle Ages. Another such topic is human sexuality. Any discussion of the sexual practices of the Victorian Age must be set against the durable sexual relations that, in significant ways, changed little in the course of millennia. In social history, then, what has not changed is often more important than what has changed, making it difficult for the social historian to decide where to divide, cut off, or end a subject.

As a way out of this difficulty, social historians have come to favor a simple division between premodern (or traditional or preindustrial) society and the modern (or industrial) world. This split has several advantages. First, it clearly indicates that the Industrial Revolution constituted a watershed, affecting lifestyles and human relationships throughout society. The Industrial Revolution raised new problems and new questions involving workers' movements, nationalism, mass democracy, and women's emancipation, to name just a few topics. In the industrial era, developments occurred more rapidly than in preindustrial society, where dietary habits, family relationships, and work patterns, for instance, had changed more slowly over time. Second, the terms *traditional* and *premodern,* on the one hand, and *modern,* on the other hand, are general enough to permit historians to use the words while disagreeing about their meanings. What, exactly, does it mean to be *modern?* What is the process of modernization? Were people in the nineteenth century modern?

I have grouped the selections in this volume into four parts. Part One, "Early Modern Europe: Sixteenth and Seventeenth Centuries," begins with the European invasion of the Americas and continues to the end of the seventeenth century, with some overlap into the eighteenth century. Part Two, "The Old Regime," focuses on the eighteenth century, although because social history does not adhere to individual dates, some articles go back into the seventeenth century and one goes forward into the nineteenth century. Part Three, "The Nineteenth Century," begins with the Industrial Revolution. But because the Industrial Revolution actually began in England in the late eighteenth century, a few of the articles start there. Part Four, "Contemporary Europe," treats World War I as a great divide. Here again, some essays go back in time to discuss the prior century and traditional Europe. In sum, historians impose periods on history that are always debatable and sometimes capricious but certainly essential in providing some order to the study of the past.

In any case, well-researched and well-written social history should convey excitement, for it makes us vividly aware of the daily lives, habits, and beliefs of our ancestors. In some ways, their patterns of behavior and thought will seem similar to ours, but in other ways our predecessors' actions and values may appear quite different, if not barbaric or alien. It is important to keep in mind that the living conditions and attitudes that exist in the present are not necessarily superior to those of the distant or recent past. Social history does not teach progress. Rather than drawing facile lessons from the daily lives of those who came before us, we might, as historians, attempt to immerse ourselves in their cultures and understand why they lived and acted as they did.

THE
SOCIAL
DIMENSION
OF WESTERN CIVILIZATION
Volume 2

Readings from
THE SIXTEENTH CENTURY
TO THE PRESENT

PART ONE

EARLY MODERN EUROPE

Sixteenth and Seventeenth Centuries

Jared Diamond

Henry Kamen

Merry Wiesner

Natalie Z. Davis

Sara F. Matthews Grieco

Robin Briggs

Raffaella Sarti

Richard van Dülmen

Christopher R. Friedrichs

In one sense, history is the solving of problems. Two classic problems for historians have been the difficulty of defining *modern* and, following from that, the difficulty of determining when the modern world began. Wrangling over these issues persists, with little agreement. The Italians of the Renaissance considered themselves, with little modesty, the first modern people, more closely akin to the ancient world than to their immediate ancestors, whom they called Gothic and barbaric. Renaissance Italy saw the centuries after the fall of Roman civilization as the Middle Ages, a period between the classical world of Greece and Rome and fourteenth- and fifteenth-century Italy. In the nineteenth century, historians began to debate whether or not Renaissance Italy was indeed modern, or rather gave rise to the protomodern world, or was even medieval in fundamental ways. This debate continues today and is part of the larger problem of historic periodization. Are there actual periods in history? Or do historians arbitrarily classify certain centuries as periods, labeling them as distinct when in fact they are not?

As a way out of the dilemma, many favor the term *early modern Europe,* partly because its chronological boundaries are so vague that historians can use it when discussing very different cultures. Sometimes the early modern period in Europe refers to the years from 1400 to 1789, thus encompassing Renaissance Italy, or the years 1500 to 1789, omitting both the Renaissance and the French Revolution.

The fifteenth century began the "Age of Exploration," when Europeans explored, colonized, and conquered overseas. The Portuguese went to Africa before eventually reaching India and later the Far East. Spain, of course, dispatched ships to the New World in 1492, and soon after to East Asia as well. The results of European invasions of continents were often disastrous, especially in the Americas. Jared Diamond explains why Spaniards succeeded in the conquest of much of the New World and why Native American societies did not and could not sail to Europe and conquer Spain, for example.

European society was still predominantly rural, though urban centers increased in size. Capitalism likewise grew, though this period was surely not its heyday. Monarchy remained the political ideal and reality, though there were some calls for socialist or republican governments. The religion was Christian, though Christianity changed dramatically. In sum, the early modern era in Europe was a period of confluence of old and new, a period of rapid change in some respects, but not a period of desire for, or expectation of, change — unlike, for example, that of today's Western world.

The sixteenth and seventeenth centuries experienced the Protestant and Catholic Reformations with their attendant religious zealotry and conflict. As Henry Kamen rebuts the stereotypical view that the Spanish Inquisition was evil incarnate, he analyzes its effects on the Spanish people. With the Inquisition, Spanish Catholicism labored to eliminate "superstitions," incorrect behavior, and heterodox beliefs. Intolerance and persecution increased in both Catholic and Protestant states as religious feeling intensified and as governments developed more efficient bureaucracies able and eager to impose a greater degree of religious orthodoxy and political subservience. Merry Wiesner explains the varied impact of the Protestant Reformation on German women, and Natalie Z. Davis portrays the intensity of religious feeling in the sixteenth century in her analysis of religious riots in France. Some historians refer to this period as an age of crisis, because so much was called into question and so many institutions, beliefs, and conventions were shaken. The fear that gripped Europeans can be seen in the persecution of witches, which Robin Briggs reveals to have been endemic in the rural world. Community conflicts led to accusations of witchcraft and often to charges of consorting with Satan. Such witches, Europeans believed, worked to destroy Christian society.

Tradition, relative immobility, and privilege characterized this premodern society of the sixteenth and seventeenth centuries. In discussing women's bodies, cleanliness, beauty, and prudery, Sara F. Matthews Grieco illuminates changes that occurred in the midst of feverish efforts to preserve traditional ideas of male domination and of marriage. Raffaella Sarti's survey of homes and diet in early modern Europe uncovers important, though slow developments in living conditions.

The sixteenth and seventeenth centuries had singular accomplishments, such as the Scientific Revolution and Baroque art. These intellectual and cultural developments masked the stark reality of life for the overwhelming majority of the population, concerned with survival and with the pious hope that blessed life in the next world might compensate for the tireless and painful struggle in this existence.

Life for all but the social elite could be described in the words of the English philosopher Thomas Hobbes as "poor, nasty, brutish, and short." Condemned to hunger and cold, wracked by diseases, intensely religious if not fanatical, often violent, subject to increasing supervision by church and state, early modern Europeans could, moreover, expect a life span less than half that of ours today. Richard van Dülmen's piece points to the brutalization of life as experienced in severe and public executions. Early modern cities, Christopher Friedrichs argues, could never cope sufficiently with the problem of poverty, which was exacerbated by the influx of immigrants who swelled the numbers of vagrants, beggars, prostitutes, and the laboring poor. The age of Michelangelo, Cervantes, and Shakespeare had an unappealing underside to its glittering cultural accomplishments.

HEMISPHERES COLLIDING
Eurasian and Native American Societies, 1492
Jared Diamond

The magnitude of the Spanish conquest of much of the New World played out on 16 November 1532 when a Spanish force of 168 faced the Inca emperor Atahuallpa, supported by perhaps 80,000 fighters. At the end of the day, 7,000 Indians had been killed; no Spaniard died. Jared Diamond, professor of physiology at the UCLA School of Medicine, seeks to understand why the Spanish invasion of the Americas was so successful. He also asks why the situation was not reversed, with Atahuallpa crossing the Atlantic Ocean to invade Spain.

Diamond, a biologist, dismisses any notion of ethnic or racial superiority. The Europeans proved triumphant because of geography and biology. They lived on the largest continent, Eurasia, which allowed animals, food, and people to disperse on an east-west axis that had no impenetrable barriers. In contrast, New World cultures experienced no similar diffusion because its north-south axis precluded fauna and flora from spreading easily into different climatic and geographical zones. Proximity to large domestic animals (Eurasia had thirteen of the fourteen largest in the world, whereas the Americas had only one) allowed animal diseases to pass to humans, who gained immunities over time. Thus, measles, smallpox, and other diseases decimated sixteenth-century Native Americans. The greater number of domesticated plants and animals led to higher population densities in the Old World, which freed more people to be technology specialists and warriors. While Spaniards and Native Americans sought the reasons for European conquest in religion or in conceptions of racial superiority, Diamond's explanation for European conquest and devastation of the native population boils down to location, to the edge that millennia of living on the Eurasian continent gave to Europeans.

What specific agricultural advantages did Europeans have? In what areas of technology did Europeans excel? How did European political organization facil-

Jared Diamond, *Guns, Germs, and Steel: The Fates of Human Societies* (New York: Norton, 1997), 354–375.

itate conquest? Why did the first Eurasian endeavor — by the Norse (Vikings) — to colonize the Americas fail? Does Diamond's conclusion about human biology have possible implications for the twenty-first century?

The largest population replacement of the last 13,000 years has been the one resulting from the recent collision between Old World and New World societies. Its most dramatic and decisive moment . . . occurred when Pizarro's[1] tiny army of Spaniards captured the Inca emperor Atahuallpa,[2] absolute ruler of the largest, richest, most populous, and administratively and technologically most advanced Native American state. Atahuallpa's capture symbolizes the European conquest of the Americas, because the same mix of proximate factors that caused it was also responsible for European conquests of other Native American societies. Let us now return to that collision of hemispheres. . . . The basic question to be answered is: why did Europeans reach and conquer the lands of Native Americans, instead of vice versa? Our starting point will be a comparison of Eurasian and Native American societies as of A.D. 1492, the year of Columbus's "discovery" of the Americas.

Our comparison begins with food production, a major determinant of local population size and societal complexity — hence an ultimate factor behind the conquest. The most glaring difference between American and Eurasian food production involved big domestic mammal species. . . . Eurasia . . . [had] 13 species, which became its chief source of animal protein (meat and milk), wool, and hides, its main mode of land transport of people and goods, its indispensable vehicles of warfare, and (by drawing plows and providing manure) a big enhancer of crop production. Until waterwheels and windmills began to replace Eurasia's mammals in medieval times, they were also the major source of its "industrial" power beyond human muscle power — for example, for turning grindstones and operating water lifts. In contrast, the Americas had only one species of big domestic mammal, the llama/alpaca, confined to a small area of the Andes and the adjacent Peruvian coast. While it was used for meat, wool, hides, and goods transport, it never yielded milk for human consumption, never bore a rider, never pulled a cart or a plow, and never served as a power source or vehicle of warfare.

That's an enormous set of differences between Eurasian and Native American societies — due largely to the Late Pleistocene[3] extinction (extermination?) of most of North and South America's former big wild mammal species. If it had not been for those extinctions, modern history might have taken a different course. When Cortés[4] and his bedraggled adventurers landed on the Mexican coast in 1519, they

---

[1] Francisco Pizarro (ca. 1470–1541), Spanish soldier and conqueror of Peru.

[2] Emperor of the Incas, defeated and executed by Pizarro in 1533.

[3] Before 10,000 B.C.E., at the end of the last ice age.

[4] Hernán Cortés (1485–1547), Spanish soldier and conqueror of Mexico.

might have been driven into the sea by thousands of Aztec cavalry mounted on domesticated native American horses. Instead of the Aztecs' dying of smallpox, the Spaniards might have been wiped out by American germs transmitted by disease-resistant Aztecs. American civilizations resting on animal power might have been sending their own conquistadores to ravage Europe. But those hypothetical outcomes were foreclosed by mammal extinctions thousands of years earlier.

Those extinctions left Eurasia with many more wild candidates for domestication than the Americas offered. Most candidates disqualify themselves as potential domesticates for any of half a dozen reasons. Hence Eurasia ended up with its 13 species of big domestic mammals and the Americas with just its one very local species. Both hemispheres also had domesticated species of birds and small mammals — the turkey, guinea pig, and Muscovy duck very locally and the dog more widely in the Americas; chickens, geese, ducks, cats, dogs, rabbits, honeybees, silkworms, and some others in Eurasia. But the significance of all those species of small domestic animals was trivial compared with that of the big ones.

Eurasia and the Americas also differed with respect to plant food production, though the disparity here was less marked than for animal food production. In 1492 agriculture was widespread in Eurasia. Among the few Eurasian hunter-gatherers lacking both crops and domestic animals were the Ainu of northern Japan, Siberian societies without reindeer, and small hunter-gatherer groups scattered through the forests of India and tropical Southeast Asia and trading with neighboring farmers. Some other Eurasian societies, notably the Central Asian pastoralists and the reindeer-herding Lapps and Samoyeds of the Arctic, had domestic animals but little or no agriculture. Virtually all other Eurasian societies engaged in agriculture as well as in herding animals.

Agriculture was also widespread in the Americas, but hunter-gatherers occupied a larger fraction of the Americas' area than of Eurasia's. Those regions of the Americas without food production included all of northern North America and southern South America, the Canadian Great Plains, and all of western North America except for small areas of the U.S. Southwest that supported irrigation agriculture. It is striking that the areas of Native America without food production included what today, after Europeans' arrival, are some of the most productive farmlands and pastures of both North and South America: the Pacific states of the United States, Canada's wheat belt, the pampas of Argentina, and the Mediterranean zone of Chile. The former absence of food production in these lands was due entirely to their local paucity of domesticable wild animals and plants, and to geographic and ecological barriers that prevented the crops and the few domestic animal species of other parts of the Americas from arriving. Those lands became productive not only for European settlers but also, in some cases, for Native Americans, as soon as Europeans introduced suitable domestic animals and crops. For instance, Native American societies became renowned for their mastery of horses, and in some cases of cattle and sheepherding, in parts of the Great Plains, the western United States, and the Argentine pampas. Those mounted plains warriors and Navajo sheepherders and weavers now figure prominently in white Americans' image of American Indians, but the basis for that image was created only after 1492. These examples demonstrate that the sole missing ingredients required to sustain food production in large areas of the Americas were domestic animals and crops themselves.

In those parts of the Americas that did support Native American agriculture, it was constrained by five major disadvantages vis-à-vis Eurasian agriculture: widespread dependence on protein-poor corn, instead of Eurasia's diverse and protein-rich cereals; hand planting of individual seeds, instead of broadcast sowing; tilling by hand instead of plowing by animals, which enables one person to cultivate a much larger area, and which also permits cultivation of some fertile but tough soils and sods that are difficult to till by hand (such as those of the North American Great Plains); lack of animal manuring to increase soil fertility; and just human muscle power, instead of animal power, for agricultural tasks such as threshing, grinding, and irrigation. These differences suggest that Eurasian agriculture as of 1492 may have yielded on the average more calories and protein per person-hour of labor than Native American agriculture did.

Such differences in food production constituted a major ultimate cause of the disparities between Eurasian and Native American societies. Among the resulting proximate factors behind the conquest, the most important included differences in germs, technology, political organization, and writing. Of these, the one linked most directly to the differences in food production was germs. The infectious diseases that regularly visited crowded Eurasian societies, and to which many Eurasians consequently developed immune or genetic resistance, included all of history's most lethal killers: smallpox, measles, influenza, plague, tuberculosis, typhus, cholera, malaria, and others. Against that grim list, the sole crowd infectious diseases that can be attributed with certainty to pre-Columbian Native American societies were nonsyphilitic treponemas. (. . . [I]t remains uncertain whether syphilis arose in Eurasia or in the Americas, and the claim that human tuberculosis was present in the Americas before Columbus is in my opinion unproven.)

This continental difference in harmful germs resulted paradoxically from the difference in useful livestock. Most of the microbes responsible for the infectious diseases of crowded human societies evolved from very similar ancestral microbes causing infectious diseases of the domestic animals with which food producers began coming into daily close contact around 10,000 years ago. Eurasia harbored many domestic animal species and hence developed many such microbes, while the Americas had very few of each. Other reasons why Native American societies evolved so few lethal microbes were that villages, which provide ideal breeding grounds for epidemic diseases, arose thousands of years later in the Americas than in Eurasia; and that the three regions of the New World supporting urban societies (the Andes, Mesoamerica, and the U.S. Southeast) were never connected by fast, high-volume trade on the scale that brought plague, influenza, and possibly smallpox to Europe from Asia. As a result, even malaria and yellow fever, the infectious diseases that eventually became major obstacles to European colonization of the American tropics, and that posed the biggest barrier to the construction of the Panama Canal, are not American diseases at all but are caused by microbes of Old World tropical origin, introduced to the Americas by Europeans.

Rivaling germs as proximate factors behind Europe's conquest of the Americas were the differences in all aspects of technology. These differences stemmed ultimately from Eurasia's much longer history of densely populated, economically specialized, politically centralized, interacting and competing societies dependent on food production. Five areas of technology may be singled out:

First, metals — initially copper, then bronze, and finally iron — were used for tools in all complex Eurasian societies as of 1492. In contrast, although copper, silver, gold, and alloys were used for ornaments in the Andes and some other parts of the Americas, stone and wood and bone were still the principal materials for tools in all Native American societies, which made only limited local use of copper tools.

Second, military technology was far more potent in Eurasia than in the Americas. European weapons were steel swords, lances, and daggers, supplemented by small firearms and artillery, while body armor and helmets were also made of solid steel or else of chain mail. In place of steel, Native Americans used clubs and axes of stone or wood (occasionally copper in the Andes), slings, bows and arrows, and quilted armor, constituting much less effective protection and weaponry. In addition, Native American armies had no animals to oppose to horses, whose value for assaults and fast transport gave Europeans an overwhelming advantage until some Native American societies themselves adopted them.

Third, Eurasian societies enjoyed a huge advantage in their sources of power to operate machines. The earliest advance over human muscle power was the use of animals — cattle, horses, and donkeys — to pull plows and to turn wheels for grinding grain, raising water, and irrigating or draining fields. Waterwheels appeared in Roman times and then proliferated, along with tidal mills and windmills, in the Middle Ages. Coupled to systems of geared wheels, those engines harnessing water and wind power were used not only to grind grain and move water but also to serve myriad manufacturing purposes, including crushing sugar, driving blast furnace bellows, grinding ores, making paper, polishing stone, pressing oil, producing salt, producing textiles, and sawing wood. It is conventional to define the Industrial Revolution arbitrarily as beginning with the harnessing of steam power in 18th-century England, but in fact an industrial revolution based on water and wind power had begun already in medieval times in many parts of Europe. As of 1492, all of those operations to which animal, water, and wind power were being applied in Eurasia were still being carried out by human muscle power in the Americas.

Long before the wheel began to be used in power conversion in Eurasia, it had become the basis of most Eurasian land transport — not only for animal-drawn vehicles but also for human-powered wheelbarrows, which enabled one or more people, still using just human muscle power, to transport much greater weights than they could have otherwise. Wheels were also adopted in Eurasian pottery making and in clocks. None of those uses of the wheel was adopted in the Americas, where wheels are attested only in Mexican ceramic toys.

The remaining area of technology to be mentioned is sea transport. Many Eurasian societies developed large sailing ships, some of them capable of sailing against the wind and crossing the ocean, equipped with sextants, magnetic compasses, sternpost rudders, and cannons. In capacity, speed, maneuverability, and seaworthiness, those Eurasian ships were far superior to the rafts that carried out trade between the New World's most advanced societies, those of the Andes and Mesoamerica. Those rafts sailed with the wind along the Pacific coast. Pizarro's ship easily ran down and captured such a raft on his first voyage toward Peru.

In addition to their germs and technology, Eurasian and Native American societies differed in their political organization. By late medieval or Renaissance times, most of Eurasia had come under the rule of organized states. Among these, the Habsburg, Ottoman, and Chinese states, the Mogul state of India, and the Mongol state at its peak in the 13th century started out as large polyglot amalgamations formed by the conquest of other states. For that reason they are generally referred to as empires. Many Eurasian states and empires had official religions that contributed to state cohesion, being invoked to legitimize the political leadership and to sanction wars against other peoples. Tribal and band societies in Eurasia were largely confined to the Arctic reindeer herders, the Siberian hunter-gatherers, and the hunter-gatherer enclaves in the Indian subcontinent and tropical Southeast Asia.

The Americas had two empires, those of the Aztecs and Incas, which resembled their Eurasian counterparts in size, population, polyglot makeup, official religions, and origins in the conquest of smaller states. In the Americas those were the sole two political units capable of mobilizing resources for public works or war on the scale of many Eurasian states, whereas seven European states (Spain, Portugal, England, France, Holland, Sweden, and Denmark) had the resources to acquire American colonies between 1492 and 1666. The Americas also held many chiefdoms (some of them virtually small states) in tropical South America, Mesoamerica beyond Aztec rule, and the U.S. Southeast. The rest of the Americas was organized only at the tribal or band level.

The last proximate factor to be discussed is writing. Most Eurasian states had literate bureaucracies, and in some a significant fraction of the populace other than bureaucrats was also literate. Writing empowered European societies by facilitating political administration and economic exchanges, motivating and guiding exploration and conquest, and making available a range of information and human experience extending into remote places and times. In contrast, use of writing in the Americas was confined to the elite in a small area of Mesoamerica. The Inca Empire employed an accounting system and mnemonic device based on knots (termed quipu), but it could not have approached writing as a vehicle for transmitting detailed information.

Thus, Eurasian societies in the time of Columbus enjoyed big advantages over Native American societies in food production, germs, technology (including weapons), political organization, and writing. These were the main factors tipping the outcome of the post-Columbian collisions. But those differences as of A.D. 1492 represent just one snapshot of historical trajectories that had extended over at least 13,000 years in the Americas, and over a much longer time in Eurasia. For the Americas, in particular, the 1492 snapshot captures the end of the independent trajectory of Native Americans. Let us now trace out the earlier stages of those trajectories.

Historical Trajectories of Eurasia and the Americas

Approximate Date of Adoption	Eurasia		
	Fertile Crescent	China	England
Plant domestication	8500 B.C.	by 7500 B.C.	3500 B.C.
Animal domestication	8000 B.C.	by 7500 B.C.	3500 B.C.
Pottery	7000 B.C.	by 7500 B.C.	3500 B.C.
Villages	9000 B.C.	by 7500 B.C.	3000 B.C.
Chiefdoms	5500 B.C.	4000 B.C.	2500 B.C.
Widespread metal tools or artifacts (copper and/or bronze)	4000 B.C.	2000 B.C.	2000 B.C.
States	3700 B.C.	2000 B.C.	500 A.D.
Writing	3200 B.C.	by 1300 B.C.	A.D. 43
Widespread iron tools	900 B.C.	500 B.C.	650 B.C.

This table gives approximate dates of widespread adoption of significant developments in three Eurasian and four Native American areas. Dates for animal domestication
neglect dogs, which were domesticated earlier than food-producing animals in both Eura-

The table summarizes approximate dates of the appearance of key developments in the main "homelands" of each hemisphere (the Fertile Crescent[5] and
China in Eurasia, the Andes and Amazonia and Mesoamerica in the Americas). It
also includes the trajectory for the minor New World homeland of the eastern
United States, and that for England, which is not a homeland at all but is listed
to illustrate how rapidly developments spread from the Fertile Crescent.

This table is sure to horrify any knowledgeable scholar, because it reduces exceedingly complex histories to a few seemingly precise dates. In reality, all of
those dates are merely attempts to label arbitrary points along a continuum. For
example, more significant than the date of the first metal tool found by some ar-
chaeologist is the time when a significant fraction of all tools was made of metal,
but how common must metal tools be to rate as "widespread"? Dates for the appearance of the same development may differ among different parts of the same
homeland. For instance, within the Andean region pottery appears about 1,300
years earlier in coastal Ecuador (3100 B.C.) than in Peru (1800 B.C.). Some dates,
such as those for the rise of chiefdoms, are more difficult to infer from the archaeological record than are dates of artifacts like pottery or metal tools. Some of
the dates in the table are very uncertain, especially those for the onset of American food production. Nevertheless, as long as one understands that the table is a
simplification, it is useful for comparing continental histories.

The table suggests that food production began to provide a large fraction of
human diets around 5,000 years earlier in the Eurasian homelands than in those

---

[5] The land between the Tigris and Euphrates rivers, where the first civilization began.

Historical Trajectories of Eurasia and the Americas (continued)

| | Native America | | |
Andes	Amazonia	Mesoamerica	Eastern U.S.
by 3000 B.C.	3000 B.C.	by 3000 B.C.	2500 B.C.
3500 B.C.	?	500 B.C.	—
3100–1800 B.C.	6000 B.C.	1500 B.C.	2500 B.C.
3100–1800 B.C.	6000 B.C.	1500 B.C.	500 B.C.
by 1500 B.C.	A.D. 1	1500 B.C.	200 B.C.
A.D. 1000	—	—	—
A.D. 1	—	300 B.C.	—
—	—	600 B.C.	—
—	—	—	—

sia and the Americas. Chiefdoms are inferred from archaeological evidence, such as ranked burials, architecture, and settlement patterns. The table greatly simplifies a complex mass of historical facts: see the text for some of the many important caveats.

of the Americas. A caveat must be mentioned immediately: while there is no doubt about the antiquity of food production in Eurasia, there is controversy about its onset in the Americas. . . . Still, even if plant domestication did begin earlier in the Americas than the dates shown in the table, agriculture surely did not provide the basis for most human calorie intake and sedentary existence in American homelands until much later than in Eurasian homelands.

. . . [O]nly a few relatively small areas of each hemisphere acted as a "homeland" where food production first arose and from which it then spread. Those homelands were the Fertile Crescent and China in Eurasia, and the Andes and Amazonia, Mesoamerica, and the eastern United States in the Americas. The rate of spread of key developments is especially well understood for Europe, thanks to the many archaeologists at work there. As the table summarizes for England, once food production and village living had arrived from the Fertile Crescent after a long lag (5,000 years), the subsequent lag for England's adoption of chiefdoms, states, writing, and especially metal tools was much shorter: 2,000 years for the first widespread metal tools of copper and bronze, and only 250 years for widespread iron tools. Evidently, it was much easier for one society of already sedentary farmers to "borrow" metallurgy from another such society than for nomadic hunter-gatherers to "borrow" food production from sedentary farmers (or to be replaced by the farmers).

Why were the trajectories of all key developments shifted to later dates in the Americas than in Eurasia? Four groups of reasons suggest themselves: the later start, more limited suite of wild animals and plants available for domestication, greater barriers to diffusion, and possibly smaller or more isolated areas of dense human populations in the Americas than in Eurasia.

As for Eurasia's head start, humans have occupied Eurasia for about a million years, far longer than they have lived in the Americas. According to the archaeological evidence . . . , humans entered the Americas at Alaska only around 12,000 B.C., spread south of the Canadian ice sheets as Clovis hunters[6] a few centuries before 11,000 B.C., and reached the southern tip of South America by 10,000 B.C. Even if the disputed claims of older human occupation sites in the Americas prove valid, those postulated pre-Clovis inhabitants remained for unknown reasons very sparsely distributed and did not launch a Pleistocene proliferation of hunter-gatherer societies with expanding populations, technology, and art as in the Old World. Food production was already arising in the Fertile Crescent only 1,500 years after the time when Clovis-derived hunter-gatherers were just reaching southern South America.

Several possible consequences of that Eurasian head start deserve consideration. First, could it have taken a long time after 11,000 B.C. for the Americas to fill up with people? When one works out the likely numbers involved, one finds that this effect would make only a trivial contribution to the Americas' 5,000-year lag in food-producing villages. The calculations . . . tell us that even if a mere 100 pioneering Native Americans had crossed the Canadian border into the lower United States and increased at a rate of only 1 percent per year, they would have saturated the Americas with hunter-gatherers within 1,000 years. Spreading south at a mere one mile per month, those pioneers would have reached the southern tip of South America only 700 years after crossing the Canadian border. Those postulated rates of spread and of population increase are very low compared with actual known rates for peoples occupying previously uninhabited or sparsely inhabited lands. Hence the Americas were probably fully occupied by hunter-gatherers within a few centuries of the arrival of the first colonists.

Second, could a large part of the 5,000-year lag have represented the time that the first Americans required to become familiar with the new local plant species, animal species, and rock sources that they encountered? If we can again reason by analogy with New Guinean and Polynesian hunter-gatherers and farmers occupying previously unfamiliar environments — such as Maori colonists of New Zealand or Tudawhe colonists of New Guinea's Karimui Basin — the colonists probably discovered the best rock sources and learned to distinguish useful from poisonous wild plants and animals in much less than a century.

Third, what about Eurasians' head start in developing locally appropriate technology? The early farmers of the Fertile Crescent and China were heirs to the technology that behaviorially modern *Homo sapiens*[7] had been developing to exploit local resources in those areas for tens of thousands of years. For instance, the stone sickles, underground storage pits, and other technology that hunter-gatherers of the Fertile Crescent had been evolving to utilize wild cereals were available to the

---

[6] Paleo-Indians who take their name from Clovis, New Mexico, where their artifacts were found.

[7] Our species, *homo sapiens,* emerged between 400,000 and 200,000 years ago; fully modern humans, however, appeared approximately 125,000 years ago.

first cereal farmers of the Fertile Crescent. In contrast, the first settlers of the Americas arrived in Alaska with equipment appropriate to the Siberian Arctic tundra. They had to invent for themselves the equipment suitable to each new habitat they encountered. That technology lag may have contributed significantly to the delay in Native American developments.

An even more obvious factor behind the delay was the wild animals and plants available for domestication. . . . [W]hen hunter-gatherers adopt food production, it is not because they foresee the potential benefits awaiting their remote descendants but because incipient food production begins to offer advantages over the hunter-gatherer lifestyle. Early food production was less competitive with hunting-gathering in the Americas than in the Fertile Crescent or China, partly owing to the Americas' virtual lack of domesticable wild mammals. Hence early American farmers remained dependent on wild animals for animal protein and necessarily remained part-time hunter-gatherers, whereas in both the Fertile Crescent and China animal domestication followed plant domestication very closely in time to create a food producing package that quickly won out over hunting-gathering. In addition, Eurasian domestic animals made Eurasian agriculture itself more competitive by providing fertilizer, and eventually by drawing plows.

Features of American wild plants also contributed to the lesser competitiveness of Native American food production. That conclusion is clearest for the eastern United States, where less than a dozen crops were domesticated, including small-seeded grains but no large-seeded grains, pulses, fiber crops, or cultivated fruit or nut trees. It is also clear for Mesoamerica's staple grain of corn, which spread to become a dominant crop elsewhere in the Americas as well. Whereas the Fertile Crescent's wild wheat and barley evolved into crops with minimal changes and within a few centuries, wild teosinte[8] may have required several thousand years to evolve into corn, having to undergo drastic changes in its reproductive biology and energy allocation to seed production, loss of the seed's rock-hard casings, and an enormous increase in cob size.

As a result, even if one accepts the recently postulated later dates for the onset of Native American plant domestication, about 1,500 or 2,000 years would have elapsed between that onset (about 3000–2500 B.C.) and widespread year-round villages (1800–500 B.C.) in Mesoamerica, the inland Andes, and the eastern United States. Native American farming served for a long time just as a small supplement to food acquisition by hunting-gathering, and supported only a sparse population. If one accepts the traditional, earlier dates for the onset of American plant domestication, then 5,000 years instead of 1,500 or 2,000 years elapsed before food production supported villages. In contrast, villages were closely associated in time with the rise of food production in much of Eurasia. (The hunter-gatherer lifestyle itself was sufficiently productive to support villages even before the adoption of agriculture in parts of both hemispheres, such as Japan and the Fertile Crescent in the Old World, and coastal Ecuador and Amazonia in the New

---

[8] A tall Central American grass related to corn.

World.) The limitations imposed by locally available domesticates in the New World are well illustrated by the transformations of Native American societies themselves when other crops or animals arrived, whether from elsewhere in the Americas or from Eurasia. Examples include the effects of corn's arrival in the eastern United States and Amazonia, the llama's adoption in the northern Andes after its domestication to the south, and the horse's appearance in many parts of North and South America.

In addition to Eurasia's head start and wild animal and plant species, developments in Eurasia were also accelerated by the easier diffusion of animals, plants, ideas, technology, and people in Eurasia than in the Americas, as a result of several sets of geographic and ecological factors. Eurasia's east–west major axis, unlike the Americas' north–south major axis, permitted diffusion without change in latitude and associated environmental variables. In contrast to Eurasia's consistent east–west breadth, the New World was constricted over the whole length of Central America and especially at Panama. Not least, the Americas were more fragmented by areas unsuitable for food production or for dense human populations. These ecological barriers included the rain forests of the Panamanian isthmus separating Mesoamerican societies from Andean and Amazonian societies; the deserts of northern Mexico separating Mesoamerica from U.S. southwestern and southeastern societies; dry areas of Texas separating the U.S. Southwest from the Southeast; and the deserts and high mountains fencing off U.S. Pacific coast areas that would otherwise have been suitable for food production. As a result, there was no diffusion of domestic animals, writing, or political entities, and limited or slow diffusion of crops and technology, between the New World centers of Mesoamerica, the eastern United States, and the Andes and Amazonia. . . .

Thus, we have identified three sets of ultimate factors that tipped the advantage to European invaders of the Americas: Eurasia's long head start on human settlement; its more effective food production, resulting from greater availability of domesticable wild plants and especially of animals; and its less formidable geographic and ecological barriers to intracontinental diffusion. A fourth, more speculative ultimate factor is suggested by some puzzling non-inventions in the Americas: the non-inventions of writing and wheels in complex Andean societies, despite a time depth of those societies approximately equal to that of complex Mesoamerican societies that did make those inventions; and wheels' confinement to toys and their eventual disappearance in Mesoamerica, where they could presumably have been useful in human-powered wheelbarrows, as in China. These puzzles remind one of equally puzzling non-inventions, or else disappearances of inventions, in small isolated societies, including Aboriginal Tasmania, Aboriginal Australia, Japan, Polynesian islands, and the American Arctic. Of course, the Americas in aggregate are anything but small: their combined area is fully 76 percent that of Eurasia, and their human population as of A.D. 1492 was probably also a large fraction of Eurasia's. But the Americas, as we have seen, are broken up into "islands" of societies with tenuous connections to each other. Perhaps the histories of Native American wheels and writing exemplify the principles illustrated in a more extreme form by true island societies.

After at least 13,000 years of separate developments, advanced American and Eurasian societies finally collided within the last thousand years. Until then, the sole contacts between human societies of the Old and the New Worlds had involved the hunter-gatherers on opposite sides of the Bering Strait.

There were no Native American attempts to colonize Eurasia, except at the Bering Strait, where a small population of Inuit (Eskimos) derived from Alaska established itself across the strait on the opposite Siberian coast. The first documented Eurasian attempt to colonize the Americas was by the Norse at Arctic and sub-Arctic latitudes. . . . Norse from Norway colonized Iceland in A.D. 874, then Norse from Iceland colonized Greenland in A.D. 986, and finally Norse from Greenland repeatedly visited the northeastern coast of North America between about A.D. 1000 and 1350. The sole Norse archaeological site discovered in the Americas is on Newfoundland, possibly the region described as Vinland in Norse sagas, but these also mention landings evidently farther north, on the coasts of Labrador and Baffin Island.

Iceland's climate permitted herding and extremely limited agriculture, and its area was sufficient to support a Norse-derived population that has persisted to this day. But most of Greenland is covered by an ice cap, and even the two most favorable coastal fjords were marginal for Norse food production. The Greenland Norse population never exceeded a few thousand. It remained dependent on imports of food and iron from Norway, and of timber from the Labrador coast. Unlike Easter Island and other remote Polynesian islands, Greenland could not support a self-sufficient food-producing society, though it did support self-sufficient Inuit hunter-gatherer populations before, during, and after the Norse occupation period. The populations of Iceland and Norway themselves were too small and too poor for them to continue their support of the Greenland Norse population.

In the Little Ice Age that began in the 13th century, the cooling of the North Atlantic made food production in Greenland, and Norse voyaging to Greenland from Norway or Iceland, even more marginal than before. The Greenlanders' last known contact with Europeans came in 1410 with an Icelandic ship that arrived after being blown off course. When Europeans finally began again to visit Greenland in 1577, its Norse colony no longer existed, having evidently disappeared without any record during the 15th century.

But the coast of North America lay effectively beyond the reach of ships sailing directly from Norway itself, given Norse ship technology of the period A.D. 986–1410. The Norse visits were instead launched from the Greenland colony, separated from North America only by the 200-mile width of Davis Strait. However, the prospect of that tiny marginal colony's sustaining an exploration, conquest, and settlement of the Americas was nil. Even the sole Norse site located on Newfoundland apparently represents no more than a winter camp occupied by a few dozen people for a few years. The Norse sagas describe attacks on their Vinland camp by people termed Skraelings, evidently either Newfoundland Indians or Dorset Eskimos.

The fate of the Greenland colony, medieval Europe's most remote outpost, remains one of archaeology's romantic mysteries. Did the last Greenland Norse starve to death, attempt to sail off, intermarry with Eskimos, or succumb to disease or Eskimo arrows? While those questions of proximate cause remain unanswered, the ultimate reasons why Norse colonization of Greenland and America failed are abundantly clear. It failed because the source (Norway), the targets (Greenland and Newfoundland), and the time (A.D. 986–1410) guaranteed that Europe's potential advantages of food production, technology, and political organization could not be applied effectively. At latitudes too high for much food production, the iron tools of a few Norse, weakly supported by one of Europe's poorer states, were no match for the stone, bone, and wooden tools of Eskimo and Indian hunter-gatherers, the world's greatest masters of Arctic survival skills.

The second Eurasian attempt to colonize the Americas succeeded because it involved a source, target, latitude, and time that allowed Europe's potential advantages to be exerted effectively. Spain, unlike Norway, was rich and populous enough to support exploration and subsidize colonies. Spanish landfalls in the Americas were at subtropical latitudes highly suitable for food production, based at first mostly on Native American crops but also on Eurasian domestic animals, especially cattle and horses. Spain's transatlantic colonial enterprise began in 1492, at the end of a century of rapid development of European oceangoing ship technology, which by then incorporated advances in navigation, sails, and ship design developed by Old World societies (Islam, India, China, and Indonesia) in the Indian Ocean. As a result, ships built and manned in Spain itself were able to sail to the West Indies; there was nothing equivalent to the Greenland bottleneck that had throttled Norse colonization. Spain's New World colonies were soon joined by those of half a dozen other European states.

The first European settlements in the Americas, beginning with the one founded by Columbus in 1492, were in the West Indies. The island Indians, whose estimated population at the time of their "discovery" exceeded a million, were rapidly exterminated on most islands by disease, dispossession, enslavement, warfare, and casual murder. Around 1508 the first colony was founded on the American mainland, at the Isthmus of Panama. Conquest of the two large mainland empires, those of the Aztecs and Incas, followed in 1519–1520 and 1532–1533, respectively. In both conquests European-transmitted epidemics (probably smallpox) made major contributions, by killing the emperors themselves, as well as a large fraction of the population. The overwhelming military superiority of even tiny numbers of mounted Spaniards, together with their political skills at exploiting divisions within the native population, did the rest. European conquest of the remaining native states of Central America and northern South America followed during the 16th and 17th centuries.

As for the most advanced native societies of North America, those of the U.S. Southeast and the Mississippi River system, their destruction was accomplished largely by germs alone, introduced by early European explorers and advancing ahead of them. As Europeans spread throughout the Americas, many other native societies, such as the Mandans of the Great Plains and the Sadlermiut Eskimos of the Arctic, were also wiped out by disease, without need for military action. Populous native societies not thereby eliminated were destroyed in the same way the Aztecs and Incas had been — by full-scale wars, increasingly waged by professional European soldiers and their native allies. Those soldiers were backed by the political organizations initially of the European mother countries, then of the European colonial governments in the New World, and finally of the independent neo-European states that succeeded the colonial governments.

Smaller native societies were destroyed more casually, by small-scale raids and murders carried out by private citizens. For instance, California's native hunter-gatherers initially numbered about 200,000 in aggregate, but they were splintered among a hundred tribelets, none of which required a war to be defeated. Most of those tribelets were killed off or dispossessed during or soon after the California gold rush of 1848–1852, when large numbers of immigrants flooded the state. As one example, the Yahi tribelet of northern California, numbering about 2,000 and lacking firearms, was destroyed in four raids by armed white settlers: a dawn raid on a Yahi village carried out by 17 settlers on August 6, 1865; a massacre of Yahis surprised in a ravine in 1866; a massacre of 33 Yahis tracked to a cave around 1867; and a final massacre of about 30 Yahis trapped in another cave by 4 cowboys around 1868. Many Amazonian Indian groups were similarly eliminated by private settlers during the rubber boom of the late 19th and early 20th centuries. The final stages of the conquest are being played out in the present decade, as the Yanomamo and other Amazonian Indian societies that remain independent are succumbing to disease, being murdered by miners, or being brought under control by missionaries or government agencies.

The end result has been the elimination of populous Native American societies from most temperate areas suitable for European food production and physiology. In North America those that survived as sizable intact communities now live mostly on reservations or other lands considered undesirable for European food production and mining, such as the Arctic and arid areas of the U.S. West. Native Americans in many tropical areas have been replaced by immigrants from the Old World tropics (especially black Africans, along with Asian Indians and Javanese in Suriname).

In parts of Central America and the Andes, the Native Americans were originally so numerous that, even after epidemics and wars, much of the population today remains Native American or mixed. That is especially true at high altitudes in the Andes, where genetically European women have physiological difficulties even in reproducing, and where native Andean crops still offer the most suitable basis for food production. However, even where Native Americans do survive, there has been extensive replacement of their culture and languages with those of the Old World. Of the hundreds of Native American languages originally spoken in North America, all except 187 are no longer spoken at all, and 149 of these last 187 are moribund in the sense that they are being spoken only by old people and no longer learned by children. Of the approximately 40 New World nations, all now have an Indo-European language or creole as the official language. Even in the countries with the largest surviving Native American populations, such as Peru, Bolivia, Mexico, and Guatemala, a glance at photographs of political and business leaders shows that they are disproportionately Europeans, while several Caribbean nations have black African leaders and Guyana has had Asian Indian leaders.

The original Native American population has been reduced by a debated large percentage: estimates for North America range up to 95 percent. But the total human population of the Americas is now approximately ten times what it was in 1492, because of arrivals of Old World peoples (Europeans, Africans, and Asians). The Americas' population now consists of a mixture of peoples originating from all continents except Australia. That demographic shift of the last 500 years — the most massive shift on any continent except Australia — has its ultimate roots in developments between about 11,000 B.C. and A.D. 1.

THE SPANISH INQUISITION
AND THE PEOPLE
Henry Kamen

Many people think the Spanish Inquisition (a tribunal created in 1478 to combat heresy, or unorthodox beliefs) was a cruel and barbaric establishment persecuting, torturing, and burning thousands of victims who thought or behaved
contrary to the autocratic Catholic Church or who were Jews or Muslims. This
one-sided and erroneous image owes much to the so-called "Black Legend"
spawned by the propaganda of Protestants, especially in England, and originated in the sixteenth century when Protestant England and Catholic Spain were
at war. Protestants linked the often bestial Spanish treatment of Indians in the
New World to the alleged obscurantism and inhumanity of Spaniards and their
institutions, notably the Inquisition and Roman Catholicism. Indeed, in the nineteenth and even in the twentieth century, historians shared this interpretation,
even if their writings were usually nuanced.

Henry Kamen, professor of the Higher Council for Scientific Research in Barcelona, wrote in 1965 a revisionist book, *The Spanish Inquisition,* where he argues that the Inquisition was not so evil, efficient, and bloodthirsty as previously
thought. He compares the Spanish Inquisition favorably to other legal systems,
even in Protestant countries. Not all historians accept his arguments and some
contend that he pushes his points in challenging the standard conception of the
Spanish Inquisition. However, his command of archival sources and the cogency
of his arguments force us to reevaluate the stereotypical image of the Inquisition.

The excerpt below comes from the third edition of Kamen's book on the
Spanish Inquisition, where he tones down some of his initial views and presents
a lucid picture of its procedures and limitations. It is clear from Professor
Kamen's research that the Spanish Inquisition was not monolithic or all-powerful,
that it primarily affected urban centers, that many Spaniards did not encounter
its courts, that its activities changed over time (particularly after the fifteenth
century, when it had persecuted vigorously converted Jews), that it used torture
sparingly, and that it did not cause Spanish intellectual decline. What offenses

Henry Kamen, *The Spanish Inquisition* (London: Weidenfeld & Nicolson, 1997), 255–282.

did the Inquisition try before its tribunals? What major problems did the Inquisition see among the people and the clergy? How religious were the people? What did the Spanish population think of the Inquisition? Do you know of current societies in the world today whose religious courts search out and punish people for their beliefs rather than for any criminal activities? In what areas of life do political and religious leaders in the West seek to impose a single, "correct" way of thinking?

Because the Inquisition had been brought into existence to combat the "heretical depravity" of judaizers,[1] for a long time it paid little attention to other offences. Secondary offences were always listed in accusations, but mainly to back up the main crime. The Aragonese notary Dionis Ginot, burnt in effigy at Saragossa in 1486, was condemned for both Judaism and bigamy. Inevitably, judaizers were frequently accused of a wide range of other offences such as atheism and usury. When dealing with these matters, the Inquisition came into contact with the ordinary misdemeanours of the mass of the Spanish people.

Conversos[2] were often accused of atheism, a perfectly credible accusation in view of the strange cultural situation in which many found themselves, living . . . "neither in one law nor the other." . . . Indeed, what was particularly alarming was not simply that true religion may have been perverted by heresy, but that in many parts of Spain it could be doubted whether there was any true religion at all.

It was this realization that moved one inquisitor to argue in 1572 that Galicia should have its own Inquisition:

> If any part of these realms needs an Inquisition it is Galicia, which lacks the religion that there is in Old Castile, has no priests or lettered persons or impressive churches or people who are used to going to mass and hearing sermons. . . . They are superstitious and the benefices so poor that as a result there are not enough clergy.

"If the Holy Office had not come to this realm," a local priest wrote later, "some of these people would have been like those in England."

The judgments of the inquisitor obviously called in question both the nature and the depth of religious belief in Spain. Centuries away from that time, it is difficult to assess the true situation. Over much of Spain Christianity was still only a veneer. The religion of the people remained backward, despite gestures of reform by Cisneros[3] and other prelates. It was still a period of vague theology, irregular religious

---

[1] Former Jews who practiced Judaism secretly.

[2] "Converts," Spanish Jews and Muslims who converted to Catholicism and their descendants; also known as New Christians.

[3] Cardinal Francisco Jiménez de Cisneros (1436–1517), archbishop of Toledo and inquisitor general (head of the Spanish Inquisition) from 1507.

practice, non-residence of both bishops and clergy, and widespread ignorance of the faith among both priests and parishioners. Over vast areas of Spain . . . the people combined formal religion and folk superstition in their everyday attempt to survive against the onslaught of climate and mortality. The standard religious unit was the rural parish, coinciding normally with the limits of the village. Over four-fifths of Spain's population lived in this environment, beyond the reach of the big towns to which villagers only went on market days to sell their produce. As religious reformers and inquisitors quickly found out, the rural parishes were close-knit communities with their own special type of religion and their own saints. They were also hostile to any attempt by outsiders — whether clergy or townspeople — to intrude into their way of life.

Clergy recognized that the people were lax in their observance of religion, and woefully ignorant about their faith. In Vizcaya in 1539 an inquisitor reported that "I found men aged ninety years who did not know the Hail Mary[4] or how to make the sign of the cross." In the town of Bilbao, stated another in 1547, "the parish priests and vicars who live there report that one in twelve of the souls there never goes to confession." In the north of Aragon, reported another colleague in 1549, there were many villages "that have never had sight of nor contact with Church or Inquisition."

The Holy Office[5] was far from being the only institution interested in the religious life of Spaniards. Already by the late fifteenth century there had been three major channels through which changes were being introduced into peninsular religion: the reforms of religious orders, instanced on one hand by the remarkable growth of the Jeronimite[6] order and on the other by imposition of the reformist Observance[7] on the mendicant orders;[8] the interest of humanist bishops in reforming the lives of their clergy and people, as shown for example by the synodal decrees of the see of Toledo under Alonso Carrillo[9] and Cisneros: and the new literature of spirituality exemplified in García de Cisneros'[10] *Exercises in the Spiritual Life* (1500). As elsewhere in Catholic Europe, humanist reformers were well aware that theirs was an elite movement that would take time to filter down into the life of the people. Efforts were, however, being made by the orders. From 1518 the Dominicans[11] were active in the remote countryside of Asturias. The principal

---

[4] A Roman Catholic prayer to the Virgin Mary, known as the Angelic Salutation.

[5] Another name for the Inquisition.

[6] Established in Spain in the fourteenth century, the Jeronimites (the order of St. Jerome) forbade after 1485 the entry into the order of conversos or their descendants.

[7] Members of the Franciscans (see note 15) who strove to "observe" the severe rule of St. Francis (1182–1226).

[8] Catholic religious orders that could not own property in common and whose members (friars) were not tied to a monastery, but were allowed to beg or work to support themselves.

[9] 1410–1482, cardinal and archbishop of Toledo.

[10] Gárciá de Cisneros (ca. 1456–1510), an abbot.

[11] The Dominicans were a Roman Catholic religious order founded in 1220.

impulse to popular missions came from the growth of the Jesuits[12] in the 1540s. At the same time, several reforming bishops tried to introduce changes into their dioceses. It was an uphill task. In Barcelona, Francisco Borja,[13] at the time Duke of Gandía and viceroy of Catalonia, worked hand in hand with reforming bishops but commented on "the little that has been achieved, both in the time of queen Isabella[14] and in our own."

From the early century a patient effort of evangelization was made. In America in 1524 a group of Franciscan[15] missionaries, numbering twelve in deliberate imitation of the early apostles, set out to convert Mexico. In 1525 the Admiral of Castile, Fadrique Enríquez, drew up a plan to recruit twelve apostles to convert his estates at Medina de Rioseco to Christianity. The problem in both cases was perceived as being the same: there were "Indies" of unbelief no less in Spain than in the New World. From the 1540s at least, the Church authorities became concerned not only with the problem of converting the Moriscos[16] but also with that of bringing the unchristianized parts of the country back into the fold. In Santiago in 1543 the diocesan visitor reported that "parishioners suffer greatly from the ignorance of their curates and rectors";[17] in Navarre in 1544 ignorant clergy "cause great harm to the consciences of these poor people." Many rural parishes lacked clergy, particularly in Catalonia and the Basque country, where ignorance of the language made it difficult for priests to communicate with their flock. The immense confusion of jurisdictions presented a major obstacle: churches, monasteries, orders, secular lords, bishops, towns, the Inquisition — all disputed each other's authority.

The piecemeal efforts to reform religion in the early century were given a unity of purpose by the coming of the Counter Reformation[18] and the issue in 1564 of the decrees of Trent.[19] Concerned to keep religious change under his control, the king in 1565 ordered the holding of Church councils in the principal sees of the monarchy. Subsequent proposals for reform involved the collaboration of the Inquisition.

The visitations made by inquisitors were not an isolated effort. Over the same period many Spanish clergy also began carrying out visitations of their dioceses

---

[12] Members of the Society of Jesus, a Roman Catholic religious order established in 1540.

[13] After a political career, he joined the Jesuits, worked to establish the order in Spain and Portugal, and subsequently became general (head) of the Society of Jesus (1510–1572).

[14] Isabella I (1451–1504), queen of Castile; ruled Spain with Ferdinand of Aragon after their marriage in 1479.

[15] The Franciscans were a Roman Catholic religious order founded in 1209.

[16] Moors who converted to Catholicism.

[17] A curate was a clergyman who assists the rector, the chief priest of a parish.

[18] The Roman Catholic Church's reform movement and resurgence that combated the Protestant churches in the sixteenth century.

[19] The Council of Trent, Roman Catholic Church council (1545–1563) that clarified doctrines and reformed the church.

and religious houses. The tasks did not overlap. Bishops were primarily concerned with getting good clergy and decent churches; the Inquisition was concerned with getting orthodox worshippers. Jesuits made Spain into a mission field. "This land," a canon of Oviedo wrote in 1568 to Borja, "is in extreme need of good labourers, such as we trust are those in the Society of Jesus." Another wrote in the same year: "There are no Indies where you will suffer greater dangers and miseries, or which could more need to hear the word of God, than these Asturias." The mission field soon encompassed all of Spain. The Jesuit Pedro de León, who worked all over Andalusia and Extremadura, wrote that "since I began in the year 1582, and up to now in 1615, there has not been a single year in which I have not been on some mission, and on two or three in some years." The need was stressed by an earlier Jesuit, reporting on the inhabitants of villages near Huelva: "many live in caves, without priests or sacraments; so ignorant that some cannot make the sign of the cross; in their dress and way of life very like Indians."

By venturing into the mission field, the Inquisition began to take cognizance of some offences that had formerly been poorly policed. . . . [W]hereas in the first phase of its history the tribunal had been concerned almost exclusively with conversos, in the next century its attention was focused primarily on Old Christians.[20] Nearly two-thirds of those detained by the Holy Office in this period were ordinary Catholic Spaniards, unconnected with formal heresy or with the minority cultures. The new policy of directing attention to Old Christians cannot be viewed cynically as a desperate move to find sources of revenue. The prosecuted were invariably humble and poor, and the tribunal's financial position was in any case better after the mid-sixteenth century.

The almost entire absence of heresy in much of Spain during the peak years of religious conflict in Europe, can be illustrated by . . . diagrams . . . showing the activity of the Inquisition among Catalans.

The Catalans represented just over half of the cases dealt with by the Inquisition in those years. Yet allegations of heresy were never made against them, only against the French and others of non-Catalan origin. A fifth of the Catalans were accused of sexual offences (mainly bigamy, bestiality and rash statements), 15 per cent were accused of blasphemy ("moral control"), 19 per cent were clergy who had seduced women or said offensive things in their sermons, 13 per cent were laymen who had made anticlerical statements or robbed churches, 11 per cent were people who had dabbled in witchcraft, a further 20 per cent represented officials of the Inquisition who had committed offences or laymen who had impeded them in their duties, and two per cent were guilty of stealing horses.

By its collaboration with the campaigns of bishops, clergy and religious orders among the native population, the Inquisition contributed actively to promoting the religious reforms favoured by the Counter Reformation in Spain. But its role was always auxiliary, and seldom decisive; it helped other Church and civil

---

[20] Not conversos; Spaniards not descended from Jewish and Muslim converts.

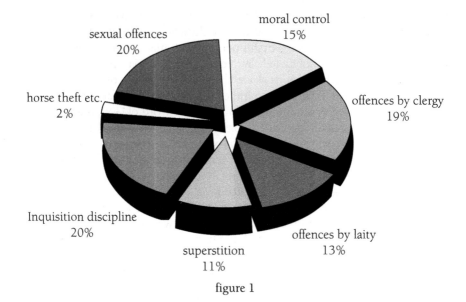

figure 1

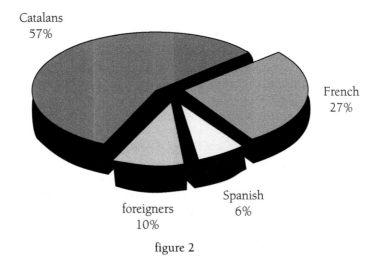

figure 2

Tribunal of Barcelona, showing 1,735 cases tried over the years 1578–1635. Figure 1: the offences of 996 Catalans; figure 2: the 1,735 cases by national category

courts to enquire into certain offences, but seldom claimed exclusive jurisdiction over those offences. As a result, it is doubtful whether its contribution was as significant or successful as that of other branches of the Church. . . . Because prosecutions in the Inquisition were initiated from below, the tribunal was in a peculiarly strong position to affect and mould popular culture, and the volume of prosecutions in some areas may suggest that it was carrying out its task successfully. The Holy Office, however, suffered from at least one major advantage: it was always an alien body. Bishops, through their parish priests, were directly linked to the roots of community feeling, and were able to carry out a considerable programme of religious change based on persuasion. The Inquisition, by contrast, was exclusively a punishing body. It was operated, moreover, by outsiders (often unable to speak the local language), and though feared was never loved. As a result, its successes were always flawed.

When not directly occupied with the alleged heresies of conversos and Moriscos, the Holy Office during the sixteenth and seventeenth centuries dedicated itself in great measure to disciplining the Old Christian population. It paid attention, above all, to the attitudes, beliefs and actions of lay people; but it also looked at the role of the clergy in these same matters. Its activity was, in the Europe of that day, by no means exceptional. Many Protestant churches, above all the Calvinists, also tried to enforce norms of belief and conduct. Their methods were sometimes harsh, and often criticized as "inquisitorial."

The entry of the tribunal into the area of disciplining the laity can be dated with some precision. From the mid-sixteenth century reformist clergy in Spain, inspired in part by the Jesuits, became concerned about the low levels of moral and spiritual life. A few tribunals, led by that of Toledo, showed that they were willing to take action against non-Christian conduct. From the 1560s, prosecutions multiplied.

The overwhelming bulk of prosecutions was for purely verbal offences. The inquisitors themselves classified these as "propositions." Ordinary people who in casual conversation, or in moments of anger or stress, expressed sentiments that offended their neighbours, were likely to find themselves denounced to the Inquisition and correspondingly disciplined. A broad range of themes might be involved. Statements about clergy and the Church, about aspects of belief and about sexuality, were among the most common. In particular, persistent blasphemy and affirmations about "simple fornication" were treated seriously. The offence arose less with the words than with the intention behind them and the implicit danger to faith and morals.

We should be clear about the place of verbal offences in traditional culture. In a large pre-literate age, all important social affirmations — such as personal pledges or court testimony — were made orally. "Whole aspects of social life," it has been pointed out for mediaeval Europe [by historian Marc Bloch in *Feudal Society*], "were only very imperfectly covered by texts, and often not at all . . . The majority of courts contented themselves with purely oral decisions." A man's spoken word was his bond. Judicial evidence consisted of what some people said about others. By the same token, negative declarations — insults, slander — were usually verbal. Verbal statements directed against one's neighbours and against God or religion were treated with severity by both state and Church authorities, for they disturbed the peace of the community. All legal tribunals of the day, including the Holy Office, therefore paid attention to the consequences of the spoken word. The inquisitors never went out looking for "propositions." Their job was not the wholly impossible one of regulating what Spaniards said. Nor were they trying to impose a form of social control. In practice, it was members of the public who, out of malice or (very occasionally) out of zeal, took the trouble to report offensive statements. Nearly one-third of the 996 Catalans disciplined by the Inquisition between 1578 and 1635, were in trouble for what they had said rather than for anything they did.

In many cases the Inquisition was called in as a social arbiter, to keep the peace or to resolve disputes. It was a valuable function that more normally was performed by the Church, but which in special cases might call for the intervention of the inquisitors. In 1632, for example, they were asked to intervene in a village near Montserrat (Catalonia), where bitter personal quarrels erupted one day into scandalous conduct at Sunday mass. In the same year they intervened in a quarrel between the parish priest of a village near Girona, and the local familiar. Both men were summoned and ordered to mend their conduct to each other.

The Inquisition joined other Church authorities in demanding more respect for the sacred. Blasphemy, or disrespect to sacred things, was at the time a public offence against God and punishable by both state and Church. In time, the tribunal gave the term a very broad definition, provoking protests by the Cortes[21] of both Castile and Aragon. The Cortes of Madrid in 1534 asked specifically that cases of blasphemy be reserved to the secular courts alone. The Holy Office continued, however, to intervene in the offence, punishing bad language according to the gravity of the context. Blasphemous oaths during a game of dice, sexual advances to a girl during a religious procession, refusal to abstain from meat on Fridays, obscene references to the Virgin, wilful failure to go to mass: these were typical of the thousands of cases disciplined by the Inquisition. . . .

The attempt to discipline words and actions was time-consuming, and formed the principal activity of inquisitors during their visitations in this period. The problem was particularly grave in rural areas. In Galicia in 1585, for example, the inquisitors admitted that doubts about the presence of Christ in the sacrament were widespread, but "more out of ignorance than malice," and that questioning of the virginity of Mary was "through sheer thickheadedness rather than out of a wish to offend." They had the case of the man in a tavern who, when a priest present claimed to be able to change bread into the body of Christ, exclaimed in unbelief, "Go on! God's in heaven and not in that host which you eat at mass!" In Granada in 1595, a shepherd from the village of Alhama claimed not to believe in confession and said to his friends: "What sort of confession is it that you make to a priest who is as much of a sinner as I? Perfect confession is made only to God." The inquisitors concluded that "he seemed very rustic and ignorant and with little or no capacity of understanding," and sent him to a monastery to be educated. Rather than making its sentences lighter because of the low degree of religious understanding in rural areas, the Inquisition increased its punishments in order to achieve greater disciplinary effect. Thus every type of expression, whether mumbled by a drunkard in a tavern or preached by an ignorant priest from the pulpit, that was considered offensive, blasphemous, irreverent or heretical, was — if denounced — carefully examined by the Holy Office. It was at the level of ver-

[21] Representative assembly.

bal offences rather than heretical acts that the Inquisition came most into contact with the ordinary people of Spain for the greater part of its history.

For those who were arrested instead of being simply penanced during a visitation, there was normally a close examination in the basic elements of belief. Prisoners were asked to recite in Castilian the Our Father, Hail Mary, Credo,[22] Salve Regina[23] and the ten commandments, as well as other statements of belief. The interrogatory seems to have come into use in the 1540s, and provides useful evidence of the extent to which ordinary Spaniards were instructed in the faith. An analysis of 747 interrogations from the tribunal of Toledo suggests, it has been argued, that there was an improvement in knowledge of the essentials during the late sixteenth century. Before 1550 only about forty per cent of those questioned were able to repeat the basic prayers; by the 1590s this had risen to nearly seventy per cent. Since the test was not carried out on the same people in both periods, however, no reliable comparison can be made. In default of statistical proof, we must fall back on simple impressions. Evidence from the Toledo Inquisition papers of the late seventeenth century suggests that levels of religious knowledge were fairly high. Scores of accused from the lower classes and from rural areas enjoyed a basic knowledge of the prayers of the Church, and all were able to recite the Our Father and Hail Mary. . . .

If an improvement in elementary religious knowledge really happened, it was certainly not general. In parts of Spain that did not enjoy the density of clergy and schools to be found in Madrid and Toledo, ignorance was still the order of the day. The Church set up schools, made sermons obligatory and enforced recitation of prayers at mass. Even in its negative disciplinary role, the Inquisition made some contribution to the evolution of Spanish religion. It attempted to impose on Spaniards a new respect for the sacred, notably in art, in public devotions and in sermons. This can be seen in the other side of the tribunal's disciplining activity: its attempt to control the clergy.

Clergy were encouraged to put their churches in order. Diocesan synods at Granada in 1573 and Pamplona in 1591 were among those which ordered the removal and burial of unseemly church images. The Inquisition, likewise, attempted where it could to censor religious imagery. In Seville in the early seventeenth century it recruited the artist Francisco Pacheco[24] to comment on the suitability of public imagery. The attempt to regulate art was usually futile; there was no obvious way to influence taste. . . .

Public devotions were generally under the supervision of the bishops, but here too the Inquisition had a role. It helped to repress devotional excesses, such as credulity about visions of the Virgin. The celebration of pilgrimages and of fiestas such as Corpus Christi[25] was regulated by the episcopate. But written works,

---

[22] The Apostles' Creed, the Roman Catholic profession of faith.

[23] "Hail, Holy Queen," a Catholic hymn.

[24] Spanish painter, 1571–1654.

[25] A Roman Catholic festival instituted in the thirteenth century to honor the Blessed Sacrament (believed to be the body of Jesus).

such as the text of *autos sacramentales*[26] (plays performed for Corpus), normally had to be approved by the Inquisition, creating occasional conflicts with writers. On the other hand, the tribunal steadfastly refused to be drawn into the debate over whether theatres were immoral and should be banned. It is well known that substantial Counter-Reformation opinion, especially among the Jesuits, was in favour of shutting theatres; and indeed they were shut periodically from 1597 onwards. But theatres were normally under the control of the council of Castile, not of the Holy Office, and the only way the latter could express an opinion was when plays were printed. Even then it kept clear of the theatre, and the major dramatists of the Golden Age[27] were untouched. No play by Lope de Vega,[28] for example, was interfered with until 1801. When the Inquisition did tread into the field, by requiring expurgations (in the 1707 Index)[29] in the Jesuit Camargo's *Discourse on the Theatre* (1689), it explained that the ban was "until changes are made; but the Holy Office does not by prohibiting this book intend to comment on or condemn either of the opinions on the desirability or undesirability of seeing, reading, writing or performing plays."

A highly significant area of activity was sermons. No form of propaganda in the Counter Reformation was more widely used than the spoken word, in view of the high levels of illiteracy. Correspondingly, in no other form of communication did the Inquisition interfere more frequently. Sermons were to the public of those days what television is to the twentieth century: the most direct form of control over opinion. The impact of the Holy Office on sermons — among those denounced to it were sermons by Carranza[30] and Fray Francisco Ortiz[31] — was perhaps even more decisive than its impact on printed literature. Bishops normally welcomed intervention by the inquisitors, for they themselves had little or no machinery with which to control some of the absurdities preached from the pulpits of their clergy. Occasionally, inquisitorial intervention took on political tones. The tribunal of Llerena in 1606 prosecuted Diego Díaz, priest of Torre de Don Miguel, for preaching (in Portuguese) that God had not died for Castilians: and the tribunal of Barcelona in 1666 prosecuted a priest of Reus for having declared that "he would prefer to be in hell beside a Frenchman than in heaven beside a Castilian." More normally, the problem lay in preachers who got carried away by their own eloquence or who were shaky in their theology, such as the Cistercian[32] Maestro Cortes who in 1683 put the glories of Mary above those of the Sacrament,

---

[26] "Sacramental ordinances," entertainment similar to English morality plays.

[27] Sixteenth and early seventeenth centuries.

[28] Felix Lope de Vega Carpio (1562–1635), playwright and poet.

[29] A list of prohibited books issued by the Roman Catholic Church.

[30] Bartolomé Carranza (1503–1575), archbishop of Toledo; the Inquisition arrested him on suspicion of Lutheranism.

[31] Sixteenth-century Franciscan preacher and mystic.

[32] A strict Roman Catholic religious order founded in 1098.

or the priest in Tuy who on Holy Thursday told his flock that in the Sacrament they were celebrating only the semblance of God, whose real presence was above in heaven.

Both laity and clergy were affected by another major sphere into which the inquisitors intruded: their sexual life. Bishops after the Council of Trent made extensive efforts in Spain to impose the official view on the sanctity of matrimony. In Barcelona after 1570, for example, licences to marry could not be issued without both parties being formally instructed in religion, and the bishops issued decrees against the common practice of young people living together after betrothal. The Inquisition, for its part, enforced post-Tridentine morality by attempting to stamp out the widespread conviction that "simple fornication" was no sin, and it also prosecuted various sexual offences including bigamy.

"Simple fornication," in early modern Spain, was voluntary intercourse between two unmarried adults. The Inquisition took an interest in this and other sexual questions not because of the sexual act in itself but because of the implied disrespect for the sacrament of matrimony. In pre-Tridentine Spain, a low level of religious awareness and the persistence of traditional moral practices combined to produce far greater sexual freedom among all age groups than is commonly imagined. This was reflected in the remarkably widespread view that sex ("simple fornication") was not wrong if it broke no rules. By extension, concubinage was not wrong, nor was it wrong for an unmarried adult to have sex with a prostitute. The absence of sexual guilt was shared by laity and clergy alike. The inquisitors of Toledo were actively preoccupied with the problem, and from 1573 the Suprema[33] encouraged other tribunals to pursue the matter. In Toledo prosecutions for statements about simple fornication constituted a fifth of all prosecutions in 1566–70, and a quarter in 1601–5. An indication that the imposition of the new morality was, in some measure, an imposition of urban rigour on rural laxity comes from Galicia, where propositions on fornication (such as that of Alonso de Meixide, who maintained "that in his village it had never been a sin to have carnal intercourse between unmarried men and women") were more commonly found among the peasantry. This was so much the case that the inquisitors there explained in 1585 that "the reason why we are less strict with fornicators is because we know from experience that most of those we arrest in these lands, where there is a great lack of doctrine especially in the rural areas, speak from stupidity and ignorance and not from a wish to commit heresy."

In Barcelona in 1599 a man warned a prostitute that what she did was a sin, to which she replied that "it is no sin since we are both unmarried." He promptly denounced her to the inquisitors, who dismissed the matter but warned her "to learn the catechism and come to the Inquisition every two weeks until she has learnt it." The problem, evidently, arose from the existence of brothels, which operated with public licence in most parts of Spain. Since the city authorities continued to permit them, and they did their best business during religious festivals,

---

[33] "The Council of the Supreme and General Inquisition," located in Madrid after 1608.

all that the clergy could do was to try to convince both prostitutes and their customers of the sinfulness of their actions. It did not help when priests with ulterior motives told attractive women in the parish that "fornication is no sin."

The Inquisition continued its sexual campaign with a drive against bigamy. Because the offence was normally punishable in civil and Church courts, there were constant protests against the Inquisition's interference. The Catalan concordia[34] of 1512, for example, laid down that bishops alone should try bigamy cases unless heresy was involved. The Inquisition, however, argued that bigamy implied a measure of heresy, since it questioned the sacredness of matrimony; it therefore continued its activity despite repeated protests from the Cortes of Aragon. Nor was the Holy Office wasting its time on an offence of negligible importance. Bigamy was surprisingly frequent, possibly because it represented, in a society that did not permit divorce, one alternative to an unsatisfactory marriage. In most tribunals, about five per cent of cases tried by the Inquisition were for bigamy. From the mid-sixteenth century five years in the galleys became the standard punishment for men, a much lighter penalty than that meted out by secular courts. Women, no less than men, were frequent bigamists. Many did not feel they were committing wrong. . . .

The moral behaviour of clergy had preoccupied Church reformers through the centuries, and bishops were happy to obtain the cooperation of the Inquisition. The Council of Trent had placed clerical reform at the forefront of its programme. Bishops defined the duties of priests strictly and cut back their public role (they could no longer, for example, go to taverns or wedding-feasts). It was inevitably easier to pass decrees than to enforce them, and clergy continued to use their privileged position to disport themselves, break the laws and seduce parishioners. They also continued the long-standing custom of keeping women. The problem, attended to by both Church courts and Inquisition, was insoluble. In the two years 1561–2 the vicar general[35] of Barcelona had to issue fifty-seven warnings to clergy of the diocese over their concubines. . . .

The Inquisition was particularly interested in the problem of solicitation during confession. The confession-box as we know it today did not come into use in the Church until the late sixteenth century, before which there was no physical barrier between a confessor and a penitent, so that occasions for sin could easily arise. The frequent scandals caused Fernando de Valdés[36] in 1561 to obtain authority from Pius IV[37] for the Inquisition to exercise control over cases of solicitation, which were interpreted as heresy because they misused the sacrament of penance. Though accused confessors were usually guilty it is quite clear that the confessant was sometimes to blame. . . . In Valencia the parish priest of Beniganim was tried in 1608 for having solicited twenty-nine women, most of them unmar-

---

[34] Agreement.

[35] A priest whom a bishop appoints to represent him in the administration of the diocese.

[36] 1483–1568, archbishop of Seville and inquisitor general since 1547.

[37] Pope from 1559 to 1565.

ried, "with lascivious and amorous invitations to perform filthy and immoral acts."

There were many cases of marginal sexuality in which the Inquisition also intervened. Sodomy was the most significant. Homosexuality in the Middle Ages was treated as the ultimate crime against morality: the standard definitions of it refer to the "abominable" or the "unspeakable" crime. The usual punishment was burning alive or, in Spain, castration and stoning to death. Under Ferdinand[38] and Isabella the punishment was changed to burning alive and confiscation of property. Since the mediaeval Inquisition had exercised jurisdiction over sodomy, the Spanish tribunal seems to have begun to do so; but in 1509 the Suprema ordered that no action was to be taken against homosexuals except when heresy was involved. Here a curious split in policy seems to have occurred, because although the tribunals of Castile never again exercised jurisdiction over sodomy, the Inquisition in Aragon now officially adopted powers over this very crime. On 24 February 1524 the pope, Clement VII,[39] issued a brief granting the Inquisition of the realms of Aragon jurisdiction over sodomy, irrespective of the presence of heresy. From this time onwards the Aragonese inquisitors kept their new authority, which they never gave up, despite the typical complaints raised by the Cortes of Monzón in 1533. Aragon was unique in this matter, for not even the Roman Inquisition exercised jurisdiction over sodomy. The punishment laid down by the law, and rigorously enforced by the state, was death by burning.

The Inquisition was harsh to sodomizers (both men and women), but tended to restrict death by burning only to those aged over twenty-five. Minors, who were inevitably a high proportion of those arrested, were normally whipped and sent to the galleys. A certain liberality on the part of the Suprema can be seen in the fact that some death sentences were commuted, and mildness was also shown to clergy, who were always a high proportion of offenders. The treatment of bestiality, usually placed in the same category as homosexuality, altered this picture somewhat, for it was almost invariably punished ruthlessly. Those guilty of it were normally marginalized people of poor intelligence, but this appears not to have helped them. By contrast, some highly placed homosexual offenders were more favourably treated. The most famous case was that of the Valencian grandee Pedro Galcerán de Borja, grand master of the chivalric Order of Montesa. In 1572 he was arrested by the Inquisition of Valencia on charges of sodomy. His case dragged on for some three years; he was heavily fined, but subsequently returned to active political life. . . .

The campaign against popular superstition was a broad one, marginal to the Inquisition's concerns in the sixteenth century but more significant in the seventeenth, when in some tribunals it accounted for a fifth of all prosecutions. Popular cul-

---

[38] Ferdinand II of Aragon (1452–1516); ruled Spain with Isabella of Castile after their marriage in 1479.

[39] Pope from 1523 to 1534.

ture, especially in the rural areas, had always sought unorthodox cures to daily afflictions. Villages had their wise men or wise women (*curanderos*) who could offer
medicinal ointments, find lost objects, heal wounded animals, or help a girl to win
the affections of her loved one. Cures might take the form of potions, charms,
spells or simply advice. It was a subculture that coexisted with and did not try to
subvert official Catholicism, although in certain New Christian areas the Christian content of the spells was doubtful. In rural areas the world of magic even entered the Church, with many clergy incorporating folk practices — rites, prayers,
offerings, dances — into the normal liturgy. All this was stamped on firmly by reforming bishops, post-Tridentine clergy and the Inquisition. In the process of
contrasting the dark world of primitive superstition with the illuminated world
of the gospel, unfortunately, preachers and learned men unduly simplified the
forces at work and helped to create fears of "witchcraft."

The role of the Inquisition in cases of witchcraft was much more restricted
than is commonly believed. In 1370 and 1387 the laws of Castile declared that
sorcery was a crime involving heresy, for which laymen would be punished by the
state and the clergy by the Church. Well after the foundation of the Inquisition,
jurisdiction over sorcery and witchcraft remained in secular hands. . . . By the
early sixteenth century, when the Holy Office began enquiries into the heresy of
witchcraft, repression of the offence was still normally in the hands of the state
courts. The Inquisition's reluctance to interfere was motivated in part by doubts
whether any heresy was involved. Certain types of popular superstition, "sorcery," and the whole range of astrology, were ill-defined areas in which many
learned men and clergy themselves dabbled. . . .

Throughout the sixteenth century the Inquisition seems to have maintained
its hostility to persecution of witches. Juana Izquierda, tried before the Toledo tribunal in 1591, confessed to taking part in the ritual murder of a number of children. Sixteen witnesses testified that the children had in fact died suddenly, and
that Izquierda was reputed to be a witch. What would in any other European
country have earned Izquierda the death sentence, in Spain earned her nothing
more than abjuration de levi[40] and 200 lashes. . . .

. . . [T]he Inquisition since 1526 had turned its face against the traditional
death sentence for witches; . . . more and more letrados,[41] rather than theologians,
were becoming inquisitors; and . . . the best informed opinion in Spain was in
favour of scepticism over the reality of witchcraft. . . .

On 29 August 1614 the Suprema issued authoritative instructions that reaf-
firmed the policy of 1526 and were to remain the principal guide to the future policy of the Inquisition. . . . Although the Inquisition was still obliged to follow
European opinion and regard witchcraft as a crime, in practice all testimony to
such a crime was rejected as delusion, so that Spain was saved from the ravages

---

[40] The punishment of penance, the mildest the Inquisition prescribed, whereby the sinner had to
abjure the offenses and pledge to avoid such sins in the future.

[41] University-educated lawyers.

of popular witch-hysteria and witch burnings at a time when they were prevalent all over Europe. . . .

We have seen that a good part of the Inquisition's zeal for religion was little more than active xenophobia. This was ironic, since Spain's imperial expansion took thousands of Spaniards abroad and brought them in touch with the rest of the world on a scale unprecedented in their history. The imperial experience did nothing to change the xenophobia of the inquisitors. From 1558 the Lutheran scare was used as a disincentive against contact with foreigners. A common accusation levelled against many accused was that they had been to a *tierra de herejes*,[42] which in inquisitorial parlance meant any country not under Spanish control.

All properly baptized persons, being *ipso facto* Christians and members of the Catholic Church, came under the jurisdiction of the Inquisition. Foreign heretics, therefore, appeared from time to time in autos held in Spain. The burning of Protestants at Seville in the mid-1500s shows a gradual increase in the number of foreigners seized, a natural phenomenon in an international seaport. Of those appearing in the Seville auto of April 1562, twenty-one were foreigners — nearly all Frenchmen. At the auto of 19 April 1564 six Flemings were "relaxed"[43] in person, and two other foreigners abjured de vehementi.[44] At the one on 13 May 1565 four foreigners were "relaxed" in effigy, seven reconciled and three abjured de vehementi. One Scottish Protestant was "relaxed" at the Toledo auto of 9 June 1591, and another, master of the ship *Mary of Grace,* at the auto of 19 June 1594.

The harvest reaped by the Inquisition was by now greater from foreign than from native Protestants. In Barcelona from 1552 to 1578, the only "relaxations" of Protestants were of fifty-one French people. Santiago in the same period punished over forty foreign Protestants. These figures were typical of the rest of Spain. . . . [U]p to 1600 the cases of alleged Lutheranism cited before the tribunals of the peninsula totalled 1,995, of which 1,640 cases concerned foreigners. Merchants from countries hostile to Spain ran the risk of having their crews arrested, their ships seized and their cargoes confiscated. . . .

Foreign visitors who publicly showed disrespect to acts of Spanish religion (refusing to take off one's hat, for example, if the Sacrament passed in the street) were liable to arrest by the Inquisition. This happened so frequently that nations trading to Spain made it their primary concern to secure guarantees for their traders before they would proceed any further with commercial negotiations. . . .

In general, since the late sixteenth century the authorities in Spain's principal ports had turned a blind eye to the trading activities of foreign Protestants, mainly English, Dutch and Germans. The peace treaties with England in 1604 and with the Dutch in 1609 merely accepted the situation. Some French merchants

---

[42] Land of heretics.

[43] Released to the secular authorities to be executed.

[44] "Vehemently," an abjuration (recantation) similar to the *abjuration de levi,* but where the offense was more serious and where the penitent faced formidable punishment if the sin were repeated.

continued to fall foul of the tribunal. In broad terms, however, the resolution
of the council of state in 1612, accepted by the Inquisition, was that English,
French, Dutch and Bearnese Protestant merchants not be molested, "provided
they cause no public disturbance." Commercial realities imposed the need for
toleration. . . .

Foreign Protestants did not normally appear in autos de fe[45] at the end of the
seventeenth century, but the pressure on them continued, especially in the ports.
Catalonia, for example, experienced the presence of foreigners in the form of
sailors in the ports, soldiers in foreign regiments of the Spanish army and French
immigration across the Pyrenees. The Barcelona tribunal had regular numbers of
"spontaneous" self-denunciations from foreigners wishing to become Catholics. In
the 1670s and 1680s there were about a dozen cases a year, often outnumbering
prosecutions of native Spaniards. In the record year 1676 no fewer than sixty-four
foreigners came before the Inquisition there, renounced the heresies they had
professed and asked to be baptized. There were still unfortunate cases — such as
the twenty-three-year-old Englishman who was arrested for public misbehaviour
in Barcelona in 1689 and died in the cells of Inquisition — but in general the Holy
Office was both lenient and tolerant. It is significant that after the long war of the
Spanish Succession from 1705 to 1714, when thousands of heretical (Huguenot,
English and German) troops had been captured by Spanish forces on Spanish territory, not a single fire was lit by the Inquisition to burn out any heresy that might
have entered the country. . . .

A kaleidoscopic survey of the Holy Office, such as the present one, runs the risk
of presenting a view only from above. The presence, and therefore the impact, of
the Inquisition appears unquestionable. It is logical to conclude (as some do)
that the Inquisition imposed fear and uniformity throughout Spain. The tribunal
itself never ceased to proclaim its successes. At the auto de fe in Barcelona in 1602,
reported the inquisitors with considerable satisfaction (but doubtful veracity),
"our procession caused terror in the people." Many historians have assumed that
the Inquisition was an effective weapon of social control, keeping the population
in its place and maintaining social and religious norms.

There is little evidence to support this contention. In their daily lives Spaniards, like others in Europe, had to deal with many authorities set over them. They
contended with secular lords, royal officials, Church personnel, religious communities, and urban officials. The Holy Office also was one of these authorities.
But except at times when the inquisitor came round on his visitation, the people
had little contact with him. The presence of a local familiar[46] or comisario[47] did

---

[45] "Act of faith," an elaborate public sentencing of convicted heretics that included sermons, a
Mass, and processions of penitents. The Inquisition turned those sentenced for heresy over to the secular authority. The heretics were then burned at the stake.

[46] Lay official of the Inquisition. (Author's note.)

[47] Select local clergy who helped the Inquisition in administrative matters. (Author's note.)

not affect the situation; their job was to help the inquisitor if he came, not to act as links in an information network.

The likely degree of contact, in a world where (unlike our own today) control depended on contact, is in effect a good guide to whether the Inquisition managed to have any impact on the ordinary people of Spain. The evidence from the tribunal of Catalonia is beyond question. No proper visitations were made here by the inquisitors during the early sixteenth century. In the second half of the century sixteen visitations in all were made, but they were always partial visits done in rotation, and limited to the major towns. These towns might be visited once every ten years. The people out in the countryside, by contrast, were lucky if they managed to see an inquisitor in their entire lives. There were large areas of the principality that had no contact with the Inquisition throughout its three centuries of history. Three-quarters of all Catalans prosecuted by the Inquisition in the years 1578–1635 came from the capital, Barcelona. The activity of the tribunal, in short, was restricted to the city (where its influence was notoriously small). Out in the countryside it had neither activity nor influence. The degree of social control was negligible.

After generations of living with the Holy Office the people accepted it. No demands for its abolition were made before the age of Enlightenment. In many cases, the existence of the Inquisition was even welcomed, for it offered a disciplinary presence not often found in the society of that time. People with grudges or complaints, particularly within families and within communities, could take their problems to the tribunal and ask for a solution. "You watch out," an angry housewife in Saragossa screamed at her inn-keeper husband (in 1486), "or I'll accuse you to the inquisitor of being a bad Christian!" A court of this type could conceivably be welcomed by some Spaniards even in the twentieth century. Acceptance was probably greater in the cities, where the numerous clergy gave it active support in their sermons and where the tribunal from time to time put on autos de fe to reaffirm its role. But even in the unexplored countryside it could sometimes have a positive role to play. The documents record many cases of village conflict and tension that in the last resort looked for a solution to one or other of the disciplinary tribunals in the city.

Hostility to the tribunal was, for all that, commonplace. There were three main reasons for this. First, the Inquisition was a disciplinary body, and therefore (like any similar body, even in the twentieth century) resented by ample sectors of the population. Its policing duties were modest, but excited the hostility of other policing officers from other jurisdictions; and of those who by definition did not like police intrusion. In moments of anger, such people could not refrain from cursing the Holy Office. Where possible, the Inquisition tried to protect its reputation against them. The "propositions" that they prosecuted offer useful evidence of what some Spaniards felt. The archives contain hundreds of statements expressing rage or contempt, ample material with which to prove the hostility of the Spanish people. "I don't give a damn for God or for the Inquisition!" "I care as much for the Inquisition as for the tail of my dog!" "What Inquisition? I know of none!" "I could take on the whole Inquisition!" "The Inquisition exists only to rob people!" The multitude of oaths, however, no more prove hostility than their absence in the late eighteenth century proves support. Enmity to the tribunal was common, but most oaths were uttered out of habit or when drunk or in moments of anger or stress. The brawling and the swearing demonstrate a lack of respect, but otherwise prove little more than that Spaniards have never inertly accepted the political or religious systems imposed on them.

The second reason for hostility was when jurisdictions clashed. No other tribunal in all Spanish history provoked so much friction with every other authority in both Church and state. The conflicts were particularly intense in the realms of the crown of Aragon. In Catalonia the inquisitors complained more than once, and apparently with good reason, that the Catalans wanted to get rid of them. In 1632 the inquisitors of Barcelona complained that "among the travails suffered by this Inquisition and its officials the most serious are the contempt and scorn they face in public and in private, on every occasion and in every way." But, despite all the fury, its opponents never once questioned the religious rationale of the Holy Office.

In *ancien régime*[48] Spain, no popular movements attacked the Inquisition and no rioters laid a finger on its property. The exceptions, to be found only in the fuero[49] provinces of Spain, are notable. In 1591 the tribunal of Saragossa intervened rashly . . . in the Antonio Pérez affair and was directly attacked by the angry mob. In the revolutionary Barcelona of 1640 the mob, informed that Castilian soldiers were lodged in the Inquisition, burst into the building, smashed down the doors, threatened the inquisitors and took away documentation. Especially in the crown of Aragon, the tribunal never ceased to be regarded as a foreign institution.

The third reason for hostility was the frequently alien character of the tribunal. The inquisitors were Castilians, unable to speak the languages or dialects of the rural communities into which they intruded. They were city men, unwelcome in the quite different environment of country villages. Their visits, we have seen, were very rare indeed. In contrast to the welcome they usually gave to wandering preachers, villages were seldom pleased to see an inquisitor. In sixteenth-century Galicia, a parish priest begged his congregation to be deaf and dumb when the inquisitors visited. "Let us be very careful tomorrow," he said, "when the inquisitor comes here. For the love of God, don't go telling things about each other or meddle in things touching the Holy Office." In seventeenth-century Catalonia the parish priest of Aiguaviva publicly rebuked the comisarios of the Inquisition when they came to check the baptismal records in order to carry out a proof of limpieza.[50] "He told them not to write lies, and that it would not be the first time they had done so, by falsifying signatures and other things."

---

[48] Old Régime, the two centuries before the French Revolution of 1789.

[49] Those provinces (such as Aragon, Catalonia, Mallorca, Sardinia, and Valencia) whose laws (*fueros*) monarchs pledged to preserve.

[50] Short for "limpieza de sangre," "purity of blood," meaning having no heretics or Semites among one's ancestors.

The effective contact of the tribunal with the people was at all times, outside the big towns, marginal. In sixteenth-century Mexico, "95 per cent of the population never had any contact with the Inquisition."[51] A similar situation can be found in much of Spain. In Catalonia, "in over 90 per cent of the towns, during more than three centuries of existence, the Holy Office never once intruded."[52] We have seen already that the rarity of visits throughout the countryside by inquisitors in effect cut off much of Spain from contact with the Inquisition. In the heartland of Castile, by contrast, communications were better and contact more effective. But even in Toledo five times as many townspeople as peasants were tried by the tribunal, testimony to the difficulties of dominating the much larger rural population. Though the Inquisition was singularly effective in its initial campaign against alleged judaizers, therefore, there is good reason to conclude that it failed when it turned to matters that were not directly questions of heresy.

---

[51] Richard Greenlief, cited in *Historia de la Inquisitión en España y America,* ed. J. Perez Villaneuva and B. Escandell Bonet (Madrid, 1984–93), II, 665.

[52] Henry Kamen, *Crisis and Change in Early Modern Spain* (Aldershot, 1993), 436.

NUNS, WIVES, AND MOTHERS: WOMEN AND THE REFORMATION IN GERMANY
Merry Wiesner

In a famous essay, a historian argues persuasively that there was no Italian Re-naissance for women, that the cultural flowering in the fourteenth and fifteenth centuries scarcely affected women's lives. According to this perspective, hu-manism, artistic innovations, and political experimentation did not improve the status of women in law, in the home, or in the workplace. In fact, the condition of women may even have worsened during the Renaissance. Merry Wiesner, professor of history at the University of Wisconsin at Milwaukee, finds that — unlike the Italian Renaissance — the sixteenth-century German Reformation made an appreciable difference to women, improving the lot of some while ad-versely affecting that of others. She bases her conclusions principally on the writ-ings of the Protestant reformers as well as of women themselves, and on laws.

On the eve of and during the Protestant Reformation, German society placed social and political restrictions on women. What impediments closed possible avenues of advancement to women? Moving beyond these hindrances, Wiesner sketches neatly the impact of religious change on women according to their sta-tus in three categories: as members of female religious orders, as single or mar-ried, and as workers. Within these broad categories, different groups existed. It is important to understand how the religious transformation from Catholic to Protestant marked the lives of these various groups.

The Protestants closed convents, forcing nuns and lay sisters to fend for themselves or marry. The Reformation altered the lives of other women as well, whether single or married. How did the reformers view marriage and the rela-tionship between wife and husband? Were women any less subordinate in the Protestant denominations than in Catholicism? Society regarded religious tol-eration as an evil and so reformers discussed marriages in which each spouse

Merry Wiesner, "Nuns, Wives, and Mothers: Women and the Reformation in Germany," in *Women in Reformation and Counter-Reformation Europe: Private and Public Worlds,* ed. Sherrin Marshall (Bloomington: Indiana University Press, 1989), 8–26.

belonged to a different religion. What, then, was a Protestant wife to do when her husband, to whom she owed obedience, was Catholic?

There is a difference, to be sure, between the ideas of Protestant theologians on the nature of women, their proper place, and their duties, on the one hand, and the translation of those ideas into actual practice, on the other hand. Protestant states passed laws modifying the behavior of women in marriage and in religion. Wiesner rightly stresses that women reacted to the Reformation; they were not just acted upon. How did women — both aristocrats and commoners — contribute to the religious developments sweeping Germany? Overall, did the Reformation improve the status or situation of any groups of women?

It is in many ways anachronistic even to use the word "Germany" when discussing the sixteenth century. At that time, modern-day East and West Germany were politically part of the Holy Roman Empire, a loose confederation of several hundred states, ranging from tiny knightships through free imperial cities to large territorial states. These states theoretically owed obedience to an elected emperor, but in reality they were quite independent and often pursued policies in opposition to the emperor. Indeed, the political diversity and lack of a strong central authority were extremely important to the early success of the Protestant Reformation[1] in Germany. Had Luther[2] been a Frenchman or a Spaniard, his voice would probably have been quickly silenced by the powerful monarchs in those countries.

Because of this diversity, studies of the Reformation in Germany are often limited to one particular area or one particular type of government, such as the free imperial cities. This limited focus is useful when looking at the impact of the Reformation on men, for male participation and leadership in religious change varied depending on whether a territory was ruled by a city council, a nobleman, or a bishop. Male leadership in the Reformation often came from university teachers, so the presence or absence of a university in an area was also an important factor.

When exploring the impact of religious change on women, however, these political and institutional factors are not as important. Except for a few noblewomen who ruled territories while their sons were still minors, women had no formal political voice in any territory of the empire. They did not vote or serve on city councils, and even abbesses were under the direct control of a male church official. Women could not attend universities, and thus did not come into contact with religious ideas through formal theological training. Their role in the Refor-

---

[1] The sixteenth-century split in western Christianity between the Roman Catholic Church and a variety of Protestant denominations.

[2] Martin Luther (1483–1546), initiator of the Protestant Reformation in Germany.

mation was not so determined by what may be called "public" factors — political structures, educational institutions — as was that of men.

Women's role in the Reformation and the impact of religious change on them did vary throughout Germany, but that variation was largely determined by what might be termed "personal" factors — a woman's status as a nun or laywoman, her marital status, her social and economic class, her occupation. Many of these factors, particularly social and economic class, were also important in determining men's responses to religious change, but they were often secondary to political factors whereas for women they were of prime importance.

The Protestant and Catholic reformers recognized this. Although they generally spoke about and to women as an undifferentiated group and proposed the same ideals of behavior for all women, when the reformers did address distinct groups of women they distinguished them by marital or clerical status. Nuns, single women, mothers, wives, and widows all got special attention in the same way that special treatises were directed to male princes and members of city councils — men set apart from others by their public, political role.

It is important to keep in mind that although a woman's religious actions were largely determined by her personal status, they were not regarded as a private matter, even if they took place within the confines of her own household. No one in the sixteenth century regarded religion or the family as private, as that term is used today. One's inner relationship with God was perhaps a private matter (though even that is arguable), but one's outward religious practices were a matter of great concern for political authorities. Both Protestants and Catholics saw the family as the cornerstone of society, the cornerstone on which all other institutions were constructed, and every political authority meddled in family and domestic concerns. Thus a woman's choice to serve her family meat on Friday or attend the funeral of a friend whose religion was unacceptable was not to be overlooked or regarded as trivial.

Although "personal" is not the same as "private" in Reformation Germany, grouping women by their personal status is still the best way to analyze their role in religious change. This essay thus follows "personal" lines of division and begins with an exploration of the impact of the Reformation on nuns, Beguines,[3] and other female religious. It then looks at single and married women, including a special group of married women, the wives of the Protestant reformers. Although the reformers did not have a special message for noblewomen, the situation of these women warrants separate consideration because their religious choices had the greatest effect on the course of the Reformation. The essay concludes with a discussion of several groups of working women whose labor was directly or indirectly affected by religious change.

Women in convents, both cloistered nuns[4] and lay sisters, and other female religious, were the first to confront the Protestant Reformation. In areas becom-

---

[3] Roman Catholic lay sisterhoods.

[4] Confined to a convent and therefore secluded from the world.

ing Protestant religious change meant both the closing of their houses and a nega-
tion of the value and worth of the life they had been living. The Protestant reformers encouraged nuns and sisters to leave their houses and marry, with harsh
words concerning the level of morality in the convents, comparing it to that in
brothels. Some convents accepted the Protestant message and willingly gave up
their houses and land to city and territorial authorities. The nuns renounced their
vows, and those who were able to find husbands married, while the others returned to their families or found ways to support themselves on their own. Others did not accept the new religion but recognized the realities of political power
and gave up their holdings; these women often continued living together after the
Reformation, trying to remain as a religious community, though they often had to
rely on their families for support. In some cases the nuns were given a pension.
There is no record, however, of what happened to most of these women. Former
priests and monks could become pastors in the new Protestant churches, but former nuns had no place in the new church structure.

Many convents, particularly those with high standards of learning and morality and whose members were noblewomen or women from wealthy patrician
families, fought the religious change. A good example of this is the St. Clara convent in Nuremberg, whose nuns were all from wealthy Nuremberg families and
whose reputation for learning had spread throughout Germany. The abbess at the
time of the Reformation was Charitas Pirckheimer, a sister of the humanist
Willibald Pirckheimer and herself an accomplished Latinist. In 1525, the Nuremberg city council ordered all the cloisters to close; four of the six male houses in
the city dissolved themselves immediately, but both female houses refused. The
council first sent official representatives to try to persuade the nuns and then
began a program of intimidation. The women, denied confessors and Catholic
communion, were forced to hear Protestant sermons four times a week; their servants had difficulty buying food; people threatened to burn the convent, threw
stones over the walls, and sang profane songs when they heard the nuns singing.
Charitas noted in her memoirs that women often led the attacks and were the
most bitter opponents of the nuns. Three families physically dragged their daughters out of the convent, a scene of crying and wailing witnessed by many Nurem-
bergers. The council questioned each nun separately to see if she had any complaints, hoping to find some who would leave voluntarily, and finally confiscated
all of the convent's land. None of these measures was successful, and the council
eventually left the convent alone, although it forbade the taking in of new novices.
The last nun died in 1590. . . .

The Jesuits[5] and other leaders of the Catholic Reformation[6] took the opposite
position from the Protestants on the value of celibacy, encouraging young women
to disobey their parents and enter convents to escape arranged marriages. Although

---

[5] Members of the Society of Jesus, a Roman Catholic religious order established in 1540.

[6] The Roman Catholic Church's reform movement and resurgence in reaction to the Protestant
Reformation during the late sixteenth century.

they did not encourage married women to leave their husbands, the Jesuits followed the pre-Reformation tradition in urging husbands to let their wives enter convents if they wished.

The Counter-Reformation church wanted all female religious strictly cloistered, however, and provided no orders for women who wanted to carry out an active apostolate; there was no female equivalent of the Jesuits. The church also pressured Beguines, Franciscan tertiaries,[7] and other sisters who had always moved about somewhat freely or worked out in the community to adopt strict rules of cloister and place themselves under the direct control of a bishop. The women concerned did not always submit meekly, however. The Beguines in Münster, for example, refused to follow the advice of their confessors, who wanted to reform the beguinage and turn it into a cloistered house of Poor Clares.[8] The women, most of whom were members of the city's elite families, appealed to the city council for help in defending their civil rights and traditional liberties. The council appealed to the archbishop of Cologne, the cardinals, and eventually the pope, and, though the women were eventually cloistered, they were allowed to retain certain of their traditional practices. . . .

Of course most of the women in sixteenth-century Germany were not nuns or other female religious but laywomen who lived in families. Their first contact with the Reformation was often shared with the male members of their families. They heard the new teachings proclaimed from a city pulpit, read or looked at broadsides attacking the pope, and listened to traveling preachers attacking celibacy and the monasteries. . . .

The Protestant reformers did not break sharply with tradition in their ideas about women. For both Luther and Calvin, women were created by God and could be saved through faith; spiritually women and men were equal. In every other respect, however, women were to be subordinate to men. Women's subjection was inherent in their very being and was present from creation — in this the reformers agreed with Aristotle[9] and the classical tradition. It was made more brutal and harsh, however, because of Eve's responsibility for the Fall — in this Luther and Calvin[10] agreed with patristic[11] tradition and with their scholastic and humanist predecessors.

There appears to be some novelty in their rejection of Catholic teachings on the merits of celibacy and championing of marriage as the proper state for all individuals. Though they disagreed on so much else, all Protestant reformers agreed on this point; the clauses discussing marriage in the various Protestant confessions

---

[7] A group of laywomen attached to the Franciscan order, a Roman Catholic religious order founded in 1209.

[8] An order of Franciscan nuns.

[9] Greek philosopher (384–322 B.C.E.).

[10] John Calvin (1509–1564), French Protestant theologian, founder of Calvinism and religious leader of Geneva.

[11] Referring to the fathers, or theologians, of the early Christian Church.

show more similarities than do any other main articles of doctrine or discipline. Even this emphasis on marriage was not that new, however. Civic and Christian humanists also thought that "God had established marriage and family life as the best means for providing spiritual and moral discipline in this world," and they "emphasized marriage and the family as the basic social and economic unit which provided the paradigm for all social relations."

The Protestant exhortation to marry was directed to both sexes, but particularly to women, for whom marriage and motherhood were a vocation as well as a living arrangement. Marriage was a woman's highest calling, the way she could fulfill God's will: in Luther's harsh words, "Let them bear children to death; they are created for that." Unmarried women were suspect, both because they were fighting their natural sex drive, which everyone in the sixteenth century believed to be much stronger than men's, and because they were upsetting the divinely imposed order, which made woman subject to man. . . .

The combination of women's spiritual equality, female subordination, and the idealization of marriage proved problematic for the reformers, for they were faced with the issue of women who converted while their husbands did not. What was to take precedence, the woman's religious convictions or her duty of obedience? Luther and Calvin were clear on this. Wives were to obey their husbands, even if they were not Christians; in Calvin's words, a woman "should not desert the partner who is hostile." Marriage was a woman's "calling," her natural state, and she was to serve God through this calling.

Wives received a particularly ambiguous message from the radical reformers. . . . Some radical groups allowed believers to leave their unbelieving spouses, but women who did so were expected to remarry quickly and thus come under the control of a male believer. The most radical Anabaptists were fascinated by Old Testament polygamy and accepted the statement in Revelations that the Last Judgment would only come if there were 144,000 "saints" in the world; they actually enforced polygamy for a short time at Münster, though the required number of saints were never born. In practical terms, Anabaptist women were equal only in martyrdom.

Although the leaders of the Counter Reformation continued to view celibacy as a state preferable to matrimony, they realized that most women in Germany would marry and began to publish their own marriage manual to counter those published by Protestants. The ideal wives and mothers they described were, however, no different than those of the Protestants; both wanted women to be "chaste, silent, and obedient."

The ideas of the reformers did not stay simply within the realm of theory but led to political and institutional changes. Some of these changes were the direct results of Protestant doctrine, and some of them had unintended, though not unforeseeable, consequences. . . .

Every Protestant territory passed a marriage ordinance that stressed wifely obedience and proper Christian virtues and set up a new court or broadened the jurisdiction of an existing court to handle marriage and morals cases which had previously been handled by church courts. They also passed sumptuary laws that regulated weddings and baptisms, thereby trying to make these ceremonies more purely Christian by limiting the number of guests and prohibiting profane activities such as dancing and singing. Though such laws were never completely successful, the tone of these two ceremonies, which marked the two perhaps most important events in a woman's life, became much less exuberant. Religious processions, such as Corpus Christi[12] parades, which had included both men and women, and in which even a city's prostitutes took part, were prohibited. The public processions that remained were generally those of guild masters and journeymen, at which women were onlookers only. Women's participation in rituals such as funerals was limited, for Protestant leaders wanted neither professional mourners nor relatives to take part in extravagant wailing and crying. Lay female confraternities, which had provided emotional and economic assistance for their members and charity for the needy, were also forbidden, and no similar all-female groups replaced them.

The Protestant reformers attempted to do away with the veneration of Mary and the saints. This affected both men and women, because some of the strongest adherents of the cult of the Virgin had been men. For women, the loss of St. Anne, Mary's mother, was particularly hard, for she was a patron saint of pregnant women; now they were instructed to pray during labor and childbirth to Christ, a celibate male, rather than to a woman who had also been a mother. The Protestant martyrs replaced the saints to some degree, at least as models worthy of emulation, but they were not to be prayed to and they did not give their names to any days of the year. The Protestant Reformation not only downplayed women's public ceremonial role; it also stripped the calendar of celebrations honoring women and ended the power female saints and their relics were believed to have over people's lives. Women who remained Catholic still had female saints to pray to, but the number of new female saints during the Counter Reformation was far fewer than the number of new male saints, for two important avenues to sanctity, missionary and pastoral work, were closed to women.

Because of the importance Protestant reformers placed on Bible-reading in the vernacular, many of them advocated opening schools for girls as well as boys. The number of such schools which opened was far fewer than the reformers had originally hoped, and Luther in particular also muted his call for mass education after the turmoil of the Peasants' War.[13] The girls' schools that were opened stressed morality and decorum; in the words of the Memmingen school ordinance from 1587, the best female pupil was one noted for her "great diligence and application in learning her catechism, modesty, obedience, and excellent penmanship." These schools taught sewing as well as reading and singing, and religious instruction was often limited to memorizing the catechism.

---

[12] A Roman Catholic festival instituted in the thirteenth century to honor the Blessed Sacrament (the term used for the sacrament of the Eucharist and especially for the consecrated bread and wine, which the Roman Catholic Church believes to be the body and blood of Jesus).

[13] Uprisings in central and southwest Germany (1524–1525), inspired by the Reformation leaders' defiance of authority.

Along with these changes that related directly to Protestant doctrine, the Reformation brought with it an extended period of war and destruction in which individuals and families were forced to move frequently from one place to another. Women whose husbands were exiled for religious reasons might also have been forced to leave. Their houses and goods were usually confiscated whether they left town or not. If allowed to stay, they often had to support a family and were still held suspect by neighbors and authorities. A woman whose husband was away fighting could go years without hearing from him and never be allowed to marry again if there was some suspicion he might still be alive.

Women were not simply passive recipients of the Reformation and the ideas and changes it brought but indeed responded to them actively. Swept up by the enthusiasm of the first years of the Reformation, single and married women often stepped beyond what were considered acceptable roles for women. Taking literally Luther's idea of a priesthood of all believers, women as well as uneducated men began to preach and challenge religious authorities. In 1524 in Nuremberg, the city council took action against a certain Frau Voglin, who had set herself up in the hospital church and was preaching. In a discussion after a Sunday sermon by a Lutheran-leaning prior, a woman in Augsburg spoke to a bishop's representative who had been sent to hear the sermon and called the bishop a brothel manager because he had a large annual income from concubinage fees. Several women in Zwickau, inspired by the preaching of Thomas Müntzer,[14] also began to preach in 1521.

All of these actions were viewed with alarm by civic authorities, who even objected to women's getting together to discuss religion. In their view, female preachers clearly disobeyed the Pauline injunction[15] against women speaking in church and moved perilously close to claiming an official religious role. In 1529, the Zwickau city council banished several of the women who had gathered together and preached. In the same year, the Memmingen city council forbade maids to discuss religion while drawing water at neighborhood wells. No German government forbade women outright to read the Bible, as Henry VIII[16] of England did in 1543, but the authorities did attempt to prevent them from discussing it publicly.

After 1530, women's public witnessing of faith was more likely to be prophesying than preaching. In many ways, female prophets were much less threatening than female preachers, for the former had biblical parallels, clear biblical justification, and no permanent official function. . . .

With the advent of the religious wars, female prophets began to see visions of war and destruction and to make political, as well as religious and eschatological,[17] predictions. Susanna Rugerin had been driven far from her home by imperial

---

[14] Radical religious leader who led a peasant rebellion in 1524–1525.

[15] "[W]omen should keep silence in the churches. For they are not permitted to speak, but they should be subordinate. . . . [I]t is shameful for a woman to speak in church" (1 Corinthians 14, 34 ff).

[16] King from 1509 to 1547.

[17] Having to do with death, final destiny, the end of the world.

armies and began to see an angel who revealed visions of Gustavus Adolphus.[18] The visions of Juliana von Duchnik were even more dramatic. In 1628 she brought a warning from God to Duke Wallenstein, a commander of imperial troops, telling him to leave his estate because God would no longer protect him. . . .

The most dramatic public affirmation of faith a woman could make was martyrdom. Most of the female martyrs in Germany were Anabaptists, and the law granted women no special treatment, except for occasionally delaying execution if they were pregnant. Women were more likely to be drowned than beheaded, for it was thought they would faint at the sight of the executioner's sword and make his job more difficult. Some of them were aware that this reduced the impact of their deaths and wanted a more public form of execution. A good indication of the high degree of religious understanding among many Anabaptist women comes from their interrogations. They could easily discuss the nature of Christ, the doctrine of the Real Presence,[19] and baptism, quoting extensively from the Bible. As a woman known simply as Claesken put it, "Although I am a simple person before men, I am not unwise in the knowledge of the Lord." Her interrogators were particularly upset because she had converted many people: they commented, "Your condemnation will be greater than your husband's because you can read and have misled him."

Although most of the women who published religious works during the Reformation were either nuns or noblewomen, a few middle-class women wrote hymns, religious poetry, and some polemics. Ursula Weide published a pamphlet against the abbot of Pegau, denouncing his support of celibacy. The earliest Protestant hymnals include several works by women, often verse renditions of the Psalms or Gospels. . . .

Seventeenth-century women often wrote religious poems, hymns, and prose meditations for private purposes as well as for publication. They wrote to celebrate weddings, baptisms, and birthdays, to console friends, to praise deceased relatives, to instruct and provide examples for their children. If a woman's works were published while she was still alive, they included profuse apologies about her unworthiness and presumption. Many such works were published posthumously by husbands or fathers and include a note from these men that writing never distracted the author from her domestic tasks but was done only in her spare time. Unfortunately, similar works by sixteenth-century German women are rare. Thus, to examine the religious convictions of the majority of women who did not preach, prophesy, publish, or become martyrs, we must look at their actions within the context of their domestic and community life.

Married women whose religious convictions matched those of their husbands often shared equally in the results of those convictions. If these convictions con-

---

[18] Protestant king of Sweden from 1611 to 1632; defeated the Catholic imperial forces in Germany during the Thirty Years' War (1618–1648).

[19] That the body and blood of Jesus is actually present in the sacrament of communion (the Eucharist).

flicted with local authorities and the men were banished for religious reasons, their wives were expected to follow them. Because house and goods were generally confiscated, the wives had no choice in the matter anyway. Women whose husbands were in hiding, fighting religious wars, or assisting Protestant churches elsewhere supported the family and covered for their husbands, often sending them supplies as well. Wealthy women set up endowments for pastors and teachers and provided scholarships for students at Protestant, and later Jesuit, universities.

Many married women also responded to the Protestant call to make the home, in the words of the humanist Urbanus Rhegius, "a seminary for the church." They carried out what might best be called domestic missionary activity, praying and reciting the catechism with their children and servants. Those who were literate might read some vernacular religious literature, and, because reading was done aloud in the sixteenth century, this was also a group activity. . . .

There are several spectacular examples among noble families of women whose quiet pressure eventually led to their husbands' conversions and certainly many among common people that are not recorded. But what about a married woman whose efforts failed? What could a woman do whose religious convictions differed from those of her husband? In some areas, the couple simply lived together as adherents of different religions. The records for Bamberg, for example, show that in 1595 about 25 percent of the households were mixed marriages, with one spouse Catholic and the other Lutheran. Among the members of the city council the proportion was even higher — 43 percent had spouses of a different religion, so this was not something which simply went unnoticed by authorities. Bamberg was one of the few cities in Germany which allowed two religions to worship freely; therefore, mixed marriages may have been only a local phenomenon. This, however, has not yet been investigated in other areas.

Continued cohabitation was more acceptable if the husband was of a religion considered acceptable in the area. In 1631, for example, the Strasbourg city council considered whether citizens should lose their citizenship if they married Calvinists. It decided that a man would not "because he can probably draw his spouse away from her false religion, and bring her on to the correct path." He would have to pay a fine, though, for "bringing an unacceptable person into the city." A woman who married a Calvinist would lose her citizenship, however, "because she would let herself easily be led into error in religion by her husband, and led astray."

As a final resort, a married woman could leave her husband (and perhaps family) and move to an area where the religion agreed with her own. This was extremely difficult for women who were not wealthy, and most of the recorded cases involve noblewomen with independent incomes and sympathetic fathers. Even if a woman might gather enough resources to support herself, she was not always welcome, despite the strength of her religious convictions, for she had violated that most basic of norms, wifely obedience. Protestant city councils were suspicious of any woman who asked to be admitted to citizenship independently and questioned her intensely about her marital status. Catholic cities such as Munich were more concerned about whether the woman who wanted to immigrate had always been a good Catholic than whether or not she was married, particularly if she wished to enter a convent.

Exceptions were always made for wives of Anabaptists. A tailor's wife in Nuremberg was allowed to stay in the city and keep her house as long as she recanted her Anabaptist beliefs and stayed away from all other Anabaptists, including her husband, who had been banished. After the siege of Münster, Anabaptist women and children began to drift back into the city and were allowed to reside there if they abjured Anabaptism and swore an oath of allegiance to the bishop. Both Protestant and Catholic authorities viewed Anabaptism as a heresy and a crime so horrible it broke the most essential human bonds.

It was somewhat easier for unmarried women and widows to leave a territory for religious reasons, and in many cases persecution or war forced them out. . . .

Women who worked to support themselves generally had to make special supplications to city councils to be allowed to stay and work. Since they had not been trained in a guild in the city, the council often overrode guild objections in permitting them to make or sell small items to support themselves and was more likely to grant a woman's request if she was seen as particularly needy or if her story was especially pathetic. A woman whose husband had been killed in the Thirty Years' War asked permission in 1632 to live in Strasbourg and bake pretzels; this was granted to her and several others despite the objections of the bakers because, in the council's words, "all of the supplicants are poor people, that are particularly hard-pressed in these difficult times." . . .

One of the most dramatic changes brought about by the Protestant Reformation was the replacement of celibate priests by married pastors with wives and families. Many of the wives of the early reformers had themselves been nuns, and they were crossing one of society's most rigid borders by marrying, becoming brides of men rather than brides of Christ. During the first few years of the Reformation, they were still likened to priests' concubines in the public mind and had to create a respectable role for themselves. They were often living demonstrations of their husbands' convictions and were expected to be models of wifely obedience and Christian charity; the reformers had particularly harsh words for pastors who could not control their wives. . . .

Pastors' wives opened up their homes to students and refugees, providing them with food, shelter and medical care. This meant buying provisions, brewing beer, hiring servants, growing fruits and vegetables, and gathering herbs for a household that could expand overnight from ten to eighty. . . .

Other pastors' wives assisted in running city hospitals, orphanages, and infirmaries, sometimes at the suggestion of their husbands and sometimes on their own initiative. . . . Wealthy women set up endowments for pastors and teachers and provided scholarships for students at Protestant, and later Jesuit, universities.

Neither the Protestant nor the Catholic reformers differentiated between noblewomen and commoners in their public advice to women; noblewomen, too, were to be "chaste, silent, and obedient." Privately, however, they recognized that such women often held a great deal of power and made special attempts to win them over. Luther corresponded regularly with a number of prominent noblewomen, and Calvin was even more assiduous at "courting ladies in high places."

Noblewomen, both married and unmarried, religious and lay, had the most opportunity to express their religious convictions, and the consequences of their actions were more far-reaching than those of most women. Prominent noblewomen who left convents could create quite a sensation, particularly if, like Ursula of Münsterberg, they wrote a justification of why they had left and if their actions put them in opposition to their families. Disagreements between husband and wife over matters of religion could lead to the wife being exiled, as in the case of Elisabeth of Brandenburg. They could also lead to mutual toleration, however, as they did for Elisabeth's daughter, also named Elisabeth, who married Eric, the duke of Brunswick-Calenburg. She became a Lutheran while her husband remained a Catholic, to which his comment was: "My wife does not interfere with and molest us in our faith, and therefore we will leave her undisturbed and unmolested in hers." After his death, she became regent and introduced the Reformation into Brunswick. . . . Several other female rulers also promoted independently the Reformation in their territories, while others convinced their husbands to do so. Later in the century noble wives and widows were also influential in opening up territories to the Jesuits.

Most of these women were following paths of action that had been laid out by male rulers and had little consciousness of themselves as women carrying out a reformation. Others as well judged their actions on the basis of their inherited status and power, for, despite John Knox's[20] bitter fulminations against "the monstrous regiment of women," female rulers were not regarded as unusual in the sixteenth century. Only if a noblewoman ventured beyond summoning and protecting a male reformer or signing church ordinances to commenting publicly on matters of theology was she open to criticism as a woman going beyond what was acceptable. . . .

Like noblewomen, women engaged in various occupations did not receive any special message from the reformers. Even Luther's harsh diatribe against the prostitutes of Wittenberg was addressed to the university students who used their services. This is because in the sixteenth century, women who carried out a certain occupation were rarely thought of as a group. A woman's work identity was generally tied to her family identity.

This can best be explained with an example. For a man to become a baker, he apprenticed himself to a master baker for a certain number of years, then spent several more years as a journeyman, and finally might be allowed to make his masterpiece — a loaf of bread or a fancy cake — open his own shop, marry, and hire his own apprentices and journeymen. He was then a full-fledged member of the bakers' guild, took part in parades, festivals, and celebrations with his guild brothers, lit candles at the guild altar in Catholic cities, and perhaps participated in city government as a guild representative. He was thus a baker his entire life and had a strong sense of work identity.

For a woman to become a baker, she had to marry a baker. She was not allowed to participate in the apprenticeship system, though she could do everything

---

[20] Leader (ca. 1505–1572) of the Protestant Reformation in Scotland.

in the shop her husband could. If he died, she might carry on the shop a short time as a widow, but, if she was young enough, she generally married again and took on whatever her new husband's occupation was. She had no voice in guild decisionmaking and took no part in guild festivals, though she may have actually baked more than her husband. Changes in her status were not determined by her own level of training but by changes in her marital or family status. Thus, although in terms of actual work she was as much a baker as her husband, she, and her society, viewed her as a baker's wife. Her status as wife was what was important in the eyes of sixteenth-century society, and, as we have seen, many treatises and laws were directed to wives.

Although female occupations were not directly singled out in religious theory, several were directly affected by changes in religious practices. The demand for votive candles, which were often made and sold by women, dropped dramatically, and these women were forced to find other means of support. The demand for fish declined somewhat, creating difficulties for female fishmongers, although traditional eating habits did not change immediately when fast days were no longer required. Municipal brothels were closed in the sixteenth century, a change often linked with the Protestant Reformation. This occurred in Catholic cities as well, however, and may be more closely linked with general concerns for public order and morality and obsession with women's sexuality than with any specific religion.

Charitable institutions were secularized and centralized, a process which had begun before the Reformation and was speeded up in the sixteenth century in both Protestant and Catholic territories. Many of the smaller charities were houses set up for elderly indigent women who lived off the original endowment and small fees they received for mourning or preparing bodies for burial. They had in many cases elected one of their number as head of the house but were now moved into large hospitals under the direction of a city official. The women who worked in these hospitals as cooks, nurses, maids, and cleaning women now became city, rather than church, employees. Outwardly their conditions of employment changed little, but the Protestant deemphasis on good works may have changed their conception of the value of their work, particularly given their minimal salaries and abysmal working conditions.

Midwives had long performed emergency baptisms if they or the parents believed the child would not live. This created few problems before the Reformation because Catholic doctrine taught that if there was some question about the regularity of this baptism and the child lived, the infant could be rebaptized "on the condition" it had not been baptized properly the first time; conditional baptism was also performed on foundlings. This assured the parents that their child had been baptized correctly while avoiding the snare of rebaptism, which was a crime in the Holy Roman Empire. In 1531, however, Luther rejected all baptisms "on condition" if it was known any baptism had already been carried out and called for a normal baptism in the case of foundlings. By 1540, most Lutheran areas were no longer baptizing "on condition," and those persons who still supported the practice were occasionally branded Anabaptists. This made it extremely important that midwives and other laypeople knew how to conduct correctly an emergency baptism.

Midwives were thus examined, along with pastors, church workers, and teachers, in the visitations conducted by pastors and city leaders in many cities, and "shocking irregularities" in baptismal practice were occasionally discovered. . . .

In areas of Germany where Anabaptism flourished, Anabaptist midwives were charged with claiming they had baptized babies when they really had not, so that a regular church baptism would not be required. In other areas the opposite seems to have been the case. Baptism was an important social occasion and a chance for the flaunting of wealth and social position, and parents paid the midwife to conveniently forget she had baptized a child so that the normal church ceremony could be carried out.

Despite the tremendous diversity of female experience in Germany during the Reformation, two factors are constant. First, a woman's ability to respond to the Reformation and the avenues her responses could take were determined more by her gender than by any other factor. The reformers — Catholic and Protestant, magisterial and radical — all agreed on the proper avenues for female response to their ideas. The responses judged acceptable were domestic, personal, and familial — prayer, meditation, teaching the catechism to children, singing or writing hymns, entering or leaving a convent. Public responses, either those presented publicly or those which concerned dogma or the church as a public institution, shocked and outraged authorities, even if they agreed with the ideas being expressed. A woman who backed the "wrong" religion was never as harshly criticized as a man; this was seen as simply evidence of her irrational and weak nature. One who supported the "right" religion too vigorously and vocally, however, might be censured by her male compatriots for "too much enthusiasm" and overstepping the bounds of proper female decorum. Thus, whatever a woman's status or class, her responses were judged according to both religious and sexual ideology. Since women of all classes heard this message from pamphlet and pulpit and felt its implications in laws and ordinances, it is not at all surprising that most of them accepted it.

Second, most women experienced the Reformation as individuals. Other than nuns in convents women were not a distinct social class, economic category, or occupational group; thus, they had no opportunity for group action. They passed religious ideas along the networks of their family, friends, and neighbors, but these networks had no official voice in a society that was divided according to male groups. A woman who challenged her husband or other male authorities in matters of religion was challenging basic assumptions about gender roles, and doing this alone, with no official group to support her. Even women who reformed territories did so as individual rulers. Men, on the other hand, were preached to as members of groups and responded collectively. They combined with other men in city councils, guilds, consistories, cathedral chapters, university faculties, and many other bodies to effect or halt religious change. Their own individual religious ideas were affirmed by others, whether or not they were ultimately successful in establishing the religious system they desired.

The strongest female protest against the Reformation in Germany came from the convents, where women were used to expressing themselves on religious matters and thinking of themselves as members of a spiritual group. Thus, although the Protestant reformers did champion a woman's role as wife and mother by closing the convents and forbidding female lay confraternities, they cut off women's opportunities for expressing their spirituality in an all-female context. Catholic women could still enter convents, but those convents were increasingly cut off from society. By the mid-seventeenth century, religion for all women in Germany, whether lay or clerical, had become much more closely tied to a household.

THE RITES OF VIOLENCE: RELIGIOUS RIOT IN SIXTEENTH-CENTURY FRANCE
Natalie Z. Davis

Eight religious wars rocked the kingdom of France from 1562 to 1598. Spurred by the grandiose ambitions of the leading aristocratic families and fueled by the religious fervor so characteristic of the Protestant and Catholic Reformations, these civil wars became international wars as Spain sought to dismember its northern neighbor — and nearly succeeded. The devastation was enormous, as Huguenot (French Protestant) and Catholic armies crisscrossed France. Indeed, by the late 1580s, there were three competing factions: Protestant, ultra-Catholic (receiving support from Spain), and the French who placed the state above religion. No wonder, then, that during these ungodly four decades of turmoil, violence and brutality were endemic.

Natalie Z. Davis, a historian of early modern France and former president of the American Historical Association, is professor emeritus from Princeton University. Here she explores one aspect of violent behavior in late-sixteenth-century France — the religious riot — and analyzes the patterns of riot behavior. Her sources include memoirs, journals, correspondence, sermons, contemporary books and pamphlets, and literary works. Davis does not see the riots as class warfare; they drew legitimacy from religious rituals and beliefs. Most notorious of the riots was the St. Bartholomew's Day Massacre of 23–24 August 1572, when Catholics killed perhaps two thousand Huguenots in Paris and, later, approximately three thousand in other parts of France. Davis goes beyond this well-known event to the dynamics of religious riots, and in so doing she raises important questions. What claims to legality did the rioters have? We are often tempted to dismiss rioters out of hand as lawbreakers, but sixteenth-century participants in crowd violence had other perspectives. Were the participants the very poor, hoping to profit from the occasion, or better placed social groups, sin-

Natalie Zemon Davis, "The Rites of Violence: Religious Riot in Sixteenth-Century France," *Past and Present: A Journal of Historical Studies* 59 (May 1973): 51–91.

cerely committed to specific goals? Did the rioters simply lash out at random, or were they organized, planning their acts of desecration, brutality, and death?

Davis's examination of the idea of pollution places us in the midst of the religious crowd. Sixteenth-century Catholics were certain that Protestants profaned god and the community by their actions and even by their very existence. Protestants believed the same about Catholics. The French felt an obligation, a duty to society and to god, to remove the uncleanliness and profanation. Sincere Christians in the sixteenth century could not permit defilement by others who threatened to overturn society, to rupture what should be, according to both Catholics and Protestants, a society unified by the one faith and only one faith. French people did not believe in the virtue of religious tolerance. In fact, they considered religious tolerance injurious to god and to god's plan. What were the differences between Catholic and Protestant riots, and how did the belief system of each religion affect the types of violence practiced by its adherents? Do you think religious violence was extraordinary or usual in Reformation France?

Arguably, the Bible commands Jews and Christians to smite the followers of false gods, just as the Koran orders Muslims to do so. Should historians condemn societies that obey such literal biblical commands?

> These are the statutes and judgements, which ye shall observe to do in the land, which the Lord God of thy fathers giveth thee. . . . Ye shall utterly destroy all the places wherein the nations which he shall possess served their gods, upon the high mountains, and upon the hills, and under every green tree:
> And ye shall overthrow their altars, and break their pillars and burn their groves with fire; and ye shall hew down the graven images of their gods, and destroy the names of them out of that place [Deuteronomy xii. 1–3].

Thus a Calvinist pastor to his flock in 1562.

> If thy brother, the son of thy mother, or thy son, or thy daughter, or thy wife of thy bosom, or thy friend, which is as thine own soul, entice thee secretly, saying Let us go serve other gods, which thou hast not known, thou, nor thy fathers . . . Thou shalt not consent unto him, nor hearken unto him . . . But thou shalt surely kill him; thine hand shall be first upon him to put him to death, and afterwards the hand of all the people. . . .
> If thou shalt hear say in one of thy cities, which the Lord thy God hath given thee to dwell there, saying, Certain men, the children of Belial are gone out from among you, and have withdrawn the inhabitants of their city, saying Let us go and serve other gods, which ye have not known . . . Thou shalt surely smite the inhabitants of that city with the edge of the sword, destroying it utterly and all that is therein [Deuteronomy xiii. 6, 8–9, 12–13, 15].
> And [Jehu] lifted up his face to the window and said, Who is on my side? Who? And there looked out to him two or three eunuchs.[1] And he said, Throw

---

[1] Castrated men.

her down. So they threw [Jezebel] down: and some of her blood was sprinkled on the wall, and on the horses: and he trode her under foot. . . . And they went to bury her: but they found no more of her than the skull and the feet and the palms of her hands. . . . And [Jehu] said, This is the word of the Lord, which he spake by his servant Elijah . . . saying, In the portion of Jezreel shall dogs eat the flesh of Jezebel: and the carcase of Jezebel shall be as dung upon the face of the field [II Kings ix. 32–3, 35–7].

Thus in 1568 Parisian preachers held up to their Catholic parishioners the end of a wicked idolater. Whatever the intentions of pastors and priests, such words were among the many spurs to religious riot in sixteenth-century France. By religious riot I mean, as a preliminary definition, any violent action, with words or weapons, undertaken against religious targets by people who are not acting *officially and formally* as agents of political and ecclesiastical authority. As food rioters bring their moral indignation to bear upon the state of the grain market, so religious rioters bring their zeal to bear upon the state of men's relations to the sacred. The violence of the religious riot is distinguished, at least in principle, from the action of political authorities, who can legally silence, humiliate, demolish, punish, torture and execute; and also from the action of soldiers, who at certain times and places can legally kill and destroy. In mid sixteenth-century France, all these sources of violence were busily producing, and it is sometimes hard to tell a militia officer from a murderer and a soldier from a statue-smasher. Nevertheless, there are occasions when we can separate out for examination a violent crowd set on religious goals. . . .

. . . We may see these crowds as prompted by political and moral traditions which legitimize and even prescribe their violence. We may see urban rioters not as miserable, uprooted, unstable masses, but as men and women who often have some stake in their community; who may be craftsmen or better; and who, even when poor and unskilled, may appear respectable to their everyday neighbours. Finally, we may see their violence, however cruel, not as random and limitless, but as aimed at defined targets and selected from a repertory of traditional punishments and forms of destruction. . . .

. . . My first purpose is to describe the shape and structure of the religious riot in French cities and towns, especially in the 1560s and early 1570s. We will look at the goals, legitimation and occasions for riots; at the kinds of action undertaken by the crowds and the targets for their violence; and briefly at the participants in the riots and their organization. We will consider differences between Protestant and Catholic styles of crowd behaviour, but will also indicate the many ways in which they are alike. . . .

What then can we learn of the goals of popular religious violence? What were the crowds intending to do and why did they think they must do it? Their behaviour suggests, first of all, a goal akin to preaching: the defence of true doctrine and the refutation of false doctrine through dramatic challenges and tests. "You blaspheme," shouts a woman to a Catholic preacher in Montpellier in 1558 and, having broken the decorum of the service, leads part of the congregation out of the church. "You lie," shouts a sheathmaker in the midst of the Franciscan's Easter sermon in Lyon, and his words are underscored by the gunshots of

Huguenots waiting in the square. "Look," cries a weaver in Tournai, as he seizes the elevated host from the priest, "deceived people, do you believe this is the King, Jesus Christ, the true God and Saviour? Look!" And he crumbles the wafer and escapes. "Look," says a crowd of image-breakers to the people of Albiac in 1561, showing them the relics they have seized from the Carmelite monastery, "look, they are only animal bones." And the slogan of the Reformed crowds as they rush through the streets of Paris, of Toulouse, of La Rochelle, of Angoulême is "The Gospel! The Gospel! Long live the Gospel!"

Catholic crowds answer this kind of claim to truth in Angers by taking the French Bible, well-bound and gilded, seized in the home of a rich merchant, and parading it through the streets on the end of a halberd. "There's the truth hung. There's the truth of the Huguenots, the truth of all the devils." Then, throwing it into the river, "There's the truth of all the devils drowned." And if the Huguenot doctrine was true, why didn't the Lord come and save them from their killers? So a crowd of Orléans Catholic taunted its victims in 1572: "Where is your God? Where are your prayers and Psalms? Let him save you if he can." Even the dead were made to speak in Normandy and Provence, where leaves of the Protestant Bible were stuffed into the mouths and wounds of corpses. "They preached the truth of their God. Let them call him to their aid."

The same refutation was, of course, open to Protestants. A Protestant crowd corners a baker guarding the holy-wafer box in Saint Médard's Church in Paris in 1561. "Messieurs," he pleads, "do not touch it for the honour of Him who dwells here." "Does your God of paste protect you now from the pains of death?" was the Protestant answer before they killed him. True doctrine can be defended in sermon or speech, backed up by the magistrate's sword against the heretic. Here it is defended by dramatic demonstration, backed up by the violence of the crowd.

A more frequent goal of these riots, however, is that of ridding the community of dreaded pollution. The word "pollution" is often on the lips of the violent, and the concept serves well to sum up the dangers which rioters saw in the dirty and diabolic enemy. A priest brings ornaments and objects for singing the Mass into a Bordeaux jail. The Protestant prisoner smashes them all. "Do you want to blaspheme the Lord's name everywhere? Isn't it enough that the temples are defiled? Must you also profane prisons so nothing is unpolluted?" "The Calvinists have polluted their hands with every kind of sacrilege men can think of," writes a Doctor of Theology in 1562. Not long after at the Sainte Chapelle,[2] a man seizes the elevated host with his "polluted hands" and crushes it under foot. The worshippers beat him up and deliver him to the agents of Parlement.[3] . . .

One does not have to listen very long to sixteenth-century voices to hear the evidence for the uncleanliness and profanation of either side. As for the Protes-

---

[2] A Gothic church in Paris, built in the thirteenth century to house relics.

[3] The Parlement of Paris, a sovereign judicial court with jurisdiction over approximately one-half of France.

tants, Catholics knew that, in the style of earlier heretics, they snuffed out the candles and had sexual intercourse after the voluptuous Psalmsinging of their nocturnal conventicles.[4] . . . But it was not just the fleshly licence with which they lived which was unclean, but the things they said in their "pestilential" books and the things they did in hatred of the Mass, the sacraments and whole Catholic religion. As the representative of the clergy said at the Estates[5] of Orléans, the heretics intended to leave "no place in the Kingdom which was dedicated, holy and sacred to the Lord, but would only profane churches, demolish altars and break images."

The Protestants' sense of Catholic pollution also stemmed to some extent from their sexual uncleanness, here specifically of the clergy. Protestant polemic never tired of pointing to the lewdness of the clergy with their "concubines."[6] It was rumoured that the Church of Lyon had an organization of hundreds of women, sort of temple prostitutes, at the disposition of priests and canons; and an observer pointed out with disgust how, after the First Religious War,[7] the Mass and the brothel re-entered Rouen together. One minister even claimed that the clergy were for the most part Sodomites. But more serious than the sexual abominations of the clergy was the defilement of the sacred by Catholic ritual life, from the diabolic magic of the Mass to the idolatrous worship of images. The Mass is "vile filth"; "no people pollute the House of the Lord in every way more than the clergy." Protestant converts talked of their own past lives as a time of befoulment and dreaded present "contamination" from Catholic churches and rites.

Pollution was a dangerous thing to suffer in a community, from either a Protestant or a Catholic point of view, for it would surely provoke the wrath of God. Terrible wind storms and floods were sometimes taken as signs of His impatience on this count. Catholics, moreover, had also to worry about offending Mary and the saints; and though the anxious, expiatory processions organized in the wake of Protestant sacrilege might temporarily appease them, the heretics were sure to strike again. It is not surprising, then, that so many of the acts of violence performed by Catholic and Protestant crowds have . . . the character either of rites of purification or of a paradoxical desecration, intended to cut down on uncleanness by placing profane things, like chrism,[8] back in the profane world where they belonged. . . .

For Catholic zealots, the extermination of the heretical "vermin" promised the restoration of unity to the body social and the guarantee of its traditional boundaries:

---

[4] Secret religious meetings.

[5] The Estates in French provinces were assemblies that maintained relations with the central government and dealt with provincial affairs.

[6] A concubine is a woman who cohabits with a man to whom she is not married.

[7] 1562–1563.

[8] Holy oil used in Christian ceremonies.

And let us all say in unison:
Long live the Catholic religion
Long live the King and good parishioners,
Long live faithful Parisians,
And may it always come to pass
That every person goes to Mass,
One God, one Faith, one King.

For Protestant zealots, the purging of the priestly "vermin" promised the creation of a new kind of unity within the body social, all the tighter because false gods and monkish sects would no longer divide it. Relations within the social order would be purer, too, for lewdness and love of gain would be limited. As was said of Lyon after its "deliverance" in 1562:

. . . When this town so vain
Was filled
With idolatry and dealings
Of usury and lewdness,
It had clerics and merchants aplenty.

But once it was purged
And changed
By the Word of God,
That brood of vipers
Could hope no more
To live in so holy a place.

Crowds might defend truth, and crowds might purify, but there was also a third aspect to the religious riot — a political one. . . .

. . . When the magistrate had not used his sword to defend the faith and the true church and to punish the idolators, then the crowd would do it for him. Thus, many religious disturbances begin with the ringing of the tocsin,[9] as in a time of civic assembly or emergency. Some riots end with the marching of the religious "wrongdoers" on the other side to jail. In 1561, for instance, Parisian Calvinists, fearing that the priests and worshippers in Saint Médard's Church were organizing an assault on their services . . . , first rioted in Saint Médard and then seized some fifteen Catholics as "mutinous" and led them off, "bound like galley-slaves," to the Châtelet prison.

If the Catholic killing of Huguenots has in some ways the form of a rite of purification, it also sometimes has the form of imitating the magistrate. The mass executions of Protestants at Merindol and Cabrières in Provence and at Meaux in the 1540s, duly ordered by the Parlements of Aix and of Paris as punishment for heresy and high treason, anticipate crowd massacres of later decades. The Protestants themselves sensed this: the devil, unable to extinguish the light of the Gospel through the sentences of judges, now tried to obscure it through furious war and

---

[9] Bell used to sound an alarm.

a murderous populace. Whereas before they were made martyrs by one executioner, now it is at the hands of "infinite numbers of them, and the swords of private persons have become the litigants, witnesses, judges, decrees and executors of the strangest cruelties."

Similarly, *official* acts of torture and *official* acts of desecration of the corpses of certain criminals anticipate some of the acts performed by riotous crowds. The public execution was, of course, a dramatic and well-attended event in the sixteenth century, and the wood-cut and engraving documented the scene far and wide. There the crowd might see the offending tongue of the blasphemer pierced or slit, the offending hands of the desecrator cut off. There the crowd could watch the traitor decapitated and disemboweled, his corpse quartered and the parts borne off for public display in different sections of the town. The body of an especially heinous criminal was dragged through the streets, attached to a horse's tail. The image of exemplary royal punishment lived on for weeks, even years, as the corpses of murderers were exposed on gallows or wheels and the heads of rebels on posts. . . . [C]rowds often took their victims to places of official execution, as in Paris in 1562, when the Protestant printer, Roc Le Frere, was dragged for burning to the Marché aux Pourceaux,[10] and in Toulouse the same year, when a merchant, slain in front of a church, was dragged for burning to the town hall. "The King salutes you," said a Catholic crowd in Orléans to a Protestant trader, then put a cord around his neck as official agents might do, and led him off to be killed.

Riots also occurred in connection with judicial cases, either to hurry the judgement along, or when verdicts in religious cases were considered too severe or too lenient by "the voice of the people." Thus in 1569 in Montpellier, a Catholic crowd forced the judge to condemn an important Huguenot prisoner to death in a hasty "trial," then seized him and hanged him in front of his house. . . . And in 1561 in Marsillargues, when prisoners for heresy were released by royal decree, a Catholic crowd "rearrested" them, and executed and burned them in the streets. . . .

The seizure of religious buildings and the destruction of images by Calvinist crowds were also accomplished with the conviction that they were taking on the rôle of the authorities. When Protestants in Montpellier occupied a church in 1561, they argued that the building belonged to them already, since its clergy had been wholly supported by merchants and burghers in the past and the property belonged to the town. . . .

To be sure, the relation of a French Calvinist crowd to the magisterial model is different from that of a French Catholic crowd. The king had not yet chastised the clergy and "put all ydolatry to ruyne and confusyon," as Protestants had been urging him since the early 1530s. Calvinist crowds were using his sword as the king *ought* to have been using it and as some princes and city councils outside of France had already used it. Within the kingdom before 1560 city councils had

---

[10] Pig market.

only *indicated* the right path, as they set up municipal schools, lay-controlled welfare systems or otherwise limited the sphere of action of the clergy. During the next years, as revolution and conversion created Reformed city councils and governors (such as the Queen of Navarre) within France, Calvinist crowds finally had local magistrates whose actions they could prompt or imitate.

In general, then, the crowds in religious riots in sixteenth-century France can be seen as sometimes acting out clerical rôles — defending true doctrine or ridding the community of defilement in a violent version of priest or prophet — and as sometimes acting out magisterial rôles. Clearly some riotous behaviour, such as the extensive pillaging done by both Protestants and Catholics, cannot be subsumed under these heads; but just as the prevalence of pillaging in a war does not prevent us from typing it as a holy war, so the prevalence of pillaging in a riot should not prevent us from seeing it as essentially religious. . . .

So long as rioters maintained a given religious commitment, they rarely displayed guilt or shame for their violence. By every sign, the crowds believed their actions legitimate.

One reason for this conviction is that in some, though by no means all, religious riots, clerics and political officers were active members of the crowd, though not precisely in their official capacity. In Lyon in 1562, Pastor Jean Ruffy took part in the sack of the Cathedral of Saint Jean with a sword in his hand. Catholic priests seem to have been in quite a few disturbances, as in Rouen in 1560, when priests and parishioners in a Corpus Christi[11] parade broke into the houses of Protestants who had refused to do the procession honour. . . .

On the other hand, not all religious riots could boast of officers or clergy in the crowd, and other sources of legitimation must be sought. Here we must recognize what mixed cues were given out by priests and pastors in their sermons on heresy or idolatry. . . . However much Calvin[12] and other pastors opposed such disturbances (preferring that all images and altars be removed soberly by the authorities), they nevertheless were always more ready to understand and excuse this violence than, say, that of a peasant revolt or of a journeymen's march. Perhaps, after all, the popular idol-smashing was due to "an extraordinary power *(vertu)* from God." . . .

The rôle of Catholic preachers in legitimating popular violence was even more direct. If we don't know whether to believe the Protestant claim that Catholic preachers at Paris were telling their congregations in 1557 that Protestants ate babies, it is surely significant that . . . Catholic preachers did blame the loss of the battle of Saint Quentin[13] on God's wrath at the presence of heretics in France. . . . And if Protestant pastors could timidly wonder if divine power were not behind

---

[11] A Roman Catholic festival instituted in the thirteenth century to honor the Blessed Sacrament of the body of Jesus.

[12] John Calvin (1509–1564), French Protestant theologian, founder of Calvinism and religious leader of Geneva.

[13] Spanish victory over the French in 1557.

the extraordinary force of the iconoclasts, priests had no doubts that certain miraculous occurrences in the wake of Catholic riots were a sign of divine approval, such as a copper cross in Troyes that began to change colour and cure people in 1561, the year of a riot in which Catholics bested Protestants. . . .

In all likelihood, however, there are sources for the legitimation of popular religious riot that come directly out of the experience of the local groups which often formed the nucleus of a crowd — the men and women who had worshiped together in the dangerous days of the night conventicles, the men in confraternities, in festive groups, in youth gangs and militia units. It should be remembered how often conditions in sixteenth-century cities required groups of "little people" to take the law into their own hands. Royal edicts themselves enjoined any person who saw a murder, theft or other misdeed to ring the tocsin and chase after the criminal. Canon law allowed certain priestly rôles to laymen in times of emergency, such as the midwife's responsibility to baptize a baby in danger of dying, while the rôle of preaching the Gospel was often assumed by Protestant laymen in the decades before the Reformed Church was set up. . . .

. . . [T]he occasion for most religious violence was during the time of religious worship or ritual and in the space which one or both groups were using for sacred purposes. . . .

Almost every type of public religious event has a disturbance associated with it. The sight of a statue of the Virgin at a crossroad or in a wall-niche provokes a Protestant group to mockery of those who reverence her. A fight ensues. Catholics hide in a house to entrap Huguenots who refuse to doff their hats to a Virgin nearby, and then rush out and beat the heretics up. Baptism: in Nemours, a Protestant family has its baby baptized on All Souls' Day[14] according to the new Reformed rite. With the help of an aunt, a group of Catholics steals it away for rebaptism. A drunkard sees the father and the godfather and other Protestants discussing the event in the streets, claps his sabots[15] and shouts, "Here are the Huguenots who have come to massacre us." A crowd assembles, the tocsin is rung, and a three-hour battle takes place. Funeral: in Toulouse, at Easter-time, a Protestant carpenter tries to bury his Catholic wife by the new Reformed rite. A Catholic crowd seizes the corpse and buries it. The Protestants dig it up and try to rebury her. The bells are rung, and with a great noise a Catholic crowd assembles with stones and sticks. Fighting and sacking ensue.

Religious services: a Catholic Mass is the occasion for an attack on the Host or the interruption of a sermon, which then leads to a riot. Protestant preaching in a home attracts large Catholic crowds at the door, who stone the house or otherwise threaten the worshippers. . . .

But these encounters are as nothing compared to the disturbances that cluster around processional life. Corpus Christi Day, with its crowds, coloured banners and great crosses, was the chance for Protestants *not* to put rugs in front

---

[14] Commemoration of the souls of the departed, celebrated on 2 November.

[15] Cheap wooden shoes worn by peasants and workers.

of their doors; for Protestant women to sit ostentatiously in their windows spinning; for heroic individuals, like the painter Denis de Vallois in Lyon, to throw themselves on the "God of paste" so as "to destroy him in every parish in the world." Corpus Christi Day was the chance for a procession to turn into an assault on and slaughter of those who had so offended the Catholic faith, its participants shouting, as in Lyon in 1561, "For the flesh of God, we must kill all the Huguenots." A Protestant procession was a parade of armed men and women in their dark clothes, going off to services at their temple or outside the city gates, singing Psalms and spiritual songs that to Catholic ears sounded like insults against the Church and her sacraments. It was an occasion for children to throw stones, for an exchange of scandalous words — "idolaters," "devils from the Pope's purgatory," "Huguenot heretics, living like dogs" — and then finally for fighting. . . .

The occasions which express most concisely the contrast between the two religious groups, however, are those in which a popular festive Catholicism took over the streets with dancing, masks, banners, costumes and music — "lascivious abominations," according to the Protestants. . . .

As with liturgical rites, there were some differences between the rites of violence of Catholic and Protestant crowds. . . .

. . . [T]he iconoclastic Calvinist crowds . . . come out as the champions in the destruction of religious property ("with more than Turkish cruelty," said a priest). This was not only because the Catholics had more physical accessories to their rite, but also because the Protestants sensed much more danger and defilement in the *wrongful use of material objects*. . . .

In bloodshed the Catholics are the champions (remember we are talking of the actions of Catholic and Protestant crowds, not of their armies). I think this is due not only to their being in the long run the strongest party numerically in most cities, but also to their stronger sense of *the persons of heretics* as sources of danger and defilement. Thus, injury and murder were a preferred mode of purifying the body social.

Furthermore, the preferred targets for physical attack differ in the Protestant and Catholic cases. As befitting a movement intending to overthrow a thousand years of clerical "tyranny" and "pollution," the Protestants' targets were primarily priests, monks and friars. That their ecclesiastical victims were usually unarmed (as Catholic critics hastened to point out) did not make them any less harmful in Protestant eyes, or any more immune from the wrath of God. Lay people were sometimes attacked by Protestant crowds, too, such as the festive dancers who were stoned at Pamiers and Lyon, and the worshippers who were killed at Saint Médard's Church. But there is nothing that quite resembles the style and extent of the slaughter of the 1572 massacres. The Catholic crowds were, of course, happy to catch a pastor when they could, but the death of any heretic would help in the cause of cleansing France of these perfidious sowers of disorder and disunion. . . .

. . . [T]he overall picture in these urban religious riots is not one of the "people" slaying the rich. Protestant crowds expressed no preference for killing or assaulting powerful prelates over simple priests. As for Catholic crowds, contemporary listings of their victims in the 1572 massacres show that artisans, the "little people," are represented in significant numbers. . . .

. . . Let us look a little further at what I have called their rites of violence. Is there any way we can order the terrible, concrete details of filth, shame and torture that are reported from both Protestant and Catholic riots? I would suggest that they can be reduced to a repertory of actions, derived from the Bible, from the liturgy, from the action of political authority, or from the traditions of popular folk justice, intended to purify the religious community and humiliate the enemy and thus make him less harmful.

The religious significance of destruction by water or fire is clear enough. The rivers which receive so many Protestant corpses are not merely convenient mass graves, they are temporarily a kind of holy water, an essential feature of Catholic rites of exorcism. . . .

Let us take a more difficult case, the troubling case of the desecration of corpses. This is primarily an action of Catholic crowds in the sixteenth century. Protestant crowds could be very cruel indeed in torturing living priests, but paid little attention to them when they were dead. (Perhaps this is related to the Protestant rejection of Purgatory and prayers for the dead: the souls of the dead experience immediately Christ's presence or the torments of the damned, and thus the dead body is no longer so dangerous or important an object to the living.) What interested Protestants was digging up bones that were being treated as sacred objects by Catholics and perhaps burning them, after the fashion of Josiah in I Kings. The Catholics, however, were not content with burning or drowning heretical corpses. That was not cleansing enough. The bodies had to be weakened and humiliated further. To an eerie chorus of "strange whistles and hoots," they were thrown to the dogs like Jezebel, they were dragged through the streets, they had their genitalia and internal organs cut away, which were then hawked through the city in a ghoulish commerce.

Let us also take the embarrassing case of the desecration of religious objects by filthy and disgusting means. It is the Protestants . . . who are concerned about objects, who are trying to show that Catholic objects of worship have no magical power. It is not enough to cleanse by swift and energetic demolition, not enough to purify by a great public burning of the images, as in Albiac, with the children of the town ceremonially reciting the Ten Commandments around the fire. The line between the sacred and the profane was also re-drawn by throwing the sacred host to the dogs, by roasting the crucifix upon a spit, by using holy oil to grease one's boots, and by leaving human excrement on holy-water basins and other religious objects.

And what of the living victims? Catholics and Protestants humiliated them by techniques borrowed from the repertory of folk justice. Catholic crowds lead Protestant women through the streets with muzzles on — a popular punishment for the shrew — or with a crown of thorns. A form of charivari[16] is used, where

---

[16] Davis defines this elsewhere as "a noisy, masked demonstration to humiliate some wrongdoer in the community."

the noisy throng humiliates its victim by making him ride backward on an ass. . . . In Montauban, a priest was ridden backward on an ass, his chalice in one hand, his host in the other, and his missal at an end of a halberd.[17] At the end of his ride, he must crush his host and burn his own vestments. . . .

These episodes disclose to us the underlying function of the rites of violence. As with the "games" of Christ's tormentors, which hide from them the full knowledge of what they do, so these charades and ceremonies hide from sixteenth-century rioters a full knowledge of what they are doing. Like the legitimation for religious riot . . . , they are part of the "conditions for guilt-free massacre." . . . The crucial fact that the killers must forget is that their victims are human beings. These harmful people in the community — the evil priest or hateful heretic — have already been transformed for the crowd into "vermin" or "devils." The rites of religious violence complete the process of dehumanization. So in Meaux, where Protestants were being slaughtered with butchers' cleavers, a living victim was trundled to his death in a wheelbarrow, while the crowd cried "vinegar, mustard." And the vicar of the parish of Fouquebrune in the Angoumois was attached with the oxen to a plough and died from Protestant blows as he pulled.

What kinds of people made up the crowds that performed the range of acts we have examined in this paper? First, they were not by and large the alienated rootless poor. . . . A large percentage of men in Protestant iconoclastic riots and in the crowds of Catholic killers in 1572 were characterized as artisans. Sometimes the crowds included other men from the lower orders. . . . More often, the social composition of the crowds extended upward to encompass merchants, notaries and lawyers, as well as clerics. . . .

In addition, there was significant participation by two other groups of people who, though not rootless and alienated, had a more marginal relationship to political power than did lawyers, merchants or even male artisans — namely, city women and teenaged boys. . . .

Finally, as this study has already suggested, the crowds of Catholics and Protestants, including those bent on deadly tasks, were not an inchoate mass, but showed many signs of organization. Even with riots that had little or no planning behind them, the event was given some structure by the situation of worship or the procession that was the occasion for many disturbances. In other cases, planning in advance led to lists of targets, and ways of identifying friends or fellow rioters. . . .

That such splendor and order should be put to violent uses is a disturbing fact. Disturbing, too, is the whole subject of religious violence. How does an historian talk about a massacre of the magnitude of St. Bartholomew's Day? One approach is to view extreme religious violence as an extraordinary event, the product of frenzy, of the frustrated and paranoic primitive mind of the people.

A second approach sees such violence as a more usual part of social behaviour, but explains it as a somewhat pathological product of certain kinds of child-rearing, economic deprivation or status loss. This paper has assumed that conflict is peren-

---

[17] A combined spear and battleaxe.

nial in social life, though the forms and strength of the accompanying violence vary; and that religious violence is intense because it connects intimately with the fundamental values and self-definition of a community. The violence is explained not in terms of how crazy, hungry or sexually frustrated the violent people are (though they may sometimes have such characteristics), but in terms of the goals of their actions and in terms of the rôles and patterns of behaviour allowed by their culture. Religious violence is related here less to the pathological than to the normal.

Thus, in sixteenth-century France, we have seen crowds taking on the rôle of priest, pastor or magistrate to defend doctrine or purify the religious community, either to maintain its Catholic boundaries and structure, or to re-form relations within it. We have seen that popular religious violence could receive legitimation from different features of political and religious life, as well as from the group identity of the people in the crowds. The targets and character of crowd violence differed somewhat between Catholics and Protestants, depending on their perception of the source of danger and on their religious sensibility. But in both cases, religious violence had a connection in time, place and form with the life of worship, and the violent actions themselves were drawn from a store of punitive or purificatory traditions current in sixteenth-century France.

In this context, the cruelty of crowd action in the 1572 massacres was not an exceptional occurrence. St. Bartholomew was certainly a bigger affair than, say, the Saint Médard's riot, it had more explicit sanction from political authority, it had elaborate networks of communication at the top level throughout France, and it took a more terrible toll in deaths. Perhaps its most unusual feature was that the Protestants did not fight back. But on the whole, it still fits into a whole pattern of sixteenth-century religious disturbance.

This inquiry also points to a more general conclusion. Even in the extreme case of religious violence, crowds do not act in a mindless way. They will to some degree have a sense that what they are doing is legitimate, the occasions will relate somehow to the defence of their cause, and their violent behaviour will have some structure to it — here dramatic and ritual. But the rites of violence are not the rights of violence in any *absolute* sense. They simply remind us that if we try to increase safety and trust within a community, try to guarantee that the violence it generates will take less destructive and less cruel forms, then we must think less about pacifying "deviants" and more about changing the central values.

THE BODY, APPEARANCE, AND SEXUALITY
Sara F. Matthews Grieco

One of the most dynamic areas of recent scholarship is the history of the body. Not only have people changed physically over time, but representations of the body have varied in the cultures that make up Western civilization. The body has symbolized different meanings — such as social rebellion or protest (as at Carnival) — and has allowed the individual to present him- or herself to society in many ways. Professor of history at Syracuse University (Florence), Sara F. Matthews Grieco specializes in the ideology of gender, the representation of women, and sexual roles in sixteenth-century Italy and France. Art, diaries, medical and theological writings, and literature lead Grieco to discern two conflicting attitudes toward the body: basic mistrust for its weaknesses and sexuality, and veneration of its physical beauty and opportunity for perfection.

The sixteenth- and seventeenth-century elite were hygienic, but their notion of cleanliness differed from ours today. How did early modern Europeans maintain their waterless cleanliness, and why was a faultless appearance so important?

What constituted a beautiful and feminine body, and how did women attempt to improve their appearances? Beauty was, of course, linked to love and sexuality. What was the "renaissance of prudery," and how did it affect women's status and condition? What types of sexuality did religious and political authorities consider proper and improper?

Grieco sees the eighteenth century as a watershed in the history of the body. What changes occurred in the eighteenth century with respect to marriage, sexuality, and the proper care of one's body? In what ways do standards of beauty today compare to those of early modern Europe?

Two conflicting attitudes toward the body characterize the early modern period. On the one hand, the Renaissance inherited from the Middle Ages a basic mistrust

Sara F. Matthews Grieco, "The Body, Appearance, and Sexuality," in *A History of Women in the West,* ed. Natalie Z. Davis and Arlette Farge, vol. 3 of *Renaissance and Enlightenment Paradoxes* (Cambridge: Belknap Press of Harvard University Press, 1993), 46–73, 76–84.

of the body, its ephemeral nature, its dangerous appetites, and its many weaknesses. This heritage of suspicion and diffidence carried over into the Protestant Reform[1] and the Catholic Counter-Reformation;[2] accordingly, sixteenth- and seventeenth-century Europeans were encouraged in prudery with respect to the body, its appearance, and its sexuality. On the other hand, the Renaissance also brought the rediscovery of the nude and a rehabilitation of physical beauty. The artists and humanists of the Italian peninsula disseminated throughout Europe classical ideals of physical and spiritual perfection as well as Neoplatonic[3] justifications for earthly love and beauty that were to form the basis for the aesthetic canons and elite mores of the early modern period. But it was also from Italy that the dual scourges of plague and syphilis reached the rest of Europe, causing the closure of most public baths and brothels, the rejection of water for bodily hygiene, and the promotion of marital sexuality at the expense of all other sexual practices. Attitudes toward the body and sexuality were thus marked by an unceasing dialectic between the obsession with erotic love and the obligations of social and religious duty. This same paradoxical dialectic was to define women's bodies and their sexuality for almost three hundred years.

Women's social identity has long been conditioned by their culture's perception of their bodies. Whether they be considered "imperfect males" or "walking wombs," earthly reflections of divine beauty or lascivious lures in the service of Satan, their lives are dominated as much by their society's attitudes toward the body in general as by its more specific definitions of gender. In order to understand both the social and imaginary dimensions of women's lives from the sixteenth through the eighteenth centuries, it is therefore essential to understand how the body was perceived and treated. What was considered necessary for its protection, hygiene, and maintenance? Above all, what were the criteria according to which women constructed their appearance, and what purposes did this appearance serve? Canons of feminine beauty and norms of physical hygiene underwent a series of significant changes between the end of the Middle Ages and the end of the early modern period. These evolutions in practice and taste reflected, however, more than just changes in the concept of the body and the appearance of women. In a period of chronic social instability and political and religious conflict, they also expressed a constant and overwhelming concern for order and clearly defined social boundaries in which the concept of gender played a ubiquitous and determining role.

Cleanliness and personal hygiene are relative concepts that underwent a radical transformation from the early Renaissance through the eighteenth century.

---

[1] The Protestant Reformation, the sixteenth-century split in western Christianity between the Roman Catholic Church and a variety of Protestant denominations.

[2] The Roman Catholic Church's reform movement and resurgence in reaction to the Protestant Reformation during the late sixteenth century.

[3] Relating to the third-century pagan philosophy that emphasized spiritual purity.

Formerly dependent on regular baths and the luxury of the steam room, bodily hygiene in the sixteenth and seventeenth centuries became a waterless affair. Clean linen replaced clean skin. A new fear of water gave rise to substitutes such as powder and perfume, which in turn created a new basis for social distinction. More than ever before, cleanliness became the prerogative of the wealthy.

During the sixteenth and seventeenth centuries the custom of bathing, either in public establishments or in the privacy of the home, virtually disappeared. Fear of contagion (plague and syphilis) and more stringent attitudes toward prostitution (a sideline of many baths) accounted for the closure of most public bathing establishments. In private homes, growing distrust of water and the development of new, "dry," and elitist techniques of personal hygiene brought about the disappearance of the bathing tub.

The deliberate elimination of public baths constituted an act of social and moral hygiene. Far from being devoted solely to personal cleanliness, these establishments also offered services that civil authorities regarded as a threat to the moral tenor of the cities. Wine and meals were served to bathers in or out of the water, and beds were available for those who wished to rest after their ablutions, to meet their lovers, or to be entertained by a prostitute. Although many bathing facilities allocated different rooms or separate bathing pools to men and women (some even alternated men's and women's days or served one sex only), most public baths were places of pleasure, associated with brothels and taverns in the minds of contemporaries. Preachers thus inveighed against the evil habits of young men who wasted their time and their patrimony in visiting "brothels, baths and taverns." Similarly, Albrecht Dürer's[4] careful accounts of travel expenses list his baths (often taken with friends) among the costs of other pastimes such as gambling and drinking.

Moral depravity was not, however, the only ill associated with those naked or scantily clad bodies that mingled in the intimacy of the steam room, partaking of the often boisterous pleasures of the collective tub. Like taverns and brothels, baths were among the first establishments to be closed in times of plague, in accordance with the prevailing belief that any gathering of people would facilitate the spread of the dread disease. Doctors and public health officials also discouraged bathing of any sort during epidemics for fear that the naked skin, its pores dilated by hot vapors, would become more vulnerable to the pestiferous "miasmas"[5] that were credited with carrying sickness. Throughout the sixteenth and seventeenth centuries, belief in the permeability of the skin and the threat that bathing presented for health in general continued to furnish medical texts with a variety of arguments against the evils of public baths and the dangers of water. In the sixteenth century, fear of syphilis joined that of other contagious diseases in the stock arguments against promiscuous baths, along with other, more fanciful but equally important fears such as that of "bath pregnancies," whereby women

---

[4] German painter and engraver (1471–1528).

[5] Bad-smelling vapors.

were supposedly inseminated by adventurous sperm wandering about in warm waters. . . .

Slowly baths became a medical rather than a pleasurable or hygienic practice, accompanied by the use of cupping-glasses[6] to draw off harmful humors and inevitably surrounded by a series of precautionary measures. The body was considered "open" and vulnerable when wet, "closed" and protected when dry; whence the development of new, waterless techniques to ensure the niceties of personal hygiene and presentability.

Scholars long believed that the disappearance of water from daily ablutions in the early modern period constituted a lapse into a universal state of grease and grime. This was not entirely true. Although the filth of the lower social orders remained, in this period, as much a characteristic of their inferior status as the dingy homespun garments on their back, those who could afford to do so tended to pay increasing attention to the care and appearance of their person, or at least to those parts visible to the public eye.

Where water disappeared, wiping and rubbing, powdering and perfuming took over. Courtesy books[7] such as Erasmus's[8] influential *De civilitate morum puerilium*[9] (1530) not only described the proper way to blow one's nose or to sit at table but also mandated the cleansing of the body and its orifices, thus emphasizing new social imperatives that distinguished the elite from the "vulgar." . . .

In accordance with the new norms of civility, more attention was paid to the parts of the body that were not covered: the face and the hands. But whereas in the sixteenth century water was still used for morning ablutions on these two parts of the body, by the seventeenth it was considered fit only for rinsing the mouth and the hands — and only on condition that its potentially harmful effects be tempered by the addition of vinegar or wine. Courtesy books especially discouraged the use of water on the face because it was believed to harm eyesight, cause toothache and catarrh,[10] and make the skin overly pale in winter or excessively brown in summer. The head was to be vigorously rubbed with a scented towel or sponge, the hair combed, the ears wiped out, and the mouth rinsed. Powder made its initial appearance as a kind of dry shampoo. Left on the head overnight, it was combed out in the morning along with grease and other impurities. By the end of the sixteenth century, however, perfumed and tinted powders had become an integral part of the daily toilet of the well-to-do, men and women alike. This visible and olfactory accessory not only proclaimed the privilege of cleanliness enjoyed by its wearer but also his or her social standing, for fashion was also a privilege of the wealthy. By the seventeenth century, powder had so conquered the

---

[6] Small glasses used to draw blood from the body.

[7] Works explaining proper manners and behavior.

[8] Desiderius Erasmus (ca. 1466–1536), Dutch humanist.

[9] *On Civility in Children.*

[10] Inflammation of the nose or throat.

upper classes of Europe that no self-respecting aristocrat would be seen in public without it, and by the eighteenth century young and old sported white heads of hair, either wigs or their own silvered locks. An absence of powder came to signal not only a dual impropriety (hygienic and social) but also social inferiority: it was the bourgeois[11] and their inferiors who had "black and greasy hair."

Perfume was likewise credited with a number of virtues, the most important of which were the aesthetic elimination or concealment of unpleasant odors and the hygienic functions of disinfection or purification. Scented towels were used for rubbing the face and the torso, especially the armpits. Long used by the rich to disinfect houses, furniture, and textiles in times of plague, incense and exotic scents were also used in clothing chests to "cleanse" their contents. . . . Like powder, perfumes became a sign of social standing, and the distance between "good" and "bad" odors increased to the extent that in 1709 the French chemist Nicolas Lémery[12] proposed three categories of scent: *parfum royal, parfum pour les bourgeois,* and a *parfum des pauvres*[13] made of oil and soot, whose sole purpose was to disinfect the air. Whence another class privilege, for perfume not only protected the body but also ensured good health. . . .

The new rules of propriety, which dictated that the visible parts of the body be inoffensive to the eye and pleasing to the nose, were more concerned with appearance than with hygiene. A clean appearance was a guarantee of moral probity and social standing; whence the importance of white linen, whose candid surface was identified with the purity of the skin below. Body linen, this "outer envelope" or second skin, also served as a protection for the "inner envelope" or epidermis, and in this respect it progressively came to act as a substitute for all other cleansing functions. White cloth was especially valued, not only because it absorbed perspiration but also because it was supposed to attract impurities and thus preserve the health of the wearer. As of the early seventeenth century a change of shirt or chemise[14] was an essential element of daily hygiene for both the bourgeoisie and the aristocracy — so much so that Savot,[15] in his 1626 treatise on the construction of châteaus and townhouses, pointed out that bathing facilities were no longer necessary "because we now use linen, which helps us keep our bodies clean better than the tubs and steam baths of the ancients, who were deprived of the use and convenience of undergarments."

In the late fifteenth century, shirts and chemises began to peek more and more boldly out from under the garments of men and women. By the end of the sixteenth century, touches of lace or a ruffle at neck and wrist had expanded into fanciful collars and ruffs, spreading into elegantly embroidered expanses that flowed

---

[11] Middle class.

[12] French physician and chemist (1645–1715).

[13] Literally, royal perfume, perfume for the middle class, and perfume of the poor.

[14] A woman's shirt-like, loose-fitting undergarment.

[15] Louis Savot (1579–1640), French physician and author of *French Architecture.*

over shoulder, breast, and forearm in the seventeenth, and turning into cascades of lace and transparent finery in the eighteenth. Throughout the Renaissance, the use of body linen thus increased significantly, in inverse proportion to the use of water and baths. . . .

Body linen and undergarments did not become widely used until the eighteenth century, when the standards set by the ruling classes not only filtered down to servants, salaried workers, and artisans but also inspired a proliferation and diversification of undergarments in which feminine fashion played a decisive role. . . .

Drawers[16] are reputed to have been an Italian invention, introduced to France by Catherine de Médicis[17] in order to ride a horse *à l'amazone* (sidesaddle) without transgressing the rules of decorum. Many contemporaries approved of this feminine adaptation of a male garment insofar as it both preserved "those parts that are not for male eyes" in case of a fall from a horse and protected women from "dissolute young men, who put their hands under women's skirts." The preservation of feminine modesty was not, however, the only function of this unusual garment. Noblewomen had their *caleçons* or *calzoni*[18] made from rich materials, thus adding yet another weapon to their intimate arsenal of suggestion and seduction. That drawers were considered a rather daring addition to the panoply of feminine lingerie is further attested by the fact that courtesans[19] were repeatedly condemned for wearing similar "masculine" articles of dress. Though popular with these ladies' admirers, pantalettes[20] not only transgressed ecclesiastical rulings against cross-dressing but also were suspected of constituting a concession to male homosexuality in that they made their wearers look like boys. Even in the eighteenth century only actresses, window-washers, prostitutes, and aristocrats wore drawers, whose primary functions remained, paradoxically, the protection of modesty and stimulation of the erotic imagination. It would take the hygienic revolution of the nineteenth century to impose underpants as a basic element of the feminine wardrobe.

Although water continued to be credited with many harmful powers and regarded with much suspicion throughout the early modern period, the bath made a comeback in the eighteenth century, both as a luxurious pastime and as a means of a therapeutic exercise. In the 1740s aristocrats began to construct luxurious bathrooms in their palaces and townhouses; some were embellished with fountains and exotic plants. Although most immersions were still surrounded by precautionary measures (a purge beforehand, bedrest and a meal afterward), the practice began to catch on. . . .

---

[16] Underpants.

[17] (1519–1589), queen of France and regent.

[18] Women's underpants.

[19] Prostitutes who have wealthy clients.

[20] Long underpants with a frill at the bottom of each leg.

It was the location and the temperature of the water, however, that determined both the purpose of a bath and its impact on the body. Hot baths in private homes were voluptuous events practiced by indolent women (and men), often in preparation for an amorous encounter. Elsewhere, hot baths could serve a curative function. In 1761 a bathing establishment was built on the banks of the Seine where the wealthy (a bath there cost the equivalent of a week's salary for an artisan) could be "cured" close to home by the virtues of river water. Cold baths became increasingly popular after 1750, following a rash of monographs and medical studies on the value of bathing in maintaining health: a properly taken bath was believed to help the humors circulate, tone up the muscles, and stimulate the functioning of the organs. A new generation of physicians waxed enthusiastic about the tonic qualities of cold water, which contracted the body and increased its vigor. Cold baths were therefore considered useful, not because they cleansed the body, but because they strengthened it. On the whole, those who took cold baths did so as much out of a kind of ascetic morality as for health reasons. Favored by a rising bourgeoisie whose energy disdained aristocratic languor, the cold bath became the symbol of a new, "virile" class in opposition to an old, "effeminate" aristocracy whose delicacy was the proof of its decadance.

Beauty has always been just as relative a concept as personal cleanliness. From the end of the Middle Ages to the end of the early modern period the canons of feminine beauty and the ideal womanly form underwent a series of radical transformations. From svelte to plump and from fresh to painted, the female silhouette and complexion responded to changing conditions of diet, status, and fortune, creating new standards of appearance and taste, new ideals of the beautiful and the erotic.

The medieval ideal of the graceful, narrow-hipped, and small-breasted aristocratic lady gave way in the sixteenth century to a plumper, wide-hipped, and full-breasted model of feminine beauty that was to remain valid until the late eighteenth century. This change in body aesthetics corresponded with a significant evolution in the alimentary habits of the elite. Cookbooks of the fourteenth and fifteenth centuries show a marked preference for sour and acid sauces, containing neither sugar nor fats, whereas those of the sixteenth and seventeenth centuries abound in butter, cream, and sweets. Were women of the ruling classes fatter than their medieval forebears, and did fashion thus adapt itself to a changing physical reality? Or did Renaissance women deliberately develop a rounded silhouette to emulate the current ideal of beauty? In any case a "healthy" plumpness, like cleanliness, was generally reserved for the wealthy; thinness was considered ugly, unhealthy, and a sign of poverty. After all, the majority of women — peasants, servants, and artisans — ate less well than their menfolk, the best and the most food being reserved for the male members of the family, the children, and the women, in that order. European women also grew smaller as a result of an economic and agricultural crisis that persisted from the fourteenth through the eighteenth centuries. Another consequence of female undernourishment was a significant change in the age of puberty, which fluctuates as a function of the ratio between age and body weight. In the Middle Ages girls matured between twelve and fifteen. In the seventeenth and eighteenth centuries, however, the average age at puberty moved up to sixteen, being slightly lower for city dwellers and slightly higher for the peasantry.

Rickets, scurvy, and a variety of unsightly ills followed in the path of chronic undernourishment. No wonder that women of the upper classes took care to distinguish themselves from their less fortunate sisters, cultivating vast expanses of milky flesh in contrast to the haggard, brown, and emaciated physiques of those whose hard lives made them not only ugly in the eyes of contemporaries, but also prematurely old. . . .

The Renaissance was not only a period in which women of the ruling classes distinguished themselves from their social inferiors by means of their well-fed physique and the pristine whiteness of their body linen; it was also a period in which it became more important that women be "different" from men in all aspects of dress, appearance, and behavior. The vestiary[21] revolution of the late Middle Ages consisted in the differentiation of male and female clothing. Men's robes were shortened to reveal their legs, and the codpiece[22] was invented, destined to become increasingly prominent and beribboned in the sixteenth and seventeenth centuries. Women, on the other hand, tended to remain more chastely dressed. Their long and voluminous robes revealed a waist made even more slender by the use of a busk[23] and, more liberal mores permitting, might even disclose a pair of milky breasts, suitably powdered and rouged. Every movement, every gesture had to reflect the delicacy and tenderness now expected of women as opposed to the energetic virility of men. . . .

From the fifteenth century on, treatises on the family, courtesy books, and even medical literature all insisted upon the fragility of the female sex and the duty of men to protect women from their own innate weaknesses by ruling them with a gentle, if firm, hand. Gone were the courtly models of gender relations according to which the knight obeyed his mistress and served her as his sovereign. The Renaissance brought with it a desire for clearly defined social boundaries and immutable hierarchies (including gender hierarchies), a desire that became all the more important as the reality of economic and political life confused class distinctions and created new elites to challenge the old. Sumptuary laws[24] also reflected a chronic concern for issues of social status, sexual identity, and dress. Cross-dressing, for example, was universally condemned — a fact that did not prevent women from repeatedly affecting articles of male costume, much to the horror of their contemporaries. Vestiary legislation also denounced the "mad expenditure" of vain women and accused them of being the cause of a spectrum of

---

[21] Relating to clothing.

[22] A stuffed, penis-shaped bag attached to the front of men's tight-fitting breeches.

[23] Stiffening for corsets.

[24] Laws regulating the style and quality of clothing.

ills, from the ruin of the national economy to demographic crisis and their husbands' homosexuality. . . .

Although clerical culture throughout the early modern period tended to fear feminine charms and the power they gave women over men, Renaissance Neoplatonism specifically rehabilitated beauty by declaring it to be the outward and visible sign of an inward and invisible goodness. Beauty was no longer considered a dangerous asset, but rather a necessary attribute of moral character and social position. It became an obligation to be beautiful, for ugliness was associated not only with social inferiority but also with vice. Were not prostitutes rendered unsightly by syphilitic sores, and the degenerate poor monstrous by skin afflictions and mange? The body's outer envelope became a window through which the inner self was visible to all.

Feminine beauty was not only extolled as being a guarantee of moral probity and an inspiration for those who had the privilege of gazing upon a pretty countenance; it was also codified by a massive production of love poems, courtesy books, and collections of recipes for cosmetics. Beauty followed a formula, and women went to a great deal of trouble and expense to make their appearance conform to standards that remained virtually unaltered throughout the early modern period. In Italy, France, Spain, Germany, and England the basic aesthetic was the same: white skin, blond hair, red lips and cheeks, black eyebrows. The neck and hands had to be long and slender, the feet small, the waist supple. Breasts were to be firm, round, and white, with rosy nipples. The color of the eyes might vary (the French were fond of green; the Italians preferred black or brown), and occasional concessions might be made to dark hair; but the canon of feminine appearance remained essentially the same for some three hundred years. . . .

How did women achieve the perfection required of them? With the invention of printing in the mid-fifteenth century, books of "secrets" and recipes for perfumes and cosmetics (some of which had already circulated in manuscripts in the Middle Ages) began to appear throughout Europe, reinforcing and enriching an oral tradition handed down from mother to daughter, from apothecary to son. Written mostly by men, whose criteria of beauty were thus implicitly imposed on their feminine readers, these collections were rarely restricted to beauty secrets. Their contents were eclectic, often gathering medical information, kitchen recipes, natural magic, astrological tables, and various other arts (such as physiognomy) all between the covers of one book. Who read these books? Women (and men) of a certain social standing, of course, who were educated enough to know how to read. Not all, however, were necessarily members of the ruling classes. . . . Outside certain elite circles, where cosmetics were as essential an accessory as powder, perfume, and body linen, paints and creams were considered to be a sign of vanity and an incitation to lust. Yet women of all social classes persevered in "improving" their appearance by means of cosmetic concoctions, some of which ended up doing more harm than good. . . . A sixteenth-century *Tracte Containing the Artes of Curious Paintinge, Carvinge & Buildinge* dedicates an entire section to the nature of certain cosmetics then in daily use, since women were supposedly unaware of their ingredients and the ill effects they had on their users. The section begins with a gruesome description of the harmful effects of sublimate of mercury, which may have been partially responsible for the fast fading of youth and beauty bewailed by the ladies of Queen Elizabeth's[25] court. . . .

Warnings about the long-term effects of cosmetics were not the only argument used against makeup. Women who painted themselves were also accused of "altering the face of God" (was not humanity made in the image of the Lord?). In *A Treatise against Painting and Tincturing of Men and Women* (1616), Thomas Tuke[26] wondered how ladies were able to pray to God "with a face, which he doth not owne? How can they begge pardon, when their sinne cleaves onto their faces?" Beneath many criticisms of paint also lay a masculine fear of deception. Was the youthful beauty they desired not perhaps an old hag or a disease-ridden body, artfully camouflaged? Besides which, those who made cosmetics were often suspected of dabbling in the magic arts, for many recipes contained incantations to be recited during preparation and ingredients such as earthworms, nettles, and blood.

Despite repeated cautions, masculine accusations of adultery and deception, and daily examples of the untoward effects of cosmetics, women persevered in "improving" their appearance with the help of powders, creams, and paints. In sixteenth-century Italy it was said that all women in cities used makeup, "even the dish-washers." . . .

Most books on cosmetics and feminine beauty focused on the hair, the face, the neck, the breasts, and the hands — all parts of the body visible to the public eye. The recipes that filled these books generally fulfilled one of two functions: to correct existing faults or to improve upon nature. Hair, for example, was better if blond, thick, wavy, and long, whence the long hours Italian women spent bleaching their hair in the sun (their snowy complexions protected by the *solana,* a wide-brimmed sunhat without a crown), washing it in the juice of lemon or rhubarb, or applying other, more elaborate concoctions made with sulfur or saffron. . . . After the hair was bleached, the hairline was carefully plucked or treated with a depilatory cream in order to create the high, domed foreheads that were still fashionable in the sixteenth century. The eyebrows were also plucked, sometimes entirely, and sometimes just enough to make two thin, wide-spaced arcs that were then blackened to contrast with the hair and make a frame for the eyes. Eyelashes, on the other hand, were considered unaesthetic and were either left unadorned or entirely pulled out. . . .

The face, neck, breasts, and hands were supposed to be creamy white, enlivened by rosy hues in strategic places. White was the color associated with purity, chastity, and femininity. It was the color of the "female" heavenly body, the moon, as distinct from the more vibrant hues of the "masculine" sun. A white complexion was also the privilege of the leisured city dweller as distinct from the

---

[25] Queen of England from 1558 to 1603.

[26] Royalist theologian (d. 1657).

sunburnt skin of the peasant. . . . The ivory complexion so prized by women was not, however, a uniform white. The cheeks, ears, chin, nipples (when displayed), and fingertips were touched with rouge to give an impression of health and attract the eye. . . .

Over and above the role played by cosmetics in the social and moral obligation women felt to look beautiful, makeup was a necessary signifier of social rank. Paint was the "clothing" of the visible parts of the body, distinguishing its wearer as much as rich materials, fine linens, and expensive ornaments revealed the wealth and status of their owner. Cosmetics were the ultimate accessory, without which an elegant woman did not feel herself dressed. . . .

If early modern hygienic and cosmetic practices were motivated by a variety of beliefs and concerns, ranging from an acute interest in health to the social imperatives of physical appearance, perhaps the most universal purpose to which these practices were applied was the service of Eros. In seventeenth-century Europe, the few remaining public baths still served two main purposes, and he who did not bathe for reasons of health was most probably preparing for an amorous encounter. Similarly, feminine cosmetics were universally decried for their uncanny powers of seduction, which, according to moralists and theologians alike, lured men to their perdition in the sweet throes of lust. Ever present, and increasingly policed, sexuality became one of the bugbears of both secular and religious authorities. Authorized only in the context of marriage, and then solely in the function of procreation, sex was subject to a wave of control and repression that strove to mold the mores of urban and rural populations along lines strictly defined by both church and state.

Whereas the Middle Ages had witnessed the formulation of a sexual ethic based on the refusal of pleasure and the obligation of procreation, it was not until the sixteenth century that a coherent campaign was launched against all forms of nudity and extraconjugal sexuality. Between 1500 and 1700, new attitudes toward the body and new rules of behavior gave rise to a radical promotion of chastity and modesty in all areas of daily life. Brothels were closed, bathers were obliged to retain their shirts, and the nightgown replaced the birthday suit as approved sleeping apparel. The lower half of the body became a world apart, a forbidden territory that the seventeenth-century Précieuses[27] refused to name. Under the dual influence of the Protestant Reformation and the Catholic Counter-Reformation, artists relinquished their hard-won battle to display the human form, and a multitude of accidental draperies, leaves, and fortuitous shrubs once again veiled the nude. Nudity became vulgar, something only apprentices inflicted upon the public eye as they sported in the river on a hot summer's day; and even then they might find themselves in trouble, as did eight young men in Frankfurt in 1541, who ended up being condemned to a month in prison on

---

[27] "Precious Women," women who led a literary and linguistic movement to purify the French language in the mid-seventeenth century.

bread and water. In the seventeenth and eighteenth centuries refined Parisian ladies fainted at the sight of naked male bodies on the banks of the Seine, while even their occasional private bath was clouded with milk or a handful of bran in order to preserve their nudity from their servants' eyes. Modesty became a sign of social and moral distinction, especially dear to the middle ranks of society, who condemned both the uncouth physicality of the lower orders and the libertine nonchalance of the aristocracy.

The first victims of the new wave in social morality were women. Long decried by misogynist theologians and sexually frustrated clergy as the daughters of Eve, women were represented as insidious temptresses whose primary object in life was to seduce unsuspecting men and deliver them to Satan. Medical science reinforced this voracious vision of female sexuality by declaring erotic fulfillment to be a biological necessity for women. Not only did their "hungry" wombs ever clamor to be filled, but dire disorders would attend upon those who ignored the "natural" imperative of reproduction. Hysteria, a malady whose origin lay in the uterus, was accounted responsible for delusions of diabolic possession and other forms of mental illness. Another factor that strengthened the equation between women, sex, and sin was the appearance and rapid spread of syphilis in the late fifteenth century. Although the most virulent epidemics had abated by the 1550s, the disease had come to stay, indelibly imprinted on the contemporary imagination as a terrestrial punishment for the sin of lust and, above all, as a consequence of frequenting houses of ill repute.

Municipally owned or authorized brothels were a common feature of late medieval European towns and cities. Prostitution was encouraged and protected not only in order to meet the needs of growing numbers of sexually mature adolescents, unattached apprentices, and men who were marrying at a later and later age, but also to combat male homosexuality, considered to be one of the greater social ills of the time and responsible for various manifestations of divine wrath such as plague, famine, and war. In the sixteenth century, however, the same municipalities that had encouraged prostitution closed their official brothels. Accused of spreading lechery and disease, fomenting brawls and other forms of civil disturbance, leading young men astray, facilitating adultery, and ruining family fortunes, prostitutes became one of the "criminal" populations (along with vagabonds and witches) destined for elimination by both secular and religious authorities. . . .

In the eyes of both religious and secular authorities, there existed two basic types of sexual behavior, one acceptable and the other reprehensible. The first was marital and was practiced in the service of procreation. The second was governed by amorous passion and sensual pleasure, its outcome malformed or illegitimate, its logic that of sterility. Guilty outside of wedlock, sensual passion became all the more blamable within the bounds of matrimony, where it threatened not only the controlled, contractual concept of conjugal affections and the health of offspring conceived in the heat of amorous excess, but also the couple's ability to love God, contaminated as they were by terrestrial rather than spiritual love.

Despite the normative prescriptions of theologians, physicians, and civil officials, young people did not always wait for marriage to experiment with erotic pleasures. Since men and women married at an increasingly late age throughout the early modern period (an average of twenty-five to twenty-eight years), they were sexually mature for a good decade before being able to experience sex legitimately. Historians differ as to the extent of sexual activity in these years: was Europe swept by a wave of chastity, or did erotic needs find alternative outlets? The closure of the vast majority of brothels and a record low birthrate of illegitimate children from the sixteenth to the mid-eighteenth centuries have led some historians to postulate a mass internalization resulting in widespread sexual continence. Other scholars have asserted important changes in sexual behavior, ranging from an increase in masturbation to the spread of rudimentary contraception. Scholars do agree, however, on the existence of one well-documented sexual practice. Under circumstances subject to various controls, young men and women of the lower social orders could indulge in a certain amount of sexual experimentation as well as "try out" potential marriage partners without suffering moral censure.

Known as "bundling" in England, . . . various forms of parentally authorized premarital flirtation, sexual experimentation, and even cohabitation were practiced throughout Europe. Bundling generally involved paying court to a girl at night, in a room apart from the rest of the family, in bed, in the dark, and half-naked. However, although it involved two young people spending the night together, talking and petting, bundling did not lead to much pregnancy. In the Vendée in France, . . . couples of lovers [stayed] in the same room or even in the same bed, where they could control any one of their number who threatened to get carried away. In Savoy, the boy had to swear to respect the girl's virginity before bedding with her. In Scotland, the girl's thighs were symbolically tied together. What bundling did lead to were marriages based on affection and sexual attraction. It provided an opportunity for the two parties to explore each other's minds and characters in some depth as well as to obtain sexual satisfaction in the decade between maturity and matrimony without running the risk of an unwanted pregnancy or an ill-fated marriage. . . .

Neither Protestant nor Catholic authorities regarded such carryings-on with an indulgent eye. In the sixteenth century, and especially after the Council of Trent[28] (1563), the Roman church began to wage a systematic struggle against all forms of prenuptial sexual relations. Episcopal ordinances mark the progress of this battle in France. Young people in Savoy lost their right to albergement[29] in 1609. In the Pyrenean dioceses of Bayonne and Alet, intercourse during the period of *fiançailles*[30] remained customary until 1640, when it suddenly became grounds for excommunication. In Champagne boy-girl encounters in the

---

[28] Council (1545–1563) that clarified doctrines and reformed the Roman Catholic Church.

[29] Bundling.

[30] Betrothal, engagement.

escraignes[31] became liable to the same penalty in 1680. Similarly, nocturnal visits were still being attacked in the Protestant county of Montbéliard by the civil magistrate, the Duke of Württemberg, in 1772.

Despite numerous and repeated attempts to suppress premarital sex and cohabitation, rural areas long resisted the "approved" model of marriage, according to which all matches were to be arranged by parents. . . . In the cities, however, where wealth weighed more heavily in the balance, parental influence in the choice of marriage partner became absolute. Sixteenth- and seventeenth-century Europe saw a rash of rulings against marriage without parental consent progressively deprive young people of the right to choose their helpmate, even if they had previously exchanged vows, given each other rings, or had sexual relations. Particularly efficient in urban areas, where marriage strategies played a key role in the social, economic, and political ambitions of the middle and upper ranks of society, the paternalist model of marriage remained unchallenged until the eighteenth century. . . .

There are several features of sexual behavior peculiar to early modern Europe. The first is the average interval of ten or more years between puberty and marriage. This gap, which tended to be larger among the lower social orders than among their betters, continued to widen throughout the seventeenth and eighteenth centuries. Moreover, a significant number of people never married at all, ranging from about 10 percent among the peasantry and urban poor to as much as 25 percent among the elites. A second unique feature is the superimposition of the notion of romantic love on the biological constant of sexual drive. Beginning as a purely extramarital ideology in troubadour literature[32] of the twelfth century, the concept of romantic love spread via the printing press and the increase in literacy in the sixteenth and seventeenth centuries, inspiring poetry, plays, and novels until it finally found its way into real life in the mid-eighteenth century. The third and last feature is the predominance of Christian ideology in the legitimation and practice of sexuality. Though somewhat mitigated by humanist and Protestant efforts to replace the medieval ideal of virginity by that of holy matrimony, the dominant attitude toward sexuality remained one of suspicion and hostility. . . .

Religious authorities considered any sexual act committed outside marriage to be a mortal sin, as well as any conjugal act not performed in the interest of reproduction. Saint Jerome[33] had declared the husband who embraced his wife overly passionately to be an "adulterer" because he loved her for his pleasure only, as he would a mistress. Restated by Saint Thomas Aquinas[34] and echoed end-

---

[31] Cottages.

[32] Lyric poetry written in the vernacular of southern France.

[33] Scholar and Bible translator (ca. 340–420).

[34] Saint and theologian (ca. 1225–1274).

lessly by authors of confession manuals throughout the sixteenth and seventeenth centuries, the denunciation of passion in marriage condemned the amorous wife as much as the libidinous husband. Even the positions adopted by the couple were subject to strict controls. The *retro* or *more canino*[35] position (not to be confused with sodomy) was declared to be contrary to human nature because it imitated the coupling of animals. *Mulier super virum*[36] was equally "unnatural" insofar as it placed the woman in an active and superior position, contrary to her passive and subordinate social role. All erotic acrobatics other than the approved formula — the woman supine and the man above her — were considered suspect in that they privileged pleasure at the expense of procreation. The only position that favored the planting of the male seed was the one metaphorically associated with the plowing of the earth by the laborer.

Medical texts supported theological rulings with respect to the optimum conditions for creating offspring in terms of both the moderation of passion and the most favorable position, threatening that any deviation from the norm might well result in deformed or deficient progeny. Both groups of authorities also stipulated a variety of days on which sexual intercourse was to be avoided. For the pious, fast days were also chaste days, as well as all religious holidays such as Sundays, Christmas, Good Friday, and Easter. Continence was also recommended throughout Lent, although early modern theologians no longer expected the faithful to be capable of total abstinence. Over and above the 120 to 140 days of religious observance during which sex was discouraged if not expressly forbidden, couples were urged to avoid intercourse during the hot summer months and during the wife's various periods of indisposition. Not only was intimacy during the monthly cycle or during the 40 days of "impurity" after childbirth considered potentially hazardous to the husband's health, but sexual relations during pregnancy and nursing were believed to threaten the child's chances for survival. A growing concern for the well-being of infants, whose mortality rate was extremely high in the first two years of life, led a number of physicians and religious authorities to forbid intercourse throughout the breast-feeding period. . . .

No doubt many women, worn out by numerous pregnancies and the care of many children, would willingly have availed themselves of the medieval right to refusal of the *debitum conjugale*,[37] especially as marital chastity was considered desirable once a good-sized family had been created. Theologians in the sixteenth, seventeenth, and eighteenth centuries, however, were not so quick to permit either partner to neglect the other's sexual needs. No longer seen solely in the light of reproduction or as a second-rate solution for concupiscence, conjugal sexuality was increasingly considered to be a legitimate remedy for a natural physical drive, the refusal of which might drive the frustrated partner into the greater sins of adultery or "pollution" (masturbation).

---

[35] Having sex dog-style.

[36] Having sex with the woman on top.

[37] The marital obligation to have sex.

The crime of Onan (who was struck down by God for having spilled his seed upon the ground) became one of the major obsessions of early modern religious and medical authorities. . . . Along with *coitus interruptus*,[38] homosexuality, and bestiality, masturbation was one of the four sexual sins that defied nature's reproductive imperative in the name of "perverse" pleasures. Although this solitary practice was too widespread to merit the exemplary punishments reserved for sodomy and bestiality, it caused a great deal of anxiety on the grounds that bad habits acquired in youth might continue into adulthood, either polluting the marriage bed or even replacing marriage altogether. . . .

. . . Whatever pre- or extramarital behavior patterns may have been, it is likely that fear of the dangers of childbirth and the economic burdens of a growing brood of children also motivated many married couples to limit the size of their families through these prohibited practices. Of course the practice of *coitus interruptus* requires a considerable amount of control on the part of the man and affords little pleasure to the woman, who is often left sexually aroused but frustrated. But even within the context of procreational sex, the male tendency to hasty ejaculation would also have left many female partners unsatisfied. If one adds to this tendency the experience of some ten years' self-manipulation and the loveless matches that characterized both the aristocracy and the bourgeoisie, the chances for mutually satisfying sexual relations within the framework of marriage must have been very low indeed.

The only form of masturbation authorized by both physicians and Catholic confessors was feminine self-manipulation, either in preparation for intercourse (to facilitate penetration) or, after the husband had prematurely ejaculated and withdrawn, in order to reach orgasm, "open" the mouth of the womb, and release the female "seed," which, according to seventeenth-century medical authorities, was as useful to the act of procreation as that released by the male. Although the feminine "right to orgasm" continued to be debated in confession manuals well into the eighteenth century, the majority of theologians accepted Galenist medical theory[39] with respect to the desirability of female satisfaction: would God have given women this source of pleasure without a purpose? A snag in this logic was the fact that women could conceive passively and without pleasure, in which case their "semen" would be wanting. Never at a loss, medical science came to the aid of doctrine and declared the function of feminine seed to be auxiliary to that of its masculine counterpart. If emitted at the same moment as the man's, it would create more beautiful offspring. . . .

Outside marriage, there was no licit sexuality. The ascending scale of sexual crimes was defined in terms of the number of infractions committed against the three basic justifications for authorized physical relations, namely, the obligation to procreate, conformity to "natural" laws, and a sacramental concept of marriage. A "first-degree" infraction would be simple fornication between unmarried individuals who had not taken vows of chastity. The crime could be judged more

---

[38] In sexual intercourse, withdrawal before ejaculation.

[39] Medical theory based on the writings of the Greek physician Galen (ca. 130–ca. 201).

or less severe according to the age and social station of the two parties. The rape of a virgin, for example, was generally considered worse than that of a widow. Similarly, the threat of violence or a promise of marriage by the man would constitute a mitigating circumstance in the woman's favor. The "second degree" of sexual sin was adultery. Simple adultery implied only one married person; double adultery involved two. Incest was also considered a form of adultery, as was the seduction of a nun, "bride" of Christ.

The third and worst type of sexual infraction involved crimes "against nature," which surpassed the former two insofar as they precluded reproduction. Masturbation, homosexuality, and bestiality haunted churchmen, civil magistrates, and medical doctors throughout the early modern period. . . . Sodomy was "complete" if it entailed homoerotic relations, and "incomplete" if it described extravaginal heterosexual relations. Bestiality, on the other hand, was the sin "without a name." Always mentioned in Latin, even in the least prudish texts or manuals of confession, it not only reduced men to the level of animals but also was suspected of resulting in hybrid monsters.

Our knowledge of extraconjugal relations is based largely on historical records related to their fruit, although the actual birthrate of illegitimate children is hardly an indicator of the frequency or the quality of unauthorized sexuality. Extramarital pregnancy was, more often than not, an undesired complication, and studies of illicit relations in an age that knew neither effective contraception nor antibiotics have shown that various forms of sexual play could be preferred to coitus. Fear of venereal disease, pregnancy, and even emotional or legal entanglement was the cause of a great deal of fondling, groping, and mutual masturbation. And because a single act of intercourse had little chance of resulting in pregnancy, even relationships that did not rely upon some form of birth control (generally withdrawal; the prophylactic sheath was a rarity until the eighteenth century) stood an equally good chance of remaining undetected. The major source of information on illicit fornication during the ancien régime[40] is formal complaints, to civil or religious authorities, made by women who had been impregnated by men who would not or could not marry them. Known in France as the *déclaration de grossesse*,[41] these documents contain precious information on the mother and purported father of the child as well as on the circumstances of their relationship.

Three distinct patterns of illicit relationships can be discerned in the déclarations de grossesse. The first is the relationship between unequals, in which the man was generally the social and economic superior of the woman. Sometimes the seducer was the employer of his sexual partner, and in some cases he offered her a job, money, or food in exchange for her favors. Lower-class women were especially vulnerable to this sort of exploitation, not only because they earned less than men in whatever calling they practiced, but also because masters had a lingering

---

[40] Old Régime, the centuries before the French Revolution of 1789.

[41] Statement about the circumstances of pregnancy.

traditional right to the bodies of the women they employed. Servants were doubly vulnerable in this respect insofar as they not only depended upon the head of the household for their livelihood but also lived in daily proximity with a number of men: masters, sons, and other male servants. Women who took part in relations of inequality tended to be under twenty-five years of age, and ten to thirty years younger than the men they accused. This fact may indicate that women in their late teens or early twenties were more naive, and therefore more easily seduced. It may also indicate a preference among older men for girls. Not all of these women were innocent victims, however; calculating gold-diggers appear in all places at all times. Nor were all of the seducers heartless satyrs, but sometimes lovers or common-law husbands of long standing who promised to "take care" of their child. The keynote in relations of inequality, however, is the very different consequences they had for men and women. For men, there seems to have been little social opprobrium associated with paternity suits. For women, the consequences of an illicit affair were usually disastrous. Publicly disgraced, discharged from their job, and in some cases even sent to a house of correction, they would often be forced to choose between abandoning their child or turning to prostitution to support the two of them.

The second type of relationship that appears in official declarations of pregnancy is one of equality. Most women who appeared before the courts had had relationships with men of equal social standing whom they accused of having promised them marriage. Whereas women who were involved in relationships of inequality could hardly have hoped for legitimation of them, those who had relationships with their social equals generally believed (or pretended to believe) that theirs was a prebridal pregnancy gone wrong. The pattern seems to have been one of promise of marriage (often accompanied by a betrothal present), ritual rape, sexual relations approved by the woman's family, followed by desertion. Every step but the last was probably fairly typical of prenuptial behavior in the lower social orders in both city and country up through the eighteenth century. This situation would explain why the women's versions of the relationships tended to insist upon marriage promises and presents, whereas the men's focused on the sexual promiscuity of their partners and denied any serious intentions on their own part.

The third and last type of illegitimate relationship is the short-term, chance encounter. In this case the pregnancy was attributed either to an alleged rape or to the promiscuous behavior (or even prostitution) of the woman. The rapists were usually "unknown" men, identified from their clothing as soldiers or itinerant farm hands who had taken advantage of peasant girls or servants sent alone on errands. Inn servants and part-time prostitutes also had a hard time identifying the father of their child, given their tendency to have single encounters with different men. . . .

To what extent did women take pleasure in these encounters? Even with allowances made for the voluntary censorship and manipulation of information that undoubtedly characterize such autobiographical recitals, there is little evidence of a search for sexual fulfillment in the *déclarations de grossesse*. It would seem that most sexual relations were short and frequently brutal. Men apparently made little attempt to ensure the enjoyment of their partner, and foreplay was so rare as to be practically nonexistent. The stock description, "he threw me on the ground, stuck a handkerchief in my mouth, and lifted my skirts," is a constant of both legitimate and illegitimate relations, and even if force was not used, the threat of violence was always present. For most women, it would seem that sexual relations were instrumental and manipulative rather than affective. They were a means to an end — marriage, money, or simply survival — rather than an end in themselves.

The repression of concubinage[42] and all forms of nonmarital sex in the sixteenth and seventeenth centuries had a decisive influence on the birthrate of illegitimate children, which was under 3 percent of all births until the mid-eighteenth century. This low figure almost certainly reflects, over and above a stricter observance of premarital chastity, a significant rise in contraceptive practices, abortion, and infanticide. With the decline of medieval tolerance of bastard children and concubinage, there remained only the déclaration de grossesse and the paternity suit to protect unmarried women and preserve the lives of their babies. After all, the greater the social opprobrium attached to a fault, the greater the temptation to suppress the evidence; whence the proliferation of laws against infanticide, the creation of new foundling homes, and the new obligation of pregnancy declarations by single women, which automatically assumed that the unwed mother of a stillborn child was a murderess unless she had previously declared her pregnancy. . . .

The history of adultery is the history of a double standard: the extraconjugal affairs of men were tolerated, whereas those of women were not. One explanation for this disparity lies in the value attached to female chastity in the marriage market of a patriarchal and propertied society. Virginity was expected of a bride on her wedding night, and marital fidelity ever after, so as to ensure her husband of legitimate heirs. . . .

The view that masculine fornication and adultery were but venial sins to be overlooked by the wife was reinforced by the fact that before the eighteenth century, most middle- and upper-class marriages were arranged by parents in the interests of family economic or political strategies. Not only did neither bride nor groom have much opportunity before the wedding to get to know each other, but emotional attachment after marriage was considered inconvenient, indeed almost indecent. Male adultery with servants and lower-class women was therefore seen as normal, although some women protested the double standard and the wounds a husband's infidelity could inflict on feminine feelings. By the early seventeenth century, however, both Counter-Reformation and Puritan[43] sexual standards imposed greater secrecy on adulterous liaisons. Concubines and mistresses were not flaunted as openly as in the past, nor was the fruit of such relationships systematically provided for in wills.

---

[42] The cohabitation of a man and a woman not married to each other.

[43] Relating to English religious reformers of the late sixteenth and early seventeenth centuries who wanted to purify Christianity of any beliefs and practices not contained in the Bible.

A second explanation for the prevalence of the double standard lies in the fact that women were considered the sexual property of men, and their value would be diminished if they were used by anyone other than the legal owner. From this point of view, masculine honor became dependent upon female chastity. The cuckold was not only someone whose virility was in question because he was unable to "maintain" his property adequately (that is, sexually satisfy his wife), but he was also incapable of ruling his own household. In many countries, uxoricide[44] was pardonable if committed in *delictum flagrans*[45] and very lightly punished if motivated by adulterous conduct. This is all the more understandable if one remembers that an unfaithful wife was often considered a disqualifying factor for public office and other honors. In rural areas, village communities took matters into their own hands by subjecting cuckolded husbands[46] and their wayward wives to public shame rituals in churches and raucous skimmington[47] rides.

Only among the aristocracy did the otherwise universal double standard not prevail. Attractive court ladies were practically pushed into their sovereign's bed in order to advance their husbands' ambitions, while others felt at liberty to take lovers once they had performed their conjugal duty by providing their husbands with a legitimate male heir. Furthermore, few men of wealth and fashion were willing to risk their lives in a duel to avenge a wife's compromised honor. . . . Moreover, not all the ladies courted by aristocratic men were either married or noble. The end of the early modern period saw improved education of bourgeois daughters, together with a lack of career opportunities for genteel women suddenly impoverished by the economic uncertainties of their families' professional or mercantile fortunes. The result was a pool of good-looking and well-mannered mistresses who could be shown in public to the credit of their current lovers. . . .

For most women, however, illegitimate love remained an area in which the price to be paid for disposing of their own bodies and affections was much heavier than that paid by men. Less and less protected against the consequences of seduction and concubinage, women were equally discriminated against in the long-lived double standard for adultery. . . .

In the sixteenth and seventeenth centuries two stereotypes of sexual conduct predominated: temperate, and often loveless, conjugal intercourse aimed at producing a male heir, whereas extramarital relations provided an arena for both sentimental love and sexual pleasure. In the lower classes, mutual affection, sexual compatibility, and marriage were more easily reconciled thanks to courtship practices that permitted couples to get to know each other intimately before betrothal. In

---

[44] The murder of a wife by her husband.

[45] In the very act of committing a crime.

[46] Husbands whose wives have been unfaithful.

[47] The English equivalent of a *charivari* — a ceremony, especially in peasant societies, in which a community attempts to impose its values on deviant members by means of raucous music, public humiliation, and crowd intimidation.

the eighteenth century, however, the rise of illegitimate births in this same social bracket would seem to indicate a widening gap between love and marriage, with the penalty for aspiring to a union based on mutual inclination heavily visited upon mothers who remained unwed. The pattern was just the opposite in the middle and upper classes. Although the double standard with respect to premarital chastity and conjugal fidelity persisted throughout the early modern period, the eighteenth century saw the rise of a more affective model of conjugal relations based on compatibility of sentiment and mutual sexual attraction. This change, as well as the greater autonomy accorded to young men and women in their choice of marriage partner, encouraged the reshaping of the ideal model for wifely behavior to include carnal and emotional functions previously performed by the mistress. In the realm of extramarital sensuality, more tolerant mores also encouraged the proliferation of adulterous liaisons, prostitution, and homosexuality as well as the development of a number of sexual devices and diversions such as dildoes and pornography. In terms of sexual attitudes, however, the most radical change lay in an elite reconciliation of love, sex, and marriage that was to form the basis for our concept of marriage today.

THE WITCH-FIGURE AND THE SABBAT
Robin Briggs

During the age of the witch-hunts, which lasted from approximately 1450 to 1650 in western Europe and into the eighteenth century in eastern Europe, European courts condemned to death between forty thousand and fifty-three thousand people by burning, strangulation, or hanging. One-half of those died in Germany alone. Courts exiled or sentenced to prison countless others, many of whom had been tortured brutally. Some accused witches lucky enough to earn acquittal returned to their community only to be treated as outcasts.

In the last thirty years, a number of historians have researched witch-hunts, adding greatly to our knowledge of the alleged witches and those who persecuted them. But much about the period of the witch-hunts is still unclear. For example, historians disagree about why the hunts began during the Renaissance and the scientific revolution, supposed periods of intellectual advance. Certainly the belief in witches was not new, yet the so-called medieval Dark Ages witnessed no hunts for witches. Some scholars locate the origins of the hunts in folklore, theology, heresy, and changes in the law. Others look to the practice of ceremonial magic among socially prominent individuals, or to the development of a fictitious stereotype of a small, secret sect of night-flying witches who strove to destroy Christian society and who met regularly with the aid of the devil to engage in ritual murder, cannibalism, incest, and other antihuman activities.

Robin Briggs, senior research fellow at All Souls College in Oxford, takes a different approach to European witchcraft. Briggs questions why some areas of Europe escaped witch-hunting and, if there was such fear of diabolical witches, why courts did not condemn hundreds of thousands of alleged witches. Briggs consults contemporary writings about witchcraft and exploits trial records in Lorraine (now an eastern province of France) to show that witchcraft was, above all, a village crime: Neighbors knew well those whom they accused. How did an accusation of witchcraft come about, and what was the profile of the average witch?

Briggs is especially interested in understanding the European belief system. What motivated the witches who signed pacts with Satan? The sabbat, an

Robin Briggs, *Witches and Neighbors: The Social and Cultural Context of European Witchcraft* (New York: Viking, 1996), 17–26, 28, 31–32, 34–35, 38, 40–41, 49, 51–59.

organized gathering of witches, was central to the idea of diabolical witchcraft. How did belief in the sabbat encourage witch panics, and how did the sabbat vary across Europe? What does Briggs mean when he refers to the sabbat as "the ultimate anti-world"? What was the role of torture in witch trials, and why did some accused witches freely confess without having been tortured?

In July 1596 the *prévôt* (the local administrator and law enforcement officer) of the small Lorraine town of Charmes reported the arrest of Barbe, wife of Jean Mallebarbe. This old woman of about sixty had fled Charmes some months earlier after being called witch in public, just as legal proceedings were being started against her. She evidently hoped that feelings would have calmed down in her absence, particularly since the old *prévôt* who had been very hostile to her had just died. When she found this was not the case, Barbe plainly wanted to get the inevitable over as quickly as possible — she even tried in vain to hang herself in prison, then asked to be put to death without being tortured. Few of the thousands of people executed as witches can have been more eager to please, or to confirm the beliefs of their persecutors. Her original confession had been simple and to a degree self-exculpatory. She and her husband of some twenty-seven years had always been day-labourers; more recently they had been forced to sell some small plots of land and, being left with only a house and garden, were increasingly dependent on charity (the husband was said to be old and crippled). Six months earlier Barbe, angry after a beating from her husband, had been seduced by "master Percy," as the Devil was often named in Lorraine, who promised her "money in abundance." The Devil gave her two sacks of powder, but she threw these in a stream, and had done no-one any harm. The judges were unimpressed, for they knew there were plenty of witnesses who thought they had suffered very real harm at her hands. They threatened Barbe with torture, beginning a process which over the next two weeks (ending with a session when she was lightly racked) would see her story become steadily more elaborate. Although to our eyes this was a parody of justice, with relentless pressure applied to a defenceless old woman, it was also, in its way, a negotiation. The questions indicated the kind of answers required, but the details were supplied by the accused, drawing on a common stock of stereotypes.

Barbe's culpability grew, until she was admitting to at least twenty years in the Devil's service. Early admissions to killing the cows of men against whom she had grievances, and a horse at each of three houses where she was refused alms, did not satisfy the court. The accused was pressed to admit that she had harmed people, responding with a story about how she had killed her neighbour Claudon Basle, with whom she had quarrelled, and who had called her an "old bigot and witch." Barbe's revenge was to throw powder down her neck, inflicting an illness which killed Claudon 18 months later; Barbe asserted that she had not wished to cure the sick woman, who in any case had never asked that she should heal her.

The imminent prospect of torture drew out a new series of confessions to crimes against those who had offended her. Some had been given lingering illnesses, so that their limbs were twisted and they became permanently crippled, while others were killed. Among these was a servant she met in the woods with a cart and horses; after he refused her some bread she heard the crows by the track calling to her "kill him, and break the necks of his horses," advice she duly followed. She had been changed into the form of a cat by her master, so that she could try to strangle the wife of Claude Hullon, after he had accused her of causing a fog on the lake. When she found she did not have the power to carry out this plan she still terrified the victim by speaking to her, then attacking her in her cat-form. After Laurent Rouille called her "old witch" and accused her of stealing wood from his barn she wanted to kill him too, but a wind had come in her ear telling her she had no power over him, so she had to be content with killing an ox and two cows. The torture produced a final batch of admissions of using her powder to kill men, women and children after she was refused alms. Barbe knew she must name accomplices she had seen at the sabbat,[1] where witches met, so identified three other women, two of whom were quickly arrested and tried after she maintained her accusations against them to the last.

Like many other witches, Barbe claimed she had simply been unable to escape the clutches of the Devil once she took the fatal decision to enter his service. On the other hand, in the imaginary world she had constructed to offer some kind of explanation for her supposed misdeeds, she was not completely subservient to him. When the *receveur*[2] of Charmes, meeting her by chance on the road, called her an old witch, Percy urged her to avenge herself — but she remembered that he was often charitable to her and would not harm him despite beatings from her angry master. She suffered similar attacks at the sabbat, when she resisted plans to harm the crops, because of the prospect of death and hardship for the poor. When one male witch (recently executed nearby) wanted to cause a hailstorm, she accused him of hoping to raise the price of the grain he had in store, only to be kicked in the backside by Percy and propelled an incredible distance. Asked if the Devil spoke to them gently, she replied "ho, what gentleness, seeing that when he commanded us to cause harm and we did not want to obey his wishes, he would beat us thoroughly." With no more than the minimum of suggestion from her judges, whose questions are carefully recorded, Barbe was able to produce an extensive confession that included just about every stereotypical feature of general beliefs about witches. Unlike most other accused, she had not heard the specific charges against her because she had started to confess before the witnesses had been summoned. Her widespread anger and malevolence was something she either recalled or invented without specific prompting. Witnesses only entered the proceedings at the final stage, to confirm some of the quarrels and deaths she had already reported.

---

[1] An organized gathering of witches, presided over by the devil.

[2] Tax collector.

"La Mallebarbe" cannot be regarded as "typical," any more than any other individual witch. As we shall see, many different types of people were accused, while the charges might vary widely. Nevertheless, her pathetic story of deprivation, insults and resentment was a familiar one across most of Europe during the hard decades of the late sixteenth and early seventeenth centuries. These, rather than grand theories about diabolical conspiracies, were the common currency of witchcraft as it was actually experienced and punished. They were stories anyone could tell, drawing on a great reservoir of shared beliefs and fantasies, endlessly recycled as part of everyday experience. Those who accused their neighbours could easily become suspects in their own turn, caught up in the same remorseless machinery of local conflicts and rumours. Even when reading the actual documents, it can be hard to believe that such trials really happened, that real people, flesh, blood and bone, were subjected to appalling cruelties in order to convict them of an impossible crime. If torture was barely used in this case it was only because the accused was already so frightened that she confessed without direct coercion. On 6 August 1596 Barbe was bound to the stake at Charmes, allowed to feel the fire, then strangled before her body was burned to ashes. The two other old women with whom she used to go begging and whom she had denounced as accomplices, Claudon la Romaine and Chesnon la Triffatte, followed her to the stake on 3 September of the same year. The sceptical English gentleman Reginald Scot[3] had written angrily a decade earlier, with reference to a scabrous passage in the early witch-hunting manual the *Malleus Maleficarum*,[4] "These are no jests, for they be written by them that were and are judges upon the lives and deaths of those persons." Elsewhere he had asked "whether the evidence be not frivolous, and whether the proofs brought against them [the witches] be not incredible, consisting of guesses, presumptions, and impossibilities contrary to reason, scripture, and nature." Indeed they were, but we have to go beyond indignation and horror to understand why just about everyone believed in witches and their power and why, within their own thought systems, it was neither irrational nor absurd for them to do so.

Modern ideas of the witch have been simplified to the point of caricature. . . . A fascinating collection of descriptions from modern Newfoundland includes the following quite typical portrait of the witch as

a creature with long, straight hair, a very sharp nose, and long slender fingers. She has a big mouth with pointed teeth. She dresses in black. Her dress is black and she wears a pointed black felt hat on her head. A witch usually sails through the air on a long broom and is always accompanied by a fierce-looking cat.

The crude woodcuts which accompanied early witchcraft pamphlets are very similar, although contemporaries would have seen nothing odd about the dress

---

[3] Author (1538–1599) of *The Discoverie of Witchcraft* (1584), which ridiculed the belief in diabolical witchcraft and denounced the persecution of witches.

[4] *The Hammer of Witches* (1486), a demonology that two inquisitors wrote to serve as a handbook for witch-hunters.

or the hat, which were the normal attire of older women. In 1584 Reginald Scot described the Kentish suspects he knew as "women which be commonly old, lame, blear-eyed, pale, foul, and full of wrinkles"; they were also "lean and deformed, showing melancholy in their faces to the horror of all that see them." . . . Around 1600, therefore, this image was already in existence in most essentials. . . . This familiar portrait is nevertheless highly misleading as a guide to the people persecutors thought they had to deal with. It was the small group of sceptical writers on witchcraft, notably Johann Weyer[5] and Scot, who picked on the fact that many of the accused were pathetic old women whom their neighbours found obnoxious. Their aim was to ridicule the extravagant claims made for this secret resistance movement recruited by the Devil, whose chief accomplishment was apparently to kill a few cows and impede the making of butter or beer. . . .

Those writers who pleaded for greater severity were usually careful to avoid any suggestion that witches could be typecast in such a facile manner. . . . The typical approach was to stress the seriousness of the diabolical fifth column, the secrecy with which it operated and its closeness to the centres of political and social power. Even those such as Jean Bodin,[6] who asserted (quite wrongly) that almost all witches were women, still made much of the minority of powerful male figures among them. The Catholic zealots of the Holy League,[7] who sought to overthrow King Henri III[8] of France, circulated pamphlets claiming to have found evidence that he was a witch himself. It was easier to argue that the Devil was successful up to the highest level because a number of early trials had been political set-ups directed at powerful individuals. The demonologists,[9] who openly plagiarized one another, made repeated reference to these cases. Fantasies about satanic conspiracies on a national or international scale could gather around the occasional elite victim, like Louis Gaufridy (a priest from Aix-en-Provence burned in 1611). Two years later the exorcists who had "unmasked" him had moved on to extract tales from possessed nuns in the Spanish Netherlands who described how Gaufridy presided as prince at great sabbats.

Early pictures of witches convey the same message. Old hags are usually present among them, but they mix with nubile young women, men and children. Witchcraft was neither gender nor age specific for these artists, any more than it was confined to one social class. In reality members of the elite were rarely brought to trial, outside such exceptional pandemics as afflicted the German prince-bishoprics of Bamberg, Trier, and Würzburg. Nevertheless, there were enough

---

[5] A German physician (1515–1588) who argued in his book *On Magic* (1563) that most accused witches were mentally disturbed.

[6] French political philosopher and demonologist (1530–1596). His *Demonomania of Witches* (1580) advocated the prosecution of alleged diabolical witches.

[7] The Catholic League, an uncompromisingly anti-Protestant faction during the French Wars of Religion (1562–1598).

[8] King of France from 1574 to 1589.

[9] Theologians and lawyers who specialized in the study of the diabolical.

scattered cases and, no doubt, more extensive rumours, to keep the notion of hidden satanists in high places alive well into the seventeenth century. A high proportion of those concerned were men, with clerics prominent among them. The exceptional rarity of men among those accused in England, coupled with misogynistic statements by various demonologists, has encouraged an uncritical belief that nearly all the accused were women. In many parts of Europe men comprised 20 or 25 per cent of those charged; in some, including large areas of France, they actually formed a majority. There does seem to have been a widespread conviction that women were specially vulnerable to the wiles of the Devil, so that most confessing witches said they were more numerous at the sabbat; however, a fair number insisted there was parity of the sexes, or even a preponderance of men.

For persecutors and general populace alike then, the stereotype of the old woman as witch had no more than a marginal purchase on their minds. Some old women who found themselves accused complained of their special vulnerability, and where statistics are available they bear this out to an extent, in that older women and widows are heavily over-represented among the sample. . . . [T]he statistics need careful handling; we have to remember that many of those who came to court had been suspected for ten, fifteen or twenty years. Therefore their reputations very often went back to middle life or earlier, while relatively few first attracted suspicion as elderly crones. . . .

The popular image of the witch was that of a person motivated by ill-will and spite who lacked the proper sense of neighbourhood and community. Suspects were often alleged to have shown themselves resentful in their dealings with others and unwilling to accept delays or excuses in small matters. There seems little doubt that some of them were notoriously quarrelsome, although it is less clear whether this carried any *necessary* imputation of witchcraft. Indeed, to some extent such behaviour must have been as much the result as the cause of reputations, for there could hardly have been a more effective way of damaging communal or personal relationships than calling a neighbour a witch. There is a strong impression when studying larger groups of trials that such personal characteristics were commonly brought into play to reinforce suspicions which began for other reasons. Those who conciliated others were liable to find themselves described, like Marguitte Laurent, as "fine and crafty, careful not to quarrel with people or threaten them," while a failure to react was readily interpreted as betraying vengefulness. A particularly damaging charge was that the accused had talked of concealing anger until the moment for revenge had come. Jehenne la Moictresse was alleged to have told another woman that she should imitate her practice of giving no sign when angry, while Mengeotte Lausson claimed that when she had been angered she remembered it seven years later, without giving any sign. . . . The commonest of all remarks attributed to witches were those on the lines of "you will repent" or "you had better watch out," much of whose meaning depended on the context in which they were made. In many cases it was also said that the accused had taken no notice or pretended not to hear, when called a witch in public. In theory the proper response was to seek damages for slander, but suspects must have been very reluctant to embitter relationships further by such action.

Popular descriptions of witches do not therefore give any very certain guide to the reasons why they were identified; they are simply too flexible and circumstantial. Close analysis of the trials reveals why this was bound to be the case. There was no single or dominant reason why individuals fell under suspicion, while reputations were built up piecemeal over time and could incorporate very disparate elements. In consequence, supposed witches were a very heterogeneous group, even in the broadest terms. They were more often poor than rich, old rather than young and female rather than male, but there were quite numerous exceptions to all these tendencies. At any one time a particular community probably had a small group of strong suspects, with a much looser periphery of marginal ones; the latter were probably only known to individual families or close neighbours, and were not yet the subject of general village gossip. . . . For other members of the community, the witch appears to have alternated between being a terrifying enemy who could bring ruin or death and a pathetic figure to be despised and insulted.

One very powerful link did unite many of the accused; that of family and heredity. The idea that a "race" was either sound or tainted was much employed, both in self-defence and in accusations. To be the child of a convicted or reputed witch was inherently dangerous; in one pathetic case in Lorraine a young couple were both accused, and it emerged that they had decided to marry after attending the execution at the stake of their respective parents, "so that they would have nothing to reproach one another with." There are signs that as persecution became established in some areas this element was progressively strengthened, with a growing proportion of victims having such antecedents. How far this was just a natural statistical outcome of the situation is harder to determine; here we still lack good comparative information for different regions. The possibility remains open that in areas of endemic persecution this tended to concentrate increasingly on a self-defining group of "witchcraft families." It is also unclear how far the popular ideas on the subject implied some kind of congenital weakness, as opposed to the notion that parents might deliberately initiate their children as witches. Judges certainly showed considerable interest in the latter possibility, but it is less obvious in the testimony of witnesses. Confessing second-generation witches, who quite often blamed their parents for their initial seduction, are probably best seen as trying to displace responsibility rather than as expressing general beliefs.

Everyone seems to have known how the Devil carried out his seductions. Once witches decided to confess they told similar stories, with very little prompting, which rarely changed much over time. The Devil normally appeared unbidden to someone who was in a receptive psychological state. This might involve anger against relatives or neighbours, despair caused by poverty or hunger, or anxiety at being called a witch. He offered consoling words, a gift of money and assurances that his followers would not want for anything. He might also promise that they would have power to avenge their wrongs, often providing a powder with which such revenge could be effected. Once the prospective recruit agreed to renounce God and take the Devil for master, the latter gave symbolic force to the change of allegiance. This normally meant touching the new witch to impose the mark, leaving either a visible blemish on the skin or an insensible place. At the same time the chrism[10] given at baptism was supposedly removed. With women the Devil then took possession of them sexually, an experience they often described in vivid terms as a virtual rape, made more unpleasant by the glacial coldness of his penis. Any remaining illusions were shattered when the money turned out to be leaves or horse-dung, at which point the witches knew they had been cheated. . . .

. . . Once the witch had been lured into this disastrous error there was thought to be no way back. A handful of the accused claimed they had made some attempt to reintegrate themselves within the church, but all had apparently found this impossible. Catherine Charpentier tried to take advantage of the special terms available to penitents during the Jubilee[11] of 1602 by confessing her apostasy to a friar at St. Nicolas. He made her promise to abandon the Devil, then absolved her, after which she felt the Devil leave her. She was also to carry holy bread and candle wax with her, then make a full confession to her own *curé*[12] the following Easter, with three-monthly confessions thereafter. Unfortunately, although at the outset she was determined to comply, "once she was at home and the time arrived to make her confession to the *curé*, the shame of revealing herself to him, together with her fear that he would expose and defame her, overcame her to such an extent that she did not say a word to the *curé*." The Devil saw his opportunity, duly appearing to reclaim her allegiance. . . .

. . . The diabolical pact was a very ancient story that all concerned were readily able to manipulate. The narratives combined elements of folklore and official demonology, which were fitted around social and psychological determinants. The Devil stood for the temptation to reject the normal constraints and obligations which regulated personal relations. In a society where communal norms were so coercive and privacy so elusive, the related stresses must have been peculiarly intense. The fantasy of the pact brought together an inner drama experienced by individuals with the judges' requirements for clear cut offences. As the ultimate treason against God and man it could be held to justify an automatic death sentence, even the bending of normal rules of procedure. . . .

In many accounts the pact was followed by the sabbat; either immediately after the seduction or within a few days, the Devil would lead the new witch to a meeting with others. This too was a notably malleable set of ideas, which formed part of the same narrative and overlapped with other elements in it. . . . It is impossible to determine how far these confessions sprang from an exceptionally rich local folklore and how far they were generated by a very active group of clerical and lay persecutors. Certainly the witchcraft panic in both French and Spanish Navarre in 1609–11 produced some of the most sensational testimony about

---

[10] Holy oil used in Christian ceremonies.

[11] In Roman Catholic practice, a year, coming once every quarter century, during which believers gain full remission of the punishment of their sins.

[12] Chief parish priest.

the sabbat, whose influence has been remarkably durable. The French judge Pierre de Lancre[13] was largely responsible for this, for he wrote the statements up in a suitably lurid fashion. In a famous purple passage he described the purposes of those attending the sabbat as being

> to dance indecently, to banquet filthily, to couple diabolically, to sodomize execrably, to blaspheme scandalously, to pursue brutally every horrible, dirty and unnatural desire, to hold as precious toads, vipers, lizards and all sorts of poisons; to love a vile-smelling goat, to caress him lovingly, to press against and copulate with him horribly and shamelessly.

The idea of secret meetings where orgies take place and evil is planned must be one of the oldest and most basic human fantasies. Charges of nocturnal conspiracy, black magic, child murder, orgiastic sexuality and perverted ritual were nothing new in Europe when they were applied to witches. They had been used against early Christians and then against heretics, Jews and lepers. In the fourteenth century they were made against popes, bishops and the great Crusading order of the Knights Templar.[14] The stereotype is obvious; it consisted of inverting all the positive values of society, adding a lot of lurid detail (often borrowed from earlier allegations), then throwing the resulting bucket of filth over the selected victims. A kind of scholarly pornography was generated, while the use of torture secured the required confessions. It was also in the fourteenth century that humble people started to be convicted for witchcraft, at first in very small numbers; initially they were simply charged with causing harm to their neighbours by occult means, with no mention of devil-worship. This was quickly added to, however, drawing on a range of popular beliefs about nocturnal activities, mostly ascribed to women. Some were negative; stories of cannibalistic women who flew by night, killing and eating children in particular. Others were positive, concerning various forms of guardian spirits who were dangerous if not treated with respect, but essentially acted as protectors of people, animals and crops. The stories of the sabbat represented a fusion between the persecuting stereotypes elaborated by clerics and judges and the various older folkloric traditions of the peasantry. . . .

. . . The belief in witchcraft was plainly widespread in Europe, leaving the way open for persecution to feed on itself. Each witch who came to trial might be tortured, then denounce several others seen at the sabbat, in a kind of infernal, elaborate domino effect. Although there does seem to have been a small peak of trials in the 1480s, it was not until the late sixteenth century that denunciations came to function widely in this way. In fact it looks as if the idea of the sabbat was slow to spread from its Alpine origins. The great early witch-hunter's manual of 1486, the *Malleus Maleficarum,* hardly mentions the sabbat; although the authors are evidently quite well aware of the idea that witches meet in assemblies, the rigid

---

[13] A demonologist and judge (1553–1631) who was responsible for the execution of more than eighty accused witches.

[14] A religious order of knights, founded to protect Jerusalem from the Turks.

scholastic format of the work somehow prevents them putting any emphasis on this. When Bodin wrote his *Démonomanie des Sorciers*[15] in 1580 he felt it necessary to offer extensive proofs that witches really were transported to the sabbat, while commenting angrily on the way some judges and others ridiculed the whole notion. It can in fact be argued that the idea of the sabbat discouraged the elites from taking witchcraft seriously, because it was thought too implausible and too much tainted by popular credulity. In other words, for the better part of a century the destructive potential of the belief in groups of night witches failed to operate as might have been expected. Furthermore, even in the peak decades of persecution the role of the sabbat remains very ambiguous.

When trials did multiply, notably from the 1580s, there were numerous areas of Europe where the full-blown version of the sabbat was very slow to emerge from the trials or indeed never did so. Around this time the early critics of witchhunting, such as Weyer and Scot, were already raising the question of whether such confessions did not merely demonstrate that their makers must be deluded. This was simply a more vigorous expression of long-standing uncertainties, for, in what may well have been the first formal discussion of the new crime of diabolical witchcraft, John Nider[16] seemed to imply that the sabbat was some kind of diabolical illusion. . . . Another idea shared by intellectuals and ordinary suspects was that some kind of substitution took place when the witch went to the sabbat; either their body stayed behind in bed, or a diabolical illusion took its place. Evasive reasoning of this kind, all too common, was really a sign of weakness faced with the implausibilities of the standard myth. . . .

Like other myths of its type, the sabbat worked on the basic principle of inversion; it presented a mirror image of the Christian world in which people actually lived. Familiar practices and relationships remained quite recognizable, but in distorted or parodic forms. . . .

The norm itself is very clear. Witches went to the sabbat under orders, often carried by their master or on a broom, even when it was so close that these methods of transport were gratuitous. Sometimes they returned on foot, which emphasized how the outward journey by air was a detail intended to stress the abnormality of the whole affair. Symbolically it expressed the extraordinary character and difficulty of transfer between the normal world and another opposed antiworld. Night flying could also explain large meetings of witches coming from long distances, but such big gatherings were rare events which appeared in few confessions. In a parody of a village festival the witches danced back to back, consumed horrible food and made hail, frosts or caterpillars which damaged their own crops. Sexuality and cannibalism were only mentioned in a handful of cases. This was an anti-fertility rite conducted on the familiar principle of inversion. Many accounts had the participants concealing their identity by wearing masks, aided by the fact it was night. . . . Nearly all the standard features of the sabbat

---

[15] *Demonomania of Witches.*

[16] A theologian (ca. 1380–1438) and author of a demonology, *The Anthill* (1455).

could be reinverted — in the odd aberrant confession the witches even enjoyed a good meal or went by day. These symbolic constituents were apparently not very firmly grasped by a significant minority of those who confessed. Although the idea that witches held secret meetings was well established in popular folklore, the formal structures of inversion seem to have been rather insecurely attached to this central theme.

The really constant element in the confessions is harming the crops, occasionally omitted but never reversed. Just as the main purpose of most communal Christian rites was to protect the crops and encourage fertility, so the diabolical festivals sought to destroy them. This fundamental inversion was never misunderstood. That this was the primary meaning of the sabbat is emphasized by the numerous accounts of disputes between rich and poor witches over such plans. Catherine Charpentier claimed that the rich "who said that they still had enough grain in store, wished and suggested that they should make hail and destroy the grain and the other fruits of the earth. As for her, she had never wished to agree, because of her fear of being in want, knowing as she did the poverty of her husband, also, she had several times been beaten by her said master Persin, who supported the wishes of the others." This is a very common theme recounted by the witches, one which plainly expressed the basic social divisions of the local community. High prices meant desperate times for the poor but profits for those with a surplus of grain to sell, who were also likely to take advantage to increase their land holdings. Here inversion normally stopped in the fantasies, for only in a few cases did the rich not get their way at the sabbat as they did in the real world. Occasionally the poor won the argument; more often they managed to sabotage the hail-making in some way — perhaps by upsetting the pot being used — at the price of a beating from the Devil. . . .

. . . Like so much else in the concept of witchcraft, the sabbat was primarily concerned with power. Such visions were of course fundamentally deceptive. They could only be fulfilled in negative terms, through the destruction of the basic assets of rural society, the reverse of bringing any improvement to the lives of participants. A curious logic is evident, whereby the Devil needs the witches in order to produce corporeal effects and so uses a mixture of false promises, threats and compulsion to obtain their presence at his disgusting ceremonies. The betrayal which begins with the seduction and the pact is completed at the sabbat, where nothing is quite what it seems. The food, instead of being merely repellent might be entirely illusory, as for Hellenix Horrin, who reported that Persin "had promised to give her a meal, but did no such thing, and those who had already eaten said that when they left they were dying of hunger." The basis for virtual enslavement to this deplorable master was never really explained, except as a result of the witches' own pathetic gullibility and the pact they made. As for the proceedings at the sabbat, these appear to prefigure Hell itself, in which respect at least we may fairly see the sabbat as the gateway to the land of the dead. For those who made the confessions death loomed in a very real sense, although many seem to have felt that by making a clean breast of their sinful relations with the lord of the underworld they ensured ending up in the other place. . . .

If the sabbat myth appeared in some form virtually everywhere witches were detected, it was still very far from presenting a uniform pattern. . . . It was mostly in German cities that the juridical, political and social peculiarities of virtually independent urban communities interacted to generate terrifying outbreaks of persecution. The cities involved had populations of only a few thousand, and functioned as market, legal and clerical centres for the surrounding countryside. Surviving examples suggest a rather claustrophobic environment, with narrow houses packed tightly within the medieval walls to make an ideal setting for a satanic thriller. Small Catholic cities ruled by bishops also had abnormally large clerical populations, and would have been filled with the sounds and symbols of belief, yet also with petty rivalries and jealousies. While the dramatic episodes that took place against such a background only made up a relatively small proportion of known European trials, they have inevitably dominated most later thinking about witchcraft. The unrestrained use of torture to extract confessions and denunciations horrified many contemporary observers. In fact these persecutions turned out to be self-limiting, for they created such social instability and general fear that finally the ruling groups brought them to an end. It should be added that major cities and centres of government were never involved; the places concerned were always relative backwaters, where small groups of zealots could have disproportionate influence. The most spectacular cases of all were in some prince-bishoprics — Trier in the 1590s, Bamberg and Würzburg around 1628–31, Cologne in the 1630s — but Protestant towns were also affected. There are striking similarities with earlier persecutions of Jews on charges of the ritual murder[17] of children and both types of outbreak brought efforts by the Emperor and his jurists to enforce higher judicial standards.

These intense persecutions were necessarily built around the sabbat, for it was only through the identification of numerous accomplices that the panic could spread as it did. It is also noticeable that as accusations spread to clerics and other members of the elites the confessions became more elaborate, with much emphasis on complex diabolical rituals at the sabbat. The poor might go on brooms or pitchforks, but the rich allegedly travelled in silver coaches or other luxury conveyances. A particularly unpleasant feature of these outbreaks was the way in which children became involved in large numbers as both accusers and victims. This . . . was to be a major factor in the Swedish witch-hunt of 1668–76. In this last instance the confessions made much of the legend of Blåkulla (the blue mountain), a Swedish equivalent of the German peak known as the Brocken, which shared the reputation of the latter as a meeting place for witches. The children elaborated this into stories of a great hall where devils and angels alternated amidst a series of bizarre and often playful inversions, intermixed with devil-worship and scenes of punishment. Here the meshing together of demonology and local tradition is particularly obvious, alongside the fertile qualities and dan-

---

[17] The belief, held by Christians, that Jews sacrificed Christian children during the Passover holiday.

ger of juvenile fantasy. The children were grouped together in special houses, supposedly for their protection from the witches, and this encouraged them further in their role as mouthpieces for local opinion. Although there was considerable elite scepticism from the start, the local clergy and community leaders took up the hunt with enthusiasm; the persecution was only stopped after it spread to Stockholm. Only at this point did the government itself come to appreciate the dangers properly. Under hostile questioning the whole great edifice of fantasy collapsed as the children admitted their stories were lies from beginning to end. Over the previous years they had brought terror and panic to large areas of northern Sweden. Yet because there were dissenting voices and there was no systematic use of torture, less than 15 per cent of those accused were put to death, with the total number of executions being around 200.

In Sweden it was only during this late outbreak that ideas of the sabbat contributed much to witchcraft persecution. There were many other regions in Europe where the sabbat played a marginal role at best, appearing in small minorities of trials in other parts of Scandinavia or in Aragon and Hungary, for example. It is no surprise to find that it made only fleeting appearances in connection with Dutch witchcraft, while its absence from most English cases is often noted. In this context England seems much less exceptional than was once thought, and indeed the sabbat did creep gradually on to the English scene albeit in a rather tame and homely form. It surfaced hesitantly in the Lancashire trials of 1612 and 1634; these were unusually large group trials for England, and particularly good evidence has survived from the first, when nineteen persons were tried and most of them convicted and hanged. In 1634 an even larger group was tried, with seventeen known convictions, but intervention by king and council first stopped the executions, then finally exposed the main accuser, a boy named Edmund Robinson, as a fraud. . . .

In north-western Europe the sabbat appears to have enjoyed greatest prominence in Denmark and Scotland, where there is a rather odd relationship. Danish witches often confessed to meetings with the Devil in their local churches and this has been plausibly linked with the wall-paintings in the churches, where scenes of temptation were commonplace. When King James VI[18] of Scotland married Anne of Denmark in 1590 the storms which troubled the return voyage were ascribed to witchcraft in both countries. In Scotland around a hundred individuals, supposedly led by the Earl of Bothwell,[19] were accused of high treason through meetings with the Devil in the kirk[20] at North Berwick. This bizarre affair took the sabbat into Scottish witchcraft trials, where it subsequently cropped up in numerous confessions. . . . Scottish witches were rather well behaved and in fact inversion played rather a limited role in most stories. In a society where

---

[18] James VI was king of Scotland from 1567 to 1625 and, as James I, king of England from 1603 to 1625.

[19] James Hepburn, earl of Bothwell (ca. 1536–1578), third husband of Mary, Queen of Scots.

[20] In Scotland, the parish church.

almost all forms of spontaneous festivity were banned, the idea of disorderly gatherings was perhaps sufficient evidence of depravity on its own. In the coastal villages where many trials took place it was the sinking of ships, rather than the spoiling of crops, which exemplified the treason to the community. . . .

Such links between different countries crop up in various contexts. The account of the Swedish trials in Glanvill's *Sadducismus Triumphatus*[21] evidently influenced the New England clergyman Cotton Mather,[22] and may have had some indirect bearing on events in Salem Village.[23] The behaviour of the possessed girls during this famous episode has obvious parallels with that of the children in Sweden, although there is no sign of direct imitation. The sudden appearance of the sabbat in New England in 1692 remains mysterious; the children's stories have too much in common with European accounts not to have some literary or folkloric source whose exact nature is now impossible to recover. In comparison with their counterparts in the Old World, the authorities in the New came out remarkably well. Not only did they bring the trials to a close much more quickly and with a modest number of executions, they also sponsored public penitence for the wrongs committed, and ultimately rehabilitated both the accused and the dead. Whereas the Swedes executed four of the accusers, including a boy of thirteen, in Massachusetts the girls were left to wrestle with their own consciences. Another who engaged in painful self-examination was Cotton Mather, much troubled by his failure to intervene earlier and stop the persecution yet still fascinated by what he called "the wonders of the invisible world." For men like Mather, the Devil's anti-world remained a vital part of their cosmology, even when they saw how easily the great enemy could lead them astray.

In a very different context, the Inquisitors[24] in the extreme north-east of Italy were confronted by a strange nocturnal world in the beliefs of the *benendanti*[25] of Friuli, peasants with a peculiar folklore of their own. These belonged to at least one widespread belief system, for they were allegedly marked out by an accident of birth, having been covered by the caul (or amniotic membrane) at the moment of delivery. Various similar chances — birth at a particular time or at a particular place in the family — were supposed to confer special powers of insight or healing elsewhere in Europe. In Friuli the *benendanti* went out in dreams to fight the witches and ensure the fertility of the crops; some of them also claimed the power to identify witches and treat their victims. The Inquisitors tried with some success to assimilate these local traditions to orthodox demonology, turning the dream

---

[21] Joseph Glanvill (1636–1680) confirmed the reality of witchcraft in *Sadducismus Triumphatus, or full and plain evidence concerning witches and apparitions* (1681).

[22] New England Puritan preacher and demonologist (1663–1728), author of *Wonders of the Invisible World* (1693).

[23] A town in Massachusetts, site of witchcraft trials in 1692.

[24] Members of the Inquisition, a tribunal engaged in combating beliefs opposed to those of the Roman Catholic Church.

[25] Do-gooders.

meetings of the anti-witch cult into versions of the sabbat. However by the time they had achieved this, around 1650, the sceptical attitudes of both the Roman authorities and the Venetian secular administration averted the danger of an ensuing persecution. While male *benendanti* allegedly fought witches, women seem to have been more concerned to make contact with the souls of those recently dead, bringing back reports of their condition and their needs. There are hints of similar beliefs elsewhere, but nothing remotely as complex or systematic as this strange corpus of folklore. If most scholars have seen the *benendanti* as an exceptional local case rather than the tip of a submerged iceberg, this must of necessity remain a matter of opinion. Where there is certainly no problem is in linking them to the role of the sabbat as an anti-fertility rite, for their stories exemplify this in a particularly vivid fashion. . . .

We must also suppose that a wide range of local folklore was caught up in the judicial machinery, through whose distorting lens it is preserved. The complex process of interaction . . . provides a general model within which these beliefs can to some extent be reintegrated; it seems unlikely we shall ever be able to reconstruct them fully. What we do not need is any pseudo-empirical explanation, whether in the form of . . . pagan covens or . . . early drug cults. . . . It was often claimed in the course of trials that witches smeared themselves or the objects on which they flew with ointments, while there was quite widespread knowledge of various medical plants, including some hallucinogens. Dream experience is likely to have played a significant part in validating personal stories; it is even possible that some of it was drug-induced, perhaps by fungi with psychotropic qualities. When one looks in detail at the stories about ointments however, it becomes plain that the ingredients were usually magical in a quite different sense, for they only acquired their virtue by being placed in a symbolic system, through preparation at particular times and so forth. Powerful magical qualities were frequently accorded to human grease, simply because it carried such a charge of the forbidden. Wherever there is clear evidence about the alleged ointments they turn out to be harmless substances, identified or even deliberately manufactured to support confessions. It is hardly credible in any case that drugs could have produced specific visions of goats sitting on thrones or of perverted rituals; at most they could be linked to general sensations like that of flying through the air. To give them more importance requires us to homogenize the confessions in disregard of the endless local variations. This would be to repeat the error of demonologists like the Jesuit Martin Del Rio, whose enormous compendium on magic and witchcraft argued that the similarity of the confessions showed the sabbat was no illusion. . . .

While confessions were normally extracted under thumbscrews, rack, strappado or other refinements of the torturer's art, a certain proportion of the accused made "free" confessions, which in some cases did not reflect even the implicit threat of torture. . . . Such confessions no longer seem as puzzling as they once did; some recent cases of alleged satanic abuse have provided yet more evidence of the way individuals placed under extreme stress will manufacture preposterous stories, apparently coming, at least for a while, to believe that they must be true. They mingle themes from their cultural milieu with elements derived from dream and fantasy, to generate self-incriminating narratives which have their own psychological significance. . . . Those witches who made a clean breast of such imaginary turpitudes were engaging in a form of self-purification, just as they should have done when they confessed to the priest, if they were Catholics. In the face of a terrifying situation, which saw them excluded and vilified by their own community, the confession represented an appeal for forgiveness and reintegration. The judges frequently emphasized the importance of a complete account, including all separate acts of witchcraft, as the condition for being received back into the church and rendered eligible for salvation. In practice they were very careless about enforcing this, but such exhortations produced statements such as that made by Claudatte Jean, who

> prayed for the honour of God that she should be put to death as soon as possible for the salvation of her soul, and wished that there might be no more witches in the world, but that she might be the last, so that the fruits of the earth might be more abundant than they had been, because so much and so long as there were witches it would be a great evil for the poor people. She then prayed she might have a good confessor to secure the salvation of her soul, and begged all those she had offended to pardon her.

. . . [O]thers were better aware of the fictitious nature of their accounts, to the extent that they could explain how they had concocted them. We should also remember such terrible stories as that of mayor Junius of Bamberg,[26] who wrote to his daughter explaining how the executioner — either very sly or unusually merciful — begged him to confess, rather than oblige him to inflict endless torment. These German witch-hunts were very different in some respects; since the accusations were spread by denunciations made under torture, the arbitrary nature of the process was far clearer to the accused and they were rarely suspected until the last moment. . . .

The detailed accounts of the pact and the sabbat evidently reflect the everyday cultural and social concerns of their tellers, however fanciful the imaginary packaging may appear. They also reaffirm the creativity and significance of human fantasy, through which the juxtaposition of real and imaginary worlds took place. For their neighbours and the judges it was the witches who bridged the gap between the worlds, with the sabbats as the ultimate anti-world, hovering uneasily between diabolical illusion and some kind of perverted reality. Stories that the Devil incited those present to do wrong, then distributed the necessary powders or other poisons, sought to link the secret nocturnal meetings back to the *maleficium*[27] the witches operated in the ordinary sphere of village life. The weakness or absence of this element in most accounts of the sabbat suggests how imperfectly this element was ever integrated into popular thinking. One must add examples,

---

[26] Johannes Junius, famous for his tearful letter to his daughter after a court unjustly sentenced him to death as a witch in 1628.

[27] Harmful or evil magic.

such as that of England, which demonstrate how persecution and witch beliefs could function perfectly well without the sabbat at all. It is not a case of there being a "classic" type of European witchcraft built around the pact and the sabbat, with a few deviant types in peripheral regions; the picture is much more varied and the sabbat was only the central basis for persecution in a small number of extreme cases. What this complex superstructure does do is to give us enormously helpful insights into the minds of those concerned. Only so long as it is placed firmly in the mind, and allowed its full range of local variants, will its great symbolic richness help rather than hinder our understanding.

MATERIAL CONDITIONS
OF FAMILY LIFE
Raffaella Sarti

Raffaella Sarti, researcher in early modern history at the University of Urbino in Italy, examines people's homes and diet in the sixteenth, seventeenth, and eighteenth centuries, thereby allowing us to appreciate the immediate environment of Europeans' daily lives and rudimentary existence. Wills, inventories taken after death, personal writings (such as correspondence and memoirs), art, and architecture enable historians to reconstruct the material conditions of life. Approximately a half-century ago, the French historian Lucien Febvre wrote that the two greatest concerns of early modern Europeans were cold and hunger. Sarti depicts how Europeans coped with those two dangers.

These premodern centuries prior to the Industrial Revolution saw momentous developments in living conditions, though not at the more rapid pace that we in the contemporary world have come to expect. The study of material culture, the objects of the past that people produced and used, offers insight to fundamental living conditions. Sarti assays changes in home construction that affected the degree of comfort in Europeans' lives, the extent of personal privacy, and differing gender roles. She contrasts modes of life between the elite and those in lower social groups and between rural and urban areas. What people ate and what they used to eat their food illuminates social health, happiness, and values. Here the impact of the New World on the Old World is evident.

In what ways did home construction and interior design, food, and drink change during the early modern centuries? How did food delineate social distinctions? What evidence supports the notion of the birth of consumerism and of a consumer revolution? How did daily lives become more comfortable and less nasty? Did changes in material life widen the differences between rich and poor and between men and women?

Raffaella Sarti, "The Material Conditions of Family Life," in David I. Kertzer and Marzio Barbagli, *Family Life in Early Modern Times: 1500–1789* (New Haven: Yale University Press, 2001), 3–23.

THE HOME

Living Conditions in Rural Areas

A family huddled together in semi-darkness around a smoking fire lit in a hole in the ground, with the animals nearby for warmth. The house has one or two rooms, walls made of wood or vegetable matter mixed with mud or clay, a roof of straw or reeds, a floor of beaten earth and frequently no windows: such scenes were common during cold nights in rural parts of Europe during the late Middle Ages. In early modern times, however, some important changes took place.

First, the fire. The fireplace built into a side wall, probably invented in Venice in the twelfth or thirteenth century, became a common feature of houses. True, it wasted a lot of heat, but it guaranteed a much less smoky atmosphere. Even better in this respect was the closed stove, which also utilized the heat in a more rational manner. These stoves — built of simple masonry or tiled — were also on the increase. They were often located between two rooms, heating both simultaneously; around the stove were benches on which people could keep warm, sometimes in crowded conditions. An Italian traveling in Poland in the sixteenth century spent his nights in houses where the whole family slept around the stove on benches covered in furs. He took advantage of the lack of privacy to make advances to some of the women. Stoves of this kind were popular in Central and Eastern Europe. From the seventeenth century onward, there were also stoves of cast iron. Fireplaces predominated in Italy, France, Portugal, Norway, and England. In the southern Slavonic areas open fires continued to be the norm. In Spain braziers were preferred, but in the Tierra de Campos and the Tierra del Pan straw was burned in underground ducts.

Transformations such as the removal of the hearth from the center of the room to one wall, the addition of extra fireplaces or the concealment of the fire inside the stove imply a radical alteration of the way people lived, and of the way living was perceived. The symbolic balance of the house was thus transformed, as were (more prosaically) the materials from which it was constructed. It was no coincidence that changes in the way a house was heated should combine with other changes. In the early modern period dwellings like the ones described above were with increasing frequency abandoned, demolished, replaced, rebuilt, or used for other purposes. New houses were more spacious and higher and the interior space was divided more clearly. Especially since the eighteenth century houses were usually built of stone or brick, with roofs of tiles or slates. They were much less flammable, more solid and more durable. They offered less shelter to mice and insects. On the other hand they were liable to cost 15 times as much as a house made of wood or other plant material. The quality and cost of a house did not depend solely on the materials used. Even the humblest dwellings were made of stone where this was in plentiful supply (in the Mediterranean area, in Brittany, Cornwall, Burgundy, the Ile-de-France, etc.). The *Fachwerkhäuser*[1] of Central and

---

[1] Thatched-roofed houses.

Northern Europe, although consisting of a wooden structure filled in with wat-
tles and daub, clay and straw, or some similar mixture, could evidently be both
elegant and comfortable.

Well-known architects were hired by Italian landowners keen to make the
most of their estates also by rebuilding their country houses. In sixteenth-century
France a new architectural genre appeared, albeit one with familiar antecedents.
This new type of house was called the *maison rustique*[2] by the humanist Charles
Estienne,[3] whose precepts were to influence house-building for more than two
centuries. From the late sixteenth century onward, intense building activity in
England, particularly in the Midlands and the south, made cottages consisting of
one or two rooms much scarcer.

These transformations generally first affected the prosperous echelons of rural
society in wealthy areas, then the lower social strata and the poorer areas. . . . The
Heuerlinge[4] of north-western Germany . . . lived in miserable hovels near the
houses of the *Altbauern*,[5] who gave them land in exchange for labor. The miners
of the Auvergne lived in wretched one-roomed hovels (*barriades*), and agricultural
day laborers in Sicily suffered a similar fate.

In fact, houses differed according to where they were situated, and also according to the social status of their inhabitants and the functions they had to fulfil. For day laborers they were often no more than a refuge; for richer folk they
were a status symbol and an investment. For farming families, they were a tool of
their trade. Farmhouses in central Italy had storage space for grain, olives, grapes,
etc., and places where these crops could be processed, according to what was cultivated. Big houses, with various wings, were built as they were because they had
to fulfil a variety of functions, not necessarily because they housed a large and
complex family. These multifunctional homes, however, be they the palaces of the
nobility or large farmhouses in central Italy, were frequently inhabited by large,
often complex, families, sufficient in number to perform all the various tasks.

Let us now pay a visit to a house inhabited by prosperous peasants, for example the large *Fachwerkhaus* belonging to Jacob Grösser and Agatha Deuggerin
in about 1625, in the German village of Jungingen (Zollernalbkreis). The front
door opens on to a space which leads to another door. Propped against the wall,
or hanging from it, there are various agricultural tools. On the left hand side are
store-rooms and perhaps a laundry room; on the right is the stable. Under the
staircase a glimpse might be caught of a hen coop, a cage with some piglets in it
and a stake for slaughtering animals. On the first floor the *Stube*[6] is large and
bright. It has two rows of windows, almost certainly glazed. From the late Mid-

---

[2] Country house.

[3] French physician (1504–1564) and writer.

[4] Day laborers.

[5] Old, established peasantry.

[6] The best room.

dle Ages glass began to spread from churches and the grandest palaces to ordinary homes. The *Stube* is heated by a tiled stove, surrounded by benches. In the opposite corner near the window stands a table. There are benches fixed to the wall and a large chest for sitting on. There are shelves bearing dishes, jugs, and the Bible. Clothes and utensils hang on the wall. Somewhere there is probably a candlestick or a lamp holder. A spinning wheel dominates one corner of the room and we can imagine Agatha sitting there spinning. The *Stube* is not only used as a place to eat, or for social life but also for work: here textiles are spun, clothes are sewn, tools are mended.

Let us have a look at the kitchen: there is probably a cupboard, there are iron and copper pans, dishes of terracotta and wood, baskets, a container for water, a churn, a bottle of cider, a knife and wooden block for the preparation of meat, a pile of wood. There is also the opening through which the stove in the *Stube* is stoked and this is probably where the cooking is done — there is no chimney. There are a few openings in the ceiling to allow the smoke to rise through the loft and out of the thatched roof. The smoke dries the grain and fruit stored in the loft, and also protects the beams from infestation. Beneath the loft, on the first floor, are some more (unheated) rooms, probably three. They are bedrooms. Agatha and Jacob possess three beds at most. But the family consists of five people and two servants. Seven people in three beds? Sharing a bed was perfectly normal: a bed with a mattress, sheet, and blankets was more or less as valuable as a cow.

On the whole, Jacob and Agatha's house was comfortable. At that time, small animals often lived in the main room. The stables were frequently located right next to the living room so that none of the heat from the animals was wasted, and they could be minded without anyone having to venture outside. In Brittany, for example, until quite recently, people and animals lived under the same roof in longhouses, the people separated from the animals by just a few pieces of furniture. Sometimes the intimacy was even greater. According to a late eighteenth-century source, crofters[7] in the Outer Hebrides shared their home with chickens, sheep, goats, and cows, whose combined excrement was removed only once a year. Moreover between 1650 and 1700 in the Vale of Berkeley, in Gloucestershire, and in East Kent (one of the richest parts of Britain, with bountiful agriculture and well-developed commercial and craft activities in small towns and villages) 50 percent of the poorest households possessed no chairs, although the majority had a table, and about 80–90 percent a bedstead. Every household, however, owned at least a mattress to lay on the floor as was the custom in the sixteenth century.

A few decades later, seats became the norm in almost all English houses. In the early modern period the availability of consumer goods went through a period of extended growth, although the pace of the growth quickened or slackened from time to time. It is not easy to give an exact date for the beginning of this expansion. Some scholars maintained that "there was a consumer revolution in eighteenth-century England." In their eyes modern consumerism was born there.

---

[7] Those who rented and worked small farms.

Others noted that Renaissance Italy experienced a spectacular growth both of material culture and consumption: "Modern consumer society, with its insatiable consumption setting the pace for the production of more objects and changes in style, had its first stirrings, if not its birth, in the habits of spending that possessed the Italians in the Renaissance." Thus more recent research concludes that "the emergence of a consumer society was by no means sudden — certainly not confined to the late eighteenth and early nineteenth century — nor was it limited geographically to Britain." Sometimes growth continued in spite of general economic decline. In any case, different parts of Europe developed at different rates. In the valley of the Duero, in Spain, in the poorest households chairs were a rarity even as late as 1750. In the Plain of Caen at the beginning of the eighteenth century there were chairs in three-quarters of the houses; by the end of the century every household owned chairs. (In the early part of the century every family owned a bed. Tables became universal 50 years later.) This expansion was not uniformly spread through society, nor were the wealthiest people necessarily the most innovative.

Smaller possessions multiplied, as well as furniture: the acquisition of consumer goods stimulated and satisfied new needs and habits. In the Tuscan countryside, the number of sheets owned by every family doubled between the sixteenth and the eighteenth century. In Normandy during the periods 1700–1715 and 1770–1789, inventories listing at least one tablecloth, glasses, and forks increased respectively from 61 to 76 percent; from 28 to 50 percent; and from 4 to 60 percent.

Living Conditions in Urban Areas

The conditions of life described so far existed predominantly in rural or semi-rural areas. The material life of someone living in the country, however, is different from that of someone living in a town, even though in the countryside large houses and mansions belonging to wealthy people existed alongside the homesteads of peasants and artisans. What were conditions like in the city at this time? In the three centuries we are looking at, houses grew taller and more densely crowded together because of population growth. In Naples, Genoa, Venice, and Rome buildings divided into apartments became more common during the sixteenth century; in seventeenth-century Amsterdam the number of four-storey houses increased. In Paris an edict of 1667 forbade the erection of buildings more than 15.6 meters high, and in 1783 the requirement to respect the ratio between the width of the street and the height of buildings was introduced. During the eighteenth century, however, buildings were rising to six storeys in height and sometimes (according to one witness) as high as nine. In some areas of the city the density of population was about 500 people per hectare.[8] In some parts of London it was 800. Urban growth was due predominantly to immigration, as the mortality rate in the

---

[8] 2.471 acres.

city was higher than it was in the country. Such density of population encouraged the spread of illness and it also made the disposal of waste difficult, even though much of it was recycled. The dung of animals kept in interior courtyards, or of animals used for transport, the contents of chamber pots emptied into the street and other refuse made the urban habitat unhealthy.

Liquid from this refuse percolated down into the aquifers, which were also threatened by the increasing number of septic tanks. By the end of the eighteenth century there was at least one lavatory in nearly all buildings, usually in the courtyard or in the common areas. Wells, frequently polluted, at which women and children often waited in line for hours at a time, were one of the main sources of water. In London, where in the sixteenth and seventeenth centuries pumps and piped water were introduced, to have water brought directly to your house remained the privilege of the few. In Paris, even after the brothers Perrier[9] had inaugurated their domestic water deliveries in 1782, there were around 20,000 water carriers and vendors in the town; the water came from the polluted Seine river. Not surprisingly, the average daily consumption of water at the beginning of the eighteenth century in Paris was less than 5 liters per head; by the end of the century it had risen to 10 liters. (In 1976, in cities with more than 10,000 inhabitants, the daily consumption was estimated at more than 400 liters per head.) In Bologna, Italy, where a system of sluices delivered water to many cellars in town, in summer the water used for laundry was dark and muddy.

In the second half of the eighteenth century, however, perceptions of health and hygiene began to change. For doctors, hygienists, and administrators, washing the streets to clear the air, and opening cities to wind and light became urgent necessities. In addition to being dirty, cities were dark: although as early as the sixteenth century streets were widened to allow carriages to use them, and to provide an appropriate setting for new architecture, in general the urban landscape was characterized by narrow streets running between houses piled one on top of another.

The problem of nocturnal darkness was also being tackled: in Paris there were 2,736 lamps in public places in 1697, and at least 7,000 in 1766. Lighting began to lose its reputation as a luxury reserved for the few. The means of illumination, mainly candlesticks, increased in private houses, particularly after 1750–1760. In eighteenth-century Paris there were on average five per apartment. They were in widespread use among the lower classes too. The lights of the city were in sharp contrast to the darkness of the countryside. In the Plain of Caen, for example, between 1700 and 1715 only 57 percent of all families possessed a candlestick (by 1770–1789 this had risen to 88 percent).

The lighting of the interior of the house was improved by an increase in the number of windows, in Paris particularly notable from the 1720s and 1730s onward. Relatively large panes of translucent glass replaced paper and oiled canvas

---

[9] The brothers Auguste Charles and Jacques Constantin Périer (1742–1818) installed steam-driven pumps to provide Paris with a water supply.

or small panes of glass. Only the richest, however, were able to flood their rooms with light through really generous windows.

The desire for sunlight conflicted with the need for warmth, even in the wealthiest households. In 1695 in Versailles water and wine froze on the king's dining table. Humbler dwellings, which were small and crowded, were sometimes less cold. In Bologna in the eighteenth century, the *camino* (i.e. "hearth," a room with a fireplace) represented the minimum space that was normally rented. In eighteenth-century Paris there was an average of one fireplace for every two rooms. One-roomed dwellings nearly always had one, but a house with more than 20 rooms might only have four. In the houses of the rich the servants' rooms seldom had a fireplace: being warm was a prerogative which employers tended to keep for themselves. After 1720, however, technical developments improved the output of heat. New houses were more likely to have one fireplace per room. In the second half of the century, in Paris as in Turin, stoves began to become more widespread. Even as late as the French Revolution the poorest were still warming themselves at dangerous braziers, and this was in Paris where, in spite of the problems of procuring and storing fuel, people were generally better heated than they were in the countryside and in other French cities.

The need to survive the cold makes the importance of the bed comprehensible. A bed was often brought to a marriage by the bride, along with the chest containing her trousseau, and was another focal point (with the hearth) of family life. This is why in many wealthy Dutch houses in the seventeenth century it took pride of place in the middle of the room. In Parisian probate inventories of the period it is usually the first item of furniture to be listed, and also the one described in most detail. On average its value represented about 15 percent of the estate of a poor man or woman. Among wage earners a bed represented 25 percent of the cost of furnishing a dwelling, or 39 percent among domestic servants. Every household possessed at least one, but they could vary from a simple mattress to a four-poster bed with hangings. The differentiation between beds developed especially in the fifteenth century when the custom of sleeping on straw or on a palliasse[10] laid on the ground, or on planks, began to decline. In the period between 1690 and 1789, a sample of more than 3,000 beds in Paris reveals that 72.5 percent had curtains round them which created a sort of "house within a house." Sometimes the bed was placed in a niche with a curtain or a door.

In the country it was common for people to share a bed. What about the town? In Norwich, at the end of the seventeenth century, it seems that almost everyone, apart from couples and children, had a bed to him or herself. There were differences between the social groups all the same. In Paris between 1695 and 1715 among domestic servants each bed housed an average of 1.9 people, 2.3 among wage earners. By 1780 the figures were, respectively, 1.8 and 1.9. Poor families often snuggled up in a single bed. In wealthy families in the eighteenth century, on the other hand, even the children often had their own beds. Couples

---

[10] A straw mattress.

frequently shared a bed with their youngest children in spite of the risk of suffocation. Upper-class husbands and wives often had separate beds, even separate bedrooms. The nobility would sometimes receive visitors and friends in bed, particularly in France, where the king received ministers, and — so to say — governed the country from his bed. The opulent beds from which such social activities took place were not the beds in which their occupants slept: they were "ceremonial beds," in use especially in the second half of the seventeenth century.

Besides the bed, in urban interiors there were other items of furniture. Houses in towns were generally better furnished than peasant houses in the country, where in the eighteenth century many dwellings were still without tables and chairs. In Paris such things abounded: while stools and benches were declining, armchairs and sofas were becoming more common. A certain abundance characterized lower strata homes as well: often there were more seats to sit on than there were inhabitants. In addition to three or four tables, often collapsible, there was an average of a dozen seats per dwelling. One-roomed dwellings, which accounted for 31 percent of homes, were generally lived in by two to three people; dwellings with two or three rooms (42 percent) by three or four people and the same number for dwellings with four to seven rooms (20 percent). Only larger houses (7 percent) housed a greater number of people, most of them domestic servants. The large number of chairs probably indicates a busy social life: we can imagine lower-class homes full of friends or relations sitting on rush-seated chairs chatting, playing games, or listening to one member of the company reading. Or drawing rooms belonging to highly educated society hostesses where guests, seated on elegant chairs, made conversation while sipping the fashionable beverage of the day from decorated cups.

Pots, pans, and cutlery were on the increase and were changing. Stoneware, glass, pottery, earthenware were coming into use, replacing wood and, to some extent, metal. Many items cost less than they had in the past, and were more numerous. New consumer goods were emerging too, linked to new habits (such as tea, coffee, and chocolate services, with their sugar bowls). The taste for comfort and elegance was increasing: comfortable, handsome easy chairs, small tables, knick-knacks, porcelain, clocks, mirrors, paintings, hangings, and tapestries for decorative purposes and to insulate rooms against the cold. Moreover, new items of furniture were invented in which the growing volume of domestic objects could be neatly put away: the old chests in which everything used to be piled were replaced by cupboards, chests-of-drawers, bookshelves, and wardrobes. In the kitchen the crockery and cooking pots were no longer scattered around the fireplace, thanks to the presence of kitchen cupboards; there were tripods with space for burning embers over which caldrons could be placed; stoves built into the wall and, from about 1750, heavy metal kitchen ranges. It became possible to cook without squatting on the floor.

The increase in the number and specialized function of furnishings was accompanied by specialization in the use of rooms. Even in the Middle Ages the elite used particular rooms for particular purposes. Kitchens are one example. For a long time, nevertheless, activities generally carried out today in separate rooms were all pursued in the same room. In seventeenth-century London, where the process of reserving rooms for particular uses was fairly well advanced, to the extent that upstairs rooms were mainly bedrooms while food was usually prepared in the kitchen, there were beds in shops, kitchens, and halls. They could also be found in the most unexpected places in eighteenth-century Paris. Rooms were often partially multifunctional even in the spacious palaces of the nobility. This explains why Madame de Maintenon[11] undressed, with the assistance of her chambermaids, and went to bed in the very room where Louis XIV[12] was deep in discussion with his ministers separated from his mistress only by the bed curtains. It was during his reign, in fact, that the upper classes began to have "dining rooms"; *salons*[13] spread from the 1720s to 1730s onward, while rooms defined as "bedrooms" became more common during the second half of the eighteenth century.

For a long time there was no special place to eat. During the Middle Ages, tables would be set upon trestles, generally in the main room, and these would be dismantled after the meal. In the palaces of the Renaissance, however, rooms began to appear, called *salette* or *salotti,* where the master of the house's family could be accommodated for the meals, even if they could eat elsewhere as well: in the main hall, antechambers, private apartments. . . . In the English country house in the seventeenth century the hall ceased to be the place where the whole family ate and lived, and where some of the servants slept, because the master's family began to take their meals in a room set aside for the purpose. The hall degenerated into a refectory for the servants. Then, when a room where servants could eat became the norm, it became simply the entrance to the house.

Obviously the development of specialized rooms did not involve the whole of society at an equal pace. In late eighteenth-century France, the middle classes had no dining room or drawing room. In Paris only one tenth of the population had a real bedroom, and only the same proportion a kitchen used solely for preparing food. Many families adapted the space under the stairs, or storerooms and closets outside the apartment itself, to make small rooms within which a bit of intimacy could be enjoyed. This helped to demarcate the boundaries between inside and outside more clearly. Until about 1750, the rooms inhabited by a family were spread over various floors. Therefore even the growing popularity of the "horizontally" arranged apartment in the second half of the century contributed to this developing demarcation.

The disposition of available space was subject to increasing attempts to use it more rationally from the fifteenth century onward, but in the early modern period it changed in a number of different ways. In the Renaissance palaces of Italy (which were imitated all over Europe) service areas, reception areas, and private areas began to be differentiated. For the master of the house, then for other mem-

---

[11] Françoise d'Aubigné, Marquise de Maintenon (1635–1719), second wife of King Louis XIV of France.

[12] King of France from 1643–1715.

[13] Sitting or living rooms.

bers of his family, apartments consisting of a series of connecting rooms were developed: one or more antechambers, a bedroom, a few small rooms (a study, a wardrobe, a lavatory). Proceeding through these rooms one entered spaces of an increasingly personal and private nature. At the end there was generally a door or a concealed staircase by means of which the master of the house could come and go without passing through the public rooms.

In order to facilitate movement around the house, the number of doors increased — a rational measure in dwellings with connecting rooms where, in order to move from one room to another, all the rooms in between had to be crossed. In dwellings like this — and they were extremely prevalent in the period we are describing — any activity might be interrupted by someone passing through. Members of the family ran into one another as they moved about. The corridor changed this state of affairs. The first modern corridor probably appeared in a residence in Chelsea designed by John Thorpe[14] in 1597. The (gradual) introduction of the room with a single door opening on to a corridor transformed each room into an isolated space, decreased casual encounters, and facilitated communication that had a particular aim. This transformation embodied and reinforced the growing preference for choosing the people with whom one had relations, a new sense of modesty, and an increasing need for solitude.

In the seventeenth century . . . the corridor . . . prevented the servants from having to pass through the parts of the house where the owners spent their time. Some categories of domestic servant had lived in very close contact with their masters for centuries, although in the larger palaces of the Renaissance they had their own quarters. Louis XIV had a manservant who slept in the same room as he did. In 1751, when the first wife of the nobleman Francesco Albergati requested the annulment of her marriage on grounds of her husband's impotence, the *marchese's*[15] manservant was able to testify to his master's virility because, while helping him to dress in the morning, he had sometimes seen him with an erection. As time passed, however, the need for privacy prevailed over the need to have domestics close at hand, ready to serve. The spatial segregation of servants and masters consequently grew ever greater. The servants may also have come to appreciate their own private space. From the later years of the seventeenth century, fewer male servants seem to have lived with their masters (on the other hand, the female servants continued to live in the master's house for a long time).

In conclusion, new boundaries appeared in domestic space, which over the years became more clearly divided from external space; interior space was organized into specialized areas dedicated to private activities (such as sleeping) or more public activities (such as receiving guests). Of course, a proportion of the population, larger or smaller according to location and period, was completely uninvolved in such changes, or at least only very minimally. Where they did take place, however, the change in function of the various rooms and in their spatial

---

[14] English architect, ca. 1570–1618.

[15] Italian title equivalent to a marquis, a nobleman below the rank of a duke.

arrangement was the physical embodiment of changes taking place in interpersonal relations, and these in their turn were affected by the domestic changes. Having discussed the spread of tables and chairs, the increase in the use of saucepans and cutlery, and the identification of a room for use as a dining room, and bearing in mind that "the most important social relations are expressed at table," let us now focus our attention on food and eating.

EATING

. . . In the eyes of many members of the middle and upper strata, . . . the scarcity of crockery and cutlery (as well as of food) of many rustic households was taken as evidence of the alleged crude nature of the peasantry. Knowing how to behave "correctly" at table was a strong social identifier. Nevertheless in France as late as 1730 the use of the fork was uncommon even at court. The fork appears to have been invented in Byzantium[16] and to have appeared in Italy in the tenth or eleventh century, but its use became widespread in the thirteenth or fourteenth century. From the Italian peninsula it spread gradually to other European countries. On the other hand, the plate quite rapidly replaced the medieval wooden platter. From the sixteenth century onward, every guest (in decent society) was given a plate, a glass, a spoon and knife and, possibly, a fork of his own. The old "convivial promiscuity" was on its way out: now everyone could eat from his own plate and drink from his own glass.

What did eating together signify? One author [Renée Valeri] has said that "commensality is a sign of trust and fraternity, or of proximity of status." Nearly all marriages were celebrated with a banquet. "Eating together" could be one of the characteristic features of a genuine family: to live *a uno pane e uno vino* (i.e. "with the same bread and wine"), as the Tuscan saying goes. Conversely the breakup of a family unit could be reflected in eating separately: Roman Catholicism does not permit divorce, but the separation of "bed, *table* and dwelling" is possible. "We have one hearth between us, but each does his own cooking," a woman from a village on Lake Lugano explained in 1769; she was in conflict with her daughter-in-law. Social hierarchies were manifest at table, as were hierarchies of gender and generation. The Tyrolean mountain folk reserved their wine and their solitary seat for their important visitor. Basque tradition forbade women from sitting at the table of the paterfamilias.[17] Similarly, in other parts of Europe men ate sitting down while the women and/or children stood, and often were not served until after the men had finished. In northern Germany several methods of eating meals have been described: in the first, probably the oldest, women and children stood; in another, all the members of the family, including servants, sat at the table. The

---

[16] Present-day Istanbul, formerly capital of the Byzantine (Eastern Roman) Empire, named Constantinople in 330 C.E.

[17] Father of the family; head of the household.

head of the family sat at the top and the highest-ranking servants and older children were placed closest to him, with women and men on opposite sides; in the last, the master and family ate separately, the servants being relegated to another table in another room. In aristocratic households in the modern period it was the custom to have separate tables. In 1782, in the summer residence of the nobleman Francesco Albergati, there were at least four: one for the *marchese,* his wife, their two children, the children's tutor, and the resident violinist; one for the female domestics at which the valet also ate once he had served at the master's table; one for the steward and his wife, in their private apartment and one (or more) in the kitchen where the remaining servants ate.

There were no women in the Albergati kitchen. In elite families all those entrusted with important jobs such as the preparation and cooking of food were men, often men of relatively high class, especially those serving at table in princely houses at the beginning of the early modern period. Poisoning was greatly feared. It is interesting to note that, in Italian, the word for both the piece of furniture on which cold food and dishes were placed, and for the method of proffering food without touching it with the hands, was *credenza,* derived from the Latin *credo,* I trust. The success of a banquet, an important opportunity for members of the upper classes to display their wealth and power, depended on the skill of the domestic staff. A "normal" meal for the Czar of Russia consisted of 150 different dishes, 50 types of strong drink, 10 varieties of beer, and kvass.[18]

Although customs differed in different parts of Europe, in general it was not until the eighteenth or nineteenth century that elite kitchens were populated by female cooks. In France the first cookery book for women appeared in 1746. In just over fifty years, about 93,000 copies were printed. Appropriately enough it was called *La Cuisinière bourgeoise.*[19] In the eighteenth century, *haute cuisine*[20] in France (admired all over Europe) developed a certain simplicity: "bourgeois" food prepared at home by housewives or household servants came into fashion. Because cookery was an important factor in family wellbeing, the preparation of food in middle- and lower-strata families was delegated less frequently to servants than were the cleaning and washing. However this probably varied according to where you were: in England it appears that women of relatively high class were expected to know how to cook, whereas in Italy and France cooking was regarded as the work of the maidservants and ladies took no part in it. . . .

Food itself was a tremendous clue to social class and hierarchy. It was held that all should eat according to their "quality," i.e. according to their social condition (as well as according to their constitution, state of health, age, and sex). The Italian writer Giulio Cesare Croce[21] tells the story of a peasant, Bertoldo, who was

---

[18] A slightly fermented beverage made in Russia from mixed cereals.

[19] *The Bourgeois* [middle-class] *Cook.*

[20] Gourmet food; artful, elaborate food preparation.

[21] An Italian street musician (1550–1609) who wrote a comic romance about the peasant Bertoldo.

obliged to eat dainty foodstuffs when he unexpectedly embarked on a career at court: "He died in severe pain because he could not eat turnips and beans." Along these lines, at the beginning of the early modern era it was considered that birds and fowl were suitable fare for the upper classes and turnips for peasants, since up was considered positive and down negative. Poultry was thought to enhance sexual excitement: widows, who were supposed to be chaste, were discouraged from eating chicken. Servants and masters living under the same roof (and even domestics of different rank) usually ate different food. Today "family pack" indicates inexpensive food in large quantities, not always of the best quality; this derives from "family wine," the wine given to the servants. Similarly a "family loaf" was a loaf of low quality. In the early modern period people seated at the same table might be offered different food: the best bits went to the most important people.

Food was different in town and country too. In town even the middle and lower strata ate bread made of wheat, although the bread grew whiter as it rose through the social scale. The bread eaten by peasants was generally dark in color and made of inferior cereals, chestnut or lupin flour, or flour made of a mixture of whatever was locally available. In addition, city dwellers, particularly the middle and upper classes, ate fresh bread every day, made in a bakery or at home (in the latter case, it might be taken to the bakery to be baked). To save time and fuel, and in order to eat less, peasants baked rarely. In some Alpine areas, bread was baked only twice a year. Cereals that were too unsuited to bread-making were made into pap, farinaceous foods, and polenta.

Modern attitudes to nutrition in Europe derived from a combination of the Roman diet, centering around bread, wine, and oil (enriched by milk, cheese, vegetables, and meat), and the "barbarian" diet of meat, dairy products, beer, and cider combined with oat porridge and flat barley bread. The success of the Germanic tribes in battle had persuaded everyone of the value of eating meat, while the "success" of bread was linked to the spread of Christianity: bread, with wine and oil, occupied a central role in Christian worship. Interestingly, the Reformation also affected diet. The Protestants rejected the dietary practices of the Roman Catholic Church, with its fast days. Ancient differences between Northern and Southern Europe re-emerged: in fact they had never completely disappeared. The north was more carnivorous, the south more vegetarian; the eating of meat and animals in the Catholic south was prohibited on about 140–160 days in the year. Fast days were even more numerous in Orthodox Europe: there were about 200 in the Russian calendar. Jews, scattered throughout various European countries, also had their own dietary laws.

While religious beliefs and customs dictated what could or could not be eaten, the opportunity to satisfy one's hunger depended on the availability of food. After the catastrophic plague of 1347–1351, until about the middle of the sixteenth century, the European diet was, in general, rather adequate and balanced. After that, however, it became impossible to adapt resources to the requirements of a growing population. It was not until the eighteenth century that innovations designed to increase agricultural productivity caught on and trade in foodstuffs intensified. Most people were then forced to eat less meat and more bread. The quality of bread deteriorated, however. Even in the cities, where white bread had been eaten since the thirteenth century, wheat was mixed with inferior cereals or pulses — or even sometimes replaced by them. Apart from Norway and Iceland, where the diet was predominantly fish, for many people in Europe cereals provided more than 80 percent of their caloric intake. A poor harvest was enough to cause famine. To confront a famine situation, people began growing plants which previously had been little cultivated in Europe, such as rice and buckwheat, or new plants recently arrived from America (peppers, capsicums,[22] tomatoes, beans, maize, and potatoes).

Maize was imported into Europe by Columbus in 1493 and spread rapidly in many regions of Spain, Portugal, south-western France, the Veneto, the Balkan peninsula, and Hungary. For a long time it was used only as fodder, or was cultivated only in kitchen gardens. The transition to the cultivation of maize in fields took place mainly at moments of crisis, particularly in the eighteenth century. In the Balkans, for example, this happened after the famine of 1740–1741. In various parts of northern Italy maize polenta became the staple food of the peasantry, to the extent that deficiency of niacin in a monotonous diet dominated by maize provoked the spread of pellagra.

The potato was known in Peru in 1539, but for a long time Europeans viewed it with profound suspicion. Only hunger, particularly during the famine of 1770–1772, encouraged its wider cultivation. In fact, the potato has almost twice the yield of grain. In addition, because potatoes grow underground, the harvest of a field of potatoes is assured, even if an army camps on it for months on end. War encouraged the spread of the potato, particularly in the northern part of Central Europe.

By the end of the eighteenth century, therefore, the geography of vegetable foodstuffs looked different from the way it had looked two or three centuries earlier: north Central Europe was predominantly potato eating, whereas in Southern and Southeastern Europe there were large areas where polenta was very common. In the mountainous areas of the Mediterranean, chestnuts were the main food (dried, boiled, or ground into flour to make bread, *ciacci* or polenta). In spite of its appearance, the chestnut is a nourishing food. In southern Italy pasta became an important element in the diet of the poor from the seventeenth century onward.

Although potatoes and maize helped increase the availability of food, they also contributed to the deterioration in nourishment suffered by the majority of Europeans between the sixteenth and eighteenth centuries, causing the decrease in average height revealed by recent research. In the eighteenth century, peasants in the Veneto, who ate only polenta, suffered a fate similar to that of the first English industrial workers who lived on bread and sweet tea.

Sugar originated in India and was used in Europe from the Middle Ages onwards. In the sixteenth century it became a luxury seasoning for all types of meal (the passion for sweet-sour food died away in the seventeenth/eighteenth cen-

---

[22] Chilies.

tury). As production increased, sugar became more widely available. Tea, Chinese in origin, arrived at the beginning of the seventeenth century. It became popular in England, winning favor first with the elite, then with the populace at large. In the second half of the seventeenth century the first coffee shops appeared. Here the beverage introduced from the Middle East and familiar to the Venetians as early as the 1570s could be sampled, and here too a new form of social life was born. Coffee was a stimulating drink, the symbol of bourgeois rationalism and efficiency — in contrast to chocolate, which was popular particularly among the aristocracy or as a drink to be enjoyed while fasting (it came from America).

Like tea, cocoa, and coffee, spirits were first used pharmaceutically. From the seventeenth century on, however, they were drunk along with more traditional drinks, i.e. wine and beer. Wine was predominant in Mediterranean Europe, but the elite enjoyed wine everywhere. Beer was the favorite in Central Europe and was also drunk widely in the Iberian peninsula. Although the poorest of the poor often drank plain water, the consumption of alcoholic drinks was presumably very high. It seems that anyone who drank wine would drink at least a liter a day, although the alcoholic content was often low. In English families in the seventeenth century adults and children daily drank probably about 3 liters of beer per head. Alcoholic drinks were drunk because drinking-water was difficult to come by. Liquid was needed to supplement the diet, to assist with the mastication of stale bread, and to quench the thirst caused by very salty food (salt was used to preserve meat and fish and to add flavor to cereals and pulses). People also drank in order to forget the rigor of their harsh lives, or to dispel the memory of hunger pains (they took hallucinogenic plants for the same reason). Throughout the early modern period hunger, whether experienced or feared, was central to the lives of a large proportion of the population. The excess that was part of the feasting on high days and holidays helped to exorcize the specter of hunger.

Nevertheless, the peasant diet was not necessarily one of total deprivation. Women used aromatic plants in the kitchen to prepare tasty food even if they could not perform miracles. Kitchen gardens provided vegetables and fruit: soups were prepared from onions, pulses, cabbage, potatoes, turnips, often mixed with cereals or stale bread, dressed with butter, lard, dripping, or oil and if possible enriched with a little meat. Turnips and cabbage were ubiquitous. In Central Europe, where there were no fresh vegetables in winter, sauerkraut was an essential part of the diet; in Southern Europe salads were vital, and in fact were often all there was to eat. According to one witness, Tuscan peasants in the late eighteenth century had three meals a day: one consisted of polenta and salad, one of bread and boiled beans and other vegetables dressed with a little oil, and the third of soup. A little meat was eaten on Sundays. In Mediterranean countries olives, dried figs, and fruit were very common; some of the peasants of southern Italy survived in winter on nothing but bread and figs. Apples, pears, and cherries were widely eaten in Central and Eastern Europe: dried, they were sometimes used as a substitute for bread. Nourishment was also derived from nuts: almonds, pine nuts, hazelnuts, walnuts. It was also obtained from hunting (or poaching) and fishing, from stable and farmyard, although eggs, poultry, and rabbits were mainly reserved for the landowners or for sale.

It was usually the women who looked after the kitchen garden and farmyard. In many areas, including England, women were also responsible for making butter and cheese. In other countries this was man's work, work that was sometimes central in defining gender: among the Basques of Saint-Eugrâce only sexually mature males were allowed to make cheese. Those too old to beget children were not allowed into the mountain huts where the milk was processed for cheese; they stayed at home with the women and children and were assimilated back into their midst.

The division of labor according to sex varied from place to place. It was usually quite rigidly observed, but not immutable. Women's tasks were many: it has been calculated that, in Britain, on average, the preparation of food took three to four hours a day, fetching water and wood about one hour, one hour was spent keeping the fire going and suckling or feeding children. Women then worked in the kitchen garden (one hour), saw to the animals and milked them (two or three hours), made bread and beer (three hours per week for each activity) and sometimes preserves. Not counting any work done outside the home, women expended their energy on doing the washing (four hours per week), cleaning the house (two hours a day), spinning for clothing (two hours), looking after children (three hours). A male cook is preferable to a female, wrote Vincenzo Tanara[23] in the mid-seventeenth century, because "the female puts the pot on the fire . . . and while the food is cooking . . . she spins." It is not difficult to believe that for many women this is the way things were. As the English folk-song says: "A woman's work is never done." . . .

---

[23] Italian agronomist, d. 1667.

RITUALS OF EXECUTION
IN EARLY MODERN GERMANY
Richard van Dülmen

Basing his study on the court records of major German cities, Richard van Dülmen, professor of modern history at the University of the Saarland, Germany, describes a society that, lacking a police force and a prison system, imposed social
control by means of rituals of torture and grisly public executions. A veritable
"theatre of horror" (the title of the book from which this selection is drawn)
maintained social order. Governments ordered corporal punishments — such as
mutilation, branding, flogging — and the pillory that meant public disgrace.
The criminal's public confession, which courts demanded, legitimized the sentence and execution and offered a moral lesson to the audience. There were also
ecclesiastical punishments, which emphasized public shame, but secular court
systems eventually incorporated these as early modern states sought to limit the
ability of churches to act with any independence. Medieval legal systems had
stressed the public nature of trials. Early modern courts, however, removed the
public from the process of determining guilt and instead insisted on the public
spectacle of execution and on the ritual of social purification. Courts even ordered the execution of the corpses of criminals, thus underscoring the necessity
of the execution ritual and the accompanying cleansing of society.

The poor suffered more than the elite from the system of punishments; the
latter's social status elicited more humane methods of execution. German courts,
reflecting the anti-Semitism that pervaded early modern society, likewise treated
Jews more brutally than Christians. Men and women often experienced different forms of execution (the latter being burned, drowned, or buried alive). Why
does van Dülmen refer to these practices as rituals of purification? Why did
courts demand such severe retribution?

The number of executions and the harshness of punishment peaked in the
sixteenth century, in part owing to the Protestant and Catholic religions' new
concern for the purification of morals. Why do you think horrific methods of execution, although they continued to exist, began to lose favor in the seventeenth
and eighteenth centuries?

Richard van Dülmen, *Theatre of Horror: Crime and Punishment in Early Modern Germany,* trans.
Elisabeth Neu (Cambridge: Polity Press, 1990), 88–97, 99, 101–106.

Do you think that brutal and public executions were justified because they brought the community together by reinforcing contemporary morality and social standards? To what extent do you believe such executions acted as an effective deterrent to criminals?

Early modern Europeans were accustomed to violence and brutality. Do you think the callous disregard for pain inflicted on others has been a constant in Western civilization, or do you find that attitude peculiar to certain centuries or regions or social groups? How much of the brutality in sixteenth- and seventeenth-century German executions was a result of German law and culture, or was that ferocity simply a natural part of the human condition?

The traditional rituals of execution were burning, drowning and burying alive. Documented abundantly for the sixteenth century, and in part also practised in the early seventeenth century, they subsequently lost their significance. In so far as their objective was the radical extermination and annihilation of a malefactor of whom no trace — either memory or grave — must remain, these forms of execution can be viewed as society's rituals of purification. Society cleansed itself of crimes, especially of those that violated the religious and moral order in a way that brought fear of harm to the community if they were not punished accordingly. These punishments were mainly inflicted upon women. Death was not brought about by the executioner's hand, but without bloodshed by forces of nature, through fire, water or earth, to which specially destructive or purifying powers were attributed. To a certain extent hanging can be included, as the delinquent was abandoned to the power of air — that is, to the weather and the birds. With the authorities' increasing control over penal practice and executions designed for theatricality, intimidation and moral edification, "purificatory" rituals became more and more disfunctional in the eyes of the authorities and were substituted for the main part by the "deterrent" punishment of the sword.

Being buried alive was deemed a particularly horrific and severe punishment for a variety of sexual offences such as adultery, murder of one's spouse and infanticide, but it also punished cases of grand larceny. It was used mainly as a punishment for women, as a counterpart to breaking on the wheel for men. The delinquent was generally undressed and laid on her back in a pit beneath the gallows, bound, covered with thorns and buried from the feet upwards. This was often combined with impalement — that is, a pale was driven from above through the heart, navel or chest. This might be carried out before or after burial. The symbolism is not completely clear; obviously a return was to be rendered impossible and at the same time impalement prevented slow suffocation. One of the last and most famous cases of a delinquent being buried alive is documented for Frankfurt in 1585. A woman had killed her husband in bed, stabbing him sixty-four times. Burying her alive and driving "a long, pointed spike through her body" was considered the most appropriate punishment for her crime. Burying alive was practised frequently in the fifteenth and early sixteenth centuries, but is considerably less often documented than burning or drowning. It was deemed a particularly horrific punishment which occasionally resulted in pitiful scenes and it was therefore — often through the executioner's initiative — abandoned early on. In 1497 a woman in Nuremberg was buried alive beneath the gallows for grand larceny. "But the poor creature showed herself to be so resilient during the burying that her skin on hands and feet gashed open so that she aroused great pity in the people." She had obviously defended herself vigorously. After this, the council decided no longer to bury women alive, but rather to drown them, "and so it happened afterwards that those who had stolen in this way, had their ears cut off or were drowned." Despite this note in the records, burying alive continued to be carried out in Nuremberg. A last case is documented as late as 1522: a woman who had poisoned her husband and granddaughter was "chained to a cart at the hands and neck, led outside and pinched with red-hot tongs, then a spike was driven through her heart and afterwards she was buried alive under the gallows."

The far more widespread punishment of drowning was likewise mainly inflicted upon women. But occasionally men also were put to death in this way. Predominantly offenders who violated moral norms or the order of the church were drowned; child murderers, adulterers and heretics. Many Anabaptists[1] had to suffer this death. But if there was no river in the vicinity, drowning was replaced by other punishments. Besides the idea of annihilation, the purificatory power of water symbolizing the washing away of guilt played a significant role. There was a preference for running water. The courts made use of drowning throughout the sixteenth century. Although gradually abandoned in the seventeenth century, it was once more increasingly employed in Prussia and Saxony, mainly in the struggle against infanticide. Drowning was also considered a horrific punishment which — because of the relatively uncertain outcome — still retained many elements of a trial by ordeal.[2] The execution was generally carried out on a bridge. The malefactress was partially undressed, forced to squat so that a stick could be put through the hollows of her knees and then her hands and feet were tied together behind the stick. She was thrown into the water and an assistant of the executioner pushed her underneath the surface with long poles. There were other variations: for instance the so-called "sacking," originating in Roman law. The condemned person was put into a sack together with three or four animals. Justice required that these should be a dog, a cockerel,[3] a snake and a monkey. But since monkeys were hard to come by here and snakes were also rarely at hand, instead of the monkey a cat, and for the snake a painted image of a snake, were put into the sack. The meaning of these additions is not altogether clear. Perhaps they signified a refinement of the punishment or served to indicate especial shame. . . .

---

[1] Radical Protestants who denied the doctrine of the Trinity, believed that only adults should be baptized, and refused to cooperate with the government.

[2] Used in the Middle Ages, a method of determining guilt by making the suspect undergo a test such as carrying a red-hot iron bar.

[3] Young rooster.

Another variation strongly reminiscent of trial by ordeal was found mainly in Switzerland. The executioner drew the malefactress into the water by means of a rope and pulled her out on the other shore. If she survived, she was free. Sources speak of "drifting downstream." Another variation consisted of the malefactress being bound and thrown into the water without a rope and left to drift. If the fetters loosened in the water and she could swim to the shore, she was also pardoned. We read in a document of 1521 from Elbing: "So she was carried along to the red fisherman's hut and thrown onto the shore still alive. The hangman's assistant wanted to push her into the river again, but the spectators, who had followed, rescued the woman from his hands and freed her from her bonds as they had seen the clear proof of her innocence." It was a tacit rule that a punishment that had been properly carried out, but failed to kill the delinquent, should not be repeated. The people wished to see this right retained, whereas the judicial authorities were increasingly successful in insisting on a repetition of the punishment.

The third, and in a sense most complete, form of punishment by annihilation and purification was burning. Predominantly those convicted of witchcraft, heresy, brewing poison, sodomy and forgery were burned. The punishment was inflicted upon men and women alike. Burning was most frequent during the sixteenth century, the time of the Counter-Reformation and the rigid enforcement of church morals. Afterwards, in so far as burnings continued to take place, the malefactor was strangled beforehand or a little sachet of gunpowder was put around his or her neck so that death would occur before fire consumed the body. Burning, especially if the fire was set badly, could last for a very long time and be extremely painful. It was always an intricate ritual of punishment. Usually, a post was rammed into the ground and bundles of brushwood, straw and wood piled round it. The condemned person was fastened to the post with an iron chain round neck or trunk. He or she could either be placed on the pyre or be set on a stool. The fire burned as long as it took to reduce everything to ashes. If the bones did not burn, they were eventually ground to powder. Then either all remains were buried underneath the gallows or thrown into a river. The killing was to result in total extermination and annihilation "so that the memory of this shameful deed may for ever be eradicated," as it is phrased in the sentence, or "so that the wrath of God and His punishment may be averted from the town and the land."

In 1659 in Nuremberg a young shepherd, "a cruel and abhorrent sodomite had to sit on the pyre made for this purpose and be burnt alive by fire and sent from life to death and executed, for him a well-deserved punishment, and since this horrible vice is strongly increasing and becoming more widespread, as a warning, abhorrence and example for others to beware all the more of such shameful misdeeds and reprovable crimes." A witness tells us that the shepherd died an extremely "pitiful and cruel" death because "not only the bonds and ropes burnt down along his hands and feet, but also when the fire cracked open his hands, feet and body, he was still alive." In cases of sodomy the animal was also burnt. Although burning was considered a death penalty with a secure, predictable outcome, as with burying alive or drowning, unexpected events could occur which would result in a "frightful and pitiful death" for the delinquent. It is understandable that the executioner, who had to prepare the fire, wished to see this punishment replaced by others, as he could be held responsible for a failed burning. Hence prior strangulation or the little sachet of gunpowder round the delinquent's neck was not only based on humane considerations, but also on the wish for a smooth execution.

Breaking on the wheel, quartering and dismemberment were also among the traditional execution rituals. These bloody butcherings fulfilled no purifying function, but translated *par excellence* the idea of retaliation into action and therefore corresponded to the older punishments of mutilation. They were predominantly inflicted upon men, but there were cases when they were also suffered by women. Severe crimes, such as multiple murder or treason, were punished by the wheel or by quartering. Although often threatened, quartering was rarely carried out in Germany and hardly ever inflicted from the sixteenth century onwards. But if it took place, the effect on the public was all the greater. Breaking on the wheel, however, remained a fairly widespread punishment for murder until well into the nineteenth century. However, the delinquent was often beheaded or strangled before being tied to the wheel.

Only a few instances of quartering are documented, but their descriptions are all the more vivid. Quartering was considered the cruellest punishment, and imposed mainly on traitors and regicides. . . . In the cases we know of, . . . the executioner and his assistants put the delinquent naked onto a wooden bed — often on a large scaffold in the middle of the town — and tied up all his limbs. The executioner then cut the chest from below with a large knife designed especially for this purpose, removed all the entrails together with the heart, lungs and liver and "all the contents of the body," "hurled them unto the mouth" of the culprit and subsequently buried the organs. The man was then put on a table, bench or block, his head struck off with a special axe and the body hacked into four pieces which were later nailed to oak columns or gibbets standing along the main roads.

Of the cases known to us, the execution of the noble conspirator Grumbach[4] in 1567 is the most instructive. The event was nothing more than butchery, witnessed by "a horribly large number of people, of princes, counts, noblemen, men of war, citizens and peasants." Six executioners erected a large scaffold in the market-place in Gotha, described in contemporary sources as a wooden bridge of blood or a shambles.[5] Many accounts circulated in public afterwards. The entire procedure of the execution of Grumbach and his five fellow conspirators lasted two hours. Two troops of soldiers surrounded the scaffold. The imperial provost with cavalry and trumpeteers led the condemned conspirators one by one from the town hall — Grumbach himself was brought from the castle. As Grumbach suffered from gout, eight gaoler's assistants had to carry him on a stool. The exe-

---

[4] Wilhelm von Grumbach (1503–1567), German knight who led a revolt in Saxony against the Holy Roman Emperor.

[5] Butcher shops.

cution was staged as a sovereign act. Each convict was read his sentence by the clerk of the criminal court, sitting high upon his horse. The confessions followed just as solemnly. Grumbach admitted his guilt and asked everyone he had harmed to forgive him. . . . He was then undressed, bound and his heart cut out and hurled by the executioner at Grumbach's mouth with the words "Behold, Grumbach, your false heart!" The executioner then hacked his body into four pieces. Grumbach's chancellor Brück suffered the same fate. He had come to his execution in a black cloak of mourning, with a black ribbon on his black hat. His sentence was also read aloud. He too apologized and asked everyone for forgiveness. As his heart was cut out and slapped many times across his mouth, he is reported to have screamed "horribly and for a very long time." The other four conspirators suffered "more lenient" punishments which illustrate the complete range of possible executions. The first was decapitated and then quartered; the second had also been sentenced to death, but subsequently had his sentence commuted to incarceration, the third was decapitated in "magnificent" clothes and the last was hanged. After the execution, those who had been quartered were thrown onto a cart and their limbs [were] nailed to twelve pillars on the four roads leading to the gates of the city. . . .

Breaking on the wheel was considered a horrific, severe and disgraceful punishment. It was practised almost exclusively on men and predominantly served to punish robbery with murder or the murder of one's spouse. But from the seventeenth century delinquents were often beheaded or strangled beforehand. This act of mercy did not minimize the effect of deterrence. The public rarely knew anything of the strangling. No other punishment was as effective as a deterrent as breaking on the wheel. . . . Usually the condemned person was tied naked on the ground on spikes and a heavy wheel was thrust onto his limbs or he was put on a wheel-shaped base and his limbs were crushed either from the feet up or the head down. If a malefactor had not been strangled beforehand, a *coup de grâce*[6] might be administered if he so wished. The wheel had to be unused. A display of the wheel on which the dying malefactor was bound formed part of the ritual. Like that of those hanging on the gibbet, the corpse was now left to the birds. In St. Gallen a murderer and robber murderer was sentenced to death by the wheel in 1596. He was dragged head down on a hurdle[7] to the place of execution. There he was tied to a wooden bed and each of his four limbs was broken twice with the wheel, i.e. above and below the knees and elbows. A *coup de grâce* by the knife, which he begged of the executioner, ended his torments. Finally the corpse was bound to the wheel in an upright position "so that the birds may fly below and above the wheel." The number of thrusts was precisely laid down in the sentence and often corresponded to the number of offences committed.

Like every ritual of execution, breaking on the wheel might be intensified by additional punishments. It might be preceded by dragging the delinquent to the

---

[6] A deathblow administered as an act of mercy.

[7] Rectangular wooden frame on which traitors were dragged to execution.

place of execution, by pinching him with red-hot tongs, or followed by beheading and burning. Here the head was stuck on a pole above the wheel or the entire body was burnt. The boundary between quartering and breaking on the wheel was reached when the delinquent's limbs were not only broken, but subsequently torn from the body and displayed individually; this might be combined with removing the entrails, but this variation is rarely documented. These cases present not so much a refinement of punishments as already forms of cumulative punishments. If, for instance, a malefactor was accused and convicted of murder as well as of grand larceny and incest, an attempt was made to express this in the ritual of punishment in the way that breaking on the wheel was combined with hanging or burning. Either a gibbet was constructed above the wheel or the crushed body was burnt afterwards. Criminal courts in Switzerland were especially inventive in this respect. A criminal convicted of church robbery, murder, arson and rape — he had buried women alive after raping them — was punished in St. Gallen in 1600 as follows: he was dragged to the town hall on a hurdle and there pinched with red-hot tongs once on his chest and six times on each arm. The same procedure was repeated on his thighs in the market-place. At the place of execution he was put on a wooden plank, his arms and legs were crushed above and below the joints and he was tied to the wheel so that his head was in the gallows' noose without strangling him. Finally the wheel was displayed and everything burnt to ashes. At times special emphasis was put on burning the delinquent very slowly. . . . Such spectacles of execution were consciously staged by the authorities and attracted many spectators from far and near. Broadsheets ensured that news of the event was well publicized. Only a few representatives of the enlightened intelligentsia condemned these spectacles, but not because of the severity of the punishment. Their concern was rather the brutalization of the people through these spectacles and at the same time they disputed the value of such executions to the state. . . .

Hanging and beheading were the most frequent capital punishments. They had always existed, but gained dominance in the seventeenth century when the authorities became the sole organizer of executions. The most common offences, larceny and murder, were punished by the sword or by the rope.

The capital punishment most frequently carried out, at least in early times, was by hanging from the gallows. It was usually a punishment for grand larceny and fraud and was mainly designated for men. Because of its disgraceful character, hanging was replaced from the seventeenth century by beheading. Hanging was the most disgraceful punishment: it not only took the life and honour of the delinquent, but also put his entire family in disgrace. So relatives often sought commutation of the punishment to execution by the sword. In later times especially, residents and members of the upper strata of society were granted this relief. Hanging was deemed an indelible disgrace; moreover — and this was no less devastating at the time — exposure of the corpse to the birds meant that the delinquent was refused burial and his soul would not be granted peace. In this respect there was a correspondence between hanging and breaking on the wheel, where the body was left to decompose on the wheel. . . . Hanging was carried out in a variety of ways, but two methods prevailed. Either a delinquent, bound, had to mount the ladder backwards, the hangman put a noose round his neck and then pushed him off the ladder. Or the condemned person was pulled up by means of a strap by the hangman's assistants, the noose put round his neck before he was pushed down. . . .

According to the gravity of the offence, variations might be introduced into the process of hanging. It was, for instance, stipulated precisely how long an offender had to remain on the gallows. If the time was too long, there was a danger that the body might fall down or be stolen — or that at least several of the limbs would be removed. Although this was often done by those who placed great hopes in the healing powers of parts of the body, it was mainly family members who stole the entire corpse to wipe out the shame and grant their relative peace for the soul through burial. Moreover, the position on the gallows or the height of the gallows might be stipulated. Being hanged from the middle of the cross beam of the gallows was deemed especially disgraceful, as was being hanged very high. "The higher anyone was hanged, the more humiliating was the punishment."

The execution of the Jew Süss Oppenheimer[8] in Stuttgart in 1738 was a spectacle of a particular kind. Convicted of treason, fraud, incest and other crimes, Süss was hanged not only from unusually high gallows but also in a large cage which projected over the gallows. During the trial he had stated: "You cannot hang me higher than the gallows." The court had spared no cost in answering this challenge and succeeded in hanging Süss higher than the gallows before a large crowd of spectators. . . . A large number of soldiers marched in and many boxes had been especially erected for cavaliers and their ladies. Booths offered wine and beer. Street traders sold broadsheets with a picture of Jew Süss and derisory verses. It was an exciting, festive scene when Süss, who had stubbornly resisted both the court and the repeated attempts of Protestant ministers to convert him, put up a last desperate resistance to the hangmen when they tried to slip the noose round his neck. The convict had been driven through the city to the place of execution on a high knacker's[9] cart. He was clad in a scarlet mantle and had been allowed to keep a precious, conspicuous ring. As he was pulled up, the vicar of the city shouted at the dying man: "The devil take you, stubborn knave and Jew"; while Jews who had accompanied Süss prayed aloud "Jahve Adonai[10] is one God and eternal."

Occasionally a malefactor sentenced to hanging had to wear a placard round his or her neck on which either the stolen object was depicted or the offence proclaimed. The punishment was refined by the hand being struck off and stuck onto

---

[8] Joseph Süss Oppenheimer (1698–1738), financial advisor to the Duke of Württemberg; the Nazis made an influential anti-Semitic film, *Jud Süss* (1940), about his life.

[9] Dealer in horse carcasses.

[10] Lord Yahweh, the Jewish god.

a pole. Hanging might also qualify as an accumulation of punishments, as in the examples above. Subsequent burning is frequently documented.

The execution of Jews was a special ritual. They were hanged by the feet, flanked by two dogs. Often death did not occur for a number of days. These executions were mostly carried out in an open field on three- or four-legged gallows.

Although hanging may appear simple at first sight, it demanded great concentration on the executioner's part. If the rope was too short, painful strangulation ensued, which could lead to arguments between executioner and spectators. These might likewise occur if the rope was too long and therefore broke when the delinquent was pushed down, which meant that the execution had to be repeated. If an execution failed, an accusation of cruelty was voiced by the spectators and by the convicted person's family, who could then insist on mercy.

From the seventeenth century the predominant form of execution was beheading by the sword, the least severe and most acceptable form of capital punishment. As a rule, members of the nobility and persons of rank were beheaded. As before a hanging, the delinquent was blindfolded, his or her hands were tied behind and the neck bared so that the blow could be aimed with precision. The delinquent awaited beheading either standing, kneeling or sitting on a stool. Most delinquents wanted to be beheaded as it was the least painful way of dying. Yet to sever the head in one single blow was not an easy task. The audience was satisfied when blood gushed forth and the head fell after the first blow. But the delinquent might suddenly move his or her head, and therefore the executioner tried to gain the condemned person's assent beforehand. If the executioner's attempt was unsuccessful, his life was at risk, while a "masterly" stroke was met with appreciation by authorities and people. . . .

Criminals convicted of manslaughter, robbery, incest, infanticide (from the seventeenth century) and severe fraud were beheaded. Whether a delinquent was buried beneath the gallows after decapitation, handed over to the anatomists . . . or granted burial in a church yard often depended upon the verdict, or rather the mitigation of the verdict. It was deemed a special mercy if a delinquent could be buried by his or her friends and family immediately after the beheading. After a Franconian nobleman was executed for murder in Frankfurt in 1618 "on a particular scaffold on a black cloth by the sword, from life to death," he was placed in a coffin by soldiers "and carried in the customary funeral procession headed by a cross into the church of St. Niclas: there he lay until the following Sunday when he was fetched by his family who took him away." It was likewise deemed a great mercy if the delinquent was spared the executioner's touch. But not only were there various means of commuting punishments; equally numerous were combinations of punishments, whether enforced as refinements or as part of other forms of execution. The head that had been struck off might be stuck onto a pole or the gallows, the body might be put on the wheel or buried beneath the gallows. But this was generally the fate of delinquents who had been reprieved from death on the wheel. A normal case may illustrate this: a city messenger had insulted the council and citizens of Frankfurt in 1607. As a punishment, the two fingers of his right hand with which he had sworn were cut off in front of the town hall, then his head was struck off and together with the two fingers stuck on a pole "and the head had its face turned towards the street and then the dead body was buried beneath the gallows." Many kinds of combinations existed, yet they frequently bore traces of the intention of mirroring the crime in the punishment.

Alongside these forms of execution with their individual refinement or accumulation of punishments, there were execution practices that, although they were unique and comprehensible only in the context of the crime, bore characteristic traits of the penal practice of the early modern age. Two cases might be mentioned here. Both date from the sixteenth century, the century showing the most resourceful inventiveness in forms of punishment. Our examples pertain to executions immediately after the Peasants' War[11] and the collapse of the Anabaptists' revolt in Münster,[12] but remain atypical of the steps taken by the authorities against leaders of the peasants and Anabaptists, who on the whole were punished far more leniently than the average robber murderer or blasphemer.

Jäcklein Rohrbach, the leader of the Neckar revolt,[13] and the piper Melchior Nonnenmacher were arrested, Nonnenmacher because as a former piper to the nobility he had piped them to their death, Rohrbach for forcing noblemen to run the gauntlet.[14] Both were sentenced to death by burning. They were chained to a tree so that they were allowed some freedom of movement. Wood was piled round the tree. The convicted men could move within the ring of fire, but their chains were too short to allow them to curtail their agonies by jumping into the fire. Noblemen themselves set the fire, which slowly burned Rohrbach and Nonnenmacher to death. This execution was clearly an act of revenge on the part of the noblemen. Another special case, full of symbolism, is the execution of the Anabaptist leaders Jan van Leiden,[15] Bernd Knipperdolling[16] and Bernd Krechting[17] in 1536 in Münster. The Bishop of Münster ordered a large stage to be constructed in front of the town hall to which all three Baptists and rebels were chained by iron collars. The executioner pinched them with red-hot tongs "on all the fleshy and veined parts" of their bodies "so that from each part touched by the tongs, a flame blazed out and such a stench filled the air that nearly everyone standing in the market-place was unable to bear it in their noses." After this lengthy torture — which they survived — their tongues were torn out with red-hot tongs and a long dagger thrust deep into their heart "so that the seat of life was

---

[11] A massive rural uprising in 1525 that threatened the social order.

[12] A group of Anabaptists took over the city government of Münster in 1534 and attempted to establish a theocracy.

[13] Jäcklein Rohrbach, an innkeeper, led the peasants of the Neckar Valley in revolt in 1525.

[14] A military punishment whereby the victim was forced to run between two rows of men who beat him as he passed.

[15] A Dutch tailor (1509–1536) who became the leader of the Münster Anabaptist revolt.

[16] Wealthy cloth merchant and Jan van Leiden's prime minister (ca. 1490–1536).

[17] Prominent supporter of Jan van Leiden.

wounded and they would lose the very thing all the more quickly." Finally the bloody corpses were locked into cages especially constructed for the occasion and hung high from the spire of St. Lamberti to be seen as a warning from far away.

But it is not only these special cases, which do not correspond to any pattern, that should be mentioned. We must finally consider the phenomenon of executing corpses. This does not mean executions in which a delinquent was beheaded or strangled before being put on the wheel, burnt or quartered and the entire procedure of torture exerted on the dead body, but rather those cases in which delinquents who were already dead were put on trial or the punishment to which the court had sentenced them before death was executed after their demise. . . . In 1690 an entire gang of church robbers was tried. When during his execution the Jew Jonas Meyer, "to the greatest annoyance of the bystanders and other Christians delivered very shameful and blasphemous speeches against our Saviour and Redeemer Jesus Christ," a second trial was instigated against him — or rather against his corpse. The sentence commended the tearing out and burning of his tongue and a second hanging, this time head down, next to a dog.

There are many more cases of criminals who before their apprehension or when already incarcerated committed suicide and the intended sentence was subsequently enforced on their bodies. Suicide in itself was deemed a crime and as a rule the offender was either burnt by the executioner, stuffed into a barrel and thrown into the river or buried beneath the gallows. But a prisoner who committed suicide might face a much more severe punishment. Some examples from Frankfurt may illustrate this. In 1685 a man who had often lived in disharmony with his wife had murdered her and then wounded himself so badly in his house that he died in the main watch house. The sentence prescribed that his corpse should be dragged publicly to the place of execution. There his head was struck off and stuck onto a pole while his body was put on the wheel. This was the punishment for murdering one's wife. A maid who, after killing her child, jumped into a well and drowned suffered the same fate in Frankfurt in 1690. The great procession leading to the execution of a footpad and citizen of Frankfurt in 1690 was arranged on purpose as a gruesome spectacle. While in prison, he had taken his life "intentionally." As punishment, he was dragged past his house to the place of execution. There his head was struck off with an axe, stuck onto a pole and his body put on the wheel for general abhorrence. Until the eighteenth century suicide was considered "one of the most severe and dangerous kinds of manslaughter since by committing it one shamefully depraves body and soul." If a sentence had been passed before the delinquent's suicide, "the very one must be executed, as far as possible, on the dead body, serving as a deterrent to others." We read this in the enlightened Prussian *Allgemeines Landrecht* of 1794.[18]

Although the original, cruel methods of execution such as quartering, burning, burying alive and breaking on the wheel were carried out, they do not entirely define the penal practice of the early modern age, not even that of the sixteenth

---

[18] Prussian code of criminal and civil law.

century. The same applies to commuted punishments carried out upon delinquents already beheaded or strangled. By the sixteenth century, and certainly in the eighteenth century, hanging and beheading became the prevailing forms of execution. Cruel methods did not disappear altogether, and existed in the eighteenth century, but more in theory. They were, however, frequently threatened. Yet everyone could easily witness a hanging or a beheading in their lifetime. Both forms served predominantly as a more or less disgraceful liquidation without torture, but might be intensified by torments or defilement before or after death. . . .

We should not deduce from this that the intention of fitting the punishment to the crime — which was obviously achieved best in the cruel variations — was completely abandoned with the decrease in horrific methods and the increase of hanging and beheading. It was only the character of the punishment fitting the crime that altered. Despite all restraint, there were plenty of opportunities to emphasize traces of traditional rituals of punishment through refinement or diverse combinations of punishments. Hanging might be combined with fixing placards, or even the burning of the delinquent's corpse. Beheading did not exclude the possibilities of the head being stuck onto a pole or the hand being cut off. Although traditional penal forms were increasingly obscured, important traces of the old system survived until the end of the eighteenth, and even into the early nineteenth, century.

A third, instructive fact survived in the criminal penal system. Punishments were inflicted not only upon the living, but also — and consciously — upon the dead body. We have to differentiate between two dimensions. When hanging a delinquent, it was decisive for how long he or she remained on the gallows, which was of no importance to the dead offender, but considered a part of the punishment in legal practice and by the public. Equally, torture continued whether or not the convicted person died with the first thrust of the wheel. The corpse was crushed further, then put on the wheel or gutted and beheaded. In these cases torture before or after execution was an integral part of the punishment. Obviously the aim was not only to kill the delinquent, but to exercise on him or her a punishment that corresponded to the offence, but bore no direct relation to the individual criminal. Moreover, it made no difference whether the punishment was inflicted upon the living or upon the dead body. Punishments were designed to create a horror of the crime as well as to provide examples of the penalties for a crime.

In whatever different ways the corpse might be included in the execution ritual, for a long time no clear distinction was made between living and dead. The idea that a person and his or her criminal activities could still be punished by inflicting torture upon the corpse lasted up to the nineteenth century.

POVERTY AND MARGINALITY IN THE EARLY MODERN CITY
Christopher R. Friedrichs

Jesus said, "The poor ye have always with you." Some of his followers interpreted this remark to mean that there is no point in trying to eliminate poverty — it is simply part of life. Nevertheless, many individuals, groups, and governments have tried to help the poor, or at least some of the poor, often in the name of Christian charity and good will.

Christopher Friedrichs, professor of history at the University of British Columbia, observes that Christianity long has commanded charity. Theologians held that the rich should give some of their surplus to the poor. Because Jesus denounced wealth, praised the poor in his Sermon on the Mount, and lived a life bereft of riches, Christians believed that poverty could be next to godliness. Poverty, for instance, was one of the vows that monks took. St. Francis of Assisi gave away his possessions and raised poverty to an ideal lifestyle that he and his new religious order of the Franciscans followed. There are many other such examples of Christian commitment to a life of poverty in medieval and early modern Europe. But this ideal soon clashed with reality as large numbers of poor poured into cities.

Poverty, Friedrichs says, was both a religious challenge and a social problem. Early modern cities had to balance a religious duty to help the poor with the fear that poverty and vagrancy would overwhelm urban resources. How did cities deal with the problem of poverty? What were the causes of urban poverty? What were the different types of "poor"? Which urban groups attempted to cope with the growing presence and problems the poor represented? Did Protestant and Roman Catholic attitudes toward the poor differ? To what extent were cities successful in dealing with the unemployed, beggars, and vagrants? How do opinions about poverty today compare to those in early modern Europe?

Christina Bobingerin was desperate. She was 19 years old in the summer of 1601, a peasant girl from the village of Göggingen just outside the walls of Augs-

Christopher R. Friedrichs, *The Early Modern City, 1450–1750* (New York: Longman Publishing, 1995), 214–229, 234–235.

burg. One day in June she sneaked into the city, trying to locate the soldier with whom she had been living some months earlier. He had long since abandoned her, but she had heard that he was in Augsburg and she thought if she found him he would have to take her back. As soon as she got into the city, however, Christina was arrested and jailed. Two days later she was interrogated.

This was not the first time Christina had been detained as an unwelcome visitor to Augsburg. At least half a dozen times before she had been arrested, whipped, led to the city gate and warned never to return. Knowing that she was unwanted, why did she insist on coming back? "Do you really think," the authorities asked her gravely, "that we should have to suffer such defiance from you?"

Christina's answer was simple. Sheer need had driven her to sneak into the city. No, she was not a prostitute, nor was she a thief. She had simply come to find her soldier or, failing that, to beg. But she was allowed to do neither. Once again she was banished from the city.

Christina's story was repeated not hundreds but thousands of times in European cities of the early modern era. Every city had its share of male and female beggars and vagrants who were desperately trying to make a living while eluding the authorities. Almost every city also had its beadles and beggar-wardens whose job was to apprehend vagrants and lock them up, kick them out, or — occasionally — permit them to carry on with their activities. Yet public begging was, in turn, only part of a vastly greater structural problem of urban poverty in early modern Europe. For countless people in the early modern city, life was not a struggle for power or prestige nor even for economic security: it was simply a struggle to survive from day to day.

"Countless" is said advisedly, for the numerical dimensions of urban poverty in early modern Europe can never be determined. Many of the poor, after all, belonged to the least systematically documented members of urban society. We may know how many households a city had, how many families paid taxes, how many people took communion, how many were born or died. Sometimes we even know how many families received welfare payments or how many beds were occupied in civic institutions. But we can never know for sure how many vagrants were living furtively in cellars or sleeping in sheds or huddled outside the city walls hoping to slip inside when the gates were opened. Nor did the size of this floating population remain constant. In times of distress — especially during wars or famine — the number of vagrants ballooned as outsiders flooded into the city in search of food or money.

Nor could the permanent residents of the city be divided with certainty into those who were poor and those who were not. Poverty itself is always difficult to define. Certainly a family which could not support its members without sustained recourse to private or public assistance would always be included among the poor. To some analysts, however, this group — the truly indigent — represented only the most extreme form of poverty; the urban poor can also be said to have included many householding families who, in normal times, seemed to be economically independent. For often these people were able to support themselves and their families only so long as they — and the local economy — remained in good health; they were liable to slip over the edge into destitution as soon as they faced some unmasterable catastrophe — a sudden collapse in the market for the goods they made, a sudden rise in the price of bread, the onset of a disabling illness, the death of a provider, or the birth of yet another dependent. In late fifteenth-century Nuremberg a city ordinance required that labourers in the building industry be given their daily wages in the morning, so that they could bring the money to their wives when they went home for a midday snack. People like this obviously lived perilously close to the margins of poverty; even when they were able to support themselves, they were bound to be conscious of indigence as a constant, looming threat.

Yet members of even the most modest householding families in the early modern city did have some resources with which to cope with the fear or fact of poverty. Every such family belonged to a network of institutions and relations which could be drawn upon for assistance. The best strategy, of course, was to anticipate and minimize economic distress in advance. Here the guilds[1] played a central role, by protecting the right of each member to earn a living and fighting to preserve traditional markets and monopolies. In addition to this, guilds often provided short-term assistance to distressed members or their widows. Sometimes confraternities[2] played this role, for often the strongest charitable impulses within the brotherhood were directed towards its own members. There were certainly cases in which poor citizens joined confraternities chiefly as a form of social insurance, knowing that in cases of illness or unemployment they would have the first claim on assistance from the richer brethren. Family relations provided another resource: in times of need, people borrowed from their relatives, or moved in with them. Only social custom could reinforce a sense of obligation between siblings or cousins, but the law often imposed an obligation among closer relatives. In some communities, for example, adult children were required to support indigent parents.

On top of all this, cities had long-established systems of private, church and municipal charity to which poor people could turn in times of need. Both the organization and the philosophy of urban charity underwent significant changes during the early modern period, but certain principles remained unchanged. Charity could take different forms, involving the distribution of food, clothing, firewood or money. But whenever possible, established residents were to be supported in their own homes. If householders were ashamed to let their neighbours know that they had become dependent on charity, discreet means of providing as-

---

[1] Economic and social associations of people who plied a specific craft or trade; such associations regulated the quality and output of goods and limited competition in order to maintain prices and so guarantee their members a secure living.

[2] Religious associations of laymen, often from the same occupation, that provided for the religious well-being of their members.

sistance were often arranged. Only in extreme cases would a person be removed from his or her own home to be looked after in a hospital or other institution.

In every city it was understood that recognized members of the community had a legitimate claim on the community's resources. This view of things owed much to the teachings of the church, but it was reinforced by the communal philosophy that lay behind the organization of the guilds and the very concept of citizenship. In fact the various forms of organized charity which had developed in European cities by the end of the middle ages would almost certainly have been sufficient to alleviate poverty without undue strain on local resources if cities had maintained a closed, stable population. But this was never the case. Urban poverty was always a serious social problem, and there is every indication that it became steadily more acute in the course of the early modern era. In city after city, the number of poor people and the desperation of their circumstances seemed to be growing. New measures to deal with poverty were constantly being devised and some of them were actually implemented. But they were never adequate, for the problem always ran far ahead of the solution.

The reason for this was simple: immigration. Not all of the poor were immigrants, and not all immigrants were poor. But immigration and poverty were always linked. Every community recognized that some immigration was inevitable and immigrants were often a valuable resource. Many male immigrants did well in the city, arriving as apprentices or journeymen and moving successfully into the ranks of householding artisans. Some even ascended into the urban elite. Many female immigrants also prospered: arriving in most cases as servants, they acquired husbands and founded stable households. Even immigrants with less promising prospects could still fill important niches in the urban economy as long-term servants or unskilled labourers. But the supply of immigrants always exceeded the city's capacity to absorb them effectively into the urban economy.

Immigration flows were never constant. The overall volume of migration to cities probably increased substantially in the sixteenth century, when the population of Europe as a whole was rapidly growing. It may have dropped somewhat during parts of the seventeenth century when the rate of demographic growth declined. But municipal authorities were little aware of any long-term trends. They were far more conscious of seasonal shifts or sudden increases in the migration rate during times of crisis. And they always felt, year after year, that far too many immigrants were turning up.

In theory only immigrants with the requisite wealth or skills would be allowed to stay in the community and settle down as permanent residents. In practice this was impossible to enforce, for the distinction between temporary and permanent residents was often blurred. This was especially the case in the rapidly expanding metropolitan centres with their sprawling outer districts — the suburbs and *faubourgs*[3] outside the walls where work and residence patterns were par-

---

[3] Outskirts; suburbs.

ticularly hard to control. Unlicensed artisans and unskilled workers abounded in these outer neighbourhoods, where overlarge parishes and underdeveloped institutions made it difficult to keep track of exactly who lived there. But even within the city walls, municipal governments found it hard to keep a close grip on the number of inhabitants. Every market-day, every seasonal fair brought a host of travellers. Not all of them left again. Innkeepers and citizens were constantly warned not to provide accommodation to visitors without notifying the authorities. It never helped. There always seemed to be more and more people in the city — and many of them, far from contributing to the urban economy, were in desperate need of help.

When all else fails, people beg. There had always been beggars in the European city, and what they did was powerfully sanctioned by medieval theology and social practice. To give alms to a beggar was the classic good work, as beneficial to the soul of the giver as it was to the body of the recipient. But the beggar did something good too: not only did his prayers aid the donor, but also his very existence gave donors the opportunity to do good by giving alms. In addition, the presence of mendicant religious orders,[4] whose members were supposed to support themselves by seeking alms, powerfully legitimized begging as a social activity. Nobody really imagined that all beggars were tinged with holiness and every act of giving sanctified the donor; people of the late middle ages were robust realists who knew that not every intimidating beggar who demanded a handout would ever remember the benefactor in his prayers. Occasional legislation condemning the idleness of vagrants and beggars can be traced back to the fourteenth century. Until the sixteenth century, however, such laws were largely ignored. For even when the recipient was not worthy, the act of giving was. And begging itself was still a legitimate enterprise in many communities. . . .

As long as begging remained socially and spiritually acceptable, every random act of almsgiving was regarded as commendable. But much charity was also given in the form of bequests after death, for this too could help speed the donor's soul heavenward. Clothing, food or cash could be distributed at the deceased's funeral. Yet other, more lasting forms of posthumous charity were also common. Testaments often included bequests to support existing institutions in their work of charity or to establish new ones. Many of these institutions were of course religious, but it was by no means uncommon to bypass the church and establish a private charity to be administered by the secular authorities. By the start of the sixteenth century, every sizeable European city had a hodgepodge of hospitals, leper-houses, pilgrim hospices and other philanthropic institutions, supported largely by rents or other forms of income bequeathed by the faithful in their wills. Nobody had to restrict his or her bequest to existing institutions; any sincere gift would be equally commendable. In the early sixteenth century, for example, the Frankfurt merchant Jacob Heller bequeathed funds for the estab-

---

[4] The Franciscans and Dominicans, founded in the 1200s, who practiced strict rules of poverty.

lishment of a public warming-house in the city. Every year from November to February this house was to be open from dawn to dusk, with a two-hour closure at midday, as a place where beggars and other poor people could find relief from the chills of a German winter. Where the visitors would spend the night was not considered; this was a day-time facility, not an attempt to deal with poverty on a structural level. But it was a classic act of traditional Christian charity.

Poverty, then, was a religious challenge. But it was also a social problem. Its dimensions could be masked by almsgiving and charity, but whenever a sudden crisis occurred the full extent of human need became glaringly apparent. In the late 1520s, for example, all over northern Italy a cycle of severe famines compounded by the disruptions of warfare drove huge masses of peasants into the cities in search of succour. A patrician of Vicenza described the situation in 1528:

> Give alms to two hundred people, and as many again will appear; you cannot walk down the street or stop in a square or church without multitudes surrounding you to beg for charity: you see hunger written on their faces, their eyes like gemless rings, the wretchedness of their bodies with the skins shaped by bones. . . . Certainly all the citizens are doing their duty with charity — but it cannot suffice.

Indeed it could not. Yet it was in exactly these years, beginning in the 1520s, that all over Europe a sudden burst of interest in the reform of poor relief became apparent. This movement began in cities, but it engendered widespread discussion among thinkers and policymakers and in some countries contributed to the enactment of new legislation on the national level. The details differed from one community to the next, but municipal leaders avidly followed what was happening in other cities, and the reforms had much in common. The most fundamental principle, reiterated in almost every community that drafted new poverty legislation, was the prohibition of indiscriminate public begging. The scattered complaints about dishonest beggars and occasional laws against public begging were consolidated into a universal condemnation of the practice. Everyone understood, of course, that some people were driven by desperate need to engage in begging. But the beggar would no longer be regarded as a universal category. Instead, each case would be assessed on an individual basis. Those who were entitled to assistance would receive it. Those who were not would not.

To implement this principle required new administrative arrangements. Commissions were appointed to distinguish between those who deserved aid and those who did not. The deserving poor were identified and listed; in many communities they were required to wear badges so that all could know who they were. They would no longer have to beg, for they and their needs were now clearly recognized, and they could wait at home for food or money to be delivered. The undeserving were also identified. Once they were, they might also be marked — generally with a whipping — before they were sent back to their home towns or simply led to the city gates with a warning never to return.

The commitment to support all the deserving poor called for a higher level of coordination than had formerly been the case. The money previously handed to individual beggars was now to be deposited in poor-boxes and offering plates or collected by officials who went from house to house. The money thus gathered would then be distributed to the deserving poor according to their needs. This often required the establishment of a new municipal agency. In addition, many city governments set up systems of inspection and supervision to ensure that existing charitable institutions were fulfilling their responsibilities in a fiscally sound manner. Sometimes the municipal government went even further, taking over existing charities to consolidate them into larger, more efficient units under the direct control of the city council.

In many cities of central Europe, the reform of poor-relief systems went hand in hand with the introduction of the Protestant Reformation. Certainly Protestant theology, with its rejection of salvation by works, saw no spiritual benefit in the act of giving alms to a beggar — and a rationally organized welfare system corresponded closely to the Protestant vision of the godly community whose members obeyed God's commands not in hopes of grace to come but in gratitude for blessings already received. There were practical reasons, too, why so many Protestant communities reorganized their welfare systems: when monasteries, convents and other church institutions were disbanded, it was only natural for municipal governments to take over some of their functions along with all of their revenues. But there was nothing inherently "Protestant" about the wave of welfare reforms which swept across Europe beginning in the 1520s. In Protestant cities they were often part of a larger package of ambitious social, political and educational reforms associated with the optimistic mood of the early Reformation. But in Catholic cities very similar welfare reforms were often enacted in response to a specific social or economic crisis — typically a severe famine which drove up food prices for the inhabitants while simultaneously flooding the city with refugees. One of the most characteristic manifestations of the new approach, for example, was the famous *Aumône-Générale*[5] established by the predominantly Catholic leaders of Lyon in the 1530s. This municipal agency was set up to receive charitable donations in lieu of the alms formerly given directly to beggars. Once a week, the *Aumône-Générale* distributed bread and money to the city's deserving poor, who were listed on the basis of careful house-to-house surveys.

Unlike Protestants, Catholic theologians were deeply divided over the issue of begging: some insisted that the spontaneous relationship between almsgiver and recipient must be retained, while others held that a less personal but more effective gift was equally meritorious. Virtually all Catholic theologians would have agreed, however, that alms must be given voluntarily. The idea of a compulsory poor-rate[6] imposed on all prosperous householders — as was implemented in England by the end of the sixteenth century — would not have appealed to Catholic thinkers. But heavy moral suasion to pressure donors to give something was acceptable. In any case there were certainly enough Catholic theologians

---

[5] Literally, "General Charity."

[6] A local property tax that funded welfare for the poor.

who favoured the thrust of the new approach to inspire or at least endorse the efforts of municipal leaders intent on welfare reform in cities like Lyon. . . .

. . . Much attention was focused on hospitals: old ones were reformed and new ones founded. Traditionally hospitals had served a variety of different purposes, in most cases reflecting the wishes of their original founders or subsequent benefactors. Some hospitals took in the sick of every description, others accepted only victims of a specific disease. Some were primarily rest-houses for travellers, some functioned as homes for aged paupers, some took in well-to-do widows or widowers who paid for their room and board. But before the sixteenth century, nobody expected hospitals to do more than relieve distress on an incidental basis. Now some reformers saw in hospitals a potential solution to broad social problems. If banishing beggars did not work, perhaps confining them to hospitals would. In 1581 a beggars' hospital was founded in Toledo. Public begging was forbidden and beggars were ordered to check into the new institution where all their needs would be met. Many chose to leave the city instead — and wisely so. Funding for the new hospital never lived up to expectations, and within a few years the project collapsed.

But the idea of confining the unstable elements of society survived. In the course of the seventeenth century, increasingly many institutional solutions to the problem of poverty were advanced. Workhouses were introduced. A hospital merely succoured the beggar; in the workhouse he or she would be taught some skill and, it was hoped, be habituated to a more industrious way of life. Closely linked in spirit to the workhouse was the orphanage, where the child who lacked parents would be introduced to good work habits before being put out as a servant or apprentice. Some workhouses even accommodated children whose parents were still living but could not afford to raise them. In the English town of Salisbury the tiny workhouse established to confine twelve adults in 1602 was expanded two decades later to include lodgings for poor children who would be taught the rudiments of a trade before being bound over as apprentices. At the same time, the city financed a programme under which masters in the textile trades would put poor people to work in their own shops, keeping them occupied with relatively unskilled tasks like spinning and knitting. But it soon became apparent that both funds and employment opportunities were too limited to make the programme a success; the workhouse survived, but the training programmes collapsed.

All such schemes turned out to be inadequate to the need. Yet in city after city, a new generation of municipal leaders would tackle the problem with a fresh burst of optimism. The vision of a comprehensive institution to combine confinement and training was particularly powerful in French towns of the seventeenth century. This normally took the form of an *hôpital-général*[7] which would enclose the ill, the aged, the orphaned, the insane and the idle all at once, providing palliative care or disciplined training as appropriate to each category. Many such

---

[7] General hospital; a refuge for those who were terminally ill, destitute, homeless, or aged.

institutions were proposed and quite a few were actually founded in the course of the seventeenth century. The *Hôpital-Général* of Paris, which was launched in 1657 with a spectacular round-up of beggars from the streets of the city, may have housed close to 10,000 inmates at a time. Smaller but similar institutions were founded in many provincial cities, often in the hope that systematic confinement would finally eliminate social disorder and wipe out habits of idleness among the poor. But even so it was never more than a small fraction of the rootless poor who were effectively confined. The costs were too high and the potential clients, in many cases, preferred the risk of remaining free to the punitive security of institutional confinement.

Begging could not be eliminated. No matter how many vagrants were banished or confined, desperate people still found their way on to the streets of the city, determined to collect whatever they could while staying out of the beadle's[8] sight. Catholic town-dwellers continued to believe that handing alms directly to a beggar was a work of mercy; even in Protestant cities it was hard for inhabitants to resist the insistent appeal of the outstretched palm. Completely consistent policies were impossible to enforce. Even communities which tried to maintain a general policy of expelling or confining beggars often made exceptions for special cases, for example by granting crippled or blind vagrants permission to beg in the streets. But the real problem was that no amount of charity, private or public, would ever be sufficient to cope with the dimensions of poverty.

Everyone agreed that scarce resources should be directed primarily to the deserving poor. But establishing exactly who was "deserving" was not a simple matter. Three intersecting systems of categorization were involved. One category was geographical: the local person — especially someone actually born in the community — was always more deserving of support than the outsider. A second category was physical: the person unable to work due to illness, youth or age was more deserving of aid than the person who had the physical capacity to earn a living. The third category was moral: the person who was willing to work was more deserving than the shirker. The "sturdy beggar" — the healthy person who was able to work but unwilling to do so — was a popular target of fierce moralizing and repressive legislation. In fact everyone knew, or could have known, that many such people were idle not by choice but by circumstance. But this was often ignored. For there was little that could be done even for paupers who were willing and able to work. Occasionally the physically able beggars were commandeered for public works projects such as rebuilding or reinforcing the city fortifications. But such undertakings and the funds to support them were usually short-lived. Nor was it easy to arrange private employment for the poor. Even when the law provided that local orphans were to be put out as apprentices, the guilds sometimes raised objections. The likelihood that outside beggars could be converted to productive workers with an accepted niche in the local economy was always slight. It was altogether easier to act on the premise that beggars were deliberate

---

[8] A minor parish officer responsible for keeping order and for dealing with petty offenders.

shirkers, constitutionally unwilling to submit to the discipline of labour. Vagrants were depersonalized, seen not as distressed individuals but as a collective threat to the city's well-being. The city had to protect itself against the "plague of beggars" by quarantine measures not unlike those which were applied in the case of contagious illnesses. In actual fact, beggars were as hard to stop as infectious diseases. Many a gate-keeper or beadle found it convenient or even lucrative to let a beggar elude his notice. But whenever the authorities found the beggars too bothersome, it was easy to solve the problem: with a little effort, the current crop of beggars could always be apprehended, whipped, banished and forgotten.

The local poor, by contrast, could be neither removed nor ignored. The social obligation to meet their needs was conceded by all. But cities did everything they could to restrict their number. In many German towns, anyone who applied for citizenship or even just for local residence rights had to give evidence of an adequate degree of wealth before being accepted. Sometimes the applicant also had to promise to make no claim on the city's welfare institutions for a specific number of years. In England, where poor-rates were collected and distributed on the parish level, there were even obstacles to moving from one parish to another within the same city. Newcomers were often asked to post a bond to cover the initial costs of any poor-relief they might incur; if they failed to do so, they could be sent back to their original parish. In seventeenth-century Southwark, just south of London Bridge, a parish "searcher" promptly visited every new arrival who took up residence in the district. Anyone who lacked obvious means of support or refused to post a bond was quickly evicted by the constable.

Even in the face of such measures, however, every European city had an irreducible core of impoverished inhabitants — the "house poor" or "parish poor" who enjoyed an undisputed right to live in the community yet could not support themselves without assistance. How many people belonged to this category? Naturally the proportion varied enormously from town to town, and it could rise or fall drastically within a given community as economic conditions changed. A few examples can, however, give some evidence of the extent of poverty.

Start with the well-recorded case of Augsburg. For the year 1558 the tax register recorded a total of 8,770 citizen households. Of these, a total of 4,161 households — about 47 per cent — were listed as "have-nots." This was a tax category, not an indication of total destitution — but it does show that almost half the householders in Augsburg lacked any property worth taxing and lived almost entirely off their income. Many of them could not break even: in the same year exactly 404 households, containing a total of 1,038 men, women and children, received regular support in the form of bread, lard, firewood and other supplies from the city alms office. Thus, in 1558 about one out of every twenty citizen households were living in definite poverty. . . .

In every town, in fact, there would have been a similar difference between the number of "structural" poor who were permanently dependent on relief and those who needed assistance only in times of famine or other crisis. This was vividly apparent, for example, in the English town of Warwick. In 1582 St. Mary's parish, which encompassed most of the town, had a total of 373 families. Of these, only

42 families, or 11 per cent, actually received poor-relief. But another 68 families were said to be at risk of decaying into poverty. Precisely this happened to many of them five years later when a drastic famine hit the town, for in 1587 a total of 93 families in St. Mary's parish — close to a quarter of the total — stood in urgent need of assistance. A number of London neighbourhoods in the same era showed a similar pattern, with 5–10 per cent of the parish families regularly receiving relief and a second group, perhaps twice as large, needing assistance in times of crisis. Much the same applies to late sixteenth-century Lyon: it has been estimated that in normal years 6–8 per cent of the city's population needed poor relief, but in times of famine 15–20 per cent of the inhabitants required support. . . .

Early in the year 1635, the authorities in Salisbury undertook — not for the first time — a survey of the poor in each parish of the city. In one parish, St. Martin's, the enumerators even distinguished between two levels of poverty. Thirty-three households were listed as regularly receiving alms. One was headed by a man, three were headed by married couples, and fully twenty-nine were headed by women — widows, spinsters or wives whose husbands had abandoned them. Among the much larger group of 174 parish households which, though poor, did not need regular alms, 105 were headed by married couples. Among the rest, 48 were headed by women and only 21 by bachelors and widowers.

. . . Women were, by and large, less mobile than men — and more economically vulnerable. An unmarried man was more likely than an unmarried woman to leave his home town, whether as a journeyman, a soldier, a sailor or even a vagabond. Among married couples, husbands abandoned their families far more often than wives. But above all, the poor widow was a much more common phenomenon than the poor widower. A man's chances of remarrying were normally greater, and even if he did not remarry his economic resources were normally larger. It is true that among the social elite, widowhood could open up opportunities for a woman to deploy her property independently and find a new marriage partner of her own choosing. Among the poor, however, widowhood was always a disaster. The paltry dowry a poor woman had brought into her marriage — if it was even intact — offered no economic security, and her opportunities to continue to earn a living were always circumscribed. Even if the law guaranteed a widow the right to continue operating her husband's shop, in practice most poor women lacked the capital and the contacts to do so effectively.

Yet the "house poor" widow may still have been regarded with envy by some other women in the community. She at least had a recognized claim on a modest degree of social assistance. Women who had never established a household in the first place were often even more vulnerable. Among these were servants. To be sure, not all servants, male or female, were ill-treated. Some worked for patriarchal masters who recognized an obligation to care for those who had loyally served them. But mistreatment of servants was no less common, and female servants ran the additional risk of being subjected to sexual exploitation. In early modern Bordeaux many a last will included bequests for servants, often with a specific reference to the recipients' faithful service. But evidence from the same city also illustrates the risks that female servants faced. In the 1620s about thirty babies were abandoned by their mothers every year, to be taken in by the Jesuit[9] foundling hospital.[10] Generally, of course, babies were abandoned in secret, but occasionally the hospital staff was able to identify the parents. Looking after foundlings was an expensive proposition — in each case a willing wet-nurse had to be found and paid — and whenever possible the authorities hoped to pin the expenses on the responsible party. The fathers who were traced came from every social level — but ten of the eleven mothers whose circumstances were recorded were listed as domestic servants. In most such cases, a master had made his servant pregnant and then fobbed her off with a promise of regular child support — and when the payments eventually tapered off, the mother could see no other recourse than giving up the baby. . . .

One of the most famous of William Hogarth's[11] "progresses" was the set of twelve engravings issued in 1747 under the title "Industry and Idleness." This series compares the careers of two imaginary apprentices of London: the industrious Francis Goodchild, whose hard work and good conduct result in economic success and political eminence, and Tom Idle, whose laziness and irreligion lead via petty crime and underworld activity to the scaffold at Tyburn.[12] The whole series, like most of Hogarth's work, is didactic, moralistic and ironic all at once. The contrast between the careers is unrealistically extreme. Yet the point Hogarth made was a valid one: that for any young person arriving in London, or indeed in any city of early modern Europe, many options were still open. Whether the newcomer would eventually rise into the more secure world of the established householders or would sink into permanent marginalization was, in many cases, determined by economic factors far beyond his or her control. But personal conduct could make a difference. Parents, church, school and guilds all promoted values of hard work, deference and sexual morality which are easy to interpret as instruments of social control. But these were also values which helped the young adult to maximize his or her chances of securing a foothold on the social ladder — and by doing so to climb into the circle of established householders who formed the core of every urban community. . . .

---

[9] The Society of Jesus, a Roman Catholic religious order established in 1540.

[10] Orphanage.

[11] English painter (1697–1764) known for satirical pictures of eighteenth-century lowlife.

[12] Field in London where public executions were held until 1868.

PART TWO

THE OLD RÉGIME

John McManners
Robert Darnton
Olwen Hufton
Dominique Godineau
Keith Wrightson

Politically, the Old Régime was the Age of Absolutism, the era before the French Revolution; intellectually, it encompassed the Scientific Revolution and the Enlightenment; artistically, the Baroque and Rococo styles set the tone. The seventeenth and eighteenth centuries saw the nobility as preeminent over other social groups. Most people were poor physical specimens who worked hard, suffered from vitamin deficiency and malnutrition, and lived short lives. Although it is often difficult to read the minds of people who left few records of their feelings, one can suppose that happiness and enjoyment seemed out of the reach of the majority of Europe's population, save for that happiness that accompanies survival or the brief interlude of an exceptional occasion, such as a religious feast, a wedding, or some small victory extracted from a harsh and severe world.

Essays in this section on the Old Régime convey the violence, uncertainty, and desperation that marked the lives of most Europeans. In his essay, "Death's Arbitrary Empire," John McManners paints a riveting picture of the prevalence of disease, of the wracked condition of bodies, and of the vulnerability of most people to the vagaries of food production, weather, war, and the lack of healthy living conditions. Perhaps the greatest privileges of the wealthy were security from hunger and a diet that offered them better resistance to disease. The print-shop workers in eighteenth-century Paris could engage in an ephemeral revolt — a massacre of cats — against their boss, as Robert Darnton shows, but those workers had little hope of improving their social position. Working-class women had an active role in the economy, but Olwen Hufton concludes that their toil was unrelenting and their prospects for financial security dim, especially if they were single or widowed. Keith Wrightson's survey of infanticide throughout Europe reveals that some women believed they had little choice but to murder their infants because of the infamy associated with illegitimate births. Judges, exclusively male, did not exercise undue mercy toward women convicted of infanticide, a crime linked always to mothers, never to fathers.

As a rule, early modern Europeans revered unity and hierarchy, and abhorred dissent and pluralism. Although there were, to be sure, some outside the Christian fold — Jews, Muslims, and a sprinkling of atheists — nearly all Europeans were Christians. After the Protestant Reformation had torn apart a relatively united Christendom in western Europe in the sixteenth century (the Eastern Orthodox

Church had split from western Christianity in 1054), most states maintained an established church and discriminated legally against Christians who belonged to other denominations. Christians venerated order and authority, and they found them in a church, in the pope, or in scripture. The body politic likewise signified harmony and obedience. Monarchy mirrored god's supremacy over the cosmos.

Deference and order characterized the social structure as well. Kings governed subjects, lords dominated peasants, men ruled women, and parents regulated their children's lives. Rank in the Old Régime was everything, and it certainly had its privileges. If men of commerce and industry rose in stature — in Great Britain and the United Provinces, for example — this social mobility in no way weakened the belief that hierarchy provided the ideal basis for society. Throughout most of Europe, the aristocracy stood at the pinnacle of the social pyramid, and in many places — some as far apart as France and Russia — the nobles experienced a resurgence of power and prestige. The aristocratic ethos offered a standard of behavior and a set of values that few non-nobles could emulate. Only a small number of individuals, primarily intellectuals or those on the fringes of society, dreamed of a democratic revolution that would sweep the aristocracy and their perquisites into the dustbin of history.

The Old Régime therefore possessed a certain unity in the midst of great diversity, a unity grounded in the respect, even glorification, of religious, political, and social order. Though changing, the Old Régime signified a stability that accompanied faith in respected institutions. The preferred form of change was individual change, a modest improvement in one's personal fortunes or those of one's family. Such alterations of status, however, did little to dispel the terrible and brutal conditions of daily existence that faced the vast majority of Europe's population.

During the Middle Ages and the early modern period, Europeans had looked to the past for inspiration — religiously to the time of early Christianity and culturally to classical antiquity — and had grown accustomed to gradual change. The Industrial Revolution, however, increased dramatically the pace of change and brought the expectation of future improvement in social and economic life. Furthermore, the French Revolution put Europeans on notice that anything was possible, that the political and social order could be altered fundamentally according to human effort and will. The Parisian women whom Dominique Godineau describes influenced greatly the course of politics during the French Revolution. Although their political clubs were suppressed and their efforts to achieve their political, social, and legal goals stymied, their political militancy in the French Revolution foreshadowed later developments throughout the Western world.

The deluge of the Industrial and French Revolutions helped create a new régime in which modern technology ushered in the idea of progress and where political and social experimentation could occur.

DEATH'S ARBITRARY EMPIRE
John McManners

The eighteenth century is known as the Enlightenment, the Age of Reason, or the Age of Voltaire. John McManners, an Anglican priest and former Regius Professor of Ecclesiastical History at Oxford University, reveals the underside of that epoch of cultural achievement, a world where, for most people, death triumphed early. Observers who lived during that era, including physicians, give vivid accounts of the deplorable physical condition of the French populace. When McManners reviews the history of eighteenth-century France in terms of medicine, disease, and mortality, he finds ill-health, violence, and misery to have been as characteristic of the age as enlightened reason and Voltairian wit.

During the eighteenth century, the high rate of infant mortality was the primary reason for a short life expectancy. Why did so many infants and children die? What, if anything, could people have done to improve their children's health and longevity? Orphans were less likely to survive childhood than any other group. The presence of orphanages, however, suggests that society attempted to care for orphans. If that is true, why did so many die so young?

McManners paints a bleak picture of physicians and their ability to treat illness and disease. Why were medical doctors so ineffective? Surely we cannot place all of the blame on physicians, because their patients, even in the best of times, were models of poor health. The living conditions in towns (such as overcrowding and the lack of sanitation), an insufficient and poor diet, the dangers of the workplace, the vagaries of the weather, even the clothing — all made people easy prey for disease. And where could one be safe? Not in an institution, for hospitals, army barracks, and asylums were dangerous places. The economic elite, healthier because of a better diet, certainly fared better than most, but even the rich suffered from disease and illness to an extent scarcely imaginable to us in our era of antibiotics and long life expectancy. In the eighteenth century, death's empire was whimsically arbitrary.

Nothing, not even youth and robust health, could give security from suffering or early death, for eighteenth-century France was a violent society. Highwaymen, domestic violence, wild animals, and rural conflicts were omnipresent.

John McManners, *Death and the Enlightenment: Changing Attitudes to Death among Christians and Unbelievers in Eighteenth-Century France* (New York: Oxford University Press, 1981), 5–23.

Often hungry, cold, sick, and frightened by forces seemingly beyond their control, the overwhelming majority of people had little time to marvel at Voltaire's wit. How would current Western societies fit into the model of social deprivation that McManners details? In what areas of life today have conditions improved and where in Western civilization do we find life to be as bleak as in eighteenth-century France?

In eighteenth-century France, "death was at the centre of life as the graveyard was at the centre of the village." Speaking in averages, and confounding in one the diversity of the whole country and the fortunes of all classes, we find that something like a quarter of all babies born in the early years of the century died before reaching their first birthday, and another quarter before reaching the age of eight. Of every 1,000 infants, only 200 would go on to the age of fifty, and only 100 to the age of seventy. A man who had beaten the odds and reached his half-century would, we may imagine, have seen both his parents die, have buried half his children and, like as not, his wife as well, together with numerous uncles, aunts, cousins, nephews, nieces, and friends. If he got to seventy, he would have no relations and friends of his own generation left to share his memories. If this is a description of the average, what can we say of the unfortunates whose sombre ill luck weights down the figures to this mean? . . .

A new understanding of the eighteenth century comes to us when we review its history in terms of disease and mortality. In narrow fetid streets and airless tenements, in filthy windowless hovels, in middens and privies, in undrained pools and steaming marshes, in contaminated wells and streams — and, for that matter, in the gilded corridors of Versailles, where excrement accumulated — infections of every kind lurked. The files of the administrators, more especially those of the Royal Society of Medicine at the end of the *ancien régime*,[1] are full of information sent in by medical experts about local epidemics and peculiar illnesses, but it is often difficult to deduce from their accounts what the specific diseases were. They spoke essentially of symptoms. Fevers were "bilious," "putrid," "autumnal," "red," "purple," "intermittent," "malignant," "inflammatory." The spitting of blood so often mentioned could have been the result of cancer of lungs or larynx, infection of the trachea, or pulmonary tuberculosis; their "scurvy," deduced from bleeding gums and painful joints, could include arthritis and pyorrhoea. An autopsy frequently produced a report of "worms" in lungs or stomach, without any other evidence to bring precision. . . . "With their bodies assaulted on all sides, these people were carried off before the more subtle disorders had a chance to strike." The main killers were influenza and pulmonary infections, malaria, typhoid, typhus, dysentery, and smallpox, striking in waves across a debilitating pat-

---

[1] Old Régime, the two centuries before the French Revolution of 1789.

tern of routine afflictions — mange, skin disorders, gout, epilepsy. The grimmest scourge of all was smallpox, which seems to have become a more common and more virulent disease from the late seventeenth century. A doctor of Montpellier in 1756 described it as being "everywhere," as it were "naturalized" and "domesticated," especially at Paris, "where it never relaxes its grip." . . . Not surprisingly, then, the army records on new recruits continually speak of marked faces. . . . This was, indeed, a disease which destroyed the beauty of so many of those it did not slay. . . .

   . . . There were two seasons when mortality was at its highest, winter and early spring on one hand, and autumn, especially the month of September, on the other. In some places, winter was the cruellest season, in others autumn. From December to March, pneumonia and pulmonary afflictions abounded, and the sheer cold took its toll of those who were ill-clothed and lacked the means to keep warm. And these were numerous. Wood was in short supply in the cereal-growing plains and in the cities. Heating arrangements were rudimentary; even in Versailles, wine froze at the royal table in winter, and the heavily padded and decorated coats of courtiers were not just for display. Clothing passed from upper to lower classes and from older to younger generations, getting more and more threadbare on its journey. The poorer streets of cities were a motley pageant of rags, anonymous or with prestigious social origins. There were peasants who never changed their linen, and when they discarded it, it was too worn to be sent to the paper-mills. Even the more prosperous peasants . . . made do with two shirts and two coats a year, and a cloak every five. There was not much in the wardrobe to keep them warm and dry in the snow or rain of winter. In August, September, and October, dysentery would strike, and before illnesses encouraged by the excessive heat had declined, there would come the onset of those which flourished in the ensuing dampness. . . . These were fevers — malaria (coming, as contemporaries noted, with the floods), typhoid, and "purple fever" which was often confused with the ubiquitous scarlatina or measles. Generally, it was adults, especially the aged, who succumbed in winter, and the younger children in the autumn — though there were exceptions: the cold in some places carried off more babies under the age of one than the intestinal infections of the hotter weather. Superimposed upon this yearly cycle of menace was the arbitrary onslaught of great epidemics, sometimes driving the death rate up to double and treble the monthly average; there was the dysentery in Anjou in 1707 and 1779, highly infectious and lethal within two or three days, the influenza in the same province which caused devastation in 1740, the typhoid and enteric fever in Brittany from 1758 onwards which was largely responsible for reducing the population of that province by 4 per cent; there were more localized outbreaks, like the military fever in Pamiers in 1782 which killed 800 people.

   Being born was a hazardous business for both mother and child. "Don't get pregnant and don't catch smallpox" was Mme. de Sévigné's[2] advice to her married

---

[2] Famous writer of letters (1626–1696).

daughter . . . although she had only simple ideas of how to avoid either. The proverbial pride in pregnancy of primitive societies was overwhelmed, in eighteenth-century France, by fear. Medical manuals considered a pregnant woman to be suffering from an illness, and even cited Scripture in ascribing the pains of childbirth to the transgression of Eve. Many women, especially those of the poorer classes, came to their ordeal in wretched health, and the prevalence of rickets caused deformities which made delivery difficult. There were hardly any hygienic precautions, the technique for arresting haemorrhages was not yet developed, and the manipulation of forceps (supposed to be limited to qualified surgeons alone) was clumsy. Until the reign of Louis XVI, there was hardly any attempt to train midwives. In reporting to their bishops or to the secular authorities, parish priests described how the office of midwife came to be filled in their parish. . . . A *curé*[3] in the diocese of Boulogne in 1725 said that his midwife inherited the job from her mother — "the women have a reasonable amount of confidence in her." Another *curé* said that "ours has worked here for thirty years: she took up the office of her own accord, the women of the parish accepted her, and it has not been thought fitting to oblige her to undergo further training." Horror stories about midwives abound — beating on the stomach to "hasten delivery," cutting the umbilical cord too close or failing to tie it, forgetting the placenta, crippling babies by rough handling, and — even — showing off by turning the infant round so that the feet emerged first. Louis XIV made a clean break with tradition when he called in a man, the surgeon Jacques Clément, to the *accouchement*[4] of the Dauphine in 1686. . . . But were surgeons much more use than midwives? Clément bled his patient, wrapped her in the skin of a newly flayed sheep, and kept her in a dark room for nine days without so much as a single candle. And how good was the gynaecologist whose advertisement in Paris has been preserved as a curiosity? — "Montodon, ci-devant pâtisseur, boulevard Bonne Nouvelle, est actuellement chirurgien et accoucher."[5] In fact, there was little that even the most expert practitioner could do if things went wrong. If the baby's head stuck, there would be a week of agony and the vileness of gangrene before inevitable death. The Caesarian section without anaesthetics left one chance in a thousand for the women. . . . Many babies were stillborn, or died within a few days, or were maimed for life. A memoir to an intendant in 1773 describes young people coming out of a parish mass, marked by inexpert deliveries — atrophied, hunchbacked, deaf, blind, one-eyed, bandy-legged, bloodshot of eye, lame and twisted, hare-lipped, "almost useless to society and fated for a premature end." Many women too were killed, or crippled, or mentally scarred; a *curé* blames the rise of contraceptive practices in his parish on the neurotic determination of so many women never to undergo the experience of childbirth again.

---

[3] Chief parish priest.

[4] Parturition.

[5] "Montodon, former pastry cook, boulevard Bonne Nouvelle, is currently a surgeon and obstetrician."

. . . Between 20 and 30 per cent of babies born died in their first year: in a particularly wretched hamlet in the early part of the century, over 32 per cent died in their first year and over 22 per cent in their second. There were, of course, healthy and unhealthy areas, depending on the peculiar combination of advantages and disadvantages in food supplies, geographical features, and climate. The national average in the eighteenth century for children surviving to the age of ten was, roughly, 55 per cent; at Crulai in Normandy it was 65 per cent; in poverty-stricken villages amidst the stagnant malarial pools of the Sologne or of the Mediterranean littoral, it was 40 per cent. . . . The deadly season of the year for infants was early autumn, when heat, humidity and flies, and unhygienic ways of living brought the intestinal infections for which no remedy was known. These visitations were facilitated by the custom, prevalent among richer people and town dwellers, of sending infants away to be nursed by foster mothers. Towards the end of the century, of the 21,000 babies born each year in Paris, only 1,000 were fed by their mothers, another 1,000 by wet-nurses brought into the home, 2,000 to 3,000 were sent to places near the city, and the rest to more distant localities — concentric circles within which the proportion of deaths became higher as the distance from home increased. . . . For families of the urban working class, like small shopkeepers or the silk workers of Lyon, it was an economic necessity to get the wife back to counter or loom quickly. For the leisured class, a satisfactory explanation is harder to find; a certain harshness of mind, an unwillingness to become too attached to a pathetic bundle whose chances of survival were so limited, the desire to resume sexual relationships as soon as possible, the belief that loss of milk diluted the quality of the blood of the mother, a reliance on the therapeutic qualities of country air to give the baby a good start or (very doubtfully) some subconscious reaction against an infant's "oral sadism" — whatever the reasons, a compelling social custom had arisen. In 1774, a reformer, appealing to have children "brought up in the order of Nature," described the sensation when a mother declares her intention of breast-feeding her first child: protests from her parents, and all the ladies lamenting to see her risking her life for a new-fashioned theory. Given the demand, around the cities a wet-nursing "industry" had arisen. In some villages near Limoges, girls married earlier to qualify. Such glimpses as we get of this peculiar interchange between town and country show an unfeeling and mercenary world — women who take on two or three babies in addition to their own, knowing that there will be competition for survival, who go on drawing their pay when they know their milk is drying up and their client's infant will have no chance. . . . These practitioners are preying on legitimate children, with parents to look after their interests and hoping against hope that they will be trundled back home in nine months' time. What then of the illegitimate ones, the multitude of foundlings, the *enfants trouvés?*[6]

The fate of these unhappy infants throws a harsh, cold light on the cruel underside of the century of crystalline wit and rococo delicacy. Increasing numbers

---

[6] Orphans, foundlings.

of children were being abandoned. An average of 2,000 a year came to the Enfants Trouvés of Paris in the 1720s, rising to a record total of 7,676 in 1772; thereafter, royal edicts forbade the bringing-in of foundlings from the provinces, and the Parisian total stabilized at about 5,800 a year. In Bordeaux at the mid-century, there were about 300 admissions annually; in Metz, in the winter of 1776, no less than 900. . . . These numbers swamped the organizational abilities of the *ancien régime,* . . . and the hopeless problem they presented deadened the charitable instincts of those who cared. A Genevan doctor reports a nun of the Parisian foundling hospital taking refuge in the reflection that these innocent souls would go straight to eternal bliss, since the revenues of her institution could not feed any more of them anyway. There was a prejudice against making immoral conduct easier by spending money on those "unhappy fruits of debauchery" (though it is true that some children were abandoned by married parents who were too poor to maintain them). Many illegitimate children were doomed before ever they reached the shelter of an institution — physically impaired by the mother's attempts to conceal her pregnancy or to produce an abortion, infected with venereal disease, or hopelessly weakened by a journey from some distant place, crowded in baskets on the back of a donkey, or of a porter travelling on foot, or jolting in a wagon. The infants who got through the crucial first week in which so many died had to survive the grim and crowded conditions in the hospital, and the rigours of the system of putting out to nurse (with private families paying more to preempt the healthiest and most reliable foster mothers). Only one foundling in ten lived to reach the age of ten: nine had perished. Such survivors as there were would live gloomily learning a trade in some institution full of prostitutes, layabouts, and madmen, or in some ruthlessly disciplined orphanage; a very few might be found again by their parents or left with some sympathetic country family — but the chances of a decent existence were infinitesimal. One who did get through the hazards and succeeded was the *philosophe* and mathematician d'Alembert,[7] left as an infant on the steps of the church of Saint-Jean-la-Ronde. An expert on the calculus of probabilities, he must often have reflected on the odds that he had beaten.

Driven to despair by poverty, some parents abandoned their children: there were suspicions that others did not strive officiously to keep them alive. The synodal statutes of various dioceses ordered the *curés* to warn their flocks against the dangerous practice of putting children to sleep in the beds of their parents, where so often they were suffocated. . . . A surgeon described the injuries suffered by babies in the vineyard country around Reims: while their mothers toiled among the vines they were sometimes attacked by animals — eyes pecked by turkeys, hands eaten off by pigs. And for the healthy grown-up, the ordinary routines of life were precarious. Society was ill-policed, unable to take effective measures to suppress highwaymen and discipline vagabonds. Rural life was violent. Wife-beating was common. Unpopular *curés* were kept awake by nocturnal *tapages*[8] which could

---

[7] Jean le Rond d'Alembert (1713–1783).

[8] Rows.

degenerate into riots. There were affrays with cudgels and clubs at fairs. In Languedoc, where the hunting rights of the lords had been bought off, peasants went around with guns; poachers returned the fire of gamekeepers; and pot-shots were taken at *seigneurs*[9] and other unpopular local worthies. The youths of villages were organized, quasi-officially, into bands, the *"garçons de paroisse,"*[10] who fought pitched battles with those from other places at fairs, marriages, and the draw for the *milice*,[11] or when communities quarrelled over boundaries or grazing rights. . . . In towns, the police force was inadequate to maintain order at festivals or to organize precautions against accidents. A panic at the fireworks in Paris for the marriage of the Dauphin in 1770 led to more than 1,000 being trampled to death; two years later, the great fire at the Hôtel-Dieu claimed many victims. There were, indeed, few precautions against fire — for long the only Parisian fire brigade was the Capuchin friars, swarming into action in frocks and cowls, with axes and ladders. Narrow streets, ramshackle buildings, and an abundance of wooden construction made the old parts of cities hopelessly vulnerable, tinder dry in summer, and underpinned with extra fuel in winter when the cellars of the rich were crammed with firewood and grain. . . . Buildings, especially the parish churches for whose maintenance a local rate had to be levied, were often left unrepaired and dangerous; every year there were floods from unbanked rivers, wreaking devastation and leaving legacies of fever. In the streets and in the countryside, savage dogs, some with rabies, wandered; in remote areas wolf packs hunted — there was a government bounty for each one killed, the parish priest to issue a certificate on the production of the ears; in 1750, 126 were killed in the province of Anjou alone. Our modern concept of "accident" as some technical failure — burnt-out wire, slipping flange, broken lever — obtruding into well-organized habitual comfort, was almost unknown in the eighteenth century. Life was hazardous throughout. . . .

Up to the last two decades of the *ancien régime*, hardly anything was done to regulate dangerous trades or to prevent industrial accidents. . . . Even so, though nothing was being done, contemporaries were becoming aware of the terrifying hardships which crippled industrial workers and abbreviated their lives. . . . Conditions in French mines were grim enough: twelve hours a day underground, in continual danger from explosions (because fires were burning to suck air along the galleries) and from flooding (if the horse-turned pumps failed). The workers who polished mirrors, their feet continually in water and hands continually getting cut, were worn out by the interminable pushing to and fro of the heavy weight; printers received fractures and bruises from the levers of their presses; candle makers stifled in the heat around the furnaces; hemp crushers invariably got asthma; gilders became dizzy within a few months from the mercurial fumes which eventually poisoned them; workers who handled unwashed wool were

---

[9] Lords.

[10] Boys of the parish.

[11] Militia.

recognizable by their pale and leaden countenances, upon which would be superimposed the permanent stains of the colours used in dyeing. Alarming examples of the effect of bad conditions of working and living on mortality rates can be studied in the armed forces. In war, few sailors were killed by cannon-balls. The seventy-four-gun ship *Ajax* patrolled in the Atlantic and Indian Oceans from February 1780 to June 1784; during that period 228 of her crew of 430 died. Battle accounted for only thirty (and of these half perished from the explosion of one of the ship's own cannon); nine were drowned . . . ; no less than 185 were killed by diseases: scurvy, dysentery, malaria — infections that ran riot among men cooped below decks for most of their time afloat, and living on food lacking in indispensable vitamins. . . . It could be said that war killed soldiers, but essentially indirectly. The mortality rate in a particular regiment from 1716 to 1749 was five times higher in war years than in those of peace, but the deaths occurred principally from December to April, when the troops were in winter quarters. In the barracks built in the eighteenth century (always at the expense of the local authorities, not of the Crown), the standard size for a room was 16 by 18 feet, to contain thirteen to fifteen men crammed into four or five beds. These stifling conditions, rampant epidemics, the cold outside, and venereal disease killed many more in winter quarters than the shot and steel of the enemy in the summer campaigning season. It was a rule under the *ancien régime* that life in State institutions was abbreviated. When *dépôts de mendicité*[12] were set up in 1767 to clear vagabonds off the roads, the inmates died off rapidly. . . . At Rennes, of 600 initially arrested, 137 died within a year, though it is true there were a lot of infections about at the time. At Saint-Denis, the death rate in the *dépôt* was consistently double that for the town, not excepting the high infant mortality from the latter total.

. . . [D]eath was not without deference to rank and possessions, to the well-to-do with their log fires, warm clothing, protein diet, and spacious houses. . . . True, in this age of multitudinous servants, it was difficult to erect effective barriers of unofficial quarantine — in the last resort, infections got through. . . . No doubt there were special afflictions to descend upon the self-indulgent; moralists (with some injustice to the sufferers) liked to instance apoplexy, paralysis, and gout. Cynics would add the dangers from the medical profession; the peasant, who distrusted blood-letting and could not afford to pay the surgeon to do it, was at least free from his attentions. Even so, the life expectancy of the rich was much better than that of the poor, and the men of the eighteenth century knew it. In statistical terms, we might guess that the advantage was something like ten years above the average and seventeen years above that of the very poor. Peasants, living crowded together in single-roomed cottages, were very vulnerable, and even more so were the poor of the towns, whose debilitating conditions of working were allied to crowded, insanitary accommodation. Disease spread quickly where there was only one bed for a family. A doctor in the countryside complained of the way in which people "occupy the beds of those who are dead of the malady

---

[12] Workhouses.

[typhoid] on the same day the corpse is taken out of it," and it was well known that the communal bed was one of the reasons why the great plague of 1720 in Provence so often swept off a whole family. . . . The church-wardens of the poverty-stricken parish of Saint-Sauveur in Lille complained that the death rate of their parishioners in the epidemic of 1772–3 had been much higher than in the wealthy parish of Saint-André. "The higher numbers here," they said, "can only be because the inhabitants are poor, more numerous and crowded into little houses, often occupied by many families, and situated in very narrow streets called alleyways . . . , they breathe the less pure air here, and because of the dirt which is virtually inseparable from poverty, they propagate all the diseases which catch a hold among them." In Lyon, the silk workers lived twelve to fifteen in a garret, forty to fifty families in a house in the tall buildings around sunless courts, stinking of the chickens, pigs, and rabbits that they reared, and of latrines. . . .

When the Royal Council on 29 April 1776 set up its commission to investigate epidemic diseases in the provinces, one of the questions it posed was: "Why do epidemics sometimes seem to spare a particular class of citizens?" Probably, the intention was not to look at the obvious overcrowding of the slums, but at the food and water supplies and at the dietary habits of the different classes. Seventy years earlier, during the misery at the end of the reign of Louis XIV, the economist Boisguilbert, in a burning tirade, had censured the maldistribution of food supplies which cut short so many lives. There are men, he said, who sweat blood in their toil, with no food other than bread and water, in the midst of a land of abundance, who "perish when only half their course is run," and whose children are "stifled in their cradles." . . . Estimates . . . — at Arles in 1750, by the agricultural society of La Rochelle in 1763, by the owner of a carpet factory in Abbeville in 1764 — show that the poorer peasants and urban workers, though far from being reduced to bread and water, lived all their lives on the margins of danger: any loss of working days had to be paid for by starvation later. There was a cycle of illness, debt, and hunger which made death almost certain on the next round of visitation, and it was not unusual for wretches who had struggled fiercely against starvation to give up on hearing that they had caught some disease, knowing that the future had little hope.

Most people in France lived on cereals, because this was what they could afford. A modern attempt to work out a typical budget for a family of the poor majority in an ordinary year, suggests 50 per cent of expenditure on bread, 16 per cent on fats and wine, 13 per cent on clothing, and 5 per cent on heating. So far as the proportion on bread is concerned, eighteenth-century estimates studied more recently confirm the generalization. The ration in hospitals was one and a half *livres* a day, and this was the amount an employer generally allowed to a servant in Paris. . . . Judged on the scale of calories, in a fair year, the workers of France were fed efficiently, so far as potential energy was concerned, but, as more than 90 per cent of these calories came from cereals (including maize porridge in the south and beer in the north), the dietary deficiencies are obvious. The food consumption of the inmates of the hospital of Caen (bread, and the unusual advantage of plenty of Norman cider), of the conscripts doing guard duty at the citadel of Saint-Malo in the mid-century (unimaginative bread, biscuits, and salt meat, with none of the coastal fish which ought to have diversified their diet), of the peasants of Périgord (chestnuts and maize in fearful stews kept simmering all day), of the peasants of Basse-Auvergne (bread, soup of nut oil, and water tinctured with wine) — all show the same deficiencies: a lack of meat, fish, dairy produce, and fresh vegetables. That meant a deficiency of vitamins, animal fats, calcium, and trace elements, leaving the way open for rickets, scurvy, skin eruptions, loss of teeth, the breaking down of the natural power of resistance to cold, and the stunting of growth, both physical and mental. It was a matter for wonder that men from mountain areas (where the pastures offered milk and meat) were so tall — as in Auvergne, where they towered over the puny inhabitants of the cereal-growing plain. . . . The ill effects of the inevitable deficiencies were increased by ignorance. . . . [T]here was little knowledge of what constituted a balanced diet. Even the rich did not know what was good for them. They ate a large amount of meat. . . . But an analysis of the meals eaten by a magistrate of Toulouse and of the pupils at a boarding-school for young nobles shows, even so, a lack of calcium and some vitamins. The food available to ordinary people was not always wisely used. The regulation stew-pot of the peasants boiled away the vitamins. . . . Fresh bread was unusual, since for economy, huge loaves which lasted for two or three months were baked in communal ovens. The oft-recorded obstinacy of peasants in refusing to eat unusual food like potatoes, even when starving, is paralleled by the refusal of the Parisians to accept the government economy bread of wheat, rye, and barley, invented during the dearth of 1767. And of course, the people were spendthrift; living on crusts and onions all week, they would go to drinking booths on Sunday night, or swig a tot of *eau-de-vie*[13] on their way to work in the mornings. But statistics of vitamin, calcium, and trace-element deficiencies can prove too much. Like the analysis of wages in eighteenth-century France, they go to show that half the population ought not to have been alive at all. Life, for these people, was "an economy of makeshifts," patching up a living by all sorts of incongruous combinations of earnings; no doubt they supplemented their food supplies by tilling odd corners, keeping animals in hutches, gleaning in hedgerow and common, begging, poaching, and pilfering. That was why it was so dangerous to become institutionalized, whether shut up in a *dépôt de mendicité*, a hospital, a madhouse, or on shipboard. Survival became difficult when there was no scope for enterprise.

    Whatever mysterious and useless medicines they prescribed, the doctors of eighteenth-century France knew the primary importance of sound nourishment to aid the sick to recovery. Meat soup was the standard prescription for all convalescents. . . . "Remedies and advice are useless unless there is a foundation of solid nourishment," said a physician called in to investigate the outbreak of dysentery in Anjou in 1707, and he asked for "bouillons" to be dispatched daily to all who had been afflicted. "Bread, wine, and blankets" were the prescriptions of the doctors of Anjou who dealt with epidemics of dysentery in 1768 and typhus in

---

[13] Brandy.

1774. In times of dearth, the poor were driven to eat contaminated or unripened grain, and were poisoned in consequence. . . . Officials in Brittany in 1769 and 1771 reported diseases (one called them of an "epileptic" kind) which were sweeping the provinces because the crop failures had driven the people to eat grain that had been damp when stored and had fermented and grown musty. . . . In the Sologne, there were outbreaks from time to time of ergotism caused by infected grain — the disease was called "St. Anthony's fire" and "dry gangrene": it led to the loss of fingers, noses, or whole limbs, and eventually to madness. And the greatest killer of all was contaminated water. Springs and wells would become infected as they dried up or floods overflowed them from dubious catchment areas, or were permanently dangerous because of defective masonry in cisterns, or because animals had access to them. Typical complaints concern effluent from flax-crushing or animal manure getting into drinking supplies, or froth from the oxen's mouths still floating on the top of buckets brought in for domestic consumption. In some villages without a well, water was collected in shallow holes dug here and there and had to be filtered through linen. And any Parisian who gave a thought to where his water supply came from would confine himself to drinking wine always — if he could afford it.

Certain seasons of the year brought the shadow of food shortages. There were the dangerous months . . . from April to July, when the previous year's grain was being used up, and before the new crop was harvested. There was a danger period too in winter, especially for townspeople, for freezing weather might ice up the canals along which the supply barges came, or stop the watermills from grinding the flour. And, worst of all, the crop might fail, damaged by unseasonable cold or rain or hail; rumour would race ahead of truth, encouraging the hoarding which transformed fear into the first instalment of grim reality.

It is generally said that the era of great famines ended in 1709; thereafter came shortages, serious indeed, but not deadly. . . . "In the seventeenth century people died of hunger: in the eighteenth they suffered from it." This is true so far as dying as a direct result of starvation is concerned, though local historians can always find a catastrophic year to form an exception worthy to qualify as the last of the crises. . . . A common-sense review of the probabilities of dying might suggest a logical sequence: famine, hunger weakening the resistance of the population, the resort to contaminated food causing illness, the onset of some killing disease, and the starving poor forced into vagabondage acting as carriers for the infection. In practice, in the eighteenth century this proposed pattern of death's operations is only occasionally borne out by comparisons of the graphs of corn prices, illness, and mortality. At Dijon in the 1740s, it seems clear that famine must have been the essential cause of the increase in the number of deaths, though an epidemic could strike at a particular place with an overwhelming impact only explainable by its own virulence. . . .

It has been argued, with eighteenth-century England as the example, that malnutrition does not weaken resistance to disease, except in the case of afflictions arising directly from deficiencies of diet, and tuberculosis and dysentery. A historian who has never known what it is to be hungry for very long instinctively feels inclined to doubt this assertion. True, studies of the Third World today show how deprived peoples can sometimes maintain themselves in calorific and protein balance on a diet that would mean starvation to the inhabitants of advanced countries. While bodily size and appearance are affected by the food supply, the same does not necessarily apply to resistance to infection. But there is a distinction to be made. While the nutrition taken by individuals seems not to have much effect on their chance of becoming infected with most diseases, it is of the utmost importance in deciding what their ultimate fate will be. "Malnutrition does not particularly favour or impede the acquisition of infection, but it goes a long way to determine the course of the resulting disease." The relationship between dearth and epidemic among the poorer classes of eighteenth-century France is not so much a short-term correspondence, but a general pattern of attrition by the alternations and the accumulated onslaughts of hunger and disease. The point may be taken, however, that pathogenic bacteria and viruses do not need to wait to find a human population weakened by famine before they strike; some apparently hopeless human groups may have built up an immunity, while some apparently flourishing ones may be unprotected. One disease may fade out, leaving the weak as predestinate victims for another; thus the plague vanished from Languedoc after 1655, and malaria took over, its victims forming a new reservoir of infection to pass on to future generations. We may picture death as vigilant but unhurried and patient. Sometimes hunger served its purposes, as in the terrible dearth in the spring of 1740 in Auvergne, where a *curé* reported that the women let their children die so that the adults could live, and the men, to avoid conceiving children, resorted to unnatural practices with animals. Sometimes some overwhelming contagion, like the plague of Marseille, swept away all human defences. It could be, in these disasters, that the swift succumbing of the physically weak was a precondition for a widespread pattern of infection which trapped the rich, who might otherwise have escaped. . . . More often, the continuing cycle of disease, hunger, renewed disease, and despair brought life to an end. There is a story of Louis XV encountering a funeral procession and asking what the man had died from. "Starvation, Sire." It was an indictment of his government, and the answer would have been true, indirectly, of many other deaths from infections and accidents. "C'est de misère que l'on meurt au dix-septième siècle."[14] . . . Though the situation was changing in the eighteenth century, this grim generalization was still broadly applicable. Particular diseases were the indispensable infantry in Death's dark armies, but his generals were Cold and Hunger.

---

[14] "It was destitution that brought on death in the seventeenth century."

THE GREAT CAT MASSACRE
Robert Darnton

Robert Darnton, Shelby Cullom Davis Professor of History at Princeton University, examines a slice of eighteenth-century daily life as seen through the eyes of Parisian workers. Although the history of humor and insult remains to be written, Darnton's essay suggests how rich, varied, and important that subject is. Darnton uncovered a bizarre incident in which a Parisian printer's apprentices and journeymen massacred cats. He wondered why those workers thought the slaughter hilarious and what else lay behind their deed besides a morbid sense of humor. This incident reveals the strained relationship between workers and their employer. Darnton also analyzes the importance of cats as historical symbols of sexuality and explores the economic and social divisions that separated artisanal workers from the bourgeois establishment. Darnton thus links humor to popular culture, labor conflict, and the relationships between different social groups and animals. He brings the reader face-to-face with the thinking and actions of eighteenth-century people, which are quite different from our own.

Why did popular culture tolerate the torture of animals? Why do you think the print-shop workers found the torture and killing of the cats to be gleeful? Why did the print-shop owner and his wife feel humiliated by the cat massacre? What sexual meanings and symbolism infused the workers' massacre of the cats? Do we use sexual symbolism in our political discourse?

The funniest thing that ever happened in the printing shop of Jacques Vincent, according to a worker who witnessed it, was a riotous massacre of cats. The worker, Nicolas Contat, told the story in an account of his apprenticeship in the shop, rue Saint-Séverin, Paris, during the late 1730s. Life as an apprentice was hard, he explained. There were two of them: Jerome, the somewhat fictionalized version of Contat himself, and Léveillé. They slept in a filthy, freezing room, rose before dawn, ran errands all day while dodging insults from the journeymen and abuse from the master, and received nothing but slops to eat. They found the food

Robert Darnton, *The Great Cat Massacre and Other Episodes in French Cultural History* (New York: Basic Books, 1984), 75–83, 85, 89–92, 94–101.

especially galling. Instead of dining at the master's table, they had to eat scraps from his plate in the kitchen. Worse still, the cook secretly sold the leftovers and gave the boys cat food — old, rotten bits of meat that they could not stomach and so passed on to the cats, who refused it.

This last injustice brought Contat to the theme of cats. They occupied a special place in his narrative and in the household of the rue Saint-Séverin. The master's wife adored them, especially *la grise* (the gray), her favorite. A passion for cats seemed to have swept through the printing trade, at least at the level of the masters, or *bourgeois* as the workers called them. One bourgeois kept twenty-five cats. He had their portraits painted and fed them on roast fowl. Meanwhile, the apprentices were trying to cope with a profusion of alley cats who also thrived in the printing district and made the boys' lives miserable. The cats howled all night on the roof over the apprentices' dingy bedroom, making it impossible to get a full night's sleep. As Jerome and Léveillé had to stagger out of bed at four or five in the morning to open the gate for the earliest arrivals among the journeymen, they began the day in a state of exhaustion while the bourgeois slept late. The master did not even work with the men, just as he did not eat with them. He let the foreman run the shop and rarely appeared in it, except to vent his violent temper, usually at the expense of the apprentices.

One night the boys resolved to right this inequitable state of affairs. Léveillé, who had an extraordinary talent for mimickry, crawled along the roof until he reached a section near the master's bedroom, and then he took to howling and meowing so horribly that the bourgeois and his wife did not sleep a wink. After several nights of this treatment, they decided they were being bewitched. But instead of calling the curé[1] — the master was exceptionally devout and the mistress exceptionally attached to her confessor — they commanded the apprentices to get rid of the cats. The mistress gave the order, enjoining the boys above all to avoid frightening her *grise*.

Gleefully Jerome and Léveillé set to work, aided by the journeymen. Armed with broom handles, bars of the press, and other tools of their trade, they went after every cat they could find, beginning with *la grise*. Léveillé smashed its spine with an iron bar and Jerome finished it off. Then they stashed it in a gutter while the journeymen drove the other cats across the rooftops, bludgeoning every one within reach and trapping those who tried to escape in strategically placed sacks. They dumped sackloads of half-dead cats in the courtyard. Then the entire workshop gathered round and staged a mock trial, complete with guards, a confessor, and a public executioner. After pronouncing the animals guilty and administering last rites, they strung them up on an improvised gallows. Roused by gales of laughter, the mistress arrived. She let out a shriek as soon as she saw a bloody cat dangling from a noose. Then she realized it might be *la grise*. Certainly not, the men assured her: they had too much respect for the house to do such a thing. At this point the master appeared. He flew into a rage at the general stoppage of

---

[1] Chief parish priest.

work, though his wife tried to explain that they were threatened by a more serious kind of insubordination. Then master and mistress withdrew, leaving the men delirious with "joy," "disorder," and "laughter."

The laughter did not end there. Léveillé reenacted the entire scene in mime at least twenty times during subsequent days when the printers wanted to knock off for some hilarity. Burlesque reenactments of incidents in the life of the shop, known as *copies* in printers' slang, provided a major form of entertainment for the men. The idea was to humiliate someone in the shop by satirizing his peculiarities. A successful *copie* would make the butt of the joke fume with rage — *prendre la chèvre* (take the goat) in the shop slang — while his mates razzed him with "rough music." They would run their composing sticks across the tops of the type cases, beat their mallets against the chases, pound on cupboards, and bleat like goats. The bleating (*bais* in the slang) stood for the humiliation heaped on the victims, as in English when someone "gets your goat." Contat emphasized that Léveillé produced the funniest *copies* anyone had ever known and elicited the greatest choruses of rough music. The whole episode, cat massacre compounded by *copies,* stood out as the most hilarious experience in Jerome's entire career.

Yet it strikes the modern reader as unfunny, if not downright repulsive. Where is the humor in a group of grown men bleating like goats and banging with their tools while an adolescent reenacts the ritual slaughter of a defenseless animal? Our own inability to get the joke is an indication of the distance that separates us from the workers of preindustrial Europe. The perception of that distance may serve as the starting point of an investigation, for anthropologists have found that the best points of entry in an attempt to penetrate an alien culture can be those where it seems to be most opaque. When you realize that you are not getting something — a joke, a proverb, a ceremony — that is particularly meaningful to the natives, you can see where to grasp a foreign system of meaning in order to unravel it. By getting the joke of the great cat massacre, it may be possible to "get" a basic ingredient of artisanal culture under the Old Regime.[2]

It should be explained at the outset that we cannot observe the killing of the cats at firsthand. We can study it only through Contat's narrative, written about twenty years after the event. There can be no doubt about the authenticity of Contat's quasi-fictional autobiography. . . . Because printers, or at least compositors,[3] had to be reasonably literate in order to do their work, they were among the few artisans who could give their own accounts of life in the working classes two, three, and four centuries ago. With all its misspellings and grammatical flaws, Contat's is perhaps the richest of these accounts. But it cannot be regarded as a mirror-image of what actually happened. It should be read as Contat's version of a happening, as his attempt to tell a story. Like all story telling, it sets the action in a frame of reference; it assumes a certain repertory of associations and responses on the part of its audience; and it provides meaningful shape to the raw

---

[2] The two centuries before the French Revolution of 1789.

[3] Typesetters.

stuff of experience. But since we are attempting to get at its meaning in the first place, we should not be put off by its fabricated character. On the contrary, by treating the narrative as fiction or meaningful fabrication we can use it to develop an ethnological *explication de texte.*[4]

The first explanation that probably would occur to most readers of Contat's story is that the cat massacre served as an oblique attack on the master and his wife. Contat set the event in the context of remarks about the disparity between the lot of workers and the bourgeois — a matter of the basic elements in life: work, food, and sleep. The injustice seemed especially flagrant in the case of the apprentices, who were treated like animals while the animals were promoted over their heads to the position the boys should have occupied, the place at the master's table. Although the apprentices seem most abused, the text makes it clear that the killing of the cats expressed a hatred for the bourgeois that had spread among all the workers: "The masters love cats; consequently [the workers] hate them." After masterminding the massacre, Léveillé became the hero of the shop, because "all the workers are in league against the masters. It is enough to speak badly of them [the masters] to be esteemed by the whole assembly of typographers."

Historians have tended to treat the era of artisanal manufacturing as an idyllic period before the onset of industrialization. Some even portray the workshop as a kind of extended family in which master and journeymen labored at the same tasks, ate at the same table, and sometimes slept under the same roof. Had anything happened to poison the atmosphere of the printing shops in Paris by 1740?

During the second half of the seventeenth century, the large printing houses, backed by the government, eliminated most of the smaller shops, and an oligarchy of masters seized control of the industry. At the same time, the situation of the journeymen deteriorated. Although estimates vary and statistics cannot be trusted, it seems that their number remained stable: approximately 335 in 1666, 339 in 1701, and 340 in 1721. Meanwhile the number of masters declined by more than half, from eighty-three to thirty-six, the limit fixed by an edict of 1686. That meant fewer shops with larger work forces, as one can see from statistics on the density of presses: in 1644 Paris had seventy-five printing shops with a total of 180 presses; in 1701 it had fifty-one shops with 195 presses. This trend made it virtually impossible for journeymen to rise into the ranks of the masters. About the only way for a worker to get ahead in the craft was to marry a master's widow, for masterships had become hereditary privileges, passed on from husband to wife and from father to son.

The journeymen also felt threatened from below because the masters tended increasingly to hire *alloués,* or underqualified printers, who had not undergone the apprenticeship that made a journeyman eligible, in principle, to advance to a mastership. The *alloués* were merely a source of cheap labor, excluded from the upper ranks of the trade and fixed, in their inferior status, by an edict of 1723.

---

[4] A detailed analysis of a literary work.

Their degradation stood out in their name: they were *à louer* (for hire), not *compagnons* (journeymen) of the master. They personified the tendency of labor to become a commodity instead of a partnership. Thus Contat served his apprenticeship and wrote his memoirs when times were hard for journeymen printers, when the men in the shop in the rue Saint-Séverin stood in danger of being cut off from the top of the trade and swamped from the bottom. . . .

Contat . . . began his description of Jerome's apprenticeship by invoking a golden age when printing was first invented and printers lived as free and equal members of a "republic," governed by its own laws and traditions in a spirit of fraternal "union and friendship." He claimed that the republic still survived in the form of the *chapelle* or workers' association in each shop. But the government had broken up general associations; the ranks had been thinned by *alloués;* the journeymen had been excluded from masterships; and the masters had withdrawn into a separate world of *haute cuisine*[5] and *grasses matinées.*[6] The master in the rue Saint-Séverin ate different food, kept different hours, and talked a different language. His wife and daughters dallied with worldly abbés.[7] They kept pets. Clearly, the bourgeois belonged to a different subculture — one which meant above all that he did not work. In introducing his account of the cat massacre, Contat made explicit the contrast between the worlds of worker and master that ran throughout the narrative: "Workers, apprentices, everyone works. Only the masters and mistresses enjoy the sweetness of sleep. That makes Jerome and Léveillé resentful. They resolve not to be the only wretched ones. They want their master and mistress as associates (associés)." That is, the boys wanted to restore a mythical past when masters and men worked in friendly association. They also may have had in mind the more recent extinction of the smaller printing shops. So they killed the cats.

But why cats? And why was the killing so funny? Those questions take us beyond the consideration of early modern labor relations and into the obscure subject of popular ceremonies and symbolism.

Folklorists have made historians familiar with the ceremonial cycles that marked off the calendar year for early modern man. The most important of these was the cycle of carnival and Lent,[8] a period of revelry followed by a period of abstinence. During carnival the common people suspended the normal rules of behavior and ceremoniously reversed the social order or turned it upside down in riotous procession. Carnival was a time for cutting up by youth groups, particularly apprentices, who organized themselves in "abbeys" ruled by a mock abbot or king and who staged charivaris or burlesque processions with rough music in order to humiliate cuckolds,[9] husbands who had been beaten by their wives,

---

[5] Gourmet food.

[6] Sleeping in; getting up late.

[7] Abbots. *Abbé* was also a courtesy title given to all ecclesiastics.

[8] In the Christian calendar, forty days of penitence and fasting before Easter.

[9] Husbands whose wives are having affairs.

brides who had married below their age group, or someone else who personified the infringement of traditional norms. Carnival was high season for hilarity, sexuality, and youth run riot — a time when young people tested social boundaries by limited outbursts of deviance, before being reassimilated in the world of order, submission, and Lentine seriousness. It came to an end on Shrove Tuesday or Mardi Gras,[10] when a straw mannequin, King Carnival or Caramantran, was given a ritual trial and execution. Cats played an important part in some charivaris. In Burgundy, the crowd incorporated cat torture into its rough music. While mocking a cuckold or some other victim, the youths passed around a cat, tearing its fur to make it howl. *Faire le chat*,[11] they called it. The Germans called charivaris *Katzenmusik*,[12] a term that may have been derived from the howls of tortured cats.

Cats also figured in the cycle of Saint John the Baptist,[13] which took place on June 24, at the time of the summer solstice. Crowds made bonfires, jumped over them, danced around them, and threw into them objects with magical power, hoping to avoid disaster and obtain good fortune during the rest of the year. A favorite object was cats — cats tied up in bags, cats suspended from ropes, or cats burned at the stake. Parisians liked to incinerate cats by the sackful, while the Courimauds (*cour à miaud* or cat chasers) of Saint Chamond preferred to chase a flaming cat through the streets. In parts of Burgundy and Lorraine they danced around a kind of burning May pole with a cat tied to it. In the Metz region they burned a dozen cats at a time in a basket on top of a bonfire. The ceremony took place with great pomp in Metz itself, until it was abolished in 1765. The town dignitaries arrived in procession at the Place du Grand-Saulcy, lit the pyre, and a ring of riflemen from the garrison fired off volleys while the cats disappeared screaming in the flames. Although the practice varied from place to place, the ingredients were everywhere the same: a *feu de joie* (bonfire), cats, and an aura of hilarious witch-hunting.

In addition to these general ceremonies, which involved entire communities, artisans celebrated ceremonies peculiar to their craft. Printers processed and feasted in honor of their patron, Saint John the Evangelist,[14] both on his saint's day, December 27, and on the anniversary of his martyrdom, May 6, the festival of Saint Jean Porte Latine.[15] By the eighteenth century, the masters had excluded the journeymen from the confraternity[16] devoted to the saint, but the journeymen

---

[10] In the Christian calendar, a festival the day before Lent.

[11] Playing games with cats.

[12] Cat music, caterwauling.

[13] In Christian legend, Jesus' cousin.

[14] Supposed author of the fourth Gospel and the Book of Revelation in the New Testament.

[15] Feast commemorating the legend that the aged John the Evangelist was thrown into a boiling cauldron outside the Latin Gate at Rome, survived, and went into exile.

[16] Religious association of laymen, often from the same occupation, that provided for the religious well-being of its members.

continued to hold ceremonies in their chapels. On Saint Martin's[17] day, November 11, they held a mock trial followed by a feast. Contat explained that the chapel was a tiny "republic," which governed itself according to its own code of conduct. When a worker violated the code, the foreman, who was the head of the chapel and not part of the management, entered a fine in a register. . . . On Saint Martin's, the foreman read out the fines and collected them. The workers sometimes appealed their cases before a burlesque tribunal composed of the chapel's "ancients,"[18] but in the end they had to pay up amidst more bleating, banging of tools, and riotous laughter. The fines went for food and drink in the chapel's favorite tavern, where the hell-raising continued until late in the night. . . .

So much for ceremonies. What about cats? It should be said at the outset that there is an indefinable *je ne sais quoi*[19] about cats, a mysterious something that has fascinated mankind since the time of the ancient Egyptians. One can sense a quasi-human intelligence behind a cat's eyes. One can mistake a cat's howl at night for a human scream, torn from some deep, visceral part of man's animal nature. . . .

This ambiguous ontological position, a straddling of conceptual categories, gives certain animals — pigs, dogs, and cassowaries[20] as well as cats — in certain cultures an occult power associated with the taboo. That is why Jews do not eat pigs . . . and why Englishmen can insult one another by saying "son-of-a-bitch" rather than "son-of-a-cow." . . . Certain animals are good for swearing. . . . I would add that others — cats in particular — are good for staging ceremonies. They have ritual value. You cannot make a charivari with a cow. You do it with cats: you decide to *faire le chat,* to make *Katzenmusik.*

The torture of animals, especially cats, was a popular amusement throughout early modern Europe. You have only to look at Hogarth's *Stages of Cruelty*[21] to see its importance, and once you start looking you see people torturing animals everywhere. Cat killings provided a common theme in literature, from *Don Quixote*[22] in early seventeenth-century Spain to *Germinal*[23] in late nineteenth-century France. Far from being a sadistic fantasy on the part of a few half-crazed authors, the literary versions of cruelty to animals expressed a deep current of popular culture. . . . All sorts of ethnographic reports confirm that view. On the *dimanche des brandons*[24] in Semur, for example, children used to attach cats to poles and roast

---

[17] Bishop of Tours and a patron saint of France (d. 397).

[18] Workers with seniority.

[19] Something that cannot be explained fully.

[20] Large flightless birds related to the ostrich.

[21] English painter (1697–1764) known for satirical pictures of eighteenth-century lowlife. *Stages of Cruelty* (1751) tells the story of a sadist's progress from torturing animals to murder.

[22] The Spaniard Miguel de Cervantes's (1547–1616) satirical novel (1605).

[23] The French writer Émile Zola's (1840–1902) novel (1885) about a coal strike.

[24] Sunday of the firebrands.

them over bonfires. In the *jeu du chat*[25] at the Fete-Dieu[26] in Aix-en-Provence, they threw cats high in the air and smashed them on the ground. They used expressions like "patient as a cat whose claws are being pulled out" or "patient as a cat whose paws are being grilled." The English were just as cruel. During the Reformation in London, a Protestant crowd shaved a cat to look like a priest, dressed it in mock vestments, and hanged it on the gallows at Cheapside. It would be possible to string out many other examples, but the point should be clear: there was nothing unusual about the ritual killing of cats. On the contrary, when Jerome and his fellow workers tried and hanged all the cats they could find in the rue Saint-Séverin, they drew on a common element in their culture. But what significance did that culture attribute to cats?

To get a grip on that question, one must rummage through collections of folktales, superstitions, proverbs, and popular medicine. The material is rich, varied, and vast but extremely hard to handle. Although much of it goes back to the Middle Ages, little can be dated. It was gathered for the most part by folklorists in the late nineteenth and early twentieth centuries, when sturdy strains of folklore still resisted the influence of the printed word. But the collections do not make it possible to claim that this or that practice existed in the printing houses of mid-eighteenth-century Paris. One can only assert that printers lived and breathed in an atmosphere of traditional customs and beliefs which permeated everything. . . .

First and foremost, cats suggested witchcraft. To cross one at night in virtually any corner of France was to risk running into the devil or one of his agents or a witch abroad on an evil errand. . . . Witches transformed themselves into cats in order to cast spells on their victims. Sometimes, especially on Mardi Gras, they gathered for hideous sabbaths at night. They howled, fought, and copulated horribly under the direction of the devil himself in the form of a huge tomcat. To protect yourself from sorcery by cats there was one, classic remedy: maim it. Cut its tail, clip its ears, smash one of its legs, tear or burn its fur, and you would break its malevolent power. A maimed cat could not attend a sabbath or wander abroad to cast spells. Peasants frequently cudgeled cats who crossed their paths at night and discovered the next day that bruises had appeared on women believed to be witches — or so it was said in the lore of their village. Villagers also told stories of farmers who found strange cats in barns and broke their limbs to save the cattle. Invariably a broken limb would appear on a suspicious woman the following morning.

Cats possessed occult power independently of their association with witchcraft and deviltry. They could prevent the bread from rising if they entered bakeries in Anjou. They could spoil the catch if they crossed the path of fishermen in Brittany. If buried alive in Béarn, they could clear a field of weeds. They figured as staple ingredients in all kinds of folk medicine aside from witches' brews. . . .

---

[25] Cat play.

[26] The feast of Corpus Christi, a Christian holiday commemorating Holy Communion.

There was a specific field for the exercise of cat power: the household and particularly the person of the master or mistress of the house. Folktales like "Puss 'n Boots"[27] emphasized the identification of master and cat, and so did superstitions such as the practice of tying a black ribbon around the neck of a cat whose mistress had died. To kill a cat was to bring misfortune upon its owner or its house. If a cat left a house or stopped jumping on the sickbed of its master or mistress, the person was likely to die. But a cat lying on the bed of a dying man might be the devil, waiting to carry his soul off to hell. . . . Cats could harm a house. They often smothered babies. They understood gossip and would repeat it out of doors. But their power could be contained or turned to your advantage if you followed the right procedures, such as greasing their paws with butter or maiming them when they first arrived. To protect a new house, Frenchmen enclosed live cats within its walls — a very old rite, judging from cat skeletons that have been exhumed from the walls of medieval buildings.

Finally, the power of cats was concentrated on the most intimate aspect of domestic life: sex. *Le chat, la chatte, le minet* mean the same thing in French slang as "pussy" does in English, and they have served as obscenities for centuries. French folklore attaches special importance to the cat as a sexual metaphor or metonym. As far back as the fifteenth century, the petting of cats was recommended for success in courting women. Proverbial wisdom identified women with cats: "He who takes good care of cats will have a pretty wife." If a man loved cats, he would love women; and vice versa: "As he loves his cat, he loves his wife," went another proverb. If he did not care for his wife, you could say of him, "He has other cats to whip." A woman who wanted to get a man should avoid treading on a cat's tail. She might postpone marriage for a year — or for seven years in Quimper and for as many years as the cat meowed in parts of the Loire Valley. Cats connoted fertility and female sexuality everywhere. Girls were commonly said to be "in love like a cat"; and if they became pregnant, they had "let the cat go to the cheese." Eating cats could bring on pregnancy in itself. Girls who consumed them in stews gave birth to kittens in several folktales. Cats could even make diseased apple trees bear fruit, if buried in the correct manner in upper Brittany.

It was an easy jump from the sexuality of women to the cuckolding of men. Caterwauling could come from a satanic orgy, but it might just as well be toms howling defiance at each other when their mates were in heat. They did not call as cats, however. They issued challenges in their masters' names, along with sexual taunts about their mistresses: "Reno! Francois!" "Où allez-vous? — Voir la femme à vous. — Voir la femme à moi! Rouah!" (Where are you going? — To see your wife. — To see my wife! Ha!) Then the toms would fly at each other like the cats of Kilkenny,[28] and their sabbath would end in a massacre. The dialogue dif-

---

[27] A children's story about a cat that dresses in his master's clothes.

[28] A nursery rhyme about cats who fought so fiercely that one could not tell where one cat ended and the other began.

fered according to the imaginations of the listeners and the onomatopoetic[29] power of their dialect, but it usually emphasized predatory sexuality. "At night all cats are gray," went the proverb, and the gloss in an eighteenth-century proverb collection made the sexual hint explicit: "That is to say that all women are beautiful enough at night." Enough for what? Seduction, rape, and murder echoed in the air when the cats howled at night in early modern France. Cat calls summoned up *Katzenmusik,* for charivaris often took the form of howling under a cuckold's window on the eve of Mardi Gras, the favorite time for cat sabbaths.

Witchcraft, orgy, cuckoldry, charivari, and massacre, the men of the Old Regime could hear a great deal in the wail of a cat. What the men of the rue Saint-Séverin actually heard is impossible to say. One can only assert that cats bore enormous symbolic weight in the folklore of France and that the lore was rich, ancient, and widespread enough to have penetrated the printing shop. In order to determine whether the printers actually drew on the ceremonial and symbolic themes available to them, it is necessary to take another look at Contat's text.

The text made the theme of sorcery explicit from the beginning. Jerome and Léveillé could not sleep because "some bedeviled cats make a sabbath all night long." After Léveillé added his cat calls to the general caterwauling, "the whole neighborhood is alarmed. It is decided that the cats must be agents of someone casting a spell." The master and mistress considered summoning the curé to exorcise the place. In deciding instead to commission the cat hunt, they fell back on the classic remedy for witchcraft: maiming. The bourgeois — a superstitious, priest-ridden fool — took the whole business seriously. To the apprentices it was a joke. . . . Not only did the apprentices exploit their master's superstition in order to run riot at his expense, but they also turned their rioting against their mistress. By bludgeoning her familiar, *la grise,* they in effect accused her of being the witch. The double joke would not be lost on anyone who could read the traditional language of gesture.

The theme of charivari provided an additional dimension to the fun. Although it never says so explicitly, the text indicates that the mistress was having an affair with her priest, a "lascivious youth," who had memorized obscene passages from the classics of pornography . . . and quoted them to her, while her husband droned on about his favorite subjects, money and religion. During a lavish dinner with the family, the priest defended the thesis "that it is a feat of wit to cuckold one's husband and that cuckolding is not a vice." Later, he and the wife spent the night together in a country house. They fit perfectly into the typical triangle of printing shops: a doddering old master, a middle-aged mistress, and her youthful lover. The intrigue cast the master in the role of a stock comic figure: the cuckold. So the revelry of the workers took the form of a charivari. The apprentices managed it, operating within the liminal area where novitiates traditionally mocked their superiors, and the journeymen responded to their antics in the tra-

---

[29] Naming an action or thing by the sound associated with it.

ditional way, with rough music. A riotous, festival atmosphere runs through the whole episode, which Contat described as a *fête*:[30] "Léveillé and his comrade Jerome preside over the *fête*," he wrote, as if they were kings of a carnival and the cat bashing corresponded to the torturing of cats on Mardi Gras or the *fête* of Saint John the Baptist.

As in many Mardi Gras, the carnival ended in a mock trial and execution. The burlesque legalism came naturally to the printers because they staged their own mock trials every year at the *fête* of Saint Martin, when the chapel squared accounts with its boss and succeeded spectacularly in getting his goat. The chapel could not condemn him explicitly without moving into open insubordination and risking dismissal. . . . So the workers tried the bourgeois in absentia, using a symbol that would let their meaning show through without being explicit enough to justify retaliation. They tried and hanged the cats. It would be going too far to hang *la grise* under the master's nose after being ordered to spare it; but they made the favorite pet of the house their first victim, and in doing so they knew they were attacking the house itself, in accordance with the traditions of cat lore. When the mistress accused them of killing *la grise,* they replied with mock deference that "nobody would be capable of such an outrage and that they have too much respect for that house." By executing the cats with such elaborate ceremony, they condemned the house and declared the bourgeois guilty — guilty of overworking and underfeeding his apprentices, guilty of living in luxury while his journeymen did all the work, guilty of withdrawing from the shop and swamping it with *alloués* instead of laboring and eating with the men, as masters were said to have done a generation or two earlier, or in the primitive "republic" that existed at the beginning of the printing industry. The guilt extended from the boss to the house to the whole system. Perhaps in trying, confessing, and hanging a collection of half-dead cats, the workers meant to ridicule the entire legal and social order. . . .

Cats as symbols conjured up sex as well as violence, a combination perfectly suited for an attack on the mistress. The narrative identified her with *la grise,* her *chatte favorite.*[31] In killing it, the boys struck at her: "It was a matter of consequence, a murder, which had to be hidden." The mistress reacted as if she had been assaulted: "They ravished from her a cat without an equal, a cat that she loved to madness." The text described her as lascivious and "impassioned for cats" as if she were a she-cat in heat during a wild cat's sabbath of howling, killing, and rape. An explicit reference to rape would violate the proprieties that were generally observed in eighteenth-century writing. Indeed, the symbolism would work only if it remained veiled — ambivalent enough to dupe the master and sharp enough to hit the mistress in the quick. But Contat used strong language. As soon as the mistress saw the cat execution she let out a scream. Then the scream was smothered in the realization that she had lost her *grise.* The workers assured

---

[30] Festival.

[31] Favorite pussy.

her with feigned sincerity of their respect and the master arrived. "'Ah! the scoundrels,' he says. 'Instead of working they are killing cats.' Madame to Monsieur: 'These wicked men can't kill the masters; they have killed my cat.' . . . It seems to her that all the blood of the workers would not be sufficient to redeem the insult."

. . . By assaulting her pet, the workers ravished the mistress symbolically. At the same time, they delivered the supreme insult to their master. His wife was his most precious possession, just as her *chatte* was hers. In killing the cat, the men violated the most intimate treasure of the bourgeois household and escaped unharmed. That was the beauty of it. The symbolism disguised the insult well enough for them to get away with it. While the bourgeois fumed over the loss of work, his wife, less obtuse, virtually told him that the workers had attacked her sexually and would like to murder him. Then both left the scene in humiliation and defeat. . . .

. . . The question remains, however, what precisely was so funny about the cat massacre? There is no better way to ruin a joke than to analyze it or to overload it with social comment. But this joke cries out for commentary — not because one can use it to prove that artisans hated their bosses (a truism that may apply to all periods of labor history, although it has not been appreciated adequately by eighteenth-century historians), but because it can help one to see how workers made their experience meaningful by playing with themes of their culture. . . .

. . . [I]t seems clear that the workers found the massacre funny because it gave them a way to turn the tables on the bourgeois. By goading him with cat calls, they provoked him to authorize the massacre of cats, then they used the massacre to put him symbolically on trial for unjust management of the shop. They also used it as a witch hunt, which provided an excuse to kill his wife's familiar and to insinuate that she herself was the witch. Finally, they transformed it into a charivari, which served as a means to insult her sexually while mocking him as a cuckold. The bourgeois made an excellent butt of the joke. Not only did he become the victim of a procedure he himself had set in motion, he did not understand how badly he had been had. The men had subjected his wife to symbolic aggression of the most intimate kind, but he did not get it. He was too thick-headed, a classic cuckold. The printers ridiculed him in splendid Boccaccian[32] style and got off scot-free.

The joke worked so well because the workers played so skillfully with a repertory of ceremonies and symbols. Cats suited their purposes perfectly. By smashing the spine of *la grise* they called the master's wife a witch and a slut, while at the same time making the master into a cuckold and a fool. It was metonymic[33]

---

[32] Ribald and boisterous, from Giovanni Boccaccio's (1313–1375) collection of stories, the *Decameron*.

[33] A figure of speech that uses the name of one thing for something else with which it is associated.

insult, delivered by actions, not words, and it struck home because cats occupied a soft spot in the bourgeois way of life. Keeping pets was as alien to the workers as torturing animals was to the bourgeois. . . .

The workers also punned with ceremonies. They made a roundup of cats into a witch hunt, a festival, a charivari, a mock trial, and a dirty joke. Then they redid the whole thing in pantomime. Whenever they got tired of working, they transformed the shop into a theater and produced *copies* — their kind of copy, not the authors'. Shop theater and ritual punning suited the traditions of their craft. Although printers made books, they did not use written words to convey their meaning. They used gestures, drawing on the culture of their craft to inscribe statements in the air.

Insubstantial as it may seem today, this joking was a risky business in the eighteenth century. The risk was part of the joke, as in many forms of humor, which toy with violence and tease repressed passions. The workers pushed their symbolic horseplay to the brink of reification, the point at which the killing of cats would turn into an open rebellion. They played on ambiguities, using symbols that would hide their full meaning while letting enough of it show through to make a fool of the bourgeois without giving him a pretext to fire them. They tweaked his nose and prevented him from protesting against it. To pull off such a feat required great dexterity. It showed that workers could manipulate symbols in their idiom as effectively as poets did in print.

The boundaries within which this jesting had to be contained suggest the limits to working-class militancy under the Old Regime. The printers identified with their craft rather than their class. Although they organized in chapels, staged strikes, and sometimes forced up wages, they remained subordinate to the bourgeois. The master hired and fired men as casually as he ordered paper, and he turned them out into the road when he sniffed insubordination. So . . . they generally kept their protests on a symbolic level. A *copie,* like a carnival, helped to let off steam; but it also produced laughter, a vital ingredient in early artisanal culture and one that has been lost in labor history. By seeing the way a joke worked in the horseplay of a printing shop two centuries ago, we may be able to recapture that missing element — laughter, sheer laughter, the thigh-slapping, rib-cracking Rabelaisian[34] kind, rather than the Voltairian[35] smirk with which we are familiar.

---

[34] Coarse satire and humor, as in the works of the French novelist François Rabelais (ca. 1494–ca. 1553).

[35] Characterized by sardonic humor, as in the works of Voltaire (1694–1778), the French intellectual.

WOMEN AND WORK
Olwen Hufton

The idea of equal pay for equal work did not exist in early modern Europe. Using autobiographies, letters, and quantifiable sources (such as demographic information), Olwen Hufton, Leverhulme Research Professor, Merton College, University of Oxford, shows that European women had more difficulty finding employment than did men, that their work was often harder, and that their pay was always less. Women helped propel the economy, but their diligence did not relieve them of constant worry, long hours, and low wages. Moreover, the slightest economic downturn brought them less work and more suffering, for they inevitably lost their jobs before men did.

Although she explains the economic situations of aristocrats and women of middling families, Olwen Hufton concentrates on working-class women. On the one hand, she offers a depressing account of the wretched reality of their existence. For example, single women toiled for years to accumulate dowries and work skills so that they could attract husbands. On the other hand, resourcefulness pervaded women's lives as they attempted to cope with the labor market and their own circumstances, whether they were single, married, or widowed.

Note how the work life of married women could vary significantly from that of single women and how marriage influenced women differently according to a husband's social status. Hufton states that economic considerations were the major factor in the choice of a marriage partner. In fact, marriage was a significant goal for single working women, whereas widowhood and spinsterhood often doomed women to poverty and economic insecurity. Hufton thus depicts bleak economic lives for most women in early modern Europe, despite their active engagement in the economy. Accordingly, the adage that "a woman's work is never done" rings true, for a woman, in addition to long hours of work outside the home, had other responsibilities, including helping a husband in his business and running a household.

How did social and economic developments, such as the population increase from the sixteenth through the eighteenth centuries, affect women's work?

Olwen Hufton, "Women, Work, and Family," in *A History of Women in the West,* ed. Natalie Zemon Davis and Arlette Farge, vol. 3 of *Renaissance and Enlightenment Paradoxes* (Cambridge: Belknap Press of Harvard University Press, 1993), 15–34, 38–45.

Do you think women fared better in farm work, in domestic service, or in industrial labor? Women made up most of the labor force in certain sections of the economy, as servants or in the silk and lace industries, for example. What factors determined the employment opportunities for women in towns and in the countryside? What are the similarities and differences between the eighteenth-century and the present-day working-class family?

When the essayist Richard Steele sought in 1710 to define woman, he did so in a terse but, by the standards of the day, fully acceptable manner: "A woman is a daughter, a sister, a wife and a mother, a mere appendage of the human race. . . ."

A good woman, one such as to merit the praise of men, might find herself commemorated as did the Elizabethan noblewoman Marie Dudley on her funeral monument in St. Margaret's Westminster:

> Here lyeth entombed Marie Dudley, daughter of William Howard of Effingham, in his time Lord High Admiral of England, Lord Chamberlain and Lord Privy Seal. She was grandchild to Thomas Duke of Norfolk . . . and Sister to Charles Howard, Earl of Nottingham, High Admiral of England by whose prosperous direction through the goodness of God in defending his lady Queen Elizabeth,[1] the whole fleet of Spain was defeated and discomforted.[2] She was first married to Edward Sutton, Lord Dudley and after to Richard Monpesson Esquire who in memory of his love erected this monument to her.

From the moment a girl was born in lawful wedlock, irrespective of her social origins she was defined by her relationship to a man. She was in turn the legal responsibility of her father and her husband, both of whom, it was recommended, she should honor and obey. Father or husband, it was assumed, served as a buffer between her and the harsh realities of the violent outside world. She was expected to be the economic dependent of the man who controlled her life. The duty of a father, according to the model, was to provide for his child until her marriage, when he, or someone on his behalf, negotiated a settlement for his daughter with a groom. A husband expected to be compensated at the outset of marriage for taking a particular woman to wife. Thereafter he was responsible for her well-being, but her contribution at the moment of marriage was critical in the establishment of the new household.

This model had rigorous application in upper- and middle-class society throughout the early modern period. Marriage settlements for children were interpreted, in the language of the day, as "the weightiest business" a family could undertake. Ideally, the money and resources that a female child took from her family purchased her future well-being and enhanced the standing of her kin through the new alliance. A woman's dependency was a closely negotiated item.

---

[1] Elizabeth I (1558–1603) established Anglicanism and led England to victory over Spain.

[2] Disheartened or sorrowful.

For most women, the model could not be so completely applied. Women of the working classes were expected to work to support themselves both when single and when married. . . .

Notwithstanding the obligation to labor in their own support, society did not envisage that women could or should live in total independence. Indeed, the independent woman was seen as unnatural and abhorrent. It was assumed that father and husband would provide her with a home and hence contribute in some degree to her maintenance. This assumption was reflected in customary female wages: a woman could be paid less for her labors because a man put a roof above her head. If a woman could not find work to keep her in her own home before marriage, a substitute protective environment must be sought for her. She must enter her employer's home. He would assume the role of protective male figure and be responsible for the costs of feeding and sheltering her and would stand *in loco parentis*[3] until she left to work elsewhere, to return home, or to marry. The wages he paid her would reflect the fact that she was fed and sheltered. Ideally, she would spend as little of these wages as possible, and her employer would save them for her and place them in her hands when she left his home.

The target of the single woman's working life was thus explicit: while sparing her own family the cost of feeding her, she was in the business of accumulating a dowry and work skills to attract a husband. When no more than a child, she was taught by her family and the society in which she lived that life was a struggle against grinding poverty and that for long-term survival she needed a husband to provide shelter and aid. Such realizations were what impelled about 80 percent of country girls to leave home at about age twelve — two years before their brothers did so — to begin equipping themselves for the time when they might hope to marry. From the moment of her departure, the average European girl began a ten- or twelve-year phase of her working life, upon the success of which her future depended. The prospect may have been daunting and frightening, and the pitfalls were known to be many. Childhood was brief for the daughters of the poor.

The female children of smallholders, agricultural laborers, or odd-job men commanded few skills beyond those transmitted by their mothers — perhaps no more than the ability to sew, spin, perform simple farm tasks, or care for younger children. Demand for work as a residential farm servant was very high, far outstripping the supply. Residential work for women in the agricultural sector was limited to large establishments, especially dairy farms, where milking and cheese and butter making were the work of women. There was great competition for farm jobs because they offered servant girls the chance to remain near their families and to avoid an abrupt change in their way of life. . . .

Throughout Europe, family contacts accounted for most placements in farm jobs. In some regions of France, such as Champagne, the spread of cottage industry led to an increase in the number of farm servants because it made possi-

---

[3] In the place of parents.

ble ancillary industrial labor that contributed to a girl's keep during the dead season. The availability of farm work thus varied from region to region. But overall,
by the end of the eighteenth century this kind of work became increasingly scarce,
in part as a result of demographic growth, in part as a result of the emergence of
larger commercial farms and greater regional specialization. In other areas the
overproliferation of smallholdings as a result of population growth reduced the
keeping of livestock and the ability to maintain a female servant. When the cow
was missing from the landscape, there were few female farm workers.

The girl who could not find farm work near home looked townward, although she did not necessarily have to go very far; the nearest town of five or six
thousand might afford her work as a maidservant, ranging from the lowest resident drudge, who carried heavy loads of laundry to and from the local washplace
or loads of vegetables from the market and emptied privies, to cook and cleaner.
The demand for urban domestic service appears to have increased considerably
throughout the early modern period, reflecting both growing affluence in some
sectors of urban society and the cheapness of the labor on offer. Again, the best
jobs came through family and village contacts.

The potential for local jobs was usually exhausted before a young girl ventured farther afield. When she did so, it was usually along a well-established
route, and at her destination she would find neighbors' daughters and kinsfolk in
the vicinity. In short, young girls were rarely pioneers. Sometimes they followed
an established migratory flow set up by male seasonal migrants, like the girls of
the Massif Central[4] who went down to Montpellier or Béziers to work as servants
and whose brothers came down every year to the region to pick grapes; or those
of South Wales who stayed in the London area as maidservants after accompanying their male relatives to work in the market gardens of Kent and who made
contacts while ferrying fruit and vegetables to Covent Garden.[5]

Female servants constituted the largest occupational group in urban society,
accounting for about 12 percent of the total population of any European town or
city throughout the seventeenth and eighteenth centuries. . . . [I]n 1806 . . . London had as many as 200,000 servants of both sexes but . . . there were twice as
many women as men. . . .

Types and conditions of service must have varied widely. Much depended
upon the status of the employer. Servants were an indicator of social standing, and
since female labor was cheap and abundant, it was one of the first luxuries even
a modest family permitted itself. But although certain ducal families such as the
House of Orleans[6] or the Dukes of Marlborough[7] counted their household servants in hundreds, it was unusual for even the most extensive aristocratic house-

---

[4] Large plateau in south central France.

[5] London's main fruit and vegetable market.

[6] Junior branch of the French royal family.

[7] Descendants of John Churchill (1650–1722), brilliant British general during the War of the
Spanish Succession (1702–1714).

hold to employ more than thirty servants of both sexes. The gentry and affluent merchants in the great cities might have six or seven. Indeed, one definition of a poor noble throughout the period was someone who had only three servants. In seventeenth-century Amsterdam, however, which had more than its share of wealthy merchants, one or two servants was the norm; and this was perhaps the commonest urban model. The fewer the number of servants, the likelier it was that all the servants would be women.

In the hierarchy of employees of both sexes maintained by an aristocratic household — cooks, coachmen, footmen, butlers, ladies' maids, chambermaids, laundrymaids, grooms, scullery maids, and so on — women held many of the jobs at the bottom. Modest households employed a maid of all work — for which there is an equally cumbersome phrase in most European languages. Tradesmen might employ a girl both to work in the shop and to run errands delivering and picking up work; tavernkeepers employed girls as barmaids, waitresses, and washers up; busy housewives helping in family businesses such as cookshops and bakeries employed girls to do anything from turning a hand in commercial food production to taking the family's washing to the washplace, carrying or pumping water, or lighting and maintaining ovens and fires.

The best jobs were gained through contacts and by ascending the servant hierarchy as one acquired experience and skill. However, a great deal depended upon good fortune and the kind of qualifications one had at the outset. Employers were concerned that a girl have an honest background and would not open the door to a pack of thieving relatives or disappear into the night with the family silver. . . .

The girl who entered a multiple-servant household at the bottom could expect to come by a variety of skills in kitchen service and in laundry work, tending and repairing linen. After a few years of washing dishes and scrubbing floors, lighting fires, and fetching and carrying coal, water, and slops, if she maintained a neat air and had a degree of good looks and a trim figure, she might advance to parlormaid. With a measure of good luck, which might include resisting the advances of employer or, more probably, fellow servant, she might find her way upstairs to chambermaid or lady's maid.

However, at each stage of the upward journey, she faced competition or came up against the limited demands of the household of which she was a member. If she was ambitious she must move "for her preferment." Hence the intense mobility within the world of domestic service by the end of the eighteenth century and the fading image, much bemoaned and exaggerated by the affluent, of the long-term retainer. Mobility was made possible by contact and recommendation and, in Britain, the newspaper. However, competition at the upper end of the scale was intense; one advertisement for a lady's maid would bring scores of applicants.

There were many girls, however, who could not compete in the career structure of service, and the immiseration of certain regions as a result of demographic growth in the sixteenth and eighteenth centuries brought many from the countryside into the towns. These girls were chronically poor, undernourished, rickety, pockmarked, dirty, and lice-ridden. They lacked the training that fitted them for employment in even a modest household. Girls from entire regions — and, in the case of Ireland, from an entire nation — who arrived in British cities seeking work were automatically excluded by the very poverty of their backgrounds from anything approaching a respectable situation as a servant.

Service, then, embraced a vast range of conditions. For a small minority it had a career structure, and in her mid-twenties a maidservant who had managed to become a chambermaid or lady's maid would have a respectable capital sum, the amount depending upon her ability to accumulate without cutting into her wages to help her family or to cope with periods of illness or unemployment. At the other end of the scale were the vast majority of women whose work was wretched, volatile, dependent upon the honesty of the employer and upon staying constantly in work so that they did not eat into their reserves. A maidservant who became pregnant was simply dismissed. In the middle were those who by their mid-twenties might have fifty pounds to their names, a modest sum but a personal triumph.

In some industrial areas, which relied on a reservoir of cheap female labor, the domiciled servant was in fact the resident textile worker. Cheap female labor was critical in the development of European textile industries, such as the silk industry at Lyons. Silk was a costly delicate fabric intended for the wealthy and prepared from start to finish in urban workshops under the supervision of a master. Female labor was used to empty the silk cocoons, twist the thread, wind the shuttles, and draw them through the loom to achieve patterned effects of great complexity. The work of men was to set up and pull the loom. Every workshop included a minimum of three to four girls, a male apprentice, the master, and his wife. Over the industry as a whole, female workers outnumbered males by five to one. . . . Girls of twelve and fourteen started work in the lowest job, that of cocoon unwinder, sitting over basins of scalding water into which they plunged the cocoons to melt the sericine, the sticky substance binding the cocoon together. Their clothes were continually damp, their fingers lost sensitivity, and tuberculosis was rampant. Still, if she could survive without long periods of unemployment — during the frequent slumps, girls were unceremoniously shown the door — and advance to draw girl, then after about fourteen years a female silk worker had not only a sum of money but also a wide range of industrial skills. She was the ideal wife for the ambitious apprentice because she could provide him with the lump sum to pay for his mastership and contribute to the running of a new workshop.

The lace industry, too, could be organized on a resident basis to help young girls accumulate a dowry. From the purchase of raw thread through the actual fabrication to the sale of the finished product to the wholesaler, the lace industry tended to be entirely in the hands of women — an unusual state of affairs in European handicrafts. Lace was the costliest textile commodity in Europe. . . . The value lay entirely in the handiwork, and many years were required to learn the skill. Yet the remuneration was at the lowest level of female wages: in France a day's labor might provide a couple of pounds of bread. In lace areas tens of thousands of women were involved in production. In some of these areas, notably in Flanders, where the best lace was made, and in the Pays du Velay in France, philanthropic effort achieved the seemingly impossible and converted lace production into a small dowry-raising enterprise. In Flanders convents taught lacemaking to children for nothing and, when they were proficient, put aside a little of their wages to help them accumulate a small lump sum. When they married they could become outworkers or come to the convent workshops, where they did not have to pay lighting and heating costs. In the Velay there were no such convents, but groups of pious women called Béates,[8] backed by some philanthropic money, ran lace dormitories in the city of Le Puy free of charge and negotiated the sale of work with the merchants to see that the lacemakers got the best price. After a small deduction for food, they held onto the proceeds of the sale to help the girls accumulate their precious dowries. After marriage these young women could work at home, and the Béates, by invitation of the villages, ran communal houses where the village women could congregate and share lighting costs and a common soup pot.

Silk and lace production were thus tailored to bring girls into the towns, teach them a craft, and help them with their dowries. . . .

Except in a few industrial cities, a girl born of working-class parents in a town or city was unlikely to become either a domestic servant or a textile worker. Instead, as censuses make clear, she pursued one of a limited number of options in the garment trades (as seamstress, mantua maker,[9] milliner,[10] glove stitcher, embroiderer) or service trades (as washerwoman, street seller, stall operator). Or, perhaps most commonly, she contributed to a family business, working at home.

In most European towns girls' work options were limited by the restrictions of the guilds, which regulated the urban world of skilled work with varying comprehensiveness. The daughters and wives of tradesmen involved themselves in aspects of artisanal production, but most guilds resisted women's attempts to enter their specialties. Resistance to women in guild-regulated production often came less from the masters than from their workmen, who were afraid that women would work for less and hence undercut journeymen's wages. When work was plentiful and labor scarce, the guilds were relatively tolerant and turned a blind eye to women's activities in their sphere; but when times were hard, attitudes changed. . . .

By the late eighteenth century the guilds were fast disappearing in Britain and France. Even so, women existed most easily in newer trades such as millinery and mantua making, which had no medieval antecedents. During the eighteenth century work became more plentiful, particularly in the garment trades, but as the number of women seeking such employment increased, the work became iden-

[8] Blessed ones.

[9] Dressmaker.

[10] Maker of women's hats.

tified as "women's work," and wages fell accordingly. *Campbell's Directory of London* in 1762 placed all the garment trades practiced by women in the category of pauper work, exposing the incumbent to dire necessity and providing the recruiting ground for prostitution.

At a somewhat lower level than that of the solid artisan family the mother was more likely than the father to shape the choice of a daughter's job. The washerwoman's daughter became a washerwoman, the seamstress' daughter a seamstress, and the innkeeper's daughter stayed at home and served the beer and victuals. The tendency of urban parents to absorb their female children into a work pattern perhaps explains the relatively small number of recorded formal apprenticeships for women. Indeed, those who sought such apprenticeships were likely to be either orphans, on whose behalf orphanages sought guaranteed work and protection, or girls whose parents were in work that could not absorb them and who lacked relatives such as a seamstress aunt who could provide structured help. These two categories sought formal apprenticeship not because the training would guarantee a girl a better job but because they needed assurance of continuous training leading to regular employment. . . .

Most women in fact married as the model insisted they should. Between 1550 and 1800 the proportion of women who died above the age of 50 in the celibate state varied from 5 to 25 percent. The highest levels occurred in the mid-1600s but fell dramatically over the next century; permanent spinsters constituted something under 10 percent of the population by the end of the eighteenth century. In the seventeenth century more French women married than English women, but thereafter the number of French spinsters began to rise, and by 1789 about 14 percent of those dying over the age of 50 had never married. In the seventeenth century, English women married on average at the age of 26, but by the end of the eighteenth century at just over 23. In France, women's average age at marriage at the beginning of the seventeenth century, 22, rose gradually to 26.5 on the eve of the Revolution. . . .

Whom one married depended upon one's class, in some instances upon birth position — the oldest daughter of an upper-class family usually had priority — and upon the size of one's dowry. Most women did not marry beneath themselves. An aristocratic heiress had the pick of the market. The daughters of clergymen, doctors, and lawyers married men in the same profession as their fathers and thus cemented business connections. Farm servants married farm laborers and hoped to set up with their accumulated resources on a small farm. Sometimes girls who had gone to work in town as servants returned home with their little sums and set up as smallholders' wives. But those who had emigrated to town from an area of large farms were unlikely to return to their native villages. . . .

Of the young people who did not return home to marry, a minority of servant girls married other servants, and of these a minority may have remained in service, although demand for a resident couple was limited. The logical course for a servant girl upon marriage was to use her portion and her husband's contribution to set up in business of some kind, running a drink shop or a café bar, or for the pair to go into the catering business. Often the maidservant's main social contacts with the opposite sex had been with apprentices delivering goods to the back door. Tavern servants married construction workers. Other servants married tradesmen and opened lodginghouses. In industrial areas, spinners married carders or weavers. The large unskilled and largely urban female work force of flower sellers, peddlers of haberdashery, load carriers, and the like who had no dowry on marriage, or those who had failed to amass a dowry because of illness or unemployment, were not precluded from finding a marriage partner; but, lacking capital or a substitute skill, they could expect to marry only a man in a similar position.

The evidence everywhere points to economic considerations as the main determinant in the choice of partner, although this fact need not have precluded romantic considerations as well. Marriage was interpreted as an institution designed to furnish succor and support to both parties, and a clear perception of economic imperatives was essential to survival.

Marriage was seen not merely as woman's natural destiny but also as a metamorphic agent, transforming her into a different social and economic being as part of a new household, the primary unit upon which all society was based. The husband's role was that of provider of shelter and sustenance. He paid taxes and represented the household in the community. The role of the wife was that of helpmate and mother. . . .

Generally, although the labors of a wife were deemed essential for the wellbeing of a family and an idle wife was seen as a curse upon her husband, her work was rarely estimated in monetary terms. Even in areas where countrywomen were able to work in domestic industry, in agriculture, or even on the roads for pay, they were seen not as generators of money but as providers of largely unremunerated support services within the family.

Married countrywomen with children and encumbered with the work of a holding did not take on more paid work than they regarded as strictly necessary to the subsistence of their families. They defined need by reference to an adequate diet, warmth, and the ability to ward off debt. In short, they sought outside work only when the family was in need. Otherwise the arduous, long, and physically unpleasant work related to family and holding was paramount. Women carried water to steep mountain terraces in areas where the terrain was difficult and water scarce. In many cases the terraces themselves had been constructed from earth carried there in buckets by women. They cut and dried turf, collected kelp, firewood, weeds by the roadside to feed rabbits. They milked cows and goats, grew vegetables, collected chestnuts and herbs. The commonest source of heating for British and some Irish and Dutch farmers was animal turds, which were gathered by hand by women and received their final drying out stacked near the family fire. Haymaking and harvesting involved heavy spells of work, and weeding had to be done in all weather. Small wonder that women liked spinning: it gave them the chance to sit down for a few hours while productively occupied.

By the end of the eighteenth century the work patterns of the countrywoman had changed in many areas. One reason was population growth, which reduced the number of available subsistence units, depressed wages in the agricultural sector, pushed up prices, and inspired commercially minded landlords to curtail commons and gleaning rights. Growing numbers of married women tried to become casual daylaborers, hoeing and weeding vegetables on large properties in the appropriate season. In Britain, however, the introduction of heavier farm tools curtailed their labors as harvesters. Everywhere a potential labor force of married women seems to have been anxious to perform industrial work, leaving the running of the smallholding to husbands and perhaps abandoning the keeping of livestock or time-consuming agricultural work. . . .

Generally, when farms in arid or mountainous regions could no longer feed a family, women assumed responsibility for the farming for months or even years while their husbands worked as seasonal laborers or even emigrated for a time. Sometimes the woman ran the farm only between planting and harvest, and when the man returned from his seasonal job as, say, a chimney sweep, he performed the more difficult chores. Occasionally migration occurred in winter: peasants from Auvergne, Savoy, Tuscany, the Pyrenees, or Ireland went to the city — Paris, Bordeaux, Saragossa, Valladolid, Livorno, or London according to the traditions of their region — and looked for work on the docks or hauled coal or wood. Others went off in the summertime, like those peasants of the Massif Central who traveled south to Mediterranean regions to help with the grape harvest. Sometimes they stayed away for several years. In Corrèze and Aveyron a considerable number of married men as well as bachelors walked to Spain to offer their services in the ports. Their wives took over all farm work. Irish peasants also left for long periods, but of course potato farming was work that could easily be done by women. The men's remittances would pay the rental on holdings and the return fare across the Irish Sea, but the work of the farm was done by women. Everywhere, women's activity was deemed needful to hold a farmstead together and feed the children.

The role of married townswomen in the family economy does not lend itself to easy generalization; much depended on the town and the potential it offered. There, too, however, most married women filled roles complementary to their husbands'. In a family business, such as a printing shop or a drapery, a woman might function as an organizer, a fellow worker (mixing ink, cleaning letters, measuring cloth or ribbon), or, more often, a bookkeeper. Many mercantile houses in cities such as Amsterdam and London drew on the bookkeeping services of the merchant's wife. . . . Lower down the social scale, women appear to have virtually monopolized the actual sale of objects made by their husbands. Or they operated in their own right as petty traders in the market or shop or merely on street corners. In many towns, married women were prevented through borough custom, guild regulations, or municipal laws from trading in their own right. . . . Nevertheless, women did the actual work of selling even though the shop or stall was leased in their husband's name. Hence the fishwives of Amsterdam, Marseilles, Paris, Glasgow, Edinburgh, and London dealt with customers in the market while the fishmongers handled the wholesale trade. While butchers were responsible for slaughtering cattle and preparing joints of meat, their wives and daughters were frequently involved in taking the money from customers and in selling tripe, sausage meat, and black puddings (blood sausages). Covent Garden and Les Halles[11] were packed with women selling all kinds of food, from eggs and cheese to fruit. They also played a role in the sale of grain and flour. . . .

One form of selling in which married women were preponderant and which was quite independent of the activities of their husbands was the secondhand clothes trade. The importance of this traffic in early modern Europe should not be underestimated. A substantial proportion of the population did not purchase new clothing. Children wore hand-me-downs or cut-down adult clothing. In times of hardship, the poor parted with their clothes (outerwear first) and acquired others from secondhand dealers when times improved. Paris in the 1760s had 268 registered secondhand clothes dealers, all of whom were married women or widows. The business needed little capital input and involved transactions primarily among women. Mothers exchanged children's clothing with appropriate compensation to a middlewoman; maidservants bartered employers' castoffs; the clothes of a deceased person were exchanged for money or other garments by the inheriting relatives. These businesswomen seldom encountered opposition from male guilds. . . .

Many married women in town and country were multioccupational, with no single aspect of their work occupying them full time. They might operate as saleswomen only on market days, or as washerwomen by arrangement with specific families only a few times a month. Other responsibilities always waited: caring for children, shopping, carrying water, and perhaps organizing older children into some kind of remunerative activity, such as selling pies or commodities made by the parents. Frequently entire families performed one set of tasks during the day and another in the evening — like the Spitalfields silkworkers who made fireworks when they went home or the silk seamstresses of the Leicester area who supplied fine condoms for Mrs. Phelp's[12] mail-order service. In the economy of expedients that characterized the way most families lived in early modern Europe, the woman was likely to be the pivotal figure. While her husband performed the single job of agricultural laborer or casual worker she might be engaged in very different tasks at different seasons. Unlike her husband's tasks, which were clearly demarcated and began and ended (unless at harvest) at a specific time and usually permitted him some leisure to spend in the tavern or village square, "a woman's work was never done." If her man fell ill, was suddenly unemployed, failed to return from his seasonal migrations, or died, her work must expand to cover the deficit created in the family economy. In his lifetime she may have been an ancillary worker, but she was nonetheless crucial to the survival of the family unit. . . .

If her child survived infancy, a mother assumed the role of educator, although what that meant varied with social class, time, and place. A mother taught her

---

[11] The central market in Paris.

[12] Eighteenth-century pornographer and brothel-keeper.

child to negotiate the world in which they both lived. Notwithstanding the battery of servants, nannies, nurserymaids, and governesses available in aristocratic households, memoirs of aristocratic mothers frequently reveal concern for the advancement of their daughters and for equipping them for the marriage market. A daughter's success reflected upon the mother: in addition to some acquaintance with vernacular literature she needed to know how to present herself, dress, manage a household of servants, dance, embroider, play a musical instrument, and speak French. Lady Mary Wortley Montagu[13] considered the upbringing of three daughters a full-time occupation. A middle-class girl accompanied her mother on charitable errands, learned how to keep household accounts, and knew about pickling, preserving, and other methods of food preparation appropriate to the season even if she herself was not the cook. A daughter reflected the image of the household. . . .

Along with cooking, a mother was expected to teach her daughter needle skills. Fine needlework marked a great lady. A woman, however high her rank, was expected to produce baby bonnets and layettes and embroidered waistcoats to offer at Christmas to her husband or brother. Lower down the social scale, the emphasis was on hemming, seaming, mending, and darning. Shirts, petticoats, children's garments, and smocks were all made by women at home. Girls were also taught all tasks designated as female around the home. They assisted in the care of younger children. They helped to prepare food for their brothers and stitched their clothing. . . .

At the lowest levels of society the expedients for maintaining a frail livelihood involved close cooperation among family members, but the partnership between mother and daughter in the work force was perhaps the most striking. Girls learned survival skills from their mothers. Mothers and young daughters together sold milk, crockery, and vegetables in the markets; they also begged together. The economy of the poor was invariably a delicate balancing act, and those who lost their footing and fell into the ranks of the destitute were numerous. Where to turn in hard times was valuable knowledge. . . .

. . . Every mother knew that her daughter needed material assets on marriage and that the more she had, the higher her standing would be in the community and in the eyes of her husband's family. To assist in the important process of dowry accumulation, mothers put aside some of their work profits when they could, perhaps from the sale of eggs, a pot of honey, or a fattened pig that had been the runt of the litter, as a cumulative contribution. Or mother and daughter might rear rabbits on hand-picked weeds for the same purpose. Many mothers directed their young daughters' needlework toward making quilts and household articles either from scraps or from bits of raw wool picked from hedgerows and converted over the years into cloth. This collaboration in the accumulation of a dowry helped to cement the mother-daughter relationship and perhaps also helped it to survive physical distance. . . .

---

[13] English traveler and writer (1689–1762).

The loss of a husband in a society that defined a woman in terms of her relationship to a man was obviously an event that carried immense social, economic, and psychological consequences for a woman. The higher the social standing of the family, perhaps the less the upheaval. An aristocratic woman was, at least theoretically, in command of her jointure, the income guaranteed to her when she brought her dowry into the marriage to sustain her in her lifetime in the event of her husband's death. Furthermore, the aristocratic widow was usually delegated rights in the wardship of her children. Hence she passed into a directorial capacity and became arbiter of her own destiny, unrestrained by any tutelage. . . .

Most widows, however, were left in middle age with adolescent families and insufficient means to indulge their whims. Society expected the widow to bury her husband with decorum or honor; doing so might entail expenses that she could ill afford. . . .

No one ever assumed that a widow could do as well as her husband had done. Hence journeymen and servants to whom debts were due now demanded settlement, adding further to the widow's problems. Many had to default, and the most conspicuous sufferers were servant girls, who failed to realize their accumulated wages. Once debts had been paid, the widow had to decide at what scale she could continue to operate. . . . Taken overall, the need to make good the husband's labor by paying for a substitute probably stripped over 90 percent of artisans' widows of the ability to keep their husband's business fully functioning.

Best tailored to cope with the eventuality of a husband's death was the family economy that included a small business, especially a tavern, a café bar, a victualler's shop, cake, pie, or muffin production, or a lodginghouse. Most of these activities lay outside guild regulation. . . . [A] large number of taverns, cabarets, and refreshment stands were run by widows, with large numbers of widows' children selling hot pies and sweetmeats from trays in the street.

The widow thrown back on the work of her hands with children to support probably sank as low as it was possible to sink in the European economic hierarchy. She was heavily represented on poor lists and records of charities, and if charity was to be had — and there was nothing automatic about this — she was the most conspicuous candidate whose claims were universally acknowledged. . . .

Permanent spinsters were not much better off than widows unless they had family members to provide support. The low level of female wages precluded an independent existence. Many single women clustered in towns, sharing garrets and sparse lodgings and serving as support networks to one another. Their exiguous wages left them with little or nothing to buttress them during sickness, unemployment, or old age. Some might find shelter in a brother's dwelling or serve as mother substitute to a relative's orphaned family, but the prospects were bleak, even for those with more than a rudimentary education. . . .

POLITICAL CULTURE
AND FEMALE SOCIABILITY
IN THE FRENCH REVOLUTION
Dominique Godineau

One of the great watersheds in history, the French Revolution signaled the passing of the Old Régime. Monarchy, hierarchy, and privilege — all pillars of the
social order — came under attack, not only in France, but throughout much of
Europe. French armies crisscrossed the continent attempting to spread revolutionary ideals of "liberty, equality, and fraternity" and in the process inadver-
tently awakening the most potent of nineteenth-century ideologies, nationalism. Historians have entered seemingly interminable debates concerning the
French Revolution, questioning, among other things, whether or not it was favorable to liberty, or to capitalism, and which social groups benefitted the most
from the Revolution.

In recent decades, women's historians and then historians of gender have
moved beyond seeing the French Revolution as a male event to examining the
importance of women in the social and political world of the Revolution. This
revision at first involved the study of important female participants and then
evolved to an examination of power relationships wherever they existed and to
the realization that politics extended to clubs and other organizations beyond
the traditional governmental institutions previously studied by historians.

In a book originally published in French in 1988, Dominique Godineau, professor of social sciences at the Université de Rennes 2, takes aim at those who,
consciously or unconsciously, have written histories of the French Revolution
without due attention to revolutionary women's social and political lives and
roles. Relying heavily on police records (reports of spies, for instance), she finds
that many women were not on the periphery of events but were activists who
were motivated by the extraordinary opportunities and possibilities that the
Revolution opened up. In the section from her book excerpted here, we can appreciate the women's fervor and their intense involvement in political life (even

Dominique Godineau, "Political Culture and Female Sociability in the French Revolution," in Dominique Godineau, *The Women of Paris and the French Revolution* (Berkeley: University of California Press,
1998), 179–220.

after the banning in 1793 of their clubs). What was the debate about female participation in clubs? In a historical context, how radical was the participation of women in the revolutionary process? To what extent was there a separate world of men and a world of women during the French Revolution? How was the female popular class politicized? How do you explain the attendance of such women in the galleries of assemblies and clubs day after day, month after month, despite their daily work and care of children? Can you think of examples in the recent past where ordinary women have been as politically passionate and steadfast during revolutionary upheavals? Why have men been so eager historically to exclude women from meaningful participation in the political process?

"Women, whose moral education is almost nonexistent, are less enlightened in principles [than men]. Their presence in popular clubs would thus give an active role in government to people who are more vulnerable to error and seduction," asserted Amar[1] on 9 Brumaire Year II[2] (30 October 1793) before an audience of deputies who were eager to believe him. . . .

A "nonexistent moral education?" Were women permanent minors, deprived of all intelligence and all political sense, so fragile and so frivolous that they were ready to follow the first demagogue who appeared? If we accompany police informers to revolutionary assemblies, cabarets, or the courtyards of popular homes, if we leaf through the statements of commissioners, then Amar's allegation requires serious corrections. Glancing through police reports and registers, we find on the contrary a female Parisian population actively acquiring a true political education. This knowledge was certainly neither uniform nor bookish. Its stages were often modeled on those of militant engagement and came from the simple knowledge of the Declaration of the Rights of Man and the Citizen[3] through the regular reading of living theoreticians of the Revolution such as Robespierre,[4] and even in certain exceptional cases the theories of Enlightenment philosophers. This education was not limited to theoretical knowledge. A popular and political female socia-

---

[1] Jean-Baptiste Amar (1755–1816) was a lawyer known for his denunciation of the king and a member of the Committee of General Security, a government institution with broad police powers created in 1792.

[2] The French Revolution introduced a new calendar on 5 October 1793 and dated the year I from 22 September 1792, with the proclaiming of the French Republic. There were new names for the months (such as Messidor, Prairial, and so forth), each with thirty days. Five days were added at the end of the year (six in leap years). Brumaire was the month of mist (fog).

[3] Revolutionary document issued on 27 August 1789 that guaranteed basic rights of liberty, equality, and property. Two years later, Olymphe de Gouges (1748–1793) wrote a Declaration on the Rights of Women, but no government agreed to it.

[4] Maximilien Robespierre (1758–1794), leader of the most extreme political faction during the Reign of Terror (September 1793–July 1794), when thousands of the Revolution's enemies were executed.

bility also played an intrinsic part in it. Militant women combined a desire to participate in the Revolution with a desire to go beyond the secondary place assigned to women in the Sovereign People. The roads that they took to accomplish this were often crooked and even more frequently full of pitfalls. . . .

In revolutionary Paris, there were many opportunities for all men and women who wished to perfect their political knowledge. Since 1789, women had pursued their political apprenticeship in the galleries of various revolutionary assemblies. Their strong presence was remarked in the galleries of the general assemblies of the sections[5] and the meetings of section societies or popular clubs, the most representative expressions of the sansculottes[6] movement.

Almost all sections reserved a gallery for their female residents who wished to attend the general assemblies. Like any other member of the social body, female citizens could present themselves to a general assembly in order to expedite workaday matters such as requests for passports, certificates of public spiritedness, and so on. Like many Parisians, they had the habit of discussing their private and public affairs there, in the spirit of fraternity, solidarity, and "publicity" (in the sense of making public) characteristic of the sansculottes movement. But female citizens crowded into the galleries in order to follow the proceedings about the political life of the nation and the sections. According to the informer Bacon, who specialized in section life and who repeatedly indicated the importance of the female public in general assemblies, many women attended. (Given the lack of statistics on the number of those present, we must content ourselves with his assessments.)

Normally, women had neither the right to vote nor the right to deliberate in these assemblies and were separated from male citizens of the section. But in hours of crisis, such as the spring or summer of 1793, they left their galleries and joined the men to participate in the verbal or physical fight. In some sections, or under exceptional circumstances, women were allowed to speak. They also intervened during the assembly by their comments and their signs of approval or disapproval, especially at decisive moments.

Bacon often described the cries and applause that came from the galleries of women. On 15 Ventôse Year II (5 March 1794), he was obliged to leave the gallery where he attended the Bon-Conseil assembly, because the women's mutterings prevented him from hearing. This didn't matter, he thought; he would go do his work in a neighboring section assembly. But he was scarcely more successful in the Amis-de-la-Patrie assembly, which was stormy because a male citizen had just been denounced. "Noise . . . Noise . . . As the women make a great uproar new sentries have been stationed." The "uproar," "hubbub," and invectives were not signs of women's frivolity or lack of discipline. They were the only way these

---

[5] In June 1790, Paris was divided into forty-eight sections (units of local government), which held regular meetings. Militant revolutionaries dominated the meetings beginning in 1792.

[6] Workers, artisans, and shopkeepers distinguished by their dress (long pants and a red bonnet), behavior, and attitudes (radical and egalitarian). They supported the Reign of Terror.

women, who were denied the rights to deliberate and vote, had to make their opinion known. . . .

The general assembly was not the only place where Parisian women could keep up to date on political life. Many women attended the proceedings of popular societies. Dating sometimes from the first years of the Revolution, these clubs dedicated themselves to educating the people and overseeing the course of the Revolution. They multiplied in the sections during the summer and especially during the autumn of 1793 in order to circumvent the decree passed on 9 September that limited the number of general assemblies to two per week. Thus each section soon had its club which met on days when the general assembly did not take place. Only its members could deliberate, but in the public galleries men and women attended the debates and listened to the reading of patriotic newspapers or to speeches delivered to the Convention[7] and to the Jacobins.[8] Thus, on 28 Pluviôse Year II (16 February 1794), the Faubourg-Montmartre[9] popular society opened its meeting with the reading of political articles from the *Journal de la Montagne:*[10] "Women listened with great interest for they themselves imposed silence." The female spectators praised popular clubs that lived up to their expectations. On 9 Pluviôse Year II (28 January 1794), young female citizens who were "electrified" by the republican teachings that had been read in the Lazowski club (Finistère section) said, "We would be very aggravated if we had to miss the popular assembly even just once. At least there we improve our knowledge." "By coming here, we become educated and we learn news," asserted women from the galleries of the Maison-Commune popular club.

From their galleries, female spectators remarked on the political situation or the progress of the meeting. If they asked to speak, they were permitted to do so more easily than in the general assemblies. And most important, some sexually mixed popular clubs admitted female citizens as full-fledged members. It is difficult to say how often this happened because we do not possess all the regulations for these clubs, which were usually silent on the subject of women. Early fraternal clubs, which were frequently open to women, disappeared or merged in 1793 with new section clubs and lost their mixture of both sexes as members; these included the Fraternal Society of les Halles, Nomophiles, Minimes, and perhaps that of the Fontaine-de-Grenelle section. What became of the Fraternal

---

[7] Name of the governmental assembly that first met on 21 September 1792 and established a republic.

[8] Members of republican clubs during the French Revolution who supported the Mountain (*Montagne;* followers Montagnards), the left wing in the Revolution's governments, dominated by Robespierre during the Terror. Originally moderate, the Jacobins became increasingly radical and prevailed in the government during the Terror.

[9] The Montmartre suburb of Paris.

[10] *Newspaper of the Mountain,* which supported the political views of the left-wing group known as the Mountain.

Society of the Women Citizens of Unité section that contributed significantly both to the Assembly of Republican Women[11] on 24 February 1793 and the "war of the cockades"?[12] Its case is unique because it appears that this club was not really sexually mixed but composed of two parts, one male, the other female, each possessing its own officers and members. Did it merge in the autumn of 1793 into the new Popular and Republican Society of Unité section, which was not sexually mixed? Was it dissolved as a women's club after the decree of 9 Brumaire?[13] Or did it assume again the old name of the Society of the Indigent, which in the winter of Year II included women? . . .

Among the sexually mixed Parisian clubs, only the Social Harmony club in the Arsenal section, which dedicated itself primarily to education, admitted women as a matter of principle: "Article II: the principles of social Equality should be solemnly established and practiced, the right to acquire and spread instruction and enlightenment useful to the Public Good belongs equally to both sexes, female citizens will be admitted equally and without distinction from male citizens, to share the patriotic works of the club."

The Luxembourg Society set a quota of one fifth for its female members; in addition, although male citizens were admitted from the age of seventeen years, female citizens had to wait for their twenty-first birthday before they could become members. . . .

Female members could be assigned to fulfill different duties than men. In the Luxembourg section, they did not hold office but were eligible for three seats on the committee composed of fifteen commissioners. In the Hommes-Libres Society, four female citizens formed one third of the purification committee (which reviewed the political conduct of members). . . . In addition, all the sexually mixed clubs made it a rule to always include a certain number of women in their deputations, in proportions that varied from a fifth to a third, and even close to a half for the Panthéon section. (In contrast, in all the ceremonies of the cult of the martyrs Marat[14] and Lepeletier,[15] the delegations were predominantly female.) In spite of this unequal representation, female commissioners were not tokens. They were not figureheads who had to limit themselves to listening to the men speak. On the contrary, they were frequently designated by the entire deputation to "act as a spokesperson" even in the most important circumstances. Thus, during the strug-

---

[11] Club established on 22 February 1793 by female *sansculottes* in response to the economic crisis resulting from the high price of food.

[12] The cockade was a revolutionary emblem, worn on the red "liberty cap" (the ancient symbol of freed slaves). Some fought the wearing of the bonnet and cockade, perceived as a symbol of *sansculottes* women and female political participation.

[13] Law prohibiting women's clubs, 30 October 1793.

[14] Jean-Paul Marat (1744–1793), journalist who published the newspaper, *L'ami du Peuple* (*The Friend of the People*), popular with the *sansculottes* for its strident advocacy of democracy.

[15] Louis-Michel Lepeletier (LePeletier) de Saint-Fargeau (1760–1793), former magistrate and educational reformer. Like Marat, he was assassinated; both became revolutionary martyrs.

gle over section power during the summer of 1793, it was the female speaker of a deputation of the Social Harmony club who caused the Fédérés[16] section, up until then held by the moderates, to tip over to the side of the sansculottes.

From twenty to thirty women were enrolled in each of these clubs. . . .

Popular clubs . . . "constituted from the autumn of 1793 to the spring of Year II, the framework of the popular movement." In fact, in many sections these clubs replaced the general assemblies, which followed their orders. They censured section officials, distributed certificates of public spiritedness,[17] and controlled and directed local political life. This created an astonishing situation in which female citizens, who were excluded from all political rights, were able to participate in the power of the sections. Contemporaries were perfectly aware of this paradox. The Fraternal Society of Both Sexes of Panthéon-Français section came the closest to an egalitarian sexual mix. It also attracted the most criticism when popular clubs were attacked as organizations that were too independent of the most radical sansculottes. The difficulties it experienced illustrate the problems created by women's activity in sexually mixed popular clubs.

During the winter of the Year II, contemporaries protested loudly over the eminent role that women held in the Panthéon club. They were initially angry that female citizens had the right to deliberate and to vote there and that they took advantage of this right to pass extreme measures. On 1 Nivôse Year II (21 December 1793), two police informers reported that a "deputation of both sexes" of the club had presented itself to the general assembly of the section to inform them of a decree it had passed against "former priests, nobles, and lawyers." The female speaker of the deputation "expanded on the decree by a more than revolutionary speech, claiming that it was necessary to expel all of them from assemblies." Women were thus accused of preaching dissension or of seeking "to make all those who had places lose them." Like many other sections, the Panthéon section was riven during the winter by quarrels between the "patriots of '89" and the "patriots of '93." The conflict opposed militant revolutionaries of 1789, former active citizens,[18] to revolutionaries of more modest birth who appeared in section organizations after 10 August 1792.[19] Justice of the Peace Hû became the spokesperson for the first group and fought with the club, which he accused of dividing citizens and of fostering "hatreds and calumnies against patriots who since 1789 have served the cause of the people." To this conflict between militant revolutionaries of different social origins was added the conflict that divided the partisans and adversaries of political participation by women. Foremost among Hû's

---

[16] "Federates"; name of a section from August 1792 to 4 July 1793.

[17] "The certificate of public spiritedness, which was usually issued by general assemblies, testified to the patriotic conduct of its holder. Those who were refused one were, according to the law, considered suspect." (Author's note.)

[18] The constitution of 1791 divided adult males into "active" and "passive" citizens. Only active citizens had the right to vote.

[19] The date of the overthrow of the French monarchy.

recriminations were those against the club's sexual mix. On 17 Pluviôse (5 February), he declared that he had "merited the honor of persecution and that he owed this to the hermaphrodite club of Panthéon [section]," where "intriguers tyrannized their brothers and were themselves enslaved by libertine women who shared with them the honors of office." Not a single attack against the club spared its female members. The occasion was too good an opportunity, given that a large proportion of the population opposed all political activity by women. But the flights of oratory against "libertine women" were not a mere tactic. Wounded in his pride and his male ego, Hû was sincere when he said "that he had seen the dignity of men offended by undergoing the censure of some women in order to be admitted as members of this club." These women questioned "educated citizens who needed certificates of public spiritedness on political and dogmatic matters" and refused them "according to whim." His double grievance is obvious: people without enlightenment had power over educated people! Worse, women, who were by definition without enlightenment or reason, had power over educated men!

After the banning of women's clubs on 9 Brumaire (30 October), many had believed that women were now excluded as members from all clubs. On 30 Brumaire Year II (20 November 1793), when a deputation of the Fraternal Society of Panthéon section led by a woman presented itself to the general assembly of this section, "citizens claimed that a women did not have the right to speak, to deliberate in assemblies, according to the law." And on 26 Pluviôse (14 February), the general assembly of the Panthéon section was thrown into tumult. A deputation of the Amis-de-la-République club, interpreting the decree of 9 Brumaire, was astonished that the section of Panthéon "had maintained up to this day" the rights granted to women in its Fraternal Society when the Convention had forbidden women to meet. The speech of the spokesman for the deputation was interrupted by applause several times, and only when Paris, a club member and elected municipal official, intervened to defend the contrary opinion was the situation restored in favor of the club.

Not all members of the club were themselves persuaded of the validity of its sexual mixture, but its leaders, among whom were women, defended the policy fiercely. Members had their membership cards revoked, one "for having made a motion aimed at expelling female citizens," another for having asserted that women "should not be allowed to deliberate on section affairs, nor should they be permitted to purge section members." "How do you feel about female members?" asked the (sexually mixed) committee of purification when it wished to ascertain the revolutionary opinions of a member, and a hostile response to this question led to expulsion. Replying to the accusations of Justice of the Peace Hû, the officers of the club wrote: "Why do some individuals show so much bad temper against hermaphrodite clubs, whereas city hall, composed of patriots, welcomes them? It is because women can size people up with an accuracy of judgment that frightens intriguers."

This last phrase illustrates perfectly the imbrication[20] existing between membership of women within the club, which shocked some, and the difficult positions that women defended there. There was no question for women of making themselves forgotten in order to be accepted. The most frequently expressed grievance against women of the club was that they only sparingly awarded certificates of public spiritedness. . . .

Though in other sexually mixed clubs the stir provoked by women's participation did not attain these heights, it existed nevertheless. At the time women's clubs were banned, the Hommes-Libres Society in the Pont-Neuf/Révolutionnaire section asked if female citizens who were not wives of male members should be excluded. During the winter, a female resident of this section rebelled against the vote of four female citizens sitting on the purification committee. She wrote that she found the vote to be illegal because the law forbade women to express their views. And the crucial question of certificates of public spiritedness, a revealing stumbling block in the ties between radical and nonradical members of popular clubs, continued to raise concern. A report of 3 Nivôse (22 December), is instructive on this matter. "There are complaints that the citizens wearing red caps gather in clubs and take names worthy of them, such as 'hard hitter,' 'terrible brother,' and similar ones. It is greatly feared that these clubs are more counterrevolutionary than revolutionary. It has been asserted that they initiate female citizens in their clubs, who have the right to speak in their deliberations."

Wishing to argue that these men were too "extreme" to be revolutionaries, the observer wrote that women participated in their clubs, linking successfully by this absence of transition the militant women and the avant-garde of the sansculottes movement. In general assemblies and in popular clubs that were not sexually mixed, women were often conspicuous by their support for the most radical causes.

How can we explain this female extremism? Was Amar correct when he asserted that women were more vulnerable to error and seduction (meaning the seduction of revolutionary individuals)? Should we subscribe to the idea that women are prone to follow extremists on any side because they are not guided by their reason but by a sort of exaltation that is "natural" to them? It is necessary to take our sources into account: these documents were written by men and probably exaggerate this attraction to extreme positions by focusing on it in order to emphasize its scandalous aspect. The opportunity to denigrate groups by insisting on their shocking behavior is too tempting to pass up. This phenomenon is emphasized even more by an almost total inability to see the female sex other than globally. Extremists among the women were mentioned in reports under the generic title "women," even if they were far from representing the majority of female citizens in a section or a popular club. All French women have red hair; all women are extremists. But these exaggerations derive from a reality. It was the politically engaged female sansculottes who attended revolutionary assemblies. It is

---

[20] Overlapping.

not surprising that when, as in the winter of the Year II, part of the sansculottes movement grew more radical, some of the women also became more radical. . . . [I]t was among the radical sansculottes that we find the most supporters, perhaps not so much of a theory of equality between the sexes as of the political participation of women. Thus militant women turned toward and supported the people whose ideas they shared and who welcomed them (relatively) favorably.

The offensive against popular societies and clubs, which were often accused of Hébertism,[21] redoubled in the spring of the Year II (1794) during the repression following the Cordelier trial.[22] Even the Fraternal Society of Patriots of Both Sexes,[23] which since 1790 had welcomed women, was affected by the disrepute that fell on popular clubs, particularly those that were sexually mixed. Up until then the club had escaped the attacks against clubs open to women. In autumn of 1793, it had prudently distinguished itself from the Society of Revolutionary Republican Women. Without being established in a section, and thus without local power, it had not suffered much from the oppositions during winter. However, it was undermined by uncertainty, and in the spring it split into proponents and opponents of sexual mixing. Did the law that forbade women to deliberate apply also to the club? Should it thus revise its statutes? Each time the questions were raised, the proponents of sexual mixing won, but the dissension was such that on 21 Germinal (10 April) its purification commission asked the legislation committee for an interpretation of the law. The club began to split apart. In addition, like other popular clubs, it purged itself to excess in order to return to the Jacobins' good graces. . . .

Thus, six months after the banning of women's clubs, popular clubs that had sometimes welcomed women were in turn attacked as organs of the sansculottes movement, an attack that emphasized the place that they gave to women. Yet in most cases, women had only one place — not as actors but as active spectators, just like in section general assemblies. As in the spring, summer, or autumn of 1793, militant women were conspicuous both for their sex and for the extreme positions that they often took. The popular Parisian clubs almost all ended by dissolving themselves in Prairial Year II (May 1794), leaving the stage clear for the Jacobins. . . .

The membership of the Jacobin club was exclusively male and of a higher social level than the membership of popular clubs. However, a large public attended

---

[21] Extremist views associated with René Jacques Hébert (1757–1794), a journalist popular with the *sansculottes*. An ardent revolutionary, Hébert and his followers were executed by Robespierre for allegedly plotting a revolt.

[22] The Cordeliers constituted a club to the left of the Jacobins. Hébert was a leader of the Cordeliers, which was destroyed with the Hébertists.

[23] Founded in 1790, this, as the name states, was a sexually mixed political club whose beliefs were close to the Cordeliers.

their meetings from the galleries. One gallery was particularly filled with female citizens. Woe to those women who "did not have a good reputation," who were suspected of being aristocrats, or who had made "feeble jokes" about men of color: they were driven out without consideration, unless indeed a hand that was a little too quick struck their cheeks. The female spectators had the right to request permission to speak by writing to the president. They more frequently burst out with exclamations. However, impressed and less at ease than in section assemblies, their behavior was for the most part more reserved. The Jacobins paid attention to the women's attendance. On 15 October 1793, they distributed to all members of the club as well as male or female citizens in the galleries a calendar of meetings, and they never forgot to invite them to their demonstrations.

Most women present were habitual attendees, and it was not without reason that during the Year III they were described as "regulars of the Jacobin galleries." Claire Lacombe was one of the regulars, as were many obscure female militants: the female citizen Maubuisson, the widow Salignac, the wife of Villarmée, the widow Sergent, the female citizen Dubouy, and the wives of Huzard, Fragère, and Lance acknowledged in the Year III that they had attended almost every day. The wife of Boudray, one of the oldest and most faithful spectators, attended all the meetings and even had a "reserved" place "in the gallery to the right of the president, in front of the speaker," where she did not lose a word of the debates. The reputations of revolutionary female zealots began in these galleries, and political friendships formed there. . . .

Female Parisians could also "educate themselves," listen to great speakers, and keep up to date on the sudden shifts in politics from the galleries of the Convention, city hall, and the revolutionary tribunal. These revolutionary bodies deliberated under the eyes of the public, the people. Occupying the Convention's galleries constituted one form of women's actions in times of crisis. When the situation grew calmer, women went to these meetings occasionally, when they knew "there would be something good." The deliberations of the General Council of city hall attracted a large public. The police spy Rolin remarked on this subject on 8 Pluviôse Year II (27 January 1794): "There are many more women than men at the meetings of the General Council. Does patriotism bring them? Do they come out of simple curiosity? God knows." However, these women were not welcomed with open arms by Chaumette,[24] the chief spokesman for Paris city government, who never lost an opportunity to fulminate against them. A municipal official proposed that they give an indemnity of one hundred livres[25] to a "female gallery regular" who had been burglarized while she was at the council, because her misfortune was caused only by her public spiritedness. After Chaumette's intervention, the General Council moved on to the expected order of the day, given that "the

---

[24] Pierre Gaspard Chaumette (1763–1794), Cordelier, leader of the Paris city government (the Commune); executed by Robespierre.

[25] A *livre* (pound) was a monetary unit.

female citizen would be perhaps more useful in her household than in the galleries of the General Council" that she troubled everyday by her chatter. . . .

Though the meetings of the clubs and popular societies took place in the evening, the Convention, the city government, and the tribunal deliberated during the day. Contemporaries were surprised that many women, who should have been occupied with their household or their work, attended these meetings. But keeping up the bedroom or two rooms of a lower-class family was not really a burden. And work conditions help to explain these crowds of women on the benches of public galleries. Women who earned their living through sewing could work while attending the debates. In addition, rampant unemployment often drove female workers without work to the meeting rooms. This was the answer given on 21 Nivôse (16 January) to the police informer Monic, who was astonished at the number of female workers who "wasted their time" at the revolutionary tribunal and was surprised that they did not have enough work to be busy every day. Likewise, a female seamstress working for the government attended the judgment of Carrier in Frimaire Year III (November 1794), because "work was rare and [she] had nothing urgent to do." And it was common for a peddler, a seamstress, or a washerwoman returning with work to go around to the public galleries if she passed them on her way.

The sansculottes did not consider attendance in the galleries of various governmental authorities to be a passive act but an active way to exercise popular control over elected officials, who were agents of the Sovereign People. Thus a mailman was proud that his wife attended the meetings of the revolutionary tribunal every other day, for "it is necessary that there are always good patriots at the tribunal to impress the judges." In this sense, the substantial presence of women in the galleries, which constituted one of the particularities of their political practice, rose from a desire to exercise concretely a part of sovereignty, even if by a roundabout path. Indeed, women shared with their companions a consciousness of forming part of the Sovereign People, as well as an active conception of sovereignty. However, unlike men, they could not express this directly. Because these women were not able to control elected officials through the right to vote and could not sit as jurors, they attempted to ensure the fidelity of the peoples' representatives from their gallery benches. Militant women developed this practice. The organization of work made this possible and the organization of politics made this necessary, and thus women could compensate for their exclusion from certain rights. In a way, they had been pushed into these galleries by their desire to participate in popular sovereignty.

In the galleries was formed the portrait of militant women as knitters who often left the Convention for the revolutionary tribunal and the revolutionary tribunal for city hall before going in the evening to the Jacobin club or to the popular assemblies. Did these women truly knit? While they listened to the debates, female citizens in the galleries sometimes did handwork — not so much knitting as sewing, or shredding linen to dress soldiers' wounds. . . .

Though they did not balk at work, were these revolutionary militant women in other respects bad mothers, insensitive to the dangers run by their children abandoned in a home that the women had deserted in order to become intoxicated on speech? This was how they were represented by their detractors from the beginning to the end of the Revolution. But whereas the sansculotte militant was a father of a family, about forty years old, the militant woman was not just a mother of a family. The average age (thirty-nine years old) of women encountered in revolutionary assemblies should not mislead us. Most of the women either had passed their fiftieth year or were not yet thirty (an age distribution that characterized the Revolutionary Republican Women as well). The militant woman was thus a young or a fairly old woman, who did not have to busy herself with many children. The maternal role allotted to women influenced heavily their revolutionary commitment. Mothers of families, however, were not markedly absent from political life and revolutionary assemblies. Though their tasks prevented them from becoming absorbed in militancy, it was not rare to pass in the galleries a woman carrying her unweaned infant in her arms and holding by the hand his older brothers and sisters. . . . And spectators frequently complained of the cries of children, who kept them from listening quietly to the debates.

No female trade appears to have been a breeding ground for militancy. If seamstresses and washerwomen predominated among the female militants, it is because they predominated in society. After them follow domestics and merchants, and closely after in no particular order come all female trades: workers in the craft industries, bookmakers, embroiderers, spinners, not to mention teachers, midwives and even the landladies of prostitutes. Many women belonged to revolutionary families who had a father, a son, or a husband in the general assembly or the popular club. The female relatives of section officials studded the audience of general assemblies, and, to a lesser degree, the Jacobin club. . . .

The presence of militant couples was a given of the Parisian popular movement. However, it was uncommon for women to go to the assemblies in their husbands' company. Then did women go there alone? Oh no! This would ignore the richness of women's social life; arm in arm with their irreplaceable neighbors, women of the people went to listen to the debates. In the Montreuil section, the wife of Lance and the wife of Pampelun were "inseparable acolytes when they went on their pilgrimages to the caves" (of the Jacobins), according to a denunciation of the Year III. Since they had met in the galleries of their section's popular club, they went together to the Jacobin club and took with them several women from their neighborhoods. The men's absence during war encouraged female political conviviality. Those who remained behind pledged revolutionary commitment in words that sometimes reveal a certain female pride: they should not leave to their husbands the glory of defending the Revolution. Arrested in Prairial Year III, the wife of Saint Prix thus wrote in her defense, "I believed that by giving myself to their lying insinuations [going to the Jacobin club and supporting them] I served my country like my husband and my children serve it in the armies."

But the war only exaggerated a situation for which it was not entirely responsible. The formation within the popular movement of separate groups of men and women was rooted in a conception of the relation between the sexes. The lines of sexual division that sometimes cut across the popular movement were the repercussion of a social and cultural distinction between a world of men and a world of women, which were "parallel" and which respected each other. Men would never dream of interfering in a brawl between two neighbor women because that "was none of their business" — and if they had, they would have been poorly received. Not that they turned away while observing an amused neutrality, but they let women settle their own affairs, even if they later testified against one or the other. In the same way, men with prestige or authority acted only as arbiters in political brawls between groups of women. . . . The Revolution indeed belonged to both men and women, even though in general women concerned themselves with political affairs among women and men among men. Thus a male citizen proposed in December 1792 "to assassinate all the nobles and the priests [and] to arm the wives of patriots so that in their turn they could cut the throats of the wives of aristocrats."

This sexual demarcation resulted partially in a male disdain of "women's quarrels." When reprimanded for counterrevolutionary opinions by their servants or their spouses, male citizens responded that "women's quarrels did not concern them" and that they paid "little attention to what a woman could say in these affairs." Individuals who had been accused asked for their freedom by arguing that their accusations rested only on the "chatter of women." But these "borders" between male and female actions were not based only on male scorn. They were also the direct consequence of an affirmation of independence by women within couples. The groups of female citizens who attended club meetings together make this clear. Likewise, in order to avoid using a public scribe who would "cost money," the wife of Despavaux asked her husband to make copies for her of a denunciation that she intended to make, but which she prevented him from signing because, in her own words, "this was not his concern." This was her business. Her husband could help her save several sous[26] but should not get involved. He worried about his action, which risked putting his wife "in a quagmire," but did not argue. Even if they shared the same ideas, both spouses led their own revolutionary life.

Whether militant or not, female citizens who crowded on the benches of the galleries were driven by a concern for independence within marriage, a hunger for education, a desire to keep up to date and to understand the Revolution, and a wish to participate in political life. They had "a mania for running to assemblies," affirmed contemporaries who did not always appreciate this activity. Despite the limitations that stemmed from their place in the Sovereign People and were imposed on them in these various assemblies, women of the people followed with interest the reading of revolutionary leaders' speeches and the debates raised by important questions. Here women got their political education. . . .

Newspapers provided an important opportunity to keep abreast of events and the diverse trends of political life. They were read everywhere, even in the most mod-

---

[26] A *sou* (singular of *sous*) was a unit of currency, a coin worth one-twentieth of a *livre* (pound).

est milieus. When searches were conducted through the papers of a female citizen or a lower-class family, commissioners often found at least one or two copies of various newspapers or pamphlets — not to mention patriotic songs. . . .

Those who did not know how to read, or whose budget was too strained by the daily purchase of a newspaper, met with tenants of the same house. All the residents, including a former cook living on her pension, a female confectioner, a female worker, and a water carrier, of 255 Rue des Fossés-l'Auxerrois (Gardes-Françaises) gathered each evening in 1793 in the porter's lodge to listen to the reading of the newspaper. In a private house of the Faubourg-Montmartre, another porter welcomed into his home the other patriotic servants of his master in order to read the newspapers. But these groups did not last long because of the political quarrels that often arose among their different members. . . .

And what evening could be more agreeable for an ardent female patriot than one spent in the company of "good women friends" in a cabaret around a bottle of wine while listening and commenting on a reading of Robespierre's latest speech? At least there the "bellowers" of the general assembly did not threaten to expel them from the meeting each time the women forcefully expressed their feelings. These cabarets were true schools of public spiritedness and patriotism, where enthusiastic hurrahs often rang out and whose lower-class customers were at least half women whom, whatever their district, the informer Bacon called on 25 Ventôse "women of the lower classes, I mean to say of the true sansculottes." All the problems of daily life were discussed, from basic necessities to the Cordelier trial. Wine helped these discussions, and the atmosphere was cordial. Thus, on 6 Ventôse (24 February), Bacon heard in a cabaret on the Rue Dominique "women of the lower classes," a little drunk, speak of the scarcity of meat and assert: "Hell, we too are Republicans! . . . As long as the Seine flows and we have bread, we will be Republicans and we are screwed for being so." While saying this, "they struck the table and cried 'Long live the Republic!'" In this place of political sociability, the newspaper, read in common, disseminated information, propaganda, and reflection. . . .

Patriotic spectacles, concerts of revolutionary songs, and free theater for the people were other opportunities for enjoyment and education, along with countless political discussions that occurred between neighbors or in groups in the street.

These different examples are astonishing if we separate them from their revolutionary context. It is difficult today to imagine a female street merchant after her day of work immersed in reading the National Assembly's[27] deliberations. During the Revolution, this was just one example among many, and the fact that it is not exceptional highlights the importance of female, popular, and political culture.

Reading and writing took on increasing importance at the end of the eighteenth century. "Papers" supposed to account for the social existence of an indi-

---

[27] Government established in June 1789.

vidual appeared: certificates of baptism, marriage, divorce, and death of parents, bread cards, membership cards in popular clubs, and proof of citizenship for men, were enclosed in a chest at home or carried in pockets. Letters exchanged with relatives who had remained in the provinces or with sweethearts, even if they were written by a public scribe and read by an educated acquaintance, familiarized people with the practice of writing. Literacy was necessary in many occupations. "Laundry books" and "conditions of linen" testify to the commercial relations between a washerwoman and her customers. The retailers of la Halle[28] had to keep a book containing the names and addresses of their suppliers. Landladies had to have their registers. It began to be dangerous to be illiterate. A female fruit merchant who wrapped her cherries in sheets of paper on which was printed a royalist appeal suffered unpleasant consequences. It was also common to read at the workplace. . . . [F]emale workers in municipal spinning workshops asked to receive the *Bulletins de la Convention nationale*[29] in the factory, and a female worker distributed "pamphlets" at the exit to the workshops of her trade.

The Revolution accentuated this familiarity with reading and writing. Individual and collective petitions were written documents. The circulation of printed material among the Parisian people . . . confirms the rapid development of reading and writing during the Revolution — a development that was reinforced by an abundant and easily accessible press and that affected a large working-class public that wished to "educate itself." Papers that specialized in political analysis and commentary were predominant. The newspapers read in cabarets or elsewhere primarily carried political analyses by journalists such as Marat, Hébert, and Desmoulins[30] or reported speeches of revolutionary orators. Here men and women of the people studied the theoretical principles that allowed them to comprehend the Revolution and to clarify ideas that they could defend with the help of solid arguments. In a society where education existed without yet being acquired by all, reading of both the press and posters was not an individual and private act but created political sociability and became integrated into a culture where orality remained privileged. The political ideas of various leaders were read together and out loud, and attempts to comprehend, to analyze, and even to criticize them were made collectively. Passersby read together and out loud a political poster around which a group would form, which might become threatening. For women of the people, who were less literate than men, this mediated access to writing was often necessary. It occurred naturally in public places, such as streets, cabarets, and workshops — spaces of female sociability, which given the interest in the revolutionary common good, became spaces of reading and political practice.

But solitary reading in private and as far as possible from city noise and the presence of others also occurred in the homes of women of the people. This sort

---

[28] The central marketplace of Paris.

[29] Reports from the National Convention.

[30] Lucie-Camille-Simplice Desmoulins (1760–1794), pamphleteer and journalist who advocated a relaxation of the Terror; executed.

of reading created other, more personal ties between a reader and the text (even if the reader was still obliged to read in a faltering manner out loud). . . .

Moreover, men and women of the people expected the Revolution to accelerate this progress and place education within the reach of all. "In 1789, the people regained their rights because they wished to educate themselves," asserted washerwomen who listened to the reading of the newspaper in a cabaret. The sansculottes were perfectly aware of the power of knowledge, and one of their most cherished demands was that education be accessible to everyone. In the society that was to be born from the Revolution, education, "necessary for all" (Declaration of Rights of 1793), should no longer be a privilege reserved for the wealthy. "The true patriot does not know how to speak well, but fifteen years from now, our children will be well educated" asserted the female spectators of a popular club. And most of the women who addressed the Convention asked in their petitions that it "concern itself immediately" with the organization of national education.

. . . As a whole, glutted with speeches, capable of conceptualization, and conscious of the stakes of the Revolution, women of the people were no more politically ignorant than the men of their milieu and certainly were not manipulated masses blindly obeying the slogans of counterrevolutionaries or extremists, as they have too often been portrayed. In order to understand the politicization of the Parisian female popular class and their political awareness, which might at times seem astonishing and appear exaggerated by the historian, one must consider the political culture acquired by female citizens. Historians tend to perceive the speeches, the articles, and the political texts of a revolutionary leader in themselves, as parts of the political and philosophical thought of a man such as Robespierre, Marat, or Saint Just,[31] or of a group such as the Girondins[32] and the Montagnards. This absolutely necessary process must not make us forget that all these texts that historians study and dissect were listened to daily during the Revolution and were studied and dissected by washerwomen, dressmakers, and so on who were sometimes illiterate but, let us repeat, perfectly capable of perceiving the texts' meanings and scope.

And their reading enabled these women to clarify and shape their aspirations, which were identical to those of men.

---

[31] Louis Antoine de Saint-Just (1767–1794), a revolutionary leader during the Terror; executed with Robespierre.

[32] Name given to a group of moderate republican deputies. They were purged from the Convention in 1793.

INFANTICIDE IN EUROPEAN HISTORY
Keith Wrightson

The practice of infanticide has existed throughout history in all civilizations. Ancient societies in western Asia as well as Greece and Rome condoned infanticide, although historians debate its frequency. In ancient western Asia, only the Hebrews condemned infanticide out of hand. Indeed, one could interpret the famous (or infamous) account in Genesis — wherein god ordered Abraham to sacrifice Isaac, his only son, before sending an angelic emissary to stop Abraham at the last moment from plunging his knife into his son — as a divine injunction against the murder of children. Christianity continued the Jewish custom of forbidding infanticide.

Keith Wrightson, professor of history at Yale University, surveys the practice of infanticide and its legal history across Europe. In doing so, he uncovers the irony that although Christianity always condemned infanticide, Christian social morality nonetheless contributed to infanticide by preaching that a woman giving birth to an illegitimate child should be shunned and ostracized and by attaching a stigma to the illegitimate offspring. What other social and economic factors might have led women to infanticide, even though they knew that, if caught and convicted, they would in all likelihood suffer public humiliation and an excruciating death? Why did the Catholic and Protestant Reformations of the sixteenth and seventeenth centuries become more interested in the pursuit of infanticides than had the medieval Church?

Which women were most likely to practice infanticide, a "horror crime"? Wrightson points out that only a small minority of single women murdered their children. Of course, historians of crime must rely on court records of depositions and trials, and we therefore have no knowledge of people who committed infanticide undetected by the criminal justice system. Beginning in the late eighteenth century, changes occurred that altered the public perception of the infanticidal mother. How did "infanticidal nursing" in the nineteenth century further modify the practice of infanticide? Finally, what factors contributed to the decline of infanticide by the end of that century?

Keith Wrightson, "Infanticide in European History," *Criminal Justice History: An International Annual* 3 (1982): 1–16.

On 5 April 1578, the burial of a child of one Marie Lyttell was recorded in the parish register of Great Hallingbury, Essex. Having borne an illegitimate child on 30 March 1578, the entry informs us, the mother "most unnaturalye by all cyrcystances murthered it, cast it in to a privie having before nyped it by the throte and sculle most lamentablie." This rare example of the parochial registration of a case of infanticide encapsulates the predominant attitude towards the crime of infanticide in early modern Europe: the deed was unnatural. The English moralist William Gouge[1] . . . described infanticidal mothers as "lewd and unnatural." The clergyman and gentleman who reported another Essex case to the authorities in 1645 wrote of it as "an unnatural and barbarous murther." Elsewhere in early modern Europe infanticide took its place among those crimes which were regarded with peculiar horror — witchcraft and heresy, parricide, incest, sodomy, arson, and murder (including infanticide); the . . . *heinous crimes* . . . which were "taken to constitute, *ipso facto*,[2] a challenge to the established political, religious or social order." So horrid did the crime of infanticide appear in the eyes of European jurists that it was frequently singled out as meriting especially appalling punishment. In late medieval France burning or burial alive, sometimes accompanied by additional torments, was the fate of convicted murderers of infants. In the Holy Roman Empire the criminal code published by the Emperor Charles V[3] in 1532 followed medieval German precedents in prescribing death by burial alive, drowning in a sack, or impaling, punishments which were replaced by decapitation after torture in the seventeenth century.

Such punishments reflect both horror at a crime deemed odious in the sight of God and a perceived need for exemplary retribution which would dissociate the Christian community from such wickedness and cleanse it of guilt. That a crime so unnatural might be the result of an unbalanced mind was also recognised, but it was long before this alternative explanation of infanticide prevailed over punitive severity in the courts of Europe. In fifteenth century France, mental disturbance was one of the grounds on which mercy might be granted to women convicted of infanticide, if only after long imprisonment. In the later sixteenth and seventeenth centuries, however, such clemency was actually more difficult to obtain for infanticide than for witchcraft. Similarly, in England, the law allowed that a person *non compos mentis*[4] should not be charged with felony for homicide, and cases survive in which such a defence was successful. Yet there are equally clear cases of the condemnation and execution of women who were almost certainly victims of severe psychological disturbance.

---

[1] English Puritan writer (1578–1653).

[2] By the very nature of the case.

[3] Holy Roman emperor from 1519 to 1556.

[4] Not of sound mind.

Explanations of infanticide in terms of either human iniquity or psychiatric disorder turn upon the connected ideas of infanticide as an unnatural and irrational act. Within the cultural tradition of Christian Europe both responses may appear to have been appropriate. Yet they are not wholly adequate to the understanding of infanticide in European history, for there are situations in which social circumstances, coupled with the absence or relative weakness of cultural and legal restraints, may render infanticide both a natural and a rational response to the problem of the unwanted child. It is well established that infanticide has been extensively practiced in human societies as a form of population control or demographic selection. Among the Tikopia[5] of Polynesia population was carefully "measured according to the food" by the smothering of unwanted children at birth. In eighteenth century Japan, infanticide was employed not only "to thin out" populations pressing too heavily upon inadequate resources, but also as an element in what has been termed "household building strategy": a means of achieving the optimum size and sex composition of a family, a desired number of heirs, higher living standards and social prestige. Whether motivated by physical need and the pressures of a marginal existence or by social aspirations, infanticide has appeared a sensible and responsible solution to difficulties threatening the welfare of the larger group.

Nor were such circumstances unknown in the European past. It seems certain that the exposure of deformed, sickly and illegitimate children was not uncommon in the Europe of antiquity. In addition, Athenian families of middling and upper rank were prepared, on occasion, to expose supernumerary children once the continuance of the line was assured, while the evidence of Hellenistic[6] inscriptions suggests that some leading families were unwilling to raise more than one daughter. In Republican and early Imperial Rome,[7] the right of life and death exercised over his children by the *pater familias*[8] was enshrined in the ritual whereby he either recognised and raised up the newborn child laid before him or ordered its exposure. Among both wealthy families and peasant proprietors, preservation of the family patrimony from the burden of too many heirs appears to have been the principal motive governing such rites and actions.

In the light of such considerations, the emergence of infanticide as one of the classical horror crimes of Christian Europe and its subsequent history and eventual reappraisal in European law become problems of considerable interest. For the history of infanticide provides examples not only of the processes by which crime is defined and redefined, but also of the complex interrelationships between law and social, moral and communal values. . . .

---

[5] A people living on one of the Pacific Solomon Islands.

[6] Relating to Greece and western Asia from the reign of Alexander the Great to the Roman Empire, 323–31 B.C.E.

[7] Roman history from the eighth century B.C.E. to the third century C.E.

[8] Father of the family; head of the household.

The initial identification of infanticide as a sinful and unnatural act and the proscription of the practice by law are customarily and correctly attributed to the influence of the early Christian Church. From the outset, the tradition of Judaeo-Christian thought was uncompromisingly hostile to the taking of infant life. Infanticide was repeatedly condemned by the councils and synods of the early Church, and their hostility was gradually embodied in legislation following the formal Christianisation of the Roman Empire. . . .

This long-term shift in attitudes and values remains obscure and deserves further investigation. It seems probable, however, that the gradual triumph of Christianity did much to enhance the security of infant life. Though the restraining force of the teachings of the Church may have been slow to develop its full strength, it seems unlikely that the systematic exposure of legitimate children (if it had ever been commonplace) long survived the effective Christianisation of European societies and the enshrinement of Christian values in law and custom. Nevertheless, that process left in its wake a persistent tension between the ideals taught by the Church and the needs of particular families, needs which might on occasion prove sufficiently urgent to break the restraints of morality and law.

Awareness of this tension led the medieval Church to view with suspicion the apparently accidental deaths of children overlain by their parents during sleep. . . . Such cases were regarded by the Church as the result of culpable negligence and were seriously investigated, both parents usually being called to answer before an episcopal court. The extent to which they represent deliberate infanticide, however, is open to debate. . . .

Where unambiguous evidence of infanticide is available, in the records of the criminal courts of late medieval and early modern Europe, it relates much more narrowly to one kind: the killing of illegitimate children. Such evidence permits, for the first time in European history, a thorough investigation of infanticide. It also raises the disturbing possibility that if Christian social morality had done much to overcome the practice of infanticide motivated by considerations of communal or familial interest, it may have exacerbated resort to it to avoid the stigma of illegitimacy.

The need to conceal illegitimate births or dispose of illegitimate offspring had its place in the history of infanticide from the earliest times, but from medieval times these motives clearly predominate in surviving historical evidence. The first asylum for exposed children, established in eighth century Milan, was intended primarily for the relief of bastard children. The records of thirteenth century exposure and abandonment cases make it clear that most of the infants concerned were illegitimate. In Germany, France, England, Scotland, Sweden, Russia and the Netherlands, women tried for murdering their children between the fifteenth and the nineteenth centuries were overwhelmingly either single women or widows, and their children illegitimate. A series of remarkably similar laws was enacted in European states between the early sixteenth and the late seventeenth centuries for the suppression of the crime. Each laid down that mothers of bastard children who had concealed their pregnancy would be assumed, should their children be found dead after birth, to have killed them. . . .

Like the harsh laws intended to suppress the crime, the circumstances of the killings of bastard children by their mothers were remarkably similar across Europe and over time. The unmarried woman would conceal her pregnancy, helped by the ample nature of traditional female dress. She would give birth in secret and, having delivered the child herself, kill it and dispose of the corpse. Recorded cases generally arose from lack of success in either bearing the child secretly or concealing its body. A representative case was cited by the seventeenth century English obstetrician Percival Willughby.[9] A young woman of Hampton Ridway, Staffordshire, attempted to conceal her pregnancy although she shared a bed with her sister. She bore her child at night in an outhouse, killed and buried it and returned to bed. She was, however, "mistrusted by her neighbours" and a woman was sent to examine her, upon which she confessed. She was hanged at Stafford in March 1670.

What motivated these women? The answer is succinctly given in the English act of 1624, which speaks of their desire "to avoyd their shame and to escape Punishment." In most of Europe the consequences of bearing (as distinct from begetting) a base child were potentially, and often actually, socially disastrous. A bastard birth dishonored the individual mother and in some societies her family too. . . .

In addition to the possibility of rejection by family and friends, the pregnant single woman also faced the likelihood of public humiliation by the Church and sometimes further punishment by officers of the state. Both possibilities became likelier from the sixteenth century on, when, in the aftermath of the Reformation and Counter-Reformation, both Catholic and Protestant nations witnessed an intensification of social regulation aimed at the reformation of popular manners. In France from the sixteenth century *curés*[10] were expected to report illegitimate pregnancies to the authorities, leading to a searching interrogation, then to a public *déclaration de grossesse*.[11] In Germany unmarried mothers were automatically excommunicated and readmitted to the Christian community only after a humiliating penance. The Kirk Sessions[12] of Presbyterian Scotland and the archdeaconry courts[13] of Anglican England also enforced public penance for illegitimacy, while in the latter country Justices of the Peace[14] might in some instances order the corporal punishment of bastard-bearers or their incarceration in a House of Correction. If all this was not enough, the unmarried mother was likely to lose her livelihood (especially if, as was common, she was a servant), and since provision for her was at best uncertain, she faced the prospects of poverty, isolation, vagrancy and perhaps prostitution.

---

[9] English writer on obstetrics (1596–1685).

[10] Chief priests of parishes.

[11] Statement about the circumstances of pregnancy.

[12] The minister and elders of a Scottish Presbyterian congregation.

[13] The lowest courts in the Church of England.

[14] English local magistrates.

These dangers, quite apart from the probability of further punishment, drove some women to kill their children, as they vividly testified. Jeanne Pion hid her pregnancy in 1450 "for fear, doubt and shame," being particularly apprehensive of the reactions of her mother, stepfather and brother. In 1473 Jeanne Hardouyn, aged 24, killed her child "fearing the shame and contempt of the world." Two centuries later an Essex servant girl hid her pregnancy and bore her child in silence in the room she shared with her mistress: "it would have been bine a griefe unto her freinds if she should have discovered it. And the other cause was that she feared she should not have bine relieved[15] if she had made it knowne that she was with child." To another English servant girl the discovery of her pregnancy in 1737 spelt "certain ruin to her for life."

These women cogently expressed their shame and anxiety but left unanswered the question of why only a small minority of pregnant single women chose to conceal their pregnancies and kill their children. . . . [W]omen formerly of excellent reputation, even possessed of unusual strength of will and determination, might be those most tempted to salvage what they could by concealment and infanticide. It is an intriguing possibility and may be true of those women who intended from the outset to dispose of their unwanted children. In most cases, however, a more satisfactory explanation may lie in the findings of a recent Swedish study which suggest that the infanticidal mother was more likely to be a person peculiarly isolated in society and bereft of any help or support in pregnancy or motherhood. For many there may have been a chain reaction set in motion by an initial concealment of pregnancy resulting more from confusion than decision. The final infanticidal impulse may have come only after an exhausting and emotionally devastating secret birth. Some may have been temporarily unbalanced by the experience, like the London girl hanged in 1688 despite her plea that at the time "she had not her Senses and was Light-headed." Others may have been forced at last to choose between abandonment of the child and infanticide and found the latter the more practical alternative.

Whatever the case, the records of this most conspicuous form of infanticide carry a significant implication. They suggest that the crime sprang not from the persistence of norms alien to the conventional morality of Christian Europe, but rather from the fact that those norms and the sanctions which upheld them made so deep an impression upon the minds of pregnant (and often servant) women, most of whom were scarcely moral delinquents. The popular culture of much of Europe allowed a degree of sexual contact during serious courtships, and bridal pregnancy was common enough. But license stopped short when mistaken trust, disappointed hopes, or foolishness turned a potential pregnant bride into an actual bastard-bearer. The known consequences were sufficiently disproportionate to the offence to terrify some who faced unmarried motherhood alone into concealment and worse.

---

[15] Received aid from the poor law.

The best documented form of direct infanticide in Europe between the fifteenth and the nineteenth centuries can thus be attributed largely to the very strength of the social sanctions, informal and formal, which served to uphold conventional morality. How common were such cases? The records of the courts would suggest that they were surprisingly rare. . . . [There were] only two cases of infanticide among the records of over 4,000 late medieval coroners' inquests for four English counties. In sixteenth and seventeenth century Nuremburg, only 42 cases were reported to the city authorities. A study of homicide indictments in the English counties of Sussex and Hertfordshire between 1559 and 1625 produced only 50 infanticide trials. . . . The Parlement of Paris[16] dealt with some 2,000 appeals in infanticide cases in the years 1565–1640, a seemingly large number. Yet when we remember that this court exercised its appeal jurisdiction over a large part of the densely populated kingdom of France, including some 500 inferior court jurisdictions, the figure is less impressive. In eighteenth century England, infanticide cases in the areas so far studied (including London) scarcely averaged one case per year. In the *présidiaux*[17] of Brittany in the same period one or two cases a year was the norm, while in Amsterdam only some 24 to 30 cases were tried in the period 1680–1811.

Given the relatively small numbers of infanticide cases recoverable from criminal records, one might wonder why such an apparently infrequent crime attracted so much attention from contemporaries, and why indeed it was the object of such Draconian laws. There are several answers to this question. In the first place, infanticide had become established as a horror crime, akin to sodomy or witchcraft in the repulsion and loathing which it commonly evoked. It was a crime to be weighed rather than counted, and in consequence we should not expect any necessary relationship to exist between public concern with the crime and its actual incidence. Moreover, for the same reason, it was a crime which attracted publicity. The Essex clergyman Ralph Josselin[18] was aware of the full details of a case in a nearby village in 1655 within a day of the event and was sufficiently shocked to enter in his diary a prayer that "the lord keepe mee and mine from any such wickedness." In the eighteenth century, newspapers assiduously reported the details of cases to a public torn between horror and fascination, thereby stimulating public awareness.

Even before the advent of the popular press there were more dreadful means of publicity. Infanticide cases, though infrequent in absolute terms, might form a relatively high proportion of all homicide cases (though these in turn were a small component of the business of the courts). In sixteenth and early seventeenth century Essex, Sussex and Hertfordshire, infanticide accounted for between 18.6% and 21.7% of all extant homicide indictments, while in eighteenth century Staffordshire the figure was 25%. Given the ease with which guilt could be proved

---

[16] A sovereign judicial court with jurisdiction over approximately one-half of France.

[17] Courts of appeal for minor civil and criminal cases.

[18] English clergyman and diarist (1616–1683).

under the discriminatory concealment laws, infanticidal mothers also made up a substantial proportion of all persons publicly executed. In the late sixteenth and early seventeenth centuries some 10 to 20% of all executions ordered by the Parlement of Paris were for infanticide. In eighteenth century Sweden infanticide was only one of 68 capital crimes in the laws, yet in the years 1759–78 it accounted for 217 of 617 executions (35%). Frederick the Great[19] informed Voltaire[20] in 1777 that in the Kingdom of Prussia infanticide was the most common single cause of executions, some 14 or 15 a year.

In a period such as the sixteenth and seventeenth centuries, when the legislators of many European states were preoccupied with the suppression of ungodliness, it is easy to see why such an emotionally charged and widely publicised crime as infanticide was singled out again and again for special treatment. The very nature of the concealment laws then adopted, however, also demonstrates a persistent suspicion that many cases of infanticide escaped prosecution. Of all forms of homicide, infanticide was perhaps the easiest to conceal. The image of latrines, drains and rivers echoing to the cries of infants cast into them to hide their mothers' shame was a popular one with the preachers of early modern France. Nor was it without foundation in fact. When a drain was uncovered following the fire of 1721 in Rennes, over eighty infant skeletons were recovered. In eighteenth century Amsterdam the paucity of infanticide trials in the court records has been revealingly set against the discovery each year of the corpses of several newborn babies in the canals and public *secreten*.[21] The numbers of such corpses increased markedly in the later decades of the century, when illegitimacy rates rose rapidly throughout western Europe. The sight of infant corpses on the dunghills of eighteenth century London was yet further disturbing evidence of the extent of infanticide (though it has been argued that at least some of these were children who had died naturally, whose parents could not afford the costs of their interment). Many cases of infanticide may have escaped discovery and prosecution. Unmarried mothers could, as we have seen, bear their children in secret and with luck a well concealed corpse might remain undiscovered, or at least fail to be traced to the mother. This was perhaps more possible in great cities than in small country villages where the attentions and suspicions of neighbors were more easily aroused. How frequently this may have occurred it is simply impossible to say. Finally, in some areas sympathetic neighbors might even have turned from or condoned the dread solution.

However, it is also true that some of the women tried and condemned for the crime were innocent. The harsh laws of the early modern period not only failed to distinguish between premeditated infanticide and acts of unbalanced mothers, but also permitted the condemnation of women who, having concealed their pregnancies, gave birth to stillborn children. It is an established fact that illegiti-

---

[19] King of Prussia from 1740 to 1786.

[20] French intellectual (1694–1778).

[21] Public toilets.

mate children are born prematurely with higher frequency as a result of inadequate prenatal care, and this alone significantly increases infant mortality. How much more might this have been so among mothers who concealed their pregnancy? The phenomenon of high rates of premature stillbirths among unmarried mothers was explored by one nineteenth century German doctor. Having considered the hypothesis that infanticide was being practiced, he rejected it and concluded that poor prenatal care and childbirth procedures were to blame. Such factors were rarely considered by the courts of early modern Europe. Percival Willughby recorded the case of a "Naturall foole" who miscarried her illegitimate child while alone. Despite his evidence at her trial, the judge insisted on the letter of the statute of 1624, the jury obediently found her guilty, and "she was, afterwards, hanged for not having a woman by her at her delivery." Some juries, however, were sympathetic to a woman's plight and refused to find her guilty. As the foreman of a Derby jury which acquitted a woman in 1647 remarked, "he thought it no reason that a woman should be hanged for a mistaken harsh word or two in the statute."

In order to avoid both judicial errors and contempt for the law, increasing emphasis came to be laid in infanticide trials upon tests to determine whether a child had been born alive, and upon evidence that its mother had intended it to live. If the lungs of the child failed to float in water, it might be concluded that it had never breathed. If its navel was tied, this was taken to be proof that there had been no murderous intention, while even the preparation of child-linen by a mother might serve to acquit her of criminal intentions. If the child's body was marked, however, this might be damning evidence that force had been used. The increasing weight given to such considerations in England and the gradual shift of public sympathy towards women accused under the concealment laws were such that whereas in early seventeenth century Essex only two-fifths of women tried for infanticide were acquitted, the acquittal rate in eighteenth century Middlesex and London had risen to approximately three-quarters of those tried.

Growing unease over the harshness of the law and concern for the plight of the infanticidal mother, from the later eighteenth century, set in motion the process of legal reform and fostered the conviction that temporary mental disturbance was the overriding cause of infanticide. From the 1770s, capital punishment for infanticide was gradually abolished in the major states of continental Europe. In Britain, where it was long retained, reprieve became virtually automatic for those convicted, the last execution for the crime taking place in 1849. Such shifts in social and judicial attitudes, however, did not affect the stubborn persistence of infanticide in its classical form wherever the social stigma of illegitimacy and the informal social sanctions against the unmarried mother retained their traditional force. The virtual elimination of infanticide in its classical form undoubtedly owes more to the gradual softening of attitudes towards illegitimacy, the availability of effective contraception and abortion, and the growth of welfare and adoptive institutions to ameliorate the position of the unmarried mother, than to changes in the attitude of the law.

From the mid-nineteenth century however, the attention of legislators was less upon the killing of illegitimate children by their mothers than upon a form of indirect infanticide which had long existed, yet had been little noticed by the law: the problem of what can be termed "infanticidal nursing." As early as the end of the twelfth century Thomas of Chobham[22] had included in his catalogue of infanticidal practices the refusal of mothers to nurse their own children. In his opinion, one frequently echoed by doctors and moralists in the early modern period, children throve best on their own mothers' milk. (This view has the support of modern evidence.) Children put out to nurse by their parents commonly suffered substantially higher rates of infant mortality than did children nursed by their mothers at home, partly as a result of inadequate child care, partly because "nurslings" were often hand- rather than breast-fed. The practice of employing nurses was, of course, common among prosperous families throughout medieval and early modern Europe, and continued to be frequent among French urban artisans well into the nineteenth century. Though mortality among "nurslings" remained disproportionately high, there is no reason to believe that the parents of these children deliberately sought their children's deaths by employing nurses. They simply conformed to a long-established custom, one found convenient for a variety of reasons and clearly expected among families of a certain rank.

The nursing industry, however, had a dark side. Parents of illegitimate or unwanted infants (and even loved ones) frequently chose, or were obliged by circumstances, to leave their children in the care of cheap "baby farmers," who at best provided poor nourishment and at worst tacitly guaranteed a child's early death. The case of a Rennes gardener's wife who in 1778 nursed seventeen bastard children, in 1779 ten and in 1780 a further three, all of whom died, is only an extreme example of a system of veiled infanticide which is well documented for early modern France and England. Indeed, the activities of baby farmers in England reached a peak only in the nineteenth century. It was the publicity given to a number of particularly scandalous cases of deliberate neglect of this kind which did much to prompt late nineteenth century legislation for the protection of infant life by the registration and control of nurses.

The number of children allowed to die as the result of the deliberate neglect of baby farmers can never be accurately assessed, though the most recent estimate attempted suggests that the annual figure for mid-Victorian England may have been a thousand or more. Whatever the actual figure, the fate of these infants reveals a marked ambivalence in attitudes towards the lives of unwanted, usually illegitimate, children. They were rarely directly killed, yet they were allowed, even encouraged, to die. The same attitudes are demonstrable on a much larger scale in the treatment of abandoned children left to the care of public charity. Though the total numbers of children abandoned might be small in relation to the total population, abandonment nonetheless constituted a serious problem. Between

---

[22] Medieval bishop and scholar (ca. 1255–1327).

two and three hundred abandoned infants were found every year on the streets of mid-nineteenth century London, most of them dead or half-dead from exposure. In eighteenth century France the situation was far worse. One parish of Angers recorded 42 children abandoned in the years 1740–64, and as many as 467 in the years 1765–89. It has been estimated that perhaps 40,000 children were abandoned each year in France as a whole during the 1780s.

The reasons for abandonment on this scale are twofold. On the one hand, there were parents who could not afford to raise their legitimate offspring. On the other hand, there was the familiar motive of disposing of an illegitimate child. Examples of both forms of behavior can be found throughout the history of Europe, but can be examined in particular detail in the records of the foundling hospitals[23] of eighteenth century France. Study after study has revealed that short term fluctuations in the frequency of abandonment in France were closely linked to times of economic distress. When the price of bread rose, or employment became scarce, temporary peaks in the statistics of abandonment swiftly followed. The longer-term upward movement of abandonment figures, however, appears to be related above all to the dramatic upswing of illegitimacy experienced throughout Europe in the later eighteenth century.

This dual causation naturally raises the question of the relative proportions of legitimate and illegitimate children among the *enfants trouvés*.[24] In most cases it would appear that the origins of the foundlings were unknown. This led to most being assumed to be illegitimate, an assumption questioned by some scholars. Where better information is available, it appears that perhaps 20–30% of abandoned children were legitimate, often significantly older than their illegitimate counterparts, most of whom were abandoned at birth.

Abandonment must be distinguished to some degree from infanticide. The fact that it existed on such a large scale in France is in part a consequence of the widespread provision of foundling hospitals in that country. French foundlings were rarely actually exposed on the streets to die. More commonly they were either born in public institutions, brought in by midwives, or delivered anonymously at the gates of the foundling hospitals. Some were accompanied by notes, naming the child, explaining the mother's circumstances, sometimes expressing the hope that the child would eventually be reclaimed, though few such reclamations ever took place. For unmarried mothers the possibility of abandoning their children at the foundling hospitals may have provided an alternative to infanticide as a way out of their predicament — one of the reasons for the foundation of these institutions in European cities. Yet in practice the distinction might mean little more than the shifting of responsibility from the individual parent to a public institution, for the mortality rate among abandoned children was appalling.

Bastards or not, the foundlings were treated in the manner usually reserved for illegitimate children; which is to say, they were not encouraged to live. The

---

[23] Orphanages.

[24] Orphaned or abandoned children.

ghastly racket in which abandoned children were transported from the French provinces to the Paris foundling hospital prior to 1779, up to nine-tenths of the infants dying on the way, was only the most blatant example of such neglect. Foundlings were generally distributed as soon as possible to the cheapest rural nurses, with minimal supervision by the authorities. Of the women of one village where children from Rheims were put out to nurse, for example, those who took foundlings were a specialist group, distinguished by their poverty.

The mortality of foundlings, not surprisingly, was disproportionately high as compared with legitimate children placed with nurses. Of the 3,558 children abandoned in Rouen in the years 1782–9, as many as 3,076 died young. Nine-tenths of those abandoned at birth failed to survive one year — and this in a city where the normal rate of infant mortality was only 18–20% in the same period. The same depressing story could be told of the children maintained by the work-houses of eighteenth century London (many of whom were illegitimate), and of the infants admitted by the foundling hospitals of Imperial Russia (which were popularly known as "angel factories"). But the point is sufficiently made. Institutional neglect by well-intentioned but overburdened and under-financed charitable institutions made what was probably the largest single contribution to infanticide in modern Europe, one which long escaped public attention and legal intervention. As in the case of private baby farming, to which it was closely related, the problem persisted until the later nineteenth century, when public opinion and then national legislatures woke up to the need to regulate nursing and protect the lives of all children, whatever their origins.

The realities of infanticide by either commission or neglect retain their capacity to shock. Yet, as Marc Bloch[25] observed, "the historian's sole duty is to understand." In the light of the evidence reviewed here, several conclusions can be suggested concerning the problem of infanticide in European history. First, consideration of the circumstances underlying infanticide draws the historian into a morass of complexity. Infanticide is not, as has sometimes been assumed, a straightforward indicator of the psychological disposition of parents towards their children. The killing of infants might spring from callous indifference to the lives of unwanted children, from the anguish of mental disturbance, from the pressures exerted by marginal subsistence and the interests of the larger group, from coldly rational calculation of familial betterment, or from the fear of harsh social sanctions against breaches of the moral norms of society. These motives can all be found in some periods of the past, yet they varied also in their relative presence and strength. Second, it seems doubtful that infanticide was ever so commonplace in European societies as has been suggested by some historians of childhood. Though infanticide was neither morally nor legally proscribed in the ancient Mediterranean civilisations, the common assumption that it was frequent, even

---

[25] An influential medieval historian of the twentieth century; executed by the Nazis for membership in the French Resistance (1886–1944).

systematic, has been brought into question. Since early medieval times it seems unlikely that infanticide has played an important role in either population control or familial strategies. When short term crises dislocated family economies, abandonment was sometimes resorted to. Evidence of parental neglect can also be cited. Yet there is no conclusive evidence that such expedients were part of the norm of parental experience. Despite the deficiencies of the information available to us, it seems clear that direct infanticide in medieval and modern Europe has been largely confined to a small minority of illegitimate children, while indirect infanticide by negligent nursing was the fate of a substantially larger proportion of abandoned nurslings.

A third conclusion is that the evidence for shifts in attitudes toward infanticide suggests that change has come very largely after a series of periods of intensified public sensitivity to the problem, each of which requires explanation and deserves further study. The first of these periods, which was both the longest and the most obscure, embraced the Christianisation of the later Roman Empire and its successor kingdoms. . . . Christian teaching on the value of infant life, expressed in both moral exhortation and law, strove to establish a strong cultural inhibition on infanticide, identifying the practice as a crime of peculiar enormity. At the same time, however, the gradual institutionalisation of the Church's moral teaching had the effect of strengthening sanctions against sexual immorality, thereby contributing to infanticide motivated by the need to conceal illegitimate births or to dispose of illegitimate children. Thereafter, the history of infanticide has been punctuated by periods of augmented public concern with the crime, each of which bred legal responses appropriate to its time and helped to shape future developments: the concealment laws of the sixteenth and seventeenth centuries; the amelioration of those laws at the turn of the eighteenth and nineteenth centuries; the attempts to regulate nursing and protect infant life in the later nineteenth century.

The precise timing of such legislative initiatives varied from country to country, in consequence, no doubt, of particular national circumstances. Yet the existence of distinct periods of heightened concern of a pan-European nature seems clear and necessitates an attempt at explanation. The answer may lie in the enormous symbolic significance which infanticide had acquired in European Christian culture. Infanticide had been identified as an unnatural act; its very existence was therefore a perennial reminder of the fragility of the prevailing moral order. In times of relative social stability this peculiar resonance may have been muted. In times of significant change, when established values appeared to be threatened, a crime like infanticide might engage attention and elicit an emotional response out of all proportion to its actual incidence. Infanticide challenged a response from both the official moralists and the governors of Europe for the simple reason that attitudes toward the crime involved a judgement of the legitimacy of the prevailing moral and social order. The result could be a powerful reassertion of established norms, in which the upholding of fundamental values in the face of changing social realities might be seen to depend in part upon the repression or containment of such symbolically charged deviance.

It is perhaps for this reason that the later sixteenth and seventeenth centuries, fraught as they were with social, economic, religious and political instability, witnessed such an urgent preoccupation with the repression of the traditional horror crimes, notably witchcraft and infanticide. In the eighteenth century such concern was fading, though the crime of infanticide stubbornly persisted. The quickening pace of social change in the late eighteenth and nineteenth centuries, however, involving as it did massive population expansion, rural congestion, urbanisation, industrialisation, and all their attendant problems, again raised fears of the disintegration of the traditional social and moral order. Attention was once more focused upon infanticide; though the independent processes of change in judicial attitudes and social institutions meant that attempts were made to come to grips with the problem by other means, means more appropriate to new conditions and new perceptions of the circumstances that underlay a crime which retained its capacity to shock and challenge the public conscience.

The history of infanticide thus provides an example of the manner in which legal definitions and redefinitions of criminality are closely linked not only to the broad processes of social change, but also to persisting elements in the self-image of society. It was the established symbolic significance of infanticide in a time of change that provoked the harsh legislation of the sixteenth and seventeenth centuries as state after state was stirred to reaffirm its commitment to traditional values. Again, it was the persisting emotional resonance of the crime that finally drew the attention of social investigators, governors and legislators to the situation of the unmarried mother and her child, setting in motion the slow process of legal, administrative and institutional change which has sufficiently alleviated their position as to render infanticide by any other than a mentally disturbed parent rare and unlikely.

PART THREE

THE NINETEENTH CENTURY

Anna K. Clark
Sidney Pollard
K. H. Connell
Peter Gay
Richard J. Evans
Zoltan Barany
Herbert S. Klein
Donna Gabaccia
Stephen P. Frank
Theresa M. McBride

Historians generally count the nineteenth century as lasting from the end of the Napoleonic Wars (1815) to the beginning of World War I in 1914. Nineteenth-century Europeans appeared to exhibit a confident optimism, if not arrogance, that rested on European scientific achievement, industrial advance, and imperial conquest. The great world fairs of the period — London, 1851; Paris, 1867; Paris, 1900 — that displayed the world's art and manufactures, and that asserted European superiority over the rest of the world, suggest how rich, powerful, self-assured, and nation-proud were the times. In short, the nineteenth century was an era of apparent greatness as Europe flexed its industrial and political muscles. Then, however, came World War I, the "war to end all wars," revealing the terrible consequences of modern technology coupled with rampant nationalism and militarism.

Not all Europeans, of course, shared or reveled in the power exercised by the leaders and the social elite of various nations. Power and wealth were not evenly distributed, and most people continued their never ending struggle for food, work, and a modicum of security.

The major socioeconomic development in this century was the Industrial Revolution, whose effects were felt throughout society. The factories and machines of the Industrial Revolution altered relations among social classes, gave rise to new types of work and workers' organizations, inspired original ideas about the reorganization of society, raised the standard of living, contributed to the formation of immense urban centers, and made change rather than stability the expected fact of life. The unequal distribution of the new riches helped to spawn class conflict, as evidenced in the programs of socialists, communists, and anarchists as well as in mass political parties that recruited the laboring classes.

One of the themes of nineteenth-century history is the development of worker consciousness (aided perhaps by growing literacy and the penny press) and the increasing politicization of the masses, who resented the lifestyles and power of the bourgeoisie. These changes occurred in the midst of the new urban landscape, transformed by technological wonders such as steel and electricity. Great new industries arose in chemicals, oil, and pharmaceuticals. At the same time, Europe's colonization of other societies was at its peak; this was the great age of European power. Textbooks sometimes stress nineteenth-century intellectual

---

and cultural movements such as Romanticism or political developments such as the unification of Italy and of Germany. These were all important in their own right, but they must be set against the background of rapid and unsettling change in the relationships, values, and beliefs of the vast majority of the population.

The essays in this section deal with the nineteenth century's profound social changes. Many historians have come to use gender as a tool of analysis in order to better understand these changes. For instance, during this era traditional male dominance sometimes clashed with socioeconomic developments. Anna K. Clark shows that the wages working-class wives earned gave them a certain independence their husbands resented, thus leading to marital conflict. Donna Gabaccia writes that capitalism and modernization did not necessarily improve the lives of Italian women, whose economic and social well-being continued to be affected by male control. Traditional patriarchal attitudes existed well into the twentieth century, as Theresa M. McBride illustrates in her analysis of the lives of female department-store clerks in Paris. Store owners thought they were obligated and entitled to regulate both the working and personal lives of female employees. Peter Gay culled thousands of personal letters and proves convincingly that Victorian middle-class spouses and lovers were not sexually inert prigs, but ardently sought sexually fulfilling relationships. Ties of affection between wives and husbands embraced emotional and physical love.

Social historians continue to uncover unattractive aspects of the Industrial Revolution. Sidney Pollard underscores the imposition of factory discipline on workers unaccustomed to such restrictions. K. H. Connell's account of the potato in Ireland points to economic causes of the great famine at mid-century that industrialized Great Britain did not prevent or alleviate. While urban centers grew exponentially, their problems did not diminish. Cities remained hotbeds of disease. In a careful study of cholera epidemics in Hamburg, Richard J. Evans explains the disastrous effects of bourgeois attitudes toward trade and the poor, which led city leaders to place the continuation of trade above all other concerns and to adopt medical explanations for cholera's spread that ignored the fetid conditions where Hamburg's down-and-out lived. The century consistently saw bourgeois disgust with the lifestyles and living conditions of those below them on the socioeconomic ladder. It might well be said that those who benefited from the Industrial Revolution kicked the ladder down behind them and tried to increase the distance between themselves and the poor, whether English factory workers, Irish peasants, or Hamburg port workers. Nevertheless, as Herbert S. Klein explains, Europeans (not Americans or Africans) were instrumental in the long struggle (which required force and the threat of force) to end the Atlantic slave trade.

Some areas of nineteenth-century Europe seemingly were little affected by industrial or political change. Zoltan Barany looks at the Austro-Hungarian and Ottoman empires, far removed from the core areas of the Industrial Revolution. These empires encompassed numerous ethnic groups, and the central governments labored to maintain control and to prevent the states from coming apart. Both empires (to different degrees) perpetuated discriminatory policies against Gypsies, and other peoples persisted in holding negative stereotypes of this historically persecuted minority group. Stephen P. Frank's account of popular justice among the Russian peasantry reveals a seemingly immobile village culture, impervious to the rapid transformations we routinely ascribe to nineteenth-century Europe.

THE STRUGGLE FOR THE BREECHES: PLEBEIAN MARRIAGE

Anna K. Clark

In nineteenth-century Great Britain, as has been the case throughout Western civilization, husbands have dominated their wives, according to law and custom. In early modern England, for example, a wife who disobeyed her husband could be charged with the crime of petty treason, analogous to a subject committing high treason by disobeying the king. Anna K. Clark, professor of history at the University of Minnesota, has concentrated on sexual politics and the influence of gender in British history. Here she examines working-class marriages during the early Industrial Revolution.

Clark paints a dark picture of the effects of industrialization on working-class life and marriage. Previous historians have sometimes praised the growth of radical politics in late-eighteenth- and early-nineteenth-century Britain, the birth of worker solidarity and consciousness, and the widening of democracy. Clark, however, asserts that the working-class culture of the era seems less harmonious and less admirable when viewed from the perspective of gender relations. Gender, she implies, should be included in any and every historical investigation of social and economic phenomena.

The ability of wives to earn wages meant that plebeian (working people's) marriages were often business partnerships, with both spouses contributing to the maintenance of the home and family. Nevertheless, husbands demanded wifely submission and control of the household. According to Clark, the clash between the old patriarchal tradition and the new family economy led to conflicts over power and the command of family resources, that is, over the struggle for the breeches ("who wears the pants"). Given the independence that wage-earning fostered, a woman often chafed under her husband's yoke. How do the autobiographies of wives and husbands differ in describing their marriages? How did popular literature (including song) satirize marriage, especially through the image of the struggle for the breeches? Clark uses court records to describe the reality of plebeian marriages, including wife-beating and murder, control

Anna K. Clark, *The Struggle for the Breeches: Gender and the Making of the British Working Class* (Berkeley: University of California Press, 1995), 63–75, 77–85, 87.

over earnings, and disputes arising because of men's leisure habits (such as drinking, gambling, and socializing with other men) and infidelities. Did the popular literature accurately reflect plebeian marital relations? How did different sectors of British society react to the abuse of wives? What factors inhibited marital equality?

The life of David Love, a peripatetic ballad-writer and former collier,[1] did not follow the pattern of his name, for he found marital happiness difficult to attain. He married his second wife expecting a docile helpmeet, but their relationship soured as the shop they kept together failed and, in his words, she "strove to be master." As he continued in his autobiography, "I would not submit; but asserted my authority, which caused great contention." However, he eventually won her over:

> With her my ground could hardly stand,
> She strove to get the upper hand;
> 'Till eight years join'd in marriage band,
>   Chang'd was her life,
>   She did submit to my command,
>   A loving wife.

In common with many religious and popular authorities, David Love believed marriage should be "patriarchal yet companionate." Contemporary moral authorities made it quite clear that husbands ought to rule — albeit with love. But they feared that submission was "directly contrary to women's inclinations, an order which could be sustained only by vigilant suppression of their unruly drives.". . . The Rev. William Secker[2] both advised husbands to love and respect their wives and stressed, "Our ribs were not ordained to be our rulers. . . . The wife may be a sovereign in her husband's absence, but she must be subject in her husband's presence." Secker warned, "Choose such a one as will be a subject to your dominion. Take heed of yoking yourselves with untamed heifers." John Stephens, a London preacher, declared that woman "is forbidden to aspire to rule, for her Maker designed her for a helper." Women must not brawl, he continued, but must submit themselves to their husbands, while men must not act bitterly or inhumanly toward their wives. The Rev. Mark Wilks, a radical Baptist minister, told men to "rule in love."

Yet as Love found, there was an essential contradiction between the patriarchal and companionate ideals. Plebeian marriage was often a business partnership, for both spouses had to contribute to the family's maintenance. But wives were not supposed to acquire equal authority thereby. The sense of independence wives

---

[1] Coalminer.

[2] Clergyman and religious writer (d. 1681?).

gained by wage-earning clashed with husbands' desire to dominate, resulting in the "struggle for the breeches" satirized in comic popular literature and more tragically evident in court records of wife-beating.

To be sure, autobiographies reveal that many plebeian partnerships were happy and harmonious, especially when husbands demonstrated respect for their wives' contributions. J. B. Leno praised his wife as "a good mother, an affectionate partner, a wise counsellor, a model of industry." Whatever the faults of his second wife, David Love valued his first wife as "a blooming young woman . . . excellent at working, careful and industrious." Similarly, John O'Neill's wife helped him in his shoemaking business by binding shoes, and he remembered her upon her death during her thirteenth confinement[3] as "a mild, sober, industrious, generous-hearted woman, a good wife, an affectionate mother, a disinterested friend." The cooper William Hart, of London, tried to set up a little shop so that he and his "beloved dear" wife could support their children. . . .

In the relative poverty of Scotland, industrious wives were prized even more than in England. As one mother in a popular chapbook[4] advised her son, he shouldn't wed a thin girl who'll "di naething but prick and sew . . . an drink tea, but you maun get ane that can card and spin, and wirk in barn and byre." Indeed, Alexander Somerville, son of farm laborers in the mid Lowlands, remembered that his mother not only made clothes and engaged in other "domestic toil," but had to "add by outfield labor to the family income," carrying haystacks and performing other heavy farm work.

Weavers and other textile workers were especially likely to seek hard-working wives, for women's work in spinning was essential to the production process, and a weaving wife could contribute even more to the family's earnings. Joseph Gutteridge described his prospective wife as "kind, truthful, and industrious, gaining her living by weaving; in fact, she was just the kind of helpmeet I needed." Joseph Livesey, a Preston weaver, praised a good wife as "sober, affectionate and industrious." In Scotland, the "'slubber spinners' who 'drew long from the Flax on the rock,' producing uneven yarn, were less likely to find husbands than the fine spinners, who . . . were the object of the pragmatically-tinged affections of males who sought the best spinners as partners, and hence a higher standard of living." A young female weaver in Spitalfields could allure potential husbands by flaunting her "showy ribbons, the ear-drops, the red coral necklaces of four or five strings" she bought with her own wages, for a man would be "disposed to consider the earnings which she can make at her loom as far more advantageous to him than all she could gain or save by the use of a needle, or could benefit him by cooking dinners which his wages do not enable him to buy." . . .

Not only wives' industry but their wisdom was valued. "The Weavers' Garland, or a New School for Christian Patience," advises a hard-pressed weaver to

---

[3] The time of a woman's giving birth.

[4] A small book or pamphlet.

abandon his drinking companions and seek solace in his wife's good counsel and industry. James Paterson, a Scottish printer, attended political meetings and holiday rambles with a cobbler and his wife who were "exemplary in conjugal felicity as they were in their habits of industry and sobriety." The Rev. Mark Wilks, a former buttonmaker, remembered of his wife that "never was an attachment founded on a greater equality of esteem, or a stronger reciprocity of friendship. . . . His wife was his companion, and his friend, and he never entered on any step without first availing himself of the benefit of her opinion."

However, wives had to ensure that their husbands did not perceive their advice as undermining patriarchal authority. David Gilmour recalled several types of overt or covert struggles for power within artisan marriages in a Baptist weaving community in Paisley, near Glasgow. Gilmour's neighbor Henry Buchan acknowledged that wives could rule their husbands through manipulation:

> In every case what maistry was contended for, the idea o' marriage in its proper sense is excluded; marriage involving the acknowledgement on the part of each that the ither had the richt to be consulted. . . . A true wife will aye see her highest wisdom in her husband's, an' a true husband will always rejoice in his wife's love o' his wisdom. Mairfortaken that love o' his wisdom gies her a pow'r tae rule owre him an' his household, which a true wife will do, while as the poet says, she 'seems to obey.'

However, this patriarchal partnership was not always so companionate. Gilmour also remembered another neighbor, a radical who "waxed eloquent now and then in defence of liberty and equality, but he was from constitutional tendencies a strong-willed aristocrat, and exercised his family headship, not as a responsibility for which he was accountable, but as an authority that ought and must be obeyed."

Most male autobiographers, unlike David Love, were reluctant to reveal marital misery. . . . [S]uch revelations would have been "undignified" for writers trying to depict self-improvement. However, children may have been able to be more critical of their parents' marriages. . . . [In] working-class autobiographies, "The father emerges almost as a stereotype — frequently a drunkard, often thoughtless and uncaring of his wife and children, bad-tempered and selfish, but occasionally over-generous and sentimental."

The very few plebeian women's autobiographies presented a different perspective from that of the men. In the examples I have found, women depict marriage as a pragmatic effort to survive. The Scottish Janet Bathgate described a youthful friendship to another girl in much more intense terms than she used for her later two marriages. Similarly, Mary Ashford remembered a strong attachment to a female fellow servant, but she expressed little emotion when describing her marriages. Ashford accepted her first husband's proposal because she had just lost a place as a servant. They promised to pool their savings and "act fair and candid toward each other." Although he had an irritable temper due to gout, he "exerted himself" on behalf of their family of six children. After her first husband died, she married the widower of a close friend, who said "he knew I should do my duty by him, and he could assist me in rearing his old comrade's children." When Mary Saxby, a peripatetic ballad-singer, left her lover for another man, she lamented, "Here I only exchanged one state of slavery for another." Ann Candler suffered in an unhappy marriage for forty years. Despite her "unbounded" affection for her husband, "he treated me in a very unbecoming manner." When she finally left him, he "wept most bitterly at parting; I was sensibly affected, but had suffered too severely to waver in my resolution." Her resolution may have been strengthened by the fact that her husband was not a good provider and drank away their money when he was not serving in the army. Candler was unusual only in that she wrote an autobiography; her experience of neglect and violence was very common among plebeian women.

Popular literature often admonished husbands and wives to respect each other and forget their quarrels, upholding the values of companionate, patriarchal marriage. "The Fair Sex Vindicated" asked,

> *Who then is your constant affectionate friend?*
> *'Tis no sottish companion, I'm sure, whose advice*
> *Has ruined your children, and cheers you in vice,*
> *But 'tis your best friend, your affectionate wife,*
> *Who values your health as she values her life.*

. . . Yet publishers aimed not to inculcate morals but to sell songs. To do so, their productions had to speak to the realities, not just the aspirations, of plebeian life. The ideal marriage was rather difficult to attain, and was in any case not a source of satirical or tragic narrative. Even when songs and tales ended with promises of harmony, they almost always began with assumptions of conflict. Many plebeians felt stuck in unhappy marriages, or at least constantly overheard their neighbors' quarrels. Yet popular songs and chapbooks about marriage did not simply reflect marital misery, either, for dreary reality would not appeal to buyers any more than moralism would.

Instead, popular literature satirized marriage through a variety of rhetorical tropes[5] and ancient images — most notably the image of the "struggle for the breeches," an ancient motif in European popular culture. . . . "Breeches represent force, dominance, freedom," a crucial yet vulnerable symbol of manhood. A thinly veiled phallic symbol, the breeches symbolized male domination. However, unlike the phallus, they could easily be removed and worn by a woman. Popular culture's representations of wives wearing the breeches evoked male anxieties that women could easily undermine their rightful power, yet also excited laughter by their incongruity. Songs upheld husbandly domination by ridiculing men who were unable to enforce their will on their wives. For example, in a Scottish song, "Will the Weaver," the hero complains,

---

[5] Figures of speech.

> *Mother dear now I'm married,*
> *I wish I had longer tarried*
> *For my wife she does declare*
> *That the breeches she will wear.*

His mother admonishes him, "Loving son give her her due, Let me hear no more from you." Similarly, the wife comes off victorious in a song about marital quarrels over the respective costs of whisky and tea. The husband threatens,

> *You impudent jade[6] take care what you say,*
> *You are bound by the laws of the land to obey,*
> *And while I am able I vow and declare,*
> *I will not allow you the breeches to wear.*

But the song warns husbands,

> *For if you should flail [wives] from head to toe;*
> *You may depend on it they'll have the last blow.*

. . . [T]he image of the violent wife could be seen as humorous because it transgressed the passive, subordinate, female role — and rarely occurred in reality.

The motif of the struggle for the breeches could appeal to female readers and purchasers of popular literature as well as to disgruntled husbands. Chapbooks presented men as desiring patriarchal marriage while women dreamed of companionate unions. In the chapbook *The Jealous Man . . .* , the wife declares, "I am your yokefellow, but not your slave; your equal, but not your vassal," and her husband retorts, "I own this all to be true, and yet the breeches belong to me. Is not man lord of the creation? . . . I work for you by day, and drudge for you by night [an allusion to her sexual demands], and yet you are not contented, without superiority over me." In the popular *New and Diverting Dialogue Between a Husband and His Wife,* an impatient woman dragging her husband out of the alehouse threatens to cuckold him when he declares he'll beat her. He accuses her of rebelling against "her lord and Master," but she retorts that he is an "unnatural monster, cruel brute, tyrant," who does not remember "that husbands are to love and cherish their wives."

Many songs, especially those from the eighteenth century, vented female discontent but upheld the overall framework of husbandly dominance. But as female literacy increased in the early nineteenth century, publishers began to circulate songs that provided women with a newly defiant rhetoric against oppressive husbands. Perhaps women sang such tunes over washtubs or at their friendly society[7] meetings, egging each other on against brutal spouses. These rather bitter ballads advised women to fight back in the sex war, to "whack him with a rolling pin," a shovel, a poker, or even a chamberpot.

---

[6] A disreputable woman.

[7] An organization that collected weekly savings to protect workers from unemployment, illness, and a pauper's funeral.

What was new was that these songs drew upon a language of tyranny and slavery familiar from the political rhetoric of the time. The simple message of one song ran:

> *I'll be no submissive wife,*
> *No, not I — no, not I;*
> *I'll not be a slave for life,*
> *No, not I — no, not I.*

Publishers tried to increase sales by exposing the sexual antagonism of plebeian life, printing misogynist anti-marriage broadsheets[8] and indignant female responses. "A Woman That Is Plagued with a Man," a retort to "A Man That Is Plagued with a Woman," warned, "A woman had better be laid in her grave / Than suffer herself to be any man's slave." "The Woman That Wished She Never Got Married" seconded this warning, proclaiming, "While you ladies do single remain, / By a tyrant you'll never be hurried."

The counterparts to women's defiance were anti-marriage songs and caricatures that most likely found their audiences in the homosocial[9] worlds of plebeian culture, the pubs and clubs where men drank, sang, and caroused, the arenas where the bachelor culture of journeymen flourished. For example, the *Trades' Newspaper* reported one story about a shoemaker who sang "The Struggle for the Breeches" to a workmate who was so struck by its resemblance to his own marital woes that he dropped dead in a fit.

In song, bachelors vowed to avoid the burdens of matrimony — the expense of childbirth and childrearing, the "self-less" labor for a family, the risk of cuckoldry, and, above all, "those termagant[10] jades who'd still wear the breeches." Men should "kiss and cuddle girls," but when they're pregnant, it's "Time to Say No!" The records of the Foundling Hospital[11] and of the Glasgow kirk sessions[12] bear witness to the reality of the problem of seduction and desertion. In song, however, bachelors adamantly celebrated their state, pointing out that in marriage,

> *There's scolding and fighting, while we're delighting*
> *Our selves with our freedom, while you have this strife.*

If men stayed single, resources could be circulated among workmates rather than being saved for the home. "Advice to Sailors" declares,

> *For we that are merry and free*
> *Carouse and merrily sing*

---

[8] Large pieces of paper with information printed on one side only.

[9] Same-sex social groups, such as fraternities and sororities.

[10] Quarrelsome, shrewish.

[11] Orphanage in London, founded in the eighteenth century.

[12] The minister and elders of a Scottish Presbyterian congregation.

For we have no wives that will scold
We can both borrow and lend.

Nonetheless, most plebeians eventually married or cohabited, but the loyalty of many husbands to their drinking mates obviously caused tensions between husband and wife. Although these clashes did not necessarily lead to violence, the husbands of popular literature often required that their wives allow them to frequent the alehouse. In radical weaver Alexander Wilson's popular song "Watty and Meg, or the Wife Reformed," Watty complains to his mates in a pub of his unhappy marriage to a scolding wife:

See you, Mungo, when she'll clash [gossip] on
   Wi' her everlasting clack [scolding],
Whyles I've had my nieve [fist], in passion,
Liftet up to break her back!

But his friend Mungo advises, "O, for gudesake, keep from cuffets, [blows]," and advises him that simply threatening to desert her will infallibly keep her in line.

Yet the "humorous" intention of popular literature allowed songs to both mock and condone wife-beating. By its title, the ambiguous "A Fool's Advice to Henpeck'd Husbands," one song ridiculed men who could not control their wives. But it also advised them,

When your wife for scolding finds pretences, oh
Take the handle of a broom,
Not much thicker than your thumb,
And thwack her till you bring her to her senses, oh.

And a misogynist streak within popular culture meant that some songs and caricatures celebrated the torture of wives as funny and as justified by their shrewishness. The early nineteenth-century Glasgow ballad-singer Hawkie drew crowds with his "Cure for Ill Wives," which advised the unhappy husband to "nail her tongue to a growing tree." Congregating outside the windows of print shops to see the latest caricatures was a favorite male recreation. One engraving, "Tameing a Shrew, or Petruchio's Patent Family Bedstead, Gags and Thumscrews [sic]" depicted a man stretching his recalcitrant wife on a rack. Another viciously portrayed "The Cobbler's Cure for a Scolding Wife" to be sewing up her mouth. . . . In the punchline to a late eighteenth-century "joke," the irate husband declares to his scolding wife, "By Gingo, I will break all the Bones in your Skin, but I'll have quiet."

The wife-beating cobbler — the protagonist of a whole genre of songs — may have appealed as an anti-hero, transgressing the patriarchal ideal of companionate partnership and instead simply celebrating the misogyny of the degraded artisan who married to obtain domestic services and insisted on retaining his bachelor freedoms. "The Bold Cobbler" declares,

I'll let the vixen know,
That I will be her Master;

When I to dine set down,
I'll no more bones picking,
I will have a bit of brown,
Or Ma'am she knaps a kicking,
All skittle grounds I'll see,
To play a cheerful rubber,
And if she follows me,
Dam'me but I'll drab her.[13]

The cobbler's popularity as a wife-beater in popular literature may, to be sure, be derived from the many puns on his trade; but the puns derived their humor from an acceptance of violence. For instance,

And when my wife began to strap
  Why I began to leather
  So where to take her down some pegs
  I drubb'd her neat and clever.

        . . .

  T'would break my heart to lose my awl,
  To lose my wife's a trifle.

When we look at the incidence of wife-beating, we will see that the violent cobbler was not only a stereotype but a reality.

The image of the struggle for the breeches buttressed male dominance by presenting patriarchal authority as the natural state of things and a wife who refused to submit as aberrant. Even one magistrate described a woman who allegedly beat her husband as wearing the breeches. Police court reporters, who sometimes spiced up their accounts with satire, could use this metaphor to discredit abused wives, ridiculing them as pugnacious termagants. For instance, a *Weekly Dispatch* reporter buttressed George Parker's claim that his wife Mary beat him by describing her as a "stalwart dame who possessed the power of 'wearing breeches' and refused him his connubial rights." However, in this case, the magistrate found her more convincing and rejected Parker's charge. Similarly, when reporting a marital brawl the *Thistle's* police court reporter observed, "The wife showed marks of no slight description, which showed her husband to be of good pluck."

The image of the struggle for the breeches concealed the reality that men assaulted women in 78 to 95 percent of the domestic violence cases reported in the courts. Many wife-beaters seemed to feel they had a right to abuse their wives, and indeed until 1853 legal authorities equivocated as to whether wife-beating constituted legitimate correction or criminal assault. The alleged ruling of Francis Buller, "Judge Thumb," that a man could beat his wife with a stick no bigger than his thumb was never a legal precedent, but it entered folklore. For instance,

---

[13] "The Bold Cobbler" states that he will give his wife a sharp kicking ("knaps a kicking") if she does not serve him beer ("a bit of brown"). If she intrudes upon his playing a game of ninepins ("skittle"), he will treat her as a whore ("drab her").

the pornographic *Rambler's Magazine* cited it as a charter for wife-beaters. Even in the 1830s, at least one Glasgow magistrate did not take wife-beating very seriously. In a case in which a man had slashed his wife's face, the magistrate told him, "If he had so beaten any other person, than his wife, he would have been punished most severely, but as it was only his wife," he was bound over to keep the peace under a penalty of five pounds if he beat her again. The magistrate next fined a carter, who had whipped his horse till it bled, ten shillings and sixpence. . . .

Many abused women, however, did not accept their husbands' right to beat them. Sometimes women themselves used the language of popular literature's sex war to express their complaints. Elizabeth Cooney testified that she had been married to John Cooney for only a week "when he began to tyrannise over her." Similarly, the wife of Henry Stracey complained that "her husband was so tyrannical, she lived in constant fear of her life." At least one woman a week appeared before the Middlesex magistrates in the late eighteenth century to complain of her husband's violence. In a three-month period in 1824, fifty-six cases appeared before the Glasgow police court — more than four a week. . . .

The root cause of domestic violence, then as now, was that abusive men wanted to dominate their wives and used violence to do so. However, to put domestic violence into historical perspective requires an examination of the specific triggers for violence in a particular era. When did husbands believe their authority was being undermined, and what inspired wives to fight back and take violent spouses to court? . . . [M]id-nineteenth-century working-class couples fought over money, drink, and authority. In late eighteenth- and early nineteenth-century Glasgow and London, conflict between plebeian husbands and wives erupted over many of the same issues, but the contradictions between patriarchal ideals, the realities of the family economy, and the pull of plebeian sociability were particular to this earlier plebeian culture.

Wife-beating was not a deviant act caused by unusual pressures of poverty and unemployment, for wife-beaters could be found in all levels of plebeian society. In Old Bailey[14] sessions trials for murders and attempted murders of wives between 1780 and 1845, clerks, tradesmen, and small shopkeepers accounted for 19 percent of the 177 cases in which occupations were known. Laborers accounted for 40 percent of the cases, but their percentage of the London work force is difficult to establish. Skilled working men accounted for 41 percent of these cases in London, and this percentage approximately matches their proportion of the population of London. Only three weavers appeared, although they were the group hardest hit by unemployment. Five carpenters and four tailors were tried, a number roughly proportional to their numbers in the population, but shoemakers were overrepresented at fourteen cases, the largest single occupational group of wife-beaters. In Glasgow, they represented 6.2 percent (16 cases) of the police court domestic-violence cases, although they made up only 2.9 percent of

---

[14] Criminal court in London.

the occupied population. The discrepancy was less marked in Lancashire, where they composed 3.6 percent (7 cases) of the wife-beaters and 2.7 percent of the occupied population. In both Glasgow and Lancashire, artisans in traditional apprenticed trades were strikingly overrepresented as wife-beaters. . . .

As in London, textile workers, especially handloom weavers, accounted for many fewer of these cases than would be expected from their representation in the population. Some textile workers did beat their wives, to be sure, but it is again possible that the sexually cooperative culture of the textile industry diminished the incidence of such violence. When husbands needed their wives' skill at weaving or spinning, domestic violence could be seen to disrupt a profitable household economy. Conversely, artisans' domestic violence may have stemmed from tensions between loyalty to the family and loyalty to the hard-drinking world of journeymen's bachelor culture.

For families in all trades, the dual responsibilities of husbands and wives in the family economy could lead to productive partnerships — or to quarrels over the amount of work each performed and the allocation of resources. Proletarianization could increase these tensions, for both partners often brought in wages, but until later in the nineteenth century, when husbands often gave their wives a set amount for housekeeping, there was no clear pattern for which spouse controlled the family budget. Plebeians knew very well that husbands legally controlled their wives' earnings, but in practice women did not surrender their wages readily. The social investigator Sir Frederick Eden[15] commented in the 1790s that the legal right of husbands to claim their wives' wages deterred many industrious women from earning money, "from a thorough conviction that her mate would, too probably, strip her of every farthing which she had not the ingenuity to conceal." Hannah More[16] painted a vivid picture of a woman whose gambling husband took the pittance she earned: "She bore with patience her husband's spending all he got upon his own pleasures, and leaving her to shift for herself; but when he came home, and tore from her what she had worked so hard for, she could not help weeping and complaining."

Popular literature and witnesses in trials echoed the concerns of social investigators. From a husband's point of view, a comic broadside mandated in a mock statute that "every Washerwoman, or any Women going out to daily work, shall keep one half of her earnings, and the other shall be given to her Lord and Master, for drinking money." When "Watty" of Alexander Wilson's famous poem finally gains dominance over his wife, he makes her promise

That ye'll ne'er, like Bessy Miller,
Kick my shins or rug my hair,
Lastly, I'm to keep the siller [silver];
This upon your soul you swear?

---

[15] Political economist and social critic (1766–1809).

[16] Writer of religious tracts for the working classes (1745–1833).

Court records reveal real-life examples. When Daniel Heath set up his wife in a milk walk,[17] he allowed her the silver she earned but kept the gold for himself. Catherine Rolph complained that her husband, a shopkeeper, not only beat her but forced her to give him the money she had earned selling stock neckties.

Women whose small savings or skills gave them independence could be exploited by irresponsible husbands. When Margaret Evans left her husband Daniel Heath on account of his ill treatment, he allowed her only eight shillings a week, although, as we have seen, he had been taking the gold she earned in her milk walk. Similarly, Benjamin Blake had his new wife mind the coal shed he bought with her savings; meanwhile, he told her he worked as a carpenter, but in fact he was spending her earnings on another woman. Although Sarah Purryer and her common-law husband made and sold mats together, he beat her as well as refused to give her money to feed the children. Finally, one night after he had gotten drunk and thrown her down the stairs, she killed him with a mallet-blow to the head. Three years after she had served two months in Newgate for manslaughter, she had established herself in partnership, rather than common-law marriage, with William Umney, a Spitalfields matmaker, and was earning enough to keep a servant.

For women who had their own craft skills, small businesses, or inheritances, marriage could be disadvantageous, but at the same time their experience of public life may have given them the courage to protest against abusive husbands. The wife of John McDonach voiced a common complaint when she told the Glasgow police court in 1829 that she had to support him and the children since he refused to work, and all she had received in return were two black eyes. She assured the justices, "I am willing still to do so," to support the family, but she added, "I think if he does not contribute, he should be bound, at least, to keep the peace." The magistrate sympathized with her but feared that any fine would merely come out of her pocket; all he did, therefore, was to admonish the man, who "went away unconcerned."

Some women went to court because they resented loss of property and independence as well as their husbands' violence. Elizabeth Sims asked a magistrate for a separation because "in the absence of her husband, which frequently happened for some considerable time, she did very well, and got forward, but whenever he returned, he beat her, spent her money, and threatened her life." Similarly, Ann Casson deposed that "prior to her intermarriage . . . she kept a grocer's shop in Edgeware Road and was doing very well when she unfortunately became acquainted with and met her said husband who had little or no property at all." Phoebe Darwell, who kept a tobacconist's shop before she married, lamented, "I had respectability and some money, when I married him; but he has blasted my character, and he has done me every public and private injury." The wife of a dyer from Hume, near Salford, prayed the court to grant her an article of the peace against her husband, who not only led an "idle and dissolute life" but beat her and

---

[17] A milk delivery route.

forced her to spend her small inheritance from an uncle on his support. For such women, husbands represented more of a liability than an asset.

But most plebeian wives, working at charring,[18] washing, or hawking, were paid wages so low that their work could not serve as an avenue to independence. For them, work was only a bitter necessity, especially when a drunken husband contributed little to the family income. "The Drunkard's Wife" complained,

> *I am forc'd to get up in the morn,*
> *And labor and toil the whole day,*
> *Then at night I have supper to get,*
> *And the bairns to get out of the way,*
> *My husband to fetch from the alehouse*
> *And to put him to bed when I go [sic]*
> *A woman can ne'er be at rest,*
> *When once she is joined to a man.*

In a real-life version of this story, a man named Devon was arrested on suspicion of cutting the throat of his wife, "a sober and industrious woman, [who] dealt in fish, but had the misfortune to live very uncomfortably with her husband." Some wives had to trade support for violence. A laborer defended himself against a charge of wife-beating by claiming that "he was a well-doing man," for in the last week he had earned five shillings and had given four of them to his wife. . . .

Alcohol, of course, loosens inhibitions and aggravates any inclination toward violence. Forty percent of the domestic violence cases in the Old Bailey sessions involved drinking by the husband, the wife, or both. The percentage was even higher in Glasgow, where the availability of cheap whisky aggravated the problem. In the Gorbals police courts, 63 percent of the domestic violence cases in 1835–1836 involved a charge of drunk and disorderly. Twenty-six percent of the male assailants in the Old Bailey sessions cases were drunk at the time they committed the assault, as were 30 percent of the women. Fifteen percent of the men and 13 percent of the female assailants used their victims' drunkenness as an excuse. Men claimed that their wives were drunkards in order to excuse violence against them, and there were cases of apparently alcoholic women who assaulted their husbands and pawned all their possessions. This problem, too, seems to have been particularly acute in Scotland, where whisky could quickly intoxicate a small woman. If a man drank, his wife might still be able to hold the household together, but if the wife was an alcoholic as well the family was doomed. Working people and social reformers alike tended to see women's drinking as pathological while viewing men's as a normal, if unfortunate, part of plebeian culture. . . .

Drinking crystallized larger issues of competition over access to plebeian sociability and over control of resources. J. P. Malcolm observed of eighteenth-century journeymen and laborers that "their domestic amusements chiefly con-

---

[18] Housecleaning.

sist in disputes with a Wife, who finds herself and children sacrificed to the brutal propensities of Drinking and Idleness; and the scene of contention is intolerable, if the lady possesses a high spirit; so entirely so [to] the husband, that he fixes himself for the evening with a party at the public house." Both men and women participated in the free and easy world of libertine plebeian culture, but wives often found their highest priority was to feed the children, while artisan husbands retained their primary allegiance to the homosocial world of workshop and pub. The wife fetching her husband home from the alehouse was the subject of two of the most popular tales about marriage, "Watty and Meg" and "A New and Diverting Dialogue Between a Shoemaker and His Wife." Husbands resented what they perceived to be their wives' "nagging" about their main pleasure in life — drinking with their mates. Archibald M'Lean beat his wife with a poker when she asked him where he had spent the evening.

In turn, women resented the enjoyment their husbands found at pubs and clubs while they starved at home. Another wife defended herself against a charge of stabbing her husband, a butcher, by declaring that he beat her and "kept herself and family without decent clothes, while he went out to the play, dressed like a gentleman, smoking cigars, and stopping out most nights of the week." One printer's wife actually prosecuted a publican for keeping his tavern open too long, because her husband "spent all his earnings at the defendant's house and only brought her three farthings last Sunday." Women resented the freedom and conviviality men found in their pubs and clubs. One woman became so enraged when her husband forbade her to smoke at home although he was enjoying a pint and a pipe at his club, that she disguised herself in his coalheaver's work clothes and went to his pub. There, after imbibing a bit too much porter and tobacco, "with great volubility [she] commenced a discourse on the rights of women." The coalheavers who surrounded her, realizing she was a woman come to spy on them, hauled her to a police court, where her husband declared that "he'd larn her to vear [sic] his breeches again." . . .

The insecurity of marriage may have intensified jealousy, for 20 percent of the protagonists and witnesses in Old Bailey trials cited this emotion as a motive for violence. As the Poor Law records and bigamy trials reveal, men often deserted their wives for other women, and it was by no means uncommon for women to desert their husbands as well. Since common-law marriages were acceptable, at least in the "libertine" sections of plebeian culture, both men and women could readily seek more suitable partners if they were discontented with their first union. For instance, the wife of William King, a working ship's carpenter, left him after his drinking had "reduced his family to indigence," and she went to live with a prosperous hatter at Wapping, who established her in a snug little cottage. Jane Rogers endured the violence of John Dennet, the greengrocer she lived with, for eight years, but finally left him to marry a gardener. Although Dennet drank their health at the wedding, he eventually murdered her. . . .

The infidelity of husbands had serious economic consequences for wives, although it was much more difficult for them than for men to draw on the power of the law or popular justice to gain redress. Mary Taylor, for instance, accused her husband of treating her with "inhumanity" by spending all his money on "naughty women" and depriving her of the "necessities of life." The magistrate allowed her a separation and ordered John Taylor to pay her 3 shillings[19] a week, which was certainly not enough for subsistence. Husbands who patronized prostitutes could contract venereal disease and then transmit the disease to their wives. Thomas Dickers, for instance, "a wild debauched profligate," consorted with prostitutes and infected his wife with "the clap." Amelia Brazier fled her husband's syphilitic embraces and charged him before a magistrate with assault, but he told the judge that "he would beat and pox his wife whenever he thought proper."

British society viewed a wife's infidelity much more seriously than it did her husband's adultery. *Conjugal Infidelity*, a popular pamphlet, warned wives with the sad tale of Maria Stent, the unfaithful wife of a butcher who stabbed her in revenge. It painted a pathetic picture of the bleeding wife proclaiming, "You, my dear Henry, were the best of husbands, the most indulgent of men. I was very wicked; O may my fate prove a salutary warning to all bad wives." A husband who claimed that his wife had been unfaithful could sometimes escape punishment for beating her. In 1804 Francis Morris was found guilty of assaulting his wife, "but it appeared the Lady was not quite so pure as she held herself out to be, he was only sentenced to pay one shilling and be discharged.". . .

Neighbors sometimes assisted abused wives, but only if they screamed particularly loudly or the violence was unusually severe. The neighbors of William Carter, a shopkeeper, insisted that he be tried for murdering his long-suffering wife, whom they had found drowned in a water tub. Men sometimes tried to prevent husbands from assaulting wives, but it was much more likely that female neighbors would interfere. When John Simpson, a Shoreditch hairdresser, was tried for the murder of his wife, Eleanor Evans testified that she had told Mrs. Simpson to leave her husband and come live with her. Elizabeth Ernby warned Abraham Winter to stop abusing his common-law wife, Mary Ann Stone, telling him, "Do not use the woman so ill, for I know to my certain knowledge that she has been a wife to you, and a mother to your children." Unfortunately, he continued beating Mary Ann, and she finally defended herself by stabbing him. When John Ruddle beat his wife for telling him to get his own dinner, a female neighbor heard the commotion and alarmed Ann Baker, whose husband worked with Ruddle. She scolded him, "I am surprized at you, Ruddle, to get ill-using of your wife." Rebecca Bishop, their landlady, also heard the quarrel. She testified, "I asked him, why he made such a noise and such a piece of work in my house for; I asked him whether or no he was not ashamed to use a poor woman so ill?" He retorted that it was none of her business and threatened her. However, neighbors, whether male or female, did not always interfere in domestic matters, and their help could not always prevent domestic homicide. Instead of rescuing Mrs. Ruddle, Mrs. Bishop went back to her own room because she feared for the safety of her infant, and Ruddle proceeded to murder his wife. In another trial, Eleanor

---

[19] A former unit of British currency; one-twentieth of a pound.

Burke failed to respond to cries for help from the wife of Edward Welch, a porter who had told Eleanor he would murder his wife, because "there were often such cries; I thought he was beating her, or pulling her hair." Similarly, Sarah Paskin heard Mary Stark cry out, but, as she testified, "it was nothing new to me, as I heard them cry out very often, I continued at my work." In one Scottish case, the plebeian neighbors of Charles Donaldson often heard him beat his wife, but said, "We paid no particular attention to his doing so, as it was his daily practice.". . .

One of the fault-lines of plebeian culture ran between husbands and wives and fissured the larger community as well. Whether expressed in physical or verbal violence, the contradiction between patriarchal ideals and the reality of the family economy resulted in a struggle for power, resources, and freedom within the family — the struggle for the breeches. Of course, husbands and wives had always struggled over these issues, if the popularity of this theme in songs is any indication, but new sources of tension arose in the late eighteenth and early nineteenth centuries. For all urban plebeians, the libertine pleasures of metropolitan life proved both tempting and perilous. Husbands and wives quarreled over who would spend money at the pub, and the increasing flexibility of plebeian morals could spark flares of jealousy and fears of abandonment. Artisans seemed particularly prone to wife-beating, a phenomenon that may have resulted from the clash between bachelor journeymen's culture and the needs of married life. Textile workers may have worked out more harmonious marriages based on partnership, but neither popular culture nor religion matched practice with an ethic of marital equality.

FACTORY DISCIPLINE
IN THE INDUSTRIAL REVOLUTION
Sidney Pollard

The nature of work and leisure time changed dramatically with the Industrial Revolution. Previously, workers could proceed at their own pace, deciding when to rest or to cease their labors for the day. After all, who would care if a woman at a loom in her own home suddenly decided to take a fifteen-minute break? Basing his research on investigative reports of parliamentary committees and royal commissions as well as on memoirs, correspondence, and business records, the English business and economic historian Sidney Pollard shows that early factory owners consciously tried to change the more relaxed work habits of preindustrial England in order to maximize productivity and profits. In the process, they aimed at nothing less than the reformation of the workers' morals and character.

What exactly was the new factory discipline, and how did it operate? The need to alter the employees' concept of work stemmed from the factories' machinery. In what ways did machinery make it imperative for workers to conform to factory discipline and to the concept of "time-thrift"?

It was not enough for the owners to demand factory discipline; they also had to force or cajole their workers to relinquish centuries-old patterns of behavior. The owners used three methods: the carrot, the stick, and "the attempt to create a new ethos of work order and obedience." How did each of these methods work, and how effective were they? Surely some of the problems of factory-operative behavior — problems from the owners' point of view, that is — still persist today. Child workers presented a special problem for the owners. Notice what methods helped ensure that the very young would become accustomed to factory discipline.

Pollard claims that the carrot, a method favored by enlightened factory owners, was successful but was not copied very much. What did the owners think of the workers' character, and why did the owners try to prohibit swearing and indecent language? Did they usually treat their workers with respect, or did they view them as mere cogs in the wheels of production?

Sidney Pollard, "Factory Discipline in the Industrial Revolution," *Economic History Review* 16 (December 1963): 254–271.

Significant economic changes require changes in work habits. How have recent developments such as the information revolution, telecommunications, and computers affected work patterns?

It is nowadays increasingly coming to be accepted that one of the most critical, and one of the most difficult, transformations required in an industrializing society is the adjustment of labour to the regularity and discipline of factory work. . . . [T]he first generation of factory workers will be examined, irrespective of its appearance at different times in different industries.

The worker who left the background of his domestic workshop or peasant holding for the factory, entered a new culture as well as a new sense of direction. It was not only that "the new economic order needed . . . part-humans: soulless, depersonalised, disembodied, who could become members, or little wheels rather, of a complex mechanism." It was also that men who were non-accumulative, non-acquisitive, accustomed to work for subsistence, not for maximization of income, had to be made obedient to the cash stimulus, and obedient in such a way as to react precisely to the stimuli provided.

The very recruitment to the uncongenial work was difficult, and it was made worse by the deliberate or accidental modelling of many works on workhouses and prisons, a fact well known to the working population. Even if they began work, there was no guarantee that the new hands would stay. "Labourers from agriculture or domestic industry do not at first take kindly to the monotony of factory life; and the pioneering employer not infrequently finds his most serious obstacle in the problem of building up a stable supply of efficient and willing labour." Many workers were "transient, marginal and deviant," or were described as "volatile." It was noted that there were few early manufactures in the seaport towns, as the population was too unsteady. . . . Thus it was not necessarily the better labourer, but the stable one who was worth the most to the manufacturer: often, indeed, the skilled apprenticed man was at a discount, because of the working habits acquired before entering a factory. . . .

. . . [I]n Scotland even the children found the discipline irksome: when the Catrine cotton mills were opened, one of the managers admitted, "the children were all newcomers, and were very much beat at first before they could be taught their business." At other mills, "on the first introduction of the business, the people were found very ill-disposed to submit to the long confinement and regular industry that is required from them." The highlander, it was said, "never sits at ease at a loom; it is like putting a deer in the plough."

In turn, the personal inclinations and group *mores* of such old-established industrial workers as handloom weavers and framework knitters were opposed to factory discipline. "I found the utmost distaste," one hosier reported, "on the part of the men, to any regular hours or regular habits. . . . The men themselves were considerably dissatisfied, because they could not go in and out as they pleased, and have what holidays they pleased, and go on just as they had been used to do. . . ."

As a result of this attitude, attendance was irregular, and the complaint of Edward Cave,[1] in the very earliest days of industrialization, was later re-echoed by many others: "I have not half my people come to work to-day, and I have no great fascination in the prospect I have to put myself in the power of such people." Cotton spinners would stay away without notice and send for their wages at the end of the week, and one of the most enlightened firms, McConnel and Kennedy, regularly replaced spinners who had not turned up within two or three hours of starting time on Mondays, on the reasonable presumption that they had left the firm: their average labour turnover was 20 a week, i.e. about 100 per cent a year.

Matters were worse in a place like Dowlais, reputed to employ many runaways and criminals, or among northern mining companies which could not guarantee continuous work: "the major part of these two companies are as bad fellows as the worst of your pitmen baring their outside is not so black," one exasperated manager complained, after they had left the district without paying their debts. Elsewhere, ironworks labourers, copper and tin miners and engineering labourers deserted to bring in the harvest, or might return to agriculture for good if work was slack.

"St. Monday" and feast days, common traditions in domestic industry, were persistent problems. The weavers were used to "play frequently all day on Monday, and the greater part of Tuesday, and work very late on Thursday night, and frequently all night on Friday." Spinners, even as late as 1800, would be missing from the factories on Mondays and Tuesdays, and "when they did return, they would sometimes work desperately, night and day, to clear off their tavern score, and get more money to spend in dissipation," as a hostile critic observed. In South Wales it was estimated as late as the 1840's that the workers lost one week in five, and that in the fortnight after the monthly pay day, only two-thirds of the time was being worked.

As for the regular feasts, "our men will go to the Wakes," Josiah Wedgwood[2] complained in 1772, "if they were sure to go to the D — l the next. I have not spared them in threats and I would have thrash'd them right heartily if I could." . . .

Employers themselves, groping their way towards a new impersonal discipline, looked backwards sporadically to make use of feasts and holidays, typical of the old order in cementing personal relationships and breaking the monotony of the working year. . . . The Arkwrights and the Strutts, standing on the watershed between the old and the new, had feasts in Cromford in 1776, when 500 workers and their children took part, and annual balls at Cromford and Belper as late as 1781, whilst in 1772 the Hockley factory had an outing, led by the "head workman" clad in white cotton, to gather nuts, and be regaled to a plentiful supper afterwards.

Other examples from industries in their early transitional stages include Matthew Boulton's[3] feast for 700 when his son came of age, Wedgwood's feast for

---

[1] Printer (1691–1754).

[2] Owner of a pottery factory (1730–1795).

[3] Inventor (1728–1809), along with James Watt, of an efficient steam engine.

120 when he moved into Etruria, . . . and the repast provided by the Herculaneum
Pottery at the opening of its Liverpool warehouse in 1813. Conversely, the
Amlwch miners organized an ox-roast in honour of the chief proprietor, the Marquis of Anglesea, when he passed through the island on his way to take up the
Lord-Lieutenancy of Ireland. 600 workmen sat down to a roasted ox and plenty
of liquor at the Duke of Bridgewater's expense to celebrate the opening of the canal
at Runcorn, and feasts were usual thereafter at the opening of canals and railways,
but within a generation it was the shareholders that were being feasted, not the
workers, whose relationship with the employers had by then taken on an entirely
different character.

Once at work it was necessary to break down the impulses of the workers, to
introduce the notion of "time-thrift." The factory meant economy of time and . . .
"enforced asceticism." Bad timekeeping was punished by severe fines, and it was
common in mills such as Oldknow's or Braids' to lock the gates of the factory, even
of the workrooms, excluding those who were only a minute or two late. "Whatever else the domestic system[4] was, however intermittent and sweated its labour,
it did allow a man a degree of personal liberty to indulge himself, a command over
his time, which he was not to enjoy again."

By contrast, in the factories, Arkwright,[5] for example, had the greatest difficulty "in training human beings to renounce their desultory habits of work, and
identify themselves with the unvarying regularity of the complex automaton."
He "had to train his workpeople to a precision and assiduity altogether unknown
before, against which their listless and restive habits rose in continued rebellion,"
and it was his great achievement "to devise and administer a successful code of
factory diligence." "Impatient of the slovenly habits of workpeople, he urged on
their labours with a precision and vigilance unknown before." The reasons for the
difference were clear to manufacturers: "When a mantua[6] maker chooses to rise
from her seat and take the fresh air, her seam goes a little back, that is all; there
are no other hands waiting on her," but "in cotton mills all the machinery is going
on, which they must attend to." It was "machinery [which] ultimately forced the
worker to accept the discipline of the factory."

Regular hours and application had to be combined with a new kind of order
in the works. Wedgwood, for example, had to fight the old pottery traditions
when introducing "the punctuality, the constant attendance, the fixed hours, the
scrupulous standards of care and cleanliness, the avoidance of waste, the ban on
drinking." . . .

Finally, "[d]iscipline . . . was to produce the goods on time. It was also to prevent the workmen from stealing raw materials, putting in shoddy, or otherwise

---

[4] Also known as the putting-out system, whereby a merchant provided raw materials to workers, who then worked in their own homes.

[5] Richard Arkwright (1732–1792), inventor of the water-frame, a spinning machine that led to
the creation of large cotton mills.

[6] A woman's loose gown.

getting the better of their employers." It allowed the employer to maintain a high quality of output. . . .

Works Rules, formalized, impersonal and occasionally printed, were symbolic of the new industrial relationships. Many rules dealt with disciplinary matters only, but quite a few laid down the organization of the firm itself. "So strict are the instructions," it was said of John Marshall's[7] flax mills in 1821, "that if an overseer of a room be found talking to any person in the mill during working hours he is dismissed immediately — two or more overseers are employed in each room, if one be found a yard out of his ground he is discharged. . . . [E]veryone, manager, overseers, mechanics, oilers, spreaders, spinners and reelers, have their particular duty pointed out to them, and if they transgress, they are instantly turned off as unfit for their situation."

While the domestic system had implied some measure of control, "it was . . . an essentially new thing for the capitalist to be a disciplinarian." "The capitalist employer became a supervisor of every detail of the work: without any change in the general character of the wage contract, the employer acquired new powers which were of great social significance." The concept of industrial discipline was new, and called for as much innovation as the technical inventions of the age.

Child work immeasurably increased the complexities of the problem. It had, as such, been common enough before, but the earlier work pattern had been based on the direct control of children and youths, in small numbers, by their parents or guardians. The new mass employment removed the incentive of learning a craft, alienated the children by its monotony and did this just at the moment when it undermined the authority of the family, and of the father in particular. It thus had to rely often on the unhappy method of indirect employment by untrained people whose incentive for driving the children was their own piece-rate payment.

In the predominantly youthful population of the time, the proportion of young workers was high. In the Cumberland mines, for example, children started work at the ages of five to seven, and as late as 1842, 200–250 of the 1,300–1,400 workers in the Lonsdale mines were under eighteen. At Alloa collieries,[8] 103 boys and girls of under seven were employed in 1780. In the light metal trades, the proportion was higher still. Josiah Wedgwood . . . had 30 per cent of his employees under eighteen, 3.3 per cent under ten years of age. The greatest problems, however, were encountered in the textile mills.

The silk mills were dependent almost exclusively on child labour, and there the children started particularly young, at the ages of six or seven, compared with nine or ten in the cotton mills. Typically from two-thirds to three-quarters of the hands were under eighteen but in some large mills, the proportion was much higher: at Tootal's for example, 78 per cent of the workers were under sixteen. Adults were thus in a small minority.

---

[7] Textile magnate.

[8] Coal mines, with associated buildings and equipment.

In the cotton industry the proportion of children and adolescents under eighteen was around 40–45 per cent. In some large firms the proportions were higher: thus Horrocks, Miller and Co. in 1816 had 13 per cent of their labour force under ten years of age, and 60 per cent between ten and eighteen, a total of 73 per cent. The proportion of children under ten was mostly much smaller than this, but in water mills employing large numbers of apprentices it might be greater: New Lanark, under David Dale in 1793, had 18 per cent of its labour force nine years old or younger.

In the flax and the woollen and worsted industries, the proportions of workers under eighteen were rather higher than in cotton, being around 50 per cent. Again individual large works show much higher figures. In John Marshall's Water Lane Mill in 1831, for example, 49.2 per cent were under fifteen, and 83.8 per cent altogether under twenty-one. Further, in all the textile branches the children were largely concentrated in certain sections, such as silk throwing and cotton spinning. In such departments, the difficulties of maintaining discipline were greatest.

These, then, were the problems of factory discipline facing the entrepreneurs in the early years of industrialization. Their methods of overcoming them may be grouped under three headings: the proverbial stick, the proverbial carrot, and, thirdly, the attempt to create a new ethos of work order and obedience.

Little new in the way of the "stick," or deterrent, was discovered by the early factory masters. Unsatisfactory work was punished by corporal punishment, by fines or by dismissal. Beatings clearly belonged to the older, personal relationships and were common with apprentices, against whom few other sanctions were possible, but they survived because of the large-scale employment of children. Since the beating of children became one of the main complaints against factory owners and a major point at issue before the various Factory Commissions,[9] the large amount of evidence available is not entirely trustworthy, but the picture is fairly clear in outline.

Some prominent factory owners . . . prohibited it outright, though the odd cuff for inattention was probably inevitable in any children's employment. More serious beatings were neither very widespread, nor very effective. . . . [L]arge employers frowned on beatings, though they might turn a blind eye on the overlookers' actions. "We beat only the lesser, up to thirteen or fourteen . . . we use a strap," stated Samuel Miller, manager of Wilson's mill in Nottingham, one of the few to admit to this to the Factory Commission, "I prefer fining to beating, if it answers . . . (but) fining does not answer. It does not keep the boys at their work." The most honest evidence, however, and the most significant, came from John Bolling, a cotton master. He could not stop his spinners beating the children, he stated, "for children require correction now and then, and the difficulty is to keep it from being excessive. . . . It never can be in the interest of the master that the children should be beaten. The other day there were three children run away; the

---

[9] Royal commissions established to investigate working conditions.

mother of one of them brought him back and asked us to beat him; that I could not permit; she asked us to take him again: at last I consented, and then she beat him."

Dismissal and the threat of dismissal were in fact the main deterrent instruments of enforcing discipline in the factories. At times of labour shortage they were ineffective, but when a buyers' market in labour returned, a sigh of relief went through the ranks of the employers at the restoration of their power. Many abolished the apprenticeship system in order to gain it, and without it others were unable to keep any control whatsoever. Where there were no competing mill employers, as at Shrewsbury in the case of Marshall and Benyon's flax mills, it was a most effective threat.

In industries where skill and experience were at a premium, however, dismissals were resorted to only most reluctantly. . . .

Fines formed the third type of sanctions used, and were common both in industries employing skilled men, and in those employing mostly women and children. They figure prominently in all the sets of rules surviving, and appear to have been the most usual reaction to minor transgressions. Where the employer pocketed the fine there was an additional inducement to levy it freely, and in some cases, as in the deductions and penalties for sending small coal or stones up in the corves from the coal face, these became a major source of abuse and grievance.

Their general level was high and was meant to hurt. Typically, they were levied at 6d.[10] to 2s.[11] for ordinary offences or, say, two hours' to a day's wages. Wedgwood fined 2s. 6d. for throwing things or for leaving fires burning overnight, and that was also the penalty for being absent on Monday mornings in the Worsley mines. At Fernley's Stockport mill, swearing, singing or being drunk were punished by a fine of 5s. and so was stealing coal at Merthyr. Miners were fined even more heavily: average weekly deductions were alleged to be as high as 1s. or 2s. out of a wage of 13s.

Deterrence as a method of industrial discipline should, strictly, also include the actions taken against workers' organizations. . . . The law could usually be assumed to be at the service of the employer, and was called into service for two types of offence, breaches of contract and trade-union organization and rioting. Workmen's combinations were widely treated as criminal offences in employers' circles, even before the law made them explicitly such, and in turn, the legal disabilities turned trade disputes easily towards violence, particularly before the 1790's. In the Scottish mines, serfdom was only just being eradicated, and in the North-East the one-year contract, coupled with the character note, could be used also to impose conditions akin to serfdom; opposition, including the inevitable rioting, was met by transportation and the death penalty not only in the mines, but even in such advanced centres as Etruria as late as 1783.

---

[10] The abbreviation for *penny*.

[11] The abbreviation for *shilling*.

Where their powers permitted, employers met organization with immediate dismissal: "any hands forming conspiracies or unlawful combinations will be discharged without notice" read one rule as late as 1833. More widespread, however, was the use of blacklists against those who had aroused the employer's disfavour. Little was heard of them, even in contemporary complaints by workmen, but their importance should not be underrated: . . . it is increasingly obvious that they were a most important prop of that reign of terror which in so many works did duty for factory discipline.

By comparison with these commonly used examples of the "stick," more subtle or more finely graded deterrents were so rare as to be curious rather than significant. John Wood, the Bradford spinner, made the child guilty of a fault hold up a card with his offence written on it; for more serious offences, this punishment was increased to walking up and down with the card, then to having to tell everyone in the room, and, as the highest stage, confessing to workers in other rooms. Witts and Rodick, the Essex silk-mill owners, made their errant children wear degrading dress. These measures presuppose a general agreement with the factory code on the part of the other workmen which today few would take for granted. . . .

Employers were as conservative in the use of the carrot as they were in the use of the stick. For a generation driving its children to labour in the mills for twelve to fourteen hours a day, positive incentives must indeed have been hard to devise and, for the child workers at least, were used even less than for adults. Much better, as in the case of at least one flax mill, to give them snuff to keep them awake in the evenings. The extent of the predominance of the deterrent over the incentive in the case of the factory children is brought out in the returns of the 1833 Factory Commission, in replies to item 57 of the questionnaire sent out: "What are the means taken to enforce obedience on the part of the children employed in your works?" . . . Bearing in mind that most respondents were merely concerned to deny that they beat their children, and that many replied with the method they thought they ought to use, rather than the one actually in use, the following proportion may appear even more surprising:

Number of Firms Using Different Means to Enforce Obedience among Factory Children, 1833

Negative		Positive	
Dismissal	353	Kindness	2
Threat of dismissal	48	Promotion, or higher wages	9
Fines, deductions	101	Reward or premium	23
Corporal punishment	55		
Complaint to parents	13		
Confined to mill	2		
Degrading dress, badge	3		
Totals	575		34

The contrast is surely too strong to be fortuitous, especially since the bias was all the other way.

For adults, there were two positive methods which formed the stock-in-trade of management in this period. One was sub-contract, the transference of responsibility for making the workers industrious, to overseers, butty-men,[12] group leaders, first hands and sub-contractors of various types. But this solution, which raises, in any case, questions of its own, was not a method of creating factory discipline, but of evading it. The discipline was to be the older form of that of the supervisor of a small face-to-face group, maintained by someone who usually worked himself or was in direct daily contact with the workers.

The other method was some variant of payments by results. This provided the cash nexus symbolic for the new age. It was also a natural derivation from the methods used in earlier periods in such skilled and predominantly male trades as iron-smelting, mining, pottery or the production of metal goods. In 1833, of 67,819 cotton-mill workers in 225 mills, 47.1 per cent were on piece-work and 43.7 per cent were paid datally,[13] the method of payment for the remainder being unknown. Labourers, children and others under direct supervision of a skilled pieceworker, and some highly skilled trades in short supply, such as engineers and building craftsmen, did, however, remain on fixed datal pay.

In many enterprises the "discovery" of payment by results was greeted as an innovation of major significance, and at times the change-over does seem to have led to marked improvements in productivity. . . .

Many of the older systems of payment by results, as in copper or tin mines, or in sinking colliery shafts, consisted of group piece-work, in which the cohesion and ethos of the group was added to the incentive payment as such to create work discipline. The newly introduced systems, however, were typically aimed at individual effort. As such, they were less effective . . . and they were often badly constructed, particularly for times of rapid technological change. There were many examples of the usual problems of this type of payment, such as speed-up and rate cutting, as at Soho and Etruria, loss of quality, and friction over interpretation and deductions. Nevertheless, it represented the major change and forward step in the employer's attitude towards labour, not only because it used cash as such but more specifically because it marked the end of the belief that workers were looking for a fixed minimum income, and a rate of earnings beyond this would merely lead to absenteeism . . . and the beginning of the notion that the workers' efforts were elastic with respect to income over a wide range.

The rise in the belief in the efficacy of incentive piece payments coincided with a decline in the belief in the efficacy of long-term contracts. These contracts were largely a survival of the pre-industrial age, adopted by many employers even during the Industrial Revolution at times of acute shortages of labour. In the north-eastern coalfield, the one-year binding had become almost universal since

---

[12] Middlemen between proprietors of coal mines and workers.

[13] Daily.

the beginning of the eighteenth century and it had spread to salters, keelmen, file-workers and others. Ambrose Crowley[14] bound his men for six months, Arkwright for three months, . . . some potteries for seven years, some cotton mills for five up to twenty-one years and the Prestonpans chemical works for twenty-one years. But any hope that these indentures would ensure discipline and hard work was usually disappointed, and the system was quickly abandoned as a disciplinary method, though it might be continued for other reasons.

A few employers evolved incentive schemes with a considerable degree of sophistication. In their simplest form, overseers bribed children to work on for fourteen or fifteen hours and forgo their meal intervals, and John Wood[15] paid them a bonus of 1d. weekly if they worked well, but hung a notice of shame on them if they did not. At Backbarrow mill, apprentices received a "bounty" of 6d. or 1s., to be withdrawn if offences were committed, and in silk mills articles of clothing were given to the children as prizes for good work; at one silk mill, employing 300 children aged nine or less, a prize of bacon and three score of potatoes was given to the hardest working boy, and a doll to the hardest working girl, and their output then became the norm for the rest. Richard Arkwright, in his early years, also gave prizes to the best workers.

Later on, these bonuses were made conditional on a longer period of satisfactory work, or modified in other ways. In the early 1800's the Strutts introduced "quarterly gift money" — one-sixth of wages being held back over three months, and paid out at the end only after deductions for misconduct. At John Marshall's the best department received a bonus each quarter, amounting to £10 for the overlooker and a week's wage for the hands, and some Dowlais men, at least, also received a bonus of £2 every quarter, conditional upon satisfactory performance. At the Whitehaven collieries, the bonus to the foremen was annual and was tied to net profits: when these exceeded £30,000, the salary of the two viewers was nearly doubled, from £152 to £300, and those of the overmen raised in almost like proportion from a range of £52–82 to a range of £90–170 — a particularly effective and cheap means of inducing industry. In other coal mines, the ladder of promotion to overmen was used effectively as an incentive. . . .

Compared with the ubiquity of financial rewards, other direct incentives were rare and localized, though they were highly significant. Wedgwood at times appealed directly to his workers, in at least one case writing a pamphlet for them in which he stressed their common interests. . . . Arkwright gave distinguishing dresses to the best workers of both sexes and John Marshall fixed a card on each machine, showing its output. Best known of all were the "silent monitors" of Robert Owen.[16] He awarded four types of mark for the past day's work to each superintendent, and each of them, in turn, judged all his workers; the mark was

---

[14] Iron smelter who pioneered the large-scale importation of Swedish ores.

[15] A worsted manufacturer who began the movement for a ten-hour day.

[16] Industrialist and social reformer (1771–1858).

then translated into the colours black-blue-yellow-white, in ascending order of merit, painted on the four sides of a piece of wood mounted over the machine, and turned outward according to the worker's performance.

There is no doubt that Owen attached great importance to this system, entering all daily marks in a book as a permanent record, to be periodically inspected by him. There is equally no doubt that, naive as they might seem to-day, these methods were successful among all the leading manufacturers named, Robert Owen, in particular, running his mills, both in Manchester and in Scotland, at regular high annual profits largely because he gained the voluntary co-operation of his workers. Why, then, were these methods not copied as widely as the technological innovations?

The reasons may have been ignorance on the part of other masters, disbelief or a (partly justified) suspicion that the enlightened employers would have been successful with or without such methods, enjoying advantages of techniques, size or a well-established market; but to limit the reasons to these would be to ignore one of the most decisive social facts of the age. An approach like Owen's ran counter to the accepted beliefs and ideology of the employing class, which saw its own rise to wealth and power as due to merit, and the workman's subordinate position as due to his failings. He remained a workman, living at subsistence wages, because he was less well endowed with the essential qualities of industry, ambition, sobriety and thrift. As long as this was so, he could hardly be expected to rise to the baits of moral appeals or co-operation. Therefore, one would have to begin by indoctrinating him with the bourgeois values which he lacked, and this, essentially, was the third method used by employers.

In their attempts to prevent "Idleness, Extravagance, Waste and Immorality," employers were necessarily dealing with the workers both inside the factory and outside it. The efforts to reform the whole man were, therefore, particularly marked in factory towns and villages in which the total environment was under the control of a single employer.

The qualities of character which employers admired have, since Weber's[17] day, been to some extent associated with the Protestant ethic. To impart these qualities, with the one addition of obedience, to the working classes, could not but appear a formidable task. That it should have been attempted at all might seem to us incredible, unless we remember the background of the times which included the need to educate the first generation of factory workers to a new factory discipline, the widespread belief in human perfectibility, and the common assumption, by the employer, of functions which are today provided by the public authorities, like public safety, road building or education. . . . [O]ne of their consequences was the preoccupation with the character and morals of the working classes which are so marked a feature of the early stages of industrialization.

---

[17] Max Weber (1864–1920), German sociologist and author of *The Protestant Ethic and the Spirit of Capitalism.*

Some aspects of this are well known and easily understandable. Factory villages like New Lanark, Deanston, Busby, Ballindaloch, New Kilpatrick, Blantyre, and . . . Antrim, had special provisions, and in some cases full-time staff, to check the morals of their workers. Contemporaries tended to praise these actions most highly, and it was believed that firms laying stress on morals, and employing foremen who "suppress anything bad" would get the pick of the labour. Almost everywhere, churches, chapels and Sunday Schools were supported by employers, both to encourage moral education in its more usual sense, and to inculcate obedience. Drink and drunkenness became a major target of reform, with the short-term aim of increasing the usefulness of scarce skilled workers . . . who were often incapacitated by drink, and the long-term aim of spreading bourgeois virtues.

In this process much of the existing village culture came under attack. "Traditional social habits and customs seldom fitted into the new pattern of industrial life, and they had therefore to be discredited as hindrances to progress." Two campaigns here deserve special mention.

The first was the campaign against leisure on Saturdays and Sundays, as, no doubt, examples of immoral idleness. "The children are during the weekdays generally employed," the Bishop of Chester had declared solemnly in 1785, "and on Sunday are apt to be idle, mischievous and vitious." This was not easily tolerated. Thus Deanston had a Superintendent of streets to keep them clear of immorality, children and drink. Charles Wilkins of Tiverton formed an "Association for the Promotion of Order" in 1832 to round up the children and drive them to school on Sundays. All the hands at Strutt's and Arkwright's under twenty had to attend school for four hours on Saturday afternoons and on Sundays to "keep them out of mischief." Horrocks' employed a man "for many years, to see that the children do not loiter about the streets on Sundays." At Dowlais the chapel Sunday school teachers asked J.J. Guest in 1818 to order his employees to attend, otherwise there was the danger that they might spend the Sabbath "rambling and playing." Even Owen expressed similar sentiments: "if children [under ten] are not to be instructed, they had better be employed in any occupation that should keep them out of mischief," he asserted.

The second was the prohibition of bad language. At the beginning of the eighteenth century, Crowley's "Clerk for the Poor," or teacher, was to correct lying, swearing, "and suchlike horrid crimes"; while at the same time Sir Humphrey Mackworth, at Neath, fined "Swearing, Cursing, Quarrelling, being Drunk, or neglecting Divine Service on Sunday, one shilling," and the Quaker Lead Company, at Gadlis, also prohibited swearing in 1708. Later this became quite regular, wherever rules were made: at Darley Abbey, in 1795, the fine was 9d. or 1s.; at Mellor, 1s.; at Nenthead, 6d.; at Galloway's where "obscene and vulgar language" was prohibited, the men themselves levied the fines. At Marshall and Benyon's also, according to Rule 4 of 1785, a jury of seven was to judge the offence of striking, abusing or harming another workman.

Again, the rules of Thomas Fernley, Jr., Stockport, cotton mills, stated: "while at work . . . behaviour must be commendable avoiding all shouting, loud talk, whistling, calling foul names, all mean and vulgar language, and every kind of indecency." Swearing, singing, being drunk were fined 5s.; overlookers allowing drink in the mills were fined 10s. 6d. . . .

This preoccupation might seem to today's observer to be both impertinent and irrelevant to the worker's performance, but in fact it was critical, for unless the workmen *wished* to become "respectable" in the current sense, none of the other incentives would bite. Such opprobrious terms as "idle" or "dissolute" should be taken to mean strictly that the worker was indifferent to the employer's deterrents and incentives. According to contemporaries, "it was the irrationality of the poor, quite as much as their irreligion, that was distressing. They took no thought of the morrow. . . . The workers were by nature indolent, improvident, and self-indulgent."

The code of ethics on which employers concentrated was thus rather limited. Warnings against greed, selfishness, materialism or pride seldom played a large part, sexual morals rarely became an important issue to the factory disciplinarians (as distinct from outside moralists) and, by and large, they did not mind which God was worshipped, as long as the worshipper was under the influence of some respectable clergyman. The conclusion cannot be avoided that, with some honourable exceptions, the drive to raise the level of respectability and morality among the working classes was not undertaken for their own sakes but primarily, or even exclusively, as an aspect of building up a new factory discipline.

Any conclusions drawn from this brief survey must be tentative and hesitant, particularly if they are meant to apply to industrial revolutions in general.

First, the acclimatization of new workers to factory discipline is a task different in kind, at once more subtle and more violent, from that of maintaining discipline among a proletarian population of long standing. Employers in the British Industrial Revolution therefore used not only industrial means but a whole battery of extra-mural powers, including their control over the courts, their powers as landlords, and their own ideology, to impose the control they required.

Secondly, the maintenance of discipline, like the whole field of management itself, was not considered a fit subject for study, still less a science, but merely a matter of the employer's individual character and ability. No books were written on it before 1830, no teachers lectured on it, there were no entries about it in the technical encyclopaedias, no patents were taken out relating to it. As a result, employers did not learn from each other, except haphazardly and belatedly, new ideas did not have the cachet of a new technology and did not spread, and the crudest form of deterrents and incentives remained the rule. Robert Owen was exceptional in ensuring that his methods, at least, were widely known, but they were too closely meshed in with his social doctrines to be acceptable to other employers.

Lastly, the inevitable emphasis on reforming the moral character of the worker into a willing machine-minder led to a logical dilemma that contemporaries did not know how to escape. For if the employer had it in his power to reform the workers if he but tried hard enough, whose fault was it that most of them remained immoral, idle and rebellious? And if the workers could really be taught their employers' virtues, would they not all save and borrow and become entrepreneurs themselves, and who would then man the factories?

The Industrial Revolution happened too rapidly for these dilemmas, which involved the re-orientation of a whole class, to be solved, as it were, *en passant.*[18] The assimilation of the formerly independent worker to the needs of factory routine took at least a further generation, and was accompanied by the help of tradition, by a sharply differentiated educational system, and new ideologies which were themselves the results of clashes of earlier systems of values, besides the forces operating before 1830. The search for a more scientific approach which would collaborate with and use, instead of seeking to destroy, the workers' own values, began later still, and may hardly be said to have advanced very far even today.

---

[18] Casually, in passing.

THE POTATO IN IRELAND
K. H. Connell

The Irish, unlike any other Western people, depended almost solely on the potato for a long time. Seldom has a single food, other than grain, so shaped a culture. K. H. Connell, a specialist in Irish economic and social history, sees the widespread use of the potato originating in the Irish landholding system and influencing, perhaps more than any other element, the fate of the Irish in the seventeenth, eighteenth, and nineteenth centuries. Connell bases his findings on census data, royal commissions, parliamentary committees, and reports of Poor Law inspectors.

Introduced to Europe from the New World in the sixteenth century, the potato became a staple crop in Ireland and, to a lesser extent, elsewhere in Europe. It is interesting that the potato's popularity had nothing to do with its taste or with the population's desire for that particular vegetable. The potato was the right food at the right time and situation. Connell blames the English for their rapacious presence in Ireland and for Ireland's dependence on a single crop. England's exploitation of the land and its people largely contributed to the great famine. To what extent, then, were the English responsible for Ireland's adoption of the potato and for the crop's failure? For Connell, the answers to these questions are fundamentally economic.

Nevertheless, the potato had certain qualities that other foodstuffs did not, attributes that convinced or compelled the Irish to grow it extensively and eat it nearly exclusively. Did the potato make the Irish a healthy people in comparison to the peasantry of western Europe?

Note how the potato affected population growth and the age of marriage in Ireland. Although the potato may have had beneficial effects, it proved to be a fragile prop to the millions of Irish in the nineteenth century. One wonders what the Irish could have done to ward off the disaster that took at least half a million lives.

How does Connell's discussion of the famine's causes differ from explanations contemporaries offered? Much of the populace returned to the potato after

K. H. Connell, "The Potato in Ireland," *Past and Present: A Journal of Historical Studies,* no. 23 (November 1962): 57–71.

the famine despite knowing that the potato might fail again. What finally motivated the Irish to vary their diet?

Connell begins this essay with landholding practices; he concludes by un-
derlining the importance of land legislation in the late-nineteenth century. How
did land acts affect the lives and foods of the peasantry?

Are there nations in the contemporary world that court disaster by relying
too heavily on a single crop?

According to Arthur Young,[1] writing in the 1770s, "The food of the common
Irish [is] potatoes and milk." Many of the uncommon Irish of Ulster and parts of
Leinster ate as much oaten bread or porridge as potatoes; they were familiar with
the taste as well as the look of butter and eggs; and in good times they expected
a daily meal with fish or bacon, even a weekly meal with meat. But for the greater
part of the country, for a century before the Famine,[2] Young's generalization will
serve: the great mass of the population had, in effect, a single solid foodstuff:
stirabout, or an oatmeal loaf, was an occasional treat: weeks or months separated
the red-letter occasions when meat was eaten: day after day, three times a day, people ate salted, boiled potatoes, probably washing them down with milk, flavour-
ing them, if they were fortunate, with an onion or a bit of lard, with boiled sea-
weed or a scrap of salted fish.

No other western people, generation after generation, has starved or survived with the bounty of the potato: why did the Irish depend on it so long, and
so nearly exclusively?

The tradition is that the first Irish potatoes were grown by Sir Walter Raleigh[3]
in 1588: certainly, by the following decade, he or another had introduced this new
crop and food. An agricultural community, isolated and backward, is likely to be
conservative in both its farming and its eating. Nonetheless, when the potato
reached Ireland the traditional foods were already being displaced — and by
forces whose persistence made the potato almost inevitably their successor. Formerly, milk and its derivatives had bulked large in the Irish dietary. No other
food may be as readily available to a nomadic, pastoral people; but a settled society, practising tillage, is likely to retain milk as its staple only while land is abundant. But land in the sixteenth century was made scarce by confiscation, the redistribution of population and the landlord's demands. Some alternative was
needed to livestock produce, some foodstuff more economical of land. Traditionally, only grain had been available, and dairy produce had given way to oaten
bread and porridge. But once the potato was known, not only milk, but grain also

---

[1] Agriculturist and traveler (1741–1820).

[2] Of 1845–1849.

[3] English soldier and explorer (1554–1618).

rapidly receded in the popular dietary. The potato, in much of the country, was a more rewarding crop than oats. An impoverished people, ill-provided with granaries, mills and ovens, welcomed a food that could be stored in earthen clamps and made edible simply by boiling. Troubled times, too, favoured the potato: it had a briefer growing season; it remained relatively safe underground while grain might be carried away, burned or trampled underfoot; and when people took to the hills with their cattle, potatoes they might grow, but hardly grain.

These, however, are incidental recommendations of the potato: essentially, it displaced the traditional foods because it provided a family's subsistence on a smaller area of land. Still, in the seventeenth century, the pressure on land was maintained by the dislocation of war; and later, in more tranquil times, by the growth of population: continuously, however, and most insistently, land was made scarce by the landlord's demands.

Irish property was rooted, much of it recently, in confiscation: sudden gains might be suddenly lost: principles of estate-management were sharpened, therefore, by the owner's desire to get the most from his property while it remained his. The grantees, moreover, might be landlords already, attached to their English estates, administering them with feeling for their tenants as well as for their rents. The Irish, if they accepted the popular view, were a barbarous people, amongst whom it was foolhardy to live: certainly they were a people alien in language, loyalty and religion. Little, therefore, induced a man with ties in England to settle on his Irish estate, to get to know his tenants and sympathize with their problems. More often, they were reduced simply to a source of rent, the landlord's refuge when creditors encroached on his English property or his thriftless living. But duty, as well as necessity, turned the screw. England, the mother-country, reckoned to profit by her colony: a landlord's leniency lightened his country's purse as well as his own. The Irish, moreover, were disaffected and lazy: they needed punishment and reform: a sharp rent was a blend of both, perhaps of more lasting benefit to the man who earned it than to the man who spent it.

The institutions of Irish landlordism were as predatory as the spirit. Land-agent, middleman and rack-renting:[4] many a head-landlord felt ill-served by this apparatus of exploitation — but rarely because it failed to impoverish his tenants. Few of them ever had the chance of getting a living in the Irish towns; emigration became a likely escape only in the nineteenth century: land, therefore, a man must have to feed his family — and for a foothold on land he offered an extravagant rent. Commonly, in the topsy-turvy Irish economy, the more onerous the rent, the less productive the farm, the landlord who exacted an elastic rent was no improver; and the tenant who paid it was neither inclined nor able to better his farming.

Spurred on, then, by the fear of eviction and the loss of his livelihood, the tenant struggled to increase his rent. But, with a stagnant technique of farming, to earn more rent meant earmarking a larger proportion of his land for rent crops —

---

[4] The practice of charging excessive rent, nearly equal to the full value of the land.

a smaller proportion, in consequence, for his family's subsistence. And the less land on which a family must grow its food, the more imperatively was the potato its staple — for on no other crop could it live more economically of land. Where landlord-tenant relationships were milder — as in Ulster — there might be supplements to the potato; where, incessantly, they were harsh, people lived, not simply on the most prolific crop, but on its most prolific varieties.

Now, if the elasticity of rent tended to make people live on the potato, it tended also to reduce them to the bare quantity that would keep them alive and working. But, in fact, until the two or three decades before the Famine, the potato was lavishly consumed: people retained more potato-land than their subsistence required. But we have not, I think, made too much of the landlord's exigence, too much of the expansiveness of rent-land. There were kind-hearted landlords; landlords restrained by leases, by the fear of violence, even by the realization that profits were related to a tenant's productivity as well as his promises. So bountiful, moreover, was the potato, that a couple of acres, even less, gave a family all it could use, and conveniently waste: a little more gave real abundance. Then there was much land, doubtfully capable of earning rent, but available for the people's subsistence: it might grow potatoes well enough, but so bulky a crop was hard to sell when most country families grew their own, and communications were poor. On the whole, too, potato harvests were good until towards the 1820s; and in the occasional bad year the pig, not his master, pulled in his belt.

Certainly until the 1820s the monotony of the Irishman's diet was usually offset by its abundance. There are scores of accounts from the late eighteenth and early nineteenth centuries of the quantity of potatoes people ate. A small farmer from co. Down told a royal commission in the 1830s that "a stone of potatoes is little enough for a man in a day, and he'd want something with it to work upon." . . . There is little doubt that, day in day out, except when the crop was poor, the adult Irishman ate some ten pounds of potatoes a day. If he ate nothing else and drank only water he was hardly disastrously undernourished: if, as commonly happened, he had a cupful of milk with each meal, to the biochemist, if not the gourmet, he was admirably nourished: he had some 4,000 calories a day, compared with the required 3,000; he had enough protein, calcium and iron; he had a sufficiency, or a superabundance, of the listed vitamins.

The Irish, then, burdened with predatory landlords, practised a primitive farming: food, clothing and shelter were about the extent of their material comfort; the potato was their food; they were clothed in rags; their hovels, not infrequently, they shared with their animals. But for all their wretchedness, they were admirably nourished — better, maybe, than the mass of the people of any other country during any recent century.

Now, for much of the time that they lived on the potato, the number of the Irish increased with astonishing vigour. The population of Ireland in 1780 was probably something over four million — much what it is today. But, sixty years later, on the eve of the Famine, the four million had doubled to eight million — and contributed nearly another two million to the population of Britain and North America. Probably in no other western country has so rapid a rate of natural increase been so long sustained. Was it fortuitous that an extraordinary dependence on the potato was accompanied by an extraordinary excess of births over deaths?

During the years of this coincidence, and drawing partly on Irish experience, Malthus[5] evolved a theory of population growth plausible enough to come rapidly into vogue: population, his contemporaries agreed, tends to increase more rapidly than the resources needed for its sustenance: unless births are checked, population is limited by premature death — the result of scarcity of food or some like calamity. Was it, then, simply the lifting of this traditional restraint that caused the population of Ireland to bound upwards towards the end of the eighteenth century; was it that a people, formerly ill-nourished, lived longer as they were plentifully fed on the potato?

We lack the statistics to answer this question with assurance. But the presumption is that the potato facilitated the growth of population less by reducing mortality than by increasing fertility — and helping then to forestall an off-setting increase in mortality. Acceptance of the potato tended, no doubt, to improve physique and lessen the incidence of deficiency disease. But, advancing piecemeal over more than a century, the potato in much of the country was all but fully accepted by the 1730s: it tended, that is, to reduce mortality too gradually and too early to be the direct cause of a sharp increase in population in the 1780s.

More probable, in the 1780s, than any reduction in mortality was an increase in fertility, the result of more-youthful marriage than had been customary. Today, the Irish marry later than any other people whose statistics are available. And latest of all to marry is the would-be farmer. He is expected to have "a hold of the land" before he thinks of marrying: a farm, that is, must be his or earmarked for him. Farms, however, are rarely divided; there is little reclamation: typically, in consequence, the only land a man can acquire is his father's, but fathers are rarely anxious to give up the reins. The transfer of the land is probably put off until the old man is in his seventies: his eldest son, by then, is probably in his mid-thirties — and 38 is the average age at which farmers' sons marry in the Republic.

Now it is plausible to argue that this kind of restraint to marriage was also felt during much of the eighteenth century — though less severely than today, for fathers, no doubt, died younger. The critical change towards the end of the century was that land became more readily available — and, therefore, youthful marriage more readily possible. By the 1780s and 1790s holdings were less commonly passed intact from father to son. It was possible, often imperative, for a father to mark off a piece of his land and make it over to a still-youthful son, and later, maybe, provide for a second, even a third, son. Essentially, this subdivision of holdings was a consequence of the extension of arable farming. Irish patriots had long pleaded for legislation to encourage corn-growing. But the Irish towns were

---

[5] Thomas Malthus (1766–1834), English economist, author of *An Essay on the Principle of Population.*

a useful market for surplus British grain; and Irish supplies would have been resented in Britain. There was, therefore, no effective legislation until the second half
of the century. By then the growth of Britain's own population was turning her
from an exporter to an importer of corn; by the 1780s constitutional changes allowed Irish patriots to try their hand at moulding the Irish economy. Foster's[6] corn
law of 1784 imposed duties on the import of grain and offered bounties on its export; war, from 1793, further inflated corn prices — the more effectively after
1806 when, at last, Irish grain entered Britain duty-free. Between the 1780s and
the early years of the new century oat prices more than doubled: on more and
more estates the tilling tenant could pay most rent; he, therefore, was preferred
by the landlord.

But more tilling tenancies meant smaller tenancies: the grassland a family
could conveniently manage was embarrassingly large to cultivate by spade or
plough; there was no class of people with the capital and the skill to manage large
arable farms; tillage, moreover, needed the labour of the larger population subdivision induced.

By the closing decades of the eighteenth century, then, tenant farmers, anxious to provide for their sons, were encouraged by their landlords to divide their
holdings. Their sons — and daughters — were scarcely aware of the inducements
in other societies to postpone marriage: with an elastic rent, there was little reward
for industry, little opportunity for thrift — almost no hope that by deferring marriage a family might be reared on a firmer foundation. Living conditions were
wretched and hopeless: marriage could hardly make them worse; it might make
them more tolerable.

When, therefore, land was within their grasp, young people seized the opportunity it offered of marrying younger than had been customary. Few of them
knew of the possibility of restricting family size: almost none wanted to do so; it
cost little to rear a child; even young children helped on the land; and, in a country without a poor law, a numerous family was some assurance against a destitute
old age. The earlier a girl married, therefore, the more children was she likely to
have; the sooner a new generation was added to the old.

Largely, then, the impetus to the rapid growth of population seems to have
come from earlier marriage facilitated by subdivision, and followed by larger families. But where does the potato come in?

The incidence of sterility and still-birth varies, no doubt, with the nutrition
of husbands and wives — and of their parents. Insofar, then, as the potato was improving nutrition — even before 1750 — it tended to increase fertility in the closing decades of the century. And, without the potato, subdivision could hardly have
persisted for some three generations until, on the eve of the Famine, half of all
holdings were of five or fewer acres. Much hilly land, mountain and bog was included: holdings so small and unrewarding could earn a rent, and support a family, only if it lived on the potato. Had the popular dietary been more varied, sub-

---

[6] John Foster (1740–1828), chancellor of the exchequer in Ireland.

division would have halted earlier; marriage, presumably, would have been delayed and fertility reduced. Already by the 1820s and 1830s, some farms were so reduced in size that nothing could be pared from them for a son wishing to marry: increasingly he was tempted to emigrate; but sometimes he settled in Ireland on a scrap of waste, otherwise of little use, but able to grow potatoes.

The potato, then, tended to increase fertility; but its significance in population history is more for what it prevented than for what it did. Malthus was an accurate observer: population in his time pressed on resources: rising fertility tended to make food scarce, and to be offset, therefore, by rising mortality. But Ireland, for some sixty years, was exceptional: not only were additional children born, but many of them survived and contributed to the astonishing rapidity of population growth: crucial to their survival was the abundance and nutritional excellence of the potato.

The effects of the potato mentioned so far — its tendency to keep mortality down and, indirectly, to increase fertility — these tendencies depended on its being steadily and abundantly available. But the perils of living on a single food are more than usually acute when this food is the potato. Its yield, maybe, is more erratic than that of oats or wheat; yet it keeps so badly that the surplus of one year does nothing directly to make good the deficiency of the next; it is bulky, too, difficult, if communications are poor, to move from areas of abundance to areas of scarcity. It is planted late — lest it be damaged by frost: usually, therefore, the season is advanced when its failure becomes apparent, too advanced for other foods to be grown. Nor, in all probability, can its victims buy a substitute: growing their own potatoes, they have no money earmarked for food; reduced to the most frugal of foods, they hardly have money at all; their society, too, will have needed — and reared — only a rudimentary food trade. And even if there is public or charitable provision of grain, their troubles are not at an end: accustomed to a crop prepared simply with a pot and a fire, they are ill-equipped with the mills to grind corn; with the ovens and skills to bake it — even with the stomachs to digest it.

The potato, then, is a capricious staple, liable to fail and hard to replace. Yet not until after 1815 were the perils of Ireland's potato economy persistently demonstrated. In 1740 — and again in 1807 — early and severe frost destroyed much of the crop while it was still undug: 1800 and 1801 were lean years for Ireland as for much of the rest of Europe. By and large, however, from the middle of the eighteenth century until after 1815, the Irishman had his fill of potatoes.

Why was the precariousness of life on the potato so long concealed? It is hardly respectable to attribute more than incidental movements in economic development to shifts in the weather. Over three-quarters of a century, nevertheless, few seasons disagreed with the potato; partly, too, it yielded well because year after year, as more people depended on it, it was planted on land, not all of it poor, on which it had never grown before. But it is easier to explain the frequency and severity of failures after 1815 than their rarity before. Again, it seems, the weather played a part: year after year, between 1820 and the Famine, the potato succumbed to cold, wet seasons; it may have succumbed also to diseases unknown in Europe until steam navigation brought them across the Atlantic. Inherently, too, it probably became less resistant to disease as old varieties degenerated, and the new were chosen for their prolificness more than their vitality. And its yield became even less certain as it was grown on old land, starved of manure and exhausted by over-cropping; on new land, recently waste and ill-adapted to its needs — on so much land that once disease appeared, it quickly spread.

In the 1820s and 1830s the potato failed, partially or locally, at least as often as it yielded well. No longer, almost certainly, was rising fertility unaccompanied by rising mortality. But, it seems, there was little slackening in the rate of natural increase. The fickleness of the potato may have been countered by increasing the area on which it was planted: certainly the agrarian troubles and the unpaid rents of these years suggest an unwonted encroachment of subsistence-land on rent-land. It is probable too — for vaccination was spreading — that rising mortality from malnutrition was offset by falling mortality from smallpox. Marriage in these decades was postponed — as subdivision reached its limits, as the supply of food became less certain: but later marriage did not necessarily mean fewer births; the abnormal number of births in the previous twenty years was followed now by an abnormal number of potential parents.

Rapid natural increase, then, depended no longer on the bounty of the potato. But more and more its effects within Ireland were offset by mounting emigration, motivated, much of it, by the treachery of the potato. It was not until after 1845 that population began to decline: then, with three failures of the potato, two of them virtually complete, the population, in five years, was reduced by a fifth: half a million, perhaps more, died of starvation and associated diseases; a round million fled, like refugees.

The victims of so vast a catastrophe speculated, of course, on its cause. Was it brought by the fairies, the weather or atmospheric electricity; by the people's saintliness or sinfulness — by God's spreading the faith by spreading the Irish, or by his chastening a people who wasted the potato in its abundance, violated their pledge of temperance, emancipated the Catholics and subsidized Maynooth?[7] In the most pervasive of the popular explanations, the Famine was the work of the British government: "the Almighty . . . sent the potato blight, but the English created the Famine."

At the time this explanation had a rational and an emotional appeal. It is true enough that there was no escape from famine unless the government provided it; and there was the ring of salvation neither in allowing the export of Irish grain, nor in public works more obviously penal than benevolent. And a people, so beset by catastrophe, shied from the further agony of self-incrimination: if England, indeed, created the Famine, its victims had no call to dwell on their own defects; not even on their tolerance of the landlordism that made them idle and improvident.

---

[7] A Roman Catholic seminary in Ireland, the permanent endowment of which was controversial in the 1840s and 1850s.

Commonly, the historians of the Famine have reiterated the indictment of England. Their sympathies, very often, have been nationalist: nationalism in Ireland has been reared less on the rights of man than on historical wrongs, and the most grievous wrong was England's murder of a million. . . .

The scholarly studies of the Famine sponsored by the Dublin government and the Irish Committee of Historical Sciences enable us to re-assess England's guilt. . . . Mr. Thomas P. O'Neill allows us to believe no longer that the government, by staying the export of grain, could have staved off the famine: there was, he makes clear, an acute shortage of food, and it was relieved, not aggravated, by trade with Britain and the outside world.

Other measures of relief failed, not because the government so willed, not even because it was callous or negligent, but simply because the Famine was an intractable problem, an insoluble problem in the knowledge and opinion of the time. Once famine was imminent, epidemics of typhus and relapsing fever were all but certain: the doctors, backed however fully by the state, could do little to arrest their spread, or cure their victims. Famine — and therefore fever — could be averted only if the potato were saved, or if, by some administrative miracle, five million people were otherwise fed. The government, without delay, sought scientific advice on the potato; but the botanists knew nothing of the cause of the blight, nothing of how its spread might be arrested or its recurrence prevented. Nor were the economists and political theorists more effectual. The rotting of the potato was no excuse for corrupting their "scientific" poor law; and it was on their principles that Russell's[8] relief works foundered, their faith in unproductivity, central control and payment by results. Their insistence on free trade ruled out what relief there was in a ban on the export of Irish grain; and back of Russell's laggardly and niggardly import of food lay their refutation of state intervention, their certainty that it must aggravate more than alleviate.

A native government, it is true, might have deferred less to politics and economics more plausible in England than in Ireland. But no government could have contained the Famine: given the dominance of the potato, some such disaster was all but inevitable; given the growth of population, the more it was delayed, the more malevolent it must be. If, indeed, "England created the famine," it was not . . . in pursuit of a "deliberate policy of extermination": it was because, centuries earlier, she had geared the Irish economy to the elastic rent which ensured the diffusion of the potato and the unbridled growth of population.

No survivor of the Famine forgot the perils of life on the potato: fifty years later, the sight of a bowl of floury potatoes could bring tears to an old man's eyes. Yet in much of the country, as the blight receded, as seed became available, the potato was restored almost — but not altogether — to its former eminence. The yellow meal, eaten at first to save life, soon was enjoyed; and turnips and cabbage also became more familiar: none of these foods strained much more than the

---

[8] Lord John Russell (1792–1878), Whig prime minister from 1846 to 1852, an exponent of free market economics.

potato the peasant's resources, or his wife's cooking: all, therefore, encroached on the potato, or eked it out in the bad year, or before the new crop was dug. In north-eastern Ulster the potato was forsaken more rapidly — because, no doubt, it was never so firmly established. But elsewhere, its real relegation began, not in the 1840s, but in the 1870s and 1880s: "it was spuds, morning, noon and night," an old Donegal man recalled of his boyhood in the 1870s: a dozen years earlier, Clare families still lived on potatoes and sour milk; still in Cork and Limerick people reckoned on their ten pounds a day. And from the western seaboard, into the present century, the smaller holders "have nothing else to rely on: potatoes are their sole support."

Now for long, in the Médoc, it had been the custom to give grapes by the roadside an unappetizing appearance by spraying them with a mixture of copper sulphate and lime. But it was not until the 1880s that a passing botanist noticed that the sprayed plants were healthier than the rest, and, after some experiments, advocated Bordeaux mixture as a preventive of blight on the potato. In the following decade the Royal Dublin Society organized tests in Ireland, and, together with government agencies, landlords, teachers and doctors, it endeavoured to overcome the peasant's reluctance to spray. Spraying, some of course thought, was "going against nature": others, having started to spray, were lulled by a good season or two; or they lost faith because their mixture was adulterated or improperly prepared; or because, too poor or too unmechanical to use a knapsack, they had ineffectively shaken the mixture from a broom, or a handful of heather. By the time of the first war, the resistance was mostly overcome; spraying was all but universal. Before then the only safeguard against the blight was to plant a resistant variety; but the resistance even of the Champion had proved to be partial and diminishing. As long, then, as the hold of the potato persisted, famine recurred: several times in the second half of the nineteenth century scenes were enacted reminiscent, if not of the forties, at least of the twenties and thirties. But by the end of the century, the failure of the potato brought acute suffering only to the poorest families, most of them in the worst-congested districts: almost everywhere else the potato — with the milk that went with it — was yielding to stirabout (made increasingly of oats, instead of Indian corn); to bread, oaten and soon wheaten; to American bacon; to sugar, jam and tea — perhaps, where smuggling survived, to coffee in place of tea. The potato, of course, has never been ousted; but, in the words of its devoted historian, "it is eaten because it is liked, not because it is necessary."

There are two problems: why, after the Famine, did people revert so largely to a food they knew might fail again; and why, by the last quarter of the century, had they reduced it to one of several staples?

For all the agony that followed its failure, there was feeling still for the potato. People accustomed to stomachs distended three times a day by three or four pounds of potatoes, felt hungry and uncomfortable, though nourished enough on porridge or bread; or they complained of their difficulty in digesting grain stuffs. After the Famine, then, they welcomed the potato; and it was, very probably, a better food than any alternative widely available. And the people sensed also that, though the potato should fail again, they would hardly suffer as in the forties: the relieved (not only the relievers) learned by their mistakes; publicity and politics increasingly loosened the purse-strings: American relatives were a growing resource; and to join them became the conventional response to hardship at home.

The potato, before the Famine, meant more than nutriment; and people were drawn back to it by more than the need for food and bodily comfort. The open door and a meal for all-comers was a custom that sprang from the heart, but depended on the potato: hearts were hardened when the potato rotted — and any traveller might bring the fever. But when famine was past, it was good once more to disregard the cost of food — to return to the potato.

In reality, no doubt, as well as in the novels and travellers' tales, the Irishman was an indolent creature — not surprisingly if his family were large and his holding small; if industry, in his society, were robbed of its reward. For the lazy man there was no crop like the potato: it needed merely a few days' planting in the spring, possibly earthing up in the summer, and some more days' digging in the winter: with another week, cutting and carrying turf, a family might be fed and warmed for the year. By reverting to the potato, people with the taste for travel could take to the road soon after St. Patrick's Day, return temporarily to cut the turf, and settle down eventually to a leisurely winter with all the comfort they knew: the restless, ambitious man could spend his summer lifting the English harvest — even hewing stone in an American quarry; his family he might send out to beg, or leave at home to win the turf — and earn the rent if there were butter to be made.

But like its original diffusion, the re-establishment of the potato after the Famine probably owed more to the landlord's exigence than to the people's inclination. In the years of unpaid rents, and heavy taxes, the debts of already-embarrassed landlords piled up. In 1848, accordingly, the Encumbered Estates Act eased the transfer of Irish property — and patriots looked to it for the return, at last, of native, benevolent landlords. Much land changed hands under the act — a third of the whole country, it is said, in three years. The buyers, too, were mostly Irish; but Irish who were the patriots' despair. Few of their countrymen in 1849 had the money and the will to play the landlord and the assurance that they could make it a paying game. Much encumbered property was bought by petty shopkeepers and land agents, by gombeen men[9] and publicans, men, it might be, who had done well in the Famine, selling grain to a people unused to buying food, buying land from a people forced to abandon it. The central tradition of Irish property was safe in their keeping — perhaps, indeed, more rigorously applied, for their properties, by and large, were smaller than their predecessors'; more of them lived on the spot, and, stemming very often from the people they exploited, they were better informed of their hidden resources. There was probably no real relaxation of the pressure of rent-land on subsistence-land until the organized withholding of rent: for every peasant, then, who willingly returned to the potato after the Famine, others went back to it willy-nilly.

---

[9] Moneylenders.

In the 1870s and 1880s, the land war was followed by the land legislation. In many respects it is this, not the more spectacular Famine that divides the nineteenth century: until then the social and economic life of the countryside was geared to an elastic rent; but the land acts first stabilized rent, then made it a dwindling real charge. With industry and its reward at last united, there was point in farming more productively. Costlier foods were now within the peasant's reach: no longer must he live on whatever supported him with the greatest economy of land. Sometimes, it is true, the tenant-at-will, blown up to be head of a landowning family, shied too far from his old improvidence: his family must eat potatoes so that he might buy more land, make a priest of his son, or dower his daughter beyond her station. But prudence so extreme was not typical: an owner-occupier had his status to think of: he looked with "modest shame" not just on the potato, but on home-baked bread: commonly, moreover, he had relatives "in emigration," brothers and sons who mocked at his potatoes and milk, who expected when they came home to find baker's bread and jam and tea.

LETTER WRITING AND
THE VICTORIAN BOURGEOIS
Peter Gay

Peter Gay, Sterling Professor of History Emeritus at Yale University, has written more than twenty books. Perhaps his masterpiece is his five-volume study, *The Bourgeois Experience: Victoria to Freud*, where Gay explodes the common misconception that views the Victorian middle class as self-serving, prudish, moralizing hypocrites. In the fourth volume, *The Naked Heart*, Gay examines Victorian introspection and finds that the bourgeoisie desired to lay bare their hearts in nineteenth-century music, history, biography, autobiography, diaries, and letter writing.

Thousands of letters bear witness to happy marriages that included sexual desire and fulfillment. Correspondence between those expecting marriage testify as well to love and sexual longing. This evidence also exhibits the sharing of deep emotions as opposed to a reticence born of a personal concern for total privacy or a cultural demand for withholding one's feelings, even from loved ones. Gay has long been interested in the social history of ideas, the rooting in society's operations and belief systems of ideas held by groups of people, as opposed to traditional intellectual history that assays the thoughts of great intellectual figures. By culling so much correspondence, Gay is able to describe cogently the feelings of the Victorian middle class, the delight of lovers in one another, the abandoning of discretion, the joy of anticipated mail, and the central importance of letters to middle- and upper-class women and men.

Is Gay correct when he calls privacy a modern invention? How did the Romantic movement affect Victorian letter writing and the values contained in personal correspondence? How did the revolutionary changes in postal service affect the way people lived and acted? Were Victorians any more preoccupied with the self than people who lived before or after the nineteenth century? Have others made the journey inward that is a motif of nineteenth-century letter writing? Will historians be able to re-create the emotions of people today, given that the telephone does not leave the paper trail that correspondence provided Gay and that electronic mail is generally unreflective and quickly deleted?

Peter Gay, *The Naked Heart* (New York: Norton, 1995), 310–329.

In the Victorian century, bourgeois turned letters and diaries into repositories for glimpses into their innermost life in unprecedented numbers and with unmatched intensity. These communications to others and to oneself could, to be sure, serve as exercises in self-protection and self-concealment. But, though intended for a carefully selected audience, they became favorite agents of self-scrutiny and, with that, of self-revelation. They attest just where bourgeois drew the line at baring their heart. It will emerge that they were far more frankly confessional than their critics have liked to imagine.

There is extensive evidence that a goodly proportion of these literally innumerable documents must have been flat in tone and stingy with self-perception.[1] But the age generated striking, at times unpredictable, variations in the quality of these private bulletins. . . . In general, the societies earliest to be won over to the ideal of marriage for love and to prize feeling above calculation allowed writers to express themselves more openly on the page than did societies keeping up the time-hallowed custom of erotic reserve and practical alliances. Beyond such distinct cultural habits, status and gender divided letter writers and diary keepers into diverse populations. The educated had more words and better models to help them gain access to their inner life — and, naturally, to veil it — than did petty bourgeois, whose personal messages, to themselves or others, were often touching in their inarticulateness. Inescapably men would record experiences different from those of women: they could write about work and business and politics, arenas of action in the world foreclosed for most women, largely confined as they were to domesticity.

Still, it will emerge that the cliché about the male as a reasoning and the female as an emotional being did not govern Victorian letters and diaries. The confidential, confessional style, available to bourgeois of all persuasions, to Protestants, Catholics, and Jews as to unbelievers, flourished among men as much as among women. Romanticism propagandizing in behalf of mutual love as the only acceptable ground for permanent commitments and for the unbuttoned outpouring of emotions was, after all, an international phenomenon with lasting consequences, encouraging its heirs not to stint their confessions — all the while remaining, of course, within proper limits.

Obviously it is impossible fully to sort out the untold millions of letters and diaries the Victorians produced; doubtless those destroyed or moldering in attics unread greatly outnumber the thousands that have come down to us. It would be hasty to assume that only the best educated left papers to archives and libraries; many documents humble enough in expression, even spelling, have found their way into public depositories. Nor can we assume that the most intimate, most

---

[1] Nothing would obviously be easier than to replace many times over the passages I shall be quoting in the pages that follow and still make the same points. I have chosen my exemplars after sampling a far larger population. (Author's note.)

candid revelations were natural casualties. The ravages of time, the inevitable losses that moving house entails, a certain degree of self-censorship of diarists purging their own entries or recipients rendering passages of letters illegible were no less significant for keeping private material from the future than the interventions of family members or friends anxious to protect the writer's good name. All played cruel games with an inquisitive posterity. But enough letters and enough diaries markedly differing from one another, including those their contemporaries would have regarded as scandalous, have survived to justify the historian's confidence that his sample is relatively representative of bourgeois sentiments. . . .

The letter has a long history. Plato[2] wrote memorable letters, as did Cicero[3] and St. Paul.[4] But their epistles differed radically from their modern counterparts. Not that they lacked feeling, but they were social documents far more than personal communications, addressed to an interested public, at times to generations to come. . . . Until recent times, no letter, except for a secret diplomatic dispatch, could have borne the writer's entreaty, so familiar to the nineteenth century, not to show it to anyone or, better, to burn it. . . .

The tide turned with the mid-eighteenth-century cult of sensibility later canonized by the romantics. . . . It was this spirit that the immensely popular epistolary novels of the day . . . at once exhibited and promoted, and that inevitably fostered the taste for more forthcoming, less formulaic exchanges. Across Europe, the molders of manners moved to replace the formal style with written speech. In 1751, Christoph Gellert, academic, playwright, novelist, famous for his versified fables, published a widely appreciated menu of specimen letters exemplifying the gospel of naturalness and disdain for affectation, and this was to become the standard recipe for letter writing and not in Germany alone. . . .

. . . In 1891, in a substantial history of the German letter, Georg Steinhausen[5] devoted much of his space to the eighteenth century, "the century of the letter." He detected a veritable "cult of the letter" that matched the cult of friendship, and offered in evidence a bouquet of emotional tributes by Goethe's[6] contemporaries to the powers of the written word. One defined the letter as the "language of the heart"; another as a "copy of the soul." . . . "I have now attained the true art of letter-writing," Jane Austen[7] wrote her sister Cassandra in January 1801, "which we are always told is to express on paper exactly what one would say to the same person by word of mouth. I have been talking to you almost as fast as I could the whole of this letter." . . .

---

[2] Greek philosopher (ca. 428–ca. 347 B.C.E.).

[3] Roman orator and politician (106–43 B.C.E.).

[4] Evangelist and founder of Christianity (ca. 10–ca. 67 C.E.).

[5] German cultural historian (1866–1933).

[6] Johann Wolfgang von Goethe, German Romantic man of letters (1749–1832).

[7] English novelist (1775–1817).

... Achim von Arnim[8] and his wife, Bettina,[9] born Brentano, those German arch-romantics, exchanged cordial erotic messages: "When I get back," he wrote her, "nothing shall stop me from diving straightways under your blanket. — Amen, amen, may it happen!" Her reply, only marginally more inhibited: "Ah, I wish I hung on your neck and could look only upon you until death." He remained her "dear, silken body"; she to be kissed "a thousand times." This rush of feeling coexisted with more mundane but no less intimate messages: "For God's sake," she reminded him, "buy yourself a pair of suspenders and bring the children some apples." ...

... After Harriet Beecher Stowe[10] had been away on one of her long stays at spas, her husband . . . reminded her in a longing letter that it had been "almost 18 months since I have had a wife to sleep with me." (Separation was the couple's only means of contraception.) "It is enough to kill any man, especially such a man as I am." He tempered, or complicated, his plea by adding, "When I get desperate, & cannot stand it any longer, I get dear, good kind hearted Br[other] Stagg to come and sleep with me, and he puts his arms round me & hugs me to my heart's content." ...

What made Victorian letter writing distinctive, then, was less style than mass. Their time welcomed, and bought, handsomely decorated volumes of letters and, as we have seen, found expansive, though often doctored, excerpts embedded in biographies. Publishers expected profits from bouquets of courtship letters, collections chattily documenting two centuries of cultural habits, or the most interesting letters of the famous. . . . [T]he age was adept at spreading among the many what had been the privilege of the few. . . . The principal agent in democratizing written testimonials to the self was technology, an unforeseen but efficient ally of the romantics' mission to put feelings on the map. The improvement in roads, the rapid spread of the railroad network with its astonishing speed and dependable schedules, transformed the mails out of all recognition. So did that humble innovation the postage stamp.

Its history is well known but deserves retelling: in 1837, the year of Queen Victoria's[11] accession, that professional, self-assured, and exceedingly difficult reformer Sir Rowland Hill[12] proposed in a famous pamphlet, *Post Office Reform: Its Importance and Practicability,* a radical reorganization of the traffic in letters. At the time he wrote, the British mails were mired in a confusion of regulations, massive inconveniences, and extortionate rates. Before the reform, "a 'single' letter," Rowland Hill's daughter recalled in an adoring biography of her father, "had to be written on a single sheet of paper, whose use probably gave rise to the practice of that

---

[8] German writer (1781–1831).

[9] Bettina von Arnim (1785–1859), German writer.

[10] American writer (1811–1896); author of *Uncle Tom's Cabin.*

[11] Reigned from 1837 to 1901.

[12] British teacher and secretary to the Post Office (1795–1879).

now obsolete 'cross' writing which often made an epistle all but illegible, to which in those days of dear postage recourse was unavoidable." Indeed, "if a second sheet, or even the smallest piece of paper, were added to the first, the postage was doubled." When Hill wrote, the price of a letter was regulated not only by numbers of sheets but by weight, distance, and local rates, and averaged, including local mail, more than six pence.[13] Distance aggravated expense: for example, the charge for a single letter between London and Edinburgh or Glasgow was 1s. 3½d.,[14] a tidy sum unthinkable for the poor and hard for most of their "betters." . . .

To make matters worse, traffic in letters was far from secure, exposed as it was to loss, pilferage, smuggling, and inordinate delays. Need spawned fraud: many communicated by sending franked newspapers in which words were picked out to make a message. The ancient privilege of franking, which allowed peers, members of Parliament, officers, and favorite friends to send letters free of charge, had survived into the nineteenth century and widened the gap between those who could easily afford to write letters and those who could not. . . . Since, for the most part, postage had to be paid by the recipients, letter carriers had to find them and collect the money due — a time-consuming and irritating procedure. "Mismanagement, waste, and fraud," Hill's daughter summed up the situation, were virtually inescapable. Analyzing it coolly, Hill made two proposals, staggering in their simplicity: all letters should be prepaid, and the post office should establish a uniform rate: a penny for letters weighing half an ounce or less.

Despite its rationality, so frequently a source of bureaucratic sabotage, Hill's penny post became a reality in 1840. The official figures for England and Wales chart the arresting results: in 1839, just before the reform, the number of letters delivered stood at some 76 million. In the following year it doubled, only to explode after that: 347 million in 1850, 564 million in 1860, 3.5 billion in 1914. Letter writing, in short, had become a major occupation among the literate: if in 1839 the average Britisher wrote three letters a year, by just before the outbreak of the First World War that figure had grown to seventy-five. . . . [T]he modern way with the mails introduced sizable segments of the public to the habit of letter writing and encouraged the educated to write frequently and regularly. . . .

Other countries promptly followed Hill's lead. . . . [I]n the decisive decade between 1845 to 1855, the number of letters mailed in the United States more than tripled, from roughly 40 million to 132 million. . . . The postcard, introduced in the Austro-Hungarian Empire in 1869 . . . did not increase the intimacy of the mails but its frequency. It was soon followed by the cheerful picture postcard, a tribute to the rise of pleasure travel among those of middling income. . . . By 1897, a German compiler of sample letters could in the opening sentence of his book state without fear of contradiction that "it should be impossible to find anyone in the wide world of civilized nations who is not daily confronted with the neces-

---

[13] A penny, a unit of traditional English currency. Twelve pennies equals one shilling (one twentieth of a pound).

[14] One shilling, 3½ pence.

sity to make a written communication." He could not have written this sixty years earlier. . . .

Writing and receiving letters, then, and indeed postcards, came to enjoy a high priority in the emotional economy of the Victorians. Far more than ever before, correspondence spawned, and sustained, the desire for reciprocity; even a letter that did not explicitly beg for a reply was an implicit demand for conversation at a distance. . . . Unnumbered millions must have felt like Joseph Selden Hunting-ton, Jr., a freshman at Yale in 1886, who confided to his diary virtually every day that each morning his first act was to walk to the post office and look for his mail. Especially men and women in love transfigured the mailman into an almost myth-ical messenger, the bringer of happiness or misery. In country after country, it be-came the custom, more honored in the observance than in the breach, for cou-ples in love, and even more for those engaged, to write one another daily.

The letters exchanged by some nineteenth-century German-Jewish couples are particularly illuminating. They attest to the spread of romantic conventions and the emergence of an international style for love letters among groups long kept isolated from the mainstream of Victorian culture. Decades before Jews were granted full legal equality in the German states, at a time when many of them were still forbidden to settle in certain cities or practice certain professions, they poured out their affection in language wholly indistinguishable from that of their often an-tagonistic hosts. They wrote middle-class letters typical in every respect; if it were not for the names of the correspondents and an occasional reference to religious matters, one would be unable to conjecture about their origins. "You, my precious, were today, as usual, my first thought," wrote the young rabbi Meyer Keyserling to his adored Bertha Philippson, on February 4, 1861, from Berlin. . . . "Around 7:30 the mailman knocked with your precious letter."

Giving was as exciting as getting. The next morning, Keyserling greeted the woman he was soon to marry: "Good morning, my heart!" All he had in mind was to "write down a morning greeting with a newly fastened pen. I so much like to occupy myself with you before I start with my work!" . . .

Couples who could not keep the demanding schedule of a daily letter steadily exhorted one another to write soon, and tried to extract promises for more as-siduous epistolary attention. "Most tenderly loved Adolph," wrote Nanny Herzberg to her fiancé, Adolph Koritzer, a fur trader in Leipzig, in May 1856. "'An upright man keeps his word!' Even though I am not an upright man and only a girl, whether upright or not I do not know, still I want to keep my word, since I once promised you to reply right after receipt of your letter." . . .

. . . [L]ove letters were at heart all alike. This can be documented with lovers writing in societies in which arranged marriages were the rule. Among strictly ob-servant eastern European Jewish families, where the young couple-to-be often did not even meet until the wedding ceremony and correspondence between the be-trothed required special permission, Eros[15] found the way. . . . [O]n rare occasions

---

[15] Physical love, originally associated with the Greek winged god of love.

two young people whom their families had brought together would fall in love literally at first sight, doubtless well prepared by their fantasies.

One remarkable instance, as eloquent as it is exceptional, is the love letter that Chonon Wengeroff, the son of a rich merchant in Konotop, Ukraine, wrote to his bride, Pauline, in July 1849. He had spoken with her only two or three times. It was a letter — the first, she recalled decades later, she had ever received — she preserved with all others for half a century. "Deeply loved and cherished Peschinke, may you live, be healthy, my only soul! . . . Only yesterday I was next to you, and I heard your sweet, dear talk! O how happy I was. . . . Now all I see is that after the two hours my father wants to spend here, I'll have to travel on and with every minute, every second, I'm farther and farther away from you, my dear Pessinju. My dear, only soul Pessunja, you can imagine how I felt when I got into the carriage to start the trip, and two seconds later I couldn't see you any more! I could fill pages with how I felt after that, but I'm afraid that you will be uneasy; only you can understand, my angel, only this can be my consolation that I'll read your dear handwriting, in which I can read your feelings for me. Oh, that will give me new birth!" . . .

In short, a letter was a token, *the* token, of true affection, proof that the other was ready to set aside valuable time to visualizing, and addressing, the loved one. Letters could express deep emotions especially between proper couples because they took it for granted — or, often, the more venturesome of the two would urge the other to practice taking it for granted — that neither would hold back anything, whether the most painful experiences or the most carefully guarded confidences. Letters were surrogates for a longed-for physical presence. "You ask me, beloved woman, whether I read your letters *several times*," Ulrich Levysohn assured his fiancée, Clara Herrmann, in 1876, the year of their marriage. "My child, every evening, when I come home, I open the letter cabinet and read them in bed over and over again." Reading her letters in bed was not a complete substitute for having her in bed, but it would have to do until marriage. . . .

Silence generated anger or anxiety. "My dear good Emilie! I just wrote you the day before yesterday and expectantly look forward to more frequent letters, I already told you, my dear, that you should write to me more often even if I fall behind a little because business matters kept me from it." Thus Marcus Pflaum, a merchant in Munich, gently reproaching his fiancée, Emilie Hoeter, in Karlsruhe, on June 11, 1833. The next day . . . the dear good Emilie launched a reproach of her own. "Although I had been quite angry at you," she wrote, "still, I will not revenge myself and therefore already reply to your *long awaited letter* today. Yes, my dear Marcus, I was quite embarrassed this time, for I had thought I would receive one as early as Sunday, and so I remained in this embarrassing situation until Wednesday. You must not do this to me any more, I think you really could devote a bit of time to me." . . .

The appetite for abandoning customary discretion was oddly nourished by that modern invention — the ideal of privacy. That, too, like so much else in the bourgeois nineteenth century, was problematic; the boundaries beyond which no one might go were uncertain, especially within the family where the need of growing boys and girls to establish their private space clashed with the parents' authority to invade their children's domain. Thus, to give but one instance, in 1849, Richard Cary Morse, an American newspaper publisher and ordained minister, wrote his wife that he expected their daughter Elizabeth to be upset by his practice of breaking the seal of letters addressed to her. She ought to know, though, that "I recognize the sacredness of a seal & the seal of her letters no less than others, & where there is reason to believe that secrecy should be regarded [I] should not feel at liberty to break the seal; nor indeed in any case, if she forbids. But I take it for granted that she has all confidence in me, & that her secrets, if I should discover them are safe in her father's keeping. Yet children can never know the interest their parents take in them. We regard our children as part of ourselves." This was no doubt obtuse; but the family battle over Elizabeth Morse's right to her privacy was symptomatic of a larger and, to many, painful shift: the increasing claim of adolescents, in defiance of time-honored parental authority, to their own feelings. And the generational struggle this entailed was frequently carried out by mail. . . .

For middle-class men and women, then, the threat of having their personal exchanges exposed came not from the police or some official but from prying families. Stratagems to escape unwelcome attentions, so imaginatively depicted in novels, were a realistic necessity: lovers enlisted discreet confidantes, leased a post office box, learned shorthand to keep their amorous exchanges from intruders, folded scraps of intimate messages into innocuous letters that could safely be shown to one's family. . . .

. . . Victorian letter writers were steadily importuned to imitate books and sacrifice homespun improvisation for genteel address. At the upper end of the scale, the educated could draw on exemplars like the letters of Madame de Sévigné.[16] . . . Others might polish their skills by consulting volumes of letters by Alexander Pope[17] or Voltaire.[18] . . .

In the lower reaches of the social scale, correspondents relatively inept with the pen — and this seems to have constituted the majority of petty bourgeois — had at their disposal a sizable literature of manuals to relieve their verbal clumsiness. For centuries, that "unpretending but useful form-book, the 'Letter-writer,'" as an American author, R. Turner, called it in 1835, had served as the scribe for those who would be more literary than they were. It strove above all for versatility, with letters to the woman one loved, the suitor one rejected, the adolescent one counseled, the nobleman one petitioned, the employer one solicited, the customer one cajoled, the duel one declined, and more. The very title of Turner's vademecum,[19] typical in an age of long titles, conveys a sense of the audience in view: *The Parlour-Letter-Writer and Secretary's Assistant: Consisting of Original Let-*

---

[16] Famous writer of letters (1626–1696).

[17] English poet (1688–1744).

[18] French intellectual (1694–1778).

[19] A handbook or manual; something carried for frequent use.

ters on Every Occurrence in Life, Written in a Concise and Familiar Style, and Adapted to Both Sexes, to Which Are Added, Complimentary Cards, Wills, Bonds etc. . . .

Necessarily these lowly, though often pretentious, guidebooks adjusted their lessons from country to country or decade to decade. But early or late, all were in agreement that a letter must, above all, shun affectation. The "fashionable world" has laid it down, Turner advised his readers, "that *letters should be easy and natural,*" since they are, after all, "*a conversation between absent persons.*" . . .

Yet these authors, like their many competitors, were caught in a conflict they could not resolve, and did not even notice. Preaching freedom, they called for discipline. Exuberance of sentiment, especially in love, was a precious but heedless quality that needed to be curbed. Thus, for all their protests, in the advice givers' scheme of things naturalness confronted, and was bound to be defeated by, artifice. Turner counseled his readers to study the art of letter writing with care to master clarity, length, consistency, purity, neatness, and simplicity. . . .

In fact, pure spontaneity was not always valued. In 1834, Joseph Huntington got this note: "Dear Friend. These lines are wrote in a hurry and are not verry good read this letter and tear it up do not let anyboddy se it it is wrote so bad." And there were letter writers for whom spontaneity was impossible. . . .

Although in the books of advice self-control triumphed over impulse every time, the samples these letter writers devised were often remarkably imaginative. *The Ladies' and Gentleman's Model Letter-Writer,* published in London in 1871, contains in addition to the obvious subjects, a letter applying "for a ticket of admission, as an indoor patient to an hospital, for a sick child," and one from "a dressmaker to a lady, excusing herself from coming at the appointed time." An earlier manual from Philadelphia dating from 1854, *The Universal Letter-Writer; or, Complete Art of Polite Correspondence,* reached higher still, with a letter "From a Daughter to her Father, wherein she dutifully expostulates against a match he had proposed to her, with a gentleman much older than herself," and one "From a Merchant's Widow, to a Lady, a distant Relation, in behalf of her two Orphans." Yet even these models, probably taken from real situations, were almost as stilted as more ordinary fare. Nor could they be otherwise, since no personal feeling had inspired the prototypes they were prodding aspiring bourgeois to imitate. Efforts to organize feelings in acceptable flowing diction, they sounded as though transcribed from cheap novels. . . .

Disregarding such advice, . . . unknown numbers of middling bourgeois conducted their correspondence without consulting anyone but themselves. . . . But cliché-ridden or articulate, tremulous or confident, their letters tackled subjects that sample books would have considered taboo. . . . They wrote about the pleasures of the marriage bed, the anguish and rewards of pregnancy, the torments of religious uncertainty; they mastered the art of lying to their parents, indoctrinating their children, exciting their spouses. Being forced back on their own resources virtually guaranteed the authenticity of their self-revelations — or the intensity of their self-concealment.

. . . One respectable middle-class woman reports to her sister a painful miscarriage she just suffered and offers to share whatever contraceptive information her physician has promised to give her. Another equally respectable middle-class husband sends his wife perverse dreams as evidence that he longs for her. A third tantalizes her husband, who is away serving in the army, by picturing for him how fresh she smells after her bath. A fourth, learning from the reserved young woman he loves that she reciprocates his affection, informs her that he has just vaulted over his sofa in sheer exuberance. In fact, when it came to writing about sexual pleasures anticipated or recalled, the more liberated Victorian couples could be almost as uninhibited as the romantics had been.

To be sure, . . . many Victorians found it inappropriate to put their erotic desires on paper. But those who did — and they were not just rare, extremist exceptions — offer suggestive clues to the salient role that sexual satisfaction, whether in reality or as hope, played in the lives of respectable women little less than of men. Even fairly inexplicit love letters, proffering epistolary kisses and recalling delightful embraces, hint at erotic appetites with their sentimental effusions and romantic flourishes. Letters, then, seemed ideally suited to the disclosure of deep feelings in the courtship dance; lovers, it seemed, found it easier to send their sentiments by mail than to express them in person. In 1862, a hopeful American suitor put the case plainly to the young lady with whom he was taken: "We men are so bold upon paper." One has the feeling that paper was indeed the only place where erotic boldness was permitted. Fiancées who begged their beloved man to come to their arms; fiancés who closed their letters with sending thousands of kisses had never gone further, if this far, in reality. Letters were a safe way of breaching the barriers of bourgeois reticence.

. . . [T]he theme that dominated the nineteenth-century personal letter was health, mainly the writer's health, seldom perfect and normally compromised by complaints described with clinical details and in a matter-of-fact tone that speaks of resignation. Illnesses were, after all, so prevalent and physicians so helpless. Many of these ailments, we can see now, were psychosomatic: fainting spells, bouts of inexplicable fatigue and lassitude, stomachaches and digestive disorders with no organic basis, at times vanishing as suddenly as they had appeared. Others were deadly enough, and when cholera epidemics struck, as they did intermittently through the nineteenth century, letter writers saw it as their duty to warn family and friends against the cities, whether at home or abroad, where the infection raged. . . .

Naturally letters also abounded in accounts just how the writer was faring in trade or on the job, particulars about the children at school, plans for visits, and whatever else exercised a correspondent's little world. But they were not all amorous expression, health bulletins, or businesslike communiqués. Apprehension, indignation, even rage, frequently tamed by familial affection, found their voice by mail. That all too common domestic drama, the conflict of generations, notably the struggle between father and son, played itself out in duels with the pen; the combatants deployed whatever weapons they could mobilize in this psychological warfare: threats, reproaches, cajolery, alibis, blackmail, even silence — letters not written could be as eloquent as letters mailed. These missives, too, were fragments of autobiography: reproaching others for their subversive or impious sentiments was a way of disclosing one's own feelings.

A telling instance of such oedipal battles is the tense correspondence that the young Austrian Hermann Bahr, on the verge of launching a career as a journalist, drama critic, novelist, and playwright, carried on with his father, Erich. In 1883, a student at the University of Vienna, he had publicly orated in behalf of "the most sacred cause," the cause of a greater German republic, and laid himself open to expulsion from the university by the skittish Hapsburg authorities. It would be cowardly to deny his convictions, Hermann told his father, and adroitly blamed him: "Why did you bring me up to be an honorable human being?" In response, his father urged him to remain politically neutral, at least until he had his degree; deploying time-honored tactics, he conveniently recalled his sickly wife, his irresponsible younger son, and the difficulties in making a decent living: "And so I enter upon my fiftieth year — I strongly hope not to have to enter upon any more of them!" We have seen it before: self-pity could be an effective form of epistolary aggression. . . .

Religion was, if anything, more explosive a subject for censorious letter writers than politics. . . . This issue, too, animated the correspondence between Selden Huntington, a Connecticut merchant and land speculator, and his son Joseph from 1833, when the boy was thirteen, at boarding school, to 1846, the year of the father's death. "I hope you will remember with thankfulness your Maker," Selden Huntington wrote Joseph in November 1833. "Do *not* fail to pray to God that you may have faith in Christ." In March of the following year, Joseph's mother weighed in with the same admonition: "Above all, my son, let me entreat you to 'Remember your Creator in the days of your youth.'" In March 1835, the father was back on the lecture platform: "Hope you will be diligent in your studies & never forget for a moment your duty to the being who made you & preserves you & continues your life." In the same year, Joseph's cousin Sybil reminded him that "we have but a short time to stay on the earth & a great preparation to make for those scenes which we shall have to pass through after we enter the Dark Valley of the Shadow of Death." Frightening a sinner into religiosity was a legitimate tactic for Victorian letter writers. . . .

Obviously enough, letter writing is virtually never an altogether solitary act. Except for the narcissist writing in effect to himself, the other is always there, a photograph on the desk, a faded flower pressed between the pages of a book, an image in the mind, waiting to be informed, corrected, pleased — above all, pleased. As we have seen, the nineteenth-century literature on letter writing, modernizing Cicero, made into a truism the truth that letter writing is a kind of conversation. But how truly unrehearsed?

This question raises difficult problems of interpretation. What price sincerity? Once a letter writer has acquired sufficient practice and knowledge of the world, pleasing formulas become second nature, so automatic as to require no reflection, no hesitation. Yet this does not mean that a practiced presentation must be an act of hypocrisy, mere playing with emotion. Nor does it necessarily leave the writer's mind opaque: the urges to compliment and cajole — or to be complimented and cajoled — are facts of mental life as open to study as any other.

That old half-serious question, How do I know who I am until I read what I have written? contains an important truth: writing letters may become an exercise in self-definition. Hence any form they take, natural or affected, may become fragments of a great confession.

These are subtle matters. But, significantly, the Victorians took little note of such intricacies. By mid-century, letter writing had become a cultural imperative for the middle classes, and correspondents took it for granted that a letter not obviously formulaic would give its recipient a glimmer of the very soul of the sender. Barbey D'Aurevilly, novelist and essayist, perhaps put it best in 1876, in a review of *La Correspondance de Balzac*.[20] These letters, he asserted, gave the world more of Balzac the man and writer than pictorial representations could ever do. They were "infinitely better than a portrait, even if done by a Michelangelo[21] or a Raphael[22] of the pen. Here is flesh and blood, head and heart, soul and life of a man who was, in literary art, the most dazzling and the most profound, was at once a Raphael and a Michelangelo." He was putting into words the inarticulate assumptions of ordinary bourgeois. If the published work was the writer booted and spurred, private letters were the man — and woman — in dressing gown and slippers, talking freely.

This sense of things helps to explain a puzzling nineteenth-century habit that has made historians of the age grateful beneficiaries. For centuries, people had kept letters, whether hidden in a desk drawer or a receptacle designed for the purpose. But in the Victorian age, recipients went further. They underscored their demands to keep their letters *"secret, secret, secret."* And they preserved letters they had been earnestly enjoined to destroy. Letters, written by hand and hence all the more eloquent witnesses of their author, seemed an essential part of an important living being. It is as though even people not superstitious obscurely felt that to burn a letter was to do the sender some unspecified harm or to deprive oneself of a cherished gift: the presence of an absent one. It followed that it was unacceptable to leave testimony of oneself entrusted to unworthy hands. The Victorians took for granted that when a couple broke off their engagement, gifts — a ring, a book, a photograph — would be returned. So, too, were the letters they had exchanged. One was almost literally getting one's own back, the self fixed on a handwritten page safe once again.

---

[20] *Balzac's Correspondence;* Honoré de Balzac (1799–1850), a prolific French novelist.

[21] Italian Renaissance artist (1475–1564), famous for his sculptures *Pietà* and *David* and for his painting of the Sistine Chapel ceiling.

[22] Italian Renaissance architect and painter (1483–1520).

THE CHALLENGE OF CHOLERA
IN HAMBURG
Richard J. Evans

Cholera first visited the German port city of Hamburg in 1832 and reappeared at various times throughout the nineteenth century. Cholera was not the most deadly disease ravaging nineteenth-century Europe (tuberculosis, smallpox, typhoid, and measles killed more people), but it was perhaps the most vile. A seemingly healthy person who contracted the cholera bacillus succumbed to diarrhea, fever, and vomiting. The body shriveled, the skin discolored, the extremities turned blue with cold, and the victim died a miserable death, albeit a quick one. Unlike other diseases, cholera was socially unacceptable. Why was this the case?

Social historian Richard J. Evans is interested in industrialization's impact on social and political inequality. Using newspapers, letters, government documents, and medical publications, Evans describes the terror that cholera epidemics inspired, especially in bourgeois society. The bacillus spread through contaminated water, food, and clothes. An individual had to ingest the bacillus to become infected. Port workers and slum residents most easily contracted the disease. Thus cholera affected the poor disproportionately.

How did the medical profession and Hamburg's leaders deal with this new disease? What explanations did physicians offer for the spread of cholera, and how did they advise the state and medical community to contain the epidemic? How did their opinions reflect bourgeois disgust with the poor inhabitants of Hamburg? Note why scientist Max von Pettenkofer's theory of cholera and a voluntaristic, individualistic approach to health and hygiene proved so attractive to the bourgeois and commercial elite that controlled the city government.

Nineteenth-century Europeans debated the extent to which states should intervene to regulate epidemics. This debate was part of a wider discussion of governments' role in society. In Hamburg, how did the association of cholera with individual morality tie in to the discussion about the city's proper role in combating the disease?

Richard J. Evans, *Death in Hamburg: Society and Politics in the Cholera Years, 1830–1910* (New York: Oxford University Press, 1987), 226–252, 254–256.

In the West today, are there diseases that carry a social stigma? What makes a disease socially unacceptable?

In the early 1830s European society was suddenly confronted by the appearance of an entirely new and very serious disease: Asiatic cholera. It came to Europe as a consequence of European mercantile and industrial enterprise, and once it had arrived, it fastened on to the industrial society that was then in the making and exploited and exaggerated many of its most prominent aspects, from urbanization and overcrowding to environmental pollution and social inequality. The disease had long been endemic on the Indian subcontinent. But the expansion of the British Empire, with its frequent and large-scale movements of goods and people, and the rapid growth in trade between India and Europe that accompanied the industrial revolution in the United Kingdom, combined in the early nineteenth century to export the disease to the rest of the world. By 1819 the major outbreak that had begun in Bengal two years before had reached Mauritius; by 1824 it covered the whole of South-East Asia. More ominously still, it had been carried by traders across Afghanistan before being halted by a military cordon sanitaire in Astrakhan in 1823. It was indeed by this route that it eventually reached the West. After a brief respite in the mid-1820s, it returned to Persia and crossed the Caspian once more, making its way north to Orenburg, at the south-western edge of the Urals, in August 1829. From this new centre it was spread by merchants travelling to and from the great annual fair in Nijhni-Novgorod, as well as making its way independently up the Volga past Astrakhan, where this time the military cordon sanitaire failed to work. In September 1830 it reached Moscow. And in 1831 a major Russian military campaign against a rebellion in Poland spread it rapidly further west. By July it had reached the port of Riga, on the Baltic.

Reports of the horrifying and deadly effects of the new disease soon began to reach Western Europe. It began to affect the victim through a vague feeling of not being well, including a slight deafness. This was followed fairly quickly by violent spasms of vomiting and diarrhoea, vast and prolonged in their extent, in which the evacuations were usually described as being like "rice-water." In this stage up to 25% of the victim's body fluids could be lost. This led, not surprisingly, to a state of collapse in which, in effect, the blood coagulated and ceased to circulate properly. The skin became blue and "corrugated," the eyes sunken and dull, the hands and feet as cold as ice. Painful muscular cramps convulsed and contorted the body. The victims appeared indifferent to their surroundings, though consciousness was not necessarily lost altogether. At this stage death would ensue in about half the cases from cardiac or renal[1] failure, brought on by acute dehydration and loss of vital chemicals and electrolytes, or the victim would recover more or less rapidly. The whole progress of the symptoms from start to finish could take

---

[1] Of the kidney.

as little as 5 to 12 hours, more usually about 3 or 4 days. Modern medical science would add that the incubation period appears to last for a minimum of 24 hours and up to a maximum of 5 days, and though the carrier state may last longer, it too is usually of similar duration (roughly 24 hours to 8 days).

The most important causative agent in the disease is now agreed to be a microscopic bacillus known as *Vibrio cholerae*. It thrives in warm and humid conditions, above all in river water (up to 20 days). It multiplies very rapidly when the water is warm, though it can survive in colder temperatures. Although the bacillus is transmitted most easily in water, it can also survive on foodstuffs, especially on fruit and vegetables which have been washed in infected water. It can live in butter for up to a month. Milk also provides a hospitable environment. These facts are important because the disease can only strike if the bacillus enters the human digestive tract. In effect, it can only be caught by putting an infected foodstuff or other substance into the mouth. It is transmitted easily enough by touching the mouth with infected hands. This opens up a further range of possibilities. The bacillus survives for up to 15 days on faeces and a week in ordinary earth dust. Infected clothes and linen, especially the bed-linen of victims, are important sources of transmission, should they be touched by others who then later unsuspectingly put hand to mouth. Person-to-person transmission usually occurs indirectly through infection of food or clothing or bathroom and toilet facilities. The bacillus can also be transmitted by flies as far as their limited range takes them. The best way to combat the bacillus is through scrupulous personal hygiene. Frequent washing of the hands, especially after contact with infected persons and things (e.g. communal lavatories), is vital. During an epidemic, bacilli in the water-supply, in milk, or on foodstuffs can be killed by heat (boiling or baking). The bacillus cannot withstand acid. This includes some gastric juices and most disinfectants. It only lasts for a few minutes in wine or spirits, a few hours in beer. It can be prevented from entering the water-supply by the process of sand filtration. This introduces hostile bacteria into the water and the cholera bacilli are quickly exterminated. It follows from all this that cholera epidemics tend to break out in warm and humid weather. They are often spread by infected water-supplies, especially if allied to inefficient sewage systems. Personal contacts also play a role. Dirty and overcrowded living conditions and shared toilet facilities are especially dangerous. On a wider geographical scale, the disease is spread by victims and carriers as they move about the country. River-water is sometimes infected and spreads the disease as it flows downstream. All these factors marked out an insanitary port city such as Hamburg as a major potential centre if the disease should continue to spread.

For nineteenth-century sensibilities, cholera was a disease truly terrifying in its effects. Society had in many ways come to terms with infant deaths and with long-term, permanently present killers such as consumption. A whole set of attitudes had evolved to help people confront the reality of such everyday deaths. This was "the Age of the Beautiful Death," . . . when literature was full of edifying death-bed scenes, in which death crept up on people slowly, transformed their physical suffering into an ethereal beauty, and lent them, in its slow but

inexorable progress, a moral purity unattainable in everyday life. Death's permanent presence in the family made its emotional costs easier to bear. In most cases
where death was exceptionally sudden and violent, as on the battlefield, it was
usually possible to come to terms with it through the ideology of heroism,
chivalry, or self-sacrifice. Even an ignominious death, by suicide or on the gallows,
had its appointed rituals — the suicide note, often with its claim to a noble motive, the last meal of the condemned, the speech from the scaffold.

Death from cholera was, almost by definition, anything but beautiful. It was
a new disease, which people found hard to fit into the patterns of coping with
death evolved across the preceding centuries. Moreover, the occurrence of cholera
epidemics was sufficiently rare for people to be able to suppress their consciousness of its visitations. The threat which it posed was not permanent, and therefore not psychologically manageable. Its impact was unpredictable, its causes unknown or disputed. It affected every group of the population. Thus when a
cholera epidemic did occur, it stamped itself on the public consciousness with all
the force of a natural disaster. Tuberculosis, though a great killer, was usually a
slow disease. It spread through the city's population at a pace so leisurely that no
one could notice whether it was increasing or decreasing in incidence. Cholera
raged through the population with terrifying speed. People could be walking
about normally, with no symptoms one day, and yet be dead the next morning.
The mere onset of the symptoms could sometimes be enough to kill. People were
appalled by the terrifying and unpredictable suddenness with which the disease
struck. A businessman could leave his house in good order in the morning and
return from work in the evening to find a note on the door saying his wife and
family had been taken to hospital after being stricken down during the day. A
woman could begin her supper in good health but not live to eat the pudding.
Such stories, and the fact of their wide circulation during epidemics, attested to
the fact that the suddenness with which cholera attacked people was one of its
most frightening aspects.

In addition, the symptoms of cholera were peculiarly horrifying to
nineteenth-century bourgeois sensibility. Consumptives exhibited few symptoms
that caused embarrassment or discomfort in the onlooker, and then only from
time to time. On the whole, they merely became pale and interesting. Even typhoid, despite some unpleasant symptoms, was considered socially acceptable
and claimed a number of prominent victims. It presented symptoms of fever that
took some weeks to progress and could be understood in terms of a drama of life
and death, so that spectators were frequently present at the bedside to watch the
whole performance and converse with the patient in his or her moments of lu-
cidity. Not so cholera. The blue, "corrugated" appearance of the skin and the dull,
sunken eyes of sufferers transformed their bodies from those of recognizable people, friends, family, relatives, into the living dead within a matter of hours. Worse
still, the massive loss of body fluids, the constant vomiting and defecating of vast
quantities of liquid excreta, were horrifying and deeply disgusting in an age
which, more than any other, sought to conceal bodily functions from itself. Bourgeois society . . . took increasing pains, as the century wore on, to make private

the grosser physical acts of daily living and to pretend that they did not exist. Cholera broke through the precarious barriers erected against physicality in the name of civilization. The mere sight of its symptoms was distressing; the thought that one might oneself suddenly be seized with an uncontrollable, massive attack of diarrhoea in a tram,[2] in a restaurant, or on the street, in the presence of scores or hundreds of respectable people, must have been almost as terrifying as the thought of death itself. It is telling that while quiet diseases such as cancer and tuberculosis were widely used as literary metaphors, cholera's appearance in the literature of the nineteenth century is rare. . . .

Such was the nature of the disease that broke out in Hamburg on 5 October 1831, when a sixty-seven year-old former sailor called Peter Petersen, who mainly lived from begging, fell ill with "violent vomiting and diarrhoea." Police surgeon Hauptfleisch found him on 6 October suffering from severe cramps, "the extremities ice-cold, hands and feet blue, and eyes sunken." At 6 P.M. on 6 October 1831, Petersen died. At this point the authorities learned of another case that had occurred on 2 October on board a barge that had travelled down the Elbe from Wittenberge. It is most likely that the disease had entered the city by this route, through infection of the river-water upstream from Hamburg, where the barge lay in quarantine in the port of Geesthacht. Probably Petersen had for some reason come into contact with the river water; or it had infected the sour milk which he often drank. Several of the 41 inhabitants of his cellar lodgings, who "consisted in their entirety of vagabonds and beggars" as a history of the epidemic written later in the same year subsequently noted, also fell ill with the same symptoms. So too did some of Petersen's companions in the begging trade. Soon cases were being reported all over the city. Already on 11 October 14 new cases were reported; on 16 October there were 44, and on the 18th day the epidemic reached its height, with 51 new cases. Thereafter it declined rapidly. Hamburg breathed again. The epidemic had, all things considered, been a good deal less severe than many people had feared.

. . . But it had not yet disappeared from Hamburg. The epidemic was officially regarded as having ended in January, and the various precautionary measures ordered by the authorities were relaxed. No cases occurred in February or March. Already on 1 April, however, a new case was reported, and eight further cases, with five deaths in all, were confirmed before the Senate, on 27 April 1832, finally concluded that cholera had broken out once more. The disease spread throughout May and June, reaching a first peak on 16 June, when 92 cases were reported within the space of a few hours. In July it declined, so that towards the end of the month there were only half a dozen or so new cases reported each day. But in August it grew in intensity once more, with 30 new cases reported on the 26th. Throughout September and October it showed no signs of departing, with anything between 5 and 15 new cases occurring each day. In November it finally began to abate. The last case was reported on 17 December. All in all, 3,349 people

---

[2] Streetcar.

in Hamburg fell victim to the disease in the epidemic of April–December 1832. 1,652 of them died. In the end, therefore, Hamburg was quite seriously affected by the epidemic of 1831–2.

How the medical profession and the authorities dealt with the new disease depended on what they thought caused it. Here opinions were divided. The obvious model to which cholera seemed to conform was the plague. . . . Two Berlin medical men, writing in 1831, argued that it was "solely and exclusively caused and transmitted by an infectious material" which was spread in people's breath, in their clothing, in their excretions, and in the things they touched. They drew optimistic conclusions from their theory. If cholera was caused by a miasma,[3] they declared, there would be no means by which the individual citizen could protect himself. A contagionist theory[4] placed the means of prevention in everyone's hands. . . .

The doctrine of contagion was a very old one. It went back at least as far as the plague writings of the sixteenth century, which postulated transmission by touch, by infected clothing or goods, and (exceptionally) inhalation of an infected atmosphere. By the 1830s, however, many medical scientists seriously doubted the adequacy of the contagionist model. A second type of theory stressed instead the importance of local miasmas, in which the air was polluted by factors peculiar to certain localities under specific conditions. This too was an old theory, with parallels in medieval plague medicine. . . . Even before the disease arrived in Hamburg the local medical profession was split over the issue. On 21 June 1831 the Doctors' Club decided to meet once a week to study and discuss the reports of cholera coming in from further east and prepare for its possible arrival. Letters from doctors in Königsberg, St. Petersburg, Warsaw, and other cities where the disease had broken out were read aloud and debated. Here the first battles took place between the "contagionists" and "miasmatists." . . .

What particularly impressed the anticontagionists was the universal failure of quarantine. Time and again this was the major reason given for concluding that the disease was not contagious. . . . So certain were some writers of the noncontagious character of the disease that they predicted in advance of its arrival that cholera would never reach Hamburg. Dr. H. W. Buek, the City Medical Officer (*Stadtphysikus*), . . . gave it as his firm opinion in December 1830 "that this oriental form of disease should appear in the heart of Germany . . . seems to me . . . to be very unlikely, indeed almost unthinkable." Yet appear it did; and soon the idea of contagion was in disrepute because quarantine had failed to work. Doctors began to be converted to the idea that cholera was produced by a miasma. F. Siemerling, writing in 1831, called it *malaria animata* or "animated swamp-air" released by rotting plants in marshy land. . . .

If cholera was caused by a local miasma, then how was the disease transmitted from place to place? One writer, Karl Preu, noting that it appeared to travel

---

[3] Bad-smelling vapor thought to transmit disease.

[4] The belief that diseases are transmitted from one person to another.

along waterways, hypothesized that the miasma was carried along by "the strong airstreams that prevail along such great rivers." From there it sank into the ground on the river banks. He denied that the miasma was produced by any particular type of weather. Dr. C. F. Nagel, writing in Altona, went further in the direction of a "contingent contagionism." He argued that the disease was in part the consequence of conditions in the ground the nature of which was not yet properly understood; it also seemed to be carried by "infection by people, perhaps also by goods and effects." However, though he practised in state-interventionist Altona rather than free-trade Hamburg, Nagel did not go so far as to argue for quarantine and isolation as preventive measures. He preferred instead to place his main emphasis on personal behaviour. "Nothing encourages the outbreak of this disease more than excessive, persistent fear of the same." If people kept calm and avoided a "disorderly . . . way of life," they would be safe. In particular dirt, damp, and neglected living conditions, and above all, the "abuse of alcoholic beverages" encouraged infection. "Old drunkards" were particularly vulnerable. Thus Nagel inserted his theory within a powerful current of opinion which ascribed disease to the moral weakness of the victims.

The tendency to ascribe infection to moral failings or psychological disturbance in the victim was very widespread. "Just don't be afraid!" people were advised, "be moderate and sober!" Fear, wrote Wilhelm Cohnstein of Glogau, in a pamphlet circulating in Hamburg before the outbreak of cholera, had a "paralysing influence on the nervous system." . . .

In general, therefore, three basic explanations of cholera seem to have been circulating in Hamburg in the early 1830s: the contagionist, the miasmatist, and the moral or psychological. . . .

However, the experience of the first epidemic was enough to persuade most medical men in Hamburg — as in other parts of Europe — that whatever else cholera was, it was not a contagious disease in the accepted meaning of the word. As Zimmermann[5] remarked in 1832, "a conviction that cholera is not contagious has become so fixed here, as everywhere, among the medical and lay public, that it would be difficult to bring them over to any other point of view." It was particularly important that the Chief Medical Officer of the city, *Stadtphysikus* Dr. Heinrich Wilhelm Buek (1796–1879), was from the outset a convinced anticontagionist; his influence was doubtless a contributing factor to the spread of anticontagionist views in the Hamburg medical profession after 1831. In his official report on the next major cholera epidemic to hit the city, in 1848, Buek repeated "that an *import,* a transmission from one victim to another, an assumption that is still to be found here and there, has *not* happened here." This was proved, he considered, by the fact that the first cases to occur broke out in different parts of the city and were thus not connected. Yet "the manner in which cholera is *spread,*" he was forced to confess, "is still a riddle, nor has the present epidemic given us any clues to it." Indeed, so insoluble did the problem seem that the Doc-

---

[5] K. G. Zimmermann, physician and chronicler of the Hamburg cholera epidemic of the 1830s.

tors' Club did not think it worth discussing at all in 1848–9. The medical profession remained anticontagionist in its majority. . . . But its unity was essentially negative: the doctors could agree on what cholera was not, but they were completely at a loss when it came to explaining what it actually was.

By 1860, however, all this had changed. A new theory of cholera had been developed which seemed to offer the answer to all these problems. Its author was the Bavarian scientist Max von Pettenkofer. . . .

. . . In his own day, and indeed in his own mind, Pettenkofer was the best-known and most implacable of the contagionists' opponents. His ideas evolved and changed in various respects over the years, but the central elements in his mature theory remained constant, and it is important to look at them briefly since their consequences proved to be practical as well as theoretical.

Pettenkofer's theories of cholera took their starting-point in the ideas of his mentor Justus Liebig.[6] These stressed, among other things, the importance of the fermentation of decomposing matter as an influence on the receptivity of a given area to epidemic diseases. Pettenkofer began to apply these ideas in his account of the 1854 epidemic in Munich, published the following year. While accepting the existence of an infectious element which enabled cholera to be transported from one place to another, he denied that the disease was spread "by contagion in the narrow sense of the word." Nor, he asserted, could it possibly be carried by drinking-water. Indeed, he wrote that "in my report in Munich, I have disposed, once and for all, of causation by drinking-water." Nor, finally, was the disease carried in infected clothes or goods. It was most probably transmitted from place to place by human beings, even those who had not suffered the symptoms of cholera. But they could have no effect unless they infected the soil with their excreta. Influenced by Liebig's work on fermentation, Pettenkofer developed over the decade 1855–65 an elaborate theory of the conditions under which a cholera miasma could arise. It depended, he argued, on a series of changes in the level of the water-table or "ground-water." The water-table would suddenly rise, and the moisture content of the soil increase. These events were followed by a dry period in which the water-table dropped and the moisture content of the soil fell. Thus a layer of soil would be left above the water-table; cholera would "germinate" in this soil, provided of course that the soil had been infected with the cholera germ. A miasma would then be created, in which the disease was transmitted through air polluted by the germination process. Thus people living on high ground, or even on the upper storeys of apartment blocks, could enjoy a relative immunity, while those living on low-lying or marshy land, in cellars, or in cramped and confined conditions, where the circulation of air was restricted, were most at risk.

Pettenkofer thus became the self-appointed champion of the "localist" school, which emphasized meteorological influences operating through changes in the water-table. Though he accepted a contagious element in cholera, he did not con-

---

[6] German chemist (1803–1873).

sider it very important, and the bulk of his writings on the subject was devoted either to proving that the disease could not be transmitted by drinking-water, or to elaborating and further refining his own "ground-water" theory and providing a statistical basis for its major assertions. On these fundamental points he did not change his mind over the decades. Pettenkofer's theory achieved widespread currency, helped by his enormous influence in the field of hygiene, a discipline of which indeed he has some claim to be regarded as the founding father. . . .

In the 1860s and 1870s, therefore, there can be little doubt that Pettenkofer's "ground-water theory," and his dismissal of the notion that cholera was a waterborne disease, dominated official and medical approaches to the cholera problem in Germany. His ideas were never undisputed, and many doctors continued to emphasize moral and other factors in the aetiology[7] of cholera. But Pettenkofer's influence is unmistakable not only in a large body of medical writings on cholera by many different commentators, but also in official policy as well. How can it be explained? Certainly it would not have been possible without his indefatigable energy and the ceaseless flow of publications on cholera that streamed from his pen. Equally certainly, it owed a lot to his enormous reputation in the field of social hygiene, with which the problem of cholera had long been recognized as having an intimate though hotly disputed connection. But there were more general reasons for Pettenkofer's influence. Pettenkofer was a pioneer of preventive medicine. He advocated a broad approach and believed strongly in public education as a means of improving public health. Against some opposition from his own university, he was a determined popularizer of his own views, both on paper and by word of mouth. He was an advocate of temperance, of cleanliness, of regular bathing, of a "rational diet," of warm clothing, and above all of fresh air. Indeed, if anyone deserved to be called a "fresh-air fanatic" it was Max von Pettenkofer. He opposed drinking not least because it took place in "the horrible atmosphere" of smoke-filled, overcrowded taverns. He maintained that "our children's health suffers when they are exposed for a number of hours to the atmosphere of ill-ventilated schoolrooms." He poured well-deserved scorn on the Germans' traditional horror of draughts. He admired the English habit of maintaining an open fire in every parlour because, as he perceptively remarked, "the English fireplace is a very poor heating device but good for ventilation." All these improvements could be achieved, he thought, by means of public education and propaganda. Legislation was not only largely unnecessary, it was also impracticable.

Pettenkofer was, to be sure, an advocate of state regulation and reform where he considered it absolutely necessary in order to reduce the possibility of creating an unhealthy miasma through contamination of the soil. He insisted on the provision of adequate sewage and waste disposal. He believed that every dwelling, even a garret apartment, should be supplied with water from a central source, because this meant people were more likely to wash frequently than if they had to fetch the water from a distance. The water, therefore, had to be clean, for if foul

---

[7] The causes of a specific disease.

water was repeatedly used for washing it could turn the surfaces which it affected into breeding-places for disease. It was largely due to Pettenkofer's insistence that a slaughterhouse was constructed in Munich in 1878, that the city acquired a new water-supply from the mountains, and that a new sewage system was installed, channelling the waste into the river downstream from the city and so preventing it from getting into the soil, where he thought it did so much harm. Pettenkofer warned against regarding sewage disposal and the provision of a fresh water-supply as all that were necessary to the improvement of public health, however. He asserted that a nutritious diet and fresh air were far more important. Moreover, he does not seem to have thought it necessary to provide a filtration system for the water-supply. It was enough for the water-supply to avoid direct contamination by contact with ground-water in the soil. Thus spring-water carried from the mountains was superior to water drawn from wells in the city. The water with which he arranged for Munich to be supplied certainly was not filtrated, and indeed, shortly after the water began flowing a massive typhoid epidemic hit the city, spread by the new supply system. Pettenkofer continued to believe none the less that epidemic diseases could not spread in water. He did advocate reducing over-crowding in houses "partly by education and partly by regulations," but again he insisted that "we do not solve the problem by providing the poor with the most necessary food, housing and clothing unless we at the same time educate them in painstaking cleanliness."

. . . Pettenkofer sought to prove that prevention would result in a massive saving in hospital costs by reducing disease. It thus offered municipal authorities a substantial return on their initial investment. He called hygiene "health economics." Such preventive measures as proper sewage disposal and the provision of drinking-water were analogous to the minimal state intervention necessary to guarantee the smooth running of the economy, rather like the standardization of weights and measures or — in Hamburg — the construction of the harbour. Once they had been provided, the real responsibility for health and well-being lay with the individual.

In keeping with this voluntaristic approach to health, Pettenkofer was opposed to the massive state intervention favoured by the contagionists. Prevention, he believed, was all: once an epidemic had actually broken out, the state could do nothing to check its progress. In a major series of articles published in 1886–7, Pettenkofer declared that quarantine measures were useless against cholera. They would always be ineffective, he said. They were irrelevant to the decisive factor, which was the condition of the soil. The isolation of cholera cases after the outbreak of an epidemic, he wrote, "is equally useless; and so is the special cholera hospital." Moreover, he added, "it is obvious that I consider the disinfection of the excreta of cholera patients to be as ineffective as the isolation of cholera patients." This was because "cholera patients produced no effective infectious material." Flight was a reasonable precaution since it removed people from the miasmatic local influences. The closing of markets, fairs, and other gatherings would achieve nothing, unless they were held in a locality where the soil factor was powerful. Finally, he continued to deny categorically that cholera was transmitted by drinking-water, so all measures during an epidemic to provide people with alternative supplies of pure or boiled water were futile.

The parallels between Pettenkofer's theory of cholera and liberal theories of the state[8] are obvious. Pettenkofer attracted the adherence of medical opinion by offering a synthesis of many previous accounts and linking it to the established scientific principle of fermentation. But his ideas also had a broader appeal. His emphasis on sanitation, cleanliness, fresh air, and a rational diet were more than welcome to the German middle classes at a time when the urban environment was rapidly deteriorating, and when bourgeois consciousness of the presence of dirt and excrement, noxious vapours, and polluted or adulterated food was growing stronger. The stress he laid on temperance and regularity accorded strongly with bourgeois values, as did the belief he expressed that hygienic improvement depended above all on the individual. But the seductiveness of Pettenkofer's theories went even further than this. As we shall now see, they found a ready response not only because of the values which they expressed and the promise of environmental improvement which they held out, but also because of the direct appeal they directed to bourgeois self-interest.

When cholera first appeared on the European scene, governments everywhere went to great lengths to try and halt its progress. In Russia, military cordons were thrown around infected areas; in the Habsburg Empire, stringent quarantine measures were introduced. These activities were almost invariably ineffective. Not only did they fail to stop the cholera, they also provoked widespread popular unrest. The government and military presence in the stricken areas, the isolation of hospitalized victims, and the sudden appearance of large numbers of doctors, including many from other areas and countries who had come to observe the disease, convinced many Russian peasants that the government was trying to kill them off. Several physicians and officials were massacred amid widespread rioting. In the Habsburg Empire castles were sacked and quarantine aid officers and doctors were slaughtered. When the disease reached Prussia, official efforts to control it met with a similar response. Popular resentment against official interference in the livelihood of journeymen, peasants, traders, and many others found symbolic expression in the belief that the disease was the product of poisoning by physicians engaged in a secret campaign to reduce the excess population. . . .

Public order was very much at the front of the mind of authority as the cholera epidemic spread across Eastern and Central Europe in 1831. Even Hamburg did not escape; in September 1830 popular unrest in the city expressed itself in prolonged though minor anti-Semitic disturbances. Nevertheless, in common with the authorities elsewhere in Europe, the government of the city-state proceeded in the summer of 1831 to impose restrictions on the movement of people and goods in an attempt to stop the approach of the cholera epidemic.

---

[8] The belief that the state should improve the population by inculcating middle-class values.

Incoming ships and river barges were subjected to medical quarantine from the summer of 1831 until the beginning of 1832. From 8 October the Senate refused to issue clean bills of health to ships leaving the port. For the duration of the 1831 epidemic, Hamburg was under medical quarantine with severe restrictions on trade.

The Hamburg Senate was no less energetic in the measures which it took to combat the disease once it actually arrived. In July 1831, indeed, well before the outbreak of the disease, it issued an elaborate set of ordinances, to come into force immediately the epidemic broke out, as it eventually did in October. A General Health Commission was established, with special local commissions for the various districts of the city. All cases were to be reported to these commissions as soon as they broke out. "Houses in which there are people stricken with cholera will be signified with a poster, on which the word 'cholera' is written, so that everyone knows that they are infected." Such houses were to be isolated and disinfected. A special commission was established, to supervise disinfection work. This included chlorine fumigation in the streets, to clean the air. The cheap lodging-house where the disease had broken out was evacuated and fumigated some five days after the first case was reported, and other affected houses were similarly treated. . . . All these measures, of course, were predicated on the assumption that cholera was an infectious disease.

But they met with increasing criticism as time went on. In the first place, they were clearly unable to prevent the arrival of the disease or its spread through the city and beyond. Secondly, in Hamburg as elsewhere, they were seen as posing a threat to public order. Like other German cities, Hamburg was walled in the 1830s, but its expansion with the growth of trade had already led to the creation of a substantial built-up area of urban settlement outside the walls, in St. Pauli and St. Georg. The inhabitants of these areas resented their exclusion from the governing institutions of the city and had been petitioning for equal rights for some time, with little success. When the General Health Commission was founded in July, the Chief of the St. Georg Battalion of the Citizens' Militia demanded a seat on it, and was dubbed a "trouble-maker" for his pains. The incident led to a series of demonstrations in which the inhabitants of the suburb attempted forcibly to prevent the nightly closure of the city gate, the symbol of their exclusion from equal participation in the city's affairs. Eventually the problem was solved, but it was now felt in the Senate that any further organizational measures against the epidemic might easily offend popular sensibilities in a similar way. Finally, the measures taken in 1831 were very expensive. They involved, for example, the employment of some 700 workers to carry out the hospitalization, quarantine, and fumigation measures ordered by the Senate, as well as the construction of the special hospitals and isolation wards where the sick were housed.

Medical and bourgeois opinion all over Europe was now mobilizing against quarantine and the other interventionist policies adopted in the face of the first cholera epidemic. Quarantine, maintained a pamphlet published in Danzig in 1831, was not only useless but dangerous. It exhausted state finances, disrupted trade, and so increased poverty. It caused terror and panic flight in the population and prevented the support of the afflicted and isolated families by welfare agencies. . . . There was thus ample support for the decision of the Hamburg authorities to drop early in 1832 all the precautions they had taken against cholera the previous year. These precautions had contributed, it was believed, to "fear and terror" among "the gentlemen who frequent our Exchange," and the sealing-off of the borders by the Prussian and Danish authorities had done untold damage to trade.

The Senate was fortified in its decision by the general swing of medical opinion against contagionism, and by the fact that the epidemic had in the end proved a good deal less severe than originally feared. The quarantine measures were thus not renewed; and the state sanitary stations (Sanitätswachen) set up to deal with the disease were disbanded. When cholera broke out with increased virulence later in the year, the burden of combating the disease was placed entirely on the medical profession. The Doctors' Club set up a sanitary station in its rooms, staffed by two physicians at a time, working shifts, during the day. There were no medical services available after 10 P.M. To the Doctors' Club also fell the task of compiling lists of the sick and the dead. It was the medical profession, not the state, that arranged for hospitalization of victims and supplied ambulancemen and nursing staff, though expenses could be claimed for these measures, in arrears, from the authorities. There were no quarantine measures and no isolation wards: cholera patients were simply put alongside the normal hospital inmates. No official announcements were made of new cases, or even of the presence of an epidemic. It was hardly surprising, therefore, that while the 1831 epidemic cost the authorities fully half a million Marks Courant,[9] that of the following year cost them only twenty thousand, even though it was considerably more severe.

The widespread concern with cholera as a problem of individual morality found its way into the handbooks of medical advice on how to prevent the disease. Disease appeared here as the consequence not so much of immorality as of emotional disorder or excitement — the very factor which was also seen as at the root of the riot and rebellion with which cholera was so often associated. Virtually all the early literature, including the official leaflet issued in 1831, prescribed personal cleanliness and much of it also offered dietary advice, including the avoidance of "acidulous, watery foods and those which cool down the stomach and abdomen." Miasmatists stressed the need for fresh air, while the widespread belief that cholera was an extreme form of "the common cold" led many to urge the importance of keeping warm. Most widespread and insistent of all was the advice to avoid physical or emotional excess. Many doctors in 1831 considered that fear of the disease was a sure invitation for it to strike. Correspondingly they urged people to lead a sober and moderate life and to avoid any kind of upset. People were told to avoid "passions," to trust in God, and to maintain an "orderly way of life." The classic formula was provided by the Prussian physician Wilhelm Cohnstein, who declared that a calm and positive frame of mind was best maintained by "unconditional trust I: in Divine Providence and II: in the orders of the authorities." . . .

---

[9] Standard marks, the basic monetary unit.

The association of cholera with individual immorality was thus expressed in the very theories which medical men developed to account for it. It was felt that emotional excess could lead to increased receptivity to infection. But there was another reason for the widespread association of cholera with lack of self-restraint. Not only did it lead to public disorder in itself, but the threat which it posed was magnified by the fact that it generally appeared at moments of tension in European society, because social and international conflict both led to large-scale troop movements which tremendously accelerated the pace and scale of epidemic infection. In 1830 these troop movements were taking place everywhere in Europe, from Poland, where the Russian army was engaged in putting down a major nationalist uprising, through to the West where military engagements were taking place in many countries in connection with the successful or unsuccessful revolutions of that year. During the revolutionary upheavals of 1848–9 there were even more extensive troop movements, with the Russian army in Vienna and the Prussians marching as far west as Baden, in the deep south-west of Germany. Similarly, Bismarck's[10] wars of 1866 against Austria, and of 1870–1 against France, both brought cholera to Hamburg and spread it to other areas as well. Because the disease was notoriously liable to appear at moments of acute political tension, it is hardly surprising that the first reaction of the authorities was to appeal for calm.

Such an appeal, understandably enough, was issued with greater force than ever in the revolutionary year of 1848. On that occasion, Dr. Friedrich Simon, a Hamburg medical practitioner, urged that inns and bars be closed early for the duration of the epidemic and urged his readers to lead "a moderate, sober, and regular life-style" and "to avoid any excesses." Not only did this mean the avoidance of alcohol. It also meant, Simon explained, that

> altogether a state of mind that is as evenly balanced as possible is an essential and important means of protection. . . . Tiring intellectual exertions, especially deep into the night, have a disadvantageous effect; but strong and long-lasting spiritual excitements of other kinds, powerful passions and changes of mood, even exaggerated joy and sprightliness, are just as much to be avoided.

In 1848 there was no doubt that for the Hamburg Senate the preservation of public order was the first priority. In July, the medical representatives on the Health Committee held a meeting to discuss measures to be taken in view of the fact that after an interval of sixteen years, cholera was once more approaching the city from the east:

> The first thing that we feel impelled to express, before anything else, is the wish that the public be alarmed and disturbed as little as possible. Therefore we would like to see the avoidance of all sensation during the preparations and right up to the actual outbreak of the epidemic. We do not want the release of public notices

---

[10] Otto von Bismarck (1815–1898), Prussian statesman who unified Germany.

calling attention to this so widely feared disease, nor, later, when the epidemic has really broken out, do we want measures to be taken which allow the disease to appear as particularly dangerous or extraordinary.

Such measures, in their opinion, would only cause panic and make things worse. The previous epidemic had, they argued, showed beyond doubt that cholera was not a contagious disease. So it was decided on these grounds not to establish a quarantine, not to isolate the sick, nor to make any special arrangements for burying the victims. Such measures, the doctors warned, "are no help at all, but rather cause endless damage by getting people excited." The most that was necessary was the printing of a pamphlet advising people what to do in the event of an epidemic, together with arrangements to feed the poor, control the quality of food in the markets, ensure the cleanliness and airiness of doss-houses,[11] and hospitalize the victims should there be any. . . .

The unusually strong concern with public order, reflecting the fact that the political conflicts and disturbances of the revolutionary year reached their height in the first week in September, just as the cholera broke out, led once more to a policy of inaction on the part of the Hamburg authorities. Clearly they were anxious not to give further cause for lower-class discontent, which had already led to barricades and demonstrations in August. As in 1832, therefore, virtually nothing was done to cope with the epidemic. . . .

The epidemics of 1832 and 1848 thus established a firm tradition in Hamburg, according to which the state did virtually nothing to prevent or combat the disease, and took no steps to confirm or announce its presence in the city. The burden of coping with cholera fell instead on the medical profession and voluntary organizations such as the Doctors' Club. Here too, as we have seen, anticontagionism reigned supreme. The Chief Medical Officer, Dr. Buek, had been an anticontagionist even before the arrival of cholera in 1831; he remained one in the epidemic of 1848. There were further minor epidemics in the 1850s . . . and more serious ones in 1859 and 1866. . . . But the tradition of inactivity was only strengthened by the appointment of Buek's successor as Chief Medical Officer, Dr. Johann Caspar Theodor Kraus, a "convinced supporter of Pettenkofer's views." . . .

One of the most striking features of the history of medical administration in nineteenth-century Hamburg was the continuity of senior personnel. Dr. Buek was closely involved in dealing with all the epidemics from 1831 to 1873; Dr. Kraus, whose first experience of cholera came in 1873, was still in office in 1892. . . . [N]othing happened between 1873 and 1892, not even Koch's discoveries,[12] to make Kraus change his mind on the subject of cholera. In 1892, as in 1873, Kraus and the medical authorities were still operating to an "absolutely definite

---

[11] Cheap, overnight shelters for homeless men.

[12] Robert Koch (1843–1910), German physician who received the Nobel Prize in 1905 for his work in bacteriology.

plan" which obliged them to deny the existence of Asiatic cholera in Hamburg until after the disease had reached epidemic proportions. This policy could be justified to some extent by the anticontagionist views which Kraus espoused, but there could be little doubt that it had its origins in the fear of the quarantine measures that would immediately loom over the city if an official declaration of a cholera epidemic was made. . . .

The influence of Pettenkofer since the 1850s had diverted the attention of the medical profession to the soil factor. In many cases, it was agreed in 1874 that "one is inclined to regard possible harmful substances in the soil as a direct cause." But Pettenkofer and his supporters never thought it was possible to eliminate these "harmful substances" altogether. Improved sewage disposal would certainly help, they thought; and indeed great improvements had taken place in this area since mid-century. The faith they placed in a centralized water-supply, uncontaminated, as drinking-wells often were, by infected "ground-water," was not matched by any corresponding belief in the importance of filtration. In most respects, the influence of Pettenkofer in Hamburg simply confirmed the existing way of doing things. In 1873, as in all previous cholera epidemics since the defeat of contagionism in 1831, the medical profession and the Senate did their utmost to avoid official confirmation of the disease's presence in the city, and once they were forced to concede this point, made no attempt to impose quarantine, to isolate the victims, or to mount a campaign of disinfection. By 1871 at least the Senate was agreeable to undertaking a limited amount of state action, lending the police to collect the sick and the dead, and providing funds to stop the contamination of the ground-water. But the avoidance of financial costs and the maintenance of public order remained the highest priorities. Those who disapproved of this policy of state inaction remained a tiny minority.

THE EAST EUROPEAN GYPSIES
IN THE
IMPERIAL AGE
Zoltan Barany

One consistent theme in Western civilization, if not in world history, has been the maltreatment of ethnic and religious minorities. So commonplace has been the persecution of minorities, ranging from the imposition of nuisance taxes and minor indignities to genocide, that we should be surprised when we discover islands of tolerance in the historical ocean of prejudice and abuse. Originally from India, the nomadic Gypsies (Rom; Roma) have been the object of mistreatment for centuries, culminating in the Nazi attempt to exterminate them during World War II.

Zoltan Barany is Frank C. Erwin Jr. Centennial Professor of Government at the University of Texas at Austin. Barany compares the treatment of Gypsies by two empires, the Ottoman and Austro-Hungarian. Barany's sources include laws, decrees, government reports, newspapers, and travel accounts. How did the governmental structure, ethnic composition, and dominant religions of these two imperial states affect policies and actions toward the Gypsies? Did their policies succeed? How do you explain the persistent reputation of the Gypsies as petty thieves and criminals? We tend to think of industrialization and modernization as beneficial phenomena. Did they increase the well-being of Gypsy societies? What economic options did Gypsies have? Why did they remain nomadic? Were Gypsies better off in the Austro-Hungarian or in the Ottoman Empire? Do you see any parallels between the treatment of Gypsies and of Jews in early modern and modern Europe?

Although the Hapsburg and Ottoman states belong to the same regime-type (that is, they were both empires), their specific policies and general approach to ethnic and other minorities diverged significantly. What is the main reason for this

Zoltan Barany, "The East European Gypsies in the Imperial Age," *Ethnic and Racial Studies* 24/1 (January 2001): 50–63.

disparity? . . . This article argues that ethnic identity was a far more important distinguishing characteristic of individuals in the Hapsburg Empire than in the Ottoman state. At the same time it should be noted that, in general, ethnic minorities are better off in empires than in authoritarian states because the imperial centre is concerned mainly with imposing political order but is "rather indifferent to the ethnosocial and ethnocultural heterogeneity of subject populations."[1] . . .

The purpose of this article is to show the differences in the marginal conditions of the East European Roma (Gypsies) in the Hapsburg and Ottoman empires. The disparate state philosophies and organizing principles of these two states created dissimilar conditions for the Roma as well as for other ethnic groups. . . .

Throughout most of the imperial period the majority of Eastern European Roma lived in lands directly ruled by the Ottoman Empire or what were its vassal states (such as the Romanian principalities). "For nearly half a millennium, . . . the Ottomans ruled an empire as diverse as any in history. Remarkably, this polyethnic and multireligious society worked."[2] . . . One of the crucial foundations of this uncommonly stable state was the millet[3] system, often cited as an important precedent and model for minority rights. . . . By the standards of the age, the Ottoman Turks devised a socio-political system that was humane and tolerant. The legal traditions and practices of religious groups were respected and protected, and, while their relations with the Muslims were firmly regulated, Christian and Jewish millets were free to run their internal affairs. . . . In essence, for minority groups the Ottoman Empire was the embodiment of relatively harmonious and enduring ethnic coexistence.

Though their social position was decidedly subordinate and marginal to that of other groups, most Gypsies fared considerably better in the Ottoman Empire than they did in other regions. They had a definite place in a society where they were accepted. At the same time, the Roma were ensconced firmly at the lowest tier of the social scale, together with "other people with no visible permanent professional affiliation."[4] . . . In areas where the number of settled Roma was substantial, cities and towns had Gypsy quarters (Sliven in Bulgaria, for example, had a 1,074-strong Romani community in 1874); elsewhere, they slept in huts and tents erected beyond a town's boundary and were required to pay for the use of the municipality's pastures. Local administrators made recurrent attempts to set-

---

[1] Joseph Rothschild, *Return to Diversity: A Political History of East Europe since World War II* (New York: Oxford University Press, 1989), 10.

[2] Benjamin Braude and Bernard Lewis, "Introduction," in *Christians and Jews in the Ottoman Empire: The Functioning of a Plural Society,* ed. Braude and Lewis (New York: Holmes and Meier, 1982), 1.

[3] Millets were autonomous religious communities in the Ottoman Empire that were responsible for taxes, internal security, and administrative functions (such as education, religion, social welfare, and so on) not carried out by the central government.

[4] Peter F. Sugar, *Southern Europe under Ottoman rule, 1354–1804* (Seattle: University of Washington Press, 1977), 77.

tle the wandering Roma in order to turn them into reliable tax payers. Tax evaders faced jail, and, in exceptional cases, were sold on slave markets.

Even in the Ottoman Empire they were subjected to widespread societal prejudice and contempt, although they were rarely physically persecuted. The Turks despised the Roma not because of their ethnicity — after all the empire was a mélange of races and religions — but because they regarded them as being less reliable and trustworthy than others. Dominant groups considered unsettled Roma to be useless parasites because they did not have stable occupations. Muslim Gypsies were taxed higher than other Muslims based on the rationale that they did not follow the rules of Islam, did not adopt Muslim lifestyles (most Romani women, for example, refused to wear the veil); in essence, their behaviour was inconsistent with the religion. At the end of the seventeenth century the hardening of Ottoman attitudes towards Gypsies manifested itself in a state campaign. This campaign accused the Roma of widespread pimping and prostitution, and steeply increased taxes were imposed on them. The Gypsies also acquired a reputation for thievery and for habitually committing other, usually petty, crimes which contributed to the deepening of negative social biases.

Thus, to say . . . that the Ottoman Empire became the promised land for the Gypsies strikes one as being rather an exaggeration until one considers that in the Romanian principalities of Moldavia and Wallachia the Roma were enslaved for centuries. . . . It is difficult to say exactly when slavery was first established in the two Romanian principalities but sources dating back to as early as 1348 mention bequests of Gypsy slaves. By the late fourteenth century slavery seems to have been firmly in place and proved to be an enduring practice. The common historical explanation for the Gypsies' bondage is that in these backward, poverty-stricken areas where skilled labour was scarce, the migration-prone Roma were enslaved in order to keep them in place and minimize the cost of their labour. But this interpretation is only partly convincing because a substantial proportion of Gypsy slaves performed menial agricultural work or domestic chores at the residences of the royal family, for landowners (*boyars*) and at monasteries. The way slaves were treated depended largely on individual owners, but they could be and occasionally were killed by their masters with impunity. In time, *tsigan* (Gypsy) and *rob* (slave) became juridically and culturally synonymous terms in the Romanian principalities. . . .

. . . Urban intellectuals had called for the abolition of slavery in the 1830s, but it was only after the reformist statesman Mihail Kogălniceanu[5] started his campaign for emancipation in 1844 that it began to seem achievable. Slave owners were finally ordered to free the Roma in 1855–1856 and emancipation was fully realized by 1864. It should be mentioned that politicians in Bucharest were strongly influenced by French criticism of Romanian slavery, especially as they looked to Paris for inspiration in developing a modern state. Thus, Western pressures had played a role in accelerating the process just as in the post-communist period they made a positive impact upon the minority policies of East European states.

---

[5] Romanian historian, democratic nationalist, and prime minister (1817–1891).

In independent Hungary, prior to 1526, the Roma were tolerated, although they did not enjoy the same freedoms as they did in the Ottoman Empire. Initially, most Roma migrated through Hungary but owing to the intense persecution and expulsion orders in Western Europe, by the fifteenth and sixteenth centuries a growing number of Gypsy groups had come to regard Hungary as a destination country. Some Roma received letters of safe conduct from the Hungarian King (and Holy Roman Emperor) Zsigmond (or Sigismund, 1387–1437) and other sovereigns. These documents lost their effectiveness, however, because anti-Roma attitudes had strengthened and because the Gypsies became quite competent at forging them. A fair number of Roma were widely respected as prized gunsmiths during the reign of King Mátyás (or Matthias, 1458–1490). Still, the plea of György Thurzö, the imperial governor of "Royal Hungary" — that remained under Hapsburg tutelage after the Turks had overrun the rest of the country in 1526 — for better understanding of the Gypsies' plight and thus encouraging the authorities to let them settle was an uncharacteristic act of benevolence. . . .

In the Hapsburg Empire the Gypsies encountered far more overt persecution, and their coexistence with the dominant populations was considerably more fraught with contention than in Ottoman-ruled lands. They did not possess equal rights with other subjects of the Hapsburg Empire and were merely tolerated by them. The majority of Roma lived outside the villages and led lives separate from the dominant groups, although commercial and social contacts assured them of a place in society. Anti-Roma prejudices were generally deep-seated and frequently culminated in well-publicized trials on absurd grounds. In 1782, for instance, in Hungary (now Slovakia) an entire Romani community was charged with cannibalism, then tortured into confessions, resulting in the execution of forty-one before an inquiry, ordered by Emperor Joseph II,[6] revealed that the presumed casualties were alive. . . .

The wave of Romanticism that swept parts of Eastern Europe following the French Revolution evoked considerable interest in the Gypsies — especially in their rich traditions, myths and mysticism — and a small measure of paternalistic compassion towards them. "The moustache," a poem by the nineteenth-century Hungarian poet, János Arany — contrasting the sly, cunning, happy-go-lucky Gypsies with the vain and stingy Magyar[7] landowner — exemplifies well this jovially condescending attitude. . . . A substantial number of Roma fought on the Hungarian side in the 1848–49 War of Independence, many of them providing music for the soldiers, thereby cementing the reputation and "acceptability" of Gypsy musicianship. Hungarian nobility employed a fair number of Romani musicians and, most exceptionally, even married Gypsy virtuosos. The rise of the musicians and, to a lesser extent, skilled craftsmen in contrast to the growing impoverishment of nomadic and/or unskilled Gypsies points to the increasing stratification within the Romani population which began in the nineteenth century.

---

[6] Holy Roman emperor, 1765–1790.

[7] The Magyars are the main ethnic group in Hungary.

After Bulgarian independence from Ottoman rule (1878) the Roma's social position declined further. About 80 per cent of them were Muslim which now became the minority religion associated with the former oppressors. As the wave of industrialization reached Bulgaria, more and more Romani craftsmen were ruined economically. Some still supplied services to the rural population and, in agricultural areas, continued to fill a role and retained a well-defined place in society. Similarly, following emancipation, many Romanian Gypsies' social situation was greatly affected by the growing anti-Gypsyism of peasants rooted partly in their own miserable conditions (that gave rise to rural uprisings in 1888 and 1907), and in the exaggerated and generalized reputation of the Roma as common criminals.

The widespread Romani perspective that considers institutionalized education a waste of time and energy was already clearly reflected in their educational attainment in the imperial age. Churches played a crucial role in public education throughout this period, but they did not concern themselves with Gypsy children until the late eighteenth and early nineteenth centuries. The system of state-supported public schools, wherever they existed, left most Gypsies unaffected; they were fortunate to reach the children of peasants. One of the imperial era's few reliable and detailed surveys, conducted in Hungary in 1893, revealed that 70 per cent of Romani children never attended school and 90 per cent of the total Gypsy population and 98 per cent of those maintaining nomadic lifestyles were illiterate. . . . Bulgaria was the first East European state to establish schools for the Roma, but in 1910 their literacy rate was only 3 per cent and it increased to only 8 per cent after World War I. . . . The increasing social stratification of Gypsy society was signalled by the drastically different educational standards of a small minority, particularly musicians, who emphasized the importance of schooling, especially in music, for their offspring. . . .

The crucial point that I wish to make in this section is that although the Roma were at the bottom of the imperial era's economic and occupational scales, they had a well-defined position in imperial economies and played useful and valuable economic roles. In general, the more backward and less developed a region, the more important was the Gypsies' economic contribution. In essence, traditional Romani skills were appropriate to pre-industrial economies, but industrialization resulted in their gradual economic displacement and increasing marginalization. In Western Europe, where urbanization and industrial development began long before it did in the East, the economic role of the Gypsies declined earlier than in the Hapsburg and Ottoman empires.

As waves of industrialization reached the states of Eastern Europe, so the relevance of the Roma to their economic lives diminished. The majority of the Gypsies under Hapsburg rule lived in Hungary and Slovakia, that is, the less developed parts of the empire. In these primarily rural, agriculture-based economies they played a consequential economic role longer than in, say, Austria, the Czech lands, or Slovenia. Because the Ottoman Empire was considerably less industrialized than the Hapsburg domain and there was a virtual absence of state-supported economic development under Turkish rule, the Roma remained valued economic contributors for a longer time. Though they customarily preferred as little unnecessary contact with the *gadje* (non-Roma) as possible, the often desperately poor Romani communities could scarcely survive without the economic benefits which commercial relations with non-Gypsies could provide. As a result, they were more dependent on the dominant population than on other, less comprehensively marginal groups. . . .

Some Gypsies were not only talented artisans and craftsmen but controlled entire trades in certain areas. In the Romanian principalities, for instance, they enjoyed a virtual monopoly in smithing. The Roma had also gained fame as splendid entertainers. Gypsy bands — generally playing the dominant group's traditional music rather than their own — had become sought after at carnivals and public events and as court musicians. Romani dancers, bear-tamers, palm-readers, and fortune tellers had also been in demand and became the indispensable part of fairs and markets, major social events of rural society at the time. Most settled Gypsies, however, typically adopted unconventional trades. Although they ordinarily enjoyed far better material conditions than their peripatetic brethren, the economic integration of settled Roma with more mainstream occupations was thwarted by the refusal of trade guilds to accept them into their membership.

For logical reasons, many occupations common among the Roma were practised on the road and required the use of minimal equipment. Their reputation as thieves, beggars and prostitutes contributed to expulsion and persecution which went hand-in-hand with the prohibition of settling and of land ownership. Thus, their traditional propensity to keep moving and engage in occupations — peddling, wood carving, bear-taming, tinkering, basket-weaving — that afforded them a certain amount of personal independence and liberty and that could be exercised while travelling, was reinforced. In their travels the Roma had ample opportunity to learn about the medicinal qualities of herbs and plants and the necessity of trying to cure their ailments. As a result of such accumulated knowledge and skill a number of Roma (mostly women) became well known as healers, herbalists and persons capable of resetting broken bones.

Although some sources suggest that the Roma were hard workers, the vast majority of chroniclers have little flattering to say about their work ethic. The Roma did participate in seasonal farm-work as hired hands, though they were "seldom industrious" in such endeavours. . . . Archduke József[8] was a noted Romanologist who corresponded with his daughter in Romani and was perhaps the most important supporter that the Roma had in nineteenth-century Hungary. But even he writes that the Roma were simply not cut out for agricultural work because they were liable to leave their jobs for long periods at a time without any explanation. . . . Their reluctance to become industrious and regular wage-earners did nothing to endear them to their neighbours.

---

[8] Archduke József (Joseph) of Austria-Hungary (1833–1905), a founding member of the Gypsy Lore Society, an international association devoted to Gypsy and Traveler studies. Scottish Travelers and Irish Travelers distinguish themselves from Gypsies but engage in similar economic activities.

An important and somewhat under-appreciated element of the Gypsies' occupational history is their involvement in military endeavours. The Roma were not
only master gunsmiths; they were also respected soldiers in many European states.
In the Ottoman Empire a considerable number of Roma provided services to the
Turkish administration, especially to the military. Those who specialized in the
manufacture and maintenance of weapons and ammunition of every kind enjoyed
a particularly good livelihood and . . . gained little from the Hapsburg recovery
of territories from the Ottomans in the late seventeenth century. . . . During the
period of the sixteenth-eighteenth centuries the finest messengers and scouts as
well as the most effective spies of Transylvanian princes were Roma. Many Gypsy
men were forced into military service across Europe; others volunteered to escape
from poverty and persecution.

The belated arrival of the industrial revolution in Eastern Europe, however,
dealt a major blow to the Romani way of life, one from which they have yet to recover. Large-scale industrial production led to falling prices of consumer products
and reduced demand for goods traditionally manufactured and/or mended by the
Roma. Ultimately, economic progress jeopardized the Gypsies' established productive status in these societies. Equally important is the fact that the vast majority
of the Gypsies — as a result of their traditional attitude towards institutionalized
education, their poverty and the majority population's discriminatory policies —
could not adapt to the emerging economic conditions which required specialized
training and education. . . .

The two major East European empires conducted quite different policies towards
the Roma. In the Hapsburg Empire, where state building developed further and
greater emphasis was put on economic and social progress, the state pursued
more intrusive and discriminatory minority policies. In contrast, the Ottoman
state did not accept "the idea of minority-majority or develop a political sense of
nationality." Had they done so, "it could easily have liquidated the patchwork of
races and religions under its rule transforming them into one homogeneous Muslim or Turkish group."[9] . . . Instead, the Ottomans viewed the conquered lands as
tax farms under Muslim rule and maintained a laissez-faire[10] perspective vis-à-vis
their subject peoples as long as dues were collected and social peace persisted.

For the Gypsies and other ethnic minorities the Ottoman conquest of their
lands rarely signified a worsening in their conditions. On the contrary, the Turks
often eliminated the local aristocracy because they were the source of potential opposition to the new rulers and were thought to be expendable by the Ottomans.
The new governors — in some cases such as Albania ethnically indigenous but
always Muslim — did not generally interfere with local affairs. Their most important functions were to guarantee law and order and the timely and full pay-

---

[9] "Leave alone"; hands-off, noninterfering.

[10] Kemal Karpat, *An Inquiry into the Social Foundations of Nationalism in the Ottoman State* (Princeton: Center for International Studies), 290.

ment of levies. Ethnic Turks, for the most part, were administrators, soldiers and members of the judiciary. The Ottomans were actually dependent on the ethnic minorities — Armenians, Bulgarians, Greeks, Serbs and so forth — for the execution of a wide range of commercial, industrial and agricultural tasks. . . .

The Ottoman Empire, with the marked absence of systematically repressive policies and legislation characteristic of the rest of Europe, was a haven for the Roma. The state fully accepted, or to put it differently, did not care about, their customs and religious identities. Although some suggest that the Ottoman state did not discriminate against the Roma at all — rather that they suffered from the pre-existing prejudices of other ethnic groups — clearly this was not the case. Muslim Gypsies were not exempt from some taxes as other Muslims were (like the Bulgarian-speaking Pomaks), and could move up the Ottoman hierarchy with greater difficulty than others. The Ottomans also subjected the Roma to forced settlement policies in order to change them into reliable and reachable taxpayers, although these efforts were less coercive and more haphazard and inconsistent than elsewhere in Europe.

When the Roma arrived in Central and Western Europe in the early fifteenth century, they initially encountered populations that were often sympathetic to their alleged religious pilgrimage and respectful of the letters that they carried requesting safe passage. This tolerance proved to be ephemeral as the Gypsies' poverty increasingly made them turn to begging and thieving. The ensuing widely chronicled brutal persecution that the Roma experienced on a massive scale in medieval Western Europe was never exceeded until World War II. In pre-Hapsburg East-Central Europe the Roma were also victims of intense persecution, with the partial exception of medieval Hungary. Already in the late fifteenth century laws of deportation were enacted in the Holy Roman Empire. By one partial tally, as many as 133 anti-Gypsy laws were written there between 1551 and 1774. . . . In Moravia the expulsion of the Gypsies was decreed as early as 1538, while in Bohemia the first anti-Roma legislation was passed in 1541, following the outbreak of fires in Prague, supposedly started by the Roma. In Poland, too, the Sejm (legislature) passed repressive laws, but some moderation (or, possibly, pragmatism) was shown by Polish kings who, in the sixteenth century, allowed the Roma to select their own leaders in order to simplify tax collection. . . . In the mid-seventeenth century the Polish monarchs nominated or confirmed the "King of the Gypsies" — initially Gypsies, but who later came from the Polish gentry.

Once they established their East European empire, Hapsburg monarchs showed little interest in understanding the Gypsies' plight. Charles VI (1711–1740), frustrated by the Roma's resistance to conform to imperial laws and norms was the most brutal among them. He ordered the extermination of all Roma in his domain, a command that was not taken seriously by those who were supposed to implement it.

Perhaps motivated by Charles's heavy-handed approach, his immediate successors — his daughter Maria Theresa (1740–1780) and her son Joseph II (1780–1790) — became the two Hapsburg emperors most keen on improving (according to their own definitions) the Gypsies' conditions. At a time when several European powers, especially Britain and Portugal, sought to rid themselves of their "gypsy problem" by deporting Gypsies to their respective colonies, Maria Theresa and Joseph, along with the Bourbons of Spain, were the only European monarchs attempting to find more rational solutions. It is worth noting, however, that unlike Spain, the Hapsburg Empire possessed no faraway colonies. Maria Theresa and Joseph regarded themselves as enlightened rulers who wanted to elevate the Roma to the ranks of "civilized" and "useful" citizens. The tens of thousands of nomadic Gypsies roaming around the empire free of any state control did not suit their ideals of absolute monarchy.

The policies of the Empress and her son comprise a textbook example of forcible assimilation. Maria Theresa's four major "Gypsy decrees" illustrate this strategy. The first edict (1758) ordered all Gypsies to settle, pay taxes, do mandatory service to churches and landowners, and prohibited Romani ownership of horses and wagons and their leaving, without permission, the villages to which they had been assigned. The second decree (1761) mandated compulsory military service for Gypsies. The third (1767) eliminated the authority of Romani leaders over their communities, banned traditional Gypsy dress and the usage of Romani language, and instructed villages to register the Roma in their jurisdiction. Maria Theresa's last major decree concerning the Roma (1773) forbade marriages between Gypsies, and ordered Romani children over the age of five to be taken away to state schools and foster homes, resulting in the virtual kidnapping of approximately 18,000 Gypsy children from their parents. The intention behind this edict was to dilute Romani bloodlines and to speed up their assimilation.

Joseph II continued and expanded his mother's assimilationist policies by extending them to Transylvania, confirming previous restrictions and adding new ones, such as ordering monthly reports on Gypsy lifestyles from local authorities, permitting the Roma to visit fairs only in special circumstances, and banning nomadism and traditional Gypsy occupations (such as smithery). Joseph also emphasized improvements in Gypsy education and health, and directed the Roma to attend religious (Roman Catholic) services every week.

Few of these policies produced the intended results. The enforcement of the imperial decrees and the attached punitive sanctions by local authorities was decidedly lackadaisical. They were concerned with the disruptions in the lives of rural society caused by the coerced in-settlement of the Roma; they needed the Gypsies' economic contribution; and military commanders were rarely enthusiastic about the forced conscription of Gypsies. In fact, only a few counties, especially in the western part of Hungary, interpreted the imperial instructions to the full. . . . By the early nineteenth century the failure of Hapsburg Gypsy policy had become apparent. Nearly all Gypsy children soon escaped from their virtual captivity back to their parents. Already under the reign of Joseph II unwanted Gypsies were shuffled between villages equally opposed to the settlement of the "undesirables."

. . . [F]ollowing the failure of these eighteenth-century policies there were no further major imperial attempts to address the Gypsies' living conditions. In the last decades of the Hapsburg Empire the Roma issue became a police question dominated by the repressive regulations of local authorities. The fact that the judicial system did not consider the Gypsies equal citizens is demonstrated by the numerous discriminatory laws and decrees enacted in this period. . . .

The two Hapsburg emperors' policies towards the Gypsies should be viewed as an early and rather crude attempt at social engineering driven by pragmatic considerations. An important pattern can be identified in the approaches of eighteenth-century European states towards the Gypsies. In more developed Western Europe, where the Gypsies' economic role had declined faster, expulsion and deportation to colonies was a common strategy but the further East one looks the more prevalent are the settlement policies. The most extreme manifestation of forced sedentarization — in large part driven by the Gypsies' still valuable economic contribution — was the enslavement of the Roma in the Romanian principalities. Moreover, intriguing parallels may be pointed out between the two late eighteenth-century Hapsburg rulers and their counterpart in Spain, a state that had increasingly found itself on Europe's socio-economic periphery. In Spain, too, particularly during the reign of Charles III (1759–1788), settlement policies were preferred to expulsion and deportation. Maria Theresa prohibited the use of the term "Gypsy" and decreed that they should be referred to as "New Peasants" . . . or "New Hungarians"; so did the King of Spain who banned the term *Gitano* in 1772 in favour of "New Castilians."

Traditionally, there has been little ethnic solidarity between disparate Romani groups. Speaking in the late nineteenth century, a Spanish Rom noted that "those who are rich keep aloof from the rest, will not speak Calo,[11] and will have no dealing but with the Busne [non-Gypsies]," a situation that cheated the Roma of their "natural" protectors and supporters. . . . Nonetheless, it is important to note the first signs of Gypsy mobilization dating from the late imperial period. In 1879 the Roma organized a conference in Hungary focusing on the political and civil rights of European Gypsies. In 1906 Bulgarian Gypsies sent a petition to the parliament in Sofia demanding equal rights. The 1913 Memorial Service that Gypsies held in honour of Kogălniceanu in Romania served to strengthen ethnic identity and solidarity. . . . Although these endeavours were predictably ridiculed in newspapers of the day, they should be appreciated as early efforts at ethnic organization accomplished against overwhelming odds. . . .

Although Gypsies were the most disadvantaged ethnic group in both empires, there were clear differences between Hapsburg and Ottoman policies towards them. Especially in the early period, the Turkish administration's treatment of the Gypsies was relatively liberal although not without discriminatory measures reserved only for them. The majority of the Romani population in the Ottoman lands adopted the Muslim religion but a sizeable group remained Christian. Their basic legal rights were identical to those of their fellow Muslims and Christians. In fact, large groups from the principalities of Wallachia and Moldavia — where the Roma were enslaved from the fourteenth century until the 1850s — managed

---

[11] Language of Spanish Gypsies.

to make their way into Ottoman-ruled lands where their conditions were far better. The half-hearted efforts of local authorities to settle them met with limited success, but as long as the Roma paid their taxes there was little overt state intervention in their affairs. Taxation was the area in which anti-Gypsy discrimination was most apparent, given that the Roma were obliged to pay higher taxes than their fellow Muslims and Muslim Gypsies had to pay some types of taxes (such as the *cizye* or poll tax) which Muslims were not supposed to pay at all.

In the Hapsburg Empire the treatment of the Roma was decidedly worse. The level of persecution varied from estate to estate and largely depended on the perceived value of the services that Gypsies provided and the temperament of the landlord. In practice, the Roma could be mistreated, even killed with impunity. The most intrusive state effort to change their lives came in the late eighteenth century when Vienna introduced a comprehensive assimilationist policy sanctioning forced settlement and, if necessary, the separation of Gypsy children from their parents, prohibiting the usage of Romani language, and encouraging the masters to beat uncooperative Roma. In many areas coercion was used to convert Gypsies to Catholicism. Although once the failure of these policies was realized such systematic persecution abated, the Roma's situation was far more precarious in the Hapsburg Empire than in the Ottoman-ruled territories.

In summary, it is clear that imperial states had pursued different policies towards their ethnic minorities especially as far as the Roma are concerned. The Ottoman Empire's respect of minority traditions, languages and religious identity contrasted sharply with the intrusive policies of Hapsburg rule. Ottoman minority policies were essentially laissez faire, whereas those of the Hapsburgs were control-seeking (and, in the second part of the eighteenth century, assimilationist). Since general tendencies associated with empires — the presumed relative tolerance of ethnic minorities by imperial states — did not account sufficiently for minority policies, we need to identify the other sources of state policy towards the Roma.

States pursue common objectives, such as self-preservation, prosperity, security, social tranquility, self-preservation and, particularly in non-democratic states, control. It is these fundamental aims that provided the most elementary stimulants for policies towards the Roma, a people who seemed indifferent to state control and threatened social tranquility. Additional factors played only subordinate roles in shaping state policy towards the Gypsies. Negative societal views of the Gypsies seem to have influenced state policy only marginally (with the partial exception of the Hapsburg Empire) because imperial states were not particularly concerned with what ordinary people might have thought.

Imperial policies were hardly affected by the Roma's socio-economic situation, although one might argue that their position as society's outcasts was a motivating force behind the assimilationist policies of the eighteenth-century Hapsburg rulers. Neither were state policies influenced by the Roma's political power because they had none. At the same time, the international environment did affect policies towards the Roma. This was clearly the case in the Romanian push to abolish slavery.

THE END OF
THE ATLANTIC SLAVE TRADE
Herbert S. Klein

For four centuries, approximately ten million African slaves were transported to the Americas in the largest forced migration in history. The need of New World plantation societies for slaves emerged from an unprecedented labor shortage brought about by the devastation of the Native American population. That demographic breakdown ensued from the diseases and policies of the European invaders after 1492.

In his survey *The Atlantic Slave Trade,* Herbert S. Klein, professor of history at Columbia University, debunks several myths: that tight packing on ships (as opposed to the length of time of voyages) contributed most to the mortality rate of slaves on board, that Europeans traded mere baubles for slaves, that the slave trade was a major cause of modern capitalism, that some European states were less inhumane than others in their care of the transported slaves, that Africans did not benefit considerably from the sale of their fellow Africans to Europeans, and that slaves were cheap commodities. In the selection here, Klein explains the abolition of the slave trade in the nineteenth century.

Slavery is as old as civilization, and nearly all civilizations have not even thought to question slavery's proper place in society. We should not then be surprised at the existence of slavery; instead we should marvel at the development of abolitionist movements and seek to understand their causes and consequences.

How did religious and economic motives influence the campaign to end the Atlantic slave trade? Were there developments within Africa that contributed to the trade's decline? What led some Europeans to lag in abolition? How did different regions of North and South America react to Great Britain's abolitionist policies? What were the effects of the end of the slave trade? The termination of slavery itself in the Atlantic world was certainly not inevitable, even with the cessation of the commerce in slaves. How did the demise of the Atlantic slave trade impact the abolition of slavery itself in Western civilization?

Herbert S. Klein, *The Atlantic Slave Trade* (Cambridge: Cambridge University Press, 1999), 183–206.

If the slave trade was profitable and the Africans were put to productive use in the Americas, then why did Europeans begin to attack the trade at the end of the eighteenth century and systematically terminate the participation of every European metropolis and American colony or republic in the nineteenth century? Most economists now seem to agree that the organization of American plantation slave labor guaranteed that this system of labor was profitable to the planters and slave owners. Moreover, prices of slave-produced American goods fell over the course of the late eighteenth and early nineteenth centuries, with the result that consumption of those products was expanding at a rapid rate. The elastic demand for sugar, coffee, and cotton, the three major slave-produced crops of America, produced profits for the planter class. Nor could any free workers, except for some indentured Chinese or part-time peasants, be found who would work under these plantation systems. The question then remains as to why the trade was finally abolished if it was still profitable and important to the American economy.

It is now believed that the campaign to abolish the Atlantic slave trade, which began in the last quarter of the eighteenth century, was the first peaceful mass political movement based on modern types of political propaganda in English history. The early literature viewed this campaign as a moral crusade that was achieved at the cost of profits and trade. Once having abolished the slave trade to the English colonies in 1808, the British then attempted to force all the other major European slaving countries to cease their trades and to force African states and rulers to stop exporting people. This campaign was seen as a costly one in terms of lost trade, the alienation of traditional allies, and the high costs of a naval blockade.

The anti-slave-trade campaign had its origin in the intellectual questioning of the legitimacy of slavery and of the slave trade, which began in the context of Enlightenment[1] thought in the eighteenth century and became a moral crusade of a small group of Protestant sects in the later decades of this century. Previously there had been a few abolitionist thinkers and people who held the slave trade to be immoral, but these were isolated voices with no serious impact on European ideology. But in the late eighteenth century writer after writer began to view slavery as antithetical to a modern market economy, or considered it a fundamental challenge to the newly emerging concept of the equality of all men, or held it to be basically anti-Christian, no matter what the Bible had decreed.

Early eighteenth-century writers such as Montesquieu[2] and Francis Hutcheson[3] condemned the institution and were followed by such seminal thinkers as

---

[1] Eighteenth-century intellectual movement that advocated the use of critical reason to challenge authority, popularized the Scientific Revolution, opposed Christianity and superstition, and championed liberty and humane reforms.

[2] Charles Louis de Secondat, Baron de La Brède et de Montesquieu (1689–1755), Enlightenment intellectual, author of *The Persian Letters* and *The Spirit of the Laws*.

[3] Scottish philosopher (1694–1746), author of *A System of Moral Philosophy*.

Adam Smith[4] and Rousseau.[5] Along with the philosophical debates came the attacks of Quakers and Protestant evangelicals, which added a special religious component to the increasing negative opinion about slavery and particularly African slavery and its accompanying slave trade. The French and Haitian revolutions of 1789 and 1791 further reinforced these new and challenging ideas. For the first time in western European thought, there now emerged a widely disseminated set of beliefs that held slavery, and even more so the slave trade, to be a morally, politically, and philosophically unacceptable institution for western Europeans. By the end of the century in Europe there were no longer any major defenders of slavery on any but pragmatic grounds.

Although the philosophical origins of the antislavery movement are fairly clear, the fact that this became a significant movement in England in the 1790s and the first decade of the nineteenth century is not as easily explained. Though English statesmen and writers portrayed their campaign as a moral one there were many who attacked their motives. Cubans, Spaniards, and Brazilians, the objects of most of the post-1808 attacks by the British abolitionists, argued that the nineteenth-century campaign was motivated by fears of competition, especially after the British abolition of slavery in 1834 when sugar became a free-labor crop in the British West Indies. The Latins argued that it was the desire to keep their more efficiently produced slave products off the European market by driving up their labor costs that motivated these anti-slave-trade campaigns. This argument was taken up by later historians of the West Indian economy who argued that even the preemancipation slave plantation system in the British islands was inefficient and in serious economic trouble. . . . West Indian historians in the twentieth century believed that economic motivations explained the wellsprings of the British abolition campaign against the foreign slave traders, because the British West Indian plantations from as early as the late eighteenth century could not compete with the French, Spanish, and Brazilian planters.

In contrast to arguments based upon economic decline, recent scholars have argued that the late eighteenth- and early nineteenth-century economy of the British West Indies was a thriving one. Even after abolition of the slave trade, both the older and newer islands were competitive on the English and European markets, and it was only ending the slave trade and more importantly the emancipation of the slaves that weakened the British West Indian economies. In fact, the newer plantation colonies within the British Caribbean zone made significant gains in the world sugar market despite the increasing labor costs, which were exacerbated by the British refusal to permit postabolition internal slave trading among the colonies. If competition and fear for their declining sugar islands did not drive the British abolition campaign, was it just a moral crusade as earlier scholars argued?

---

[4] Scottish philosopher and economist (1723–1790), known for his book *An Inquiry into the Nature and Causes of the Wealth of Nations.*

[5] Jean-Jacques Rousseau (1712–1778), Enlightenment intellectual who argued for the natural goodness of humans and the corruption caused by civilization.

Though abolition had a profound appeal because of its moral component and was clearly detrimental to British planter interests, the morality of its leaders, the so-called Saints, was not based on a pro-African stance or belief in the inherent equality of blacks. In fact, racism sometimes tinged some of the positions of these leaders. The anti-slave-trade campaign was based fundamentally on a belief in free labor as one of the most crucial underpinnings of modern society and the institution that guaranteed mankind's progress out of its medieval past. Such a position appealed not only to those wedded to free trade and laissez-faire,[6] but also to workers being integrated into the urban and increasing industrial world of nineteenth-century England. To the workers of England facing the full impact of a wage system and self-determination in modern urban society, slavery was seen as antithetical to all the values of a modern society and a basic threat to their own security, even if it was only in distant lands. While the arguments against the slave trade may have had a moral origin, they were also based on the interests of European workers and capitalists and not on any concern with the African slaves themselves. The institution and its trade might be unacceptable, but at least in the English campaign it was not fought in the name of equality for blacks.

Of all parts of the institution of African slavery, the Atlantic slave trade itself was initially held to be both the most contemptible part of the institution as well as the one easiest to attack. It began in the 1750s among the 90,000 English-speaking Quakers on both sides of the Atlantic who started forcing members to abandon both slave ownership and participation in the slave trade. This was achieved as basic policy by the American Friends as early as the 1770s. The English Quakers followed a decade later and by the 1780s were exhorting their members to desist from participation in the slave trade as well. Then in 1787 they helped start the national campaign to abolish the slave trade, which quickly moved beyond the Quakers to Methodists, and a large number of both radical and traditional Protestant churches. Between 1787 and 1792 popular antislavery clubs were established and a mass campaign of petitions to Parliament was organized. This led first to amelioration laws specifying conditions for carrying slaves. In 1788 Parliament passed the Dolben's Act, which established for England the first limits on the manner of carrying slaves aboard English slavers. This act in turn was further modified in 1799 giving greater space for each slave on English vessels.

But this was only the beginning. After several failed attempts at passing a definitive prohibition of the trade, the abolitionists in Parliament, under the leadership of William Wilberforce,[7] moved toward partial restrictions by closing down parts of the trade. In 1805 the government banned the importation of slaves into the recently acquired territories of British Guiana and Trinidad. Then in May 1806 legislation that prohibited British subjects from engaging in the slave trade with foreign colonies was passed. Finally, in March 1807 came the definitive abo-

---

[6] "Leave alone," referring to the economic system advocated by Adam Smith whereby trade operates freely and the government has a minimal role.

[7] English politician and abolitionist (1759–1833) who strove to end the slave trade and slavery.

lition of the British slave trade itself, which was forced to end by the first day of 1808.

The next major campaign in the anti-slave-trade movement was the obvious one of trying to get all other nations to desist in their participation. This became a major theme of the British abolitionist movement in the 1810s, after the end of the Napoleonic Wars. Responding to a potential reopening of the French slave trade, the English abolitionists organized another mass petition campaign in 1814, which in one month sent over 700 petitions signed by close to 1 million persons to Parliament demanding universal abolition. Under this pressure the British government negotiated a treaty with Portugal in January 1815 that immediately prohibited slave trading above the equator and promised to begin progressive abolition of the rest of the trade to Brazil. This was in addition to a treaty of 1810 that restricted Portuguese slave trading to its own possessions. At the Congress of Vienna[8] in 1815 the major continental powers agreed to abolish the trade, but France and the Iberian states refused to go along. Then after Waterloo[9] in November 1815 France was forced into the abolitionist camp. This left only Portugal and Spain as active slave-trading nations, and even Portugal had abolished the trade north of the equator.

From this period onward, British foreign policy in regard to Portugal and its colony Brazil and Spain and its American colonies of Cuba and Puerto Rico was consistently to oppose the trade and demand its abolition. At the same time the abolitionist movement finally turned on slavery in America, and not just the trade, and a series of acts pushing toward emancipation within the British islands finally got underway. First came a slave registration act in 1816; then in the 1820s and 1830s campaigns for total emancipation led to the formal abolition of slavery and the creation of an apprenticeship system whereby the former slaves were to work for their old masters for a specified period of time. This in turn ended in 1838 with the abandonment of apprenticeship and the freeing of all ex-slaves from any obligations to their masters.

Having carried the campaign so successfully against the British slave trade, and against slavery itself within the British Empire, the over 1,000 antislavery committees within the British islands kept up constant pressure on the British government throughout the nineteenth century to terminate the slave trade of all other nations. This campaign defined much of the relationship between England and the two Iberian states, and the newly established Empire of Brazil when it separated from Portugal in 1822, for the first half of the nineteenth century. In this campaign Brazil would remain defiant until the end, disagreeing with concessions made by Portugal and demanding the maintenance of the trade south of the equator. This defiant attitude finally would bring direct naval attacks on Brazilian ports in 1850. In contrast, Spain tried to placate British demands while it pro-

---

[8] Assembly (1814–1815) of the major European powers that reorganized the continent following the Napoleonic wars.

[9] Decisive battle in 1815 that defeated the French emperor, Napoleon.

crastinated as long as possible. With the loss of the bulk of its American empire in 1825, Spain became ever more dependent on the expanding sugar plantation slave economy of Cuba as a major source of funding for itself and its merchants and was loath to abandon the slave trade. Thus it was able to play a constant game of duplicity, which enabled it to maintain the trade until the late 1860s.

Given Portugal's close dependence on Britain because of the protected markets for its port wine, and on its political support in continental affairs going back to the eighteenth century and its struggles against Napoleonic invasion, the Portuguese proved to be the most sensitive to British pressure. In July 1817 there was signed a "right to search" agreement with Portugal that allowed British war vessels to stop and search on the high seas any Portuguese vessel on suspicion of carrying their slaves north of the equator. This was the first such "right to search" treaty and became the model for others signed in later years. With success seemingly assured, the British later in 1817 drafted a major treaty with Spain that immediately abolished the trade north of the equator, allowed for British search of Spanish vessels, and finally promised total abolition of the Spanish slave trade in 1820.

To enforce these treaties, Britain established an independent African naval squadron in November 1819, which took up residence off the African coast and was to be a major presence until the end of the century. But this was only the beginning. France and the United States, though agreeing to terminate their slave trades, consistently refused the right of search to the British navy. Spain itself was less sensitive to British pressure than the Portuguese. . . . Spain never enforced the total prohibition of 1820.

But the British did not desist. In the early 1820s they signed new treaties with Portugal and Spain that expanded the search provisions to allow the British to examine ships that had the equipment used in the slave trade even if not carrying slaves. They also got agreement from Portugal in this period to accept that the slave trade was now illegal for all its subjects — though this, of course, had little impact on newly independent Brazil. But British pressure on the new American empire was intense and finally in 1826 an Anglo-Brazilian anti-slave-trade treaty was signed in Rio de Janeiro that forced the Brazilians to abandon the slave trade as of March 1830. Thus for Cuba after 1820 and for Brazil after 1830 the slave trade was officially illegal.

Though the trade to Cuba and Brazil temporarily stopped in the first months of these two dates, in fact the local governments made no attempt to halt the trade. . . .

But the British did not stop their efforts on closing down these trades even when the local governments resisted. After much pressure they finally forced the French in 1833 to accept a very complete search-and-seizure treaty for vessels flying the French colors and carrying slaves or slave-trading equipment. They also obtained significant French naval support for African blockades after 1845. The flight to the Spanish flag of convenience was stopped with a complete search-and-seizure treaty signed in 1836. Then in 1839 England unilaterally declared the right to seize all suspected Portuguese slaving vessels and judge them in its own vice-admiralty courts. In late 1840 came the first landings on African soil (at Gallinas near Sierra Leone) to liberate slaves being held in pens for shipment. This new British policy of direct intervention on the African coast in turn led in the 1840s to the signing of numerous treaties with local African governments along the entire western coast in which the British obtained the right to land and search for slavers. By 1847 the West African Squadron consisted of thirty-two ships, of which half a dozen were steam-driven vessels, and was actively engaged in intervention at sea and now on land as well.

Aside from maintaining a naval squadron off the coast and signing ever more complete treaties with African, European, and American governments, the British also established mixed judicial commissions with most nations to condemn slave vessels seized by the British or other cooperating navies. . . .

The final phase began against Brazil in 1845 when the Brazilians terminated their treaty with Britain, which had given the Royal Navy the right to search Brazilian vessels. In retaliation the British abolished the mixed commissions and ordered the seizure of all Brazilian ships caught with equipment or slaves on the high seas and their automatic condemnation before exclusive British vice-admiralty courts. At this point the British were also financing Brazilian abolitionist newspapers and had the Brazilian captain of the port of Rio de Janeiro (a mulatto[10] named Leopoldo de Câmara) on its payroll. There also seemed to be a large body of popular opinion building in Brazil against the trade, which the British also supported. But the British decided that this was still too slow a process. In 1849 the stabilization of relations between Britain and the Argentine government of Manuel Rosas[11] permitted the Admiralty to finally move its South American squadron to operate exclusively off the Brazilian coast where it concentrated on trade intervention. . . . This fleet contained the latest in warships and proceeded to enter Brazilian waters with impunity. Though Great Britain was actively violating international law, no nation would support Brazil on this issue and it saw itself helpless to defend its shipping or citizens. In June 1850 came the final campaign as British ships entered Brazilian ports directly and seized suspected slavers, which resulted in British seamen and marines engaging in battle with Brazilian troops. Brazil's coastal shipping was disrupted, lives were lost and the government was faced with a virtual blockade. As no one would defend the trade internally, and no one would support the government internationally, the Brazilians finally agreed to total and effective abolition of the trade in an act of 4 September 1850. The trade was declared piracy and all slaves seized were to be reshipped to Africa at government expense. A now more powerful Brazilian government carried out the terms of its decree fully, and in alliance with the British navy the trade was brought to a virtual halt by the end of that year, with only a few isolated ships arriving in 1851. Thus after some 400 years ended the longest and largest African slave trade in history. An immediate result of the closure of the trade was the collapse of slave prices in Africa and the rise of slave prices in Brazil.

---

[10] A person of mixed Caucasian and black ancestry.

[11] Argentinian military leader and dictator, 1793–1877.

The last trade to be terminated was the forced African migration to the Spanish colony of Cuba. Whereas defiant attitudes of Brazilian officials had led to direct confrontation, the numerous Spanish governments at Madrid constantly promised to terminate the trade and thus effectively held off more aggressive British intervention. Though condemning the trade, the Spanish Crown refused to prosecute it. But it conceded the right to search for equipment for the trade on the high seas in 1835, which forced Cuban traders to adopt Portuguese colors. In 1842 the U.S. government sent a squadron to West Africa as a response to Cuban slavers using the American flag.

The fears of U.S. annexationist plans for Cuba restrained the British government from more direct intervention. But the abolition of slavery in the British islands freed British abolitionists to concentrate on the slave trade from the late 1830s onward, and the British government came under increasing pressure to move against Spain. As in Brazil, there was also a growing abolitionist sentiment developing within Cuba and Puerto Rico — Spain's other major slave colony. These movements were supported by Britain. . . .

Although the abolition of the Brazilian trade in 1850 brought renewed vigor to the Cuban campaign, the distractions of the Crimean War[12] in the 1850s and the increasing pressure of southern U.S. leaders to expand the slave system overseas to Cuba through annexation dampened Britain's ability and interest in maintaining pressure against Spain. . . . But the outbreak of the Civil War[13] in the United States finally pushed the U.S. government into signing a treaty with Great Britain in 1862 that allowed free search of all its vessels. Also, all northern ports were closed to Cuban slave trade outfitters, an important provisioning source for Cuban traders, and even southern officials agreed to oppose the slave trade. Here, as with the Brazilian trade, U.S.-built vessels and supplies had been a major factor in the nineteenth-century Atlantic slave trade. Thus with the American flag of convenience denied to them, there was no legal protection anywhere for slavers. The British and U.S. naval forces now caused the volume of the trade to decline precipitously to only a few ships per annum after 1862. With the United States and Great Britain, the two previously opposing forces, now in agreement, Spain seriously feared the loss of its colony to foreign powers and finally conceded total defeat. In 1866 came an effective Spanish anti-slave-trade act, and the last slave ship is supposed to have landed some unknown number of slaves in Cuba in 1867. Thus ended the Atlantic slave trade.

In examining the evolution of the slave trade in this last century of its existence, the most obvious factor determining its organization was its transition from a legal to an illegal trade. This direct government intervention was to have a major impact on how the trade was conducted and was to lead to certain fundamental changes in the last decades that marked this late trade as different from

---

[12] War (1854–1856) by Great Britain and France against Russia.

[13] Between the northern U.S. states (the Union) and eleven southern states (the Confederate States of America), 1861–1865.

what had preceded it. The nineteenth-century Atlantic slave trade can be divided into roughly three periods: the legal trade that continued until 1817 for all the African coast; the period of legal trading south of the equator from 1817 to 1830, in which the Spanish colonies and Brazil carried on a traditional pattern of trading; and then the post-1830 period to 1867, when it was officially illegal everywhere. In many ways the pre-1830 trade followed the patterns of the eighteenth-century trade in terms of its shipping, carrying of slaves, and commercial organization. But the post-1830 era was to experience new developments in all aspects of the trade, from the initial purchase of the slaves on the African coast to the financing of the voyages, and the final sale of the slaves. All these new strategies were designed to handle either the direct military intervention by the British and/or the necessity to bribe American officials so as to land their slaves in the Americas. These activities raised the cost of shipping considerably and, with it, the subsequent prices of Africans sold in the Americas in the last thirty years of the trade.

. . . Some 3 million Africans were shipped across the Atlantic in the nineteenth century, or about 30 percent of all those who were forced to enter the Atlantic slave trade. . . .

The volume of the transatlantic trade had reached its peak in the decade of the 1780s, when close to 80,000 slaves per annum were crossing the Atlantic to America. The shock of the Haitian rebellion[14] and the destruction of the economy in the New World's premier slave agricultural colony of Saint Domingue[15] in the last decade of the century, combined with the disruption of transatlantic trade due to the imperial and Napoleonic Wars, which lasted until the early 1810s, caused a drop in the volume of African forced migrations to some 61,000 per annum in the first decade of the new century and just 53,000 per annum in the worst of the war years in the second decade of the century. By the 1820s the trade revived to close to 60,000 per annum. But after 1830, when the trade became illegal in most places, volume declined to 55,000 per annum in the 1830s and 43,000 per annum in the following decade. The elimination of Brazil as a market after 1850 dropped the volume to less than half the previous rate. Cuba absorbed only 14,000 per annum on average in the 1850s and by the early 1860s the rate was down to less than 4,000 per year.

As several commentators have noted, this decline was not due so much to the direct naval blockade as to the declining American demand. In almost all slave zones in the Americas in the nineteenth century native slave populations began to experience positive rates of growth. . . .

. . . In the early nineteenth century, as it had for most of the eighteenth century, some 90 percent of the value of African exports were slaves. But the relative importance of slaves in the total African economy would change profoundly in the nineteenth century. In the second and third decades of the century, while slave exports were still high, Africans began finding an overseas market for peanuts and

---

[14] Successful slave revolt against France in 1804 that resulted in the independence of Haiti.

[15] Haiti.

palm oil. Thus well before final abolition of the slave trade, most of the densely populated regions of West Africa were exporting commodities that soon became more valuable than slaves. Sometimes slaves were retained in Africa to produce these new export goods, as in the case of the Biafra region, and sometimes they were produced by free peasant farmers. But everywhere African traders now engaged in multiple exports, among which slaves now were only one part. The African economic ties to the world economy were becoming more complex just as the slave trade was coming to face its most determined opposition.

The Congo and Angolan regions remained the single largest producers of slaves in the nineteenth century, as they had been throughout the whole history of the slave trade. Accounting for an estimated 37 percent of slaves shipped from the beginning to 1809, they now accounted for an even higher 48 percent of all slaves leaving Africa in the nineteenth century. . . .

The newest area to enter the trade was Southeast Africa, essentially Portuguese-controlled Mozambique, which had begun sending slaves to America at the end of the previous century. . . . [A]s the slave trade slowed, ivory and cloves quickly came to be exported from this region.

Just as the origin of slaves shifted in the nineteenth century, so too did their place of destination. Whereas the United States and the British islands were absorbing 35 percent of the slaves in the last decade of the eighteenth century, and Brazil absorbed some 30 percent, the slowly developing island of Cuba took only 9 percent of the 771,000 Africans who came to America. With the trade terminated to the British islands and with Brazilian slave immigrant absorption rising steadily each decade from 181,000 in the 1780s to 431,000 in the 1820s, it was inevitable that the direction of slaves would dramatically shift as well. . . . [T]he nineteenth century after 1808 can be defined as the century when the Iberian colonies and nations dominated the trade. In the first decade of the nineteenth century Cuba and Brazil took only 42 percent of the slaves, but in the next decade this ratio rose to over 90 percent of the Africans arriving in America and this figure rarely declined after that date. By the end of the trade period, Brazil had absorbed over 1.1 million Africans, and Cuba some 600,000 in the nineteenth century.

Of the two, it was obviously Brazil that was the dominant embarkation zone in the nineteenth century as it had been from the seventeenth century onward, though Cuba by the end had become a major importer in its own right. . . .

The only major zone of importation in the nineteenth century outside these two Iberian colonies was the French West Indies. Though the French had lost Saint Domingue definitively in 1804, and had their slave trade temporarily closed during the Napoleonic Wars, they retained the islands of Martinique and Guadeloupe. These islands, along with French Guiana, were still major sugar-producing zones and continued to attract slaves until 1830. On average, these regions were bringing in some 4,000 slaves per annum with the peak period being in the early 1820s. . . .

That the slave trade continued to function despite all the efforts of the British is due to the insatiable demands of Europeans for American plantation crops and of American producers for African slaves. Though the British expended large sums, they could not stop this trade. The British blockades that began in the 1810s and lasted in many regions to the 1860s did succeed in seizing 160,000 Africans on the high seas and in taking 1 out of every 5 slavers (or some 1,600 slave ships) operating in the period of illegal activity. All this naval intervention is estimated to have prevented about 10 percent of the potential slaves from crossing the Atlantic and clearly had an impact in raising some slave prices in the American republics and colonies that used slave labor. But the British naval intervention's major impact was to force American governments to honor their treaty commitments. The costs of evading the blockade were less than the costs of bribing Cuban officials. It was only when Brazil and Cuba agreed to terminate the trade in a definitive manner that the Atlantic slave trade formally and effectively ended.

Until that time the increasing illegal trade adopted ever newer techniques to compensate for British intervention. . . . African traders or resident American business representatives now remained on the coast over many years and developed full-time facilities to accumulate slaves in large permanent pens so that their slave ships could be loaded rapidly and leave the African coast in days instead of the traditional months that was the norm in previous years.

Because of fears of capture on the high seas, there also developed after 1830 a new type of trading vessel. Increasing use was now made of supply ships as distinct from slavers, which brought the merchandise used to purchase slaves to Africa directly from America, Europe, or Asia and returned with commodity products such as peanuts or palm oil, but which never carried slaves. . . .

Given the increasing risks of capture and loss of slaves and ships to British warships, there also developed new forms of financing of the trade. True joint-stock companies were now established to spread the risks and to concentrate the large blocks of capital needed to maintain an African presence. Previously joint-stock voyages were common in the trade, but these multiowner voyages were usually organized for only one trip, and individual merchants tended to spread their risks over several voyages with several different groups. Now companies were formed among partners willing to subsidize many ships and voyages as a stable multiowner company.

Finally control of the trade passed exclusively to Cubans and Brazilians, or Europeans resident in these countries, as European criminal law made slaving a capital crime for its own citizens. Though English credit and English and North American goods continued to fuel the trade of Brazil and Cuba, British, North American, and French merchants no longer took any direct role in the trade. . . . Thus American traders now dominated the trade as never before and, though credit and goods still came from Europe and North America, the ownership of the trade was confined to the countries that still imported slaves, a distinct change from the pre-nineteenth-century period when the Europeans had played such a prominent role. . . .

All of these changes undertaken in the period of the illegal trade had the effect of keeping the majority of the slaves and slave ships out of the hands of the English. But they had little impact in changing the types of ships used to move

the slaves, or the regions from which the slaves came. Small ships by world merchant fleet standards continued to be the norm. Mortality in the pre-1830 period
still hovered in the 6 to 13 percent range, not much different from the late eighteenth century. Though it rose slightly in the next decade, it was not until the last
two decades of the trade that it rose to the 15 to 17 percent range, levels not seen
since the mid-eighteenth century. . . . Given the increasing costs and risks of trading, however, profits did rise on individual voyages and the relative cost factors
shifted. Shipping costs rose from approximately 15 percent of the sale price when
moving slaves across the Atlantic was legal, to close to 50 percent in the illegal
trade period.

The slave traders effectively responded to the increasing Atlantic blockade of the British with new techniques and new trading practices, and American
buyers and African sellers continued to participate in the movement of Africans
to America. But if the naval blockade was only a minor deterrent to the Atlantic
trade, the political power behind that blockade was not. Not only did the British
keep the diplomatic pressure constant, but they now began to find support not
only throughout all of Europe but also within the American nations themselves.
From the northern states of the United States to the southern provinces of Brazil,
more and more leaders began to accept the end of the trade as inevitable and a
first step in the eventual abolition of slavery itself. This progressive reversal of
world opinion left Brazil and Spain with no alternatives but to accept the inevitable decision effectively to end forced African immigration to America. Even
those leaders who wanted to maintain slavery in America realized that the trade
itself was a hopeless cause and many slave owners even became abolitionists in
terms of the Atlantic trade. Thus it was not force of arms in the end so much as
a profound change in world opinion that effectively ended the Atlantic slave
trade. To one and all, this was now considered an immoral trade in human life that
could not be sustained on any grounds, including even the limited justification
of necessity or the defense of American production. . . . [A] generation before the
end of slavery in America, the Atlantic slave trade was finally destroyed.

The fact that planters and slave owners in the United States, Brazil, and Cuba
were still purchasing slaves just months before final abolition of slavery itself
occurred clearly indicated that both the trade and slavery could have survived well
into the twentieth century. In 1859, 1887, and 1889 slave owners were still buying slaves and willing to pay extra for women who were in their childbearing
years. This so-called positive price for unborn children indicated that they expected slavery to last at least another full generation.

But however much slave owners fought to retain slavery, the abolition of the
trade by the 1860s marked a clear turning point. In every region but the United
States, the total number of slaves declined. Moreover, the pressure that led to the
abolition of the trade now shifted to attacking the institution of slavery itself.
Most educated elites of Europe and America began to view slavery as a retrograde
institution that could no longer be tolerated. In countries like Brazil and Cuba the
pressure for manumission grew steadily and the number of slaves freed began to
match the numbers born. . . . Only in the United States did the rate of manu-

missions actually go in the opposite direction in the nineteenth century. This trend, plus ever higher reproduction rates, meant that the slave population of the United States was the only one that was growing in the nineteenth century.

But even as that servile population grew, the United States was beginning to resolve its never ending labor problem by turning toward European immigrants. Though migrants had been coming to North America in ever increasing numbers in the eighteenth century, the nineteenth century was the great age of immigration. . . . For the Americas as a whole, already by the 1840s free European immigrants were more numerous than the slaves and reached some 204,000 per annum in this decade. . . .

Thus the ending of the slave trade, if it did not immediately end slavery in America, marked a dramatic change for the system and clearly indicated its future demise. The steady rise of slave prices after the abolition of the slave trade was followed by universal attempts at alternative labor arrangements, mostly with indentured contract labor. Though planters were buying slaves until the last months of the slave regimes in Brazil, Cuba, and the United States, all regimes but the North American one were already experiencing sharp declines in the number of slaves because of negative growth rates and increasing manumissions. Although direct political action by the individual states was needed to end slavery, just as it had been needed to end the slave trade, slave owners had already begun to anticipate the final ending of this historic institution. The slave trade gave way to an indentured and subsidized immigrant trade, and its demise spelled the end of slavery in the Western Hemisphere.

ITALIAN WOMEN IN
THE NINETEENTH CENTURY
Donna Gabaccia

Until the twentieth century, most Europeans lived on farms. Only a few areas in the Middle Ages, such as Flanders and northern Italy, had significant urban populations. After 1750, however, cities increased exponentially, the Industrial Revolution (first in Great Britain and later on the Continent) had a more substantial effect on life than any other development since the Neolithic Revolution, and capitalism impressed life in the country and gender relations in major ways. These momentous societal changes affected Great Britain, France, and Germany before Italy, and towns before the countryside. Donna Gabaccia, Charles H. Stone Professor of American History at the University of North Carolina at Charlotte, investigates women's work and existence in nineteenth-century Italy after its unification in 1860–1861.

Relying on census data and landholding records, Gabaccia finds that the introduction of a market economy touched women's lives in complicated and surprising fashion. We may be conditioned to believe that capitalism, modernization, and economic development improve people's lives, but nineteenth-century Italian women were not consistently better off for these incursions. For example, domesticity, staying at home, did not indicate a life of leisure, but male control of female behavior and often the exclusion of women from wage-earning jobs. In what fashion did domesticity affect the economic and social status of women? Patriarchy and the ethos of Italian males trumped the possible beneficial effects that modernization had on some women in other countries. How did developments in rural Italy differ precisely from those elsewhere in Europe? How did the Italian state and the growth of capitalism influence gender relations and the division of labor? Why does Gabaccia use the term "women of the shadows"? These women were medieval survivors, unable to shake off the economic, social, legal, and gender structures that burdened their activities. How did Italian women attempt to better their lives? Overall, do you believe that capitalism,

Donna Gabaccia, "Italian Women in the Nineteenth Century," in *Connecting Spheres: European Women in a Globalizing World,* 2nd ed., ed. Marilyn J. Boxer and Jean H. Quataert (New York: Oxford University Press, 2000), 194–203.

modernization, and the nation-state have improved gender relations and women's economic situation in the nineteenth- and twentieth-century West?

Women in southern Italian life have been portrayed recently as "women of the shadows." That Italy's women should seem shadowy is not surprising. The women of the shadows are invisible not only as women, but as poor, often illiterate rural dwellers, as agricultural workers and peasants, and as residents of a region that became at most a minor power among Western nations. Thus, while historians have outlined women's new roles in the nineteenth century — as factory operative, as middle-class lady or her servant, as feminist — peasant women remain obscure. The very opposite of new, they seem left over from the Middle Ages, occupants of a traditional world untouched by the major events and transformations of the century.

In fact, as this essay will demonstrate, the women of the shadows (like other people without history) become visible precisely when we recognize that they too experienced political centralization, urbanization, and the rise of the factory system. As cities grew, the countryside fed and populated them, and as urban factories produced new and cheap products, the countryside often became an important marketplace for them. Change in the countryside might mean a new crop grown, an old trade abandoned, the search for a cash income, migration, or the loss of kin and neighbors to "better opportunities" elsewhere. Our task, then, is to outline the rural and, more importantly, the gender-specific consequences of the economic, cultural, and political transformation sometimes called "development" or "modernization." This is a worthwhile task. As late as 1890, most of Europe's population lived in the agricultural countryside, especially in Ireland, eastern Europe, the Balkans, and along the Mediterranean, but also in the hinterlands of England, Germany, and France. The average European woman of the nineteenth century was still a rural woman.

Firmly located in Europe's agricultural periphery, Italy has been viewed by scholars as a kind of "school for awakening countries" in today's Third World.[1] To northern European visitors in the nineteenth century, the land seemed astonishingly backward: "almost oriental" was a favored (and telling) comparison. "Backward" is a value-laden expression of a simple reality: the Italian peninsula before 1890 little resembled the European nations which at the time proudly proclaimed themselves models for and pinnacles of human evolution. Although Italians formed a nation-state in the years after 1860, they did not yet share a strong national identity. Even more strikingly, Italy's economy showed few signs of following the example of industrializing northern neighbors. After the commercial and industrial successes of the Renaissance, central Italian industries actually declined through the seventeenth and eighteenth centuries. Modern industrialization began

---

[1] Developing countries.

in earnest only around 1900, and only in a few central and northern areas. Until the 1950s, more than half of the Italian labor force worked in agriculture. The very importance of agriculture in Italy was sometimes taken as symbolic of the country's "backwardness." But however different from north European agricultural practice, Italy's agriculture and its countryside were not static and unchanging. Neither were the women of the shadows.

We know from studies of Britain, France, Germany, and the United States that new roles for women — "the lady" and "the mill girl" — accompanied industrialization. Recently, good studies of African, Latin American, and Asian women have told us more about the meaning of political and economic change in peripheral and agricultural regions of the world. In both cases, scholars discovered new forces that relegated women to domesticity. Clearly the policies of the nation-state or the dictates of colonial development agencies play an important role in domesticating women, often by excluding them from a male-dominated public world. (In nineteenth-century Europe, while increasing numbers of men obtained suffrage, women did not. . . .) At the same time, the transition from a semi-subsistence (or household) economy to a cash (or wage) economy redefined the meaning of work.

Changing patterns in Italian women's work hint at the complexity of domesticity in an agricultural land. In the twentieth century scholars would be puzzled that so few very poor Italian women worked outside their homes. Cultural traits — a Muslim heritage in southern provinces or a more general male obsession with controlling female sexuality — often provided an explanation for the fact that Italian women, when compared to the French or British, rarely worked for wages. Italian culture, it seemed, demanded domesticity of its women. Some scholars even suggested that Italian men's insistence on female domesticity posed an insurmountable obstacle to agricultural or industrial development.

Actually, of course, the women listed in Italian censuses as "without profession and at home" were relative newcomers to Italy, as were housewives in other countries. Only where much productive work had left the household could the housewife exist. That transformation was incomplete in rural Italy in the nineteenth century. At the time of the first comprehensive Italian census in 1871, clerks found relatively few women "without profession"; they counted 50 percent of Italian women as active workers. The large number of working Italian women in 1871 reflected the continued importance for both Italian men and women of small-scale production for family consumption. Wage-earning in Italy (unlike Britain) was not yet central to defining male or female peasants as workers. Both Italian men and women, in a sense, worked in a domestic world.

What distinguished Italy from industrializing nations was that her women became more domestic in subsequent years. While rates of female labor participation in France increased (as women found wage-earning work as textile operatives or domestic servants), rates in Italy declined to less than 30 percent in 1901. This decline was partly an illusion, the result of redefining work as wage-earning; it tells us that Italian men largely claimed wage-earning for themselves. But it is also partially attributable to real changes in women's behavior. Women were less likely to be doing productive work with or without wages in 1901 than in 1871.

A major theme in Italian economic history is the slow decline of Italy's subsistence economy, and the equally slow but persistent growth of capitalist agriculture and industry. In fact, this is the trend of economic development in all western European nations in the nineteenth century: the transition from household production to wage-earning, from production for family use to production for the market, and from small-scale peasant and artisan production to large-scale capitalist production. Focusing on the women of the shadows, however, we might emphasize other themes.

The term subsistence production conjures up images of self-contained and patriarchal peasant and artisan families, working to provide themselves food, clothing and housing, little affected by money and markets. To a degree, such families did shape reality for most Italian women in the early nineteenth century. It is unwise to exaggerate the self-sufficiency of such peasant and artisan households. And it is necessary to outline several important broad variations in how Italian men and women provided for family subsistence in the early years of the nineteenth century.

In much of Italy, peasants enjoyed secure tenure to their land, either through ownership or traditional land rights; they worked small plots of land and grew their own food. If they lived close to a town, they might market any surplus there. By contrast, in parts of southern Italy, semi-feudal social relations persisted. Peasants enjoyed no secure tenure to the land; they cultivated different plots each year on large estates utilizing a three-field system. On their small plots they produced not only staple crops for their own food and garments (oil, grain, linen, sheep), but also a surplus that the estate manager marketed and used to pay land rents to the feudal lord. In areas like these, peasant family subsistence also rested on common rights to the use of land for gathering food and fuel and for grazing small animals. In addition, all over Italy peasant families combined production of food with production of cloth. Here, too, a distinction can be noted between regions with a cottage textile industry and regions where families produced cloth strictly for their own needs.

The division of labor between Italian men and women varied from region to region in the early years of the nineteenth century. In general, married men controlled access to land; few women inherited land or enjoyed rights to its usage. Where land tenure was relatively secure and where small villages were scattered through the countryside, women became an important part of the family work force in the fields, producing food for family consumption. Both men and women marketed small surpluses of eggs, milk, corn, cheese, and so on. Where large estates, herding, and extensive production for the market and concentrated settlement were common, women's agricultural labors were more clearly demarcated from men's. Women gathered, grazed small animals, and generally exploited common usage rights, while men raised grain and herded larger animals. Only at harvest time did women join men on the large distant wheat estates of Sicily, for example, and then mainly as gleaners. The fact that fewer women worked in the fields in such regions cannot be seen simply as a consequence of patriarchal concerns about women working outside the family group, although certainly that played a role. Employers' choices, as well as the very long distances (up to ten or fifteen miles) separating wheat fields from the large compact "agrotowns" of the Italian South, must also be considered.

Almost everywhere in Italy it was women's work at spindle and loom that clothed the family. Girls and mothers worked to produce the cloth and clothing that would become the dowry of daughters at the time of their marriages. (Sons inherited house and/or land.) Where cloth was produced mainly for family needs, men did little. But where cottage industry linked rural workers to city merchants, men might turn their hands in winter to spinning or (more frequently) weaving. In general, where women did little field work, men did little textile work. Local records in such areas might call men "peasants" but women "industrial workers."

The division of labor between men and women in all rural regions changed and became more differentiated in the course of the nineteenth century. The formation of the Italian nation-state can be cited as one important spur to changes in the rural world inhabited by the women of the shadows. Of course, Italy had no formulated plan for development as did colonial agencies or newly independent nations in the twentieth century. Still, the creation of a centralized state stimulated new markets, capitalist agriculture, and greater regional specialization. All in turn encouraged a new division of labor by sex. For women, the economic consequences of unification proved mixed. The legal ending of semi-feudal practices (in the southern provinces) and new inheritance laws after unification allowed small but growing numbers of women access to land. By 1881 more than a third of Italian landowners were female. At the same time, however, the end of feudalism rendered illegal women's gathering and grazing in precisely those areas where women did little field work.

The formation of the Italian nation-state allowed the growth of a unified national market for agricultural and industrial commodities. Through its changing tariff policy (free trade before the 1880s; protection for grain and industrial products thereafter), the state also regulated commercial ties between Italy and other nations. No other events more greatly affected rural Italian women than the import of cheap manufactured cloth and the growth of capitalist agriculture, producing new crops in new ways for markets far from the local piazza.

Historians have shown how the development of the textile industry in France and Britain meant wage-earning options for women. For women in the countryside, however, factory-produced cloth meant unemployment. Although there is much we do not yet know about the decline of Italian rural industries, it seems likely that some Italian women experienced unemployment earlier than others. . . .

The exact timing of Italy's declining rural industries is not yet entirely clear. It seems likely, however, that as cottage industry declined, so too did weaving at home for family use. Folklorists . . . commented on the changing occupation of young girls, who no longer sat hours at spindle or loom producing cloth for their own trousseaux. The desire to purchase manufactured cloth probably itself became an incentive for some family members to switch their labors from subsistence agriculture to seek a cash income as either agricultural or industrial laborers. Since Italy's economy offered few rapidly expanding industrial opportunities for either men or women during these years, cash earned in agriculture became increasingly important to many families.

Although individual women may have welcomed liberation from arduous work at the loom, the purchase of cloth also posed a problem. Where would the cash come from? We may never understand precisely how men and women struggled or cooperated to answer this question. But it is possible to describe the context in which differing answers emerged. The development of capitalist agriculture, the growth or decline of local male industries, and regional customs in defining men's and women's tasks all formed parts of that context.

. . . "Capitalist agriculture" assumed many forms in nineteenth-century Italy. Essential to all forms was the rural entrepreneur who contracted with individuals or families to produce crops which he sold at a profit. The three types of capitalist agriculture . . . represent a rough continuum from less to more capitalist. In the *mezzadria* ("classic sharecropping") system, the Tuscan entrepreneur owned land, houses, vines, trees, and animals; he contracted long-term with peasant families for labor. Peasants still owned some of their own tools, and they divided crops with the landlord, rather than receiving a money payment. The *latifondo*[2] of western Sicily (and Apulia and much of Calabria) evolved from the semi-feudal estates described above. Here, the rural entrepreneur rented a large estate and found short-term sharecroppers (paid in grain) and day laborers (earning a cash wage). In the Po Valley, entrepreneurs owned large tracts of land and paid money wages and provided temporary housing for families of laborers.

Several patterns characterized Italian women's work by 1881. Where women had long worked in the fields (Turin, Abruzzi-Molise, Tuscany, and the Po Valley), they increasingly turned their attentions there as they abandoned their looms. This pattern became most obvious in areas with little capitalist agriculture, like Turin's hinterland. In both Turin and Abruzzi-Molise, women typically concentrated in subsistence production, raising food, while men took whatever wage-earning became available. Men's cash earnings bought property and cloth; women fed the family. In some areas like this, women constituted as much as 70 percent of the agricultural work force in 1881. Usually women also outnumbered men. . . . Men's quest for wages encouraged them to migrate elsewhere while wives, mothers, sisters, and dependent children of both sexes supported themselves on the land. Women in such regions had not in fact moved "beyond subsistence" — even though their work had changed. By 1901 many of the women agriculturalists in regions like these would be listed as housewives, for they worked without wages.

Capitalist agriculture meant different choices for Italian men and women. Women who abandoned their looms sometimes had a harder time finding work in the fields once rural entrepreneurs organized the conditions of employment. Previous habits also worked their influence: women in 1881 were far more likely to work among the Tuscan *mezzadri* than in *latifondo* Sicily. Still, the trend in all areas was similar and clear: growing numbers of men earned wages, providing the

---

[2] Great landed estates.

cash income that cloth (and other purchases) required, while large numbers of women already in 1881 found themselves listed in the census not as spinners, weavers, or peasants, but as housewives.

Sicily provides an extreme example of this second pattern of adaptation. By 1871, most men working in Sicilian agriculture already worked part-time as wage-earners on the large wheat estates. Their labors purchased food and (where necessary) paid rents or taxes, while women's spinning and weaving still clothed most Sicilian families. As cloth production at home declined, Sicilian women sought new work in the fields. (Within a ten-year period, Sicily's women "industrial workers" disappeared from local records to be replaced first by female "peasants" and then, rather swiftly, by "housewives.") Surprisingly, at first Sicilian women actually found work in the fields. In *latifondist*[3] Corleone, for example, women made up almost 40 percent of the agricultural work force in 1881. Thus, not all Sicilian men adamantly forbade wives or daughters to work in the fields or to earn wages. Real agricultural changes, concurrent with the collapse of home textile production, may have helped undermine any male reluctance with hopes of new prosperity, for in the years following Italian unification new crops — especially grapes and oranges, but also nuts, fruits, and olives — began to replace wheat cultivation in western Sicily. These intensively cultivated crops grew conveniently close to town; furthermore, grape and olive harvests overlapped with the wheat ploughing that occupied Sicilian men. Thus, many Sicilian women in the late 1870s and early 1880s earned wages as grape, orange, and olive harvesters, providing the additional cash revenue that cloth purchase required.

During the 1880s, however, all of Sicily's major export crops suffered severe reverses on world markets, and the Sicilian adaptation collapsed in failure. Neither Sicilian men nor Sicilian women could return to subsistence agriculture as could landowning peasants in Turin's hinterland. Not surprisingly, men monopolized wage-earning opportunities in the ensuing crisis; former female agriculturalists as well as women newly liberated from the loom found themselves "domesticated." The unemployed woman became a "housewife."

In claiming wage-earning for themselves, Sicilian men continued to provide food and rents; and in families where sons outnumbered daughters, men's cash earnings might also be diverted to cloth purchase. But in many families the wages of men would not stretch so far; the problem of cloth purchase in particular remained unresolved. Male migration was not a clear answer to this problem as it was elsewhere. Excluded both from the land and from wage-earning, Sicilian women could not easily support themselves and dependent children while men risked migration and the search for cash. A major challenge for Sicilians was the search for female employment. For this reason, Sicilian women were far more likely than other women to migrate. A number of studies of Sicilian women living in the United States point to the very large numbers of such women, even when married, who earned wages in one fashion or another.

---

[3] Characterized by big landowners.

Italy's sizeable population of housewives by 1900 included three groups of women: those who produced food without wages for their families, those whose labors in capitalist agriculture were subsumed under a family wage paid to husbands and fathers, and those who might best be considered unemployed textile workers or agricultural laborers. Although housewives, few became ladies. Most Italian men and women confronted domesticity in terms quite different from their counterparts in the middle- and working-classes of France, Britain, and Germany.

In many regions of Italy, housework continued the subsistence production practiced by peasant agriculturalists in previous centuries. While peasant men during the nineteenth century claimed wage-earning for themselves, wage-earning in no way carried with it social status, as did land ownership or secure tenure to land. Thus, the usual hope of male wage-earners was to return when possible to peasant agriculture, in part because of status considerations, in part because they could still achieve on the land a more comfortable standard of living than their wages alone provided. Obviously, the labors of wives and children on the land allowed many peasant men to pursue this hope. Furthermore, throughout much of the twentieth century the political and organizational efforts of Italian wage earners aimed at land reform. Eventually, land distribution enabled many formerly landless men to become peasant agriculturalists, involved simultaneously in production for family consumption and for the market. This means that in large parts of Italy the patriarchal authority of the father over a household economy persisted relatively unchanged. Indeed, capitalist agriculture incorporated patriarchal family traditions, for rural entrepreneurs adopted from peasant agriculture the employment of family work groups.

In other areas of Italy, however, like Sicily, housework evolved instead from women's unemployment. Domesticity and the relations between the sexes had a unique meaning in these regions. Sicilian proverbs, for example, praised housewives as efficient organizers of household consumption but also implied that most women were spendthrifts. Daughters were said to "rob the father"; brothers complained about burdensome sisters; proverbs simply wished unmarried girls dead. That domesticity might elicit male hostility is not difficult to understand. Unlike the food-producing women of the Abruzzi, the unemployed Sicilian women represented an immense cost to male wage earners. Rather than furthering men's hopes of mobility, a Sicilian woman represented a debt to be paid at the time of her marriage in the form of a dowry. Once Sicilian girls had produced their own dowries by weaving cloth and by earning with their spindles to provide for other necessities. Marriages united a girl's property (cloth, clothing, jewelry) to the house, furnishings, or bit of land owned by her bridegroom. As fewer girls labored at the loom or found agricultural wages, their fathers' and brothers' wages provided the dowry; in addition, families shifted formerly male-controlled properties, especially houses, to daughters. In doing so, they sought to compensate the bridegroom for acquiring an unemployable dependent. Men, meanwhile, married "with only their pants," but feared taunts that a wife's dowry stripped them of authority as head of the family. However blinded by their own assumptions, men like these could easily see domesticity as an important component of family poverty.

Scholars and feminists have long debated the complex and contradictory legacy of domesticity in industrializing nations. While imposing severe limits on women, domesticity also offered them an autonomous world of female solidarity and an exalted, morally superior sphere of their own. Modern feminism drew upon and reacted against both aspects of domesticity. Italian domesticity provided Italy's women of the shadows with different constraints and opportunities. Where housework continued to include subsistence production in agriculture, domesticity would never appear as an exclusively female realm as it did in England, France, Germany, or the United States — too many fathers and husbands returned to work and to rule in the domestic world. Furthermore, the status of domesticity, when it overlapped with subsistence production, was a superior one shared by the entire family, not a prerogative of women alone, but a class privilege. By contrast, in areas where peasants lived in large agrotowns far from their fields — as was true in Sicily — an urban woman's world (revolving around textile production) had preceded domesticity. Women's employment brought to this separate world none of the sentimentality associated with a lady's domestic "pedestal" in industrial nations. The most likely to be called housewives were the poorest women. Domesticity did not allow for family peace along traditional lines. Instead, it subjected women to increased male hostility even while it ironically placed in their hands more real property than in the past. Daughters bore the brunt of these changes; wives enjoyed the few benefits. Domesticity added new fuels to sexual tensions long burning in this part of the Mediterranean.

POPULAR JUSTICE, COMMUNITY, AND CULTURE AMONG THE RUSSIAN PEASANTRY, 1870–1900

Stephen P. Frank

We in the West tend to have a negative view of vigilante justice, but what the rule of law is or is not depends on a particular culture. Laws are culturally relative and differ according to people's socioeconomic status. Nineteenth-century Russian villagers frequently meted out justice according to their own community mores and values, apprehending and punishing those who had broken the law or transgressed village norms. Known as *samosud* (self-adjudication, as Stephen P. Frank defines it), this collective activity was organized, even ritualized in some instances, and certainly legitimate in the eyes of the peasants, though not according to government and judicial authorities. Frank, a historian at the University of California at Los Angeles, analyzes three types of popular justice: *charivaris* (raucous demonstrations intended to shame people who transgress community customs), the harsh punishment of serious theft, and violence against witches. Frank bases his research on newspaper accounts, legal journals, government commission reports, and materials gathered by an amateur ethnographer.

What sorts of behavior led to a *charivari?* Frank explains how the Russian *charivari* differed from its counterparts in England and France. How did villagers express their moral authority in *charivaris* and in punishments for property crimes? Did harsh violence and penalties work successfully to reinforce collective rules of behavior? Notice that villagers distinguished between insiders and outsiders when punishing victims. Why were horse thieves punished more brutally than those guilty of other crimes? Why did peasants not rely on courts to punish those who violated the law and community customs? Does anything similar to *samosud* function in present-day Western civilization?

Stephen P. Frank, "Popular Justice, Community, and Culture among the Russian Peasantry, 1870–1900," in *The World of the Russian Peasant: Post-Emancipation Culture and Society,* ed. Ben Eklof and Stephen Frank (Boston: Unwin Hyman, 1990), 133–150.

Agrafena Ignatieva was known as a sorceress and a fortuneteller in the village of Vrachev (Tikhvinskii district, Novgorod province). An impoverished widow with no means of livelihood, she was forced to beg for her daily subsistence. Unfortunately for "Grushka," as the peasants called her, an outbreak of "falling sickness" in the locality where she lived brought suspicion on her. Most people knew that such an illness resulted from a spell, or *porcha,* and Ignatieva appeared to be the most likely culprit. Early in January 1879 Grushka had asked her fellow-villager Kuzmina for some cottage cheese but was refused; shortly thereafter Kuzmina's daughter fell sick and began crying out that Grushka was the cause. With this episode still fresh in everyone's mind, the illness reached Katerina Ivanova, whose sister had died from the same affliction, also "hexed" by Grushka. Ivanova attributed her sickness to the fact that she had once forbidden her son to chop firewood for the sorceress; Grushka was obviously seeking revenge. Ivanova's husband even lodged a complaint against Ignatieva with the local constable (*uriadnik*), but few villagers expected that she would be punished.

Because of the number of misfortunes attributed to her, the peasants of Vrachev decided to burn Grushka. They made their decision during a meeting of the village assembly, which had gathered to divide the property of four peasant brothers. After settling this case, the villagers reached an agreement among themselves, took some nails, and set off to "seal" Grushka, as they put it. On reaching Agrafena Ignatieva's hut, they found the entrance shed locked and broke down the door. Four peasants entered the storeroom in search of charms and potions while six others went into the house itself. After parleying for some time with the woman, they proceeded to "seal" the house. First a pole was set into the entranceway and nailed in place. Next they nailed a plank against the larger window and sealed off two small windows with logs, so that all exits were completely blocked. At about five P.M. they set fire to a bundle of straw and rope in the entrance shed, and the hut burned to the ground while nearly 200 people from Vrachev and a neighboring village looked on. Though certain they had done the right thing to protect their village, the peasants nevertheless sent the local constable 22 rubles so he would forget the case, but he declined their offer. Those most guilty in the burning of Grushka — sixteen persons — were brought before the circuit court, where three confessed their guilt and were sentenced to church penitence, while the others went free.

Community or "mob" violence of this sort frequently found its way into the pages of Russia's urban and provincial press. It was by no means limited to persons accused of sorcery; thieves were commonly subjected to community reprisal, as were those who transgressed certain village norms of conduct. Nor was the phenomenon peculiar to backward, isolated regions. . . . [S]*amosud* (literally, self-adjudication), as educated Russians called it, was primarily an activity of rural villagers and occurred most often in areas where the effects of capitalist development had been least felt, for there the presence of police and other agents of state coercion was weak and traditional peasant institutions retained greater strength. It existed in nearly all provinces of the empire and remained widespread throughout the nineteenth century and after, accounting for as much as 1 percent of all rural crimes tried before the circuit courts.

Samosud in the Russian countryside was a far more complex phenomenon than contemporaries believed it to be. Most of Russia's educated elite saw *samosud* as little more than mob violence or lynch law, and the greatest attention was paid to just these types of extralegal reprisal. The best dictionary of the period, however, took a broader view, defining *samosud* not only as willful punishment but also as arbitrariness and "adjudication of one's own affairs." In fact, many instances of *samosud* did not involve violence but bore close resemblance to the *charivaris*, "rough music," and shivarees of Western Europe and North America. Although peasants rarely offered definitions to investigators who questioned them about their juridical beliefs and practices, they did include such nonviolent acts in their conception of *samosud*. In addition, although they did not categorize the types of *samosud* practiced in the village, close examination of the acts themselves reveals that peasants distinguished sharply between punishments inflicted on community members and those used against outsiders. With fellow villagers *samosud* took on a highly ritualized character; violent forms were reserved almost exclusively for outsiders whose crimes posed a threat to the community.

This distinction between punishing members of the community and outsiders is perhaps the most useful framework for analyzing the nature and function of *samosud* in rural Russia and for understanding such acts from the perspective of the villager rather than of the urban elite. For this reason I will consider three frequent forms of popular justice, all of which were termed *samosud* by the participants: ritualized disciplinary action such as *charivari*, in which villagers inflicted shame and public disgrace on the guilty party, usually without resorting to violence; punishment of theft, particularly the theft of horses; and, briefly, violence directed against those suspected of witchcraft. . . .

. . . Invoking the commune's moral authority was one of the most notable features of *samosud*. Peasants usually brought a case before the village assembly before inflicting punishment, especially if the offender was a community member, and the assembly frequently sentenced the guilty party to some form of *samosud*. In this way the assembly sanctioned what outsiders would deem an illegal action and lessened the chance that a criminal would complain to the authorities or seek revenge, considering that to do so challenged a decision of the assembly as well as the authority of the community itself.

Other distinguishing features of *samosud* included community participation in the punishment, a real or perceived threat to local norms or to the community's well-being, and an attempt to prevent repetition of a crime through ritualized public humiliation of the offender or, in more serious cases, by ridding the community of a criminal altogether. Because the presence of these characteristics in a given act of *samosud* depended on the nature of the crime and the offender's status as villager or outsider, they helped both to differentiate the various forms of *samosud* and to join them together in a common meaning, as we shall now see.

At its simplest level, *samosud* might be inflicted for a multitude of petty infractions such as *potrava* (damage caused to another's crops by one's livestock); it was also used to discipline minors if the case warranted serious attention. One of the most widespread types of *samosud* in rural Russia, however, was called "leading of the thief" (*vozhdenie vora,* or simply *vozhdenie*) — a punishment that had the ritualistic character of *charivari* and, unlike other acts of *samosud,* was visited only upon members of the community. Known by various names throughout Europe and North America, *charivaris* were a traditional means of public criticism or punishment in which the entire community could participate and a disciplinary technique by which family or community members were forced to follow collective rules. A strong, formal similarity existed between *charivaris* in Russia, where the practice endured as late as the 1920s, and in countries such as England, France, and Germany.

The typical Russian *charivari* consisted of parading an offender through the street either on foot or in a cart, in some cases wearing a horse collar, while villagers followed along playing *paramusique*[1] by beating upon oven doors (evidently the most favored instrument), pots and pans, washtubs, and other domestic or agricultural implements, sometimes carrying signs, mocking the victim, and singing songs. Women were often stripped naked or had their skirts raised before being led around the village; men might first be stripped, then tarred and feathered. Apart from minor differences of detail, the similarities here with European examples are striking.

. . . It is, in fact, with the function of the rituals and the victims themselves that Russian *charivaris* differed from those in other countries. The *charivari* in England and France most often expressed disapproval of marital mismatches or conjugal relations considered to be deviant, such as marriages between people of great age difference, socially ill-matched marriages, or a recently widowed villager marrying a single, younger person. Sexual offenders were also common victims of *charivaris,* as were cuckolded husbands, unwed mothers, persons (usually women) who committed adultery, wife-beaters, and household members deviating from accepted sex roles — for example, men who performed women's work or whose wives beat them.

In postreform Russia[2] we do find cases of *charivaris* involving adulteresses (and occasionally adulterers too), unwed mothers, and "immoral" women, but they account for only a small proportion of collective community actions that can be termed *vozhdeniia.* Nor did I find reports of cuckolded husbands or husbands beaten by their wives being subjected to rough music. The apparent scarcity of such cases in Great Russia[3] suggests that other matters occupied a higher priority when it came to the collective enforcement of local norms. Chief among these was petty theft.

Russian peasants treated many kinds of theft and pilfering quite leniently. Both unofficial and township courts used reconciliation far more than punishment

---

[1] Rough, raucous music.

[2] In Russian history, after the reforms enacted in the 1860s.

[3] The central and northeastern areas of Russia; home of the Russian-speaking people.

in cases of petty theft. In the Volga region, for example, a peasant who perpetrated such a crime was not always viewed as someone capable of real harm to the community — a perspective clearly expressed in the popular saying, "The thief is not a thief, but a half-thief." Yet despite their apparent leniency, villagers did not simply dismiss the crime; in many instances *charivari* was a typical punishment, and its magnitude was determined above all by the seriousness of the crime, and especially by the value of the stolen item. During *charivaris* involving petty theft, offenders would be marched through the village with the stolen object hung on them. In the village of Zabolonia, Smolensk province, for example, one peasant was caught stealing another's goose. Hanging the goose from his neck, villagers led the thief three times around the hamlet, pounding all the while upon oven doors. After this procession the thief begged forgiveness, bought drinks for everyone, and there the affair ended. In another case a woman from the village of Kozinkii, Orel province, stole a sheep from her neighbor and butchered it. She was discovered and brought before the village assembly, which sentenced her to a *charivari*. Village women gathered together with sickles, oven doors, and other "instruments," hung the sheep's head around her neck, and amid songs and banging, led the woman three times through the town before letting her go. . . .

The additional humiliation of being stripped for a *charivari* was reserved mainly for women. In one village of Novgorod province, Cherepovets district, a woman named Drosida Anisimova was caught picking berries before the time agreed on by the village assembly. A village policeman brought her before the assembly, where they stripped her naked, hung on her neck the basket of berries she had gathered, "and the entire commune led her through the village streets with shouts, laughter, songs, and dancing to the noise of washtubs, frying pans, bells and so on. The punishment had such a strong effect on her that she was ill for several days, but the thought of complaining against her offenders never entered her mind" (or so the report claimed). Likewise, Katerina Evdokimova, a peasant from the village of Ermakov, Iaroslavl province, was accused in 1874 of stealing linen. The assembly found her guilty and decided to undress her, wrap her in the stolen linen, and lead her through the streets. Evdokimova, however, pleaded not to be completely disrobed, so the assembly accommodated her by uncovering her only to the waist, then wrapping her in linen and leading her in public with her hands tied to a stake as everyone rang bells and beat upon oven doors.

Charivaris could also result from a refusal to obey the assembly's decision in a criminal case. In Orel province a peasant named Mikhail was found guilty of stealing a sheep and ordered to buy the village elder and his friends a half-bucket of vodka. This they quickly drank and demanded another, promising to forgive Mikhail afterward. But while consuming the second bucket the peasants continued berating Mikhail for his crime, and becoming concerned for his safety, he fled to his home. When they finished their vodka and noticed Mikhail's absence, the irate villagers went to the thief's house led by the elder. Demanding more vodka, they became even angrier when he called them drunks and robbers. For this new insult they took a wheel from his wagon and sold it for vodka, after which they seized Mikhail, tied a large sack of oats onto his back, and led him around the village accompanied by other peasants who beat upon oven doors while laughing and insulting the victim. When the *charivari* ended, Mikhail was forced to pawn clothing at the local tavern in order to buy the men still more vodka. With this they finally agreed to forgive him, but sternly warned that things would go much worse if he ever stole again.

Mikhail got off lightly, having not been beaten. Refusal to obey the will of the assembly could lead to more severe retribution involving violence and even expulsion from the community. To her misfortune, a peasant from the village of Meshkova, Orel province, learned this the hard way. Anna Akulicheva had been found guilty of stealing canvas, and the assembly decided to subject her to a *charivari* and then sell her own fabric for vodka. First the villagers knocked off her kerchief (a grave insult among Russian peasants) and dirtied her holiday shirt. Next they tied her sack-cloth on her back, bound her hands behind her, hitched her up, and led the woman through the village. Two peasants walked ahead beating with sticks upon oven doors while Anna followed in harness with the reins held by two others. The entire village turned out to watch and laugh, and children threw clods of dirt at her. Finally they brought her home and untied her, taking only the cloth they had placed on her back to purchase vodka. At this point, however, Anna attacked her tormenters with a chain seized in the shed and then fled the village to avoid further punishment.

On the suggestion of peasants from a neighboring village, Anna lodged a complaint with the local land captain.[4] He summoned the elder from Meshkova, who confessed in detail and was forbidden to do such a thing again. Furthermore, the land captain sentenced him to two days' arrest. When he returned home, the elder immediately summoned the assembly and told them what Anna had done. The members wasted little time in responding to this latest offense. They ruled that Anna should be whipped in public by her husband, Sergei, and that some of her clothes would then be taken to sell for vodka, after which she would undergo all sorts of public ridicule. The woman was brought before the assembly but resisted her husband's efforts to force her to lie down for the beating. Finally, other peasants threw her to the ground and held her there while Sergei administered thirty blows with a knout.[5] Following this severe punishment, he went to fetch his wife's clothes, but Anna had already taken all of her things to her family in Balasheva. As a result, Anna was ostracized. She fought with her husband daily. Worse, the community held her in contempt and mocked her, and village children pelted her on the street with clods of earth to shouts of "hurrah." At last she decided to leave Meshkova. With her husband's approval she received a passport and set off, first to the city of Orel and then to Odessa.

In all of these examples the obvious function of *charivaris* was to shame thieves so that they would not steal from fellow villagers again. With its wealth of symbolism and ritual, public humiliation of a wrongdoer brought both crime

---

[4] Supervisor of peasant workers.

[5] Whip with a lash of leather thongs twisted with wire.

and criminal before the offended community for judgment, and it was the community that oversaw conformity to established rules, thereby asserting the primacy of its authority. At the level of symbolic discourse, the *charivari* held out a threat of greater sanction, for it acted as a ritualized, though temporary, expulsion of an offender from the community and reminded all villagers — not only the thief — that expulsion could be permanent if someone repeated his or her crime or perpetrated a more serious infraction. Petty thieves were allowed to return to the collective fold only after publicly acknowledging their guilt and begging the community's forgiveness. Hence the equally symbolic payment in vodka which villagers demanded at the conclusion of a *charivari*. In "treating" the community to drinks, a thief won forgiveness and, more important, readmittance.

Beyond their immediate purpose of discipline, then, *charivaris* were a constituent element of village culture and an important means of social regulation. They played a significant role in governing behavior, regulating daily life, and ordering conduct "in a highly visible and comprehensive way." In this respect the *charivari* was only one of the tools in a village culture's arsenal of regulatory customs and rituals. *Charivaris* also helped to preserve local solidarity by preventing the taking of sides in a dispute and a subsequent development of open feuding, which would otherwise disrupt activities and social relations crucial to the peasant economy. The punishment thus acted to soothe ill feelings and hostilities by involving an entire village, often with the elder's authorization and active participation.

In the majority of recorded cases peasants first brought a thief before the local assembly for sentencing, though eight to ten assembly members together with an elder or a township headman were deemed sufficient to reach a decision. It is here, in fact, with the villagers' use of their assembly as a judicial organ, that we find the basis of the commune's exclusive right in the moral control of its members. . . . The assembly's decision legitimated a *charivari* in the eyes of all villagers and made revenge on the victim's part unlikely, because to seek retribution against the participants was tantamount to challenging the authority of the commune itself. The escalation of punishment during a *vozhdenie* resulted from just such a challenge. Similarly, escalation occurred when a demand for "payment" in vodka went unmet and the offender thereby refused to reach reconciliation with the community.

Charivaris directed against persons other than thieves do not fit so neatly into the conclusions drawn thus far. Many forms of *charivari* worked in a manner similar to the French *charivari* so often held up as a model for comparison — to maintain community norms of morality and to exert community control over sexual behavior and conjugal relations. To give one example, Evgenii Iakushkin[6] reported in 1875 that if a bride in Olonets province had not preserved her virginity until marriage, villagers would stick a peg over her door, hang a horse collar on it, and lead both her and her mother under it. Adulteresses, too, might be subjected to *charivaris*. Such events included all the common elements of *charivari*: leading offenders through the village, public derision, humiliation, and para-

---

[6] Ethnographer and jurist (1826–1905) who studied customary law among the peasantry.

music. Yet in some cases of adultery, the element of violence was used even when a victim offered no resistance; the process of escalation did not function because violence seems to have been inherent to this type of *charivari*. Thus a woman named Oksana Vereshchikha was suspected by peasants in her village of Poznanka (Volynia province) of carrying on an illicit affair with the township clerk. For this they stripped her naked, placed her in irons, and tied her to a post, where she stayed all night. In the morning the villagers returned and ordered her to buy them a pail of vodka, even though they had already pawned her kerchief and sheepskin jacket for one pail on the previous day. Because she had no money, a *charivari* was organized with "musicians" marching in front, followed by Vereshchikha, the elder, and the villagers. This was a particularly creative procession in which a garland of straw and burdocks[7] was placed on the victim's head, and she was forced to dance before the crowd. They led her seven times along the street, beating her with fists and flogging her with the birch, all the while passing vodka around. At last they took her home, beat her again, and let her go.

Charivaris of adulteresses or of housewives who somehow had failed in their domestic duties reveal the ability of communities "to compel individual family members to follow collective rules," as well as the public control to which "the deviant relations of husband and wife are subject." As with cases of theft, collective responsibility and supervision constituted the basis of *charivaris*. Yet in the Russian village, communal authority was less concerned with punishing adultery than with punishing theft; adultery involved a different set of property and power relations that rested on the generally accepted position of male domination and the husband's customary authority to punish his wife with almost complete impunity. Neighbors rarely intervened to quell domestic violence between husband and wife. Thus few *charivaris* were directed against adulteresses by Great Russian peasants because villagers usually left it to a husband to mete out appropriate punishment. The expectation of corporal punishment, in turn, may account for the use of violence in those instances when villagers did subject an adulterous woman to *charivari,* for here the community symbolically took on the role of offended spouse and punished as custom dictated. Though signs of change can be found in some areas, the persistence of such punishments helps to explain the relative scarcity of incidents in which adulteresses were victims of *charivaris.* Marital violence was especially likely to occur when a wife had committed adultery or left her husband; both deeds could disrupt the household economy and bring a loss of honor to the husband.

Evidence from township courts shows that women tried to escape domestic violence or to seek justice through formal litigation. Yet peasant judges ruled in a woman's favor primarily when they found no justification for a beating, or when they deemed that the punishment had been overly cruel. In cases of adultery or "abandonment," however, litigation had little chance of success; the husband was within his rights to punish his wife as he saw fit. . . .

---

[7] Cockleburrs.

Russian *charivaris,* then, differed in important respects from those in many countries of Western Europe. Great Russian peasants used rituals of public shaming far more to punish theft than sexual and conjugal misconduct, perhaps because of the increased significance of property relations in the postemancipation period[8] and an attendant weakening of the primacy of kinship. When villagers did punish sexual misconduct, their attention focused primarily, apart from unmarried girls, on adulteresses whose husbands were absent or, in the community's view, required assistance in controlling their wives. Finally, the Russian *charivari* sought to bring offenders back into the community rather than drive them out altogether, using the symbolic threat of expulsion together with the forced purchase of vodka (i.e., symbolic reconciliation) as its main instruments for reestablishing normal intravillage relations. This fact helps to distinguish the *charivari* from other types of *samosud,* in which ritual was largely absent, violence was prominent, and expulsion constituted the overriding objective. It is to these manifestations of *samosud* that we now turn.

A second form of summary justice that clarifies the peasants' distinction between *charivari* and *samosud* brings us back to property crime, though this time to crime of a serious rather than a petty nature. Such acts were especially likely to meet with harsh penalties if the criminal was an outsider or had repeatedly committed theft in a given locality. Popular retribution involved beatings, myriad gruesome and often lethal tortures, and outright murder. These acts were almost always carried out by a crowd but lacked the organized, ritual character of *charivari.* Although an elder might direct the violence, meetings of the village assembly were not necessary before punishing a criminal.

Peasant reprisals could be merciless, especially if their aim was to rid the community of the criminal once and for all. In one part of the Mid-Volga region, for instance, a gang of six peasants had long caused trouble among their fellow villagers by stealing property and money, but attempts by the local population to catch the thieves met with no success. When the gang turned to highway robbery, villagers grew particularly enraged and selected three men to kill them, which they finally did. One thief in Kazan province was beaten savagely and then, before a large crowd on a riverbank, he was killed by the village elder and buried in the sand. Elsewhere a peasant named Vasilii Andronov had been exiled to Siberia by communal decree from his village of Grigorev, Samara province. In 1872 Andronov escaped and returned to Grigorev seeking revenge. Once there he committed theft and arson and threatened murder. On December 3 the peasants summoned their assembly and decided to end the matter by doing away with him. "At dusk the entire assembly, led by the village elder, surrounded the house where Andronov was hiding. He was caught and killed."

Here we have cases of straightforward, premeditated, collective murder by a community. Yet summary justice also included ingenious tortures, all described in great detail by the urban press, popular writers, and scholars. In Vetluzhskii dis-

---

[8] In Russian history, after the emancipation of the serfs in 1861.

trict of Kostroma province, according to one report, "this is what they do with thieves: they drive the handle of a whip into his rectum and shake up everything there. After this the peasant weakens and dies." Variations of this punishment could be found in other areas as well, where a jagged stick might be used so that it could not be removed. Some thieves and arsonists had nails driven into their heads or wooden pins behind the fingernails; others were stripped naked in winter and drenched with cold water until they died.

Horse thieves inspired the greatest fear and hatred in the Russian countryside. They usually operated in gangs, sometimes composed of several hundred members who formed networks or "societies," dividing a territory among themselves to carry out their trade. With organizations stretching into several provinces and controlling many officers of the rural police force, horse thieves worked with little fear of capture, wielding great power among the populace. Villagers knew that revenge was likely to follow if they reported the thieves' activities in their locality. Yet for peasants a horse represented the most valuable piece of property, without which farming would be impossible, as countless sayings attest: "Without a horse you're not a ploughman"; "Without a horse you're another's worker"; or "A peasant without a horse is like a house without a ceiling." Thus villagers encountering horse thieves confronted a situation in which they were prey to a parasitic gang that stole their major means of subsistence, and all too often the peasants could take no measures to prevent this loss.

When a horse thief did fall into their hands, peasants let loose an elemental fury with often deadly results. Ivan Stepanov, for example, was a well-known thief in one of Russia's central provinces. As a fellow villager later told the court investigator, hardly a person in the village had not suffered some loss from Ivan's trade. He had been publicly whipped on numerous occasions, and the last time he was caught the village assembly warned him that if he stole again, he would be exiled to Siberia. Many peasants shouted in protest that it was not worth it to spend community funds to send him away; it would be far easier just to kill him. After this Stepanov disappeared for eight months; rumors circulated that he had taken up work as a horse thief in another locality and had even sneaked into town several times to bring his wife some money. Following one of these nocturnal visits, Stepanov was leaving the village early in the morning when he spied a foal in Dmitrii Petrov's meadow, jumped onto the horse, and rode it into the nearby forest. Unfortunately for him, Stepanov was caught by a group of peasants who grabbed him and brought him back to the village, where a search had already begun for the foal. On learning of the thief's capture, a crowd gathered and started beating Stepanov. "They beat him for a long time, and Dmitrii Petrov beat him most of all. When Stepanov already lay motionless, Dmitrii cruelly kicked him in the back and sides. Seeing that he was dead, the assembly came together to discuss the matter. Petrov, a well-to-do farmer, begged them not to ruin him by turning him in, promising to help Stepanov's widow for the rest of his life. Because the murdered man was hated by all as a thief, whereas Petrov was a young man and a good worker, the assembly took pity on him. They asked the widow, who agreed to the deal, and the assembly voted unanimously to conceal the murder from officials."

Peasants reserved their worst punishments for horse thieves, who, if caught, were castrated or beaten in the groin until they died, had stakes driven into the throat or chest, were branded with hot irons, and had their eyes put out. Two punishments appear to have been particularly widespread. In one peasants first nailed a pully high onto a gatepost. Then the thief, with his hands and feet tied together, was raised into the air by a rope running through the pully. When he hung at a sufficient height, they released the rope. "He falls to the ground, striking the lower part of his back in a terrible way. This is repeated many times in succession, and each time the snap of the poor devil's vertebrae can be heard." The punishment might continue long after he had died. Another torture consisted of stripping a thief and wrapping his torso with a wet sack. A plank was then placed on his stomach and peasants beat on it with whatever they could find — hammers, logs, or stones — "gradually destroying the unfortunate's insides." The utility of such a punishment was that it left no external signs, so whoever found the abandoned body would suspect no crime. With the introduction of coroners as part of the court investigator's office in the late nineteenth century, however, the practice became far less foolproof. . . .

Given the availability of courts for punishing these crimes, why did peasants continue to employ *samosud* knowing that, if discovered, they too could be punished? One reason was their conviction that the official courts did not punish severely enough. Even in those instances when villagers turned a criminal over to the authorities, they first inflicted their own penalty. Horse thieves and arsonists might be sentenced to several years of incarceration or exile, but eventually they regained their freedom and often took up their old trade. None knew this better than villagers who had to deal with the criminals again, especially if they returned seeking revenge, and a few years in prison did not seem a just punishment. Furthermore, peasants could never be certain the thief would be punished. The overburdened, understaffed, and inefficient rural police, even if honest, were no match for professional thieves working in large groups and living secretly in prosperous, well-protected settlements. Peasants also mistrusted the official courts and attempts by outsiders to meddle in local affairs, feeling that they best knew how to treat criminals who threatened their community. They showed particular reluctance to turn a fellow villager over to an alien authority, for as one saying went, "He's *our* criminal and it's up to us to punish him."

Russian peasants also had ways of dealing with persons whose magical powers endangered the health and welfare of community members, crops, and livestock (recall Agrafena Ignatieva!). Belief in sorcery and maleficent spells remained an active element of peasant culture throughout the period, and villagers frequently utilized practitioners of magical or healing arts for many purposes. But when some disaster such as plague, epidemic, or crop failure befell the community, blame might be placed on the very people whose powers previously had appeared beneficial. Somehow, it was believed, they had been offended and were seeking revenge on the entire village or certain of its members. It proved difficult to accuse these people in court, for official law no longer recognized witchcraft as a criminal offense and often punished the complainants themselves while the sorcerer went free. As with horse theft, then, villagers confronted with maleficent spells felt that they were unprotected by state law and had to take matters into their own hands. When the "culprit" was identified, peasants meted out punishment of similar brutality to that suffered by horse thieves, and their justice often resulted in the murder of the accused.

The link between peasant culture and *samosud* appears most dramatically in instances of popular reprisal against suspected practitioners of magic. *Samosud* of sorcerers and witches could not be written off as an aberration as long as epidemics and other natural phenomena were explained within a framework of supernatural causation, and the ease with which devious charlatans and criminals exploited peasant beliefs merely confirms that such a mode of explanation continued to operate in the countryside throughout the late nineteenth century. Cases I have examined conform to the general, Western pattern of witchcraft accusations in which the main victims were impoverished elderly persons, itinerants, and the socially isolated. Despite peasants' traditional generosity toward wanderers and beggars, when such a person depended on others in the community for daily subsistence, she or he might come to be seen as a burden and, under the proper circumstances (such as an outbreak of disease), could easily become the target of hostility. Other cases might arise from a grudge held by one villager against the "witch." Having little or no say in community affairs because of their economic (and, hence, social) position, these people were particularly vulnerable to any accusation — a fact well known to neighbors and other villagers, who may have used it to their advantage.

None of this is to say that accusations of witchcraft were only pretexts for settling preexisting conflicts in the village. Persons who accused a "witch" may have known the charge was false. Still, despite such incidents, most peasants who leveled witchcraft accusations, and those who punished the accused, were directed by their belief in the supernatural. Evidence of the widespread persistence of such belief is far too convincing for us to conclude otherwise.

It is all too easy to attribute the brutality of such punishments to the peasants' lack of "culture" or "legal consciousness" and to overlook the interaction of peasant and elite cultures that was involved. Earlier criminal codes provided for severe punishment, mutilation, or execution of horse thieves (as well as other criminals), and these punishments were carried out in public settings. Even more important was the often brutal punishment of serfs on gentry estates, which certainly contributed to the peasants' concepts and practice of justice in the village (though this influence must have worked in both directions). Official codes such as that of 1839 made corporal punishment one of the few penalties that peasant courts could impose in practice. If not directly modeled on official and gentry treatment of offenders, the punishments employed by peasants had developed as a complex mixture of official and popular forms of retribution.

In the three areas discussed in this article *samosud* was a response to threats against the community or challenges to village norms and authority. It was not "lawless violence," as outsiders claimed, but action aimed at suppressing particular forms of behavior and criminal activity that could disrupt social relations or seriously harm the village economy. With little protection against danger other than that offered by their own local rules and institutions, peasants responded with the weapons available to them: *charivaris,* public beatings, ostracism, and murder.

These weapons, however, differed in both form and purpose. Directed against village members, the *charivari* employed an array of symbols and rituals designed to reconcile criminal and community and to restore peaceful relations among villagers. Only if reconciliation was rejected did peasants resort to harsher measures, for in such cases the offender became an outsider by spurning the community itself. Violent *samosud,* in contrast, focused on outsiders — defined either as nonmembers of the community or those who, through the harm caused by their crime or because of their social isolation, removed themselves from the community, thus the absence of ritual "processions" with their symbolic expulsion and reconciliation. Outsiders, by definition, could not be brought into the community except through bonds of marriage or kinship, and when they threatened the well-being of the village, mechanisms of reconciliation did not function. The purpose of punishments used against them, therefore, was to ensure that they would pose no further threat.

Samosud also forced peasants to defend their juridical beliefs and practices before the dominant culture. Educated Russia viewed such acts not only as violations of the criminal code but as proof of the ignorance and low level of civilization in which the rural population was immersed. Villagers rejected official law on this matter, as they did on many issues that touched their lives, and continued to behave as necessity dictated, resorting to *charivaris* or violence when necessary and accepting the risks accompanying their collective actions. Peasants were clearly aware that state law forbade *samosud* because they frequently attempted to conceal the results of their popular justice, and probably succeeded more often than we would imagine. Yet their views of justice did not draw the same delimitations as official law with regard to which crimes they could and could not punish. Infractions punished by *vozhdeniia,* for example, concerned the community alone, and outsiders had no business meddling in such affairs regardless of what their law might forbid. Similarly, official courts did not punish crimes such as horse theft as severely as peasants believed they should; and in cases of witchcraft the state had ceased to regard this serious problem (as villagers saw it) to be a crime. Official law punished crimes according to an entirely different set of criteria from those used by the peasantry — criteria that often took little account of local needs and concerns; and participants in the murder of a horse thief or a witch may have found no alternative to their own methods of justice.

Peasant juridical beliefs, like *samosud* itself, were most concerned with protecting the community from disruptive and harmful forces. Their juridical practices thus developed as a body of ideas incorporating norms of behavior, rules, and principles that could best serve to maintain and preserve the community. Through the continual assertion of its principles in juridical practice, the rural community asserted and reproduced not only its worldview but also the social, economic, sexual, and cultural relations by which this very community took on meaning.

Although certain types of interaction with the dominant culture could be incorporated, transformed, or at least made manageable by the village population, other efforts to force changes on peasant views of law, crime, or justice threatened to disrupt basic mechanisms through which the reproduction of the community took place. *Samosud* was one such mechanism, and efforts to eradicate the practice highlights the larger clash between peasant and official culture. When the community's ability to preserve and reproduce itself appeared threatened by government laws or regulations, peasants resisted, rejected, or simply ignored them. No such reaction was seen when the state tampered with the township court, for its reform did not impinge on villagers' lives in significant ways. The survival of *samosud* well into the Soviet period should be viewed not merely as an indication of the tenacity of Russian peasant culture in an era of major socioeconomic change but as the continued viability of an important, local, and spontaneously generated institution designed to regulate and protect village society.

A WOMAN'S WORLD: DEPARTMENT STORES AND THE EVOLUTION OF WOMEN'S EMPLOYMENT, 1870–1920

Theresa M. McBride

A fixture of Western society today, the department store is actually a quite recent innovation. It first appeared in mid-nineteenth-century Paris and revolutionized the retail trade. Because department stores had a wide variety of products to sell and many employees, they differed greatly from traditional retail businesses. What new merchandising principles did the new stores espouse? What did the French novelist Émile Zola mean in claiming that the department store helped bring about a "new religion"? How did department stores change attitudes toward and patterns of consumption?

Theresa M. McBride, professor of history at the College of the Holy Cross, depicts the department store as the "world of women," of female customers and employees. McBride has consulted census lists, municipal statistics, contemporary publications, newspapers, police reports, and government records concerning workers and business in order to reconstruct the personal and work lives of female clerks. Who were the female clerks, and why did they choose to find employment in department stores, where hours were long, the pace often frenetic, the rules stifling, the threat of fines and dismissal constant, and the supervision intense? What could the clerks hope for in their careers?

Female employees today would not tolerate being locked up in dining halls, living in company apartments, and having their sexual lives the subject of department-store concern. But in the nineteenth century, department-store owners mixed capitalism with old-fashioned paternalism, combining the pursuit of profit with the enforcement of morality. The owners believed it was necessary to concern themselves with the after-work behavior of female clerks.

The female clerks had little time to relax or to go out, but when they could, they took advantage of the independence that wage-earning offered. Thus they

Theresa M. McBride, "A Woman's World: Department Stores and the Evolution of Women's Employment, 1870–1920," *French Historical Studies* 10 (Fall 1978): 664–683.

frequented inexpensive restaurants and enjoyed the attractions of city life. Why did other women of the same social background envy the female clerks' jobs and status? What major changes occurred by World War I that affected women's employment in department stores? Is the department store today to any extent still a "world of women"?

In the 1840s Aristide Boucicaut[1] took over a small retail shop for dry goods and clothing in Paris. This shop became the "Bon Marché," the world's first department store, and soon the idea was emulated by other commercial entrepreneurs throughout the world. The department store helped to create a "new religion," as Émile Zola[2] described the passion for consumption nurtured by the department stores' retailing revolution. As churches were being deserted, Zola argued, the stores were filling with crowds of women seeking to fill their empty hours and to find meaning for empty lives. The cult of the soul was replaced by a cult of the body — of beauty, of fashion. The department store was preeminently the "world of women," where women were encouraged to find their life's meaning in conspicuous consumption and where they increasingly found a role in selling. Thus, the department store played a highly significant role in the evolution both of contemporary society and of woman's place in that society.

The department stores came to dominate retail trade by introducing novel merchandising principles. Most obviously, they were much larger than traditional retail establishments and united a wide variety of goods under one roof; specialization was retained only in the *rayons* or departments into which the stores were divided. Department store entrepreneurs throughout the world evolved the techniques of retailing between the 1840s and 1860s, which included the important innovation of fixed pricing, and eliminated bargaining from a sale. Fixed pricing was a revolutionary concept because it altered the customary buyer-seller relationship, reducing the buyer to the role of passive consumer, whose only choice was to accept or reject the goods as offered at the set price. Even the buyer's desire for certain items was created through the tactics of large-scale retailing: publicity, display of goods, and low prices of items. The salesperson became a simple cog in the giant commercial mechanism; instead of representing the owner, the salesclerk became a facilitator, helping to create an atmosphere of attention and service while the merchandise "sold itself."

The low mark-up of the large stores allowed lower prices (hence the name — Bon Marché)[3] and helped to attract crowds of customers from throughout the city. The department stores could not simply depend upon the traditional bourgeois clientele of smaller shops (the upper classes ordered goods from their own sup-

---

[1] Merchant and philanthropist (1810–1877).

[2] Novelist (1840–1902).

[3] Cheap.

pliers) and had to attract customers from among the petite bourgeoisie.[4] By catering to the budgets and the "passion for spending" of the petite bourgeoisie, the department stores brought increasing numbers of people into contact with modern consumer society.

A significant part of the department stores' merchandising revolution was the presentation. Exhibits in the spacious galleries of the stores, large display windows, publicity through catalogs and newspaper advertising shaped illusions and stimulated the public's desires for the items offered. The salesperson was herself part of that presentation, helping to create an atmosphere of service and contributing to the seductiveness of the merchandise.

In order to attract customers and facilitate a heavy volume of sales, the department stores needed a new kind of staff. Whereas the shopkeeper could rely upon family members and a loyal assistant or two, the department store became an employer on the scale of modern industrial enterprises. In the 1880s the Bon Marché employed twenty-five hundred clerks; the Grands Magasins du Louvre . . . by 1900 had a staff of thirty-five hundred to four thousand, depending on the season. Smaller provincial stores typically employed several hundred people. The Nouvelles Galeries in Bordeaux, for example, had 554 employees in 1912, divided into sales (283), office staff (60), and stock control (211). In 1906, by comparison, more than half of all commercial enterprises in France employed no more than five people (54 per cent), and two-thirds had ten or fewer employees. The average number of employees was 2.8. With such a large number of clerks, the entrepreneur could not expect to treat them like family members nor to encourage their . . . hope that they might some day take over control of the store.

Beyond simple size, the department stores were innovators in the ways in which they recruited, trained, and treated their employees. The fixed price system and the practice of allowing customers to browse freely meant that a large percentage of the work force were simply unskilled assistants, who brought the items to the customers and took their payments to the cashiers. Costs were minimized by paying very low base salaries. But loyalty and diligence were assured by a highly graduated hierarchy in which the top ranks were achieved only through intense competition. Entrepreneurs like Boucicaut realized that in order to create the proper atmosphere in their stores they would have to reward top salespeople by the payment of commissions on sales and by allowing them to enjoy a high level of status and responsibility. The department stores formalized the system of recruitment, promotion, and rewards to create a group of employees who would espouse the interests of the firm as their own or be quickly weeded out.

Women were a crucial element in this system. In fact, although women did not form the majority of the stores' work force until after 1914, women dominated certain departments and came to symbolize the "world of women," as the department store was described. Women were both the clerks and the customers in this market place, for the mainstays of the new stores were fashions and dry

[4] The lower middle class.

goods. Women were scarcely new to commerce, but their role was expanding and changing in the late nineteenth century. A parliamentary investigation into the Parisian food and clothing industries found women clerks throughout those industries, and the report's conclusions insisted upon the importance of the unsalaried work of women who were *patronnes*[5] or who shared that responsibility with their husbands. Typically, several members of the family worked in family-run businesses, so that daughters also received some early work experience. Most shops could not have survived without the contributions of female family members. For the women themselves, this kind of work was both an extension of their domestic role and an important experience in the world of business. While the department stores involved women in commercial activity in a very different way, traditional commercial roles continued to be exercised by the wives and daughters of shopkeepers well into the twentieth century.

One of the best descriptions of the new store clerks emerges from the investigations of Emile Zola for his novel *Au bonheur des dames*,[6] in which the young heroine secures employment with a large department store closely modelled after the Bon Marché and the Grands Magasins du Louvre. Zola's heroine Denise is the carefully sketched model of the female clerk: young, single, and an immigrant to Paris from a provincial store.

Denise was hired at the store after the management assured itself of her experience and her attractiveness. In the first few days, she learned to adjust to the pace of work, the supervision of older saleswomen, and to the competitiveness of the older clerks who tried to monopolize the sales. Most beginners like Denise spent much of their time arranging displays of merchandise and delivering items to customers. During peak seasons, many clerks started as temporary help "with the hope that they would eventually be permanently hired," but only a small proportion of them survived this period of "training." During the first year, beginners received little more than room and board. But if the debutante could withstand the low salaries, long hours, and often heavy-handed surveillance of other salesclerks, she had a chance to enter the ranks of the relatively well-paid saleswomen.

At the highest level of the sales hierarchy were the department heads, *chefs de rayons,* and their assistants, whose responsibilities included not only sales but also the ordering of merchandise for their own divisions and the hiring and supervision of salespersonnel. Salespeople provided information about merchandise, and once items were sold, took them to be wrapped, and delivered the payment to the cashier. Saleswomen and men were generally divided into different departments: men sold male clothing, household furnishings, and even women's gloves and stockings, while women handled baby clothing and women's dresses, reflecting the pattern in the industry as a whole. Significantly, men made up the majority of department heads and assistants, though a few women managed to win out against the intense competition to head departments.

---

[5] Employers.

[6] *The Paradise of Women.*

Department stores employed many women who were not sales clerks. There were office staffs of women who carried on the ordering, advertising, and the mail-order business. In addition, the largest stores employed hundreds of seamstresses, who were clearly distinguished from the sales force by the designation *ouvrière*[7] (rather than "employee"). The seamstresses received none of the benefits of the employees, such as free lodging or medical care, and the market provided by the department stores for the handwork of the domestic garment-making workers kept the institution of "sweated" labor alive well into the twentieth century.

The proportion of women employed in the department stores steadily increased after a large strike by clerks in 1869. In part, employers recruited women because they represented a tractable labor force. Department stores gradually replaced some male clerks with female clerks who were more "docile" and "lacking in tradition" and who, consequently, would be less eager to strike. But there were other reasons for recruiting women clerks. Women were cheaper to hire than men and readily available because of the narrowing of other employment options for women. The spread of public education for women provided a pool of workers who were reluctant to work as seamstresses or domestics. And women workers impressed employers with their personal qualities of "politeness," "sobriety," and even a "talent for calculation."

Considering both the obvious advantages of a female work force and the important traditional role of women in commerce, it seems inevitable that women should have been hired as clerks in the new department stores. But women sales-clerks were recruited from different sources than other female workers and remained a distinctive group through the period of the First World War. Why women clerks replaced men when the occupational opportunities expanded in commerce is, then, not so simple a question.

Department store clerks were very different from the largest group of women workers in the late nineteenth century — domestic servants. The young women who came to work in the Parisian *grands magasins*[8] were recruited from the cities and towns of France, while the domestic servants came from the countryside. Over half (53 per cent) of the female clerks who lived in the Parisian suburbs in 1911 and worked in Parisian stores had been born in Paris. Zola noted that one-third of the Bon Marché's saleswomen were native Parisians and that this was a larger percentage than among the male clerks. Salesmen were undoubtedly more mobile both geographically and socially. Both male and female employees who were not native Parisians had generally moved there from some provincial city where they had completed the essential apprenticeship in another store.

Department store clerks, like other commercial employees, often came from the ranks of urban shopkeepers and artisans. Children of shopkeepers frequently worked for a time in the large stores to learn commercial skills before returning to work in the family business. Over half of the shopgirls living with parents

---

[7] Worker.

[8] Department stores.

were from employee or shopkeeping families. . . . The occupational backgrounds of French clerks were primarily the urban, skilled occupations. A few even came from possible middle-class backgrounds, having parents who were teachers or *commerçants*,[9] but these were rare. In general, a clerk was not a working-class girl working her way out of poverty but more typically a lower-middle-class girl whose father was himself commercially employed, if not a shopkeeper.

Department store clerks were young. But unlike other women workers, who might begin their working lives at eleven or twelve, store clerks were rarely under seventeen years old. The Parisian *grands magasins* selected women only after a period of training, and thus the majority of the work force were in their early twenties. . . . Domestic servants and seamstresses included a wider range of ages because women could be employed at much younger ages in those occupations and could go back to work in small shops or as charwomen or seamstresses after their families were grown.

The career of the sales clerk, however, could be very short. Apart from the attrition due to marriage, the occupation simply wore some women out. Stores rarely hired anyone over 30, and the unlucky woman who lost her job after that age might be permanently retired. Younger women were more attractive, stronger, and cheaper to employ than older, more experienced women.

The life of the department store clerk was monopolized by the store. About half of the unmarried women were housed by the stores. The Bon Marché had small rooms under the roof of the store, while the Louvre housed its employees in buildings nearby. The rooms provided by the Bon Marché for their female employees were small with low ceilings; each contained a simple bed, table, and chair. But though these rooms were unadorned and sometimes overcrowded, they were often better than the rented room a young clerk could expect to find on her own. The lodgings at the Bon Marché included social rooms, where the management provided pianos for the women and billiard tables for the men. Visitors of the opposite sex were not allowed there, not even other employees. A concièrge kept track of the employees, and her permission had to be requested in order to go out at night. Such permission was nearly always granted as long as the eleven o'clock curfew was respected. Although department store entrepreneurs were innovators in retailing practices, their attitudes toward employees retained the strong flavor of paternalism that was typical of small-scale retailing. In small shops, the woman employee was almost a domestic, living in and working with other members of the family in the shop. Store managers of the department stores acted "in loco parentis"[10] at times, too, by exercising strong control over the lives of their saleswomen to preserve respectable behavior and to protect the public image of their firms.

The practice of housing female employees on the premises illustrates a variety of capitalistic and paternalistic motivations. There was considerable advantage

[9] Tradespeople.

[10] In the place of the parents.

to having salesclerks housed nearby, given the long hours they were expected to work. Employers also expressed . . . concern about the kind of . . . behavior, such as drinking, which could result from a lack of supervision. Women and young male clerks were both the victims and the beneficiaries of this system; adult men were allowed much greater freedom. The offer of housing and other benefits was combined with the opportunity to more closely control the lives of salespeople. Because of the economic advantages of ensuring a well-disciplined work force, department store owners prolonged the paternalism of shopkeepers long after the size of the new enterprises had destroyed most aspects of the traditional relationship.

Department store clerks were surrounded by their work. Not only housed in or near the store but also fed their meals there, the women were never allowed out of the store until after closing. The large dining halls where employees took their midday meal were an important feature of the first department stores, and one contemporary described them as follows: "At each end of the immense dining halls were the department heads and inspectors; the simple male employees were seated in the center at long tables. Only the opening out of newspapers and the low hum of voices broke the silence, and everyone was completely absorbed in eating, for all were required to finish [in an hour]. . . ." Female clerks ate in a different room, separately from the men. There were three sittings to accommodate the large number of employees, the first one beginning at 9:30 A.M. The break was closely supervised, and each employee had less than an hour, calculated from the time she left her post until she returned there. Although employees only rarely complained about the food they were served, much criticism was levelled at the conditions under which employees were forced to eat. Despite protests, women employees were never allowed to leave the store nor to return to their rooms during their breaks. At the Galeries Lafayette, they were locked into their dining hall during the meal. This kind of control indicates more strongly the "severity" than the "paternal indulgence" which managerial policy espoused.

Work rules throughout the store were very strict. Employees were dressed distinctively as a way of identifying them and making them conscious of their relationship to the store. Until after 1900, male employees were required to arrive at work wearing a derby or "melon," and the women were uniformly dressed in black silk. Surveillance by inspectors and supervisors assured that employee behavior was as uniform as their dress. Employees were expected to begin work at 8 A.M., and penalties were imposed on the tardy. At the Magasins Dufayel, a clerk was fined 25 centimes for being five minutes late; if she were two hours late, she could lose an entire day's wage. The average workday lasted twelve to thirteen hours, for the department stores did not close until 8 P.M. in the winter and 9 P.M. in the summer. During special sales or while preparing displays for the new season, clerks frequently had to work overtime without any special compensation. Although clerks in small shops often worked even longer hours, work in the department stores was judged more tiring by two parliamentary investigators in 1900, who argued that the large crowds attracted to the new stores quickened the pace of work.

By 1900 the workday for most female clerks had been reduced in accordance with an 1892 law setting a ten-hour maximum for women. The length of the clerk's workday had aroused much concern about the women's health, but their situation was still . . . better than that of the thousands of seamstresses who worked in sweatshop conditions in Parisian attics for little pay. Even before the reform, the workday of the salesgirl had been the envy of domestic servants, whose freedom was much more limited and whose employers did not allow the few hours of leisure which shopgirls enjoyed.

Characteristic of the way in which reforms were effected was the campaign for Sunday closing. In the 1890s . . . the large department stores began to adopt the practice of remaining closed on Sundays, giving most of their work force a day off. Although some employees were still needed to mount special expositions, pre-pare for sales, or unload deliveries, Sunday closing assured virtually all the women clerks a day off per week. The campaign for Sunday closing . . . inspired the most significant level of employee organization seen in this period. Concerted pressure was exerted by the predominantly male unions who occasionally solicited the sup-port of women clerks and at times took up issues which were specifically female ones, such as the practice of locking up the women in their dining hall. As with other reforms, the chief opponents of reform were those who were concerned about the autonomy and survival of small shops that remained open longest in order to compete with the department stores. Overall, the challenge to the de-partment store owners' authority was slight.

The authority of the employer, evident in the rigid work rules . . . was . . . ob-vious in the firing policies. The threat of termination was an excellent tool for shaping docile, hard-working employees, and employers did not use it sparingly. At the Bon Marché, the new recruits were quickly sized up in terms of their suit-ability as Bon Marché employees; among the four hundred new employees who were hired in 1873, 37 per cent were fired in the first five years. Most firings came without warning or compensation. Commonly, employers were not required to provide their employees with advance notice of termination, and employees lived with the sense of insecurity.

In the "severe yet beneficent" approach, however, there were also sweeter in-ducements to employee loyalty. Entrepreneurs like Boucicaut of the Bon Marché or Cognacq[11] of the Samaritaine knew that the success of their ventures depended in large part upon the formation of loyal employees. The department stores offered numerous incentives of various kinds. Compensation was high compared to other female salaries. Though young clerks received little more than their room and board, the average salary of a top saleswoman was three hundred to four hundred francs per month around 1900. Even a single woman could live very comfortably in Paris on a salary of that level. By contrast, the average wage of a woman em-ployed in industry in 1902 was two francs per day, and the best industrial salaries scarcely exceeded three francs. Thus, a working woman rarely achieved an income

---

[11] T. E. Cognacq (1839–1928).

of 75 francs per month, compared to the average saleswoman's income of 75 francs per week.

Clearly the averages conceal an enormous range of salaries, since the greater part of the total was earned in commissions. All of the stores gave 1 or 2 per cent commissions on sales, . . . and, in addition, employees received discounts on merchandise purchased at the store. These incentives inspired many employees to associate their own interests with those of the firm but also to go into debt over their purchases of clothing and household items.

Long-term employees received the greatest advantages, such as the benefits from the provident fund begun by the Boucicaut family. After five years' service the store invested an annual sum on behalf of each employee. After 1886 a woman with 15 years of service could begin to draw benefits after the age of forty-five. The benefits averaged six hundred to fifteen hundred francs per year, depending on the individual's salary and length of service. . . . The fund paid death benefits to employees' families, and women clerks could draw a small sum from it when leaving the store to be married. At the Grands Magasins du Louvre, the store contributed two hundred francs per year to a similar fund. The Louvre also sponsored employee savings plans and invested in vacation homes for employees. In addition, Cognacq of the Samaritaine subsidized the building of inexpensive apartments on the outskirts of Paris, and the Boucicaut family built a hospital.

As a result, . . . department store owners earned a . . . reputation for philanthropy. . . . A parliamentary committee in 1914 reluctantly concluded that the department stores treated their employees better than family-run shops, even though the report . . . was generally hostile to large-scale retailing.

Critics of the department stores emphasized the destruction of the familial relationship between employer and employee in large-scale commerce, but store owners were scarcely indifferent to the quality of employees' family lives. Women employees received paid maternity leaves (up to six weeks at the Louvre)—an important innovation. Employers also promoted larger families by awarding gifts of two hundred francs for the birth of each child. The Samaritaine . . . ran a day nursery for the children of employees in the 1890s.

Employers took an interest in the employee's welfare to prevent harm to the public image of the firm. Disreputable or disruptive behavior by employees was punished by disciplinary action, including firing. Informal liaisons among employees were strongly discouraged, and upon discovery employees were forced to "regularize" their relationship or face immediate dismissal. Relationships among employees of the same store were not encouraged for fear that they would disrupt the work atmosphere. . . . In spite of such disapproval, marriages among employees were probably common. Once formalized, the relationship between two employees received the blessings of the management in the form of a monetary gift (generally one hundred francs). Whether employers induced women to retire after marriage is impossible to determine, but the percentage of married women in their work force was low.

Employer investment in employee productivity produced plans for paid sick leave, health care, and annual vacations. Most stores assured their employees of several sick days per year, and the Bon Marché employees could be admitted to the Boucicaut hospital for long-term illnesses. The Louvre sent several employees each year to a store-owned estate in the countryside for a "cure." Commercial employees were also among the first workers to receive annual paid vacations, although at first many of these so-called vacations were actually unpaid leaves during the dead seasons of January–February and August–September. . . . [P]aid holidays of several days to two weeks became common for department store employees in the early 1900s.

The combination of paternalistic motivations and publicity seeking also inspired the organized choral groups supported by the Bon Marché. The employee groups "le Choral" and "l'Harmonie" presented regular public concerts for employees, customers, and invited guests in the great galleries of the store. A winter concert could draw an audience of several thousand. Employees were also encouraged to participate in other uplifting types of leisure activities, such as the free language lessons offered in the evening hours.

In spite of these programs, employee life was scarcely ideal. What seemed like a life of ease and relative glamour often more closely resembled the hardships of other working-class women in the nineteenth century. Like domestic servants, shopgirls worked long hours and were heavily supervised. The lodgings in the "sixième étage"[12] of the department stores were . . . little better than that of the "chambres de bonnes."[13]

Commercial employees, like other Parisian working women, had levels of mortality which were strikingly high. Employees often suffered from tuberculosis and other respiratory diseases. The high level of mortality was not easy to explain, but no one disputed the fast pace of work and long hours, which could produce fatigue and reduce the employee's immunity to certain diseases. Thus, the first protective legislation dealt directly with the problem of fatigue, requiring that a seat be provided for every female employee in the store. The legislation could not assure, however, that the clerks would actually be allowed to rest during the day. Noted an investigator in 1910:

> Among other examples, last October I saw a new salesgirl who remained standing from 8 A.M. to 7 P.M. near a sales table full of school supplies in the midst of an indescribable jostling, in a stuffy atmosphere, without stopping, often serving several customers simultaneously, accompanying them to the cashier and hurrying to return to her station; she was constantly under the threat of a reprimand from her department head, and with all of that, she had to be always smiling, amiable, even when the excessive pace of work rendered that especially difficult.

Street sales represented the worst abuse of employees, since they required a similar regimen but completely out-of-doors, even in the winter. These sales . . .

---

[12] The sixth floor (the seventh floor, counting the ground floor).

[13] The maids' rooms.

were an important part of retailing, but the consequences for employees could be tragic. Several saleswomen wrote to *La Fronde*[14] in 1898: "One of our fellow workers died last winter from an illness contracted when she was required, as we ourselves are, to work outside exposed to all kinds of weather." Even once Sunday closing was secured, the long, unrelieved days of work contributed to tuberculosis, anemia, and a variety of nervous disorders. The pace of work and the crush of customers induced a level of stress which combined with the inadequate diet of most shopgirls gave rise to a variety of gastro-intestinal problems. The medical reports stress the obvious dangers in shop work of tuberculosis and other long-term disabilities, but they also asserted a connection between the physical environment and the morally degrading aspects of work for women.

Social observers in the nineteenth century often felt that female employment offered . . . too many opportunities for the sexual abuse of women. . . . The low salaries of most women made it impossible for them to support themselves without male companionship, which a girl acquired "at the price of her honor and her dignity." Some salesgirls could be seduced by wealthy customers or lecherous supervisors. . . . [T]he shopgirl was the victim of the role she had to play — an attractive amiable "doll," who was forced "to maintain an eternal smile." Whether or not she was sexually promiscuous, the salesgirl's role inspired moralists to imagine her debauchery.

A typical salesclerk was probably planning to marry a young employee or shopkeeper, and thus the suggestion of a sexual relationship might simply be a prelude to marriage. Salesgirls often came to the department stores with the hope of finding better suitors there. The inescapable fact that most salesclerks were young and single meant that their culture was that of young, urban, single people, whose attitudes and behavior were different from their middle-class employers.

The single state was almost a condition of employment, as it was with domestic service. Employees complained that the practice of providing housing inhibited their freedom to marry. About two-thirds of the female employees of the Louvre in 1895 were unmarried. In 1911, in the suburbs of Paris, only 14 per cent of the saleswomen were married. But the clerks hoped that work "was only a temporary occupation for them" and that they would ultimately retire from the occupation upon marriage. . . .

The young single employee . . . helped to create a new urban leisure culture in the years before the First World War. This culture included the attendance at concerts and sporting events. Employees took up bicycling, which itself allowed for freer sociability and a new style of courting. Employees also frequented cafés and certain restaurants. Musical groups and organized activities at the department stores were clearly intended to lure employees away from such public entertainments, but they did not succeed. Employees continued to use more of their leisure time in their own ways.

---

[14] The first newspaper run entirely by women.

Women employees could expect to have the use of their Sundays and a few evening hours . . . between closing and curfew time. Department store clerks generally purchased their own evening meal at a restaurant, and thus they developed the habit of public dining. Whole chains of inexpensive restaurants . . . were established to supply inexpensive meals to a new class of consumers — clerks and office employees. Cheap but respectable, such establishments catered to the limited budgets of employees and office clerks and were located near the banks and stores. Shopgirls could also dine inexpensively in the Latin Quarter, where, "needless to say, a woman alone is the commonest of sights and you will not hesitate to enter any of these establishments," according to the author of *A Woman's Guide to Paris*. Unlike the working classes, who frequented cafés mainly at mid-day, employees, especially the male clerks, were highly visible in the evenings in the cafés and restaurants of central Paris.

Leisure for the female clerk also included Sunday strolls in the parks, mixing with young soldiers, servant girls, and bourgeois families. Shopgirls were said to "shine" in their leather boots and stylish hats, which set them apart from the other working girls. The salesgirl's dress expressed the ambiguity of her position. On the street, employees' appearances showed a preoccupation with their public image; most of the women tried to dress attractively in spite of the cost. "The employees seem the queens of the urban proletariat. When one encounters them in the street, it is difficult to distinguish them from ambitious petit bourgeois: they wear hats, gloves, and fine boots. This is a necessity, it seems, in their occupation, but it costs them dearly." The stylish clothes of the shopgirl suggest two things about the experience of store clerks before 1914. The salesclerk herself was affected by the retailing revolution of the department stores and seduced by the attractiveness of current fashions. But the salesclerk's behavior was also the result of her ambiguous social position, a status which was complicated by the enormous range of salaries and benefits within the sales hierarchy. Zola suggested that the department store clerk was "neither a worker nor a lady . . . [but] a woman outside." Monsieur Honoré of the Louvre suggested that young clerks were recruited from the working classes because they were attracted by the idea of escaping a life of manual labor. But the reality is more complex than the desire of a working-class girl to become a bourgeoise. The department stores did offer their employees an important chance for mobility — the owners of the four major department stores had started their careers as simple employees. But for most clerks, and especially for a woman, the possibility of becoming a shop owner was distant. Instead, one could hope to be promoted in the store's hierarchy, although even this kind of promotion was more difficult for women to achieve than for men.

The reality of mobility is impossible to assess precisely, but one can gain an impression of what a female salesclerk may have achieved by her experience in a department store. Most salesclerks came from the petite bourgeoisie and in particular from employee families. Moreover, the young women who found suitors most often married other employees. During the 1880s, when the city of Paris gathered data on marriages, the percentage of female clerks who married male employees was between 45 and 50 per cent. The intermarriage of clerks was the result of their associations at work and also of their desire for a respectable life. Rather than raising them into the middle class, their endogamy helped to form an independent lower-middle-class culture. Through marriage, employees tied their lives and their fortunes together, forming a group whose experiences and aspirations were significantly different from those above and below them.

The transition from shopkeeping to modern merchandising did not represent an easy process for employees. It was the male department store clerks who organized the first union and mounted the largest and earliest strikes of employees. Again in 1919 and 1936, department store clerks, by this time predominantly female, contributed heavily to the labor struggles of those crisis years. Employer paternalism, which had characterized the first generation of department stores, earned the employers a reputation for philanthropy, but it . . . enclosed the salesclerk in an interlocking structure of life and work that was difficult to escape.

Inevitably, fashions in clothing and in retailing changed, and the First World War accelerated the pace of those changes. The era of live-in clerks ended. Women came to predominate in the ranks of department store employees. Declining salaries and benefits during the war years were only partially restored by the wave of strikes in 1919. Female clerks gained a forty-eight hour week in 1917 but never recovered their élite status among working women.

As department store work evolved, so did the work experience of most women. By 1920 clerical work in offices as well as shops was much more common for women. Whereas in 1906 only one woman in ten worked as an employee, by 1936 one in every three was employed as a clerk. From the feminization of clerical work resulted the "deprofessionalization" of the clerk: lower salaries, the influx of unskilled labor, and declining benefits. The evolution of department store work since the 1840s has thus been an example of broader social changes. This "paradise of women," as Zola described the department store in the 1880s, became truly feminized only after the First World War, but the experience of female salesclerks in the first generation of department stores suggests much about the changing character of work and the place of women in that transformation.

PART FOUR

CONTEMPORARY EUROPE

Alistair Horne
Alex de Jonge
William J. Chase
Christopher R. Browning
Ellen Furlough
Kristina Orfali
Norman M. Naimark

One might argue that the past century has been the worst in the history of Western civilization. Mass murder and widespread torture, made easier by new technologies, have led us to view prior epochs as remarkably humane. Totalitarianism and genocide are two of the twentieth century's contributions to humankind, and nuclear catastrophe, now a permanent specter looming ominously offstage, may be the third. Few regions of Europe have not experienced the sequence of recent horrors that include World War I, Fascist and Communist brutalities, World War II and the Holocaust, and the terrorism that currently punctuates modern life. Ethnic cleansing and mass murder and rape in the 1990s in the former state of Yugoslavia demonstrate the power of tribalism and the cruel side of human nature that Western civilization only partially veils.

These tragedies have markedly influenced the social history of contemporary Europe, for the lives of millions have been altered dramatically in short periods of time. (The significance of long durations of time — a century or more — studied analytically by historians of medieval and early modern Europe, becomes less noticeable in the contemporary era.) Indeed, warfare in this period has become total, involving entire populations, soldiers and civilians alike.

Warfare has been an endemic disease in Europe since at least the Middle Ages, but recently wars have devastated the Continent more than in previous centuries. Alistair Horne's essay re-creates the unspeakable horrors of the World War I Battle of Verdun, Christopher R. Browning tries to understand why ordinary Germans murdered Jews during the Holocaust, and Norman M. Naimark recounts the ethnic cleansing and hatreds in the wars of Yugoslav succession.

Alex de Jonge depicts vividly the hyperinflation and resulting socioeconomic disequilibrium in Germany a few years after World War I. Born in that same conflagration, the Russian Revolution promised a viable alternative to bourgeois society as well as to Fascism. In describing life in Moscow during the 1920s, William J. Chase allows us to see whether Communism did indeed bring about an egalitarian and efficient workers' society.

Because Europe has become more closely knit through economic ties, travel, and communication systems, occurrences in one country create ripples throughout the Continent. Local isolation and agricultural self-sufficiency are things of the past; changes in the economy very quickly affect everyone, and consumers nearly everywhere share a common culture and a higher standard of living than their ancestors had in preindustrial Europe. Who in Europe does not know of Coca-Cola and the ubiquitous McDonald's? One of the ideals of modern citizenship is keeping abreast of the news, made readily available by the mass media, because we have come to realize that individuals and society can no longer go their own way with impunity; we are all, in every aspect of our lives, affected by changes that take place far from us. The peasant in an isolated village, eking out an existence in total ignorance of the outside world, is fast becoming extinct, save perhaps in a few remote regions. Ellen Furlough's study of Club Méditerranée and French consumer culture emphasizes the difference between today's world and the one we have lost. So does Kristina Orfali in her depiction of recent Sweden, a culture that has repudiated many of the past characteristics of Western civilization.

In sum, the twentieth century was like no other, but remnants from earlier centuries still survive. In some ways — in regard to life expectancy and health, for example — people are better off; in others, they may be worse off, prey to new diseases and to new applications of technology that often are used to repress, oppress, and wage war. What issues do Westerners face now in the twenty-first century that are likely to haunt us in the years to come?

THE PRICE OF GLORY:
VERDUN 1916
Alistair Horne

If war is hell, then the Battle of Verdun, from February to December 1916, was its deepest circle. The French and Germans sustained approximately one million casualties. The horrors of the battle can scarcely be imagined, but Alistair Horne manages to immerse us in the sights, smells, and feelings that Verdun, the most destructive battle in history, evoked. Historians of warfare have begun to move away from descriptions of military maneuvers and biographies of generals and heroes to reconstructions of war from the perspective of the ordinary soldier. Horne takes that approach in this powerful, moving essay, part of a trilogy of books this British historian has written on the Franco-German conflict from 1870 to 1940. Horne's re-creation of the battle's horrors is especially vivid owing to his use of veterans' letters and diaries and of conversations he had with the participants and their relatives.

What was the approach march like, and how did the battlefield appear? Horne frequently refers to colors, something that historians of warfare tend to ignore, save when discussing uniforms or flags. He also speaks of the overwhelming odors of Verdun; the living mixed promiscuously with the dead. Indeed, Verdun was an open cemetery, with ghastly and mutilated corpses of both men and animals prominent everywhere. Filth and disease contributed to the enormous suffering. Above all was the nearly constant artillery bombardment raining death on those who could do little to protect themselves from indiscriminate shells. What does Horne mean by the statement that "Verdun was the epitome of a 'soldier's battle'"? What was the fate of the wounded?

Horne considers the runners, ration parties, and stretcher-bearers to have been the greatest heroes of Verdun. How did the high probability of death or mutilation and the constant, seemingly unendurable suffering affect the soldiers physically and mentally? Does the saying that "there are no atheists in a foxhole" ring true at Verdun? One wonders, after reading this selection, whether the suffering and deaths of the soldiers were meaningless, mere sacrifices on the altar of nationalism. Can you think of other, more recent wars where soldiers' deaths may well have been meaningless?

Alistair Horne, *The Price of Glory: Verdun 1916* (London: Macmillan, 1978), 185–210.

Although from March to the end of May the main German effort took place on the Left Bank of the Meuse, this did not mean that the Right Bank had become a "quiet sector." Far from it! Frequent vicious little attacks undertaken by both sides to make a minor tactical gain here and there regularly supplemented the long casualty lists caused by the relentless pounding of the rival artilleries. Within the first month of the battle the effect of this non-stop bombardment, by so mighty an assemblage of cannon, their fire concentrated within an area little larger than Richmond Park,[1] had already established an environment common to both sides of the Meuse that characterized the whole battle of Verdun. The horrors of trench warfare and of the slaughter without limits of the First War are by now so familiar to the modern reader that further recounting merely benumbs the mind. The Battle of Verdun, however, through its very intensity — and, later, its length — added a new dimension of horror. Even this would not in itself warrant lengthy description were it not for the fact that Verdun's peculiarly sinister environment came to leave an imprint on men's memories that stood apart from other battles of the First War; and predominantly so in France where the nightmares it inspired lingered perniciously long years after the Armistice.[2]

To a French aviator, flying sublimely over it all, the Verdun front after a rainfall resembled disgustingly the "humid skin of a monstrous toad." Another flyer, James McConnell, (an American . . .) noted after passing over "red-roofed Verdun" — which had "spots in it where no red shows and you know what has happened there" — that abruptly

> there is only that sinister brown belt, a strip of murdered nature. It seems to belong to another world. Every sign of humanity has been swept away. The woods and roads have vanished like chalk wiped from a blackboard; of the villages nothing remains but grey smears. . . . During heavy bombardments and attacks I have seen shells falling like rain. Countless towers of smoke remind one of Gustave Doré's[3] picture of the fiery tombs of the arch-heretics in Dante's "Hell." . . . Now and then monster projectiles hurtling through the air close by leave one's plane rocking violently in their wake. Aeroplanes have been cut in two by them.

. . . The first sounds heard by ground troops approaching Verdun reminded them of "a gigantic forge that ceased neither day nor night." At once they noted, and were acutely depressed by, the sombre monotones of the battle area. To some it was "yellow and flayed, without a patch of green"; to others a compound of brown, grey, and black, where the only forms were shell holes. On the few stumps that remained of Verdun's noble forests on the Right Bank, the bark either hung down in strips, or else had long since been consumed by half-starved pack-horses. As spring came, with the supreme optimism of Nature, the shattered trees pushed

---

[1] In London.

[2] Of 11 November 1918, ending hostilities on the western front.

[3] French illustrator and painter (1832–1883), famous for his illustrations of books, including Dante's *Divine Comedy.*

out a new leaf here and there, but soon these too dropped sick and wilting in the poisonous atmosphere. At night, the Verdun sky resembled a "stupendous *Aurora Borealis*," but by day the only splashes of colour that one French soldier-artist could find were the rose tints displayed by the frightful wounds of the horses lying scattered about the approach routes, lips pulled back over jaws in the hideousness of death. Heightening this achromatic gloom was the pall of smoke over Verdun most of the time, which turned the light filtering through it to an ashy grey. A French general, several times in the line at Verdun, recalled to the author that while marching through the devastated zone his soldiers never sang; "and you know French soldiers sing a lot." When they came out of it they often grew crazily rapturous simply at returning to "a world of colour, meadows and flowers and woods . . . where rain on the roofs sounds like a harmonic music."

A mile or two from the front line, troops entered the first communication trenches; though to call them this was generally both an exaggeration and an anachronism. Parapets gradually grew lower and lower until the trench became little deeper than a roadside ditch. Shells now began to fall with increasing regularity among closely packed men. In the darkness (for obvious reasons, approach marches were usually made at night) the columns trampled over the howling wounded that lay underfoot. Suddenly the trench became "nothing more than a track hardly traced out amid the shell holes." In the mud, which the shelling had now turned to a consistency of sticky butter, troops stumbled and fell repeatedly; cursing in low undertones, as if fearful of being overheard by the enemy who relentlessly pursued them with his shells at every step. Sometimes there were duckboards around the lips of the huge shell craters. But more often there were not, and heavily laden men falling into the water-filled holes remained there until they drowned, unable to crawl up the greasy sides. If a comrade paused to lend a hand, it often meant that two would drown instead of one. In the chaos of the battlefield, where all reference points had long since been obliterated, relieving detachments often got lost and wandered hopelessly all night; only to be massacred by an enemy machine-gunner as dawn betrayed them. It was not unusual for reliefs to reach the front with only half the numbers that set out, nor for this nightmare approach march to last ten hours or longer.

One of the first things that struck troops fresh to the Verdun battlefield was the fearful stench of putrefaction; "so disgusting that it almost gives a certain charm to the odour of gas shells." The British never thought their Allies were as tidy about burying their dead as they might be, but under the non-stop shelling at Verdun an attempt at burial not infrequently resulted in two more corpses to dispose of. It was safer to wrap the dead up in a canvas and simply roll them over the parapet into the largest shell-hole in the vicinity. There were few of these in which did not float some ghastly, stinking fragment of humanity. On the Right Bank several gullies were dubbed, with good cause, *"La Ravine de la Mort"*[4] by the French. Such a one, though most of it in French hands, was enfiladed by a

---

[4] "The Ravine of Death."

German machine gun at each end, which exacted a steady toll. Day after day the German heavies pounded the corpses in this gully, until they were quartered, and re-quartered; to one eye-witness it seemed as if it were filled with dismembered limbs that no one could or would bury. Even when buried,

> shells disinter the bodies, then reinter them, chop them to pieces, play with them as a cat plays with a mouse.

As the weather grew warmer and the numbers of dead multiplied, the horror reached new peaks. The compressed area of the battlefield became an open cemetery in which every square foot contained some decomposed piece of flesh:

> You found the dead embedded in the walls of the trenches, heads, legs, and half-bodies, just as they had been shovelled out of the way by the picks and shovels of the working party.

Once up in the front line, troops found that life had been reduced, in the words of a Beaux Arts[5] professor serving with the Territorials,[6] "to a struggle between the artillerymen and the navvy, between the cannon and the mound of earth." All day long the enemy guns worked at levelling the holes laboriously scraped out the previous night. At night, no question of sleep for the men worn out by the day's shelling (it was not unknown for men in the line to go without sleep for eleven days). As soon as darkness fell, an officer would lay out a white tape over the shell ground, and the "navvies" began to dig; feverishly, exposed, hoping not to be picked up by enemy flares and machine guns. By dawn the trench would probably be little more than eighteen inches deep, but it had to be occupied all day, while the enemy gunners resumed their work of levelling. No question of latrines under these conditions; men relieved themselves where they lay, as best they could. Dysentery became regarded as a norm of life at Verdun. Lice, made much of by combatants on other fronts, received little mention. With luck, by the second morning the trench might have reached a depth of barely three feet.

Over and again eye-witnesses at Verdun testify to the curious sensation of having been in the line twice, three times, without ever having seen an enemy infantryman. On going into the line for the first time, one second-lieutenant who was later killed at Verdun, twenty-six-year-old Raymond Jubert, recalled his Colonel giving the regiment instructions that must have been repeated a thousand times at Verdun:

> You have a mission of sacrifice; here is a post of honour where they want to attack. Every day you will have casualties, because they will disturb your work. On the day they want to, they will massacre you to the last man, and it is your duty to fall.

---

[5] From the École Nationale Supérieure des Beaux-Arts in Paris.

[6] The French Territorial Army was composed of veterans and older citizens. They usually took secondary jobs, thus freeing front-line troops for combat.

Battalion after battalion decimated solely by the bombardment would be replaced in the line by others, until these too had all effectiveness as a fighting unit crushed out of them by the murderous shelling.[7] After nights of being drenched by icy rain in a shell-hole under non-stop shelling, a twenty-year-old French corporal wrote:

> Oh, the people who were sleeping in a bed and who tomorrow, reading their newspaper, would say joyously — "they are still holding!" Could they imagine what that simple word "hold" meant?

The sensation provoked by being under prolonged bombardment by heavy guns is something essentially personal and subjective; first-hand accounts cover a wide range of experience. To Paul Dubrulle, a thirty-four-year-old French Jesuit serving as an infantry sergeant at Verdun, whose journals are outstanding for their un-embellished realism, it seemed as follows:

> When one heard the whistle in the distance, one's whole body contracted to resist the too excessively potent vibrations of the explosion, and at each repetition it was a new attack, a new fatigue, a new suffering. Under this régime, the most solid nerves cannot resist for long; the moment arrives where the blood mounts to the head; where fever burns the body and where the nerves, exhausted, become incapable of reacting. Perhaps the best comparison is that of seasickness. . . . [F]inally one abandons one's self to it, one has no longer even the strength to cover oneself with one's pack as protection against splinters, and one scarcely still has left the strength to pray to God. . . . To die from a bullet seems to be nothing; parts of our being remain intact; but to be dismembered, torn to pieces, reduced to pulp, this is a fear that flesh cannot support and which is fundamentally the great suffering of the bombardment. . . .

. . . More than anything else, it was the apparently infinite duration of the Verdun bombardments that reduced even the strongest nerves. Sergeant-Major César Méléra, a tough adventurer, who had sailed around the world in peacetime and who appeared little affected by the horrors of war, describes his experience of Verdun shell-fire initially with an unemotional economy of words: "Filthy night, shells." Three days later he was confiding to his diary that the night bombardment made him "think of that nightmare room of Edgar Allan Poe, in which the walls closed in one after the other." The following day: "Oh how I envy those who can charge with a bayonet instead of waiting to be buried by a shell," and, finally, the admission:

> Verdun is terrible . . . because man is fighting against material, with the sensation of striking out at empty air. . . .

---

[7] To us this kind of futile sacrifice symbolizes the First War mentality. Yet one must always remember the dilemma facing the French at Verdun. . . . By 1916 both sides had already experimented successfully with "thinning out" the forward areas to reduce shell-fire casualties. But in the cramped space at Verdun where the loss of a hundred yards might lead to the loss of the city the risk of any such thinning out could not be taken by the French. Similarly the Germans, always attacking, could not avoid a permanent concentration of men in the forward lines. (Author's note.)

. . . With the steadily increasing power of the French artillery, experiences of the infantryman on both sides became more and more similar. In June a soldier of the German 50th Division before Fort Vaux declared that "the torture of having to lie powerless and defenceless in the middle of an artillery battle" was "something for which there is nothing comparable on earth." Through this common denominator of suffering, a curious mutual compassion began to develop between the opposing infantries, with hatred reserved for the artillery in general. To Captain Cochin on the Mort Homme,[8] it seemed as if the two artilleries were playing some idiotic game with each other, to see which could cause the most damage to the two unhappy lines of infantrymen.

What the P.B.I. felt about their own gunners may be gauged from a French estimate that out of ten shells falling on a Verdun trench, "on an average two were provided by the friendly artillery." Sergeant Élie Tardivel tells how in June seven men from a neighbouring platoon had just been killed by a single French 155 shell:

> I met the company commander; I told him I had brought up some grenades and barbed-wire; I asked where I was to put them. He replied: "Wherever you wish. For two hours our own guns have been bombarding us, and if it goes on I shall take my company and bombard the gunner with these grenades!"

Emotions between the infantry and gunners resembled those sometimes held towards the heavy-bomber crews of World War II, whom the ground troops viewed as sumptuously quartered well away from the enemy, making brief sorties to spray their bombs indiscriminately over both lines. A French company commander, Charles Delvert, describes passing two naval batteries en route for Verdun:

> Not a single man on foot. Everybody in motors. The officers had a comfortable little car to themselves. . . . I looked at my poor troopers. They straggled lamentably along the road, bent in two by the weight of their packs, streaming with water, and all this to go and become mashed to pulp in muddy trenches.

Other infantrymen were irked by the impersonal casualness with which the heavy gunners crews emerged from their comfortable shelters to fire at targets they could not see, "appearing to be much less concerned than about the soup or the bucket of wine which had just been brought."

This picture is to some extent endorsed by the artillery themselves. Staff-Sergeant Fonsagrive, serving with a 105 mm. battery wrote in his journal during the peak of the March battle on the Right Bank, "the fine weather continues, the days lengthen; it is a pleasure to get up in the morning. . . ." Watching the planes dog-fighting overhead, there was plenty of leisure time for day-dreaming about wives and families. Later, Fonsagrive notes with some vexation:

---

[8] The "Dead Man," a hill between the town of Verdun and the front line that was the scene of ferocious combat.

One day when, quietly sitting underneath an apple tree, I was writing a letter, a 130 mm. shell landed forty metres behind me, causing me a disagreeable surprise.

. . . Not all French gunners, however, were as fortunate as Sergeant Fonsagrive. When death came from the long-range German counter-battery guns, it came with frightening suddenness. A gunner sipping his soup astraddle his cannon, a group of N.C.O.s playing cards would be expunged by an unheralded salvo. In action, the field artillery particularly had even less cover than the infantry; often reduced still further by officers of the old school of that notably proud French arm, *"La Reine des Batailles,"* [9] who believed (and there were still many like them) that to take cover under fire was almost cowardice. Casualties among some batteries were in fact often at least as high as among the infantry. Captain Humbert, a St. Cyrien [10] of the 97th Infantry Regiment, testifies to the effect of the German artillery's systematic sweeping of the back areas, knowing that the French field batteries must all be there:

Nobody escapes; if the guns were spared today, they will catch it tomorrow. . . . Whole batteries lie here demolished. . . .

Lieutenant Gaston Pastre, though also a heavy gunner, provides a very different picture to Fonsagrive. Arriving at Verdun in May, he found the unit he was relieving had lost forty per cent of its effectives; "If you stay here a month, which is normal," they warned him, "you will lose half of yours too." The reverse slopes up to Fort St. Michel on the Right Bank, where Pastre's battery was sited, were crammed with every calibre of gun; it was "nothing more than one immense battery, there are perhaps 500 pieces there. A wonderful target for German saturation fire — anything that falls between Fort Michel and the road is good." There were generally only two periods of calm in the day; between 4 and 6 A.M. and between 4 and 7 P.M. when, like subhuman troglodytes, the French gunners emerged from the ground to repair the damage. For the rest of the time, to move from one shelter to another — a distance of about twenty yards — required considerable courage. By night the solitary road from Verdun came under constant fire from the German gunners, certain that French munition columns must be coming up it nose to tail. It presented "a spectacle worthy of Hell," in which men not killed outright were often hurled off their gun carriages by shell blast, to be run over and crushed by their own caissons in the dark.

Next to the incessant bombardment, the stink of putrefaction, and the utter desolation of the battlefield, Verdun combatants testify again and again to the terrifying isolation, seldom experienced to the same degree in other sectors. Verdun was the epitome of a "soldier's battle." Within an hour or less of the launching of each organized attack or counter-attack, leadership over the lower echelons ceased to play any significant role. Company commanders would lose all but the most

---

[9] "The Queen of Battles."

[10] Someone who had attended St. Cyr, the principal French military academy.

spasmodic and tenuous contact with their platoons, often for days at a time. The situation where one French machine-gun section found itself holding a hole in the front two hundred yards wide with its two machine guns for several days in complete detachment from the rest of the army, was by no means unique. To add to this demoralizing sense of isolation, the tenacious curtain of smoke from the bombardment meant that the front line frequently could not see the supporting troops behind; nor, worse still, could their rockets of supplication asking for the artillery to bring down a barrage, or cease shelling their own positions, be seen at the rear. Countless were the true heroes of Verdun, fighting small Thermopylaes[11] in the shellholes, who remained unsung and undecorated because no one witnessed their deeds.

> After twenty months of fighting, where twenty times I should have died [Raymond Jubert admitted] I have not yet seen war as I imagined it. No; none of those grand tragic tableaux, with sweeping strokes and vivid colours, where death would be a stroke, but these small painful scenes, in obscure corners, of small compass where one cannot possibly distinguish if the mud were flesh or the flesh were mud.

Of all the participants qualifying for the title of hero at Verdun, probably none deserved it more than three of the most humble categories: the runners, the ration parties, and the stretcher-bearers. As a regular lieutenant in charge of the divisional runners at Souville stated, simply: "The bravery of the man isolated in the midst of danger is the true form of courage." With telephone lines no sooner laid than torn up by shellfire, and the runner become the sole means of communication at Verdun, the most frequently heard order at any H.Q. was "send two runners." From the relative protection of their holes, the infantry watched in silent admiration at the blue caps of the runners bobbing and dodging among the plumes of exploding T.N.T. It was an almost suicidal occupation. Few paths were not sign-posted by their crumpled remains, and on the Mort Homme one regiment lost twenty-one runners in three hours.

Perhaps demanding even more courage, though, was the role of the *cuistot*,[12] *ravitailleur*,[13] or *homme-soupe*,[14] as the ration parties were variously called, in that it was played out in the solitariness of night.

> Under danger, in the dark, one feels a kind of particular horror at finding oneself alone. Courage requires to be seen [noted Jubert]. To be alone, to have nothing to think about except oneself . . . to have nothing more to do than to die without a supreme approbation! The soul abdicates quickly and the flesh abandons itself to shudders.

---

[11] Thermopylae was a small mountain pass in Greece where the Persians in 480 B.C.E. annihilated a Spartan army to the last man.

[12] Cook.

[13] Carrier of supplies.

[14] Soup man.

On account of the shelling, motor transport could approach no closer than a cross-roads nicknamed "Le Tourniquet"[15] at the end of the *Voie Sacrée*.[16] The massacre of the horses, unable to take cover upon the warning whistle of a shell, had become prohibitive. Thus all rations for the men at the front had to come up on the backs of other men. The *cuistots,* three or four to a company, were generally selected from among the elderly, the poor shots, and the poor soldiers. One of the most moving pictures printed in *L'Illustration*[17] during the war was of one of these unhappy *cuistots* crawling on his stomach to the front at Verdun, with flasks of wine lashed to his belt. Each carried a dozen of the heavy flasks, and a score of loaves of bread strung together by string, worn like a bandolier. They often made a round trip of twelve miles every night; even though, bent under their loads, at times they could barely crawl, let alone walk, in the glutinous mud. They arrived, collapsing from fatigue, only to be cursed by comrades, desperate from hunger and thirst, on finding that the flasks of precious *pinard*[18] had been punctured by shell fragments, the bread caked with filth. Frequently they never arrived. Fixed enemy guns fired a shell every two or three minutes on each of the few well-known routes with the accuracy of long practice. . . .

For all the gallantry and self-sacrifice of the *cuistots,* hunger and thirst became regular features at Verdun, adding to the sum of misery to be endured there. Twenty-two-year-old Second-Lieutenant Campana notes how he dispatched a ration party of eight men one night in March. The following morning five came back — without rations. That night another eight set out. None returned. The next night some hundred men from all companies set forth, but were literally massacred by violent gunfire. After three days without food, Campana's men were reduced to scavenging any remnants they could find upon the bodies lying near their position. Many had been decomposing for several weeks. The experience was more the rule than the exception; so too, as winter sufferings gave way to a torrid summer, was this spectacle:

> I saw a man drinking avidly from a green scum-covered marsh, where lay, his black face downward in the water, a dead man lying on his stomach and swollen as if he had not stopped filling himself with water for days . . .

Worst of all was the lot of the stretcher-bearers, which usually fell — until the supply was used up — to the regimental musicians. The two-wheeled carts that comprised the principal means of transporting the wounded on other French sectors proved quite useless over the pock-ridden terrain at Verdun; the dogs used to sniff out the wounded went rabid under the shelling. Unlike the runners or the *cuistots,* when carrying a wounded man the unhappy *musiciens-*

---

[15] The turnstile.

[16] The "Sacred Way," the road that took the French soldiers to Verdun.

[17] A French newspaper.

[18] Wine.

brancardiers[19] could not fling themselves to the ground each time a shell screamed overhead. Often the demands simply exceeded what human flesh could obey. Response to pleas for volunteers to carry the wounded was usually poor, and the troops at Verdun came to recognize that their chances of being picked up, let alone brought to medical succour, were extremely slim.

During the Second World War, there were cases when the morale of even veteran British Guardsmen suffered if, in the course of an action, they were aware that surgical attention might not be forthcoming for at least five hours. On most Western battlefields, it was normally a matter of an hour or two. Surgical teams and nursing sisters, copiously provided with blood plasma, sulfa-drugs, and penicillin, worked well forward in the battle area, so that a badly wounded man could be given emergency treatment without having to be removed along a bumpy road to hospital. For the more serious cases, there was air transport direct to base hospital, possibly hundreds of miles to the rear. In contrast, at Verdun a casualty — even once picked up — could reckon himself highly fortunate if he received any treatment within twenty-four hours. During the desperate days of July, the wounded lingered in the foul, dark, excrement-ridden vaults of Fort Souville for over six days before they could be evacuated.

Poorly organized as were the French medical services, demand far outstripped supply almost throughout the war, but several times at Verdun the system threatened to break down altogether. There were never enough surgeons, never enough ambulances, of course no "wonder drugs," and often no chloroform with which to perform the endless amputations of smashed limbs. If a casualty reached the clearing station, his ordeals were by no means over. Georges Duhamel, a doctor at Verdun . . . , vividly describes the chaos in one of these primitive charnel houses in *"La Vie des Martyrs."*[20] Arriving during the early stages of the battle, he noted in despair, "there is work here for a month." The station was overflowing with badly wounded who had already been waiting for treatment for several days. In tears they beseeched to be evacuated; their one terror to be labelled "untransportable." These, not merely the hopelessly wounded, but those whose wounds were just too complicated for the frantic surgeons to waste time probing, or who looked as if they would be little use to the army again, were laid outside in the bitter cold. It was not long before German shells landed among this helpless pile, but at least this reduced the doctors' work. Inside, the surgeons, surrounded by dustbins filled with lopped-off limbs, did the best they could to patch up the ghastly wounds caused by the huge shell splinters.

Later Duhamel and his team were visited by an immaculate Inspector-General who told them they really ought to plant a few flowers around the gloomy station. As he left, Duhamel noticed that someone had traced *"Vache"*[21] in the dust on the brass-hat's car.

---

[19] Musician–stretcher-bearers.

[20] *The Life of the Martyrs.*

[21] Swine.

At the clearing stations the backlog of even the partially repaired mounted alarmingly as, with the constant demand of the *Voie Sacrée* supply route, all too few vehicles could be spared for use as ambulances. British Red Cross sections appeared on the front . . . and later American volunteers. Though the crews drove twenty-four hours at a stretch, unable to wear gasmasks because they fogged up, still there seemed to be more wounded than the ambulances could hold. Meanwhile in the overcrowded, squalid base hospitals, those who had survived so far were dying like flies, their beds immediately refilled. Clyde Balsley, an American very badly wounded with the "Lafayette Squadron," noted in contrast that

> the miracles of science after the forced butchery at Verdun . . . made a whole year and a half at the American Hospital pass more quickly than six weeks in the [French] hospital at Verdun.

The wounded in these hospitals lived in terror of the periodical decoration parades; because it had become a recognized custom to reward a man about to die with the *Croix de Guerre*.[22] Of slight compensation were the visits of the "professional" visitors, such as the patriotic, exquisite "Lady in Green," described by Duhamel, who spoke inspiredly to the *grands mutilés*[23] of

> the enthusiastic ardour of combat! The superb anguish of bounding ahead, bayonet glittering in the sun. . . .

Equipment in these hospitals was hopelessly inadequate, but at Verdun the situation was exacerbated still further by the poisonous environment, virulently contaminated by the thousands of putrefying corpses. Even the medically more advanced Germans noted the frequency of quite minor wounds becoming fatal. Gas gangrene, for which an effective cure was not discovered till a few weeks before the Armistice, claimed an ever-increasing toll; during the April fighting on the Right Bank, one French regiment had thirty-two officers wounded of whom no fewer than nineteen died subsequently, mostly from gas gangrene. In an attempt to reduce infection of head wounds, Joffre[24] issued an order banning beards; the *poilus*[25] complained bitterly, and still the wounded died. After the war, it was estimated that, between 21 February and the end of June, 23,000 French alone had died in hospitals as a result of wounds received at Verdun. How many more died before ever reaching hospital can only be conjectured.

So much for the physical; and what of the spiritual effects of this piling of horror upon horror at Verdun? Many were affected like the young German student, highly religious and torn with doubts about the morality of war, who wrote home shortly before being killed at Verdun on 1 June:

[22] Military Cross.

[23] Badly disabled.

[24] Joseph Joffre (1852–1931), French commander in chief, 1911–1916.

[25] French soldiers.

Here we have war, war in its most appalling form, and in our distress we realize the nearness of God.

As in every war men confronted with death who had forgotten, or never knew how, began to pray fervidly. Sergeant Dubrulle, the Jesuit priest, was revolted above all by the hideous indignities he had seen T.N.T. perpetrate upon the bodies God had created. After one terrible shelling early in the battle when human entrails were to be seen dangling in the branches of a tree and a "torso, without head, without arms, without legs, stuck to the trunk of a tree, flattened and opened," Dubrulle recalls "how I implored God to put an end to these indignities. Never have I prayed with so much heart." But, as day after day, month after month, such entreaties remained unanswered, a growing agnosticism appears in the letters from the men at Verdun. Later, on the Somme, even Dubrulle is found expressing singularly non-Catholic sentiments:

> Having despaired of living amid such horror, we begged God not to have us killed — the transition is too atrocious — but just to let us be dead. We had but one desire; the end!

At least this part of Dubrulle's prayer was answered the following year.

For every soldier whose mind dwelt on exalted thoughts, possibly three agreed with Sergeant Marc Boasson, a Jewish convert to Catholicism, killed in 1918, who noted that at Verdun "the atrocious environment corrupts the spirit, obsesses it, dissolves it."

Corruption revealed itself in the guise of brutalization. . . .

It was indeed not very exalting to watch wounded comrades-in-arms die where they lay because they could not be removed. One Divisional Chaplain, Abbé Thellier de Poncheville, recalls the spectacle of a horse, still harnessed to its wagon, struggling in the mud of a huge crater. "He had been there for two nights, sinking deeper and deeper," but the troops, obsessed by their own suffering, passed by without so much as casting a glance at the wretched beast. The fact was that the daily inoculation of horror had begun to make men immune to sensation. Duhamel explains:

> A short time ago death was the cruel stranger, the visitor with the flannel footsteps . . . today, it is the mad dog in the house. . . . One eats, one drinks beside the dead, one sleeps in the midst of the dying, one laughs and one sings in the company of corpses. . . . The frequentation of death which makes life so precious also finishes, sometimes, by giving one a distaste for it, and more often, lassitude.

A period of conditioning on the Verdun battlefield manufactured a callousness towards one's own wounded, and an apathetic, morbid acceptance of mutilation that seem to us — in our comfy isolation — almost bestial. Captain Delvert, one of the more honest and unpretentious of the French war-writers, describes his shock on approaching the Verdun front for the first time, when his company filed past a man lying with his leg shattered by a shell:

Nobody came to his assistance. One felt that men had become brutalized by the preoccupation of not leaving their company and also not delaying in a place where death was raining down.

In sharp contrast to the revolted and tortured Dubrulle, young Second-Lieutenant Campana recounts how, at the end of his third spell in the line at Verdun, he cold-bloodedly photographed the body of one of his men killed by a shell that hit his own dugout,

> laid open from the shoulders to the haunches like a quartered carcass of meat in a butcher's window.

He sent a copy of the photograph to a friend as a token of what a lucky escape he had had.

Returning from the Mort Homme, Raymond Jubert introspectively posed himself three questions:

> What sublime emotion inspires you at the moment of assault?
> I thought of nothing other than dragging my feet out of the mud encasing them.
> What did you feel after surviving the attack?
> I grumbled because I would have to remain several days more without *Pinard*.
> Is not one's first act to kneel down and thank God?
> No. One relieves oneself.

This kind of moral torpor was perhaps the commonest effect of a spell at Verdun, with even the more sensitive — like Jubert — who resisted the brutalizing tendency admitting to a congelation of all normal reactions. Jubert also recalls the man in his regiment who, returning from the front, was overjoyed to find his house on the outskirts of Verdun still intact; but, on discovering that all its contents had been methodically plundered, he simply burst into laughter.

To troops who had not yet been through the mill at Verdun, passing men whom they were about to relieve was an unnerving experience; they seemed like beings from another world. Lieutenant Georges Gaudy described watching his own regiment return from the May fighting near Douaumont:[26]

> First came the skeletons of companies occasionally led by a wounded officer, leaning on a stick. All marched, or rather advanced in small steps, zigzagging as if intoxicated. . . . It was hard to tell the colour of their faces from that of their tunics. Mud had covered everything, dried off, and then another layer had been re-applied. . . . They said nothing. They had even lost the strength to complain. . . . It seemed as if these mute faces were crying something terrible, the unbelievable horror of their martyrdom. Some Territorials who were standing near me became pensive. They had that air of sadness that comes over one when a funeral passes by, and I overheard one say: "It's no longer an army! These are corpses!" Two of the Territorials wept in silence, like women.

---

[26] The major fortress at Verdun.

Most of the above accounts come from the French sources. For, compressed in their hemmed-in salient and hammered by an artillery that was always superior, maintained and succoured by organization that was always inferior, things were almost invariably just that much worse for the French. But, as time went on, the gap between the suffering of the opposing armies became narrower and narrower, until it was barely perceptible. By mid April German soldiers were complaining in letters home of the high casualties suffered by their ration parties; "many would rather endure hunger than make these dangerous expeditions for food." General von Zwehl, whose corps was to stay at Verdun, without relief, during the whole ten months the battle lasted, speaks of a special "kind of psychosis" that infected his men there. Lastly, even the blustering von Brandis, the acclaimed conqueror of Douaumont for whom war previously seems to have held nothing but raptures, is to be found eventually expressing a note of horror; nowhere, he declares, not even on the Somme, was there anything to be found worse than the "death ravines of Verdun."

INFLATION IN WEIMAR GERMANY
Alex de Jonge

The most celebrated instance of prices spiraling out of control is the hyperinflation in Weimar Germany in 1923. At the outbreak of World War I, the dollar was worth four marks; by November 1923, a person needed four trillion marks to purchase one dollar. To put this unprecedented devaluation of Germany's currency into perspective, consider the Price Revolution of the sixteenth century. This great period of inflation began in Spain and prices rose highest there, approximately 400 percent over the course of the century. Contemporaries had difficulty understanding the causes, not to mention the effects, of that increase — significant to be sure, but small compared to the hyperinflation of 1923. Alex de Jonge, a professor of Russian and comparative literature, relies primarily on memoirs and travel accounts to re-create life in Germany during the extraordinary years of hyperinflation.

The German inflation was rapid and intense. What were the causes of the hyperinflation? The Nazis found it useful to blame the Allied powers of the First World War and the Treaty of Versailles, and many Germans came to believe the Nazi interpretation. Why would they not? After all, a man who should have known better, the director of the Reichsbank, implemented a solution for inflation that would have been laughable had it not been disastrous: the use of printing presses to churn out more and more currency.

Hyperinflation had profound effects on the German social fabric. How did hyperinflation cause social chaos and affect morality, including the Germans' sexual behavior? Why did barter become so popular? Was it a coincidence that virulent anti-Semitism appeared at this time? Alex de Jonge offers dramatic and often pitiable stories of the wreckage of lives that resulted from the economic disequilibrium. Yet some groups prospered while others suffered. What finally brought an end to the period of hyperinflation? Are you aware of any nation's recent economic collapse that has similarities with that of Weimar Germany?

The year 1923 has a special and dreadful connotation in German history, for it was the year of the great inflation. If defeat, abdication and revolution had begun

Alex de Jonge, *The Weimar Chronicle, Prelude to Hitler* (New York: New American Library, 1978), 93–105.

to undermine the traditional values of German culture, then the inflation finished the process so completely that in the end there were no such values left. By November 1918 there were 184.8 marks to the pound. By late November 1923 there were 18,000,000,000,000. Although the mark was eventually "restored," and the period of inflation succeeded by a time of relative prosperity for many people, life for anyone who had lived through the lunatic year of 1923 could never be the same again.

Such a cataclysmic loss of a currency's value can never be ascribed to a single cause. Once confidence goes, the process of decline is a self-feeding one. By late 1923 no one would hold German money one moment longer than it was really necessary. It was essential to convert it into something, some object, within minutes of receiving it, if one were not to see it lose all value in a world in which prices were being marked up by 20 percent every day.

If we go back beyond the immediate cause of hyperinflation — beyond a total lack of confidence in a currency that would consequently never "find its floor," however undervalued it might appear — we find that passive resistance in the Ruhr[1] was a major factor. Effective loss of the entire Ruhr output weakened the mark disastrously, encouraging dealers to speculate against it, since the balance of payments was bound to show a vast deficit. Confidence in the currency could only begin to be restored when resistance ended late in 1923.

It has been the "patriotic" view that reparations were also a significant factor. Certainly they constituted a steady drain upon the nation's resources, a drain for which it got no return. But reparations alone would not have brought about hyperinflation. There were still other causes. Sefton Delmer[2] believes that the true explanation lay in Germany's financing of the war. She had done so very largely on credit, and was thereafter obliged to run a gigantic deficit. There were other more immediate causes, such as a total incomprehension of the situation on the part of Havenstein, director of the Reichsbank. Failing to understand why the currency was falling, he was content to blame it upon forces beyond his control — reparations — and attempted to deal with the situation by stepping up the money supply! . . .

By October 1923 it cost more to print a note than the note was worth. Nevertheless Havenstein mobilized all the printing resources that he could. Some of the presses of the Ullstein newspaper and publishing group were even commandeered by the mint and turned to the printing of money. Havenstein made regular announcements to the Reichstag to the effect that all was well since print capacity was increasing. By August 1923 he was able to print in a day a sum equivalent to two-thirds of the money in circulation. Needless to say, as an anti-inflationary policy, his measures failed.

. . . Certainly [inflation] had its beneficiaries as well as its victims. Anyone living on a pension or on fixed-interest investments — the small and cautious in-

---

[1] Belgian and French troops occupied the Ruhr Valley early in 1923 because the Germans had not delivered coal as the reparations agreement stipulated.

[2] A German newspaper reporter.

vestor — was wiped out. Savings disappeared overnight. Pensions, annuities, government stocks, debentures, the usual investments of a careful middle class, lost all value. In the meantime big business, and export business in particular, prospered. It was so easy to get a bank loan, use it to acquire assets, and repay the loan a few months later for a tiny proportion of the original. Factory owners and agriculturalists who had issued loan stock or raised gold mortgages on their properties saw themselves released from those obligations in the same way, paying them off with worthless currency on the principle that "mark equals mark." It would be rash to suggest . . . that the occupation of the Ruhr was planned by industrialists to create an inflation which could only be to their benefit. Yet we should remember that Stinnes,[3] the multi-millionaire, had both predicted that occupation and ended up the owner of more than 1,500 enterprises. It should also be remembered that some businessmen had a distinctly strange view of the shareholder. He was regarded by many as a burdensome nuisance, a drag upon their enterprise. He was the enemy and they were quite happy to see him wiped out to their benefit. Inflation was their chance to smash him. Witness the behavior of a banker at a shareholders' meeting at which it was suggested he should make a greater distribution of profit: "Why should I throw away my good money for the benefit of people whom I do not know?"

The ingenious businessman had many ways of turning inflation to good account. Thus employees had to pay income tax weekly. Employers paid their tax yearly upon profits which were almost impossible to assess. They would exploit the situation of a smaller businessman, obliged to offer six to eight weeks of credit to keep his customers, by insisting on payment in cash. The delay between paying for the goods and reselling them eroded any profit the small man might make, while the big supplier prospered.

Whether or not the industrialists actually caused inflation, their visible prosperity made them detested by an otherwise impoverished nation. Hugo Stinnes became an almost legendary embodiment of speculation and evil. Alec Swan[4] remembers how hungry Germans would stare at prosperous fellow countrymen in fur coats, sullenly muttering "Fabrikbesitzer" (factory owner) at them. The term had become an insult and an expression of envy at one and the same time.

Hyperinflation created social chaos on an extraordinary scale. As soon as one was paid, one rushed off to the shops and bought absolutely anything in exchange for paper about to become worthless. If a woman had the misfortune to have a husband working away from home and sending money through the post, the money was virtually without value by the time it arrived. Workers were paid once, then twice, then five times a week with an ever-depreciating currency. By November 1923 real wages were down 25 percent compared with 1913, and envelopes were not big enough to accommodate all the stamps needed to mail them; the excess stamps were stuck to separate sheets affixed to the letter. Normal com-

---

[3] Hugo Stinnes, speculator.

[4] An Englishman who lived in Germany during the 1920s.

mercial transactions became virtually impossible. One luckless author received a sizable advance on a work only to find that within a week it was just enough to pay the postage on the manuscript. By late 1923 it was not unusual to find 100,000 mark notes in the gutter, tossed there by contemptuous beggars at a time when $50 could buy a row of houses in Berlin's smartest street.

> A Berlin couple who were about to celebrate their golden wedding received an official letter advising them that the mayor, in accordance with Prussian custom, would call and present them with a donation of money.
> Next morning the mayor, accompanied by several aldermen in picturesque robes, arrived at the aged couple's house, and solemnly handed over in the name of the Prussian State 1,000,000,000,000 marks or one half-penny.

The banks were flourishing, however. They found it necessary to build annexes and would regularly advertise for more staff, especially bookkeepers "good with zeros." Alec Swan knew a girl who worked in a bank in Bonn. She told him that it eventually became impossible to count out the enormous numbers of notes required for a "modest" withdrawal, and the banks had to reconcile themselves to issuing banknotes by their weight.

By the autumn of 1923 the currency had virtually broken down. Cities and even individual businesses would print their own notes, secured by food stocks, or even the objects the money was printed on. Notes were issued on leather, porcelain, even lace, with the idea that the object itself was guarantee of the value of the "coin." It was a view of the relationship between monetary and real value that took one back five hundred years. Germany had become a barter society; the Middle Ages had returned. Shoe factories would pay their workers in bonds for shoes, which were negotiable. Theaters carried signs advertising the cheapest seats for two eggs, the most expensive for a few ounces of butter which was the most negotiable of all commodities. It was so precious that the very rich, such as Stinnes, used to take a traveling butter dish with them when they put up at Berlin's smartest hotel. A pound of butter attained "fantastic value." It could purchase a pair of boots, trousers made to measure, a portrait, a semester's schooling, or even love. A young girl stayed out late one night while her parents waited up anxiously. When she came in at four in the morning, her mother prevented her father from taking a strap to her by showing him the pound of butter that she had "earned." Boots were also highly negotiable: "The immense paper value of a pair of boots renders it hazardous for the traveler to leave them outside the door of his bedroom at his hotel."

Thieves grew more enterprising still in their search for a hedge against inflation.

> Even the mailboxes are plundered for the sake of the stamps attached to the letters. Door handles and metal facings are torn from doors; telephone and telegraph wires are stolen wholesale and the lead removed from roofs.

In Berlin all metal statues were removed from public places because they constituted too great a temptation to an ever-increasing number of thieves. One of the consequences of the soaring crime rate was a shortage of prison accommodation. Criminals given short sentences were released and told to reapply for admission in due course.

It was always possible that one might discover an unexpected source of wealth. A Munich newspaperman was going through his attic when he came upon a set of partly gold dentures, once the property of his grandmother, long since dead. He was able to live royally upon the proceeds of the sale for several weeks.

The period threw up other anomalies. Rents on old houses were fixed by law, while those on new ones were exorbitantly high. As a result in many parts of Germany housing was literally rationed. If one were fortunate enough to live in old rented property, one lived virtually free. The landlord, however, suffered dreadfully: to repair a window might cost him the equivalent of a whole month's rent. Thus yet another of the traditional modes of safe investment, renting property, proved a disaster. Hitherto well-to-do middle-class families found it necessary to take in lodgers to make ends meet. The practice was so widespread that not to do so attracted unfavorable attention suggesting that one was a profiteer. . . . Real property lost its value like everything else. . . . More telling is a famous song of inflation:

> *We are drinking away our grandma's*
> *Little capital*
> *And her first and second mortgage too.*

As noted in the famous and highly intelligent paper the *Weltbühne*,[5] the song picked out the difference between the "old" generation of grandparents who had scraped and saved carefully in order to acquire the security of a house, and the "new generation" for whom there could be no security any more, who "raided capital" or what was left of it, and were prepared to go to any lengths to enjoy themselves. Where their parents' lives had been structured with certainties, the only certainty that they possessed was that saving was a form of madness.

Not all Germans suffered, of course. Late in 1923 Hugo Stinnes did what he could to alleviate the misery of his fellow countrymen by the magnanimous decision to double his tipping rate in view of the inflation. Along with rents, rail fares were also fixed and did not go up in proportion to inflation. Consequently, travel appeared absurdly cheap. Alec Swan recalls crossing Germany in the greatest style for a handful of copper coins. Yet even this was beyond the means of most Germans. A German train in 1923 would consist of several first-class carriages occupied entirely by comfortable foreigners, and a series of rundown third-class carriages crammed to bursting with impoverished and wretched Germans.

Although the shops were full of food, no one could afford it except foreigners. Germans often had to be content with food not normally thought of as fit for human consumption. In Hamburg there were riots when it was discovered that the local canning factory was using cats and rats for its preserved meats. Sausage

---

[5] The *World Arena,* a left-wing journal.

factories also made much use of cat and horse meat. Moreover, . . . some of the most famous mass murderers of the age used to preserve and sell the meat of their victims in a combination of savagery and an almost sexual obsession with food that mythologizes much of the darkness and the violence that were latent in the mood of Weimar.

If 1923 was a bad year for the Germans it was an *annus mirabilis*[6] for foreigners. Inflation restored the sinking morale of the army of occupation; small wonder when every private found himself a rich man overnight. In Cologne an English girl took lessons from the *prima donna* of the opera for sixpence a lesson. When she insisted that in future she pay a shilling, the *prima donna* wept with delight. Shopping became a way of life: "All through that autumn and winter whenever we felt hipped we went out and bought something. It was a relaxation limited at home, unlimited in the Rhineland."

Germany was suddenly infested with foreigners. It has been suggested that the English actually sent their unemployed out and put them up in hotels because it was cheaper than paying out the dole. Alec Swan stayed with his family in a pension in Bonn. They had moved to Germany because life was so much cheaper there. . . .

To find oneself suddenly wealthy in the midst of tremendous hardship proved rather unsettling. Inflation corrupted foreigners almost as much as the Germans. The English in Cologne could think of nothing else.

> They talked with sparkling eyes and a heightened color, in the banks, the streets, the shops, the restaurants, any public place, with Germans standing around gazing at them.
>
> Scruples were on the whole overwhelmed by the sudden onslaught of wealth and purchasing power beyond one's dreams.

As Alec Swan put it:

> You felt yourself superior to the others, and at the same time you realized that it was not quite justified. When we went to Bellingshausen, which was a sort of wine place near Königswinter, we would start drinking in the afternoon. I would always order champagne and my Dutch friend would shake his head in disapproval. We'd have two ice buckets: he with some Rhine wine and me with German champagne. It was really rather ridiculous for a chap of my age to drink champagne on his own.
>
> Being as wealthy as that was an extraordinary feeling, although there were many things you couldn't get in Germany. It was impossible to buy a decent hat, for instance. But you could have any food you wanted if you could pay for it. I haven't eaten anything like as well as that in my life. I used to go to the Königshalle (that was the big café in Bonn) at eleven o'clock in the morning for a *Frühschoppen*[7] and a *Bergmann's Stückchen,* a large piece of toast with fresh shrimps and mayonnaise. For a German that would have been quite impossible.

---

[6] Extraordinary year.

[7] Pint of beer.

I paid two million marks for a glass of beer. You changed as little money as you could every day. No, one did not feel guilty, one felt it was perfectly normal, a gift from the gods. Of course there was hatred in the air, and I dare say a lot of resentment against foreigners, but we never noticed it. They were still beaten, you see, a bit under and occupied.

My mother did buy meat for three or four German families. I remember I bought an air gun, and, when I grew tired of it, I gave it to my German teacher's son, with some pellets. Some time later the woman came to me in tears saying the boy had run out of pellets, and they could not afford to buy any more.

On another occasion Swan, all of twenty-two at the time, took the head of the Leipzig book fair out for a meal and looked on incredulously as the elderly and eminent bookseller cast dignity to the winds and started to eat as if he had not had a meal in months.

Stories of money changing and currency speculation are legion. *Bureaux de change*[8] were to be found in every shop, apartment block, hairdresser's, tobacconist's. An Englishman named Sandford Griffith remembers having to visit a number of cities in the Ruhr which had local currencies. He stopped at a dealer's to change some money, but when he produced a pound note the dealer was so overcome by such wealth that he simply waved a hand at his stock of currency and invited the astonished Englishman to help himself. Foreigners acquired antiques and *objets de valeur*[9] at rock-bottom prices. A favorite trick was to buy in the morning with a down payment, saying that one would fetch the rest of the money from the bank. By waiting until the new exchange rate had come out at noon before changing one's money into marks, an extra profit could be made on the amount that the mark had fallen since the day before.

The population responded to the foreign onslaught with a double pricing system. Shops would mark their prices up for foreigners. It would cost a tourist 200 marks to visit Potsdam, when it cost a German 25. Some shops simply declined to sell to foreigners at all. In Berlin a . . . tax on gluttony was appended to all meals taken in luxury restaurants.

Foreign embassies were also major beneficiaries of inflation, giving lavish banquets for virtually nothing. Indeed the *Weltbühne* noted with great resentment the presence of foreign legations of nations so insignificant that they would never hitherto have dreamed of being represented in Germany. The spectacle of foreigners of all nations, living grotesquely well and eating beyond their fill in the middle of an impoverished and starving Germany did not encourage the Germans to rally to the causes of pacifism and internationalism. The apparent reason for their inflation was there for all to see, occupying the Ruhr.

The surface manifestations of inflation were unnerving enough, but its effect upon behavior, values and morals were to reach very deep indeed, persisting for years after the stabilization of the mark, right up to the moment when Hitler

---

[8] Foreign exchange offices.

[9] Valuables.

came to power. The middle class — civil servants, professional men, academics — which had stood for stability, social respectability, cultural continuity, and constituted a conservative and restraining influence was wiped out. A French author met a threadbare and dignified old couple in spotless but well-worn prewar clothes in a café. They ordered two clear soups and one beer, eating as if they were famished. He struck up a conversation with the man, who spoke excellent French and had known Paris before the war. "Monsieur," the man replied, when asked his profession, "I used to be a retired professor, but we are beggars now."

There was a general feeling that an old and decent society was being destroyed. If the year 1918 had removed that society's political traditions and its national pride, 1923 was disposing of its financial substructure. In response, people grew either listless or hysterical. A German woman told Pearl Buck[10] that a whole generation simply lost its taste for life — a taste that would only be restored to them by the Nazis. Family bonds melted away. A friend of Swan, a most respectable German whose father was a civil servant on the railways, simply left home and roamed the country with a band. It was a typical 1923 case history. Young men born between 1900 and 1905 who had grown up expecting to inherit a place in the sun from their well-to-do parents suddenly found they had nothing. From imperial officer to bank clerk became a "normal" progression. Such disinherited young men naturally gravitated toward the illegal right-wing organizations and other extremist groups. Inflation had destroyed savings, self-assurance, a belief in the value of hard work, morality and sheer human decency. Young people felt that they had no prospects and no hope. All around them they could see nothing but worried faces. "When they are crying even a gay laughter seems impossible . . . and all around it was the same . . . quite different from the days of revolution when we had hoped things would be better."

Traditional middle-class morality disappeared overnight. People of good family co-habited and had illegitimate children. The impossibility of making a marriage economically secure apparently led to a disappearance of marriage itself. Germany in 1923 was a hundred years away from those stable middle-class values that Thomas Mann[11] depicted in *The Magic Mountain,* set in a period scarcely ten years before. Pearl Buck wrote that "Love was old-fashioned, sex was modern. It was the Nazis who restored the 'right to love' in their propaganda."

Paradoxically, the inflation that destroyed traditional German values was also largely responsible for the creation of that new, decadent and dissolute generation that put Berlin on the cosmopolitan pleasure seeker's map, and has kept it or its image there ever since. It was no coincidence that 1923 was the year that the Hotel Adlon first hired gigolos, professional male dancers, to entertain lady clients at so much per dance. It was also a period when prostitution boomed. A Frenchman accustomed enough to the spectacle of Montmartre[12] was unable to believe his

---

[10] An American writer (1892–1973).

[11] German author (1875–1955) and winner of the Nobel Prize in literature in 1929.

[12] District in Paris.

eyes when he beheld the open corruption of Berlin's Friedrichstrasse. Klaus Mann[13] remembers:

> Some of them looked like fierce Amazons strutting in high boots made of green glossy leather. One of them brandished a supple cane and leered at me as I passed by. "Good evening, madame" I said. She whispered in my ear: "Want to be my slave? Costs only six billion and a cigarette. A bargain. Come along, honey."
>
> . . . Some of those who looked most handsome and elegant were actually boys in disguise. It seemed incredible considering the sovereign grace with which they displayed their saucy coats and hats. I wondered if they might be wearing little silks under their exquisite gowns; must look funny I thought . . . a boy's body with pink lace-trimmed skirt.

Commercial sex in Berlin was not well organized and was considered by connoisseurs to be inferior to that of Budapest, which had the best red-light district in Europe. But in Berlin there was no longer any clear-cut distinction between the red-light district and the rest of town, between professional and amateur. The booted Amazons were streetwalkers who jostled for business in competition with school children. . . .

> Along the entire Kurfürstendamm powdered and rouged young men sauntered, and they were not all professionals; every schoolboy wanted to earn some money, and in the dimly lit bars one might see government officials and men of the world of finance tenderly courting drunken sailors without shame. . . .
>
> At the pervert balls of Berlin, hundreds of men dressed as women, and hundreds of women as men danced under the benevolent eyes of the police. . . . Young girls bragged proudly of their perversion. To be sixteen and still under suspicion of virginity would have been considered a disgrace in any school in Berlin at the time.

Another visitor was struck by what he referred to as Berlin's "pathological" mood:

> Nowhere in Europe was the disease of sex so violent as in Germany. A sense of decency and hypocrisy made the rest of Europe suppress or hide its more uncommon manifestations. But the Germans, with their vitality and their lack of a sense of form, let their emotions run riot. Sex was one of the few pleasures left to them. . . .
>
> In the East End of Berlin there was a large *Diele* (dancing café) in which from 9 P.M. to 1 A.M. you could watch shopkeepers, clerks and policemen of mature age dance together. They treated one another with an affectionate mateyness; the evening brought them their only recreation among congenial people. Politically most of them were conservative; with the exception of sex they subscribed to all the conventions of their caste. In fact, they almost represented the normal element of German sex life.

---

[13] German writer (1906–1949).

. . . There was a well-known *Diele* frequented almost entirely by foreigners of both sexes. The entertainment was provided by native boys between 14 and 18. Often a boy would depart with one of the guests and return alone a couple of hours later. Most of the boys looked undernourished. . . . Many of them had to spend the rest of the night in a railway station, a public park, or under the arch of a bridge.

Inflation made Germany break with her past by wiping out the local equivalent of the Forsytes.[14] It also reinforced the postwar generation's appetite for invention, innovation and compulsive pleasure seeking, while making them bitterly aware of their own rootlessness. It is not surprising that cocaine was very much in vogue in those years. The drug was peddled openly in restaurants by the hat-check girls, and formed an integral part of the social life of Berlin.

Inflation was also taken as evidence that the old order was morally and practically bankrupt. Capitalism had failed to guarantee the security of its citizens. It had benefited speculators, hustlers, con men and factory owners. It had spawned Hugo Stinnes, but had done nothing for the common good. The need for an alternative system appeared universally self-evident, and until one came along the thing to do was to enjoy oneself, drink away grandma's capital, or exchange one's clothes for cocaine: a dinner jacket got you four grams, a morning coat eight.

Inflation and the despair that it created also acted as the catalyst of aggression. It was at this time that anti-Semitism began to appear in Berlin. An attractive German lady remembers walking through a prosperous suburb with a Jewish friend when someone called to her in the street, "Why do you go around with a Jew? Get yourself a good German man." In one sense she found it understandable. The ordinary German was very slow to adjust to the special situation of inflation, and in 1923 anyone who was not very quick on their feet soon went under. Jews were better at economic survival in such situations than were other Germans — so much so, she says, that by the end of inflation they had become terribly conspicuous. All the expensive restaurants, all the best theater seats, appeared to be filled by Jews who had survived or even improved their position.

One can imagine that Germans who had lost their own status might have resented the spectacle. One old conservative I spoke to added a second reason for the rise of anti-Semitism in a Prussian society which had traditionally been quite free of it. The arguments advanced are his own, and tell us something of his prejudices. He believes that the Weimar Republic was too liberal with regard to immigration from the East, admitting thousands of Jews from Galicia and the old Pale of settlement,[15] persons who, in his words, were "Asiatics, not Jews." They found themselves in a strange anonymous town, free of all the ethical restraints imposed by life in a small community where their families had lived for several generations. They tended therefore to abandon all morality as they stepped out of their own homes, morality being strictly a family affair. They would sail as close

---

[14] A prosperous bourgeois family in novels by John Galsworthy (1867–1933).

[15] The Pale was an area where Jews were permitted to live in Russia.

to the wind as the law would allow, for they had no good will, no neighborly esteem to lose. The gentleman in question is convinced that their mode of doing business during the inflation did a great deal to create or aggravate more generalized anti-Semitic feelings.

Yet precisely these immigrants were to prove a mainstay of the republic. An old Berlin Jew who had spent some time in prewar Auschwitz told me that it was just these Eastern Jews who offered the most active and effective resistance to National Socialism. They were activists where native Berliners, Jew and Gentile alike, were more inclined to remain on the sidelines.

Certainly the period saw a rise in pro-National Socialist feelings. The first Nazi that Professor Reiff[16] knew personally was a schoolboy in his last year. The young man's father, a small civil servant, had just lost everything through inflation, and as a result his son joined the party. Pearl Buck records the views of an anti-monarchical businessman worried by inflation, who said of the Nazis: "They are still young men and act foolishly, but they will grow up. If they will only drop Ludendorff[17] and his kind, maybe someday I'll give them a chance."

For many people, who felt that they had lost all zest for a life rendered colorless by war and poverty, who could see that they lived in a world in which *Schieber*[18] won and decent folk lost, a new ideology combining patriotism and socialist anticapitalism seemed to be the only viable alternative to a totally unacceptable state of financial chaos and capitalist *laissez-faire*. The shock of inflation had made people mistrustful of the past, immensely suspicious of the present, and pathetically ready to have hopes for the future. It was perfectly clear to them that new solutions were needed, equally clear that until such solutions should appear they could put their trust in nothing except the validity of their own sensations.

The mood of the inflationary period . . . endured well beyond inflation itself to become the mood of the Weimar age, a blend of pleasure seeking, sexual and political extremism, and a yearning for strange gods.

> It was an epoch of high ecstasy and ugly scheming, a singular mixture of unrest and fanaticism. Every extravagant idea that was not subject to regulation reaped a golden harvest: theosophy, occultism, yogism and Paracelcism.[19] Anything that gave hope of newer and greater thrills, anything in the way of narcotics, morphine, cocaine, heroin found a tremendous market; on the stage incest and parricide, in politics communism and fascism constituted the most favored themes.

It was indeed a time for the revaluation of all (devalued) values.

---

[16] Professor of economics who lived in Berlin during the Weimar period.

[17] Erich Ludendorff (1865–1937), German general in World War I who helped direct the war effort. He later joined the Nazi party.

[18] Profiteers.

[19] Doctrines associated with the Swiss physician and alchemist Paracelsus (1493–1541).

The mood of 1923 persisted long after inflation ended, which is why the manner of its ending is offered here as a postscript, for nothing was restored but the currency.

Restoration of confidence was only possible when passive resistance in the Ruhr ended in the autumn of 1923. At the same time, the Reichsbank appointed Hjalmar Schacht to deal with inflation. He was an extremely able man with a clear grasp of essentials. He realized that his main problem was to restore confidence both within and without Germany, and to try to prevent people from spending money as soon as it came into their hands. He established a new currency, based on the notional sum total of Germany's agricultural wealth, the *Roggen-Mark* (rye mark). This had the effect of restoring psychological confidence in the currency. He combined the move with a gigantic bear trap laid by the Reichsbank to catch the speculators who would regularly build up huge short positions in marks, in the almost certain expectation that the mark would continue to fall against the dollar: i.e., they sold marks they hadn't got, knowing that they could buy them for a fraction of their present value when the time came to meet the demand. When the mark stopped falling, thanks to the Reichsbank's engineering, they had to rush to close their positions, and were forced to buy marks which had actually begun to go up. Many speculators lost the entire fortunes which they had built up over the year.

Schacht's measures sufficed to stop the rot, but in the period between the ordinance declaring the new currency and the appearance of the first notes, there was an interim of pure chaos in which . . . "four kinds of paper money and five kinds of stable value currency were in use. On November 20, 1923, 1 dollar = 4.2 gold marks = 4.2 trillion paper marks. But by December the currency was stable." The last November issue of the weekly *Berliner Illustrierter Zeitung*[20] cost a billion marks, the first December issue 20 pfennigs. Confidence seemed to have been restored overnight. Germany could breathe again. . . .

---

[20] *Berlin Illustrated Newspaper.*

DAILY LIFE IN MOSCOW, 1921–1929
William J. Chase

Bolsheviks (Communists) intended the Russian Revolution of 1917 to usher in a society of, by, and for the workers. Civil war and foreign invasions delayed the establishment of a proletarian system, but soon the socialist Russian state became the worldwide model for many who favored social equality and an end to the oppression of the weak by the strong. But William Chase, professor of history at the University of Pittsburgh, shows that all was not well in paradise. Contemporary newspapers and journals, police records, census and other statistical data, interviews of workers, and government reports reveal that daily life in Moscow in the 1920s was often nasty and brutish.

Chase examines in turn the standard of living, housing, family life, and relations between workers and their neighbors. Where do you see the realities of daily life falling below workers' expectations, and how do you account for the frustrations and problems that workers faced? To what extent did the government contribute to or alleviate the discomforts and indignities that so frequently beset workers? Enduring low wages, overcrowding, lack of privacy, and poor sanitation, workers sought the causes of their discontent. Whom did they blame for Moscow's problems?

If thousands of Moscow residents (Muscovites) endured substandard housing conditions, thousands more searched continuously for a place to live. Many workers and homeless took refuge in factory barracks or in overnight barracks. Because crime was also a great problem, the barracks became breeding grounds for criminality, including gangs, prostitution, and drug addiction. What was daily life like in the barracks?

Socialism preached social equality, even between men and women; the law enshrined gender equality. However, the weight of tradition bore heavily on women, as did overcrowding and the scarcity of household conveniences. Chase shows that even minor problems, such as apartment buildings having only one doorbell, eroded family and neighborly relations. Divorces as well as fights between neighbors illustrate the tensions and anxieties the deplorable living con-

William J. Chase, *Workers, Society, and the Soviet State: Labor and Life in Moscow, 1918–1929* (Urbana, IL: University of Illinois Press, 1987), 173–191, 193–199, 204.

ditions fostered. How has the end of Communisim and of the Soviet Union affected daily life in Russia?

On the one hand, this essay does not elicit envy or admiration for the impoverished lives of the overwhelming majority of Muscovites in the 1920s, although one might admire their perseverance under deplorable conditions. On the other hand, perhaps urban life in Moscow was no worse than that in other European cities in previous centuries. What developments in the lives of Muscovites do you attribute specifically to the government, the first Communist state in Western civilization?

O n the Bolshevik revolution's tenth anniversary, *Trud*[1] published an article entitled "Moscow after ten years," which noted with justifiable pride the Soviet state's many accomplishments — lower death and infant mortality rates, fewer deaths from infectious diseases and tuberculosis, easily accessible medical care, the rising standard of living, and improved working conditions. Few could argue with these successes and the ways in which they ameliorated life in Moscow. But the capital was far from problem free. Annually, deepening unemployment and housing crises engulfed the city. Its apartments were overcrowded and rife with tensions; thousands were homeless. Shortages of consumer goods and municipal services complicated many residents', especially women's, lives. Life's daily problems and strains seemed minor compared to those of the 1918 to 1921 period, but they were no less real and no less irritating. In fact, precisely because the economic recovery and improvements raised hopes and expectations, some workers found the enduring problems particularly troublesome and frustrating. More important, solutions to these problems remained beyond the control of workers and, given the NEP's[2] fiscal strictures, that of the city soviet.

Because deepening problems and mounting frustrations continually undermined improvements and successes, a ubiquitous yet rather amorphous dissatisfaction and anger tempered workers' hopes and aspirations. Outside the factories, they expressed these emotions most concretely in their complaints about housing. While they frequently criticized the city soviet for its failures and inability to overcome the shortage and poor quality of housing, workers more often vented their wrath on their well-to-do neighbors — nepmen,[3] professionals, speculators, specialists — whom they believed prospered at their expense and who enjoyed creature comforts of which workers could only dream. The steady stream of press articles which criticized these groups' behavior and activities and the official campaigns against them heightened and legitimized workers' prejudices,

---

[1] Labor union newspaper.

[2] New Economic Policy, instituted in 1921 to revive the Russian economy.

[3] Speculators and merchants who profited from the New Economic Policy.

attitudes and behavior. When the agricultural crisis struck in 1928, workers' standard of living began to plummet. Fear of a return to the deprivations of the 1918–1922 period heightened worker anger and made many receptive to the party's campaign against society's "bourgeois" elements — specialists, nepmen, and kulaks.[4]

While many issues divided the proletariat, the experiences of daily life outside the factory worked to unite them around common grievances and against common enemies. By examining workers' daily experiences and frustrations, we can refine our understanding of that class' attitudes and behavior. This [essay] focuses on the most important of these daily realities — the standard of living, housing, family life, and relations between workers and their neighbors. . . .

After years of economic collapse and deprivation, raising the workers' living standard proved to be a slow and uneven process. Until 1924, workers' standard of living improved at times and declined at others. There were several reasons for this fluctuation. One was the abandonment of natural wages[5] at a time of hyperinflation.[6] In late 1920, natural wages accounted for 95 percent of the average worker's pay; the next year the proportion fell to 85 percent. During 1922, the transition to money wages intensified. By mid-1924, wages in kind[7] accounted for only 7 percent of the average paycheck. Late that year, they were abandoned entirely. Despite the steady rise in workers' nominal wages,[8] inflation often reduced their value thereby subjecting the rise in real wages[9] to periodic reversals. Reliance on the expensive private market for many essential commodities further sapped workers' buying power.

Delayed wage payments also undermined workers' real wages. Delaying wage payments was a common practice during the early 1920s. The currency depreciation placed factory administrators in extremely awkward positions — by law their expenditures could not exceed their income, and they had to pay their workers on time. In heavy industrial enterprises that were slow to recover, the cash flow problem and shortage of capital were especially severe and intensified with the transition to cash wages. Either for lack of money or for bookkeeping purposes, many factory administrators delayed paying wages. Given the inflation rate, even a few days delay reduced workers' purchasing power. Understandably, the practice also contributed to widespread worker unrest. Nationally in 1922–1923, wage issues accounted for half of the strikes and two-thirds of the strikers. The figures for Moscow were comparable. During the summer of 1923, industrial unrest reached a peak and rumors of a general strike appear to have had some basis in fact. Most strikes were wildcat strikes organized around wage issues without the knowledge or support of the unions. . . .

---

[4] Wealthy peasants unwilling to join collective farms.

[5] The portion of output allocated to workers paid in the form of the goods produced.

[6] Rapid, uncontrolled inflation.

[7] Wages paid in the form of the goods produced.

[8] Wages defined as the face value of the money paid.

[9] Wages defined as the value of the goods and services that nominal wages can buy.

For these reasons, calculating the extent to which workers' standard of living rose between 1921 and 1924 is difficult. Contemporary officials were equally as confounded. At the Thirteenth Party Conference in January 1924, Tomskii, the trade union boss, claimed that real wages had risen during the previous year, but several delegates challenged his claim. According to one calculation, average real wages in Moscow in October 1922 stood at more than 60 percent of the 1913 level. But according to *Trud*, workers' average real wages nationwide were less than 40 percent of the 1913 wage.

After 1924, steadily rising nominal wages and the relatively stable currency and prices quickly raised workers' living standard. For all workers, the nominal wage hikes were significant. Between early 1925 and late 1928, the average Moscow worker's wage rose by about one-third. There was, however, considerable disparity from industry to industry — textile workers' wages increased by 50 percent; for printers, the figure was less than 20 percent. . . . Wages also varied with skill levels and production experience. For example, unskilled workers in 1927 earned about 70 percent of the average worker's wage, whereas older, experienced, skilled workers could earn twice the average wage. . . .

Real wages also rose steadily. In 1926, average real wages reached the prewar level. During the next two years, they increased significantly: in 1926/27, they exceeded the 1913 level by 15 percent; in 1927/28, they were more than 20 percent higher. Even for many of those whose real wages fell below the average, their standard of living after 1926 was better than before the revolution. The free social insurance system, low-cost housing, transportation and admission to social and cultural events, and, in some cases, free education translated into greater economic security and real wages than in pre-revolutionary times. The years 1925–1928 were indeed the "good years" of the NEP. But the onset of the agricultural crisis in 1928 suddenly undid these gains — food prices in the private markets soared from 100 to 200 percent higher than those in state markets and in 1929 rationing was re-introduced.

Even during the heyday, however, many working-class families found it difficult to make ends meet unless more than one member worked or they had other sources of income. In 1926, approximately one-quarter of Moscow's proletarian families had two or more members working. Factory workers' families had the highest proportion of multiple wage earners. In families where the primary wage earner was unskilled or semiskilled and hence generally earned less than the average wage, the financial pressure to have family members work was greatest. Given the unemployment rate, securing work was often difficult and hence many workers' relatives engaged in petty trade, part-time and seasonal work, and occasionally speculation. Such activities were most common among low-paid workers' families.

While workers' living standard rose until 1928, that of their bosses and many nepmen was much higher and rose more rapidly. In early 1925, the average worker's monthly wage was 64 rubles and that of the average employee was 108 rubles; by late 1928, the figures were approximately 95 and 150 rubles respectively. . . . But these averages conceal the very high salaries earned by some employees. Factory directors, engineers, and technical specialists were among the highest paid employees, and, in 1928, they earned average monthly salaries of 220 rubles. Some within this group of administrators earned much more, upward of 600 rubles in the case of "bourgeois" (as opposed to Communist) factory directors. It was these personnel who implemented unpopular labor policies and productivity campaigns in the factory. While workers labored harder with each passing year, their wages declined relative to those of their bosses. Many nepmen also earned more than workers. In 1925/26, the average monthly income of a "bourgeois" entrepreneur (a factory owner or successful trader) was 420 rubles, while that of a "semi-capitalist entrepreneur" (a small scale producer or trader) was 100 rubles.

As a class, workers earned less than any of the city's major occupational groups, significantly less in some cases. While they struggled daily to make ends meet, such "bourgeois" elements, who had been pariahs after the revolution, prospered. Their good fortune galled workers. Envy, anger, frustration, these emotions provided the backdrop against which workers and their "bourgeois" neighbors interacted. . . .

Workers' families devoted slightly less than half of their income to food. The 1922 figures reflect the expenditures for December only and are not representative of the annual average. Because of the 1921–1922 famine, until the 1922 harvest Muscovites reportedly spent upward of 95 percent of their income on food. In that year, food and rationing were the main topics of factory meeting discussions, and newspapers ran regular columns devoted to the famine and its consequences. But even after the famine, regular newspaper articles on available food supplies underscored Muscovites' and officials' ongoing concern with food.

The proportion of workers' wages spent on food varied with one's income. Throughout the 1920s, the lowest paid workers spent more than half and the highest paid workers only one-quarter of their earnings on food. As real wages rose, so too did the amount of food purchased. The quality of food consumed also improved and workers' diets became increasingly well balanced as the years passed. Among working-class families surveyed in December 1922, animal products (meat, fish, and dairy products) accounted for only 9 percent of the food consumed, grains (rye, wheat, and grits) for 47 percent, and vegetables and potatoes for 42 percent. Their average caloric intake was 3,409 calories, most of which came from bread and potatoes. Two years later, the diets had changed markedly. Meat and dairy products accounted for one-fifth of the food consumed; vegetables and potatoes for one-third. Grains remained the major staple, accounting for 43 percent of their diet. But the types of grain consumed changed somewhat. Those surveyed in 1924 ate three times more wheat and 40 percent less rye than their counterparts in 1922. Because of the reduced intake of grains and potatoes, the average worker in 1924 consumed 3,250 calories. This improved diet, which provided more protein and vitamins, remained the norm until 1928. Not everyone, however, ate such balanced diets, which obviously varied with income and personal preferences.

In the early 1920s, workers received food from three sources — rations, state stores and cooperatives, and private markets. Although rationing continued until 1924, the size of rations declined sharply after 1922. Workers purchased 60 percent of their food in September 1923 at private markets; three years later, the proportion had declined to 38 percent. Given the low cost, increased quantity and improved variety of foodstuffs in state stores, workers were able to purchase more food there per ruble with each passing year and thereby to improve their diets. Then in 1927, a war scare gripped Russia. Peasants, especially kulaks, responded to the scare and the worsening market situation by holding back their produce. Moscow quickly felt the effects. Food prices rose rapidly in 1928 and rationing was reintroduced early the next year. By late 1929, cereals, sugar, tea, butter, oil, herring, soap, eggs, meat, potatoes were rationed. After several years of steady improvement, suddenly there was less food on the workers' tables. Once again, Muscovites were forced to turn to the private market where prices went as high as the market would bear, two to three times those in state markets. Rationing and the renewed dependence on the high priced, black market triggered memories of the Civil War.[10] Justifiably fearful of a return to those days, many urban workers endorsed the party's collectivization and antikulak campaigns in hopes that they would alleviate the new crisis. Clearly, the food situation during the 1920s was a mercurial one. The uncertainty of the early 1920s gave way to several years of steady improvement; but in 1928–1929, fear and anxiety once again punctuated workers' daily lives.

After food, the average working-class family devoted the next largest proportion of their income — more than one-fifth — to clothing. Although this marked a substantial improvement over pre-revolutionary times, workers were not necessarily better dressed. The limited availability and shoddy quality of some clothing combined to restrict the upgrading of most workers' wardrobes. The presence of more than 1,900 used clothes and junk dealers in Moscow in 1926 testifies to the considerable demand for used clothing.

Prior to the revolution, rent and utilities consumed more than one-fifth of the average worker's income. In Russia in 1910, wages were lower and rents higher than anywhere in western Europe; Moscow had the country's highest rents. For this reason, many workers lived in barracks and small, overcrowded apartments. After 1917, housing costs dropped dramatically, and during the 1920s, workers' rents remained very low. Several factors determined an occupant's rent, the most important being his occupation. Workers received preferential treatment; their rents could not exceed 10 percent of their income. The 1928 rental scale used to determine rents in publicly owned housing fixed rents according to occupations. All other factors being equal, employees were to pay 28 percent more in rent than did workers, artisans/craftsmen (private operators) 175 percent more, profes-

---

[10] Struggle for control of Russia, 1918–1922, among Bolsheviks, monarchists, and liberal democrats; complicated by the armed intervention of Great Britain, France, and the United States.

sionals 324 percent more, and nonworking elements (e.g., proprietors) 934 percent more. The dwelling's size and the presence (or absence) of running water,
electricity, and/or sewer connections also affected the rent. But the extent to which
occupation-based rental scales actually determined rents is unclear. As we shall
see, many workers believed that they did not. . . .

Until 1922, the state prohibited the sale of liquor, a policy initiated during
World War I. Despite prohibition and the authorities' sustained struggle to curtail the number of boot-leggers (samogonshchiki), illegal samogon (home-brewed
vodka, generally 25 proof) was easy to find. In 1922, the state legalized the sale
of beer and wine; two years later, it did the same for hard liquor. As the availability
of liquor and the number of rural migrants increased, the problem of alcohol
abuse in the city became very serious. The increasing death toll there due to
drunkenness testifies to the problem's dimensions. In 1923, when the production
and sale of vodka were still forbidden, 16 deaths were attributed to drunkenness;
in 1926, the figure soared to 144. During the 1926 Christmas holiday alone, 30
people died from excessive alcohol consumption. The proportion of patients in
Moscow psychiatric clinics who received treatment for alcohol-related disorders
rose from 6 percent in 1924 to 25 percent in 1925. Clearly, excessive drinking was
a severe problem. . . .

On the other hand, the small proportion of income spent on entertainment
and culture masked a considerable gain. In pre-revolutionary times, many cultural
activities were beyond workers' financial means. Social pressure and barriers further reduced the number of workers who attended the opera, ballet, symphony,
museums, galleries and even films. After the revolution, admission prices to such
cultural events were very cheap and workers and their families were encouraged
to attend. Post-revolutionary Moscow also bustled with amateur and avant-garde
theatrical performances in neighborhood and factory club theaters, sporting events,
and the circus. How many workers actually attended such affairs is difficult to estimate. When they did go out for entertainment, movies, sporting events, the circus, and local taverns appear to have been the more popular affairs. But these are
impressions; a thorough study of working-class culture(s) remains to be done.

One establishment that the party and unions hoped would be a center of proletarian social and cultural life was the workers' clubs. But during the 1920s,
these clubs had limited popularity. In Moscow city and guberniia[11] in late 1923,
there were 481 clubs with approximately 150,000 members; in 1927, the city's
181 clubs had some 100,000 members. The membership figures must be viewed
with caution since many members rarely frequented the clubs or participated in
their activities. Low attendance resulted from several factors — poorly defined
and organized activities, poor organization, and a rowdy clientele.

In the early 1920s, the clubs' poorly organized activities resulted from a
shortage of competent club officials and a strident debate between Proletkul't[12]

[11] Provincial soviet.

[12] An organized movement to produce art and culture relevant to proletarian interests.

and the party over the nature of club activities. Proletkul't envisioned the clubs as "forges of the new culture" and devoted its energies to organizing various types of cultural activities such as music, art and drama. The party and unions sought to focus club activities along more utilitarian lines and sponsored lectures on hygiene and politics, literacy circles, and other practical activities that might appeal to workers and serve official policy.

Younger workers (under thirty) who participated in Proletkul't cultural activities appear to have dominated the clubs' regular patrons. But many of them engaged in rowdy, disruptive behavior, and, on occasion, young "hooligans" damaged the clubs thereby forcing factory committees to form guard teams to defend their property. Rather than endure the rowdyism and antagonism of younger workers, many older workers preferred to frequent local taverns where they could socialize and drink with their peers. Considering the atmosphere at many clubs and their refusal to sell alcohol, the taverns' popularity is understandable. . . .

Housing was justifiably the proletariat's most chronic grievance. They bore the brunt of the city's ever-deepening housing crisis. Their experience during the NEP stands in stark contrast to that during the Civil War when they were the chief beneficiaries of the massive housing redistribution. Squalid though they became as a consequence of the 1918–1921 economic collapse, the confiscated apartments into which workers moved represented a dramatic improvement over the barracks and basement dwellings which they had previously inhabited. Ironically, while the quality of their housing was poor, workers had more living space per capita in 1920 than they ever had or would again for several decades. Because the 1920s witnessed a reversal of the 1918–1921 experience, worker frustration became all the more intense.

As the city's population mushroomed after 1920, the amount of living space per person declined steadily and the competition for housing intensified. On the tenth anniversary of the revolution, many workers, especially those who moved to the city after 1921, lived in dwellings that more closely resembled those of pre-revolutionary times than those that they believed the revolution had promised. Although the need for housing became more acute with each passing year, until 1925 economic policy dictated that industrial restoration received the majority of available capital. Consequently, throughout the decade, housing construction and repair lagged far behind the rate of population increase. Between 1921 and 1926 the number of inhabitable apartments increased by 38 percent, but the city's population practically doubled.

Worker discontent with their housing surfaced early. In May 1922, A. Rosenberg, a member of the Khamovnicheskii *raion*[13] soviet, reported that the housing shortage had already become critical. Workers were fully justified, he stated, to demand the repair of their present dwellings and the construction of new ones. Unless these demands, endorsed by factory committees, *raion* soviets and party organizations, were met, workers' living conditions would continue to deteriorate.

---

[13] A political subdivision comparable to a county.

But four months later, the editor of *Rabochaia Moskva*,[14] Boris Volin, wrote that the city soviet had too few resources to meet the demand for housing construction and repair. He agreed that the situation was very poor, but counseled workers to be patient. Workers paid little heed and their complaints mounted. In October, the city soviet responded to their criticisms and demands by creating an Extraordinary Housing Commission. The commission's first act was to order that 10 percent of the city's living space be made available to housing associations . . . which were organized at the workplace. This "new" living space was to be distributed to those in need of housing on a priority basis: workers and employees without adequate housing were the first priority; the registered unemployed, the second priority.

Many residents were reluctant to give up part of their dwellings. For example, the Uritskii factory's housing association encountered resistance from two recalcitrant apartment dwellers. One was a professional who lived with his wife and fourteen-year-old daughter in a five-room apartment; the other, a nepman whose three member family also occupied five rooms. The association dismissed both protests and allocated one of the professional's large rooms to three workers and their spouses. By November 1, the Extraordinary Commission announced that the 10 percent levy had resulted in 11,341 "new" rooms which were occupied by some 21,000 people. Unfortunately, the levy did little to reduce the growing demand for housing. What it did do was expose some of the housing inequities that existed. While three workers' families shared one subdivided room, the professional's family lavished in four rooms. This case was no exception.

By 1924, there was public discussion of "the housing hunger, the housing catastrophe." The next year, a trade union official lamented that Moscow's living space was filled "to the point of overflowing." . . . These were not exaggerations. With each passing year, the amount of living space per person declined — from 9.3 square meters in 1920 to 5.5 square meters in 1927 — and the average number of inhabitants per apartment increased — from five in 1920 to nine in 1926. As the demand for housing outstripped construction, the populations of factory barracks swelled, apartments were subdivided with increasing frequency, the renting of corners became more common, and many homeless people were forced to sleep in corridors, storerooms, sheds, kitchens, bathhouses, and even asphalt cauldrons. For those who refused to live in such conditions, the only alternative was to live outside the city and commute as much as fifteen kilometers to work.

While rapid population growth and inadequate construction were the prime reasons for Moscow's housing crisis, they were not the only reasons. In fact, the city's population in 1923 was 25 percent smaller than in 1917; yet the number of apartments had diminished by only 18 percent. True, much of that housing was in disrepair and of substandard quality. But what made the crisis worse was the city soviet's desire to place workers in decent apartments and not have to reopen the accursed barracks that had housed so many before the revolution. . . . [A]t least until 1923 the soviet's housing policy produced some success. The average

---

[14] *Worker's Moscow.*

amount of living space per person that year was slightly greater than in 1912. Nonetheless, overcrowded housing remained a reality of Moscow life. In 1923, more than one-half of the residents lived in apartments with two occupants per room; another third lived in apartments with three to five people per room. Less than 10 percent had the luxury of having a room to themselves.

But the success of the soviet's policy was limited. Although many Moscow workers had more living space than they did before 1917, as a class they had the least amount of living space. That inequity remained true throughout the decade. In 1927, the average amount of living space per person (in square meters) was: workers — 5.6; artisans — 5.9; employees — 7.0; professionals — 7.1. The types of dwellings in which workers lived varied widely. The 1918–1921 redistribution primarily benefited those workers who resided in Moscow during those years. The 10 percent levy benefited those workers who returned to Moscow in 1921–1922. After that, the number of workers forced to live in factory barracks, corners of apartments, sheds and other substandard dwellings grew annually. Everything was different, but little had changed in the area of housing.

To illustrate how crowded Moscow housing was during the 1920s, consider the following examples. But first, a word of caution. Relative to most workers, especially the most recent arrivals, the housing described below was comfortable, even spacious. In 1922, warehouseman V. lived in a one-room apartment in an old wooden house with his wife, two daughters, and, for at least part of the year, his mother-in-law. The apartment had 13 square meters of living space and one window. The furnishings were meager: a bed, a couple of tables and stools, and a kerosene primus stove. Late the next year, the family moved to a newly renovated apartment, which also had one room (18.6 square meters) and one window. The parents slept in the bed and the children slept on the floor.

During the first half of 1924, textile worker O., her husband, and two children lived in a one-room apartment in a two-story house shared by four families. Their apartment had only 7.7 square meters of living space and one window. The family had two cots; the mother and daughter slept in one, the father and son in the other. They moved in 1925 to a somewhat larger and cleaner one-room apartment. The room was large enough for both O. and her husband to have their own corners. Two chairs, stools, and tables were the only furniture in the apartment. . . .

To fit such cramped conditions, it follows that most families' furniture was quite simple. That of workers V. and O.'s discussed above was typical. Stools were more common than chairs and beds were scarce. Surveys conducted in 1923 and 1924 found an average of three people per bed in Moscow. Those without beds slept on the floor, tables or makeshift plank beds. It was common for very young children to sleep in open drawers. Such conditions inspired the following popular little tune:

In Moscow we live as freely,
as a corpse in his coffin.
I sleep with my wife in the dresser,
My mother-in-law sleeps in the sink. . . .

During the early 1920s, workers also demanded an improvement in the quality of their housing. The deterioration of dwellings during the Civil War had turned many apartments into spawning areas for infections and epidemic diseases. To identify and cleanse such dwellings, in 1921 the city soviet organized volunteer health sections and public clean-up campaigns. Some 2,500 such sections existed by 1923 and their activity proved to be crucial in the struggle against epidemics. But cleaning dilapidated, substandard housing and repairing and improving that housing were two different activities. The latter proceeded extremely slowly.

The slow rate of repairs resulted from two factors — the lackadaisical attitude of some residents toward housing maintenance, and the shortage of capital. . . . The fact that housing was very cheap (rent free until 1922) and did not belong to the occupants "has killed the economic interest of the dwellers" who often mistreated their dwellings or failed to maintain them. In 1922, the Petrograd soviet lamented "the insuperable difficulties in fighting the psychology of the man in the street (obyvatel') who looks upon national property as belonging to nobody and therefore at times aimlessly destroys it." Surely the same problem existed in Moscow.

The disrepair of housing in the early 1920s testifies to the consequences of years of neglect. At factory meetings and in the press, workers constantly complained about overcrowding and the need to repair walls, windows, floors, stairs, ceilings, and water and heating systems. They recognized that the lack of capital hampered the repair process, but that in no way lessened the stridency of their demands. Frustrated by the slow pace, some workers stole factory goods and supplies with which to repair their apartments. Although discontent over the disrepair diminished somewhat after 1925, complaints continued to appear in the press.

Even if residents had adhered to the letter of the law, overcoming their housing's disrepair was beyond their financial means. Unfortunately, it was also beyond the city soviet's means. Until 1924, the inflation rate placed severe fiscal strictures on the soviet, which, in accordance with national policy, gave priority to industrial recovery and the restoration of municipal utilities. Funds for housing repair were simply insufficient to meet the demand. In 1923, the city soviet allocated less than one-tenth of the amount spent in 1913 for housing repair. This meager sum barely made a dent in the problem.

Nor was the soviet in a position to build enough new housing. No large scale housing construction took place in Moscow before 1923 and few housing units were built in 1924. Of the new housing built in 1923/24, 60 percent was built by private investors and cooperatives. Until the establishment in 1925 of a bank to finance municipal housing, the city lacked access to the credit necessary to construct the requisite new housing. The bank's creation marked a turning point in municipal housing construction. After 1925, the city soviet and state agencies built more than 80 percent of all new housing. Still, insufficient capital limited new construction. . . .

Not only was the amount of housing construction during the NEP inadequate, but what was built was often of inferior quality. A 1927 city soviet investigation of newly constructed housing revealed a host of problems. Many floors, doors, and windows were made from unseasoned wood and poor quality materials, and within a short time they warped or split, often rendering them useless. So poorly designed were many buildings that some rooms were accessible only through other rooms, making their use as individual apartments difficult and annoying to the residents. Other problems among the long "series of shortcomings" included unnecessarily congested stairwells, inadequate insulation from street noise, the absence of sufficient baths and ventilation systems, and the construction of excessively large rooms that had to be subdivided. For lack of funds, the construction of creches,[15] day-care centers, and rooms for collective use in apartment buildings had to be deferred.

Given that demand far outstripped housing construction and renovation, many workers turned to their factories in search of a place to live. Many of the city's larger factories, such as Dinamo, AMO, Trekhgornaia and Serp i molot, owned reasonably decent apartment buildings. But factory administrators often preferred to use these dwellings to attract skilled workers and *spetsy.*[16] Those apartments available to other workers were quickly filled in the early 1920s. To their newest workers, the factories offered only a place in their barracks. Precisely what proportion of the city's proletariat lived in factory barracks is unclear. Two facts appear certain: the number grew with each passing year, and the majority of them were new workers from the villages.

Despite attempts by factory and union activists to maintain certain standards of quality and cleanliness in the barracks, the conditions there were reminiscent of those in pre-revolutionary times. In 1928, *Trud* described one barracks:

> The long narrow room has only one window, which cannot be opened. Some of the panes are broken and the holes plugged with dirty rags. Near the doorway is an oven which serves not only for heating but for cooking as well. The chimney spans the entire length of the room from the doorway to the window. The smell of fumes, of socks hung to dry, fills the room. It is impossible to breathe in the closeness of the air. Along the walls are crude beds covered with dirty straw ticks and rags, alive with lice and bugs. The beds have almost no space between them. The floor is strewn with cigarette butts and rubbish. About two hundred workers are housed here, men and women, married and single, old and young — all herded together. There are no partitions, and the most intimate acts are performed under the very eyes of other inhabitants. Each family has one bed. On one bed a man, a wife and three children live, a baby occupies the "second floor" — a cot hanging over the bed. The same toilet is used by men and women.

Living in these overcrowded and unsanitary barracks affected workers in many ways. They got less sleep and became ill more often than those who had better dwellings. Consequently, they had higher absenteeism rates and were less productive than the average worker. . . .

---

[15] Day nurseries.

[16] Specialists.

As much as workers who resided in apartments or barracks had reason to complain, they enjoyed a privilege not shared by all residents — they had a place to live. For thousands of Muscovites, the search for housing was a daily ordeal. As early as September 1922, a letter to the editor of *Rabochaia Moskva* stated that "masses of people pass the night on the streets." In view of the approaching winter, the author proposed the construction of overnight lodgings. . . .

As the number of homeless Muscovites increased, so too did the number of overnight barracks. By 1929, the city operated eight such dwellings. . . .

The conditions in overnight barracks were worse than those in factory barracks. Despite regulations which stipulated that they meet certain sanitary requirements and possess certain amenities of life, the shortage of capital and uncaring attitudes of the temporary tenants meant that these ideals were rarely met. Some barracks lacked separate facilities for men and women, and most were extremely overcrowded, dirty and lacked hot water, laundry facilities, and litter baskets. The dining areas were especially unsanitary and often strewn with garbage. The food and dining conditions were often so horrible that few tenants ate there. At one lodging only four of the 120 tenants ate in the dining hall.

So large was the city's homeless population that the increasing number of night lodgings were unable to accommodate them. When the weather permitted, many people slept in parks, public gardens, cemeteries, streets, and along the river banks. During the winter months, they sought shelter in abandoned or partially constructed buildings, train stations, sheds, bathhouses, and even asphalt cauldrons. The unemployed, *besprizorniki* (homeless orphans), and recent migrants comprised the vast majority of the homeless population, although some permanent workers also populated their ranks.

From this group came the largest number of criminals. Leaving aside professional criminals, evidence of whose nefarious activities is too sparse to allow for discussion, the most visible of the city's criminals were the *besprizorniki*, the orphaned and runaway children for whom criminality was both a game and means of survival. . . .

Left to their own devices, they formed gangs that offered them protection and enhanced their criminal activities. The boys specialized in theft; the girls, in theft and prostitution. The gangs created their own communal organizations and systems for the division of their spoils. They lived where they could — in sheds, asphalt cauldrons, parks, abandoned buildings or boats, or, if they had some money, in night shelters. . . . In their social milieu, the use of drugs (especially cocaine) and alcohol were everyday occurrences, and children as young as five indulged and stole so that they could purchase more.

Orphaned girls frequently turned to prostitution. In 1927, more than one-quarter of the prostitutes arrested in Moscow were under eighteen years of age, some were as young as twelve. While some became prostitutes to sustain themselves, others did so to support their drug habit. Almost three-quarters of those arrested in 1924 regularly used cocaine, opium, or morphine. Many other women also became prostitutes. While some did so for personal reasons that will forever remain secret, many resorted to prostitution in order to survive. Unemployment, the lack of financial support, and the need to sustain their families left them no choice. Women of the street practiced their trade quite openly in several parts of town, Tverskaia and Trubny squares being the best known. In the former, the sidewalks swarmed with teenage prostitutes; in the latter, the trade was less brisk and males in search of whores had to frequent one of several large tenements, in the corridors of which hung the sweet smell of opium and where next to the doors were tacked photographs of the "fair occupant in the scantiest of costume." Those who operated out of these shabby tenements had a distinct advantage over their competitors — they had a bed. The housing shortage forced the others to ply their trade in hallways, alleys, backyards, and on park lawns and benches.

Despite the efforts of the police, party, and state agencies to eliminate crime, prostitution, and drug use and to reduce the number of *besprizorniki,* all remained common features of Moscow life. Considering the deepening housing and unemployment crises, this is hardly surprising. But the conspicuous presence of criminals, prostitutes, and drug users adversely affected the quality of life there. Because most thefts, robberies, muggings, and rapes occurred at night, men and women alike worried about venturing out alone after dark. The large numbers of homeless who passed the night in public places only heightened these anxieties. Parents were also greatly concerned for their children. This was particularly true of the parents of unemployed juveniles, who out of idleness or for want of excitement fell in with *besprizorniki* gangs and took to drinking and drug use.

Workers' relatively low wages and their overcrowded living conditions imposed severe strains on them and their families and adversely affected their lives. While daily frustrations, anxieties, and uncertainties punctuated the lives of all family members, women often bore the heaviest burden. The most obvious example of this was their role in the division of family labor.

Legally, men and women were equal. But at home, as on the job, traditional, patriarchal attitudes held sway. Shopping, cleaning, cooking, and child-care were, according to most Russian males, women's work. That many women also held full-time jobs turned most days into an exhausting experience. The scarcity of household conveniences, municipal services, electricity, refrigeration, and running water forced women to devote long hours each day to household chores. For want of refrigeration, women had to shop virtually every day, an exercise that often required traveling from store to store and waiting in queues.[17] Because cooking on portable primus stoves turns even a simple meal into a long ordeal, cooking also consumed much time. So too did cleaning the apartment and washing clothes. Less than one-fifth of the city's apartments had running water, and hence water for cleaning and cooking had to be carried from communal taps, pumps (usually located outside), or from the river or open canals. According to time-budget studies conducted in 1931, women who worked full-time jobs spent an additional five hours a day on domestic chores and child-care. This left two or three hours a day

---

[17] Lines.

at most for personal sanitation, politics, or self-improvement. Males, on the other hand, devoted only two hours a day to domestic chores and child-care.

The personal and social costs engendered by overcrowded housing conditions and the demands of daily life are difficult to estimate, but data on crime in Moscow suggest that they were substantial. Between 1923 and 1927, the crime rate among females rose more rapidly than did that of males. While males were more likely to commit crimes of property or hooliganism (often associated with drunkenness), females were more commonly arrested for attacks on people. During those years, the number of women arrested for assault and battery increased by five times; those arrested for murder and "shocks, blows, and attacks on individuals" by six times. As a proportion of all crimes, those against people soared from 10 to 40 percent. People who lived in one room or less and those without permanent residences were the most apt to commit crimes. Spouses, relatives, and neighbors were their most common victims.

Of the 202 cases of hooliganism that came before Moscow's Peoples' Courts in the mid-1920s, 25 percent of them were directly attributed to the acute housing problem. Many of those convicted were housewives, mostly workers' wives, who were found guilty of starting fights over an apartment or kitchen. Petty though the issues may seem, they provide a measure of the frustration and hostility that the strains of daily life induced.

Crime statistics measure only people's most dramatic reactions to their conditions. A host of minor problems also eroded their patience and civility. For example, consider the problems caused by so simple a device as a doorbell. Because they were formerly one-family residences, many of Moscow's apartment buildings had only one doorbell for all of the residents. So as to avoid confusion, each apartment was assigned a doorbell code usually determined by the number of rings. It goes without saying that such a system is fraught with the potential for error and, in some cases, mistakes or misuse precipitated fights and arguments.

Daily frustrations and hardships could not help but affect the stability of workers' families. Judging from the city's divorce rate, the impact was significant. Unfortunately, the nature of the data prohibits identifying the reasons for divorce and that rate among workers. But so steeply did the city's divorce rate rise that it seems inconceivable that the strains and quarrels of daily life did not contribute to its increase. In 1921, there were 5,790 divorces; in 1927, 19,421 divorces; and in 1929, 23,745 divorces.

The 1920s remains the decade of the easy divorce. After 1926, the "postcard divorce" made the dissolution of marriage especially easy. The "postcard divorce" operated in the following manner. If either spouse wished to divorce the other, that person simply went to the ZAGS office (Zapiski aktov grazhdanskogo sostoianiia, which registered all marriages and divorces) and filled out a postcard announcing that the marriage had been terminated. The divorced, and possibly unwitting, spouse received the announcement in the mail several days later.

But divorce did not always end a couple's relationship. Because of the housing shortage, many divorced couples were forced to remain room-mates. When one of them remarried or took a lover, the situation could become extremely awkward. Indeed, just such a situation formed the basis of the popular contemporary film "Bed and Sofa" in which two workers contend for the love of one's wife and the right to her bed. Then there was the case of a ballerina who surprised her husband by bringing home a new husband after divorcing the former husband in the morning. Since he could find no other housing, the rejected male had to occupy a corner in his former wife's "honeymoon suite."

Economic insecurity and overcrowded housing affected even the happily married. Nowhere is this more graphically illustrated than in the city's rising abortion rate. In 1920, the Soviet government legalized abortions performed by trained doctors in approved hospitals and clinics. During the 1920s, more and more women elected to have abortions. The number of registered abortions per 100 births rose from 19.6 in 1923, to 31.4 in 1925, to 55.7 in 1926. While some women chose abortion to terminate an unwanted pregnancy or for medical reasons, more than half of those who received abortions did so because they lacked the financial resources to support a child. Low wages, unemployment, and the shortage of housing space were major considerations for women who sought abortions.

While some party members regarded the rising abortion rate as "massive" and "horrifying," others accepted it and argued that the women's reasons for electing the operation were real and justifiable. On one fact, all agreed. The abortion law marked a significant improvement over the pre-revolutionary situation, when abortions were illegal and untrained doctors, midwives, and nurses clandestinely performed them in unsanitary conditions, situations that often resulted in infection, permanent bodily injury, or death. During the 1920s, the number of women who died from abortions, contracted postoperative ailments, or reported to hospitals with incomplete abortions contracted steadily.

The lowest average wages of the city's major occupational groups, the least amount of housing space per person, a rapidly rising crime rate directly attributable to these conditions, and the personal frustrations and anxieties that accompanied these depressing phenomena, these were the realities with which the Moscow working class struggled daily. To be sure, these were not items on that class's revolutionary agenda. What made the experiences especially galling was that their bosses and other well-to-do residents did not endure such hardships. On the contrary, they prospered and frolicked during the NEP. Their success and happiness only further angered workers. . . .

There was no quintessential working-class experience during these years. Skilled and experienced urban workers earned higher wages and generally had better apartments than did new workers whose recent arrival and lack of skills and experience translated into lower wages and factory barracks housing. But the differences between workers paled in comparison to those between workers and nepmen, "speculators, professionals, etc." When it came to wages, housing, and the other daily realities that defined their lives beyond the factory gates, workers were far more united than they were divided.

GERMAN KILLERS
IN THE HOLOCAUST:
BEHAVIOR AND MOTIVATION
Christopher R. Browning

The Holocaust, the murder of approximately six million Jews by Germany and its collaborators during World War II, is a topic unlike any other in history. Recently, there have been two widely publicized interpretations that have captured the attention of Holocaust scholars and the general public. Harvard University political scientist Daniel Jonah Goldhagen argues in his 1996 book, *Hitler's Willing Executioners,* that Germany's history of what he termed "eliminationalist" anti-Semitism was the major factor in ordinary Germans' eagerness to kill Jews. Four years earlier, Christopher R. Browning, Frank Porter Graham Professor of History at the University of North Carolina at Chapel Hill, had maintained that most ordinary Germans involved in the killing of Jews did so to further their careers or to fit in with their groups; only gradually during the war, he says, did they become resolute killers of Jews.

The selection here comes from a series of Browning's lectures published in 2000 as *Nazi Policy, Jewish Workers, German Killers.* Through an examination of German police reservists, Browning returns to the fundamental question of what motivated commonplace Germans to carry out the "Final Solution," the destruction of the Jews. His sources are the testimonies of Jewish survivors and records from a police station in Upper Silesia, letters from a member of a reserve police unit in the Baltic, and documents from a German investigation of an unplanned massacre of Jews in 1942. The result is a fascinating and intricate study of executioners, reluctant participants, and victims. How did the German police treatment of Jews in Upper Silesia compare to the treatment of Jews in the Soviet Union? What do the letters of the policeman from Bremen reveal about German attitudes toward Jews and their extermination, and about Russian partisans? What were the varying types of behavior among the police at the villages of Mir and Marcinkance? What did the German investigation of the killing of

Christopher R. Browning, *Nazi Policy, Jewish Workers, German Killers* (Cambridge: Cambridge University Press, 2000), 143–169.

Jews at Marcinkance uncover? To what extent did anti-Semitism permeate the German police whom Browning studies? To what extent did these police become willing executioners?

In what way does the recent increase in anti-Semitism, especially in some Muslim countries where religious and political leaders have called for the destruction of Israel and the murder of Jews, echo the situation in Germany and elsewhere in Europe prior to the Nazi invasion of the Soviet Union in 1941?

One of the most elusive tasks facing historians of any event is to uncover the attitudes and mind-set of the "ordinary" people who "make history" but leave behind no files of official documents and precious few diaries and letters. When "ordinary" people behave in ways completely at odds with the previous patterns of their everyday life and become the perpetrators of "extraordinary" crimes, this task becomes both more difficult and more essential to undertake. But how to undertake this task is a difficult question in its own right. In the case of Nazi Germany, one approach has been to shift the focus of study from the prominent and high-ranking perpetrators of the SS[1] to the many individuals of the bureaucracy and business community, the medical and legal professions, the German railways, and even the German churches who contributed to the implementation of Nazi Jewish policy in one way or another. Among the new subjects of study, attention has been drawn in recent years above all to the German Order Police.[2]

It is no longer seriously in question that members of the German Order Police, both career professionals and reservists, in both battalion formation and precinct service or *Einzeldienst,* were at the center of the Holocaust, providing a major manpower source for carrying out numerous deportations, ghetto-clearing operations, and massacres. The professional or career Order Police, who were merged with the SS in 1936, differed in age, career aspirations, institutional identification, training and indoctrination, and percentage of party and SS membership from the reservists. It is especially the reservists, not the career professionals, of the Order Police who could be said to be representative of "ordinary Germans." Conscripted virtually at random from the population of those middle-aged men who enjoyed no exemption for providing skilled labor essential to the war economy, they represented an age cohort that was socialized and educated in the pre-Nazi period and was fully aware of the moral norms of a pre-Nazi political culture.

What was the motivation and mind-set of the Order Police reservists who became Holocaust perpetrators? Did they come to their task possessed by virulent

---

[1] *Schutzstaffel,* the Elite Guard or Protection Guard. Originally Adolf Hitler's personal bodyguard, the SS became in 1929 the Nazi (National Socialist) elite paramilitary troops that provided police, concentration camp guards, and soldiers.

[2] Armed police acting as soldiers who have authority over civilians.

anti-Semitism and eager to kill Jews, or were they transformed by the situation in which they found themselves in eastern Europe? Did their attitude toward killing Jews differ from that toward killing other victims? Did they act with uniform enthusiasm, or did they display a spectrum of response — including evasion and nonparticipation by a significant minority — when killing?

. . . The task of the historian now is to locate and analyze rare contemporary sources that can shed additional light on these issues. For that purpose I would like to consider two other kinds of sources: first, the eyewitness accounts by Jewish survivors who possessed a unique vantage point from which to observe the internal dynamics and individual behavior of German Order Police reservists, and second, three collections of unusual documents: (1) the records of the Schutzpolizei[3] station of Czeladz, an industrial suburb of Sosnowiec, in East Upper Silesia; (2) the letters of a member of Reserve Police Battalion 105 in the Baltic; and (3) the records of a German wartime investigation of an unplanned massacre of the Jews of Marcinkance in the Bialystok district in November 1942, in which both career and reserve police participated. . . .

When East Upper Silesia was annexed to the Third Reich in October 1939, a network of German Schutzpolizei precinct stations was quickly established in the urban areas, including Sosnowiec and its industrial suburb of Czeladz. The Sosnowiec Schutzpolizei operated on the assumption that fully 70 percent of these men would be married and need family housing. A roster from August 1942 reveals that fully one half of the men in the Czeladz police station had family names of Polish origin. And the police commander in Sosnowiec had to make explicit that it was forbidden for his men to speak Polish in public while in uniform because this was damaging to the image of the police. Thus it is likely that . . . the Czeladz police were reservists from Silesia. They lived with their families in a milieu with which they were relatively familiar. They were not an isolated group of men living alone far from family and home in an alien environment. Their situation was far closer to that of reservists serving in precinct service near home in Germany than of those serving on occupied Polish and Soviet territory.

From the surviving documents of the Czeladz police station, we see that the commander of the Schutzpolizei in Sosnowiec was a stickler for ideological training and indoctrination. In this regard, he was extremely disturbed by the attitude of these men. For instance, he complained about the "previous indifference" . . . of the men toward meetings and written materials devoted to ideological indoctrination. . . .

. . . [T]he experience of the 90,000–100,000 Polish Jews of East Upper Silesia was significantly different from that of their fellow Jews in the Warthegau[4] and the General Government.[5] Many were moved into certain towns and Jewish res-

---

[3] The urban police.

[4] Administrative unit created in 1939 consisting of Polish territories annexed to Germany.

[5] The German administrative unit consisting of the areas of Poland that had not been incorporated into Germany.

idence areas within East Upper Silesia, but only a few were expelled into the General Government. Though their freedom of movement was curtailed by curfews as well as prohibitions against use of public transportation and entering certain streets and buildings in 1941, the Jewish quarters of East Upper Silesia were not transformed into sealed ghettos until the spring of 1943. Unlike the rest of Poland but instead as in pre-1939 Germany, the Jews here were not marked until September 1941. By the spring of 1942 some 6,500 Silesian Jews had been rounded up and interned in the Jewish labor camps of *Organisation* Schmelt, but prior to the deportations the majority continued to work in privately owned shops. The strongest single indicator of the stark contrast between Lodz[6] and Warsaw[7] on the one hand and East Upper Silesia on the other is that despite the discrimination, expropriation, and forced labor roundups, in the first 2 years of the German occupation of East Upper Silesia there was no significant rise in the natural death rate among the Jewish population.

In short, the reserve police in the "incorporated territory" of East Upper Silesia were more like German police serving at home than on occupied territory. And the Jews they encountered were treated more like German than Polish or Soviet Jews. How did the German Schupo[8] of East Upper Silesia react toward a Jewish population that was not stigmatized by marking, isolated by ghettoization, emaciated by starvation rations, and decimated by epidemic? Scattered references in the surviving documents hint at a very different atmosphere and rank-and-file police behavior than in the rest of German-occupied Poland. In November 1939 the commander of the Schutzpolizei in East Upper Silesia warned all of his men that "the greeting of a Jew is not to be acknowledged at all," and that any police engaged in contact with Jews outside official business could be expected to be sent to a concentration camp. This was not simply a one-time setting of policy, for the following spring, the commander of the Schutzpolizei felt compelled once again to warn his men. . . .

On the eve of the May 1942 deportations, the Schutzpolizei commander felt the need to exhort his men to be tough: "You must proceed ruthlessly in the Jewish actions. . . . Racial struggle is harsh — sentimentalism is out of place." In July 1942, however, even after the first deportation action of May–June 1942 and on the eve of the second deportation action of August, the unthinkable had happened once again — "A German police official was said to have greeted a Jew. . . . Jews should not be greeted on the open street at all." . . .

Although the Schupo commander continued to see disturbing signs of insufficient harshness and disdain toward the Jews on the part of his men, between the first and second deportation actions (May–June and August 1942) in

---

[6] City in western Poland and site of the first large ghetto, established in 1940. The ghetto ceased to exist in 1944, after all its Jews had been sent to death camps.

[7] Poland's capital and site of the ghetto holding 500,000 Jews. The Warsaw ghetto is famous owning to its Jewish revolt in 1943, after which the Germans destroyed the ghetto.

[8] The *Schutzpolizei* (urban police).

East Upper Silesia, for the first time he had also to give his attention to another phenomenon — namely, the curbing of unseemly and public police violence. In July 1942 — after some 17,000 Jews had been sent to their deaths in nearby Auschwitz–Birkenau — he advised his men that beating Poles or Jews in public was "in no way permissible." . . .

. . . In East Upper Silesia, where the police were still living as at home rather than as occupiers in a foreign land and the dehumanization of the Jews through marking, ghettoization, and starvation proceeded well behind the pace set in the Warthegau and General Government, the brutalization of the police seems also to have been a much slower process. This would suggest that imposing racial imperialism was corrupting. Acting as a "master race" on occupied territory changed attitudes and behavior, and each step in degrading and mistreating victims made the next step easier. For the policemen stationed in East Upper Silesia this process went relatively slowly, in sharp contrast to those involved in Operation Barbarossa.[9] Let us turn to the letters from Reserve Police Battalion 105 in the Baltic.

A 40-year-old Bremen salesman who had previously served as a reservist in Norway wrote his wife about the battalion's orientation on the eve of the invasion: "The major said that every suspect is to be shot immediately. Well, I'm in suspense," he noted sarcastically. . . . Not hiding his antipathy toward his officers, he suggested that they might shoot as they had in the comfort of the officers' casino in Oslo, where they had been previously stationed. . . .

Two days later, after the first execution of seven civilians, his tone changed abruptly. "In comparison to our present action," he admitted, "Norway was nothing at all." . . .

Initially he made detailed references to the Jews he encountered. Sent to a village to arrest all communists, the police rounded up 19 men and 6 Jewish girls. He fully expected to be part of a firing squad. However, after interrogation, the 6 Jewish girls and 11 men were released. The 8 remaining men — none of them Jews, he noted specifically — were taken away amidst the "terrible wailing and howling" . . . of their mothers, wives, and children. Clearly Reserve Police Battalion 105 did not enter Soviet territory with prior instructions to kill all Jews but had received the *Kommissarbefehl*[10] concerning the liquidation of communist functionaries.

In early July his company was lodged in commandeered Jewish houses, where every morning the "chosen people" . . . had to appear and work. He himself had two young Jews, a 15-year-old boy and 19-year-old girl, as his servants, but they had to be provided with identification cards or otherwise someone else would grab them. "The Jews are free game. Anybody can seize one on the streets for himself. I would not like to be in a Jew's skin." . . . The Jews had no food, he noted. "How they actually live, I don't know. We give our bread and more. I cannot be so tough," he confessed. . . . In addition to food, he noted: "One can only give the

---

[9] Code name for the German invasion of the Soviet Union, which commenced on 22 June 1941.

[10] The Commissar Order (6 June 1941) demanded the execution of all captured Soviet officials.

Jews some well-intended advice: bring no more children into the world. They have no future." . . .

Two weeks later, when the company moved to Mitau, the reserve policeman noted that there were "no more Jews" in town to act as servants. "They must be working, I suppose, in the countryside," he wrote once again with a possible tone of sarcasm.

In early August he wrote . . . "Here all Jews are being shot. Everywhere such actions are underway. Yesterday night 150 Jews from this place were shot, men, women, children, all killed. The Jews are being totally exterminated." . . .

In short, in the first month of Operation Barbarossa the Bremen reserve policeman wrote about Jews in two distinct ways. When referring to Jews in general, his tone was sarcastic and unsympathetic: "the chosen people" had had their houses commandeered, and they were presumably "working in the countryside." But when he wrote of the Jews that he actually encountered, the tone was quite different. The first Jews arrested by his company were released, and he was relieved not to be part of a firing squad. The Jewish youths working as his servants were portrayed as victims facing a pitiless future, and he confessed himself not tough enough to deny them a few handouts. One month later, when systematic killing of all Jews was clearly underway, he shifted to yet another voice — what I would call the "anonymous passive" that is so prevalent in postwar testimony as well. He openly wrote that all Jews were being shot, but without mentioning in any way his own or even his unit's participation. He expressed no feelings of his own except acceptance of the inevitable — "it must be." He urged willed indifference on his wife and silence before his eldest child. There was no celebration or boasting and even a hint of shame.

The reserve policeman wrote of Russians, especially partisans, quite differently. The partisans were "beasts" . . . "dogs" . . . and "trash" . . . who had to disappear. He provided vivid descriptions of executions that were "the order of the day." For example, "The arrested communists and snipers are made to lie facedown in graves that they have dug themselves and then shot in the neck from behind." The sight of partisans whose bodies were left hanging for "deterrence" was so common it no longer affected the men, he admitted. . . .

It is clear from the letters that the civilian population at large was not spared. His company had burned down every house and barn within 25 kilometers to deny lodging to the partisans. "We were 'arsons' in the true sense of the word," he confided. Russians were forced to march in front of patrols to set off possible mines. Any Russian found in the forest was shot out of hand. When his unit suffered casualties, he and his comrades become angry; they "would like best of all to shoot down all Russians." . . .

Now there is no "anonymous passive" voice and certainly no hint of shame. On the contrary, he was "proud of" what he had gone through and experienced. . . .

If the Bremen reservist fully identified with the regime's antipartisan policies and passively accepted the mass murder of the Jews, he maintained a critical stance in regard to the behavior of his officers. Although the company posted placards announcing that "whoever plunders will be shot," his captain filled his suitcase with whatever he could lay his hands on in the houses of the villagers, despite the tearful pleas of distraught mothers at least to leave their children's winter clothing. "Well, that's what we go through along the way, and it reflects on our officers. I can't bring myself to take anything from the poor people. But the career policemen don't even question it."

In comparison to the very gradual and belated brutalization of the reserve police in the less violent environment of East Upper Silesia, this Bremen reservist initially mocked the murderous exhortations of his officers but then adapted himself to the viciousness of the "war of destruction" on Soviet territory with breathtaking speed. Though he referred briefly and in passive voice to the mass murder of the Jews, he proudly and enthusiastically detailed and filmed his unit's antipartisan activities. Where does he fit into the spectrum of reaction among the German police? Indeed, was there even a spectrum? Let us turn to two cases in which we can identify with some precision both the entire range of behavior and the proportional distribution of the individual perpetrators along this spectrum: the village of Mir in Byelorussia (what the Germans called Generalkommissariat Weissruthenien) and the village of Marcinkance in the district of Bialystok near the Lithuanian border.

For the village of Mir there is the testimony of a survivor, Oswald Rufeisen. The special quality of his testimony derives from two factors. First, he had a unique vantage point. Born and educated in Silesia, Rufeisen spoke Polish and German without a detectable accent. Following his escape from Vilna, he was passing as a person of mixed Polish-ethnic German parentage when in November 1941 he was ordered to serve as the interpreter for the chief of the regional auxiliary police living in the village of Mir. Two months later, he was commandeered to serve as translator at the German Gendarmerie station in Mir under the command of Sergeant Reinhold Hein. For the next 7 months, until August 1942, Rufeisen slept in the house of the Byelorussian police commander at night. By day he worked at the German police station across the street and took his meals seated next to Sergeant Hein.

Second, Rufeisen's formidable memory has been tested and proved in an unusual way. He had given a detailed account of his escape from the Mir police station on several occasions. When the archives in Brest-Litovsk were finally made accessible to the west, a contemporary report by Sergeant Hein on Rufeisen's escape was found. The coincidence between Rufeisen's postwar recollections and the written report is remarkable to say the least.

The German Gendarmerie unit in Mir was composed of 2 career policemen — Sergeant Hein and his second in command, Corporal Karl Schultz — and 11 reservists from the north German region of Pommern. Hein was the only Catholic. Virtually all the men were in their forties. . . . Mealtime conversation was dull and humorless. There was no political conversation either, and Rufeisen had no idea who was or was not a party member. Hitler's name was mentioned only on the Führer's birthday. The only anti-Semitic expression Rufeisen could remember was when one of the Protestants once referred to Mary, mother of Jesus, as an "old Jewess" — a remark that was as anti-Catholic as it was anti-Semitic.

Among the 13 German Gendarmes, Hein's deputy Karl Schultz was a notorious sadist and drunkard, whom Rufeisen described as "a beast in the form of a man." He kept a notebook listing all those he had killed, a tally that reached more than 80 before Rufeisen escaped. His closest companions were Rothe and Schmelzer, whom Rufeisen did not characterize as sadists. But they also killed "without remorse or conscience." A fourth policeman, Steinbach, was also placed by Rufeisen in this group of those he considered the "worst" policemen.

In contrast, identified as the "best" policemen were the *Volksdeutscher*[11] from the Netherlands, Roth, and a man named Proksch. In his interview with me, though not in other accounts, Rufeisen also added to the list of the "best" policemen the man in charge of the kitchen, whom he remembered only by the first name of Adolf. These men did not take part in the killing of Jews, and their absence on these occasions was accepted without incident or repercussion. . . .

The remaining policemen were characterized by Rufeisen as "passive executors of orders," who killed without hate or ideological motivation. Concerning the spectrum of attitudes, Rufeisen noted:

> It was clear that there were differences in their outlooks. I think that the whole business of anti-Jewish moves, the business of Jewish extermination they considered unclean. The operations against the partisans were not in the same category. For them a confrontation with partisans was a battle, a military move. But a move against the Jews was something they might have experienced as "dirty."

Sergeant Hein was the most enigmatic figure among the 13 Germans. He, too, did not take part in the anti-Jewish expeditions and flatly told his young interpreter that he would never shoot a Jew. However, he added: "But someone must do it. Orders are orders." Thus he meticulously organized the killing expeditions that he left to Schultz to carry out. According to Rufeisen, Hein was always "very gentle" and even "reverent" toward the *Judenrat*[12] members, whose community he would eventually liquidate. When delegates of the *Judenrat* attempted to bribe Hein to spare the ghetto, he refused their gifts on the grounds that he could promise them nothing in return. When one of the Jewish leaders then asked him to see that they at least would "die a humanitarian death," Hein replied affirmatively: "I can promise you this," and showed them respectfully to the door.

Let us turn to the second example of Marcinkance, a small village and customs station in the district of Bialystok just west of the Lithuanian border. The Einsatzgruppen[13] and police battalions that passed through the district of Bialystok

---

[11] Persons of German ancestry who lived outside of Germany. Hundreds of thousands joined the German army as well as the SS.

[12] The Jewish Council, composed of Jewish leaders, that the Germans created to administer the ghetto under German authority and control.

[13] Mobile killing squads that accompanied the German invasion of the Soviet Union. Their function was to execute all Jews, as well as Gypsies, Soviet commissars (officials), handicapped people, and hospital psychiatric patients. These squads killed more than one million Jews, burying them in mass graves.

in the first month of Operation Barbarossa carried out numerous killings of Jews, but thereafter an eerie calm settled over the district. During the same months in which the bulk of Soviet and Polish Jewry were being destroyed, the Jews of the Bialystok district were being ghettoized and put to work. Finally, on November 2 and 3, 1942, all the Jews in the district except those in the two major ghettos of Grodno and the city of Bialystok itself were simultaneously rounded up and placed in transit camps, from which they were subsequently deported to Treblinka[14] and Auschwitz–Birkenau.[15]

This simultaneous roundup throughout the district stretched German manpower to the limit. In the case of Marcinkance, two career policemen from the Gendarmerie station in Sobakince — 47-year-old Sergeant . . . Albert Wietzke and 35-year-old Corporal . . . Paul Olschewski — were sent to Marcinkance, where they joined two reserve policemen stationed there — 44-year-old Wilhelm Pohl and 43-year-old Fritz Thomsch. By order of the local *Amtskommissar,*[16] Czapon, virtually every German official in town had to report for duty, in order to form a squad of 17 men, who were assigned the task of clearing a ghetto of some 200 Jews. Unlike further east, in the district of Bialystok large numbers of native auxiliary police or *Schutzmänner* had not been recruited to help the Germans in such activities, and thus the ghetto-clearing squad in Marcinkance was composed of Reich Germans.

Included were eight officials from the customs office, two officials of the forestry office, the local agricultural officer, and a railway employee. At least two were so-called old fighters, or *Alte Kämpfer* — Corporal Olschewski and the 41-year-old chief forester Hans Lehmann — who had both joined the party in March 1932. The secretary of the customs office, 40-year-old Emil Marquardt, was a 1937 joiner. The railway man, Otto Fahsing, also claimed party membership. The most recent membership of 1940 belonged to the overall commander, Sergeant Wietzke.

In short, of the 17 Germans assigned to the ghetto-clearing commando, 2 were career policemen and 2 were reserve police. The remaining 13 were drawn from five sectors of the civil administration. . . . Of the 7 known by full name, 5 were party members, including 2 "old fighters." The average age of these 7 was 40 years. These men were not a cross-section of German society in either age or party affiliation, but they were probably not untypical of Gendarmerie and civil administration personnel serving far behind the lines in the occupied eastern territories.

In fact, the ghetto-clearing squad was ultimately composed of only 15 men. After the Germans had assembled early on the morning of November 2, the *Amtskommissar* and the police sergeant ordered the Jewish council to assemble all

---

[14] Nazi death camp in Poland where 700,000 to 800,000 Jews were killed.

[15] The most notorious of the Nazi death camps, located in Upper Silesia, where 1.1 million Jews were killed. The Auschwitz complex also included concentration and forced labor camps.

[16] Subdistrict commissioner.

Jews at the ghetto entrance by 8 A.M. to be transported for "labor." The *Amtskommissar* then left to check on transportation but was unable to return "because he was summoned to a suicide of a customs official." In the entire file this suicide is referred to only once, without elaboration. Given the fact that this customs official took his life at the very moment when all customs officials were to report for the ghetto-clearing operation strongly suggests, however, that the suicide was not purely coincidental or unrelated to the task at hand.

What actually happened at Marcinkance on the morning of November 2, 1942, was the subject of a German investigation triggered not by the suicide, however, but rather by a complaining letter of the chief forester Hans Lehmann, written that very day to the *Kreiskommissar*[17] of Grodno. According to Lehmann, when the 15 Germans took up their positions around the ghetto of Marcinkance at 5 A.M., the Jews were totally unsuspecting. With the break of dawn, individual Jews who attempted to leave were easily turned back without resort to weapons. After the *Judenrat* had been informed that the ghetto was to be cleared, the Jews assembled quietly at the ghetto entrance. Then, according to Lehmann:

> Without any visible reason . . . the two Gendarmes suddenly opened fire on the densely packed mass of people. All broke into wild flight, leaving the dead and wounded behind. In panicked fright the Jews then naturally tried to break through the ghetto fence. Here they came under fire from the guards outside the fence, and there were many dead and wounded. Nevertheless given the general confusion and very thin cordon a very considerable number of Jews managed to flee into the nearby forest. . . . I am convinced that the entire shoot-out, in which above all we Germans were also greatly endangered, was completely senseless and without any reasonable cause. . . .

An investigation of Lehmann's complaint was launched immediately. Wietzke was asked to submit a written report, and a two-man commission composed of a local official of the civil administration and a lieutenant of the Gendarmerie interviewed five other participants on November 6. In his written report, Wietzke noted that before the action he had been warned that the ghetto was near the forest and poorly fenced, and he was explicitly instructed to counter any attempt at flight with use of weapons. *Amtskommissar* Czapon and he had ordered the Jewish council to assemble all Jews at the ghetto entrance for "labor" . . . , but only some 80 Jews initially appeared as ordered. Therefore, Wietzke continued, after Czapon departed to check on the train, he entered the ghetto again with Corporal Olschewski and the railway man Fahsing. They ordered the Jews they encountered to go to the assembly point, where the total number of Jews increased to some 150. When Olschewski ordered them to form up in rows of 6, the Jews "with one accord" . . . scattered in all directions, some trying to escape to the woods and others fleeing again to the houses. "Before this not a single shot had been fired," Wietzke claimed, but now he, Olschewski, and Fahsing opened fire with automatic weapons to prevent the attempted escape.

---

[17] Regional commissioner.

After the shoot-out, the same three men, joined by the customs head Marquardt, went on a house-to-house search through the ghetto, uncovering bunkers under five houses with disguised entrances sawed in the floorboards. This was proof, Wietzke wrote, that the Jews had prepared their hiding places long before. As not a single Jew could be induced to leave the bunkers either through coaxing or threat, "only the use of weapons remained to carry out the measures that had been ordered." In the end a total of 132 Jews were "shot trying to escape." . . .

When *Amtskommissar* Czapon finally returned, Wietzke continued, Lehmann left his post without orders, openly accused him of shooting "peaceful Jews" . . . , and then went home. . . . Lehmann had admitted that many Jews had escaped through the fence near him, but Wietzke had never heard a shot fired in this area. Thus Lehmann, who in any case had not brought a rifle but only a small pistol with him, had not obeyed orders to use his weapon to prevent escape. Moreover, Wietzke charged, Lehmann's position was 800 meters from the ghetto entrance, so he could not possibly have seen what had actually happened. Everyone else except Lehmann had kept their nerve and done their best to prevent "the scum of humanity, the Jews" . . . from fleeing. In conclusion, Wietzke again asserted, all his actions were in accordance with orders and no "unauthorized actions" had occurred.

The visiting commission interviewed only five men: the two reserve policemen — Pohl and Thomsch — who had been in the cordon and who were subordinate in rank to Wietzke, the two men — Olschewski and Fahsing — who had been inside the ghetto with Wietzke and taken part in the very actions for which Wietzke was being investigated, as well as the customs man Marquardt, who had joined the hunt for hidden Jews. In short, the commission did not interview anyone likely to contradict Wietzke's account and confirm Lehmann's. The strong suspicion must exist that this investigation was not an evenhanded search for the truth but from the beginning was aimed at collecting the testimony necessary to dismiss a bothersome complaint.

Reserve policeman Pohl had been in charge of the cordon on the north side of the ghetto. Around 8 A.M., he said, two or three shots rang out, and the Jews attempted to break through the dilapidated ghetto fence. As ordered, he opened fire to prevent escape and shot four Jews. "Subsequently," there was a burst of fire from automatic weapons, but he could not see who was shooting from his vantage point. Reserve policeman Thomsch was still in the police station in Marcinkance when he heard gunfire from the ghetto. He rushed to the unguarded west side of the ghetto where Jews were streaming through the fence. As previously instructed, he opened fire to prevent escape and short eight Jews. . . . Neither had joined the killing in the house-to-house search, and neither expressed any anti-Semitic sentiment to the investigators.

Fahsing and Olschewski — the two men in addition to Wietzke who had been equipped with automatic weapons and were inside the ghetto — gave such similar accounts in near identical language that it is difficult to avoid the conclusion that their testimony was coordinated beforehand. . . .

The two men also made no attempt to hide their anti-Semitic credentials. . . .

Emil Marquardt testified that from his post in the cordon he saw the Jews milling around and pressing toward the fence when, like Pohl, he heard two shots. A burst of automatic gunfire then erupted, and many Jews broke through the fence. As ordered beforehand, he opened fire on the fleeing Jews. Twenty-four Jews were killed along the fence line where he was stationed. He, too, testified that the breakout appeared to have been "planned and organized." . . .

Wietzke was fully backed by the investigating police officer, Lieutenant Porzig. . . .

. . . [T]he investigative commission, joined now by yet another police officer, Lieutenant Müller, confronted Lehmann, who initially reiterated his charge that the Gendarmes had fired on peaceful Jews for no visible reason. When pressed, Lehmann admitted that he was 300–350 meters away, too far to see what had caused the Gendarmes to open fire. . . . To Lieutenant Müller's accusation that Lehmann should view the matter from the "National Socialist standpoint," the forester allegedly replied that "if occasionally one were shot, that would not be so bad, but he could not do it. In that case he should be transferred; in that case he was not suited for this territory." . . . Lieutenant Müller then concluded in his report that according to convincing testimony, the Jews had not assembled peacefully as claimed by Lehmann but instead had milled around trying to find openings in the fence. When several shots had been fired against individual attempts to break out, the Jews had scattered in mass. As ordered beforehand to prevent escapes, the Gendarmes had then opened fire. . . . Müller ruled that his fellow Gendarmes had behaved properly, and he recommended action be taken against Lehmann for his "frivolous and totally unjustified false accusation and defamation" . . . against them.

Further up the hierarchy, *Landrat*[18] Dr. von Ploetz added to the charges against Lehmann. Not only had he made a frivolous and false accusation, which if true was of sufficient gravity to have led to Wietzke's conviction in a SS court, but Lehmann had also not performed his duty properly: he had not brought a rifle with him, he had not fired on the escaping Jews, and he had left his post early. Furthermore, he had displayed an attitude toward the Jews that was "not worthy of a high official serving in the east." *Landrat* Dr. von Ploetz concluded that Lehmann, who already had a record of run-ins with other officials, had this time gone too far. He recommended that Lehmann be taken into custody. . . .

On December 15, 1942, . . . [i]n the interests of sparing time on further investigation and restoring cooperation between the forestry office, the Gendarmerie, and the *Amtskommissar,* all sides agreed to drop their various accusations. . . . [T]he Marcinkance massacre was no longer at issue.

For the historian, it is not unuseful that the investigation was conducted by outspoken anti-Semites who made no secret of their dismay over Lehmann's complaint. Only those likely to confirm the account of the accused sergeant were interviewed. And as was not the case in postwar judicial investigations, they had

---

[18] Chief administrator of a rural district; district council head.

every incentive to boast of their anti-Semitic motivation, exaggerate their role in the killing, and provide evidence that Lehmann was an isolated troublemaker. Despite all of these biases in the investigation, what do we discover? Of the 17 Germans assigned to clear the ghetto at Marcinkance, 1 committed suicide and 1 protested openly. In addition to Lehmann, 2 other men on one side of the ghetto — the agricultural officer and one customs official — refrained from shooting at escaping Jews. And Lehmann's subordinate, the other forester, suffered a shoulder injury while trying to tackle an escaping Jew, which would indicate he, too, had been unwilling to shoot unarmed, fleeing Jews at point-blank range. Once the shooting was over, only 2 men — the senior customs official and the railway man but not the 2 reserve policemen — joined the 2 career policemen in the hunt for hidden Jews with the opportunity to continue killing. The 4 eager killers were indeed all Nazi Party members and avowed anti-Semites. It is hard to imagine that others could not have joined in the "Jew hunt" if they had wished. And it is hard to imagine that others would not have joined in the anti-Semitic denunciation of Lehmann if they, too, had found his views so alien and his behavior so objectionable.

From postwar testimony of Marcinkance survivors we learn additional relevant information. First, there is not a single reference to a planned and organized breakout, as alleged by the eager, ideological killers during the investigation. Those who survived spoke only of escape and hiding. Indeed, if there had been any such plan, the Jews would hardly have assembled at the gate first, presenting a compact target for the three Germans with automatic weapons, before making their breakout attempt. Second, 105 Jews were killed that day (Wietzke had claimed 132). Nearly 100 Jews escaped, out of whom 45 survived the war. And finally, in the winter of 1943 Jewish partisans derailed a German train in the forests of eastern Bialystok. Among those taken prisoner was Hans Lehmann. Identified by a Marcinkance escapee as having "actively" helped in the liquidation of the ghetto, Lehmann was promptly executed.

This evidence that offers rare and unusually precise insight into the behavior and attitudes of individual participants of two groups of German perpetrators suggests several conclusions. First, in each group there was a significant core of eager and enthusiastic killers — 4 of 13 in Mir and 4 of 17 in Marcinkance — who required no process of gradual brutalization to accustom themselves to their murderous task. And certainly in Marcinkance, though less in Mir, the evidence for their strong anti-Semitic convictions is clear.

In both cases there was a middle group that followed orders and complied with standard procedures but did not evince any eagerness to kill Jews. The evidence from Mir and Marcinkance does not indicate any transformation over time into eager killers, though certainly the evidence from the Czeladz Schutzpolizei and Reserve Police Battalion 105 suggests that such a process was at work among the German perpetrators elsewhere.

And finally in both Mir and Marcinkance there was a significant minority of men who did not participate in the shooting of Jews — 3 or 4 of 13 in Mir and at least 3 and perhaps as many as 5 of 17 in Marcinkance. Abstention from shooting by itself did not have disciplinary consequences for these men. Nor did the presence of this minority of nonshooters create significant tensions within the group. Their nonparticipation was both tolerated and brushed aside as inconsequential. The killing went on without them.

What did create tension and invoke disciplinary consequences was crossing the line from abstention to protest. What made the Marcinkance case so unusual was not that a number of the Germans did not fire their guns during the breakout but that one German committed suicide on the morning of the action and a second wrote a strong letter of protest. Passive abstention was one thing; an open and official challenge to the system was another. The eager killers and their supportive superiors banded together to discredit and crush their upstart accuser.

Emphasizing once again the fragmentary nature of the evidence that is therefore more suggestive than conclusive, what else can one nevertheless hazard to infer from these unusual and rare documents? In East Upper Silesia, where the pace of Jewish persecution was slower than elsewhere in eastern Europe, the hardening of police attitudes also took longer. In contrast, plunged into the murderous environment of Operation Barbarossa, the transformation of the men in Reserve Police Battalion 105 took place much more quickly. Both in this battalion and among the policeman stationed in Mir, the men were far more eager to kill those who could be classified as partisans than Jews. In Reserve Police Battalion 105 the Bremen reservist was proud of his unit's antipartisan actions, which he documented on film for his children. And at times he expressed a murderous bitterness toward the Russian prisoners of war and the Russian people as a whole. These attitudes stood in contrast to his willed indifference toward and muted acceptance of the mass murder of the Jews, about which he did not want his child to hear. Likewise in Mir, the men did not speak about the killing of Jews, which was viewed as a "dirty" task, but they spoke eagerly and proudly about their antipartisan actions.

What also emerges more starkly in these documents than in postwar testimony is the difference between career police and reservists. From the documents we see that in East Upper Silesia the commander of the Schutzpolizei was disturbed by the insufficient hostility toward and enforcement of measures aimed at Jews and furious about occasional instances of public fraternization. In Reserve Police Battalion 105 the reservist from Bremen criticized both the pompousness and hypocrisy of his officers. In Marcinkance the reserve police found things to do other than join the "Jew hunt," and their testimony was both devoid of anti-Semitic comment and less than effusive in providing support on behalf of their sergeant.

Career policemen like Sergeant Hein in Mir or Major Wilhelm Trapp of Reserve Police Battalion 101 were the exception. They clearly had no great liking for their task of killing Jews and personally distanced themselves from these actions. But simultaneously they ensured that the men under their command carried out the policies of their government and the actions that had been ordered by their superiors.

At the opposite extreme of Hein and Trapp were career Order Police officers like Fritz Jacob, the commander of 25 Gendarmerie[19] and 500 *Schutzmänner*[20] in Kamenetz–Podolsk in the south Ukraine, who wrote a series of revealing letters to one of the very highest ranking Order Police officers, Generalleutnant Rudolf Querner. Jacob's virulent hatred of Jews and commitment to the Final Solution were total. The Jews he characterized as "venereal, deformed, and feeble-minded." . . . They were "not humans but rather ape men" . . . whom he killed "without the slightest prick of conscience." . . . But Jacob was not limited to Jews in his appetite for killing. "We do not sleep here," he wrote. "Weekly 3–4 actions. One time Gypsies and another time Jews, partisans, or other riffraff."

In addition to his ideological commitment to do "practical work" for his Führer, Jacob was also an ambitious careerist. He welcomed his assignment in the east because "hopefully" he would "finally" receive advancement. . . .

Clearly the German Order Police was not monolithic, but in the end the diversity of attitudes and motives made little difference. Even if the "ordinary Germans" who were conscripted as reserve policemen did not go to the east exuding ideological commitment to National Socialism and eager for the opportunity to kill Jews, when the deportations and killing began, most did as they were told and many were changed by the actions they undertook. Both the men of the Reserve Police battalions — such as 101 in Lublin, 133 in Galicia, and 45 in the Ukraine, to name several of the most notorious — as well as the countless Gendarmerie and Schupo stations throughout the German empire in the east became efficient perpetrators of the Final Solution. A core of eager and committed officers and men, accompanied by an even larger block of men who complied with the policies of the regime more out of situational and organizational rather than ideological factors, was sufficient. Unfortunately, the presence of a minority of men who sought not to participate in the regime's racial killing had no measurable effect whatsoever.

---

[19] Rural armed police functioning as soldiers.

[20] Policemen.

PACKAGING PLEASURES:
CLUB MÉDITERRANÉE AND FRENCH
CONSUMER CULTURE, 1950–1968
Ellen Furlough

In the generations following World War II, Western societies, benefiting from improved technologies, increasing prosperity, and relative international peace, have given more attention and monies to leisure time than ever before. In a seemingly relentless pursuit of pleasure outside of work, people have flocked to new organizations and businesses that purport to convert spare time into happiness.

Ellen Furlough, a historian of modern France at the University of Kentucky, examines how one such business, Club Med, aimed to provide an "antidote to civilization" for French people. Using Club Med's own publications as well as other contemporary works, Furlough notes the paradoxes she sees in Club Med's endeavor to furnish an escape from modern consumer society. What does she see as the social appeal of Club Med?

Club Med emphasized social and behavioral roles in leisure activities that it believed to be antithetical to everyday French society. Furlough describes some interesting examples of such role-playing. There was a major emphasis on beautiful, naturally enhanced bodies, proudly adorned, and quintessentially erotic, and on exercise and hearty eating. The stress on comeliness and forthright sexuality represented a reaction to French civilization.

What were the Club Med "formula" and the "Club spirit"? What were the living conditions and the atmosphere at Club Med vacation spots? Certainly, the Polynesian and Tahitian themes affected the dress, behavior, and goals of the vacationers. What were the roles of the "congenial organizers," the GOs, and why did Club Med permit them to fraternize with the "congenial members," the GMs? What rituals did the villages perform, and how did those rituals function to close the GMs off from the outside world? One wonders whether the GMs discovered their natural selves.

The author sees incongruities in Club Med's strategies and does not believe that it was successful in providing an escape from consumer society. Some types

Ellen Furlough, "Packaging Pleasures: Club Méditerranée and French Consumer Culture, 1950–1968," *French Historical Studies* 18, no. 1 (spring 1993): 65–81.

of people took Club Med vacations and other social groups resisted the alluring appeal of Club Med's paradise vacations. Did the Club Med program bear a relationship to Western imperialism and colonization? Perhaps the little Gardens of Eden the Club intended to establish were doomed to be pale reflections of certain aspects of the dominant French culture.

Has the possibility of packaged fun (such as Club Med, cruises, and Las Vegas), welfare systems, and the lure of early retirement signaled the demise of a working culture? To what extent has leisure rather than work become a preoccupation of people today?

In the midst of the French revolution of May 1968, a crowd of student radicals targeted and shattered the glass windows of the Parisian headquarters of Club Méditerranée. Club Med epitomized all they rejected about French consumer society — huge meals, idle bronzed bodies, abundance in the midst of underdeveloped countries, and a commitment to narcissistic, apolitical hedonism. Club Med officials responded by offering some of the students free visits to Club Med vacation villages, insisting that the students would realize that Club Med was an "antidote to civilization," set apart from the values and experiences of French consumer culture.

The students' critique and Club Med's response raise the question that I will address in this article: to what extent was it possible for Club Med to be an "antidote to civilization" and to what extent was its representation in those terms the key to its consumer appeal? I will argue that Club Med was not an antithesis to "civilization"; rather, Club Med was central to and indeed helped to construct French consumer culture and consumer capitalism — the very "civilization" that it claimed to counteract. A second and related concern will be to explore the social bases for Club Med's appeal. Here I will argue that Club Med's "formula" expressed, and helped consolidate, the orienting practices, attitudes, and values of the "new" French middle class during what has been termed the "postwar regime of accumulation."

Gérard Blitz founded Club Med in the spring of 1950. Blitz had grown up in Belgium, where his father was a socialist Jewish diamond cutter with a passion for, what was called at the time, "physical culture." In 1945 the Belgian government offered Gérard Blitz, who was with the Belgian intelligence service during the war, the job of operating a center for the rehabilitation of concentration-camp survivors. Blitz spent the immediate postwar years thus engaged at a hotel in the Haute-Savoie region of France. Meanwhile, his sister Didy and his father operated a vacation club for people who shared a love of sports and a desire to break with wartime memories. As Didy later recalled, people "wanted to live/be alive after those dark times." While visiting this club, Blitz was struck by the similarities with his project in the Haute-Savoie and by the recuperative power of relaxation, play, and the sun. Unlike previous tourist enterprises which stressed moral self-improvement, education, public service, health and fitness, Blitz stressed self-indulgent physical pleasure and a break from habitual social relations. The goal was to remake the self, an especially appealing ethos for people who had lived through the sacrifices and bodily harms of the war.

On 27 April 1950, Blitz deposited the statutes for "Club Méditerranée" and placed a modest notice in the Paris metro showing the sun, the sea, and his telephone number. In the summer of 1950, some twenty-five hundred people spent two weeks at his first Club Med village, situated on the Bay of Alcudia on the Spanish island of Majorca. Socially, most in this first group were urban and middle class — primarily students and young cadres; others were secretaries, lawyers, and doctors. They hailed primarily from France and Belgium, but also from Holland, England, Switzerland, Norway, and Denmark. There was not a single building; people lived in U.S. Army surplus tents and slept on allied army cots. Blitz provided a small orchestra and sports equipment and presided with his wife Claudine, who had lived in Tahiti and regularly dressed in a Polynesian sarong. People swam, played sports, ate at tables for eight, and were entertained at night by flamenco dancers. Yet, after various troubles, including a hurricane, people demanded their money back. Blitz averted disaster by addressing the assembled guests as *gentils membres* (congenial members, hereafter GMs) and guaranteeing satisfaction or money back. Apparently, most were satisfied in the end. At regular reunions in Paris, GMs shared summer photos and danced in grass skirts and bathing suits until dawn. They also received copies of the Club's bulletin, the *Trident,* which contained news of the Club's off-season activities and of marriages and births of new GMs (children of members were, for a while in the 1950s, given free memberships), and which served as a kind of "wish book" for the upcoming summer activities. Club Med villages proliferated.

What Club Med administrators, managers, employees (*gentils organisateurs* or congenial organizers, hereafter GOs), and the GMs would soon label the *esprit du Club*[1] was being created, and it was this "esprit" that served as the basis for the Club's self-representation as an "antidote to civilization." The crucial element of this "esprit" was that it was to be diametrically different from everyday life and provide "mental and physical detoxification." Villages were seen as "closed" spaces, isolated from their surroundings and from other tourists, places where people could "rediscover the needs that urban reality repressed." The indigenous society was portrayed as a perturbation or perhaps a curiosity that one might visit later on an organized excursion. Inside, the village represented personalized and more intimate relations, intensity of life, liberty of choice, a place where people would be limited only by their capacities. Closure within the villages was not seen as a limit, but a condition of liberty. Within the villages was thus to be realized the utopian society of abundance and ease, and the operative logic inside the villages was to each his or her desires.

By the early 1950s the explicit model for this "counter-society" was a mythologized Polynesia, and this "Polynesian" theme informed the rhetoric and practices

---

[1] Club spirit.

of the Club. There were poems in the *Trident* about how the GMs, or "Polynesians," dreamed of "the arch of the beach, the Polynesian huts under the palms, and dug-out canoes, men pushing their canoe into the foam of the surf, chasing young girls wearing flowers, and fishing all day." As the army surplus tents began wearing out, they were replaced by Polynesian huts, and the costume of choice at Club Med villages became the flowered Tahitian sarong. Worn by both women and men, the sarong signified the "liberated" body and nativism, and the *Trident* obligingly provided full-page illustrations on the various ways to tie one (using "Tahitian-looking" models). By 1953 Claudine Blitz arranged for groups of Tahitian students from Paris to introduce GMs at the village on Corfu to Tahitian music and dances. Then, in 1955, Club Med established a village on Tahiti and advertised it as a "pilgrimage to the source . . . an earthly paradise." Here Club Med constructed an alternative landscape for French people confronting the implications of military defeats along with an emerging technocratic order. Representations of the "Primitive" can offer "a model of alternative social organization in which psychological integrity is a birthright, rooted in one's body and sexuality, and in which a full range of ambivalences and doubts can be confronted and defused through the culture's rituals, customs, and play."

Because villages were to be distinct from everyday life, there evolved elaborate welcoming and leaving rituals so that people would both symbolically and physically enter and leave its "closed" world. For example, GOs in sarongs greeted new arrivals with a trumpet fanfare and placed flowers around their necks. Once inside the village, physical accommodations and social activities were calculated to remind GMs that they had entered a space devoted to a "total rupture with daily habits, a period of return to the forgotten rhythms of nature." The architecture, whether the tents of the early 1950s, "Polynesian" huts from the mid-50s, or the later buildings built in "local styles," emphasized its opposition to urbanism and materialism and its connection to "nature."

More important, however, was the stated objective of erasing social barriers and distinctions. This process entailed abolishing the most visible signs of social distinction, in essence peeling away social conventions to reveal people's "authentic" selves. It was the convention in all villages for people to address each other in the familiar "tu"[2] form and to call each other by their first names. All discussions about one's occupation within "civilization" were discouraged. One of the "rules of the game" most closely attended to was a different mode of dress. Spending several weeks wearing bikinis and sarongs was seen as a "rupture with daily life," and one of the most common phrases heard in a village was that "there are no social differences when everyone is in a bathing suit." Another strategy that Club executives argued muted external signs of status was the practice of replacing cash with colored beads. In order to have a drink at the bar, for example, people detached some of the colored beads that they wore around their necks or ankles. A journalist joked, "It's so hard to carry real money in sarongs." The *Trident* called

---

[2] "You."

this the "disappearance of money," a revealing formulation that acknowledges the way this practice rendered invisible the cash nexus of the enterprise.

Another area in which Club Med positioned itself as different from "civilization" was in its emphasis on play rather than work. Even the labor of the GOs was constructed so that they would not appear to be working. A Club Med village was instead said to be a "leisure society" wherein people would rediscover their natural selves, rhythms, and desires. Sports and ludic activities were uppermost in Club Med's definition of leisure. Every village had a wide range of available sports, and there were often lessons from Olympic champions. Opportunities for play in the villages were also to be found in the nightly "animations." A favorite prank was to have a male GM lie on the floor as a squalling baby. A woman GM would change his diapers and powder his fly. The ability to participate in such playful, one might say ridiculous, activities was to demonstrate not only one's willingness to change the rules, but the ability to refuse superiority, rediscover childhood playfulness, and demonstrate that seriousness was a convention of another time and place. Ridicule was cast as a form of relaxation.

Club Med vacations were also characterized by ease rather than effort. Unlike most forms of tourism, Club Med advertising assured people that everything would be taken care of. It emphasized the convenience of the single-price format, the ease of comfortable transport, and the generally well organized nature of villages run by "specialists." Although everything was foreseen, little within the village was programmed; people could choose whether or not to participate in the village's activities. Time was to become "indefinite." Club literature deployed a language of individual choice, insisting that "how you fill your time is your business."

The result of the village's closed and controlled environment and its available experiences was to be the physical and mental well-being of the individual body. Club Med was ultimately packaging the care of the self and its recuperation through play, relaxation, and pleasure. Physical health and physical beauty were central to this vision. Outward appearance was the mark of one's personality, discipline, and inner essence. These corporeal preoccupations were shot through all aspects of Club Med, and I will only mention four aspects here. First, the Club's press constantly created a discourse of bodily description, in essence creating images of ideal — and ultimately normative — physical shapes. Club literature routinely published pictures of the managers of villages and described their bodies. And, because most managers were male, this particular discourse constructed ideal masculine bodies. Here is one description: "André Baheux, 41 years old, . . . height 1 m77, weight 60kg, spread . . . 1 m80; biceps, thighs, and calves fully formed."

A second ongoing theme concerned the making of beautiful bodies. Club literature constantly emphasized that "thanks to the numerous physical activities that we offer, you will refind, at whatever age, your shapely figure." Exercise was the dominant issue here — there was no mention of dieting. Although there were some discussions of women's bodies and exercise, the creation of beautiful feminine bodies tended to be portrayed in terms of various means of adornment that were not unlike similar discussions within other aspects of French consumer culture. There were articles in the *Trident* on "How to be Beautiful in the Village" with advice about appropriate fashions and makeup. Club Med publications encouraged women to bring beauty products with them — suntan lotion, hand cream, deodorant, indelible eye makeup, and cream to protect the skin and brown it lightly while waiting for a tan. Women's "natural" beauty was to be enhanced with beauty products and proper clothing.

A third kind of discussion about the body was overtly narcissistic and self-congratulatory. A striking example of this was the poem "Creed" published in the *Trident* in 1952. The poem has four stanzas, and the first three begin: "I love my arms," "I love my legs," and "I love my torso." These are followed by paeans to the body part in question, for example within the "I love my arms" stanza: "rippling deltoids, . . . flesh furrowed with veins which swell forth during vigorous play." The final stanza reads:

> I love my body where so many forces rest in order to rise up at my command. / I love its colors and I love its shapes as eternal things. / I love the "gay science"[3] as I love healthy life. / I love to train as I love to study. / I love competitions as I love books. / I love races as I love my poems. / I love joy as one loves a friend. / I love struggle as one loves a woman. / I love all that which is Effort and Life. / I love my body as my soul. /

And a final theme, more muted in the printed literature but central to all the others, was that of the erotic/libidinal body. An erotically charged climate was central to the "pleasures" that Club Med promised. The sexuality valorized at Club Med was predominately heterosexual, casual, spontaneous, and blurred the edges of definitions of propriety. One could, in this sense, speak of Club Med as a site for performing an expanded repertoire of sexualities and playful (and perhaps even transgressive) desires. For women, this could at once defy . . . the "highly rigid regulatory frame" of gender and sexuality and remind them of the risks involved in an era when both birth control and abortion were illegal in France.[4] Whether one chooses to interpret this erotically charged climate as "liberating" or not, it is certain that for people at the time, a Club Med vacation signified a loosening of the rules regarding sexuality. Club Med villages came to have a reputation as places with "an erotic morality" involving many "brief encounters," despite Blitz's insistence that there was "no more and no less libertinage than on any other kind of seaside holiday." Though unmarried GMs were housed in single-sex arrangements, Club conventions were that a towel folded over the outside door meant "do not disturb." A male GO boasted: "I knew the taste of all the suntan oil in the village." These four discussions were not distinct, but formed a discursive web that placed the beautiful, healthy body at its center. As the village man-

---

[3] Ellen Furlough states that the subtext of the penis is obvious here and that the phrase "gay science," difficult to translate, probably refers to the German philosopher Friedrich Nietzsche's (1844–1900) *The Gay Science*.

[4] In 1967 the Neuwirth Law authorized the sale of contraceptives, and in 1974 the law forbidding abortions was repealed. (Author's note.)

ager in Tahiti, which had the reputation of being the village with the most emphasis on physical beauty and "liberated" sexuality, asserted: "the Club was the revenge of the beautiful on the intelligent."

Despite the Club's self-representation as the "antidote to civilization," Club Med was squarely within, and constitutive of, French consumer culture and consumer capitalism. This is not to say, however, that Club Med's self-representation as the "antidote to civilization" was a kind of false advertising, but rather that the seeming contradiction between Club Med's self-representation and its realization were part of its essence and indeed crucial for its success.

Club Med's ethos as an isolated and recuperative Eden was as carefully packaged as any other consumer commodity. Club Med was, and is, a large, multinational corporation and an important player in the tourism and leisure industry. Like other institutions that construct sites for consumption, Club Med created integrated environments promising predictable pleasures. Although Club Med was originally founded in 1950 as a nonprofit association, in 1957 it was legally reconstituted as a commercial organization. . . . From the early 1960s, a significant proportion of Club Med was owned by the Rothschild bank, and its business decisions were within an economic logic that was not unlike any other consumer industry. By 1958 Club Med's business strategies were increasingly under the purview of Gilbert Trigano, a former communist who had become involved with Club Med through his family's camping supply business. After joining the Club in 1954 and moving rapidly up its hierarchy, Trigano decided that the Club needed to move into "mass" tourism, sharpen its business aspects, and attend to such issues as market segmentation. Plans for and decisions about villages were, like any other consumer commodity's design and execution, created in Parisian corporate offices and replicated in selected environments. By 1967 the club operated 31 villages in Europe and did about 20 million dollars worth of business. It had a rapidly expanding membership of over four hundred thousand, and there were around two thousand employees at the height of the summer tourist season. The Club was the largest civilian customer of the Italian State Railways and the largest short-haul charterer of Air France planes. Its expansion was further aided in 1968 by an agreement with American Express. This not only provided an important infusion of capital but guaranteed promotion of Club Med's programs throughout American Express's extensive network of travel agencies.

Like other aspects of consumer culture, and despite the Club's rhetoric, the villages were not utopian worlds without social hierarchies. In the 1950s and 1960s, Club Med was an experience constructed by and for white, economically advantaged Europeans, and later for Americans. There was no "class erosion" at work, although there may have been some mild shaking up of conventions. GMs were young (67 percent under 30 in 1961), and the largest group was drawn from middle-class salaried sectors. The largest proportions were teachers, secretaries (predominantly women), and technicians, but GMs also included cadres, people from the liberal professions (mainly doctors) and commerce, students, and a small group of workers (mostly from the relatively well-paid trades of metallurgy and printing).

The social composition of Club Med consumers drew heavily from the social group that Pierre Bourdieu[5] and others have termed the "new middle class," a group seen as a "new petit bourgeoisie"[6] of service people and technicians and the "new bourgeoisie" of cadres and "dynamic executives." It was the ethos of this new middle class that provided a template for the "esprit" of Club Med. Bourdieu argues that the "new" or renovated bourgeoisie and the "new" petit bourgeoisie "collaborated enthusiastically in imposing the new ethical norms (especially as regards consumption) and the corresponding needs." He points especially to new notions of pleasure and new perceptions of the body. In a passage strikingly similar to the ethos of Club Med, Bourdieu states that these new formulations of pleasure and the body

> make it a failure, a threat to self-esteem, not to "have fun," . . . pleasure is not only permitted but demanded. . . . The fear of not getting enough pleasure, the logical outcome of the effort to overcome the fear of pleasure, is combined with the search for self-expression and "bodily expression" and for communication with others (relating — *échange*), even immersion in others (considered not as a group but as subjectivities in search of their identity); and the old personal ethic is thus rejected for a cult of personal health and psychological therapy.

He adds that this group's conception of bodily exercise aimed "to substitute relaxation for tension, pleasure for effort, 'creativity' and 'freedom' for discipline, communication for solitude." It worked toward a "a body which has to be 'unknotted,' liberated, or more simply rediscovered and accepted." In Luc Boltanski's[7] analysis of the "cadres" (a group he argues typified the new middle class), he agrees that there was a strong link between the formation and consolidation of this new middle class and a new "lifestyle." Boltanski characterizes this lifestyle as an "easy-going American style simplicity, . . . a new, relaxed way of being bourgeois, a new way of life, . . . and a new system of values." Among those values was a "cult of the waistline and devotion to the physique." I am not arguing here that Club Med was reducible to a class phenomenon, but rather that it provided an ideal space to act out this new culture and thereby contributed to its formation. This was, in short, space for redrawing social and cultural boundaries and hierarchies rather than abolishing them. Despite such stories as the one involving GMs who struck up a friendship only to discover later that one of them was a director and the other a nightwatchman at the same factory, Club Med instead offered and helped consolidate another kind of cultural capital to be traded as a shared experience among privileged vacationers.

Club Med also reinforced, and in some cases reinvented, social hierarchies and boundaries between people in the villages and in host countries. Club executives saw the geographical locations for Club Med villages as culinary resources

---

[5] French social theorist (b. 1930).

[6] The lower middle class.

[7] French sociologist (1930–2002), author of *The Making of a Class: Cadres in French Society.*

and inspirational guides for ersatz architecture (that is, "Moorish bungalows in Morocco"), populated by people who were potentially objects for the excursions and the "tourist gaze." Club Med was, in this sense, a reconfigured colonialist adventure that could be purchased. In this period of French decolonization, Club Med vacationers could continue to partake of colonialist "exoticism" even if their country no longer controlled the region politically. One journalist who went to a Club Med village in Morocco in the mid-1960s observed an excursion to "the Club's own Moroccan village." He delineated the "modern" playful vacationers from the "natives" by describing the way the Club's beach property was carefully roped off; while the Club's vacationers were cavorting on the beach and working to tan their white bikini-clad bodies, Moroccans guarding the areas "spent most of their time inside straw beehives, in which they avoid the sun that the members have come so far to find." Like other aspects of consumer society, Club Med created and sustained hierarchies privileging those who were economically advantaged, physically vigorous, "attractive," and "modern."

Club Med's claim to be an "antidote to civilization," devoid of work, preoccupations with time, seriousness, or effort can also be seen as reinforcing the very issues from which it claimed to be separate. For example, for its employees, the villages were hardly leaving behind "work"; rather, their work environments were at the forefront of the growth and proliferation of consumer service industries where . . . "the social composition of . . . those who are serving in the front line, may be a part of what is in fact 'sold' to the customer." . . . Such services "require what can loosely be called 'emotional work' such as smiling and making people feel comfortable." This can be seen as a proliferation of "feminized" work, whether women do the majority of this labor or not, and it will tend to be low paid — a characteristic aspect of the salaries of GOs. The fantasy that Club Med was creating was one where workers did not really work and where "natives" were not really oppressed — a fantasy that masked and thus helped perpetuate power relationships. Further, to "experience" the loss of a mentality of time, seriousness, and effort means one must experience their ongoing realization "outside" the vacation experience. In other words, one kind of experience (vacations) depends on and helps perpetuate its supposed opposite (everyday life).

Another way that Club Med was constructing aspects of the "civilization" that it supposedly repudiated was that its "naturalness" always depended on certain material props. Consumers bought vacations at villages containing hair salons, sophisticated sports equipment, and stores on the premises. Not only was "materialism" never absent, but Club Med fostered a key element of tourist culture — that of the souvenir. Club Med villages regularly scheduled shopping expeditions to local markets. There one could buy souvenirs — material witnesses to the commercialized "experience" of a Club Med vacation. One's transformed body could also be seen as a souvenir — returning from vacation with a tan, for example, signified physical beauty, eroticism, and a "successful" vacation.

The materialism and the consumerist theme of abundance was especially evident regarding food, an element that figured prominently in the ambiance and imaginary of the Club. Food and wine in the villages were unlimited and included in the basic cost, and both were universally said to be excellent. Club Med also fostered materialist consumer culture in the realm of clothing. From 1959, it had its own mail-order catalogue uniquely for GMs who were registered for a village for the next summer. Tahitian sarongs figured prominently in the selection.

Finally, the Club was also involved in constructing a cultural pastiche that placed it squarely within, and helped to create, other aspects of consumer (and postmodernist) culture. Not only did Club Med evoke the "natural" in the midst of a carefully packaged environment, but cultural productions were carefully utilized to create an ambiance mixing elements of "high" and "mass" culture. For example, in 1963 Club Med introduced "The Forum" into its villages. These were cast as "occasions to follow a spectacle, to participate in it, to discuss, to understand the givens of new problems, . . . to make vacations not only a rest for the nerves and the body but also an enrichment of the spirit and of the imagination." Forum discussions included Hellenism, Italian geniuses of the Quattrocento,[8] heart surgery, and the mysteries of the universe. From the mid-1960s, there were taped concerts of classical music that included a commentary in French so "no one need wonder what to think of the music." (Here again we can see Club Med attending to cultural capital.) The Club's ambiance also incorporated aspects of popular culture. One account of a British woman's journey to Club Med noted that on the journey they "twisted into the early hours of the morning." At one village, a participant described lazing in the sun next to the bar, where "the hi-fi pipes out Jacques Brel[9] and Pete Seeger."[10] Like advertising, which is, of course, another constituent element of consumer culture, Club Med promoted a "pastiche or collage effect in which the breadth and depth of cultural values can be ransacked to achieve a desired effect."

In conclusion, Club Med emerged at a particularly promising historical moment. Culturally . . . even if the reality for French people of the 1960s was more nuanced, by the late 1960s "the imaginary had changed: consumer society was in people's heads." . . . This consumer society had its symbols (the TV, the auto, the washing machine), its privileged moments (prime time, the weekend, vacations), and its recognized places (the salon, the supermarket, beach, or camping). It fostered values of abundance, comfort, and youth, and an ideology of individual choice. Club Med was all of these things, a symbol, a place, and a set of values, and its meanings were those of the larger consumer society of which it was a part.

A central tenet of Club Med was that it proclaimed the body as a vehicle for pleasure. Club Med celebrated, permitted, promoted, and commodified, the fitness, beauty, energy, and health of the libidinal "natural" body. Club Med participants were to pay, in all senses, attention to the self, and part of the grammar of pleasure that Club Med helped create was a heightened concern with the "care of the self." One's body, in essence, was one's text to be endowed with meaning.

---

[8] Fifteenth century.

[9] Belgian singer and composer (1929–1978).

[10] American folk singer and composer (b. 1919).

Crucial to this project was (and is) the endless longing and impossibility of attaining and retaining a youthful, healthy, playful, sexy body. One could, by definition, never be satisfied. What is particularly interesting about Club Med was the way this dynamic interplay between longing and lacking was initially played out within an inventive cultural landscape laced with the "primitive" Polynesian. Here we can read the longing for a culture where one could be at one with nature and find sexual pleasure along with mental and physical health, . . . using the primitive within a "rhetoric of desire." And yet, Club Med fostered the notion that people could count on having easy access to a beauty parlor, mixed drinks, and piped music. Here again we see the ways in which Club Med's utilization of what might seem to be contradictory messages and strategies was indeed crucial for its success.

This raises questions about the relationship between the social management of pleasure for profit and the consumers themselves. Is this yet another instance of a Foucaultian[11] institution controlling and regulating a set of disciplines on the individual body? Or, do we need to analyze Club Med in terms of the ways in which people understood, enjoyed, created, and perhaps subverted those "experiences"? How can we understand and theorize the historical roles and experiences of pleasure as they adhere to consumption, and how do we differentiate . . . between "real pleasure and mere diversion"? Although answering these questions is beyond the scope of this article, it is certain that the "care of the self" was closely aligned with consumer culture's message of individualist self-determination and expression. The language of the self and of individual pleasure was crucial for the cultural consolidation of a new middle class, and it obviated a language of class linked to an oppositional spirit or an ongoing political struggle. The notion of the "new middle class" was itself politically important in the 1950s and 1960s, a time heralded by some as a new social order whose social center of gravity would be the middle class. This new middle class was portrayed as "a vast group of people leading comfortable lives, sharing similar values, and employed by large organizations — individualists governed by the competitive spirit and the drive to achieve." . . . [T]he new class would support the "end of ideology" and "alleviate class tensions" through a "more equitable distribution of consumer goods and education." Bourdieu offers another way to look at this group's "new ethic of liberation" — it could supply the economy with "the perfect consumers" who were "isolated . . . and therefore free (or forced) to confront in extended order the separate markets . . . of the new economic order . . . untrammelled by the constraints and brakes imposed by collective memories and expectations."

Club Med in particular, and tourism in general, were at the forefront of consumerism's culture of distraction, fantasy, and desire. Club Med accented, packaged, and marketed key components of an emergent consumer culture: a rhetoric

---

[11] Referring to the philosopher-historian Michel Foucault (1926–1984) who saw institutions such as the prison and the asylum as modern developments whose functions were to discipline and punish.

of longing and desire, the elevation of the autonomous, healthy and pleasurable body, a (post) modern reliance on pastiche, and a belief in (and commodification of) the recuperative necessity of non-workplace touristic "experiences." Modern "mass" tourism has been a crucial engine — both culturally and economically — for modern consumer societies. While one could argue that both Club Med and French students of 1968 were questioning disciplinary boundaries and structures, it can also be argued that to accept and experience the values, definitions, and "pleasures" that Club Med offered was to believe that the system of consumer capitalism giving rise to Club Med worked.

THE RISE AND FALL OF THE
SWEDISH MODEL
Kristina Orfali

In the years since World War II, many have viewed Sweden as a paradise, a culture worthy of emulation and envy, because of its open, progressive society and its concern for the welfare of all its citizens. With the demise of the Soviet Union — which had before provided a model society for Eastern European states, for some individuals and political parties in the West, and certainly for many Third World countries — Sweden may provide an alternative to the creeping Americanization of Europe.

A sociologist, Kristina Orfali relies on newspapers, magazines, books, and government documents to present a nuanced overview of Swedish society. She points out that Sweden has been at the forefront of progressive legislation. What are the goals of Swedish legislation? What does Orfali mean by the "antisecrecy model"? To what extent are children, minorities, and immigrants better off in the Swedish system?

Sweden has a reputation for being open sexually. How have changing mores as well as laws affected marital relations, homosexual culture, prostitution, and the distribution of sexually explicit materials?

Free access to official documents, the computerization of society, collective decision making, and the right of the state to intervene in family life (to prevent corporal punishment, for example) have made Swedish society open and transparent. Where then do Swedes find privacy? What tensions exist between communitarian impulses and individualism? Orfali makes clear that Swedish society is less than perfect, even if it is admired; problems still exist in spite of Swedish social engineering.

Are there currently other societal models in Europe?

Kristina Orfali, "The Rise and Fall of the Swedish Model," in *A History of Private Life,* vol. 5, ed. Philippe Ariès and Georges Duby, trans. Arthur Goldhammer (Cambridge: Belknap Press of Harvard University Press, 1991), 417–449.

Sweden is a country that has long fascinated many parts of the world. In the 1960s a whole generation grew up on clichés of blondness and liberation, on fantasies of a sexual El Dorado filled with shapely Ekbergs[1] and sirenic Garbos[2] — but also with Bergman's[3] anguished heroines. Little by little, however, this fantasyland metamorphosed into a dark country inhabited by bores, morbid minds, and would-be suicides, a nation of "disintegrated families," "disoriented sex," and "liberated lovers in search of love" — in short, a "paradise lost." The Swedish ideal, once the object of extravagant praise and extravagant denunciation, ultimately was converted into a hyperborean[4] mirage. The idyll was gone. The welfare state, recast in the role of meddling nuisance, no longer was a country to be imitated. Yesterday's middle way (between communism and capitalism) had become a utopian dream. Today it is fashionable on the part of many people to denounce Sweden as a "benign dictatorship" or "kid-glove totalitarianism."

There is nothing fortuitous about either the initial enthusiasm or the subsequent disillusionment. The Swedish model — in part economic and political but primarily societal — did indeed exist (and to some extent still does). The very word *model* (not, it is worth noting, of Swedish coinage) is revealing. People are apt to speak of the "Americanization of a society," of the "American myth" (that "everyone can become rich"), or even of "American values," but when they speak of a Swedish model they conjure up the image of an exemplary society. Swedish society is endowed not just with material or political content but with philosophical or even moral significance, with "the good life." As long ago as 1950 Emmanuel Mounier[5] asked himself, "What is a happy man?" The Swedes, he answered, "were the first to have known the happy city."

More than may meet the eye the Swedish model is a model of social ethics. Insofar as Sweden is a nation above suspicion, a nation that aspires to universality (in the form of pacifism, aid to the Third World, social solidarity, and respect for the rights of man), and a nation whose ideological underpinnings are consensus and transparency, it can perhaps be seen as the forerunner of a new social order. In this respect the distinction between public and private in Sweden is highly significant. Hostility to secrecy, deprivatization, public administration of the private sphere — in all these areas Sweden has shifted the boundary between public and private in noteworthy ways. But the ethos of absolute transparency in social relations and the ideal of perfect communication, both characteristic of Swedish society, are seen in many parts of today's world as violations of individ-

---

[1] Anita Ekberg, Swedish film actress (b. 1931).

[2] Greta Garbo (1905–1990), Swedish film actress, noted for her beauty and her passion for privacy.

[3] Ingmar Bergman (b. 1918), Swedish film director, famous for his complex depiction of morality and faith.

[4] The extreme north of the earth.

[5] French philosopher (1905–1950).

ual privacy. The antisecrecy model has come to be seen as an intolerable form of imperialism.

The antisecrecy model affects all areas of social life down to the most private. In Sweden, perhaps more than anywhere else, the private is exposed to public scrutiny. The communitarian, social-democratic ethos involves an obsession with achieving total transparency in all social relations and all aspects of social life.

In Sweden money is not a confidential matter. Just as in the United States, material success is highly valued and ostentatiously exhibited. Transparency does not end there. Tax returns are public documents. Anyone can consult the *taxering kalender,* a document published annually by the finance ministry that lists the name, address, date of birth, and declared annual income of each taxpayer. Turning in tax cheats is virtually an institutionalized practice. While the fiscal authorities state publicly (in the press, for example) that informing on cheats is morally reprehensible, they admit that such information is frequently used. Even in the ethical sphere the imperative of transparency takes precedence.

Another illustration of the imperative is the principle of "free access to official documents" *(Offentlighets Principen).* Under the free-access law, which derives in large part from a 1766 law on freedom of the press, every citizen has the right to examine official documents, including all documents received, drafted, or dispatched by any agency of local or national government. The law allows for examination of documents in government offices as well as for having copies made or ordering official copies from the agency in return for payment of a fee. Any person denied access to public information may immediately file a claim with the courts. In practice the right of access is limited by the provisions of the secrecy act, which excludes documents in certain sensitive areas such as national security, defense, and confidential economic information. Nevertheless, the rule is that "when in doubt, the general principle [of free access] should prevail over secrecy."

As a result of the free-access principle the Swedish bureaucracy has been exceptionally open. For a long time Sweden has been an "information society," one in which information circulates freely. Computerization has accentuated this characteristic by facilitating the exchange of large quantities of information, in particular between the private sector and government agencies. There are few other countries in which the computers of several insurance companies are closely linked to those of the vital records office. Private automobile dealers may be electronically linked to vehicle registration records; a state agency may make use of a private company's credit records. Since 1974 information stored in computers has been treated just like other public documents and thus made subject to free access.

Sweden was the first European country to establish a central Bureau of Statistics (in 1756). It was also the first to issue citizen identification numbers. Comparison of different databases has been facilitated by this assignment of a personal identification number to each citizen. The practice was begun in 1946, and the numbers were used by state agencies before being incorporated into electronic databases. They are now widely used in public and private records.

If computers make individuals transparent to the state, the machines them-selves must be made transparent to individuals. The computer security act of 1973 (amended in 1982) was the first of its kind in the West. It established the office of Inspector General for Computing Machinery with the authority to grant authorization to establish a database, to monitor the use of databases, and to act on complaints relative to such use. While authorization to establish a database is usually a mere formality, it is much more difficult to obtain when the data to be gathered includes information considered to be "private." Encompassed under this head are medical and health records, records of official actions by social welfare agencies, criminal records, military records, and so on. Only government agen-cies required by law to acquire such information are authorized to maintain these sensitive files. Finally, any person on whom information is gathered has the right to obtain, once a year at any time, a transcript of all pertinent information.

Some view this computerization of society as a highly effective, not to say dan-gerous, instrument of social control. Many foreign observers have seen it as mark-ing an evolution toward a police state in which all aspects of private life, from health to income to jobs, are subject to shadowy manipulation. Interestingly, com-puterization has aroused virtually no protest within Sweden. Everyone seems con-vinced that it will be used only for the citizen's benefit and never to his detriment. The consensus reveals a deep-seated confidence in the government (or, rather, in the community as a whole, which is ultimately responsible for control of the information-gathering apparatus). To Swedes, the whole system — private indi-viduals and government agencies alike — is governed by one collective morality.

We must guard against the simplistic notion that Swedish society is a kind of Orwellian[6] universe, a world of soulless statistics. Paradoxically, this society of numbered, catalogued, faceless individuals is also a society of individualized faces. Every daily newspaper in the country publishes a half-page of photos to mark readers' birthdays, anniversaries, and deaths. Society notes take up at least a full page, and the absence of social discrimination is striking. One obituary recounts the career of a Mr. Andersson, *Verkställande dirktör* (plant manager), while another is devoted to a Mr. Svensson, *Taxichaufför* (taxi driver). Every birthday — espe-cially the fiftieth, to which great importance is attached — is commonly marked by several lines in the paper and by time off work. This mixture of a modern, com-puterized society with still vital ancient customs is a unique aspect of Swedish society.

Transparency is also the rule in collective decisionmaking. The ombudsman is one Swedish institution that is well-known abroad. The parliamentary om-budsman, oldest of all (dating back to 1809), handles disputes over the bound-ary between public and private and is especially responsible for protecting the in-dividual's "right to secrecy." He hears complaints, takes action when the law is violated, and offers advice to government agencies. Less well known, perhaps, but

---

[6] Referring to the totalitarian future described by the English writer George Orwell (1903–1950) in his novel *1984* (1948).

just as important is the procedure of public investigation. Before any major law is enacted, an investigative committee is appointed to consider pertinent issues. The committee includes representatives of different political parties, important interest groups, and various experts such as economists and sociologists. After hearings, surveys, and perhaps on-the-spot investigation, the committee transmits its report to the legislative department of the relevant ministry, which then makes public recommendations. Any citizen may also submit advice to the ministry. Thus the most "private" subjects such as homosexuality, prostitution, violence, and the like become the focus of major public debates, on an equal footing with such "public" issues as price controls, the regulation of television, the Swedish book of psalms, or the country's energy policy.

This uniquely Swedish procedure plays an important role in the elaboration of policy decisions and in the achievement of consensus. Its existence demonstrates not only how the most apparently "private" subjects are dealt with by institutions but also how individuals can take part in the various phases of the decisionmaking process. Two key ethical imperatives are highlighted: transparency of the decision process and consensus concerning the results.

Many people are unaware that Lutheranism is the state religion of Sweden and that the Lutheran Church is the established church. (Contrast this with Italy, where Catholicism is no longer the established religion.) It was in 1523, at the beginning of the Reformation, that the Lutheran Church began to function as an integral part of the governmental apparatus. The church played an instrumental role in the political unification of Sweden, since participation in religious services was then considered to be a civic obligation. The strength of the bond between church and state is illustrated by the fact that until 1860 Swedes were not permitted to quit the church — and even then they were required to become members of another Christian community. This requirement was not eliminated until 1951. Any child born a citizen of Sweden automatically becomes a member of the Church of Sweden if either its father or its mother is a member. Thus 95 percent of the Swedish population nominally belongs to the official church.

Sweden therefore remains one of the most officially Christian of states, but it is also one of the most secular. The church is controlled by the government, which appoints bishops and some clergymen, fixes their salary, collects religious taxes, and so on. (A citizen who does not belong to the Church of Sweden still must pay at least 30 percent of the religious tax because of the secular services performed by the church.) The church is responsible for recording vital statistics, managing cemeteries, and other public functions. Thus, every Swedish citizen is inscribed on the register of some parish. The pastor who performs religious marriages is also an official of the state, so a religious marriage also serves as a civil marriage.

The institutional character of the Church of Sweden is reflected in public participation in religious ceremonies. Roughly 65 percent of all couples choose to be married in church. More than 80 percent of children are baptized and confirmed in the Lutheran Church. Some members of the official state church also belong to one of the "free," or dissident, Protestant churches that derive from the Lutheran evangelical wing of the religious awakening movement (*Väckelse rörelser*), most active in the early nineteenth century. Taken together, the free churches claim a higher proportion of the religious population in Sweden than in other Scandinavian countries.

Nevertheless, this formal presence of ecclesiastical institutions cannot hide the widespread disaffection with religion among Swedes. Fewer than 20 percent claim to be active churchgoers. In contrast, a tenacious, almost metaphysical anxiety is a profound trait of the Swedish temperament. Swedes may not believe in hell, but they surely believe in the supernatural. To convince oneself of this one need only glance at the half-pagan, half-religious festivals that fill the Swedish calendar or recall the importance of trolls and the fantastic in Swedish literature, folklore, and films. Or consider a writer as profoundly Swedish as Nobel prize winner Pär Lagerkvist, author of *Barabbas* and *The Death of Ahasuerus,* whose work is one long, anguished religious interrogation. André Gide,[7] another tormented conscience, wrote of *Barabbas* that Lagerkvist had pulled off "the tour de force of walking the tightrope across the dark stretch between the real world and the world of faith."

The reconciliation of the real with the spiritual is thus more tenuous than it may first appear. The collective religious morality of the past has been transformed into a new morality, still collective but now secular, while literature and film continue to reflect the spiritual world, the metaphysical anguish and tenacious guilt that have left such a deep imprint on the Swedish imagination.

The degree to which the private sphere is open to the public is clearly visible in the evolution of family structure. There is nothing new about the fact that in a modern state "functions" once left to the family have been taken over by the government or community. In Sweden, however, this deprivatization of the family has taken on a rather specific aspect. The point is not merely to intervene in private life but to make the private sphere totally transparent, to eliminate all secrecy about what goes on there. If, for example, an unwed or divorced mother applies to the government for financial assistance, or if a child is born in circumstances where the paternity is dubious, a thorough investigation is made to identify the father. Any man who, according to the woman or her friends, has had relations with the mother can be summoned to testify. Putative fathers may be required to undergo blood tests. If necessary the courts will decide. Once paternity is established, the father is required to provide for the child's upkeep.

The justification for such a procedure is not so much economic as ethical: every child has a right to know its true father. Clearly, however, acting on such a principle may yield paradoxical results. A single woman who wants to have a child and then raise it alone forfeits her social assistance if she refuses to cooperate with the paternity investigation. Although the 1975 abortion law grants women the right to control their own bodies, they do not have the right "to give birth without providing the name of the father." The child's rights take precedence over all

---

[7] French author (1869–1951) and winner of the Nobel Prize in literature in 1947.

others; even if the mother refuses social assistance, all available means (including the courts) will be used to force her to reveal the father's identity, on the grounds that the question is fundamental and that the child will wish to know. In paternity, therefore, there is no secrecy. Kinship is supposed to be transparent and clearly determined. The notion of legitimacy thus sidesteps the family, and the institution of marriage rests on public information, which is guaranteed by law.

Recent Swedish legislation on artificial insemination is also based on the requirement of transparency. Göron Ewerlöf, judge and secretary of the Commission on Artificial Insemination, put it this way: "It is to be hoped that future artificial inseminations will be more candid and open than they have been until now. The objective should be to ensure that birth by insemination is not unthinkable and indeed no more unusual than adoption. In matters of adoption Sweden has long since abandoned secrecy and mystery. According to specialists in adoption, this has helped to make adoptive children happier." Sweden was the first country in the world to adopt a comprehensive law governing artificial insemination (March 1, 1985). Previously, artificial insemination involving a donor had been shrouded as far as possible in secrecy. All information concerning the donor was kept hidden (or destroyed). The chief innovation of the new law — and incidentally an excellent illustration of the antisecrecy model — was to eliminate anonymity for donors. Every child now has the right to know who his biological father is and may even examine all hospital data concerning the individual. (Not even adoptive parents have access to this information.) In the past attention was focused on preventing the child from learning how it was conceived. Today it is the opposite: the primary objective is to protect the child's interest, which means not blocking access to any available information about the identity of its biological father. The commission underscored the importance of a frank and open attitude toward the child on the part of the parents. In particular, it recommended (although the law does not prescribe) that at the appropriate moment parents tell the child how it was conceived. The interest of the child was again invoked to justify the decision not to authorize artificial insemination except for married couples or couples living together as though married. It is not authorized for single women or lesbian couples. Thus the image of the standard family — father, mother, and children — has been maintained, even though the number of single-parent families in Sweden has been on the rise. Various psychological and psychiatric studies were invoked in support of this decision. The primary goal is to ensure the child's optimal development. Adoption laws are even more restrictive, and adoption is limited in most cases to married couples.

The status of the child in Sweden tells us a great deal about Swedish culture and ethics. Children are regarded both as full citizens, and as defenseless individuals to be protected in almost the same manner as other minority groups such as Laplanders and immigrants. The changing status of children is the clearest sign of deprivatization of the family. Since 1973 Sweden has had a children's ombudsman, whose role is to act as a spokesperson for children and to educate the public about children's needs and rights. The ombudsman has no legal authority to intervene in particular cases. He can, however, apply pressure to government agencies and political representatives, suggest ways to improve the condition of children, instruct adults about their responsibilities toward children, and, thanks to a twenty-four-hour telephone hot-line, offer support to individual children in distress. Thus children in Sweden enjoy specific rights and an institution whose purpose is to defend them. The objective is, while respecting the individuality of children, to make sure that they will be integrated as harmoniously as possible into the society.

The same ethic prevails in regard to immigrant children, who are entitled to receive instruction in their native language. Since 1979 the state has allocated funds to provide language lessons for immigrant children of preschool age, and nursery schools increasingly group children by native tongue. Everything possible is done to make sure that immigrant children have the tools they need to learn their mother tongue and preserve their culture by maintaining bilingual competence. Results have not always kept pace with ambitions, however. Many children have a hard time adapting to one culture or the other and a hard time mastering one of the two languages. Integration is envisioned, but respect for the immigrant's native culture is considered imperative.

Immigrants in Sweden enjoy many rights: they can vote in municipal and cantonal elections and are eligible to hold office; they are not confined to ghettos but scattered throughout the society in order to encourage integration; they receive free instruction in Swedish; and they receive the same social benefits as natives. Nevertheless, Sweden has not really been able to achieve a fusion of cultures, a melting pot in the manner of the United States.

The autonomy of the child vis-à-vis familial and parental authority is reflected in the law prohibiting corporal punishment. Since July 1979 the law governing parent-child relations has prohibited all forms of corporal punishment, including spankings, as well as mental cruelty and oppressive treatment. Examples explicitly mentioned in the law include shutting a child in a closet, threatening or frightening, neglect, and overt ridicule. Admittedly, no specific penalties for violation of these provisions have been set, except in cases of physical injury. Nevertheless, any child who is struck may file a complaint, and the person responsible cannot protest that he believed he had the right to administer a spanking. This once private right, covert yet in a sense symbolic of parental authority, no longer exists.

In various ways the political sphere controls more and more of what used to be private space. The family no longer bears exclusive responsibility for the child. The child's rights are determined not by the family but by the entire national community in the form of legal and social protections. The child therefore spends more time outside the private realm and is increasingly socialized outside the family. Parent-child relations are no longer a strictly private matter; they are governed by the public. The society as a whole is responsible for *all* its children.

This way of thinking is illustrated by the so-called parental education reform of 1980. All prospective parents were invited to participate in voluntary discussion and training groups during gestation and the first year after birth. (Those who attended these groups during working hours were entitled to compensation under the parents' insurance program.) The goal of parental training was to "help improve the situation of children and families in the society": "The community and its institutions should not themselves assume responsibility for children but should try instead to give parents the means to do the job." Interestingly, this parental training, usually administered outside the home to groups of parents, was also a way of encouraging group experience, a way of fostering solidarity among individuals faced with similar problems. Individuals were drawn into group activities, and most who began with a prenatal group continued with a postnatal one. The social reforms helped to reinforce the highly communal nature of Swedish society by emphasizing all the ways in which the individual or family cell is integrated into the larger group or society.

Because the Swedish child is considered to be a full citizen, he or she may, at an appropriate age, take legal action to alter unsatisfactory conditions. This principle applies in particular to disputes arising out of divorce. The child may be a party to hearings to determine custody and visiting rights and is entitled to legal representation. Small children may even be represented by a proxy appointed by the court. In case of separation the child may choose which of its parents it wishes to stay with, even contesting the amicable settlement reached by the parents (although visiting rights are not subject to challenge). In short, the child's opinion may be expressed and defended in exactly the same manner as that of any other citizen.

If family life is largely open to public scrutiny, so is the life of the couple. Since 1965 sexual offenses such as marital rape have been subject to criminal prosecution. Since 1981 battered women have not been required to appear in person to accuse their husband or partner; a declaration by a third party is sufficient to initiate proceedings. Of course homosexuality is no longer a crime in Sweden; criminal penalties were abolished as long ago as 1944. In 1970, following a period in which a wave of sexual liberation spread over the country, homosexuals founded the National Organization for Equality of Sexual Rights, or RFSL (Riksförbundet för Sexuellt Likaberättigande).

In 1980 the government conducted a sweeping investigation into the possibility of reforming legislation concerning homosexuals so as to prevent discrimination. The investigative commission not only proposed a series of laws guaranteeing complete equality between heterosexuals and homosexuals but also advocated active support for homosexual culture and organizations. The possibility of institutionalized cohabitation of homosexual couples conferring the same benefits as marriage was also discussed. These proposals stemmed from an official investigative commission.

Paradoxically, the proposal encountered vigorous opposition on the part of certain lesbian groups, which contended that the new laws would have the effect of forcing lesbians to accept the outmoded institution of the family, which deserved no additional support from the government. They insisted that the law concern itself not with couples, whether homosexual or heterosexual, but with individuals, regardless of their relationship. The upshot was that homosexual marriage is still legally impossible in Sweden.

Well before the sexual revolution of the 1960s sexuality had lost something of its totally private character owing to the introduction of sex-education classes in the schools. In 1933 the National Association for Sexual Information, or RFSU (Riksförbundet för Sexuellt Upplysning) was founded. The goal of this nonprofit organization was to "promote a society without prejudice, tolerant and open to the problems of sexuality and to the life of the couple." At the time the chief concern was not so much to liberalize sexuality as to combat venereal disease and abortion. Nevertheless, the effort to make sexual information widely available gradually broke down a series of taboos. In 1938 a new law on contraception and abortion struck down the ban that had existed since 1910 on distributing information about or selling contraceptives. The rules governing abortion were also modified. Abortion was authorized for three reasons: physical disability; pregnancy resulting from rape; and the possibility of serious congenital defects.

In 1942 optional sex education was made available in the schools, and in 1955 it became compulsory. Such instruction initially was quite conservative; students were told that the sole purpose of sexual relations was procreation in marriage. Soon, however, students as young as seven were studying sexuality, or what Le Monde[8] in a December 1973 headline called "la vie à deux."[9] It was stressed that "the act of love should be based on reciprocal affection and mutual respect." Nevertheless, matters as intimate as "masturbation, frigidity, homosexuality, contraception, venereal disease, and even pleasure" were discussed. By 1946 the law required pharmacies to stock contraceptives, and in 1959 the sale of contraceptives outside pharmacies was authorized.

At last sexuality was out in the open, in a quite literal sense. Finally, in 1964, advertising for contraceptives (sponsored by the RFSU) began to appear in newspapers and magazines. This advertising was meant to be informative, even technical, but frequently it adopted a playful and engaging tone, because its purpose was not only to inform but also to sell. Before long, advertising went far beyond condoms and diaphragms to include all sorts of sex-related products.

The demystification of sexuality, which initially grew out of a concern to stamp out disease, misery, and ignorance, in the 1960s came to be associated with debate about censorship. In 1951 the Swedish film Hon dansade en sommar (She Only Danced One Summer) caused a scandal because in it Folke Sundquist and Ulla Jacobsson, both stripped to the waist, are shown embracing. The film helped establish Sweden's reputation as a sexually liberated country. In 1963 the Bureau of Censorship passed Ingmar Bergman's The Silence despite numerous provocative scenes; but it prohibited screening of Vilgot Sjöman's "491" (1966) until a scene in which youths force a woman to have sexual relations with a dog had been cut. This act of censorship gave rise to an impassioned debate, until ultimately the

---

[8] The World, France's leading newspaper.

[9] "Life for two" or "conjugal existence."

uncut version of the film was allowed to be shown. Homosexual scenes began to appear on the screen in 1965.

Finally, in 1967, another Sjöman film, *I am Curious: Blue,* eliminated the last cinematic taboos. It gave rise to a polemic that resulted in its being banned for viewing by children, but the film was not cut. At this point several commissions were appointed to recommend changes in laws that were clearly outmoded. Documentaries on various sexual subjects were issued, including *The Language of Love,* which dealt with female sexual pleasure, and later, in 1971, *More on the Language of Love,* which, among other things, dealt with male homosexuality and the sexuality of the handicapped. That same year censorship of films was permanently abolished (except for scenes of excessive violence).

Pornography was to the sexual revolution of the 1960s and 1970s what sex education was to the 1940s and 1950s. Pornography is perhaps the most immediate manifestation of sexuality since, unlike eroticism, it places no mediator between the spectator and the object of desire. Nothing is suggested or even unveiled; everything is exhibited. It is interesting to note that the Swedish literary tradition contains virtually no erotic novel, no *Justine*[10] or *Histoire d'O,*[11] no equivalent to the works of Bataille,[12] the Marquis de Sade, or even Diderot in *Les Bijoux indiscrets.*[13] Sweden's only frivolous, libertine literature dates from the eighteenth century when the country was considered the "France of the North." Otherwise Swedish literature, particularly in works dealing with sex, is not much given to understatement, suggestion, or indirection. It is either overtly pornographic or resolutely didactic.

The sexual revolution seemed to sweep away the last taboos. Once the right to sexual information was established, the right to sexual pleasure was next to be proclaimed. No one was to be left out — equality for all: from homosexuality to voyeurism and zoophilia, all sexual practices were equally legitimate. The very notion of a "crime against nature" disappeared from the law and was replaced by that of "sexual offense" *(sedlighets brotten).*

A reaction was not long coming, however. Indeed, when examined closely, the sexual revolution of the 1960s and 1970s turns out to have been partly illusory. Formal taboos were eliminated, but traditional patterns remained largely untouched. At least that is the view of Swedish feminists, who vigorously attacked the portrayal of male-female relations in pornographic literature. One anecdote is worth recounting. The magazine *Expedition 66,* intended to be a female equivalent of *Playboy,* first appeared in 1964. It ceased publication fairly quickly, partly for

---

[10] Pornographic novel (1791) by the Marquis de Sade (1740–1814), author of many licentious works.

[11] *Story of O,* pornographic novel (1954) by Pauline Réage (pseudonym).

[12] Henri Bataille (1872–1922), French poet and author of psychological dramas.

[13] *The Indiscreet Jewels* (1748) is a pornographic story by Denis Diderot (1713–1784), a leading thinker of the French Enlightenment.

lack of readers but even more for lack of models. (In a gesture typical of Swedish honesty, the magazine's editor, Nina Estin, refused to use photographs from the files of homosexual magazines.) Subsequently almost all pornography was directed toward men.

An excellent illustration of the reaction against sexual liberation, and in particular of the role played by institutions in that reaction, can be found in prostitution. Rather paradoxically, it was in the early 1970s — at a time when sex ostensibly had ceased to constitute a transgression — that prostitution in Sweden increased sharply. At the peak of this phenomenon (1970–1972) more than a hundred "massage parlors" and "photographic studios" were operating in the Stockholm area alone. At the same time various voices were raised in favor of greater freedom and openness for prostitutes. . . .

In 1976 a commission was appointed to study the prostitution question, and a plan for retraining prostitutes was developed in 1980. The commission's report was extremely detailed and analyzed all aspects of the trade: prostitute, client, and procurer. It gave rise to a polemic between those who favored repression (most notably feminist groups) and those who feared that treating prostitutes as criminals would not eliminate the problem but would, by forcing it underground, render control impossible. The commission demonstrated in particular that prostitution in Sweden was closely associated with illicit drugs. Those who championed prostitution in the 1960s have therefore been forced to ask themselves whether it was truly "liberating." Finally, the commission noted that prostitution served exclusively as a means of satisfying male sexual needs. Here too the sexual revolution had not truly "liberated" women.

In the wake of this report, a series of restrictive measures was adopted. Although the new laws did not punish the client (except in cases involving sexual relations with a minor), they did provide for the prosecution of any person owning property used for the purpose of prostitution. Combined with an effective program for retraining prostitutes, the new laws have led to a marked decline in prostitution since 1980.

Laws were also passed against sexual activities involving violence, a common subject in pornographic publications. Peep shows were outlawed in 1982. The commission found that most of the patrons were older men, especially foreign businessmen, and concluded that "this was one part of the Swedish cultural heritage not really worth preserving." And so a specialty for which the country was internationally renowned came to an end. In fact, the whole flood of pornography that poured from the presses in the 1960s and 1970s has been, if not stopped, then at least channeled. Debate once focused on sex has been refocused on violence in all its forms, including sexual violence.

For all the transparency of Swedish society, certain opaque areas remain. Some things are prohibited, and because their number is small they are all the more fiercely protected. Violence, though uniformly condemned and prosecuted everywhere, is still present. Alcoholism is probably the area in which consensus is most tenuous and social control most vigorously challenged. Certain places are jealously guarded and kept strictly private: some exist in geographical space — the home, the boat, the island — while others exist only in poetry or the imagination.

The passions are soft-pedaled in Sweden. If violence is not significantly more prevalent than in other countries, when it does occur it is much more shocking. Accordingly it is sternly proscribed, even in private, as in the ban on spanking. Sometimes the obsession with preventing violence can seem rather silly. Since 1979, for example, Sweden has prohibited the sale of war toys. In 1978 an exposition on the theme "Violence Breeds Violence" lumped together allegedly violent comic books, estimates of the number of children killed annually in automobile accidents, and statistics on drug use.

The goal is not just to prohibit violence but to prevent it. The government considers open, public violence as the culmination of violence born in private, including at home and on the playing field. At a deeper level, violence, whether internal or external, private or public, constitutes a threat to order and consensus. It remains one of the last areas of Swedish life outside public control.

Another area yet to be brought under control is alcoholism. To consume alcohol in Sweden is not an innocuous act. Feelings of guilt weigh on those who drink — not just the inveterate drunkards but the average Swedes who line up furtively at the *Systembolaget* (state liquor store) and sneak away with a few bottles carefully hidden away among their other parcels. Regulations governing the sale of alcohol are very strict. Temperance is officially praised, drunkenness publicly condemned. People rarely drink in public, not only because prices are high but even more because the community quietly but firmly disapproves. Drinking is permissible — and even valued — only on specific occasions, at holidays such as Midsummer's Night or the mid-August crayfish festival; at such times one drinks in order to get drunk. According to the official morality, it is just as inappropriate to drink at home in private and for no "social" reason — that is, without a justifying ritual of communication — as it is to drink in public. A daily apéritif or glass of wine can become a reprehensible secret act, something that can produce feelings of guilt.

Swedish laws on alcohol are extremely harsh. There are heavy penalties for drunk driving, which is defined as operating a motor vehicle with a blood level of more than 0.5 grams of alcohol. Alcohol cannot be purchased by anyone under the age of twenty-one, even though the age of legal majority is eighteen. This severity is hard to understand in terms of statistics alone. Alcohol consumption in Sweden in 1979 amounted to 7.1 liters per person, compared with 17 liters for France. Sweden ranks roughly twenty-fifth in the world in per-capita alcohol consumption.

The severity of the law can be understood only in terms of history. The manufacture and sale of alcoholic beverages were regulated long before the turn of the century, but it was around then that the temperance movement, having gained a powerful position in the Swedish Parliament, won adoption of a law unparalleled elsewhere in the world — the so-called Bratt System, under which anyone who wished to purchase alcohol had to present a ration book. Even today, no issue unleashes passions as strong as those connected with the alcohol problem, largely owing to members of temperance societies, whose influence in Parliament is out of proportion with their numbers in the population. Not so very long ago one deputy in three belonged to a temperance organization, and anti-alcohol societies have traditionally been a fertile breeding ground for politicians.

Nevertheless, alcohol seems to be one area in which breakdown of consensus is possible. Swedish unanimity in opposition to alcohol is more apparent than real, for in private Swedes readily violate the ban and boast, like people everywhere, of their ability to "hold their liquor."

There is a much more solid consensus in opposition to drugs. Since 1968 laws against narcotics abuse have become stricter. Serious infractions of the narcotics laws incur one of the stiffest penalties in Swedish law: ten years in prison. Furthermore, the law does not distinguish between "soft drugs" and "hard drugs." Compared with alcoholism, however, drug abuse is quantitatively a minor problem.

Violence, alcoholism, drugs: these are the principal forms of deviant behavior in Swedish society, the last areas not entirely controlled by the political sphere, the last transgressions in a society liberated from the taboos of the past.

In such a highly communitarian society, so tightly controlled by the "public," where can the individual find a private refuge? In his home, his rustic frame *sommarstuga*[14] lost in the forest or tucked away on some lake shore. The individual home is like an island, private space par excellence, cut off and personalized. In "Scandinavian Notes" Emmanuel Mounier remarked that "the most collectivist nations — Russia, Germany, Sweden — are those in which housing is most solitary."

The dream of every Swede is essentially an individualistic one, expressed through the appreciation of primitive solitude, of the vast reaches of unspoiled nature. Often built without running water and with the most rudimentary facilities, the *stuga* enables its owner to return to his rural roots and to commune intimately with nature. Virtually no Swede will travel abroad during that beautiful time in May and June when nature, at last emerged from the interminable sleep of winter, bursts forth with a dazzling and liberating light and Sweden once again becomes the land of 24,000 islands and 96,000 lakes! The small cabin lost in the country or forest thus remains, along with the island, the archipelago, and the sailboat (of which there are more than 70,000 in the Stockholm area alone), the last refuge of individualism in a highly communitarian society.

The themes of isolation, nature, and archipelago are omnipresent in Swedish literature and film. The novel entitled *The People of Hemsö* figures as a moment of illumination in Strindberg's otherwise somber oeuvre. The beautiful film *Summer Paradise* starring Gunnel Lindblom takes place entirely in the enchanting setting of a wonderful lakeside house. Though a genuine refuge, this private space can in certain situations become a tragic trap in which individuals seek desperately to recover some lost primitive state of communication, some original purity.

---

[14] House in the woods.

. . . Crimes of passion are rare in Sweden (when one does occur, it is head-line news). People almost never raise their voices and rarely gesticulate; usually they keep silent. Curiously in this society, where all sorts of things are said out loud and with unaccustomed frankness, people have difficulty conversing. Al-though workplace relations are simple, direct, and devoid of hierarchy and every-one addresses everyone else familiarly, dinner invitations are stiffly formal and prissy, something that constantly surprises foreign visitors. It does not make con-versation any easier. In Swedes, Mounier saw "the diffuse mysticism and poetry of lonely men: the Swedish people remain, in a sense, incapable of expression."

This truly private side of a self that manifests itself not so much in action as in imagination is a good starting point for exploring Swedish society and at-tempting to grasp its paradoxes and contradictions. How else can we understand the coexistence of such highly communitarian and public feeling with such in-tensely inward individualism? The solitude of that world of silence, the Great North, the intimate communion with nature — therein lies the source of Scandi-navian individualism. Primitive solitude compensates for community in all its forms — organization, group study, celebration. Everything, from holidays to laws, is directed toward breaking down solitude, allowing each person a say, maintaining the traditional community intact as a necessary condition of physi-cal survival in the harsh world of the past and of moral survival in the harsh world of the present. What else could account for the incredible popularity of the ancient pagan festivals, generally associated with rural life but now transformed into Christian holidays? Walpurgis Night celebrates spring, Saint Lucy's Night the winter solstice, Saint John's Night the middle of summer (*Midsommar*), to name only a few of the holidays that dot an unchanging calendar. For one night everyone forgets hierarchy, social class, differences, and enmities and, in togeth-erness and unanimity, recreates the perfectly egalitarian, perfectly consensual utopian community. During one unbridled *Midsommar* Miss Julie in Strindberg's[15] play talks, drinks, sleeps, and plans a future with her father's valet. Then morn-ing comes and restores social difference, the impossibility of communication, and rebellion. A night's folly ends in death. How can one possibly understand the Swedish imagination if one sees this as nothing more than an insipid story of im-possible love between a countess and a valet?

The Swedish model can be interpreted as a "total" or "totalizing" society. It de-pends on a perfectly consensual communitarian ethic, which in turn depends on absolute insistence on transparency in social relations (from the old ritual known as *nattfrieri*[16] to the child's right to know the identity of his father today). Private life cannot escape the influence of the dominant ethos. The Swedish model com-bines yesterday's communitarian morality with the modern social-democratic ethos.

---

[15] August Strindberg (1849–1912), Swedish novelist, poet, and playwright.

[16] "Night courting," the practice whereby a man courted his sweetheart secretly at her farm on summer evenings.

In the 1930s Marquis Childs[17] referred to "Sweden, the middle way," thus characterizing the country in a manner that would influence first his fellow Americans and, later, others. Sweden's material prosperity, which as early as 1928 included "a telephone in every hotel room, a plentiful supply of electricity, model hospitals, [and] broad, clean streets," along with an almost flawless social organization, lent credence in the 1930s to the notion of a Swedish model. European countries suddenly took a lively interest in the country, hoping to unearth the secret of its astonishing material success.

Spared the ravages of the Second World War, Sweden maintained its productive apparatus intact. To much of postwar Europe it seemed utopia incarnate, and Swedes became "the Americans of Europe." In many respects Sweden was seen as a more attractive model of social organization than the United States because inequality in Sweden was less pronounced. As Queffélec[18] pointed out in 1948, the Swedes "question all this natural prosperity." Also, the country's "moral health" enabled it to "avoid the dreadful consequences of Americanization." Mounier delightedly recounted the comment of one Swedish observer who was quite appreciative of American civilization: "The Swede, however, is actually much more attached to the individual than is the American."

In the 1940s and 1950s some in the West saw the typical Swedish woman as one who was "beautiful, athletic, and healthy." While "the legendary freedom of Scandinavian morals" was taken for granted, "to the traveler these young people seem distant and not very emotional. Couples dance quite properly" (*Action*, September 1946). Louis-Charles Royer wrote in *Lumières du Nord* (*Northern Lights*, 1939): "It is extremely difficult to court women in this country, because they always treat you as a pal." In 1954 François-Régis Bastide in his book *Suède* (Sweden) asked: "What should you say to a young Swedish woman?" His answer: "Whatever you do, it is extremely dangerous to mention the well-known reputation that Swedish women have. . . . That is certain to chill things off."

The Swedish woman's reputation was no doubt associated with the campaign to provide sexual information, which since 1933 had done so much to break down sexual taboos. Sweden had provided sex education in the schools since 1942, at a time no other country had gone to such lengths. The West had confused sexual information with sexual freedom, creating an image of Sweden as sexual paradise.

In 1964 French Prime Minister Georges Pompidou visited "this strange socialist monarchy" and in a famous phrase characterized his social and political ideal as "Sweden with a bit more sun." Thus attention was once again focused on the Swedish ideal, which would attain the peak of its glory in the 1970s. During this period Sweden was in vogue; whenever it was mentioned, it was held up as an example.

---

[17] American newspaperman (1903–1990) and author of *Sweden: The Middle Way*.

[18] Henri Queffélec, French novelist and essayist (1910–1992).

Everywhere Sweden was exalted and glorified. Some had dreamed the American dream; others had idealized the Soviet Union or China or Cuba. Now the "Swedish model," the image of a just compromise, seduced Europe. Sweden became a journalistic cliché. The sexual revolution of the 1960s reinforced the myth. A cover story on "Free Love" appeared in 1965, and one French magazine devoted a special issue to Sweden. . . . Sweden was the wave of the future: the press said it, television showed it, books explained it. The "Swedish case" was analyzed and dissected. People also began to ask questions.

By 1975 articles criticizing Sweden had begun to appear. Headlines such as "Women Not Totally Free" and "The Disintegrating Family" were read. Roland Huntford launched a vigorous attack on social-democratic Sweden in his book *The New Totalitarians* (1972). The defeat of the social democrats in 1976, after more than forty-four years in power, raised questions about the political stability of Sweden. . . . Sweden was portrayed in France as a perverse model, a highly coercive society. This "prodigiously permissive" society was said to have engendered its own destruction. "Sweden: Liberated Lovers in Search of Love," was trumpeted in 1980. That same year one could read: "The Swedish mirror, much admired abroad, is broken. Something is amiss in the world's most unusual system." One headline asked, "Sweden — paradise lost?"

The Swedish model had not lived up to its promise. Racism, xenophobia, suicide, and alcoholism all existed there too. The countermodel was now at its height, even if traces of the old paradise remained. In 1984 *Le Point*[19] asked students at France's leading institutions of higher education what country best corresponded to their idea of the good society. Switzerland led the list, followed by the United States; Sweden came in fifth, behind France.

If the Swedish model had lost its appeal, it was because the country had slipped badly. Claude Sarraute[20] wrote of "incessant investigations by the tax and welfare authorities, unreasonable, Orwellian interventions in people's lives. The government keeps tabs on incomes and individuals. The meddlesome welfare state sticks its nose everywhere, even into the way you bring up your children. It encourages children to turn in 'deviant' parents." Much of the West decided it wanted no part of this "revolution in private life." Though the Swedish model may still exist, the Swedish myth is dead as a doornail.

[19] The French weekly newsmagazine, *The Point.*

[20] Journalist at *Le Monde* and author of numerous books (b. 1927).

ETHNIC CLEANSING IN THE WARS OF YUGOSLAV SUCCESSION
Norman M. Naimark

Western nations observed the terrible and murderous wars that followed the breakup of the Yugoslav state with horror and bewilderment. Many people had thought that the end of World War II and its atrocities, the gradual movement in the postwar period toward cooperation among European states, and the collapse of Communist regimes in the Soviet Union and in eastern Europe would banish wholesale violence and war from Europe. The Yugoslav wars constituted a wake-up call about the hatred among different peoples and the willingness of unprincipled leaders to use nationalism to serve their ends. The hatred among Serbs, Croats, and Kosovar Albanians for one another makes one despair about the nature of humanity and about any notion that the current generation's ethical behavior is superior to the actions of generations past. Equally disheartening is the hatred among Catholics, Orthodox, and Muslims, which raises doubts about religion's ability to sway conduct for the better. The reluctance to intervene and the eventual late intervention by other nations in the Yugoslav wars in order to lessen the bloodshed and prevent further unspeakable crimes against civilians likewise shocked those who felt a moral obligation to stop the violence.

Norman M. Naimark, a professor of history at Stanford University, examines the Yugoslav wars of the 1990s and especially the phenomenon of ethnic cleansing. His sources include newspapers, magazines, firsthand accounts (from victims, journalists, observers, and politicians), proceedings of the International Court of Justice, and government and organization reports. He disputes the notion that the bitter enmity among Balkan populations arose hundreds of years ago; instead, he locates the causes of the wars and ethnic hatreds in the twentieth century. What arguments does he offer to prove this assertion (which contradicts the beliefs not only of the various Yugoslav leaders but of the Serb,

Norman M. Naimark, *Fires of Hatred: Ethnic Cleansing in Twentieth-Century Europe* (Cambridge, MA: Harvard University Press, 2001), 139–184.

Bosnian, Croat, Slovene, and Kosovar Albanian populations as well)? What were the goals of Serbia and Croatia during the Yugoslav wars? Why did Serbs systematically brutalize and rape Muslim women in Bosnia and in Kosovo? What have been the results of ethnic cleansing in the former Yugoslavia? Where else has ethnic cleansing occurred in the twentieth century? What are the differences between ethnic cleansing and genocide? Do you think that ethnic diversity, as in the United States, Canada, and Israel, for example, is superior to ethnic homogenization, as practiced, for instance, in Japan and Saudi Arabia, not to mention in Serbia and Croatia?

Ethnic cleansing in former Yugoslavia and the genocidal attacks that have accompanied it are inextricably linked to the failure of the Yugoslav idea of the nineteenth century, the collapse of the Yugoslav state in the twentieth, and the recent wars of Yugoslav succession. Even more directly, ethnic cleansing is tied to the creation in the 1990s of new states — Serbia, Croatia, Slovenia, Macedonia, Bosnia-Herzegovina — that have succeeded the old Yugoslav federation. The process is far from complete, and additional new states — Montenegro and Kosovo, for example — could emerge from the rubble of former Yugoslavia. Both the breakdown of Yugoslavia and the creation of new nation-states in its wake are rooted in the twentieth-century history of nationalism and war in the Balkans, not — as so often proclaimed in the popular literature and press — in six hundred or more years of conflict. To be sure, as they developed in the nineteenth century, modern national movements in the Balkans contained exclusivist elements. But ethnic cleansing in former Yugoslavia is not a necessary corollary of nation-state building; it is a path chosen by governmental elites with concrete political goals in mind. The conscious choices of a Milosevic[1] or Tudjman,[2] backed by their political supporters in Serbia and Croatia, are as critical to ethnic cleansing as the more abstract processes of disintegration within the former Yugoslav state and the reconstitution of its national components in a multistate system.

In the twentieth century, two Yugoslav states have failed to meet the challenges presented by their multinational composition. The first — the Kingdom of Serbs, Croats, and Slovenes — was created in December 1918 at the conclusion of World War I. Following the collapse of the Ottoman Empire and the Habsburg monarchy, the frontiers in the western Balkans were redrawn and a completely novel

---

[1] Slobodan Milosevic (b. 1941), Serbian Communist, then ultra-nationalist and president of the Federal Republic of Yugoslavia; initiated a policy of ethnic cleansing in 1998. Charged with war crimes before the International Court of Justice in The Hague, 2002.

[2] Franjo Tudjman (1922–1999), president of Croatia from 1990 to 1999; ultra-nationalist who pursued a brutal war in Bosnia.

South Slav entity was created. After King Alexander's[3] royal coup in 1929, this country was officially renamed Yugoslavia. Between the world wars, Yugoslavia's two largest and most important component nations, the Serbs and Croats, failed to share power to the satisfaction of both, gravely weakening the country's unity. . . . [T]he incursions of Italian fascists and the Third Reich into the Balkans at the onset of World War II destroyed the fragile country. The bloody fratricidal killing that characterized the war years ended when Tito[4] and the Partisans[5] forged a second Yugoslav state. Its decentralized federal structure and highly centralized political system was designed to resolve the ethnic tensions between the various nations of Yugoslavia that had festered during the interwar period and caused such destruction and death during the war.

The breakup of communist Yugoslavia at the end of the 1980s unleashed forces of national antagonism that recapitulated, in some ways, those of World War II. Even the language of combat in the wars of Yugoslav succession harked back to the struggles of the Second World War, long mythologized in Partisan lore. Serbs claimed to be fighting Croat Ustashas[6] and Bosnian SS[7] fascists; Croats and Bosnian Muslims saw themselves confronted by Serb Chetniks.[8] Both Serb and Croat fighters donned the symbols and uniforms of their Croat Ustasha and Serb Chetnik predecessors of more than a half century ago. In so doing, they emphasized that the war in Bosnia was "a continuation of the Second World War," as the Bosnian Serb leader Radovan Karadzic expressed it. The way nationalists in former Yugoslavia remembered World War II linked ethnic cleansing in Bosnia and Kosovo to the problems of this century.

Most scholars who have written about the recent war have questioned the assertion that it was produced by "ancient hatreds," centuries in the making, between the nations of the region. As they point out, many of these "nations" were relatively recent creations with little or no premodern history of entrenched struggle with their neighbors. Even those nations with more venerable medieval origins — Serbs, Croats, and Bosnians, among them — have not been locked in struggle or mutual animosity for centuries. The widespread images in both contemporary Yugoslavia and the West of an age-old conflict between Turks and Serbs, Muslims and Orthodox, need considerable revision. The six-century-long

---

[3] King of Yugoslavia (1921–1934); became dictator in 1929 in order to unify the different ethnic groups in Yugoslavia.

[4] Josip Broz (1892–1980), Communist leader against the Germans during World War II, subsequently president of Yugoslavia. As president, he followed a Communist policy independent of the Soviet Union and enforced equality among the six Yugoslav republics.

[5] Communist fighters led by Tito against both German occupation and Yugoslavian rivals during World War II.

[6] Members of the ultra-nationalist totalitarian party that ruled Croatia during World War II.

[7] The *Schutzstaffel*, the German Nazi Elite Guard.

[8] Serb monarchists who fought against the Germans and Tito's partisans during World War II.

Pax Ottomanica[9] allowed the Balkan peoples to grow and develop within their own religious communities, the millets,[10] even though they were under Ottoman domination. Before the end of the nineteenth century, a substantial percentage of the leadership of the Ottoman ruling class consisted of converted Christians from the Balkans — Albanians, Greeks, Serbs, Montenegrins, and others. Dozens of non-Turkish grand vezirs[11] and countless Balkan generals, finance ministers, and regional governors, among others, played a critical role in the Ottoman administration. Conflicts and wars accompanied the Ottoman advance into the Balkans in the fourteenth and fifteenth centuries, and the Ottoman decline and exit from the region in the nineteenth and early twentieth centuries also precipitated clashes and unrest. But these confrontations were far less significant in their own right for the wars of Yugoslav succession in the 1990s than in the way they were commemorated and manipulated by politicians and ideologues. . . .

During the nineteenth century, most of the peoples of the region began nation-building. Serbs and Greeks moved first to establish independent entities, while Albanians and Macedonians came much later; but the pattern was very similar. First, small groups of intellectuals conceived of a national entity. Second, national movements were formed with a narrow but significant social base in the population. Third, new political leaderships at the head of the respective national movements sought political power, either within a larger multinational entity or in an independence movement. Fourth, some form of autonomous unit or independent state was formed with concrete boundaries and an ethnonational identity. Finally, the new states sought to inculcate national values into populations that had been often isolated from the processes of nation building.

For the Serbs, the now world-famous epic poetry about the Battle of Kosovo, fought on St. Vitus Day (Vidovdan),[12] June 28, 1389, provided the central metaphor for the heroism and self-sacrifice of the Serbian nation. On the Field of Blackbirds (Kosovo Polje), the noble Prince Lazar led a hopeless battle against the Ottoman sultan, Murad,[13] electing to fulfill his sacred mission and that of his nation rather than sue for peace and thus compromise Serb honor. . . .

. . . The fact that Christians and Muslims fought on both sides of the battle — that Serbs, Croats, Albanians, and Turks could be found in both armies — was quickly forgotten. That the battle was probably a stand-off, a draw, and not the

---

[9] The "Ottoman Peace," the peaceful conditions created by the Ottoman Empire throughout its regions.

[10] Millets were autonomous religious communities in the Ottoman Empire that were responsible for taxes, internal security, and administrative functions (such as education, religion, social welfare, and so on) not carried out by the central government.

[11] A grand vezir (vizier) was the chief officer of state in several Muslim countries.

[12] The Serbs' most sacred day because of its association with the 1389 battle between the Serbs and the Turks.

[13] Murad I (1362–1389).

epiphany of a tragic defeat also disappeared in the searing light of national self-sacrifice. . . . But that mattered as little to the Serb bards and Church fathers, who fostered the consciousness of a common Serb fate, as it did to Milosevic, who gathered more than a million Serbs on Kosovo Field on June 28, 1989, to commemorate the 600th anniversary of the battle.

In the 1840s, the great "prince-poet" of Montenegro, Petar Petrovic Njegos, used the Kosovo myth to construct his own vision of the history of Montenegro, "The Mountain Wreath." Here, revenge for the sacrifice of the Serbs at Kosovo served the cause of uniting Montenegrin Serbs in their battle against the Turks. In Njegos's view, the problem was not so much Islam from without but Islam within — the fact that many Montenegrin clans had converted to Islam. In the poem, Metropolitan Danilo, who ruled Montenegro from 1700 to 1735, debates with himself and his notables how to deal with the problem. In Njegos's version, Danilo wavers and pounds his chest but in the end has no choice but to order the massacre of the Montenegrin "Turks," who did not flee at the threat of extinction. One of his generals reports back: . . .

> Though broad enough Cetinje's Plain
> No single seeing eye, no tongue of Turk
> Escap'd to tell his tale another day!
> We put them all unto the sword
> All those who would not be baptiz'd: . . .

Although by the end of the nineteenth century, a single Serb national ideology is hard to identify, at the center of most of its variants was a well-developed understanding of the special role of the Serbs in defending the South Slavs from the Turks (and Orthodox Christians from Muslims). Over the course of the nineteenth century, the Serbian state fought its way free from the Ottomans, expanded its borders, and strengthened its army and bureaucracy. Using and developing the myths of Kosovo and Danilo, Serb leaders assumed the mantle of defending the South Slavs against the Ottoman Turks and Habsburgs. . . .

. . . [T]he Serb national program was inherently expansionist. . . . But in expanding its borders and including Serbs in a single state, Serbia inevitably would have to confront the presence of Croats and Muslims in Bosnia. The latter were slated in most Serb (and Croat) national programs for forced assimilation. But an uneasy tension existed in the Serb national program . . . between a "narrow ideology" of Greater Serbianism, which excluded Croats, and a desire to include all South Slavs in a single state. . . .

The very strength and intensity of national self-consciousness among the Serbian political elites and cultural producers in the nineteenth century tended to work at cross-purposes with the development of the Illyrian movement, which advocated a union of equal South Slav peoples in a single state. The Croatian lawyer and linguistic pioneer Ljudevit Gaj sought to create an Illyrian language that would unite the peoples of the region in a common movement. His proclamation of the year 1836 stated: "The discordant strings of this lyre are Carniola, Carinthia, Istria, Kranj, Styria, Croatia, Slavonia, Dalmatia, Dubrovnik, Bosnia, Montenegro, Herzegovina, Serbia, Bulgaria, and Lower Hungary. . . . Let's stop each strumming on his own string, and tune the lyre in a single harmony." The Balkan Wars[14] and World War I exacerbated the underlying contradictions between the Serbian national idea and the hopes of the other peoples of the Balkans for a "single harmony." After a "Young Bosnian" (Serb) terrorist-patriot assassinated Archduke Franz Ferdinand in Sarajevo on June 28, 1914 (the anniversary of the Kosovo battle), the Serbs once again defied a superior and alien power, the Austro-Hungarian monarchy, and sacrificed their youth to the Moloch[15] of war, suffering a bitter, if heroic, defeat. Meanwhile, the other South Slav nations, freed from Ottoman and Austro-Hungarian rule, developed their own mythologies of sacrifice and independence which insisted on an equal place in the newly constructed postwar Yugoslavia.

The first Yugoslav state was fatally flawed from the moment of its birth. The two largest and most influential of its component nations — the Serbs and Croats — looked at the new country through different historical and political lenses. The Serbs saw the state's creation as a final reward for their long history of battle and sacrifice on behalf of the South Slavs, and they assumed Serbs would govern and rule it as a unitary, centralist polity, as befitted their history and experience. From the very start, Croats and Slovenes, among others, contested this vision, looking to protect their interests through decentralization and confederation, an equal union of equal peoples. The Serbs never quite lost the habits of rule of the prewar kingdom, and they looked at Croat attempts to preserve a measure of autonomy as antiquated and unnecessary. . . .

Many Yugoslav politicians and cultural figures of all the component nationalities struggled to find a formula, a way of thinking, that would defuse the ongoing national confrontations weakening the state and threatening its future. The failure of this experiment became evident in the explosion of nationalist resentments during World War II. Croat Ustasha genocidal massacres of Serbs, Serb Chetnik collaboration with Nazis, Bosnian Muslim units in the SS, and Kosovar Albanian attacks on former Serb colonists all reflect the failures of the Yugoslav state to satisfy the needs of its component nationalities between the world wars. The very intensity with which the Yugoslavist communist Partisans attacked and eliminated "bourgeois nationalist" opponents of all stripes — Chetnik, Ustasha, Muslim — both during and after the Second World War also demonstrates the extent to which the first Yugoslavia not only failed to bridge the different visions of its component nations but the fact deepened the fatal abyss between them.

Tito's solution was to grant each nation its own territorial unit and governmental apparatus. On the Soviet model, these units would be "national in form and socialist in content," meaning that the Communist Party, representing the socialist future, would ensure unity through its Leninist principle of democratic

---

[14] Two wars (1912–1913). In the first, the Ottoman Empire lost Macedonia and Albania; in the second, the Balkan states defeated Bulgaria over the spoils of the previous wars.

[15] Or Molech, ancient god of fire (Canaanite, Phoenician, and Assyrian) to whom children were sometimes sacrificed.

centralism.[16] The "sword and shield" of the party, the secret police, would hold the nationalist deviations in check. The Yugoslav People's Army, heavily imbued with the Partisan ethos of Yugoslav patriotism, also served as an important counterweight to separatist tendencies. . . .

Like most dictators, Tito made sure that no logical successors were around to step into his shoes when he died in 1981. Instead, he set up a rotating presidency to lead the state — institutionalizing the dysfunctional bargaining between nations at the very pinnacle of the federal government. The devolution of power to the republics and the paralysis at the federal executive and legislative levels became even more pronounced, and trends toward separatism and nationalism intensified as a result. The two largest nations of Yugoslavia, the Serbs and Croats, increasingly attempted to manipulate the federal system in order to forward their own narrow national interests. Economic problems in the 1980s, including severe inflation and high rates of unemployment, were compounded by pressure from the country's creditors. This economic crisis prompted the richer republics, Croatia and Slovenia, to cut loose from the ballast of the poorer ones, including Serbia. Meanwhile, the Serbs felt they also had been dealt a bad hand by Tito and now sought to redress the balance by asserting their dominance within the federation in general and within Serbian lands in particular, especially Kosovo. Meanwhile, a sea change was occurring in the impending collapse of communism in Eastern Europe and the Soviet Union. At the time, it was hard to see that Yugoslavia would be its most bloodied victim. . . .

The acceleration of national antagonisms that drove Yugoslavia into war and ethnic cleansing from the summer of 1991 onward has a number of important reference points during the previous decade. Although few could have predicted what was to come from these events individually or collectively, no one doubted that conflict was in the air and that political leadership would have to be exerted to avoid bloodshed. Kosovo was one of these reference points, where overwhelming Serbian domination of a substantial Albanian majority — by the end of the 1980s some 90 percent of the population — could not continue indefinitely. Every attempt by the Kosovar Albanians to increase control over their own affairs met with more violent Serbian countermeasures and brutality. Student protest demonstrations in the spring of 1981 led to the declaration of a state of emergency in Kosovo and further Serbian repression against the Albanian community, which continued in one form or another throughout the decade.

The second reference point was the ongoing hostility in the Yugoslav Federation between the Serbs on the one hand and the Croats and Slovenes on the other. In 1985 and 1986 the Slovene government took unilateral steps toward assuming complete control over their own budgetary and judicial affairs. . . . By the mid-

---

[16] System in which policies are decided centrally after free discussion among the ruling elite and then are binding on everyone in the party.

1980s, the Croats also sought to introduce a genuinely confederal arrangement by which they could control more of the revenues of their profitable industries, including the booming Dalmatian tourist business. But control of the Croatian party by political conservatives and periodic repressive measures against manifestations of nationalism kept Croat dissent below the surface for most of the decade.

The third reference point, less noticed by equally important to the development of interethnic antagonisms, was the growing national consciousness of the Bosnian Muslims. The Muslim elite looked to deepen its influence on the republic's policies and institutions, and alienated both Serbs and Croats in the process. . . . Like other Muslims in Yugoslavia as a whole, the Bosnians were deeply aware of their second-class status in the communist state and were determined to express their nationality as distinct from their Serb and Croat Slavic cousins.

Developments in Kosovo, Croatia, and Bosnia were tied to nationalist rumblings in Belgrade, the fourth and most important reference point. Serbs felt a growing sense of hostility and isolation from their neighbors. Like the Russians in the Soviet Union, the Serbs understood their role as the preservers and defenders of Yugoslav unity and integrity. Also mirroring Russian attitudes about Soviet policies, the Serbs felt that their own interests had been sacrificed in the Yugoslav system. They were the ones who should complain, not the Croats, Slovenes, or Bosnian Muslims. From their point of view, they had fought two world wars on behalf of the other nations of the federation; they had lost countless sons on the battlefield; and now they were faced with criticism and accusations of hegemony. The Croats and Slovenes lived much better than they, yet both republics sought to control more of their resources. Even more galling to the Serbs was the sense that the growing nationalism of the other peoples of Yugoslavia jeopardized the life and property of Serbs who lived outside of Serbia proper. In the Croatian borderlands, in Kosovo, and in Bosnia-Herzegovina, Serbs perceived that their nation was on the defensive and in trouble.

. . . [T]he first important open manifestation of Serb nationalist rhetoric came with the release of the now infamous "Memorandum of the Serbian Academy of Sciences" in September 1996. . . . The memorandum signaled the shift from the promotion of Yugoslavism, colored with a tinge of Serbian patriotism, to outright Serbian nationalism and even pan-Serbism.

. . . "Not all the national groups were equal" in Yugoslavia, the memorandum stated. "The Serbian nation, for instance, was not given the right to have its own state. The large sections of the Serbian people who live in other republics, unlike the national minorities, do not have the right to use their own language and script; they do not have the right to set up their own political or cultural organizations or to foster the common cultural traditions of their nation together with their co-nationals."

The memorandum expressed particular resentment against the situation of the Serbs in Kosovo, who, it claims, were the subject of "genocide." Kosovo is the symbol of the Serbs' "historical defeat" in Yugoslavia. "In the spring of 1981," the memorandum asserts, "open and total war was declared on the Serbian people."

"Unless things change radically, in less than ten years' time there will no longer by any Serbs left in Kosovo, and an 'ethnically pure' Kosovo, that unambiguously stated goal of the Greater Albanian racists, will be achieved." . . .

. . . In short, the memorandum recommended removing Kosovo's autonomy and subordinating the interests of the Kosovar Albanians to those of the Serbs. Milosevic would take this fateful path in 1989, which would lead to the Serbian ethnic cleansing of Kosovo and NATO bombing of Serbia in the spring of 1999. . . .

. . . [T]he career of Slobodan Milosevic represented the marked shift of Serbian politics in a nationalist direction. Milosevic was a former law student and banker, a member and by the mid-1980s leader of the Serbian branch of the Yugoslav Socialist Party, and an ambitious and attractive politician. Some biographers attribute his drive for power to a psychosis derived from two desperately unhappy parents, both of whom committed suicide. Some emphasize the important influence of his wife, Mirjana Markovic, to whom he had been close since school days in Pozarevac and who has been his life-long political partner. Markovic is the head of her own "communist" political party, the Yugoslav United Left. When Milosevic visited the town of Kosovo Polje in April 1987, no one imagined that the visit would "change the course of history." Milosevic encouraged the ultranationalist Kosovar Serbs to take their fate in their own hands. In saying to the assembled crowd, "From now on, no one has the right to beat you!" he let the Kosovar Serbs, as well as the Serbs back in Belgrade, know that the force of the Yugoslav state would be used to maintain Serbian control of Kosovo. The crowd shouted back "Slobo, Slobo," and Milosevic understood immediately the intoxicating power of nationalist rhetoric. . . .

In a subsequent meeting with Kosovar Serbs, Milosevic raised the ante even higher, calling for active struggle against the Albanians. "This is your land, here are your houses, fields and gardens, your memories. You are not going to leave your land just because life has become difficult, because you are suffering from injustice and humiliation. It was never in the spirit of the Serb and Montenegrin people to withdraw in face of difficulties, to demobilize itself when it should fight, to become demoralized when the situation is hard. You should stay here because of your ancestors and your heirs."

Shortly after his visit to Kosovo, Milosevic seized control of the Serbian government and party apparatus. . . . Milosevic then sought to abrogate those provisions of the Serbian constitution that allowed Kosovo (and Vojvodina) autonomous status within Serbia and therefore within the Yugoslav entity as a whole. By his actions, Milosevic intended to withdraw the rights of Kosovar Albanians that they had held in the province since 1974, when they effectively were given republican status by Tito and the new Yugoslav constitution. The Kosovar Albanians protested moves to limit their autonomy, calling strikes and mass meetings around the country. That was all that Milosevic needed to send in the army and proclaim a state of emergency. By the end of March 1989, Milosevic had what he wanted. "Kosovo's 'autonomy' . . . was now reduced to a mere token."[17]

---

[17] Noel Malcolm, *Kosovo: A Short History* (New York: New York University Press, 1998), 344.

But this was only the beginning of the Kosovar's problems. Continuing clashes with police led to the arrest of large numbers of Kosovar Albanian activists. Albanian-language schools were closed down. Albanians were persecuted on the street and in their homes. Many lost their jobs. Serbs were openly favored in economic policies, Albanians clearly discriminated against. Many young and talented Kosovar Albanians left to find work and practice their occupations in Western Europe. The situation was bleak; Kosovo was effectively under martial law.

Meanwhile, Milosevic continued to ride the wave of nationalism, using it to oust his political opponents and consolidate his power. He seemed as gifted at isolating and eliminating potential centers of political opposition as he was at finding support among Serb nationalists. On June 28, 1989, the 600th Anniversary of the Battle of Kosovo, Milosevic called a mass rally on Kosovo Field, and a million Serbs showed up. . . . Milosevic arrived by helicopter amidst a throng of excited supporters to deliver a warning of war and sacrifice: "Serbs in their history have never conquered or exploited others. Through two world wars, they have liberated themselves and, when they could, they also helped others to liberate themselves. . . . The Kosovo heroism does not allow us to forget that, at one time, we were brave and dignified and one of the few who went into battle undefeated. . . . Six centuries later, again we are in battles and quarrels. They are not armed battles, though such things should not be excluded yet." Surrounded by Serbian Orthodox priests, Milosevic repeated the refrain that Serbia had suffered too much to allow Yugoslavia's component parts to fall away through autonomy or separation. Wherever Serb bones lie buried in the soil, Milosevic insisted, that was Serbian territory. Wherever Serb blood was shed, that was the Serbian patrimony. . . .

. . . The Serbian countryside also fed the upsurge of nationalist sentiment. Religious intolerance and resentment of the cosmopolitan city resonated in the villages with Milosevic's "anti-bureaucratic revolution." The unity of the folk, religion, and nation had broad appeal. Socialism and Yugoslavism belonged to the past; the failure of one meant the collapse of the other. The future would have to be negotiated with an armed and dangerous Serbia.

These changes in the thinking of Serbian politicians and intellectuals at the end of the 1980s were part of a rapid — even revolutionary — paradigm shift in both Yugoslavia and the former communist bloc. Socialism had failed as an economic and political system. People in the region had understood this fact for a long time; what now became apparent was that something could be done about it. One after another, the communist regimes in Eastern Europe were deposed in 1989 and replaced by ostensibly democratic ones. Finally, the Soviet Union itself broke apart in 1991, and in its successor states socialism gave way to "capitalism" and "democracy," at least in the minds of the new leaders. But the absence of historical experience with the marketplace or with parliamentary democracy undermined programs for a rapid transition. Even with decently functioning institutions, it was hard to change peoples' habits and thinking. Corruption flourished; the open market turned into robber capitalism; the *nomenklatura*[18] found ways to

---

[18] Those appointed to senior positions by virtue of patronage.

control natural resources and industries. As political parties proliferated and the excessive privileges among political leaders fostered suspicion, common citizens gave in to cynicism and withdrew from politics and voting. Democratization came to mean little more than freedom of movement and freedom of speech, and even these were sometimes imperiled. . . .

With their constitutions weak and their political institutions underdeveloped, with democracy and the market economy beyond their immediate reach, Yugoslavia and many of its sister socialist countries were dry kindling for the flames of nationalism. This was only somewhat less the case for Slovenia and Macedonia than it was for Serbia and Croatia. Given the problematic relations between the Croats and Serbs over the course of the century, Croatian nationalism seemed destined to come into conflict with the Serbs. . . . Full independence was on the mind of many, who felt increasingly alienated from Belgrade and the Serbs.

Among this group was the historian and former Partisan fighter, later general, Franjo Tudjman. Tudjman was a Croat nationalist and the author in 1989 of *Absurdities of Historical Reality,* which rejected Serb accusations that the Ustashas had engaged in genocide against Serbs during the war and tried to whitewash Ustasha crimes against the Jews. . . . During the election campaign of 1990, Tudjman hammered unremittingly on the anvil of nationalism. . . . Tudjman intimated that nothing short of independence would satisfy the country.

On May 30, 1990, amid a profusion of Croat nationalist symbolism, Tudjman was inaugurated as president of Croatia. . . . "The Croatian President had not yet, however, accomplished what he wanted. Just out of reach was his dream of a Croatian state. There was one problem — the Serbs."[19]

Milosevic was both very much like Tudjman and very different. The Serbian leader never quite abandoned his communist roots. After 1990 his party, the Socialist Party of Serbia, blended neo-Yugoslavism with Serb nationalism, partisan traditions with those of the Chetniks, bellicosity and aggressiveness with the pathos of victimization. He dominated the Serbian state apparatus, yet appealed to populist slogans and antigovernment sentiments among the peasants. His mix of Serbian chauvinism and Yugoslav integralism meant that non-Serb nationalisms were interpreted as reactionary and separatist. For Tudjman, the problem was the Serbs; for Milosevic, every nationality of former Yugoslavia — Croats, Slovenes, Bosnian Muslims, and Kosovar Albanians — stood in the way of his ambitions. . . .

On June 25, 1991, Slovenia declared its independence; hours later, Croatia did the same. Both were outraged by Serbia's actions in Kosovo and anxious to jump from the sinking ship of Yugoslavia while they still had a chance. Both were encouraged by hopeful signs from the European community, and especially from the Germans, that their new states would be protected by ties with Europe. They

---

[19] Laura Silber and Alan Little, *Yugoslavia: Death of a Nation* (New York: TV Books, 1995), 91–92.

were wrong. Forces of the Yugoslav Peoples' Army (JNA) moved to secure the borders and control vital transportation links. The Slovenes decided to fight, but fortunately casualties were minimal. In a short ten-day war, Milosevic and his Belgrade supporters made it clear they were not interested in a bloody clash with the Slovenes. Very few Serbs lived in the republic; the two nations had no common boundaries; and Milosevic himself indicated that he was prepared to let Slovenia secede.

Not so, however, with Croatia. Backed by the JNA, Serb militia forces began to seize control of Serb-inhabited territory inside Croatia, setting up the Republic of Serb Krajina, "cleansing" the region of Croats, and erecting armed barriers on roads to Zagreb and the coast. Former Chetnik strongholds during World War II, Knin among them, served as the most radical centers of Serbian aggression. Thousands of Croats fled from the Krajina for the coast, looking for relief from vengeful Serb militiamen. A Croat village located in the Krajina, Kijevo, was the first to be cleansed of its inhabitants in a process that became integral to the wars of Yugoslav succession. In this case, it was called "cleansing of the ground." . . . Like the later cases of ethnic cleansing in Croatia, Bosnia, and Kosovo, the expulsion of the Croats and the destruction of the village of Kijevo was planned and coordinated by the Serbian forces.

Outmanned and fearful of an outright war with the JNA, the Croats initially hesitated to fight. But facing a similar Serbian attack on Vukovar in eastern Slavonia in late August 1991, they had no choice but to organize their forces to resist the Serb militias and the JNA. If Slovenia had fought a brief war with Yugoslavia and its armed forces for the right to secede, Croatia was at war with the Serbs for control of Serb-inhabited territory in Croatia claimed by Milosevic and the Croatian Serb nationalist leadership. The Serbs claimed they needed "living space" for their people, and they intended to secure it in Croatia. The JNA itself had become an almost exclusively Serb army; members from the other nationalities either deserted or fell in line with the goals of the Serb-dominated high command.

Vukovar fell to the Serbs on November 20 after three months of bombardment and bitter fighting. . . . However, the Croats had succeeded in forming an army and offering up enough resistance to force Milosevic to accede to international pressure for placing peacekeepers between his forces and those of the Croats. Behind the lines, however, Milosevic proceeded with his plans to absorb the occupied Croatian territories into a newly constituted, Serb-dominated Yugoslavia. Zeljko Raznatovic, known as Arkan, and his paramilitary forces, the Tigers, wreaked havoc among Croatian civilians, robbing, threatening, and killing. Not only did the Serbs do everything they could to drive the Croats out of territory they claimed as their own, but they destroyed private homes, businesses, and cultural monuments as a way to make sure the Croats would never come back.

If Kijevo set a pattern for ethnic cleansing that was to repeat itself throughout the 1990s, the taking of Vukovar and occupation of eastern Slavonia introduced the element of genocide into campaigns of ethnic cleansing. On November 19, 1991, JNA soldiers and Serb paramilitary forces entered a local hospital in Vukovar. Most of the sick and the wounded were evacuated to a "detention center" located at a nearby warehouse, where the prisoners were robbed and beaten.

A number of the wounded soldiers were then transferred to a prison in Sremska Mitrovica (in Vojvodina). The next morning, according to the International Tribunal in the Hague, JNA officers separated the women and children from the remaining men, many still on stretchers, and transported them from the detention center. Many of the men, both civilians and soldiers, were tortured and beaten senseless, two of them so badly that they died. Dennis Miller, a Hague tribunal investigator, later described a regular "orgy of beatings" in Vukovar. Two hundred prisoners were then taken to the Ovcara farm outside of Vukovar, massacred, and buried in a mass grave. It was the first, though certainly not the last, time in the war that ethnic cleansing was accompanied by acts of genocide.

Both the Serbs and the Croats raised the stakes in their six-month-long war by conjuring up images of World War II. The Serbs in Krajina mobilized around the threat of a new Jasenovac, the Ustasha camp where tens of thousands of Serbs, Jews, and other opponents of the fascist regime died. "For the second time in half a century," the Serbs claimed, "Croatian government organs and their paramilitary and rebel outlaw formations have committed the crime of genocide against the Serb people in Croatia." The Serbs wildly exaggerated the number of their co-nationals killed at Jasenovac, some claiming more than half a million, others more than a million victims, when the number is likely somewhat less than 100,000. Meanwhile, the Croats focused on the Titoist massacres of Croat troops in 1945, whose numbers were also wildly exaggerated. This "verbal civil war" — reinforced by the almost complete control of the media by Tudjman and Milosevic — was reenacted by the militias on the ground. Traumatic memories of war and extermination that had been repressed in individuals and suppressed and distorted by the Titoist regime became instruments of political struggle and fratricidal war.

The bitterness of the fighting reached into the everyday life of towns and villages in the war zone. Serbs and Croats blew up one another's houses, businesses, wells, and cisterns, and poisoned one another's cattle. They destroyed graveyards, churches, and monuments. . . .

. . . [T]he brutal and uncompromising nature of the struggle in Croatia and later in Bosnia and Kosovo in the 1990s had much more to do with the history of the region since 1940 and the urban social groups that fostered Serbian paramilitaries than it did with the inheritance of the distant past. . . .

By the beginning of 1992, it became clear that Bosnia was the next crisis point on the Yugoslav agenda. Milosevic and the Serbs had arranged for the JNA units in Bosnia-Herzegovina to be manned by Bosnian Serbs. . . . The Bosnian Serbs, under the aggressive nationalist Radovan Karadzic, set up a Bosnian Serb Republic in January 1992 as a way to preempt the separation of Bosnia-Herzegovina from Yugoslavia and recognition by the European Union. If Bosnia-Herzegovina declared its independence, Karadzic warned, it would not last a single day. Alija Izetbegovic, president of Bosnia-Herzegovina and leader of the Bosnian Muslim party, nevertheless steered a reluctant course toward independence. He was determined to maintain the integrity of the republic and was uninterested in sharing power with the militant Serb minority (31 percent) and the equally nationalist

Croat minority (17 percent). Talks had been held between Milosevic and Tudjman on March 25, 1991, in which the two ostensibly antagonistic leaders agreed to the partition of Bosnia, leaving the Muslims only a small enclave around Sarajevo. At the beginning of April, open warfare began, first in Zvornik in the north and then inside Sarajevo itself. For three-and-a-half years, Bosnia was to be the scene of the worst fighting and massacres in Europe since the Second World War.

. . . Even more than the war in Croatia, the Serb attacks were accompanied by horrendous campaigns of ethnic cleansing, which quickly became the term to describe the forcible expulsion of Bosnian Muslims from towns, cities, and villages claimed by the Serbs. This nasty work of creating ethnically homogeneous Serb territory was carried out primarily by paramilitary soldiers, who systematically beat, robbed, brutalized, and expelled the Muslim population, killing and raping as they moved from region to region. The paramilitaries were joined by local re-cruits, who operated close to their own towns and villages. This made the violence up-close and personal, as old scores were settled. Serbs who tried to help their Bosnian neighbors were isolated and attacked. The idea was to instill terror in the local Muslim population and to get them to run for their lives.

It worked. By the end of 1992, two million Bosnians, the vast majority of whom were Muslims, had fled from their homes. If the Serb attacks were not enough, the Bosnian Croats got in the act toward the end of the summer of 1992. They, too, attacked Bosnian Muslims and drove them out of their towns and vil-lages in acts of ethnic cleansing. . . . In the name of Serb and Croat *Lebensraum,*[20] Bosnian Muslims were attacked, beaten, raped, murdered, and expelled.

The genocidal treatment of the Muslim population in the first months of the war was particularly focused in a series of makeshift detention facilities and pris-ons set up by the Bosnian Serbs for their victims. Ethnic cleansing is not just about attack, violence, and expulsion; in almost every case it also includes punishment. Those who are driven off are punished for their existence, for the very need to expel them. Non-Serbs in the Prijedor region were isolated and forced to wear white armbands, which left them vulnerable to abuse and attacks by local Serbs. More than 47,000 homes belonging to non-Serbs were destroyed. Women were removed to the Trnopolje camp, while some 6,000 people, mostly men, were in-carcerated at Omarska. In this terrifying camp, . . . Bosnian Muslims endured all the tortures of hell. Between May and August of 1992, according to the Hague Tri-bunal, guards "regularly and openly killed, raped, tortured, beat and otherwise subjected prisoners to conditions of constant humiliation, degradation and fear of death." Zeljko Mejakic, the commander of the camp in Omarska, was the first person indicted by the Tribunal for genocide; he remains at large.

In many ways even worse than the Omarska camp was the camp at Keraterm, outside of Prijedor. According to the Tribunal indictment, between late May and

---

[20] Living space, a term used by the Nazis to refer to the perceived need to expel entire populations to make room for Germans; here it means the expulsion of Bosnians so that Serbs and Croats could take over Bosnia.

the beginning of September 1992, some 3,000 Bosnian Muslims and Bosnian Croats from the Prijedor district were interned in this former ceramics factory and storage complex. Here, as elsewhere, Serb guards and overseers seemed to derive pleasure from regularly beating, bloodying, and humiliating their prisoners. They hit and bludgeoned them with every imaginable implement: "wooden batons, metal rods, baseball bats, lengths of thick industrial cable that had metal balls affixed at their end, rifle butts, and knives." Night after night, the beatings would take place; young, old, men, women, boys, and girls were the victims. The beatings were sometimes so severe that those who endured them were injured for life. Many died as a result; some were simply killed. The worst case of murder at Keraterm took place in late July 1992, when 140 men from Brdo near Prijedor were confined to one of the rooms in the complex. The officer on duty gave orders that the room be surrounded by guards and soldiers with machine guns. At night, they opened fire, continuing to shoot into the room on and off over a period of several hours. If there were reasons for the shootings, they remain unknown. A couple of people survived to tell the tale.

The most severe damage to life and limb in the former Yugoslavia was done by paramilitary groups based in Serbia proper. . . .

The paramilitary group commanded by the indicted criminal Zeljko Raznatovic (Arkan) was notorious for its violent actions. His "soldiers" were mostly young toughs who had earlier been members of his group of soccer hoodlums, the Warriors, which followed the Belgrade club Red Star. Now they dressed in black and khakis and wore headbands with their hair short or shaven in the style of European neo-Nazis. Their insignia read "Serbian volunteers" on the outside and had a tiger in the middle. These Arkanovci or Tigers committed an unending string of atrocities in Croatia, Bosnia, and Kosovo. . . . The crimes committed by his group were state-initiated and state-supported. . . .

The Muslims had to pay exorbitant rates to get access to the buses that would transport them out of Serb-controlled territory. Before boarding the buses, they had to wait for days or weeks in ghettos — temporary housing in schools or community centers, where they were open season for more robbery and beatings. One group of Muslims was forced to run a gauntlet to get to their temporary housing. In Sehovici, where some 3,000 non-Serbs waited for transportation, the Serbs came at night, threatening violence to the children unless they got more money. Once they got on the buses, they were beaten again until they handed over money, jewelry, and other valuables. In the case of the thirteen or so checkpoints between Prijedor and the border, the buses were stopped, boarded by young thugs, who invariably checked papers, abused women, and threatened the lives of children unless the hapless Muslims came up with even more money. In the same way that the Turks stole ceaselessly from the "rich" Armenians[21] and the Germans from the "wealthy" Jews, the Serbs also seemed to think that the Muslims were endlessly wealthy, and they stole from them until there was no more to take.

---

[21] During World War I.

The last stage of ethnic cleansing was in some ways the most trying. During the trip, men of military age were removed from the buses and trucks. Especially toward the end, very few families could come up with cash or valuables to save their sons and husbands. Muslim men were moved to prisons and recruited to labor battalions. Some unlucky ones were killed outright. Younger Croats were inducted in the Bosnian Serb army; few dared to refuse. The rest of the busloads of refugees were dumped in fields several kilometers from the border, robbed, abused, and beaten again, and left to make their way through the woods and across rivers to Bosnian Muslim territory. . . .

This particular circle of violence — beating, stealing, humiliating, beating, stealing, and humiliating again, then expelling — was hardly peculiar to Arkan and the Serbs. But somehow, in contrast to their Nazi, Polish, or Turkish predecessors, who also beat and robbed their victims, the Serb paramilitaries seem to have regular routines. They beat young men more than the old, men more than women. They had lists of names, ostensibly of Bosnian Army soldiers, government agents, spies, and their families, whom they beat more viciously than others. Serb paramilitaries also engaged in outright murder. All over Bosnia, young Muslim men were shot in groups and buried in common graves.

The most devastating case of mass shootings took place in Srebrenica in July 1995. Enough evidence has been collected by journalists, human rights activists, and the international tribunal in the Hague to reconstruct the terrible story of ethnic cleansing turned to genocide. Srebrenica was a U.N. designated "safe area," protected, in theory, by a small contingent of Dutch soldiers. On July 6 General Ratko Mladic, the swashbuckling commander of the Bosnian Serb army, led an assault on the area that ended ten days later in the capture of Srebrenica. Muslim forces in the area, commanded by the notorious Bosnian fighter Naser Oric, had abandoned Srebrenica to its fate. The Dutch U.N. peacekeepers essentially stood aside as the Bosnian Serbs advanced. Some have argued that they even helped to turn over the area (and its Muslim population) to the Serbs. . . .

Thousands of Muslims from the region of Srebrenica — men, women, children, and old people — fled through the woods and mountains for Tuzla in Bosnian Muslim territory. Most made it; hundreds, maybe a thousand, did not. They succumbed to Serb attacks, exhaustion, and sickness. In Srebrenica itself, the Bosnian Serb forces, army and paramilitary, seized men of supposed fighting age, meaning from 16 to 65, and confined them at the soccer stadium in town. Within a period of a week to ten days, they were taken to a variety of sites, killed, and buried in mass graves. During the process, they were beaten, marched about at double-pace, and forced down on their knees and told to pray to Allah. Some simply had their throats cut on the spot. . . . Busloads of men, blindfolded with their arms tied behind their backs, were transported to killing fields. There, they were executed by firing squads and buried in mass graves. . . .

Srebrenica was the site of the most serious genocidal massacre that accompanied the ethnic cleansing of Bosnia and Herzegovina. . . . But the terror of ethnic cleansing was felt throughout the territories controlled or even threatened by the Bosnian Serbs. Sarajevo faced its own peculiarly terrifying fate, as Serbian artillery lobbed shells into the city below from the heights of Mt. Igman. Designated a U.N. "safe area" like Srebrenica, Sarajevo was hit by an average of one thousand artillery shells per day, aimed primarily at civilian targets. Karadzic, in particular, was determined both to destroy the city as a home of Bosnian Muslims and to remake it as a Serb entity. . . . Sometimes completely isolated and cut off from the world, with the bare minimum of food, water, and power, Sarajevo and its citizens suffered severely during the war and are still recovering from its traumatic effects.

Banja Luka, the second biggest city in Bosnia, was turned into the "Heart of Darkness," in the words of the U.N. High Commissioner on Refugees, the "worst place in Bosnia in terms of human rights abuses."[22] From the beginning of 1992 on, Muslims and Croats in Banja Luka were intimidated, attacked, fired from their jobs, and sometimes tortured and murdered. In the city and its surrounding towns and villages, Serbian police and soldiers roused families in the middle of the night, hauled off the men to camps and labor battalions, stole from the population, and confiscated their property. . . .

. . . After the expulsion of some 200,000 Krajina Serbs by the Croats in August and September 1995 and the arrival of many of these and other refugees in Banja Luka, the pressure on the remaining Muslims and Croats grew even more pronounced. By October 1995 fewer than 15,000 non-Serbs resided in a region that had a prewar non-Serbian population of over 500,000. Of Banja Luka's 60,000 or so non-Serbs, all but a few thousand had left. Radoslav Brcanin, then director of Banja Luka television, openly advocated ethnic cleansing. No more than 2,000 or so elderly Muslims should remain in Banja Luka, he is reported to have said, "Only enough to clean our streets and clean our shoes."[23] . . .

Rape and the sexual abuse of women has been associated with cases of ethnic cleansing throughout this century. But in none of the other cases that we have examined has rape appeared to be so central to the purposes of punishing and driving out the "other" as in Bosnia. All the major parties to the war — Serbs, Croats, and Muslims — have been guilty of rape and vicious attacks on women. Although many of the women felt too shamed to report their experiences, enough have been interviewed by human rights activists to allow one to generalize about their treatment. Clearly, the victims were primarily Muslim women and the perpetrators primarily Serb army and paramilitary soldiers. The Helsinki report on Bosnia, which relied on interviews with many rape victims, states: "Soldiers attacking villages have raped women and girls in their homes, in front of family members and in the village square. Women have been arrested and raped during interrogation. In some villages and towns, women and girls have been gathered together and taken to holding centers — often schools or community sports halls — where they are

---

[22] Commission on Security and Cooperation in Europe [CSCE] Briefing, *Banja Luka: Ethnic Cleansing Paradigm, or Counterpoint to a Radical Future* (Washington, D.C., 11 June 1996), 51 n. 16.

[23] CSCE Briefing, 13.

raped, gang-raped and abused repeatedly, sometimes for days or even weeks at a time." . . . The report goes on to state that there was a political purpose behind the rapes, multiple rapes, and gang rapes of women — "to intimidate, humiliate and degrade her and others affected by her suffering." In other words, the rapes were intended to induce families to flee and never come back, not just for their lives but for the honor of their women. Yet the Helsinki report also makes clear that, as in the case of the beatings, Muslim women were also being punished for their very existence. The interviewed women described "how they were gang raped, taunted with ethnic slurs and cursed by rapists who stated their intention forcibly to impregnate women as a haunting reminder of the rape and an intensification of the trauma it inflicts." The forcible impregnation of Muslim women and, in some cases, the incarceration of pregnant women in order to compel them to carry the pregnancy to term was part of the torture to which they were subjected. All this so that the women would bear "little Chetniks." . . .

One of the complicated issues related to rape in Bosnia — as well as to the killings, beatings, and burning of houses and property — was that it occurred among former neighbors from the same villages and towns. It seemed that from the Serbs' point of view old scores were settled, old slights were repayed, and "uppity" Muslims were brought down a peg or two by these sexual assaults on neighbors. When the Serb rapists came from the outside, then the motives were different — to demoralize the Muslim fighters, who, after all, were not professional soldiers but "fathers, sons, and brothers from the region." In the rape camps, Muslim women often recognized Serbs from their home villages and begged for mercy; and sometimes, in fact, they were helped and protected. But usually the rapists prevailed, whether they knew the women or not. Sometimes they claimed they had been ordered to carry out the rape; sometimes they said nothing. One 38-year-old Muslim woman reported that her 19-year-old neighbor raped her. "So often he had sat at our place, drank coffee with us. He even worked for me," she noted. . . .

The European Union estimates that some 20,000 rapes took place; the Bosnian government claims that the number is closer to 50,000. Whatever the numbers, it is apparent that rape in Bosnia was not simply another example of the excesses of men at war or even a byproduct of ethnic cleansing as it has taken place in the course of the century. We know, for example, that Serb soldiers reported having been ordered to rape. . . . Rape was organized and directed from above for a two-fold purpose. First, because traditional Muslims, in particular, would consider the crime a blight on their family honor; the very threat of rape would drive Muslims from what the Serbs thought was their land. Thus, ethnic cleansing would be accelerated by rape. Second, the forced impregnation of Bosnian women and the attempt to force the women to give birth to the "Chetnik" babies indicated a policy that combined humiliation of the Muslim women and their families with attention to the growth of the Serbian population.

The ethnic cleansing carried out by the Serbs against the Bosnian Muslims was unmatched anywhere in the Balkans in its extent and intensity. Pointing out that

Croats also engaged in ethnic cleansing against Muslims (and Serbs) or that Muslims committed violence against Serb and Croat civilians does not in any way diminish the criminality of the Serbs. We are not dealing with equally destructive phenomena. Still, Croat attacks contributed markedly to the devastation of the region and its peoples. . . . Both Milosevic and Tudjman felt that ethnically pure states would contribute to building their political power and solidifying their rule. Muslim violence, much more limited in scale, was directed against alleged secessionists and traitors to Bosnia-Herzegovina.

Franjo Tudjman's views of the Bosnian Muslims were similar to those of his ostensible antagonist, Slobodan Milosevic. . . . If Serb nationalists claimed that Bosnians were really Serbs who had been forced to convert to Islam, Tudjman insisted that most Bosnians were converted Croats. Like the Serbs, Tudjman and his Croat underlings claimed a good part of Bosnia for their own. On March 25, 1991, at Karadjordjevo, Tudjman and Milosevic met in secret and talked about the partition of Bosnia between them. . . . Backed by Zagreb, the Bosnian Croat army, the HVO (Croat Defense Council), demanded that the Bosnian government in Sarajevo withdraw its forces from the areas to be controlled by the Croats. . . . When Izetbegovic refused, the HVO launched its own campaign of occupation and ethnic cleansing. The strategically located Lasva Valley was the Croats' primary target. . . .

In Stari Vitez and throughout the Lasva Valley, the Croats brutally expelled the Muslims. As in the Serbian case, military units were supported by paramilitary groups, which were often little more than gangs of thugs. The Knights from Croat Vitez did great damage, as did the Jokers unit, which dressed in black and wore the insignia of the Ustasha movement. "We were witnessing something [we] had never seen before and we were distressed and shocked" by "the level of destruction and violence," testified British Colonel Geoffrey Thomas. The most extreme violence took place in the undefended village of Ahmici, which was attacked by the HVO in mid-April 1993. In a familiar pattern, Muslim houses were identified by local Croats and burned to the ground. At least a hundred Muslim inhabitants were killed outright or burned to death in their homes. . . .

The Lasva Valley had its own detention camps for Muslims, where the inmates were tortured and beaten. One of the worst was in Kaonik, where prisoners were used to dig trenches, repair roads, and sometimes serve as human shields against potential Bosnian Muslim counterattacks. Just as in the Serb camps, the Croat warders sought money from the inmates and beat them regularly to get them to turn over their last valuables. Kaonik was also known for its overcrowded cells; sometimes there were up to twenty inmates in a two-by-three-meter room. Even honest and decent warders could do little about the "night calls," when drunken or drugged HVO soldiers would stop by in the middle of the night for brutal entertainments, especially with the female internees. The Croats also sometimes raped and abused Muslim women. . . .

Croat ethnic cleansing reached its pinnacle much later in the war, when it was directed against the Serbs in the Krajina. In two highly successful military operations — Flash, in western Slavonia in May, and Storm, launched at the beginning of August 1995 — the Croatian forces uprooted some 180,000 to 200,000 Serbs. Investigators from the Hague came to the conclusion that the Croatian army itself was involved in the expulsion of Serb villagers and townspeople. Croat regulars "carried out executions, indiscriminate killing of civilian populations, and 'ethnic cleansing.'"

Ethnic cleansing was an integral part of the Serb and Croat strategies for securing those parts of Bosnia they saw as their own. If they could not partition Bosnia outright, as Milosevic and Tudjman would have liked, then they would do it by violent acts on the ground. This was the main thrust of their war against the Muslims, the main reason for the attacks, the burning, the killing, the robbing, the beating, and the rape. . . . Yet unlike genocide, ethnic cleansing is as much about securing control of the land as it is attacking a group for its own sake.

Strictly speaking, the Bosnian Muslims did not engage in ethnic cleansing. Their goal was to maintain the integrity of the territory of Bosnia-Herzegovina. Any kind of partition or cantonization countered their interests as the dominant nationality in the country as a whole. They recruited Serbs and Croats to their armed forces and government apparatus and tried to maintain the ideal, backed by their NATO Allies, that Bosnia-Herzegovina could remain a multinational country. This did not mean that the Muslims did not attack Croat and Serb civilians or that they did not perpetrate war crimes, though the U.S. State Department estimates that only a handful of the documented atrocities, some 8 percent of the total number reported, were carried about by the Muslims. . . .

The ethnic cleansing that took place in Kosovo in 1998 and 1999 resembled that in Bosnia in important ways. In a systematic campaign undertaken by the Serb military, paramilitary, and police forces, Serbs attacked Albanian villages, killing, raping, and burning down homes with the purpose of forcing the Kosovar Albanians to leave. In bigger cities, like Pristina and Prizren, the Serbian authorities — like those in Banja Luka or Brcko in Bosnia — made life so unpleasant for the local Albanians that they escaped, like their cousins in the countryside, to Macedonia, Albania, and Montenegro. Forcible expulsion led to general flight, as Kosovar Albanians sought relief from Serb repression. . . . The NATO bombing that commenced on March 24, 1999, in a vain attempt to stop the Serb action dramatically accelerated ethnic cleansing. Hundreds of thousands of Kosovar Albanians left their homeland or sought refuge from Serb violence (and the bombing) by fleeing into the hills.

On June 10, 1999, after 78 days of bombing, Milosevic conceded defeat and NATO took control of Kosovo. The pattern of ethnic cleansing was now reversed, though hardly on the gargantuan scale that took place under Serbian leadership. The relatively small Serb community in Kosovo, roughly 8 percent of the total population, at the beginning of the 1990s was itself attacked and driven off by returning Albanians. In some places, notably north of the divided city of Mitrovica, small Serb communities remain. . . .

If some structural aspects of ethnic cleansing in Kosovo resemble that of Bosnia, the two experiences were also different in profound ways. Although Bosnia had been the site of fratricidal warfare between Serbs, Croats, and Muslims during World War II, for the most part the region had evolved over the centuries into a multiethnic society that tolerated cultural and religious diversity. Although professing different religions, all three groups were Slavs; they looked pretty much alike and spoke the same dialect of Serbo-Croatian. This was not the case with Kosovo, which for at least a century had been the focus of national tension between Albanians and Serbs, two very distinct peoples who speak completely different languages. . . . The Serbs seized Kosovo from the Turks in the Balkan Wars, while the creation of an independent Albania in 1912–13 did not include Kosovo inside its borders. Especially after Kosovo became part of the Kingdom of Serbs, Croats, and Slovenes (later Yugoslavia), the Serbs began an intense campaign of colonization from Serbia proper, with the intention of depriving the Kosovar Albanians of their land and discriminating against their culture, institutions, and language. During World War II, the Italian occupation of Albania and western Kosovo reversed Serbian fortunes. Now the Albanians gained the upper hand over the Serbs, expelling large numbers of colonists and other Serbs and seizing their property and landholdings.

The struggle between Serbs and Albanians over Kosovo continued into the communist period. Initially, Tito's Yugoslavia favored Serbian control of Kosovo, including a renewed campaign of colonization. But Tito's policies changed in the late 1960s, when he gave in to the growing economic, intellectual, and demographic influence of the Kosovar Albanians by recognizing their rights as a nationality in the province. The constitution of 1974 completed the process; the province was given autonomy within Serbia and a formal place within the Yugoslav commonwealth of nations. Again, the tables were turned, and Serbs complained of discrimination by the Albanians and of "ethnic cleansing" — the use of violence, rape, and job discrimination to chase Serbs from the province. . . .

For the Kosovar Albanians, Milosevic's rise to power was a nightmare from the very beginning. . . .

The Serbian authorities singled out the leaders of the Kosovar independence movement for arrest, imprisonment, and physical abuse. Discriminated against in society and systematically deprived of their jobs and livelihoods, thousands of Kosovar Albanians left their homeland to seek work in Western Europe. In March of 1991 the Albanians organized huge demonstrations on the streets of Pristina to protest against the revocation of their rights. But the demonstrations were brutally suppressed by Serbian police; thousands of demonstrators were arrested and perhaps hundreds were killed. The other republics of Yugoslavia were shocked and dismayed by these repressive actions. With the Serb showing so little respect for Kosovar claims to autonomy, the Slovenes, Croats, and Bosnians, among others, worried that the Serbs might try to limit their own. The result, as we know, was a series of declarations of independence and sovereignty at the beginning of the 1990s that triggered Serbian military intervention. In this sense, the wars of Yugoslav succession began in Kosovo and ended in Kosovo. . . .

The first phase of the war in Kosovo began on February 28, 1998, when KLA[24] fighters ambushed and killed four Serbian policemen on a deserted road between Pristina and Podujevo. The Serbs retaliated in force. . . . In what became known as the Drenica Massacre, some 85 Albanians were killed, including 25 women and children. The escalation of violence was almost inevitable. Repression of the Kosovar Albanians got worse, and more and more young men, many of them jobless and hungry, took up arms against the Serbs under the banner of the KLA. With funds from their increasingly radicalized co-nationals in Europe and America, the KLA quickly grew into a well-armed opponent of Serbian domination. Although its political organization was weak and its ranks divided into numerous factions, the KLA nevertheless was able to control almost 30 percent of the territory of Kosovo by the middle of 1998.

The Serbian response to the growth of the KLA insurgency and to increasing violence in Kosovo was predictably savage and brutal. Moreover, beginning in February 1998, Serbian military, paramilitary, and police forces began a systematic campaign of ethnic cleansing, designed, or so it seemed at the time, to secure strategic areas and force hundreds of thousands of Albanians to leave Kosovo. . . .

Complicating the picture on the ground was the introduction into Kosovo of the first contingents of OSCE monitors in October 1998. . . . Yet even with some 1,300 monitors present, the Serbs attacked and cleansed Kosovar Albanians, while the KLA continued to strike a variety of targets: Serbian policemen, government installations, and alleged Albanian collaborators. A brief OSCE-negotiated ceasefire at the end of December 1998 was broken on January 8 when the KLA seized eight Yugoslav army soldiers who had mistakenly driven their truck into KLA-controlled territory. Although the OSCE managed to get them released, the Serbs again retaliated with extreme force, attacking the "guilty" village of Racak and murdering 45 Albanian civilians. Eyewitnesses reported that they had seen the "hooded men dressed in black" who had carried out the execution-style killings.

Racak had an instantly mobilizing effect on the Allies as a consequence of their chastening experience with the Srebrenica massacre in Bosnia. NATO leaders attempted to force the Serbs and Kosovar Albanians to sign an agreement at Rambouillet (February 6–23, 1999) that gave NATO the right to control Kosovo militarily, while ensuring the Albanians that after three years they would be able to vote in a referendum for independence. Neither side was initially willing to accept the ultimatum. . . . In the end, the Albanians were convinced by the Allies to sign the agreement on March 18, and after the withdrawal of the OSCE Kosovo Verification Mission on March 19 the stage was set for the NATO bombing of Serbia and Kosovo, which proceeded on March 24.

Contrary to the expectations of Western policymakers, the Serbs did not give in and instead accelerated their campaign of ethnic cleansing during the 78 days of bombing. There was no more pretense that their goal was to hunt down KLA

---

[24] The Kosovo Liberation Army, established in 1993 by Kosovar Albanians to fight for independence from Serbia.

members and expel their supporters. Now the Serbs seemed intent on reversing the population percentages in Kosovo: what was once 90 percent Albanian and 10 percent Serbian would now be 90 percent Serbian and 10 percent Albanian. Milosevic also hoped to destabilize neighboring Albania, Macedonia, and Montenegro with a stream of refugees. . . . 800,000 to 900,000 Kosovar Albanians were expelled in this period, leaving roughly 600,000 still inside the borders, many of them in hiding, and another 400,000 abroad. . . .

Ethnic cleansing in Kosovo took on many of the patterns already established in Bosnia. Local Serbs (and gypsies) identified Kosovar Albanian homes; paramilitaries broke in, beating up the inhabitants, and forcing them to hand over their money and valuables before leaving. Houses were often burned to the ground, sometimes with families still in them. Serbs also forced Kosovar Albanians to leave their apartments in the cities. Serbian forces spread out over Pristina, shouting through bullhorns and distributing pamphlets, threatening the Albanians who remained with injury and death. Tens of thousands were detained in the Pristina Sports Complex before being moved to the trains, buses, and trucks that were to transfer them to the Macedonian border. In these cases, as in Bosnia, the Albanians were forced to pay extravagant prices for tickets and ended up in dangerously overcrowded railway cars and vehicles. In Kosovo, Serbian forces were particularly intent on confiscating the Albanians' documents. At checkpoints inside the country and at refugee camps near the border, the Serbs seized both the money and personal documents of Albanians. The idea was to deprive them of any legal claim to citizenship or property. . . . Even license plates, voter registration records, and civil registries were destroyed in the campaign of ethnic cleansing in Kosovo.

Just as in Bosnia, Serbs raped women and girls both to punish the Albanians and to accelerate the Albanians' departure. . . .

It is difficult to know the true dimensions of the problem, even after the conclusion of the war, because of the highly traditional culture of a significant portion of the Kosovar Albanian population. No woman likes to talk about being raped, and reporting the crime under any circumstances is a humiliating and psychologically painful act. But in the more traditional regions of Bosnia and particularly in Kosovo, Muslim women were very hesitant to state what happened to them. . . .

Ethnic cleansing in the former Yugoslavia has cast a pall over the end of this century. The West has been forced to face the deeply depressing fact that once again millions of Europeans — in this case Bosnians, Kosovar Albanians, Serbs, and Croats — have been chased from their homes, robbed, brutalized, raped, and killed. Once again, dominant ethnonational groups have committed crimes against humanity in their determination to rid what they consider their territory of the "other" — minorities who are culturally different and ostensibly alien. Once again, state programs of ethnic cleansing have easily accommodated genocidal actions. Hundreds of thousands have died, mostly at the hands of Serb soldiers and paramilitary, and many are buried in mass graves. Once again, rape and attacks on women have become commonplace. Serbian paramilitaries have left a trail of victims among Muslim women, who will carry these crimes and a sense of violation with them for the rest of their lives.

The states and parastates that have been formed as a consequence of the breakup of Yugoslavia seek social cohesion and political stability through ethnic homogenization. The policies of ethnic cleansing during the war have been continued in the peace. National exclusivism dominates political programs almost everywhere in the region. This is as true today for the Kosovar Albanians and Bosnian Muslims as it has been since the start of the war for the Serbs, Croats, and Slovenes. Politicians employ the state-controlled media to disseminate the message of the organic unity of their respective peoples. History is rewritten to exclude the role of minorities in the past and future. The lingering bitterness of the recent fighting provides little hope for multiethnic solutions to the region's immediate problems. . . .

The Bosnian and Kosovo cases reiterate the incapacity of the international community to do much about ethnic cleansing in this century. NATO dropped bombs to get the Serbs to sign the Dayton agreement, but only after three and a half wrenching years of ethnic cleansing that displaced over two million people. Because NATO could not muster a credible ground threat, the NATO bombing in Kosovo actually accelerated the Serbian campaign of ethnic cleansing, which concluded with nearly a million Kosovar Albanians uprooted. Perhaps the most depressing part of ethnic cleansing in the Balkans is the apparent permanence of the results. . . .

ACKNOWLEDGMENTS

Zoltan Barany, "The East European Gypsies in the Imperial Age," from *Ethnic and Racial Studies* 24/1 (January 2001). Reprinted with the permission of Taylor & Francis, Ltd., www.tandfco.uk/journals.

Robin Briggs, "The Witch-Figure and the Sabbat," from *Witches and Neighbors: The Social and Cultural Context of European Witchcraft,* Second Edition. Copyright © 1996 by Robin Briggs. Reprinted with the permission of Viking Penguin, a division of Penguin Putnam Inc.

Christopher R. Browning, "German Killers in the Holocaust: Behavior and Motivation," from *Nazi Policy, Jewish Workers, German Killers.* Copyright © 2000 by Christopher R. Browning. Reprinted with the permission of Cambridge University Press.

William J. Chase, "Daily Life in Moscow, 1921–1929," from *Workers, Society and the Soviet State: Labor and Life in Moscow, 1918–1929.* Copyright © 1987 by the Board of Trustees of the University of Illinois. Reprinted with the permission of the author and University of Illinois Press.

Anna Clark, "The Struggle for the Breeches: Plebeian Marriage," from *The Struggle for the Breeches: Gender and the Making of the British Working Class.* Copyright © 1995 by the Regents of the University of California. Reprinted with the permission of the author and the University of California Press.

K. H. Connell, "The Potato in Ireland," from *Past and Present: A Journal of Historical Studies* 23 (November 1962). Copyright © 1962. Reprinted with the permission of the Past and Present Society and Mrs. H. Connell.

Robert Darnton, "Workers' Revolt: The Great Cat Massacre of the Rue Saint-Séverin," from *The Great Cat Massacre and Other Episodes in French Cultural History.* Copyright © 1984 by Basic Books, Inc. Reprinted with the permission of Basic Books, Inc., a subsidiary of Perseus Books Group, LLC.

Natalie Z. Davis, "The Rites of Violence: Religious Riot in Sixteenth-Century France," from *Past and Present: A Journal of Historical Studies* 29 (May 1973). Reprinted with the permission of the Past and Present Society and the author.

Jared Diamond, "Hemispheres Colliding: Eurasian and Native American Societies, 1492," from *Guns, Germs, and Steel: The Fates of Human Societies.* Copyright © 1997 by Jared Diamond. Reprinted with the permission of W. W. Norton & Company, Inc.

Richard J. Evans, "The Challenge of Cholera in Hamburg," from *Death in Hamburg: Society and Politics in the Cholera Years, 1830–1910.* Copyright © 1987 by Oxford University Press. Reprinted with the permission of the publishers.

Stephen P. Frank, "Popular Justice, Community and Culture among the Russian Peasantry, 1870–1900," from Ben Eklof and Stephen Frank, eds., *The World of the Russian Peasant: Post-Emancipation Culture and Society.* Copyright © 1990. Reprinted with the permission of the author and Routledge.

Christopher R. Friedrichs, "Poverty and Marginality," from *The Early Modern City 1450–1750.* Copyright © 1995 by Longman Group Limited. Reprinted with the permission of Pearson Education Limited.

Ellen Furlough, "Packaging Pleasures: Club Méditerranée and the French Consumer Culture, 1950–1968," from *French Historical Studies,* vol. 18, no. 1 (Spring 1993). Copyright © 1993 by the Society for French Historical Studies. Reprinted with the permission of the author.

Donna Gabaccia, "Italian Women in the Nineteenth Century," from *Connecting Spheres: European Women in a Globalizing World,* Second Edition, edited by Marilyn J. Boxer and Jean H. Quataert. Copyright © 2000 by Oxford University Press, Inc. Reprinted with the permission of Oxford University Press, Inc.

Peter Gay, "Letter Writing and the Victorian Bourgeois," from *The Naked Heart.* Copyright © 1995 by Peter Gay. Reprinted with the permission of W. W. Norton & Company, Inc.

Dominique Godineau, "Political Culture and Female Sociability in the French Revolution," from *The Women of Paris and the French Revolution.* Copyright © 1997 by The Regents of the University of California. Reprinted with the permission of University of California Press.

Sara F. Matthews Grieco, "The Body, Appearance, and Sexuality," from Natalie Zemon Davis and Arlette Farge (eds.), *Renaissance and Enlightenment Paradoxes, Volume III: A History of Women in the West*. Copyright © 1993 by the President and Fellows of Harvard College. Reprinted with the permission of The Belknap Press of Harvard University Press.

Alistair Horne, "The Price of Glory: Verdun 1916," from *The Price of Glory: Verdun 1916* (London: Macmillan Publishers, 1978). Copyright © 1978 by Alistair Horne. Reprinted with the permission of PFD on behalf of Alistair Horne.

Olwen Hufton, "Women, Work, and Family," from Natalie Zemon Davis and Arlette Farge, eds., *A History of Women in the West, Volume III: Renaissance and Enlightenment Paradoxes*. Copyright © 1991 by Gius. Laterza & Figli Spa. Copyright © 1993 by the Presidents and Fellows of Harvard College. Reprinted with the permission of The Belknap Press of Harvard University Press.

Alex de Jonge, "Inflation in Weimar Germany," from *The Weimar Chronicle: Prelude to Hitler* (New York: New American Library, 1978). Copyright © 1978 by Alex de Jonge. Reprinted with the permission of the author.

Henry Kamen, "The Spanish Inquisition and the People," from *The Spanish Inquisition*. Copyright © 1997 by Henry Kamen. Reprinted with the permission of The Orion Publishing Group.

Herbert S. Klein, "The End of the Atlantic Slave Trade," from *The Atlantic Slave Trade*. Copyright © 1999 by Herbert S. Klein. Reprinted with the permission of Cambridge University Press.

Theresa M. McBride, "A Woman's World: Department Stores and the Evolution of Women's Employment 1870–1920," from *French Historical Studies* X (Fall 1978). Copyright © 1978 by the Society for French Historical Studies. Reprinted with permission.

John McManners, "Death's Arbitrary Empire," from *Death and Enlightenment*. Copyright © 1981 by John McManners. Reprinted with the permission of Oxford University Press, Ltd.

Norman M. Naimark, "Ethnic Cleansing in the Wars of Yugoslav Succession," from *Fires of Hatred: Ethnic Cleansing in Twentieth-Century Europe*. Copyright © 2001 by Norman M. Naimark. Reprinted with the permission of Harvard University Press.

Kristina Orfali, "The Rise and Fall of the Swedish Model," from Philippe Ariés and Georges Duby, eds., *A History of Private Life, Volume V: Riddles of Identity in Modern Times*, translated by Arthur Goldhammer. Copyright © 1991 by the President and Fellows of Harvard College. Reprinted with the permission of The Belknap Press of Harvard University Press.

Sidney Pollard, "Factory Discipline in the Industrial Revolution," from *Economic History Review* 16 (December 1963). Copyright © 1963. Reprinted with the permission of the author.

Raffaella Sarti, "The Material Conditions of Family Life," from David I. Kertzer and Marzio Barbagli, *Family Life in Early Modern Times, 1500–1789*. Copyright © 2001. Reprinted with the permission of Yale University Press.

Richard Van Dülmen, "Rituals of Execution: From Purification to Deterrence," from *Theatre of Horror: Crime and Punishment in Early Modern Germany*, translated by Elisabeth Neu. Copyright © 1985 by C. H. Beck'sche Verlagsbuchhandlung (Oscar Beck). Translation copyright © 1990 by Polity Press. Reprinted with the permission of C. H. Beck Verlag.

Merry Weisner, "Nuns, Wives, and Mothers: Women and the Reformation in Germany," from Sherrin Marshall, ed., *Women in Reformation and Counter-Reformation Europe: Public and Private Worlds*. Copyright © 1989 by Indiana University Press. Reprinted with the permission of the publishers.

Keith Wrightson, "Infanticide in European History," from *Criminal Justice History: An International Annual* 3 (1982). Copyright © 1982 by the Crime and Justice History Group, Inc. Reprinted with the permission of the Greenwood Publishing Group, Inc.